Beginning Visual Basic 6 Database Programming

John Connell

Beginning Visual Basic 6 Database Programming

Beginning Visual Basic 6 Database Programming

Copyright © 2003 by John Connell

ISBN (pbk): 1-59059-251-4

Printed and bound in Canada 45678910

Trademarked names may appear in this book. Rather than use a trademark symbol with every occurrence of a trademarked name, we use the names only in an editorial fashion and to the benefit of the trademark owner, with no intention of infringement of the trademark.

Distributed to the book trade in the United States by Springer-Verlag New York, Inc., 175 Fifth Avenue, New York, NY, 10010 and outside the United States by Springer-Verlag GmbH & Co. KG, Tiergartenstr. 17, 69112 Heidelberg, Germany.

In the United States: phone 1-800-SPRINGER, email orders@springer-ny.com, or visit http://www.springer-ny.com. Outside the United States: fax +49 6221 345229, email orders@springer.de, or visit http://www.springer.de.

For information on translations, please contact Apress directly at 2560 Ninth Street, Suite 219, Berkeley, CA 94710. Phone 510-549-5930, fax 510-549-5939, email info@apress.com, or visit http://www.apress.com.

The information in this book is distributed on an "as is" basis, without warranty. Although every precaution has been taken in the preparation of this work, neither the author(s) nor Apress shall have any liability to any person or entity with respect to any loss or damage caused or alleged to be caused directly or indirectly by the information contained in this work.

The source code for this book is available to readers at http://www.apress.com in the Downloads section.

Credits

Dedication

This book is dedicated to my wife Janell and my two wonderful sons Garrett and Grady. This would not have been possible without their constant support and encouragement. Thanks guys.

About the Author

John Connell is a Vice President at First Chicago NDB Bank. He has a Master's Degree in Computer Science and a Master's Degree in Business Administration. John teaches computer programming classes at DePaul University in Chicago.

John has designed and written several financial programs in Visual Basic that are currently in use in many of the largest companies in the United States.

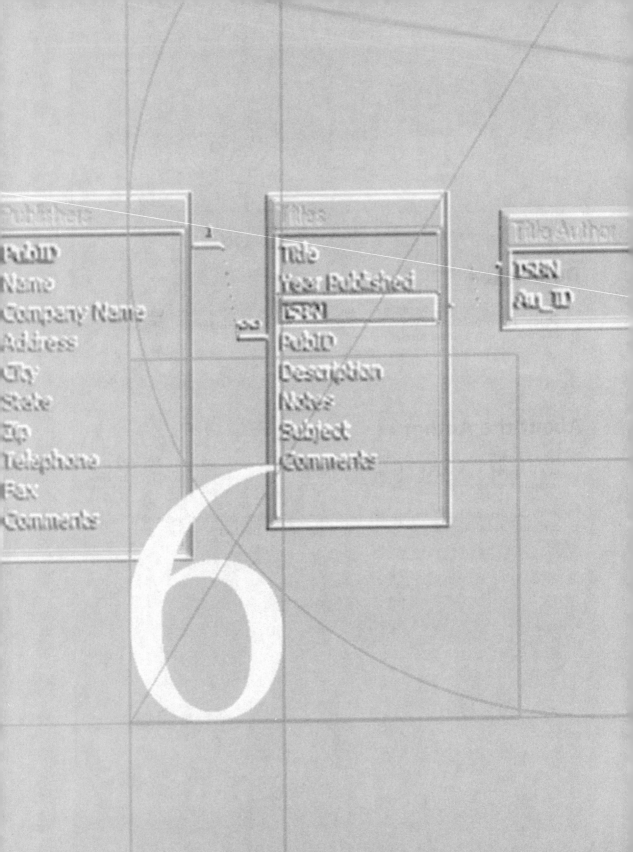

Beginning Visual Basic 6 Database Programming

What this Book is About   **1**

Who Is This Book Aimed At?   2
New Database Features in Visual Basic 6.0   2
Our Approach   3
What Do I Need To Use This Book?   3
Customer Support   4
Where To Find the Sample Code For This Book   4
Feedback and Suggestions   4
Conventions Used In This Book   4
The Road Map for This Book   6

Chapter 1: What Is a Database?   **9**

Why Use a Database?   9
What is a Database? A More In-Depth View   10
Storing Information in Our Filing Cabinet   11
Querying Our Database - Getting the Information We Need   13
Flat Files and Relational Databases   14
Relational Database Components   15
The Relational Database in More Detail   15
What Exactly is a Table?   16
Database Files and Tables   16
Our Sample Database - Biblio.mdb   16
Looking at the Data in Biblio.mdb   17
Indexes 'R' Us   18
What's a Relationship Again?   20
Relationships Between Tables   20
The Key to Successful Relationships   21
Who's Got the Key?   22
Orphaned Records   23
Normalizing Our Data   24
Moving On…   24
A Resume of Some Important Terms   24
Our Two Vehicles - Access and Visual Basic   24
Why Should We Use Access?   25
The Biblio.mdb relational database   25
Create a New Sub-Directory   25
Where Does Our VB Program Come In?   26
The User Interface   27
The Database Engine   27
Jet – A Specific Database Engine   27
DLLs – The Fuel Inside the Jet Engine   27
Jet is Self-Contained   28

The Data Store   29
Getting Our Feet Wet   29
    Tables, Records and Fields in Biblio.mdb   29
        The Publishers Table   29
        The Authors Table   30
        The Title Author Table   31
        Building a Relationship   31
The Way(s) Ahead...   32
    DAO or ADO?   33
        Beyond the DAO/ADO Conundrum   33
        Some Pros and Cons of DAO and ADO   34
        Enjoying the Complexity   34
    Choosing Your Route and Reusability   35
    The Good News Again   35
Summary   35
        Take-Home Points   36
    The Next Step   36
Exercises   37

Chapter 2: Meet the ActiveX Data Object (ADO) Data Wizard   39
What is the ADO Data Control?   40
    The Recordset   40
Meet the VB Data Form Wizard   42
    What is an Add-In?   42
        The Final Product in Design Mode   54
        The Final Product at Run-Time   56
        Navigating the Recordset   57
Looking at the Same Information in Another Way   58
        The Master/Detail Form in Design Mode   63
        The Master/Detail Form at Run-Time   64
    MS HFlexGrid Layout   65
    The MS Chart Layout   69
Pay No Attention to the Man Behind the Curtain   75
The Dark Side of the Wizard   75
A Word on Sorting   76
    ASCII Sort Order – A Primer   76
    Summary   79
    What We Learned   80
Exercises   81

Chapter 3: Programming the Data Control   83
Why Not Just Let the Wizard Do It?   83
The Data Control and Bound Controls   84
Intrinsic Controls   84
    What is a .DLL Again?   85
        Dynamic Linking   86
The Intrinsic DAO Data Control   86
What is a Recordset Exactly?   87
What is a Data Bound Control?   88
    Types of Bound Controls Available to Us   89
        Intrinsic Controls   89
        ActiveX Controls   89
Working With Data Controls   91
    Changing the Data   95
        The Sequence of Events   96
    How Does It Know That?   96

Parent/Child Data Control Relationship   98
Who Was That Masked Control?   104
Introducing the New ADO ActiveX Data Control   105
The ADO Data Control and the Bound DataList Control   106
   The Mysterious BoundColumn Property.   114
The VB 6.0 Hierarchical FlexGrid Bound Control   119
What Do All These Controls Have in Common?   122
Summary   123
What We Learned   123
Exercises   124

Chapter 4: Designing a User Interface for the Data Control   127

Designing the User Interface   127
The Visual Basic Form   128
   Properties Explained   130
   Event-Driven Programming Explained   131
   The Important Form Event Sequence   134
Into the Heart of the Data Control   134
Duplicating the Functionality of the Wizard   135
   Let's Do it Ourselves this Time   135
Bound Controls Revisited   143
   Recordsets Revisited   145
The Strange and Terrible Saga of Control Arrays   147
Under the Hood of the Data Control   148
   The BOFAction Property   149
   The EOFAction Property   150
   The Connect Property   150
Just Add Code!   151
   Reduce the Dots - Efficient Object Reference   153
   The IntelliSense Feature   155
   Why is the Code Placed in Form_Activate()?   157
   The Data Control Reposition Event   158
   Eye Candy for the User   158
   Make Some Enhancements   159
   Where Do We Go From Here?…   163
   What We Learned   163
   Onward!   163
Exercises   164

Chapter 5: Programming a Bulletproof User Interface   167

The Data Control - Right or Wrong?   167
Building an Enhanced User Interface   168
   The Class System   168
Back to the Data Control...   168
   Properties of the Data Control   169
   Methods of the Data Control   170
   Properties of the Recordset   170
   Methods of the Recordset   171
The State-Machine Concept   172
Designing a Robust User Interface   172
   Houston, We Have a Problem   178
Enhancing Record Navigation   179
A Level of Indirection   180
   Reusing the Code   180

Building the Navigation Code for the User Interface 181
Case DbEditNone - We Are Not Editing or Adding a Record 184
Build a String 185
Case dbEditInProgress - We Are Editing a Record 187
Case DbEditAdd - We Are Adding a New Record 188
The navigateButtons Sub-Routine 188
How It Works 190
Preventing Accidental Record Editing - the LockFields Subroutine 192
Locking and Unlocking Our Data Entry Fields Automatically 194
All of the 'Smarts' Have Been Added to Our Buttons 197
Adding the Interface Enhancements to our Program 198
Incorporating the updateButtons Subroutine 198
BookMarking a Record 200
Enhancing Data Manipulation Via the User Interface 200
Adding Records 200
Editing Records 202
Saving Records 202
Deleting Records 204
Undoing Changes to Records 206
Adding a Reference 208
Fun with the Object Browser 209
Summary 213
What We Learned 213
Exercises 214

Chapter 6: Completing the User Interface 217

How's It Look? 217
Unloading our Form - a Few Concerns 218
Ensuring Uniform Unloading of Our Form 219
The Lowly MsgBox Function 221
Using App.EXEName 222
Canceling the Form Unload 223
Some Data-Entry Considerations 225
What Exactly is Focus? 225
Highlighting the Right Field 227
Some More About Focus 228
Setting the Tab Order 229
Keeping Tabs on the Tabs 230
The TabStop Property 232
Ensuring the User Does Not Change the PubID 234
Using the Enter Key to Tab to the Next Control 236
Finding a Specific Record 237
How Do We Find It? 237
Adding a Code Module to Our Project 238
Creating a Generalized Find Form 239
How We'll Make This Work 239
Look Ma, No Typing! 241
Test Out the API Viewer 242
A Few Words on Global Variables 243
Why Not Use Globals? 244
Creating the Find Form 245
Why Are We Adding a "" to Each Field Anyway? 250
What Happens Next? 251
A Handle? What's a Handle? 253
Searching the Recordset to Find Our Record 256
Go Ahead and Run Your Program 257
The Find Form - Some Finishing Touches 258
Data Validation - the Programmer's Bane 261

The Validate Event 262
The Action Argument 263
The Save Argument 264
Creating Some Validation Code 264
Reflecting On the Data Control 267
Summary 268
What We Learned 268
Exercises 269

Chapter 7: Building a Data Control Class Module 271

What We'll Cover in This Chapter 271
The Joys of Repetitive Programming 271
Class Modules to the Rescue 272
Reusable Components 272
What Exactly is a Class? 273
OOP Buzzwords Revealed 274
Polymorphism 274
Inheritance 274
Encapsulation 275
VB and PIE 275
Copying Your Program 275
What We are Going to Accomplish 275
Building a Class in Visual Basic 6.0 276
Adding Code to Our Class 285
Data Encapsulation 287
Our Class's Properties 287
Assigning Values to Our Class's Properties 288
Reading Our Class's Properties 288
Setting Objects in Our dataClass 289
Making a Property Read-Only or Write-Only 289
Let's Take a Closer Look at the Properties 291
The Let Buttons Property 291
The Set dataCtl Property 291
The Let dbName Property 292
The Set FormName Property 292
The Let LabelToUpdate Property 292
The Set ProgressBar Property 292
The Let RecordSource Property 292
The Let Tag Property 294
Back to the Class Builder 294
Methods of Our Data Class 295
Adding Code to Our Class's Methods 297
Just Add Code 297
The ProcessCMD Method 297
The updateButtons Method 301
The navigateButtons Helper Subroutine 303
What We've Accomplished 309
Polishing the dataClass Class Module 310
Making Our Templates Available to All Our VB Projects 317
Data Validation...Again 326
The Object Browser - Revisited 327
Refining Our dataClass Class 328
A Parent/Child Form - the Data Control Class in Action 330
The Various Gotchas in a Parent/Child Data-Entry Form Revealed 336
Summary 339
What We Learned 339
Exercises 341

xi

Chapter 8: Getting the Data You Want from the Database   343

SQL - What's the Story?   343
Is It a Language, Is It a Technology? No, It's SQL!   344
SQL - Your Co-operative and Flexible Co-worker   344
Getting the Data We Need   345
Introducing the SELECT Statement   345
The Simplest SQL Statement - Revealed!   346
Build the SQL Query Tester   347
Selecting Specific Fields from a Single Table   353
Filtering the Returned Recordset - the Good Stuff   354
The WHERE Clause   355
Partial String Matching - the Like Clause   356
Records Within a Range - the Between Clause   357
Retrieving Records Using the IN Clause   357
Nested Conditions   358
Null Fields and You   358
The Delete Query   359
Unique or Non-Unique Fields?   359
Ordering the Returned Recordset   360
Aggregate Functions   361
Aliasing the Column Names   362
Null Values Revisited   364
A Statistical Aside   365
The GROUP BY Clause - Summarizing Values   366
Grouping With the HAVING Clause   367
Joining Tables   367
The INNER JOIN   368
The OUTER JOIN   369
The SQL Update Statement   371
"Pay no attention to the man behind the curtain"   376
Using Access-generated SQL in VB   378
Enough Theory - Let's Build a Dynamic SQL Generator!   379
What Else Can We Do With SQL?   383
Summary   384
What We Learned   384
Exercises   385

Chapter 9: Database Design, Construction and Analysis   387

When to use DAO and ADO - A Rule of Thumb   388
Giving VB 6.0 the Reference to DAO   389
The Personal Address Book   390
Normalization   392
Unnormalized Data Elements for the Address Book   392
1st Normal Form - Eliminate Any Repeating Groups   394
2nd Normal Form - Splitting Tables   395
3rd Normal Form - Eliminate Columns Not Dependent on Key   397
Creating our Database   400
How do Access, VisData, the Data Control,
Jet and DAO Relate to Each Other?   400
Guidelines for Creating Indexes   407
Creating a Database with DAO   409
ISAM File Server and Relational Client Server   410
ISAM Data Access   411
The Relational Style Client-Server Data Access   411

The DAO Object Model - what is it? 412
Objects and Collections 412
    Working with Collections 413
    Getting at and using Objects Contained in Collections 413
Database Objects 414
Connect the Dots 414
Recordset Objects 417
    Options for Opening a Recordset 418
Analyzing a .mdb File Using DAO 425
Summary 437
What We Learned 437
Exercises 438

Chapter 10: Programming The Address Book **441**

The Microsoft Tab Control 449
    The Status Bar Control 450
    The Masked Edit Control 451
Let's Write Some Code 455
    A Bit More on the Status Bar Control 461
    The clearFields Subroutine 463
    The lockFields Subroutine 464
    The updateTree Subroutine 465
    The updateForm Subroutine 470
    The setUpListView Subroutine 472
The Initialized Address Book Program 473
    The populateFields Subroutine 475
Converting Dates 477
    The populateListView Subroutine 478
    The List View Control Code 481
    Sorting the List View 482
    The Tool Bar of the Address Book 484
    Validating the Data Entry 486
    Posting the Contact to the Database 487
    Back to the Tool Bar 489
    Adding Call Notes for the Current Contact 491
The frmCall Form - Where to Log Calls 492
    Just Add Code 494
    The updatedescriptionCombo Subroutine 495
    Deleting a Call Description 498
Add a New Call or Cancel the Operation? 502
The DB Statistics Tab 504
How It All Works – A Global Recap 505
What We Learned 510
Exercises 511

Chapter 11: Universal Data Access Using ADO **513**

What's the Background to ADO? 513
    The Limitations of DAO 514
The Quest for Data 514
    Change is the Only Constant 517
    Back to the Future 517
Universal Data Access 518

Why ADO is the Cool New Way to Access Data 519
Say Hello to ActiveX Data Objects - ADO 519
OLE DB is the Answer! 520
Review of Steps to Set Up the ADODC ConnectionString 522
The ADO Data Control Properties 529
The DAO and ADO Data Control Properties Compared 529
The ADO Object Model 530
Step 1 - The Connection Object 530
Step 2 - Opening a Recordset 531
Programming with Active Data Objects 532
Creating a New Data Source 536
Using the Connection Object's Execute Method 545
Opening Recordsets 547
Fun with Schemas 548
Trawling for Data Types 553
Reacquaint Yourself With the Object Browser 555
The ADO Errors Collection 555
The Errors Collection Output 557
Finding Out All About Our Data Provider 559
A Word on Setting References 560
The ADO Object Model - Revisited 561
The Parameter Object 563
What the Heck is a Cursor, Anyway? 563
Why Cursors are Important in ADO 566
Types of Cursors 566
Opening ADO Recordsets - Syntax 568
ConnectionString Options 568
Transactions and You 569
An ADO Transaction 569
Using Transactions in Everyday Life 572
Summary 573
What we Learned 573
Exercises 574

Chapter 12: Creating ADO Data Bound ActiveX Controls 577

We Could Create ActiveX Controls Before,
Couldn't We? 578
The Holy Grail of Code Reusability 578
C++ and Visual Basic - a Short (and Partial) History 579
Time Out to Discuss Data Binding 579
Binding Datafields to Controls 581
Coding the myBoundClass Class Module 582
The Move Complete Event 585
The MoveNext Procedure 587
Showing the Status of the Move Complete 587
Coding the frmBoundExample form 588
Coding the Form Load Event 588
Showing the Reason and Status of the ADO Recordset
MoveComplete Event 589
An Easy Choice for the User 589
Running the Program 590
Let's Recap 591
Creating Our Own Data Control 592
Keeping the Control at a Constant Size 596
A Word on Declaring and Raising Events 598
Adding Properties and Methods to the Control 600

What About When Our Record Source Isn't a Table?   603
On To the cmdButton Control Array   604
Updating the User Interface   611
Enabling/Disabling the Buttons on Our Control   612
Locking and Unlocking the Bound Controls
         (AKA "How to Eliminate the Tag Property!")   613
The UserControl Properties   615
Property Pages - The Professional Touch   619
Adding an About Box   624
The ToolboxBitmap   626
Testing Our Program   627
The Bound Text Box   630
Validating Our Data   631
Our New ActiveX ADO Data Control in Action   633
Building the .OCX for Distribution   634
Our Control in the Registry   635
The Brand New VB 6.0 Data Repeater Control   637
Using the New Data Repeater Tool   637
Adding Properties to Our Control   640
Setting the Procedure Attributes   642
Check Out the Object Browser Again!   648
Summary   649
What Have We Learned?   649
Exercises   650

Chapter 13: ADO and Active Server Pages   **653**

Active Server Pages   653
Hyper Text Markup Language - or HTML   654
Enter Active Server Pages   656
Running Active Server Pages   656
How to set up PWS on Your Machine   657
Setting up a Directory for Our Examples   662
ASP, Scripts and HTML   664
What Does an ASP Script Look Like?   664
Our First ASP Script   664
The % is the Magic!   666
Let's Run Our First ASP Script   668
ASP Scripting Languages   671
A More Robust ASP Example Using ADO   671
VBScript Gets the Data and HTML Displays it   675
A Simple Client/Server ADO Application   679
Requesting Data From the Server   680
The Request Form Code   680
The Server Side   683
Persistent Client Side Data Using Cookies   687
Building an Application for Persistent Data   688
The login.asp Form in Action   690
The visitor.asp Page in Action   692
Creating the Visitors Database   696
Creating Our visitors.dll File   697
The setVisitor Function   698
The getVisitor Method   700
Saving the DLL   702
The newUser.asp Form in Action   704
The updateNewUser.asp Form in Action   706
The Application in Action   709

Summary   710
What We've Learned   710
Exercises   711

Chapter 14: Advanced ADO Programming - Data Mining   **713**

Data, Data, Everywhere…   713
Data Mining   714
   The ID3 Algorithm   715
   The Product Analysis Tool   715
ID3 Project Form and Code Initialization   721
   Opening the Database Connection   723
      How It Works   724
   Initializing Our ID3 Table   724
   Populating Our Region, Language, Country Flex Grid   729
   Performing the Analysis   738
      The Big Kahuna of SQL Statements   741
      Aggregating Data in Our ID3 Table   744
      Thinking About Exceptions   745
Determining the Entropy of the Values We Added   747
   Getting all the Entropy We Can Eat!   752
      The Scary Part   755
A Word on Creating THAT SQL Statement   760
What We Learned   761
Exercises   762

Chapter 15: Making our Data Available Universally   **765**

Exporting Recordsets to other Programs   765
   Comma Delimited Files   766
   HTML Exporting   766
   Excel Exporting   767
Exporting Our Data in a Comma Delimited File   769
   Creating a CSV Export File   770
      Taking Care of Business   774
      Running the Code   776
   The Power of CSV   780
Exporting Our Data in HTML   781
   Creating the HTML File   785
Using Objects to Send ADO Data to an Excel Worksheet   787
Late Binding   788
Early Binding   789
Sending ADO Recordset Information to Excel   790
   The Completed Project   797
Advanced ADO Techniques   798
   Learning about Advanced ADO Topics   798
   Disconnected ADO Recordsets   798
   Business Objects   799
   Remoting a Recordset   799
   Creating a Disconnected Recordset   800
   Creating a Disconnected Recordset is Simple   800
   Updating Our Database from the Remoted ADO Recordset   801
   The createRecordset Function   805
   Changing Some Data on the Client Side   807
Getting the AbsolutePosition Property   809

Another ADO 2.0 Wonder - Persistent Recordsets 811
Wrapping Up 815
Summary 815
What We Have Learned 816
Exercises 817

Chapter 16: Where Next? **819**

This Land is Your Land 819
Where We've Been 819
Where Are We Now? 820
Where Are We Going Next? 821
Next Steps 821
Finally 822

Appendix A: One Standard, Many Flavors... **825**

The [Field Name] Syntax 825
The BETWEEN Clause 826
Column Aliases 826
Joins 826
Summary 827

Appendix B: Solutions **829**

Chapter 1 829
Chapter 2 830
Chapter 3 831
Chapter 4 832
Chapter 5 833
Chapter 6 834
Chapter 7 835
Chapter 8 836
Chapter 9 837
Chapter 10 838
Chapter 11 840
Chapter 12 841
Chapter 13 842
Chapter 14 843
Chapter 15 843

Appendix C: Summary of Microsoft Access Field Types **847**

Index **849**

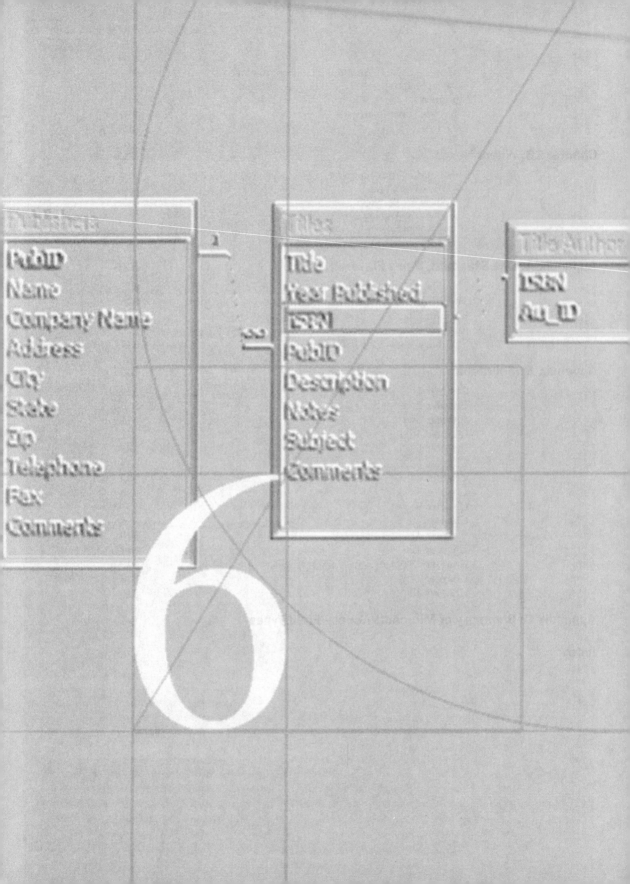

Beginning
Visual Basic 6 Database Programming

What this Book is About

This book is all about starting to use Visual Basic 6 to program databases. There are literally millions of Visual Basic programmers around the globe, and most of these programmers are like you - they need to write VB applications that store and manipulate data of some kind. These needs range from a simple desktop database for tracking friends' addresses or company products, through accessing company legacy databases, to placing database information on the World Wide Web.

These data stores are found everywhere: sitting inside desktop and home PCs; burbling away in corporate legacy systems; resting in dusty offices at the back of the store. Apart from the personal and business data we're all used to seeing and handling every day (names, addresses, prices etc.), there's a host of other data stores that are just waiting to be accessed and made useful through a visual interface: sound files, video images, e-mail archives, web pages - and more. Just thinking about all that information is enough to make your head start spinning - it's like a William Gibson sci-fi novel out there. Fortunately, we have Visual Basic at hand to aid us in making sense of all this data and to help us build the interfaces that will let us - and the users of our applications - make the most of the information that is available.

The aim of this book is to give you the background to address these twin needs: accessing data, and building interfaces to make interaction with the data simple.

Visual Basic 6, the latest incarnation of one of the most popular programming languages in the world, gives us a set of tools to develop visual interfaces to access this planet-full of data. In this book we will use the established features of VB, and the new functionality in version 6, to teach you the VB techniques for data access.

Who Is This Book Aimed At?

This book is designed to teach you how to write Visual Basic 6 programs that communicate with a database. Apress 'Beginning' series books aim to take you from the basement to the penthouse suite as quickly and easily as possible, using a wealth of examples and practical exercises to give you the core information, skills and techniques you need. This is the book for you if:

▶ You want to learn how to use Visual Basic to access databases.

▶ You have programmed before, but are new to Visual Basic - this book is written so that you can easily come up to speed. Programmers from other languages will have little trouble getting into the swing of how VB6 does things.

▶ You have used Visual Basic before. VB6 has some brand new **ActiveX Data Object (ADO)** features for accessing databases from your programs. We'll show you how to migrate existing database programs to the newly available platforms.

▶ You just need to learn what new directions VB 6 moves in within the strategic **Universal Data Access (UDA)** paradigm. We cover the new methods that help move Visual Basic towards the panacea of infinitely interchangeable data access - where any and all data sources are available to us from our programs.

You will probably have already read a 'Beginning' book on Visual Basic and are familiar with Forms, Properties, Events, and Methods. The ideal primer is Apress's 'Beginning Visual Basic 6' book. But even if you haven't used VB in a structured way, this book will still be accessible to you: it is written to use a step-by-step approach that guides you through the important information, and provides plenty of practical examples to reinforce what we're doing.

Just to give you an idea of all that is new for database programmers in Visual Basic 6.0, take a look at this table. We not only discuss each of these new features, but write practical examples to illustrate how to use them to meet your day to day business requirements. Don't worry if some of the descriptions look a bit complicated. They are all easy to use and we walk through each of them in detail so you will understand them all by the end of the book.

New Database Features in Visual Basic 6.0

New in VB 6.0	Available in which VB 6.0 Editions?	Description
ActiveX Data Objects (ADO)	All	This new data access technology is simpler than DAO and provides better integration with other Microsoft and non-Microsoft technologies. ADO sports a common interface for both local and remote data access to both relational and non-relational data.
ADO data control	All	A new data source control acts much like the intrinsic Data Control in previous versions of VB. We will use it to create database applications with a minimum of code.
Enhanced data binding	All	In previous versions of Visual Basic, it was only possible to bind controls together on a form in you knew the fields in advance. In Visual Basic 6.0, it's possible to bind any data source to any data consumer.

New in VB 6.0	Available in which VB 6.0 Editions?	Description
OLE DB Support	All	OLE DB is a set of interfaces that provide applications with uniform access to data stored in both relational and non-relational formats. We use ADO as the programmer interface to access OLE DB.
Hierarchical FlexGrid Control	All	We use this updated version of the FlexGrid control to display hierarchical recordsets (recordsets from different tables). The versatile formatting capabilities of the control allow you to present complex data hierarchies in a visually pleasing, easily understood manner.
DataRepeater Control	Professional and Enterprise Editions	We will build and insert a UserControl into the DataRepeater to create a rich view of a database. A UserControl can contain text boxes, check boxes, or any other data aware controls.
Remoting ADO Recordsets	All	You can now pass ADO Recordsets across programs and even across machines. We write a simple program that illustrates this new, efficient means for moving data between tiers in a multi-tier application.
DataGrid Control	All	This is similar to the DBGrid you are familiar with. This new control allows you to quickly build an application that views and edits recordsets.

Our Approach

Our basic approach is to assume that you have minimal experience of working with databases. This way, we can introduce database concepts and practices and get everybody up to the same level. We will then move on to look at the fundamentals of building a Visual Basic interface for database access. We then use this platform as a learning tool to develop the more detailed themes of the book - including some in-depth programming using the latest VB6 technology.

We aim to move you from the basics to the complexity in the space of this book, and provide you with a firm foundation for exploring the extensive world of data access.

What Do I Need To Use This Book?

You'll need the following tools to enjoy the full benefits of making this journey:

- A copy of Visual Basic 6 (Standard edition or higher) – this is the core requirement for this book

- A copy of Microsoft Access will let you get the most out of Chapters 8 onwards

- A copy of Microsoft Personal Web Server (PWS) is needed for creating the web/database examples in Chapter 13 (You can download PWS free from the Microsoft web site, and we provide full instructions on how to do this in the chapter)

3

Customer Support

It is standard Apress practice to provide you with all the support that you need to get as much as you can out of using this book. This means that we can supply you with the ready-made code used in the chapters that follow, and that you can contact Apress, the editors, and the author to make comments or suggest amendments for future editions.

Where To Find the Sample Code For This Book

The source code for this book is available at

`http://www.apress.com` in the Downloads section.

On our site, you will also find the details of any amendments to the code or to the book.

Feedback and Suggestions

When you buy an Apress book, you aren't just buying a product - you're also buying *in* to an organic community of authors, editors, and readers. We want to know what you thought about this book - the good, the bad, and the just plain ugly. We do whatever we can to improve the quality of our books, and the feedback that our users (that's you!) provide us with is an important part of this process. The people who produced this book will retain responsibility for its upkeep, and we need you to help us.

The quickest way to contact us is through e-mail. Send your comments to:
`http://www.apress.com`

If you find a mistake or a malfunction, please check the errata page for this book on our web site.

Conventions Used In This Book

You'll find that the text of this book is laid out in a number of different text styles. These are designed to help you find your way around and make sense of where you are in the book. Here are examples of these styles, and brief explanations of what they mean:

Try It Out - Practical Work to do Step by Step

1 Each step has a number

2 Work your way through all the steps

3 When you've finished the steps, read:

How It Works

How It Works sections explain the practical work in detail

> *Important information that you should really read appears in a gray text box like this*

FYI **Useful information appears in this style**

Background information and advice looks like this on the page

▶ Important Words are **emphasized like this**

▶ Words that appear on your monitor in menus or windows, such as in the File menu, are presented in a similar font to how they appear on screen

▶ Keys that you press on the keyboard, such as *Enter* or *F5*, are italicized like this

▶ Program Code appears in a number of formats:

▶ Blocks of code that are to be keyed in to Visual Basic or other programs appear in a gray block like this:

```
Private Sub Text1_Change()
lblTitles.Caption = "Titles published by  " & Text1
End Sub
```

▶ Any code that appears in the body of the normal text - such as **Private   Sub Text1_Change()** - is shown in this bold font.

▶ Sometimes you'll see a mixture of styles like this:

```
Private Sub Text1_Change()
lblTitles.Caption = "Titles published by  " & Text1
End Sub
```

This means that we want you to concentrate on the code that's highlighted in the gray box. We'll use this convention when we want you to add some more code to an existing program. We'll also use the gray block style to highlight chunks of code that we're explaining in the How It Works sections

5

The Road Map for This Book

As we mentioned earlier, we aim to move you up from a basic level of knowledge to a much higher plateau. By the end of this book we will be doing some pretty sophisticated things with some of the latest technologies, and you will have a feel for what can be done with data held in electronic data stores.

This approach is born out of our belief that it is much better to understand the things we are programming in as much depth as possible. So we start with simple definitions and concepts and build upon these using simple and relatively unsophisticated techniques. Then we keep building the functionality of the Visual Basic programs we're going to construct until we are well versed in the standard, tried and trusted techniques. With that knowledge under our belts (or is it under our hats?) we will then use what we've learned to apply some of the latest techniques and components.

This means that we will work our way through the well-established Visual Basic data access technology **Data Access Objects (DAO)** before moving on to the newer and strategically important **ActiveX Data Objects (ADO)**. Don't worry about these acronyms - we'll be looking at the different technologies in depth later. For the moment, just think of DAO and ADO as sets of standardized tools and components that we use in conjunction with Visual Basic to get at data.

The way that we program Visual Basic to use these two technologies is essentially the same, and the knowledge that we develop in using DAO will prepare us for the transition to ADO. DAO is a great learning tool for getting to know your way around databases and Visual Basic database programming. Additionally, DAO has a vast installed user base, and knowing the ins and outs of DAO could be useful for you in itself.

Our ultimate goal is to prepare you for your future as a Visual basic database programmer in a world where there are a lot of technologies, a lot of data, and where the technology is in constant flux. We believe that a firm grasp of the fundamentals will allow you to adapt as things change over time.

Now let's begin by moving on to Chapter 1 and establishing some common ground - just what are databases, and how are we going to use them in this book?

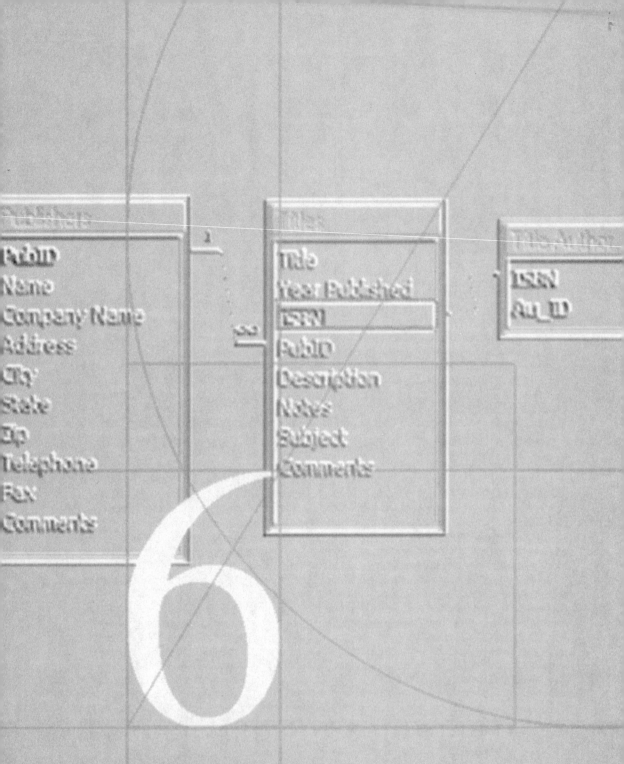

1

What Is a Database?

A **database** is a place where we store **information**. More than that, it's a place where we store **organized** information for a purpose or a set of purposes. We organize the information in our database in such a way that our programs and applications can provide useful functions for end-users.

In this chapter we'll paint the 'big picture' of what databases can do for us. We'll also explain the strengths of a very common type of database – the **relational** database – and we'll take a look at how we can use the sample relational database that comes bundled with Visual Basic. Don't worry about the terminology for the moment – all will become clear! Here's what we'll look at in this chapter:

- ▶ The components and functions of a database
- ▶ The sample relational database that's supplied with VB
- ▶ Where Visual Basic fits into the data access picture
- ▶ We'll discuss the different database access technologies available to us and see what's in store in the future

Why Use a Database?

Even before they've mastered the Visual Basic 6.0 language, many serious VB programmers come to the same conclusion; they realize that an awful lot of useful applications store and retrieve large quantities of information. Obviously, a VB program doesn't *have* to get involved in database interactions to be useful in business, but applications that *do* work with databases provide us with a lot of power and functionality. Why? Because databases allow us to read, input and store copious amounts of information that we can retrieve or change further down the line. This information can be used flexibly when needed for display or manipulation, for reports, analysis, or even to generate invoices, work orders and so on.

The bottom line is that whenever there is a substantial amount of information to organize and store, a database is the answer. Anecdotal evidence suggests that the majority of Visual Basic programs work with a database of some sort. There is a range of different situations where implementing a VB/database solution might be used, with these among them:

▶ Implementing a new application from scratch

▶ Connecting with an existing corporate database

▶ Interacting between a database and a website that takes customer orders for products directly over the Internet

The location and function of the database you're working with can be varied too:

▶ The database could be on the same machine as your program - for instance if you were building a home cataloging system for books or CDs, or creating a specialist hobbyist data store.

▶ It could reside on a server somewhere and be accessible over a local (or not so local) network - where a store of information was shared by a number of co-workers within a company, for example.

▶ In some global businesses (and with the advent of the Internet, doesn't that mean *all* businesses?) the database might be on a Web server on the other side of the globe several time zones away, catering for the needs of Internet-connected users around the world.

▶ The database could be part of a corporate legacy system that lives on in a vast, dusty mainframe, and needs a VB graphical front-end face-lift; giving data-entry or customer service staff a more flexible interface to an existing customer database, for instance.

So you can see that the combination of VB and databases makes up a vast and exciting territory. To get a tight grip on the database concepts that will help us navigate through this territory, let's look in some more detail at what a database is.

What is a Database? A More In-Depth View

The best way to start our understanding of databases is to think about how a business might store important information. In this context, a database can be thought of as an **electronic filing cabinet**. For example, a business must keep records of a number of different types of information, including some of the following:

▶ Customer information (names and addresses etc.)

▶ Product information

▶ Invoicing information

▶ Customer purchases

▶ Orders information

Without an electronic database, these paper records are filed and stored in a large metal filing cabinet. So the filing cabinet is our database. One of the filing cabinet drawers might hold all the information on our customers. Another drawer might contain all of the paper listings about our company's products and a third drawer might be used to store all of the company's invoicing information. All of the information is organized (alphabetically, for example) and different types of information are kept in different drawers.

A "NON-ELECTRONIC" DATABASE

CUSTOMERS

PRODUCTS

INVOICES

As we've thought about how we'll use our information, the database is subdivided into logical chunks: all 'Customer's' Information held together, all 'Products' Information held together and so on.

Storing Information in Our Filing Cabinet

So what happens when we want to use the information in our filing cabinet? Let's look at some of the things that happen when a customer orders one of our company's products.

An order clerk takes orders over the phone for a product and we create a new paper record containing details of the order. This sheet of paper will be stored in the filing cabinet's 'Orders' drawer. If the order were from a new customer, we'd need to create another sheet of paper listing that customer's details. Let's assume the order is from an existing customer and that we want to check out their details.

In our 'Customers' drawer there are hundreds of manila folders holding sheets of paper that store information about specific customers. Each sheet contains the customer name, address, credit information, contact names and just about anything else the business needs to know about each client. Each manila folder is considered a **record**. A record contains a logical grouping of information on a specific client. If we store the information logically it means that we don't have to hunt through different folders to find the customer's name, address and telephone number - these separate bits of information are all held together in one place so that we can get at them easily.

Let's say that we take out the manila folder from the 'Customers' drawer for the Rocket Science Propulsion Corporation. Opening up the manila folder, we pull out the form (the paper sheet) that has pre-printed boxes: one for the customer name, another for the address and a third for the telephone number - you get the picture. Each of these pre-printed boxes represents a **field** of information. So we'll have a Name field, an Address field, a Telephone Number field and so on. We can think of a field as the smallest category of information we can store in a database. A record contains many fields.

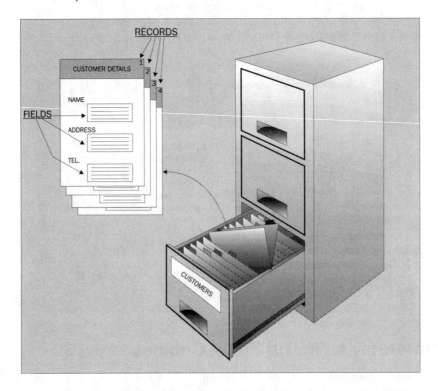

Of course, the beauty of a file cabinet is that it is organized. Let's say we get a call from Mr. John Doe at Rocket Science. He tells us that from now on, his orders should be shipped to a new warehouse location. Since our file cabinet has all its information well organized, it's easy for us to update his customer record. Here's what we need to do:

- While still on the phone, we lean over to the file cabinet
- We open the 'Customers' drawer
- Since all of our customer manila folders are arranged in alphabetic order, we quickly go to all customers whose name starts with "R" and then find the Rocket Science folder and its printed form (record)
- We take out the paper form and update the pre-printed box (field) with the new address

There, we have just updated our paper database!

Since we were smart about organizing company data, we had a major impact on productivity. We could quickly zero in on a record (the sheet of paper) containing a specific field (the pre-printed box) in our database, even though the whole database might contain hundreds of thousands of similar fields. This is something you might have done several times without even thinking about it. From a small cardboard box containing our favorite recipes, to a large filing cabinet with all the important information used to run a business, we can quickly find what we need because the records are **indexed**. Here, we have indexed our customers in alphabetic order. When we get a new client, we fill out the pre-printed form and place it in a new manila folder. We write the name of the client on the tab and insert the folder in the correct alpha order in our customer drawer. We have just indexed that customer.

Querying Our Database - Getting the Information We Need

Now the boss comes into our office and says, "I need to find out the total amount of all orders placed by Rocket Science in the last twelve months - and I need it now." Well, we first go to the 'Customer' drawer and find Rocket Science. Stapled to the back of the customer record is a list of all the invoice numbers for that company. We write down the invoice numbers for all the invoices sent in the last twelve months on a piece of paper. It turns out that Rocket Science has made four purchases from us in the last year.

We then open the 'Invoices' drawer, where our invoice folders (records) are ordered by invoice number. So we pull out the four folders that hold the invoices for Rocket Science. Each invoice record provides details about products shipped, and about payment. We grab our calculator and add up the totals for the four invoices and write the total on a piece of paper and give it to the boss.

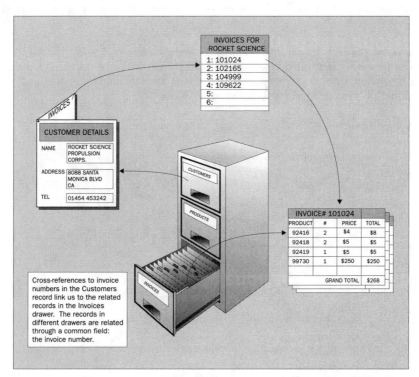

Because our business information is easy to store, access and use, we can find out what we need to know relatively quickly. We knew before we set up our filing system how different kinds of information (customers and invoices) were related to each other and we stored the information so that we could easily cross-reference it.

Next, we'll start to think about how the data storage and retrieval principles of out filing cabinet can be implemented in electronic databases. So let's get technical!

Flat Files and Relational Databases

Flat-file databases are one of the more traditional ways of storing data electronically. Essentially a flat file stores data in a single stream of bytes that can grow as large as necessary until the disk is full. As well as the file that actually holds the data you want to keep (the names, addresses, etc.), other files are required to help us get at the data; these files contain pointers which tell us the specific locations of bits of information (records and fields) in the data file.

The real headache with flat files is updating the files that contain the pointers to specific locations in the flat file. First, there is the sheer tedium of managing all the cross-reference pointers in all the different structures of the flat file. Not only that, but whenever a piece of information grows or moves in the flat file, every cross-reference offset referring to that information must be updated as well. So even if there was a small change in the shipping address of Rocket Science, it might cause changes throughout the rest of the files' internal references on where to find the specific record we are looking for. So even though this complexity is managed by the software that manages the database, you can get a sense of how complex this can be. With the evolution of database technology, this approach is no longer efficient.

Relational databases help to eliminate the inefficiencies associated with the flat-file database. There are a host of complicated rules that describe what makes a database truly relational, but the most important thing to remember is that the relational database stores and displays data in **tabular** format of **rows** and **columns**, like a spreadsheet.

CUSTOMERS DATA:
How data is stored in the tabular relational model.

COLUMNS

NAME	ADDRESS	TEL.#
ROCKET SCIENCE PROPULSION CORP	8088 SANTA MONICA BLVD,CA	01542 443315
GINA'S TIRES	222, WEST STREET, AKRON, OH	04154 453046
LARRY'S CAKESHOP	994 NORTHERN AVE. CICKELY, AK	01764 453043
SERIOUS CORPORATION	1224 BIG STREET, BOSTON MA	01021 234042

ROWS

The power of relational databases comes from their ability to store data with minimal duplication and from their ability to link (relate) data from different sources together. This latter ability is where the relational database gets its name; relational databases can easily relate two or more fields together. By linking fields, we can link entire records. In our metal filing cabinet example, we found the appropriate invoice records for a specific customer; we were able to do this because there was a logical link between records stored in the 'Customer' drawer and the 'Invoices' drawer. If you remember, the link was provided by a list of invoice numbers stapled to the customer details form. Once we knew those, we could reference the related data in the 'Invoices' drawer.

Relational Database Components

The components of the manual filing system we discussed earlier are mirrored in the relational database:

- In relational database terms, the filing cabinet, which contains *all* of the data we want, is called a **database**.

- In a relational database a **table** mirrors each of the drawers in the filing cabinet. A table stores a specific set of information - there's one table for Customers, one table for Products and one table for Invoice details, for example.

- In relational database terminology the paper sheets contained in the manila folders, which store a number of pieces of separate, but logically related information, are called **records**. So the Customer table would have a record for each customer, listing their name, address, etc.

- The individual entries on the paper sheets (the name, the address etc.) are called **fields** in a relational database. These fields are combined to form a record.

These components form the core of a relational database.

Relational databases are preferred because they use fields common to several different data files to maintain relationships among them. In fact, it is very easy to maintain multiple relationships simultaneously simply by relating one table to another by using fields that contain the appropriate information to link them. In our example, we first found the customer, grabbed the invoice numbers from the customer record and used those numbers as an index into the invoice table to retrieve the invoice records we needed.

We'll now look at the relational database concept in a bit more detail to see how it implements the needs we have for data storage, cross-referencing and easy access.

The Relational Database in More Detail

As we mentioned, a relational database is made up of tables that contain data records. Each of the records is composed of fields. A field is the smallest, 'atomic' part of a database.

What Exactly is a Table?

A **table** is a logical grouping of related information. This information is arranged in rows and columns, similar to a spreadsheet; we have a column for each category of data that we want. In our Customers table we'd want a column called 'Name', one called 'Address' and so on. Each column defines a **field**. For each customer we'd enter some data into each column and the collection of data in these fields would form that customer's **record**.

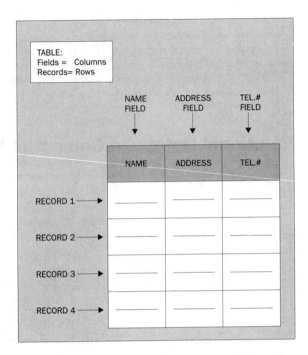

Each horizontal row is a record and the collection of records makes up the contents of the table. Next, we'll take a quick look at how the data within tables is stored.

Database Files and Tables

With the relational model, we don't have to worry about any of the physical and logical pointers that are used to link records. The relational database software is there to handle all of the low-level interaction for us. This principle extends to the way that tables and their data are physically stored. As you'll see shortly, the relational database software that we'll be using here stores the entire database as a single file. All of the tables, records and fields are invisible to us *in file terms*, since they are contained in a single *database* file sitting on our hard disk or server. This makes life easy for us in maintenance terms - the database software looks after all the file management and the details of the storage for us.

Our Sample Database - Biblio.mdb

We'll use **Biblio.mdb** to learn about relational databases. This database is large enough for us to build a fully functioning Visual Basic database program, and comes bundled with VB. Here, we'll take a quick look at some of the features of the tables contained in the **Biblio.mdb** database.

The **Biblio.mdb** database file contains four tables: **Titles**, **Authors**, **Publishers** and **Title Author**. These tables contain the data that makes up this bibliographic database. Here's a summary of the kind of information that each table holds:

▶ **Titles**: Stores data about individual books, such as the book title, publication date and ISBN number

▶ **Authors**: This table holds data about individual authors - their name, the year they were born, and a number that uniquely identifies them

▶ **Publishers**: The Publishers table stores information about individual publishing companies, such as their address and telephone number

▶ **Title Author**: This table holds fields that link together individual titles and authors - we'll see why this is useful later

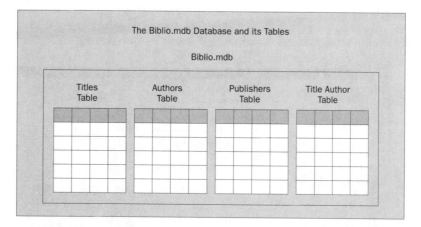

Let's take a look at some of the data held in these tables.

Looking at the Data in Biblio.mdb

FYI   We'll be using MS Access to look at the tables in the screenshots below. We'll talk about how to use Access with the `Biblio.mdb` database later. For now, trust me!

We can see some of the fields in the Titles table from this screen shot:

Title	Year P	ISBN	PubID
1-2-3 Database Techniques	1990	0-8802234-6-4	45
1-2-3 For Windows Hyperguide/Book and Disk	1993	1-5676127-1-7	192
1-2-3 Power MacRos/Book and Disk	1992	0-8802280-4-0	45
1-2-3 Power Tools (Bantam Power Tools Series	1991	0-5533496-6-X	139
1-2-3 Release 2.2 PC Tutor/Book and Disk	1990	0-8802262-5-0	45
1-2-3 Secrets/Book and Disk	1993	1-8780587-3-8	19
10 Minute Guide to Access	1994	1-5676123-0-X	192
10 Minute Guide to Access (Best Selling)	1994	1-5676145-0-7	192
10 Minute Guide to Access for Windows 95	1995	0-7897055-5-9	45

Record: 1 of 8569

The names of the fields are in the top line, just below the title bar: Title, Year Published, ISBN and PubID. A field has a name, a data type, a maximum length and other attributes. Fields can contain characters, numbers or even bitmaps. For example, the Title field uses the data type *text* and Year Published is data type *date/time*. We'll see later how to get at these attributes and use them. Also, there's a summary of MS Access field types in Appendix C.

In the screenshot below you can see that Access provides us with the ability to store just about anything we can think of in a table. If we use Access to take a peek at how the table Titles was designed, we can see the name of each field, it's data type and an optional description explaining the use of the particular field:

Indexes 'R' Us

By default, when we view the data held in a table, it is presented to us in the order that it is found in the database - all the data for a given record appears on the same row, but the records aren't sorted alphabetically or numerically. This means that we have to scroll through the entries to find the one we want. Luckily, relational databases provide us with a tool for quickly finding the precise bit of data we want - the **index**.

An index acts very much like an index in a book. Let's say you picked up a book on VB and wanted to find out about forms. You could go to the back of the book and look at the index under 'forms'. Since the index is in alphabetic order, you run your finger down the index, find the 'F's and then find Forms. There might be references to forms on page 23 and 135. So even if these references were in two different parts of the book, you could quickly find them both. An index on a table works exactly the same way. The index permits the database software to quickly locate specific records, even though they might be scattered in different parts of the table.

When we add information about a new book title, a new record is added to the database. Typically, each new record is placed at the end of the table. If we have a Titles table with over 8,500 records, we can bet the records were not entered in the database in alphabetic order. Therefore, if we wanted to select only those titles that begin with the letter L from the Titles table, the database would need to look at each and every record and gather up only those whose titles began with the letter L. This is complicated processing and can slow our application down to a crawl.

Luckily, we can create an index on any field or fields in a table that we know our users will be searching on.

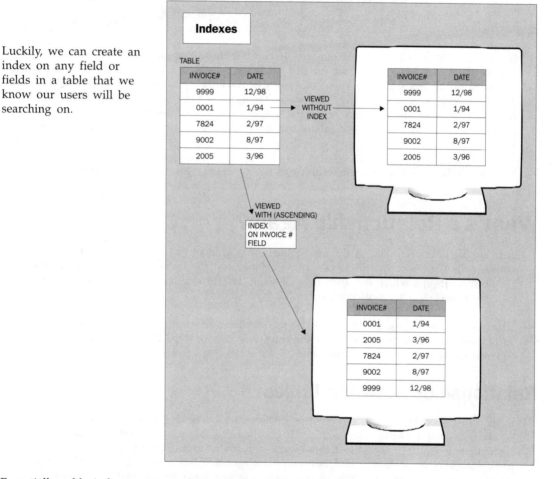

Essentially, table indexes are sorted lists that speed up the search. Each entry in the index points back to a specific row in the database. This way, when searching the database, the database software can take a quick look through an index first when looking for records. We can create an index on most types of field. Indexes speed up the search and retrieval of data tremendously and, best of all for us, we don't need to know *how* this is done. We just flag a field as an index and the database software takes care of the rest.

If we take a look at the indexes that are defined for the Titles table, we can see that there are four of them; an index can be set for any field that we think will be searched on. So when designing our Titles table, we know that we will have to search on the PubID, ISBN, Reference and Title fields - these are perfect candidates for indexes. Since an index was placed on the Title field, our database software can now very quickly isolate all titles that start with L, for example. After looking at the index, the database can zoom right to those specific records and return them to us.

Now let's take a look at the relationships of the various tables in the **Biblio.mdb** database.

What's a Relationship Again?

Relationships between data in different tables are a kind of cross-referencing, like the link between the Customer records in our filing cabinet and the Invoice records for that customer. We create relationships where we want to access the data in one table and use this data to take us to some linked data in another table.

Using Access, we can graphically see the relationships between tables in a database. Access lets us display the tables graphically and indicates any relationships that have been established between the data in the individual tables.

Relationships Between Tables

In the illustration below you can see the Publishers table linking to the Titles table. In this case we have defined a **one-to-many** relation. It is called this because **one** publisher can publish **many** book titles. It is also possible to define **many-to-many** relationships; for example, an author might work with several publishers and one publisher probably has several authors. Finally, there is the **one-to-one** relationship, where unique values in one table always map to unique values in another table.

The screenshot below shows the relationships in our four tables from `Biblio.mdb`:

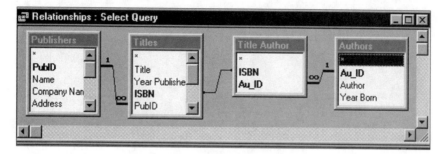

In the screenshot we have the following relationships shown:

▶ There is a one-to-many relationship between the Publishers table and the Titles table

▶ There is a one-to-one relationship between the Titles table and the Title Author table

▶ Finally, there is a many-to-one relationship between the Title Author and the Authors table

So, how do relational databases handle the relationships between tables?

The Key to Successful Relationships

If we take a step back and think, it might occur to us that if we stored everything in a single table instead of the four tables, we would have to store a lot of duplicate information. If we placed all of the information in a single table, each individual record would hold information on a book, its publisher and its author. So if a publisher published three hundred books, each of those three hundred records would contain the exact same information about the publisher. Our Publishers table has 10 fields. If we placed everything in a single table, we would have to have the exact same 10 fields replicated in each of the 300 records. We would have 3,000 fields for this information instead of just the 10 that we need. As you might imagine, this is not a good idea. You can see that this single table approach is an incredible waste of space, leads to bloated tables, redundant data, slows down processing and makes coding very difficult. Not only that, it would be more difficult for the data entry clerk to ensure that the information was added correctly.

It makes sense to avoid data duplication and find a way to store all of the information about the publisher just *once*, in the Publishers table (after all, we don't want to duplicate all of the information about that publisher each time we add a new book title issued by the publisher). What we could do then would be to relate that single publisher record to each of the three hundred books they publish (the information about the books resides in the Titles table). We could use some sort of **key** that would link the unique publisher record to the three hundred book records that relate to that publisher. So we could look at the **unique key** for that publisher in the Publishers table and round up all of the title records in the Titles table that contain that same key. That is exactly how it's done in the relational database.

RELATIONSHIPS

PUBLISHERS
TABLE

NAME	PubID
WROX	1122
A.K.PETERS	9214

TITLES TABLE

PubID	Title	ISBN	Year
1122	Beginning VB6 DB	————	———
1122	Beginning ASP	————	———
1122	Beginning VB6	————	———
1122	Professional ASP	————	———
9214	Code Writing	————	———
9214	System Design	————	———
9214	Controls	————	———
		————	———
		————	———
		————	———

> *Each table is really independent. Relating similar fields makes the relationships. So let's say that one record in the Publishers table has a "5" in the PubID field. Further, assume that ten records in the Titles table have a "5" in the PubID field. We can query the database to say, "Give me all of the records in the Titles table that have a PubID field that contains 5." This way we can retrieve all of the titles that are published by a single publisher. There is no physical link between the tables. There is only the logical relationship.*

To set up relationships, we use MS Access to establish which of the fields we want to define as our **key fields**.

Who's Got the Key?

In the index view of the Titles table, the ISBN field has a picture of a key in the leftmost column:

Indexes: Titles

	Index Name	Field Name	Sort Order
🔑▶	PrimaryKey	ISBN	Ascending
	PubID	PubID	Ascending
	Reference	PubID	Ascending
	Title	Title	Ascending

Index Properties

Primary	Yes
Unique	Yes
Ignore Nulls	No

The name for this index. Each index can use up to 10 fields.

This means that the ISBN field is used as the **primary index** key. A primary index key must always contain a unique value. It really doesn't matter what this value is, as long as it is unique. A primary index consists of one or more fields that uniquely identify each and every record in a table. So even if the name of two books that were published in the same year *could* be the same, the ISBN will *never* be the same. So it makes sense to set this field as the primary key.

The **primary key** field is defined in the 'home' table - which in this case is the Titles table. The field in the related table (the ISBN field in the Title Author table) that the primary key field refers to is called the **foreign key**.

When a field is defined as a primary index key field, each and every entry in this field must be unique. A duplicate value won't be permitted. This ensures that each record in the Titles table will be unique - because the database software ensures that each record *must* have a unique ISBN field.

Although the Titles table uses a text field for the unique primary key, numbers are typically used for this value. This is because the database software can generate them automatically for us as new data is entered and ensure that they are unique. For example, in the Publishers table, the field PubID has a number placed in this field using the AutoNumber field type. Numbers are faster to index and search, and their indexes take up less space as well.

> *We'll find that the Access AutoNumber data type comes in very handy - some programmers even consider them mandatory. If you realize that all fields in your record could possibly contain the same information, you can simply add another field to the table of type AutoNumber and name it something like tieBreaker. When the user adds a new record, the database software automatically adds a unique (sequentially increasing) number to this field. This ensures that each and every record is always unique, at least by the tieBreaker field.*

Orphaned Records

If you are still questioning why we just don't place everything in a single table and be done with it, there is another topic that we should discuss - that of **orphaned** records. A side benefit of separating the tables as we have done is that it helps us ensure the data is **synchronized**. If we didn't use relationships based upon keys, we would have to change each and every Titles record if any information in the publisher's record changed.

Let's say that the A K PETERS company moved to a new headquarters. Also, assume that there were three hundred book title records for the publisher A K PETERS in the Titles table. Now, imagine if we only updated two hundred and ninety of the three hundred records with the new address (humans being what they are, mistakes are made!). Well, if we missed ten of the three hundred records, we could never find those ten records that contained the publisher's old address. These records are **orphaned** - they have no parents. So when we wanted to find all titles published by A K Peters, we would only come up with two hundred and ninety. The other ten would be lost to us. However, with our relational approach, we can do a lot to make sure that this is unlikely to happen by establishing relationships.

Normalizing Our Data

When designing our database tables it is important for us to structure the data in a way that eliminates any unnecessarily duplicated fields. The approach we take must also provide a rapid search path to all necessary information. The process of breaking down our data into separate tables that meet these goals is called **normalization**. Normalization helps us to ensure that we store data with the minimum of duplication. A more complete discussion of the normalization process will be covered in Chapter 9, but it is important to bear these issues in mind as you go about designing your database systems.

Moving On...

We've covered a lot of ground so far and there's been a whole raft full of theory. Let's just recap where we've been.

A Resume of Some Important Terms

- A **database** is a file of **tables**.
- **Tables** consist of organized, related information. Each **table** consists of a collection of **records**.
- Each **record** contains information about a specific entity (such as a publisher or an invoice). The information for each record is contained in **fields**.
- A **field** is the basic unit of a database. It can contain text, numbers, dates, or even photographs.
- In order to organize the information in a database, we use one or more **indexes**. An **index** will keep references to the records in a sorted order so individual records can be quickly retrieved.
- **Primary** and **foreign keys** are defined in each table so that a relationship can be established between tables.

Okay, let's step back a bit from the internal logic of the relational database and see where all this fits into our job - programming VB programs that access databases.

Our Two Vehicles - Access and Visual Basic

The purpose of this book is to show you how to use Visual Basic 6.0 to program database applications. The concepts in this book are based on real world Visual Basic programs that are currently running in hundreds of large companies across the world. The database used for all of the examples in this book is Microsoft Access. This is not only because Access is a powerful and easy to use database, but because if you have Visual Basic 6.0, you already have the ability to use Access. In fact, Access does not even have to be installed on your PC. That is because we have a tool in our Visual Basic arsenal - Visdata - that will permit us to create our own database. Visdata is like a scaled down Access interface that can assist in building an Access database. You can do almost everything with Visdata that you can with Access. So if you have Visual Basic 6.0, you have everything you need to fully use the examples in the book.

The **Biblio.mdb** database was provided by Microsoft to show programmers how to use the various data manipulation techniques and it serves our purposes very nicely because the database comes pre-filled with thousands of records of data. Using this database eliminates the need to create a new database, create tables and fields and then populate it with data. Although we will cover in detail how to create and populate our own databases, by using the ready-made database we can hit the ground running.

Once you understand the concepts we will be covering, you will be able to create and work with just about any database on the market today.

Why Should We Use Access?

The image of an Access database application has evolved from only being useful for simple, specialized desktop applications, to being a standard business productivity tool used by a wide range of professional users.

Every day, more and more developers are building easy-to-use business solutions that reside on users' desktop computers. With each new release of Access, enhancements have made historically difficult database technology accessible to general business users. Whether users are using stand alone PCs, connected by a network or even to the Internet, Access ensures that the benefits of using a database can be quickly realized. We will be using Access database tables for the examples throughout the book. It is a perfect tool to learn how to program databases with Visual Basic 6.0.

Right, let's get started then!

The Biblio.mdb relational database

As we've seen, the **Biblio.mdb** database file contains four tables: Publishers, Titles, Title Author and Author. Access stores all related tables in a single file with an **.mdb** extension. The **.mdb** database is really a container for all of the various tables and the data that they contain. The **.mdb** extension stands for Microsoft Data Base if you haven't already guessed.

We'll create our own copy of **Biblio.mdb** to work on.

Create a New Sub-Directory

We will be modifying, securing, upgrading and doing all sorts of things to the database as we are learning. Therefore, I'd like you to make a separate folder (or sub-directory for you traditionalists) on your machine that can hold a copy of the **Biblio.mdb** database. You can also use the same directory for holding all of the Visual Basic projects we will be developing throughout the book. This way, if you make a mistake or just want to keep the original intact, it will be left untouched. While we're doing this we'll also copy the second sample database that's supplied with VB, the **Nwind.mdb** database. This will come in handy for us later in the book.

Try It Out – Copying the Sample Databases

1 Open up Windows Explorer and click on your hard-drive of choice (I'm using the good old **C:** drive). With the drive icon highlighted, choose File | New | Folder from the menu bar. At the prompt, type **BegDB** (for Beginner's Guide to Database Programming) and press *Enter*.

You should now have a folder with the path name **[*drive letter*]:\BegDB**.

2 Use Windows Explorer to copy, **not move**, the **Biblio.mdb** file into your **BegDB** folder. The original **Biblio.mdb** file is located in the same directory as Visual Basic on your computer. When I installed VB, I used the default directory the automatic set-up program recommended. On my machine, the database is located in **C:\ProgramFiles\DevStudio\VB98\Biblio.mdb**.

3 If you can't find the file, do a file search for **Biblio.mdb** on your local drive. If you still can't find the file, copy it from your VB CD. It is located in **[*drive letter*]\VB\progs**.

4 Copy the **Nwind.mdb** file into your **BegDB** folder.

Now our files are set up for us to use throughout the book.

Having set up the **Biblio.mdb** sample database copy, let's think about how it fits into the broader scheme of things - what are the tools that we need to get at the data and present it to users in a useful manner?

Where Does Our VB Program Come In?

When we design a VB6 database program, you can think of it as having three distinct parts: the **user interface**, the **database engine** and the **data store**. The parts relate to each other as shown:

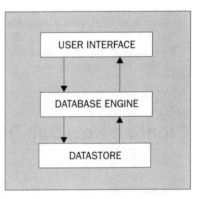

Let's talk about each of these components in turn.

The User Interface

The **user interface** is the part of the program that the user interacts with. We will develop the user interface with Visual Basic. Typically, it contains on-screen **forms** that display data and permit the user to modify that data. Along with these forms are data **modules** and **classes** that contain VB code. In this code, we will request various database services to do things like add, delete and modify records. We will also be performing queries to retrieve specific information from the database to create reports and graphs.

As you can see, we don't really directly access the database (or data store). The database requests we make in VB code are not directed to the physical data store file (which might be a database, a spreadsheet or a text file). We will use VB code to send these commands to the **database engine**. The database engine performs the requested operations on the data store and returns the results to our VB program.

The Database Engine

As we have been discussing, a database such as Access consists of tables that hold information. The database can hold our neatly organized important information. However, the database is really just a file at heart. It has no way to actually manipulate the information. Essentially, the **.mdb** file is inert.

That is where a **database engine** comes in. A database engine is the software program that actually **manages the information in the database**. So when we wish to find all book titles for a certain publisher, we really make the request to the database engine. The engine takes a look at what information we are trying to retrieve and then goes into the database and gets it. It is the database engine that manipulates the information contained in the database. When we learn to program Access, we will really be programming **Jet** - the Access database engine.

Jet – A Specific Database Engine

There are many other database engines around - but Jet is the one that is native to Visual Basic and Access. Jet can also manipulate other engines. So when we learn about Jet, we can readily take that knowledge and apply it to other engines in general. Jet is the brains of the operation.

The Jet database engine is sandwiched between our Visual Basic program and the database files. It can not only read database files, but text files and spreadsheets as well. To us, there is no change in what we do to access any of these various types of files.

To the Visual Basic programmer, the same programming techniques are used for handling any of the formats supported by Jet. You will see as we progress through the book that Jet does all of the heavy lifting for us. In case we don't happen to have Access on our machine, we will see how to create databases using both Visual Basic code and the VisData program.

DLLs – The Fuel Inside the Jet Engine

The Jet database engine is not a single program, but a group of **dynamic link library** (**DLL**) files. What are DLLs? Well, they are files that are linked to your program as it runs - i.e. **dynamically**. This is unlike the static linked libraries in the C language that are included in each and every program. Just think if you had four programs on your PC that needed to work with an Access

.mdb database. If the files were *statically* linked, the entire Jet engine suite of files would need to be incorporated into each of your four programs. Before Windows arrived on the scene that's exactly how things were done. Now, however, the **.dll**s are on disk and called as necessary by whatever programs need them. Any enhancements to Jet are placed in newer **.dll**s and any program that uses them reaps the benefits without having to change the program itself.

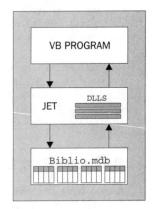

The Jet **.dll** files are automatically linked to your Visual Basic program at run time. Jet does the real work of translating our program's requests into the actual physical operations on our Access **.mdb** database or other data store.

The beauty of this separation of duties is that we can use the same code and techniques when communicating with Jet whether we operate on a database, spreadsheet or text file. Jet handles the rest - reading data and writing to the data store. Jet will also perform all the behind the scenes housekeeping tasks such as indexing the tables, security, locking and much more. We will also be using Jet's query processor that will accept our requests to retrieve data. We can request records from the database using a **Structured Query Language (SQL)** query. The SQL query will ask Jet to retrieve specific records from our database. Jet then uses a result processor to return the result of our query back to our Visual Basic program. We'll look at SQL in depth as we progress through the book.

> *Jet experts like to say that we are removed a level of abstraction from the database. For example, when driving a car, we use the interface of a steering wheel, brake and gas pedals. We don't know or care about the spark plugs firing or the gas injected into the engine. We just need to know how to drive. We are removed a level of abstraction from the details. The car is abstracted into a steering wheel and pedals. Likewise, our dealings with the database are abstracted into objects that have methods and properties. We can use a few Jet commands and concern ourselves with our Visual Basic application. We allow Jet to handle the nitty-gritty details of managing the database.*

Jet is Self-Contained

We will be using the Jet engine to interface between the data stored in our tables and our Visual Basic applications. What this means to developers is that your users do not have to have Access 7.0 loaded on their PCs. This is excellent news! Just think, if you are going to distribute 1,000 copies of your application to platforms all around the world, you can be sure that your software has everything needed to run properly. Our programs will be **self-contained**. We distribute all of the Jet and Visual Basic files in our install program. So by self-contained we mean that there is no additional software that needs to be installed on the host PC other than our files. Now, what could be easier? In fact, your users don't need to know or care about what database you are using. All of this is transparent to them.

Now, what does Jet act on?

The Data Store

The **data store** is the physical file or files on your hard drive or across the globe that contain the database tables themselves. We will be using Access **.mdb** files, since these are native to Visual Basic. If we need to communicate with another database such as Paradox, the data store might be a directory containing files with **.db** or other extensions. Your Visual Basic applications might even require access to data stored in several different database files and formats at one time. No problem. However, it's interesting to note that no matter what type of data store you are using, it is essentially **passive**. The data store contains the data, but doesn't *do* anything to it.

Getting Our Feet Wet

Okay, we've seen that we need a data store, a database engine and a user interface to build our VB database programs. To try and relate all this theory to the nuts and bolts of our database, let's revisit our sample database and get a flavor of the real data we'll be dealing with in **Biblio.mdb**.

Tables, Records and Fields in Biblio.mdb

Let's take another quick peek at what the tables contain by looking at the actual data stored in them. I've used Access to display the tables. Note that these are just screen shots so all of the fields in the tables might not be displayed, but you can get a good sense of what the tables look like.

The Publishers Table

Notice the PubID field on the far left. They just seem to contain numbers, which are in no particular order - this is because defining this field as the AutoNumber data type has generated them. The PubID is the primary key for this table and determines that this field must be unique for every record (row).

In more sophisticated tables, a primary key can consist of more than one column. This is called a **compound primary key**. In this case, duplicate values are allowed in one column, but each combination of values from all the columns defined in the primary key must be unique. If you define a compound key, the order of columns in the primary key must match the order of columns of the foreign key.

For our relationship to work, we must define a foreign key in another table. The foreign key need not contain unique values. So we might want to find all of the titles published by the A K Peters Company. Its primary key contains the unique number 624. However in the Titles table, the foreign key field is also called PubID but these do not contain unique values. So we can round up all records in the Titles table that have a value in the PubID field of 624.

The Authors Table

Although we have 6246 records in this table, it appears that most of the Year Born fields are empty. When there is no data in a field, databases use a special **NULL** value to signify that there is **no data present**. We will be discussing NULL in detail later on, but NULL does not mean an empty string. It really means **no data**.

The Au_ID is the primary key for the Authors table. Each author is unique, so the primary key identifies a single author. We can use this primary key field to index into the foreign Au_ID field in the Title Author table. This will permit us to find all books written by an individual author.

The Title Author Table

If we were interested in finding all books written by author 7576, we would need to create a **multi-table relational search** that pulled in data fields from a number of tables, each of which held information that was related to the mysterious 7576. Let's see how that might be done.

Building a Relationship

Access makes finding all books by author 7576 easy. We can draw the tables on the screen and then check the fields we wish to be displayed (don't worry about the details of doing this with Access - what we're interested in here are the *principles* involved). Notice that in the Select Query screen below the primary Au_ID key in the Authors table is shown as being related to the foreign Au_ID key in the Title Author table.

Using the intermediary Title Author table that links a unique Au_ID to an ISBN, all of the records in the Title Author table will be retrieved by matching the unique ISBN field to the ISBN field in the Titles table. So here we are performing a multi-table relational search. In our search criterion boxes at the bottom of the Select Query screen, we add the criteria of 7576 for the value of the primary key in the Authors table.

31

When we process the query, Jet takes our command, optimizes it and dives into the database to get the information we asked for. Even though the Authors table contains over 6,000 records, the Authors Title table contains over 16,000 records and the Titles table contains over 8,000 records, the Jet engine isolates and returns the records we are looking for in a fraction of a second.

Au_ID	Author	Title
7576	De Pace, M.	dBASE III : A Practical Guide
7576	De Pace, M.	The dBASE Programming Language
7576	De Pace, M.	dBASE III : A Practical Guide to Professional
7576	De Pace, M.	dBASE on a Network

Record: 1 of 4

How Does It Do That?

The mechanism behind getting the information we need is **Structured Query Language (SQL)**. We will be covering SQL in depth in Chapter 8 but if you have never used it before, here is the optimized SQL query that Jet built for us. Based on our request, Jet took the requirements and built this query that retrieves just the four relevant records out of thousands:

```
SELECT Authors.Au_ID, Authors.Author, Titles.Title
FROM Titles INNER JOIN [Authors INNER JOIN [Title Author] ON
Authors.Au_ID = [Title Author].Au_ID) ON Titles.ISBN = [Title
Author].ISBN;
```

Later on, we will show how to write dynamic SQL statements in Visual Basic. A user might have a form that displays all of the authors, for example. When an author is selected, we insert the relevant information right into an SQL query and retrieve the information the user wants. So we use VB code to build a SQL query that uses Jet to access the database.

Throughout the book we'll be revisiting these tables and using the data in them. To close up this chapter, let's step back from the nitty-gritty detail again for a moment and think about broader data access trends and techniques - these are considerations that will affect how we code our programs and what tools we use as the years roll by.

The Way(s) Ahead...

We live in a changing world and as you'll be aware, the computing world changes more rapidly than most other industries. So we need to think about the technologies that are available to us now and the ones that are up coming. This means having an overview of existing and emergent data access technologies. In our context this means **DAO** and the more recent **ADO** technologies.

DAO or ADO?

In order to program Jet and get at our data, we will use **Data Access Objects (DAO)**. DAO is a model that we can tap into for doing just about anything with the database. As we proceed through the book, we will cover the established DAO methods of accessing data. Then we will progress to the new and exciting **ActiveX Data Objects (ADO)** approach. Microsoft's vision for the future is ADO so you can be sure that the world will increasingly be accessing data using ADO.

However, DAO is *currently* the most widespread method of desktop data access and has the largest installed base of desktop database access. The pool of talented DAO programmers is enormous, but DAO's days as a cutting edge technology are probably numbered.

ADO is the successor to DAO. ADO 'flattens' the object model used by DAO. This means that it contains fewer objects and more properties, methods and events. Much of the functionality contained in DAO was consolidated into single objects, making for a much simpler object model. Because of this some DAO programmers might initially find it difficult to find the appropriate ADO object, collection, property, method or event. It should also be noted that ADO currently doesn't support all of DAO's functionality.

So we are lucky to find ourselves at an exciting turning point as Visual Basic programmers. The question in front of us is: do we use the tried and true, mature, solid and robust DAO methodology? Or do we say that it's clear that ADO is the wave of the future so we might as well write our applications for the future and ride that wave?

Actually, this is not as difficult a question as you might imagine - there are ways through it.

Beyond the DAO/ADO Conundrum

If you are trying to create a desktop solution, then the traditional DAO approach is the way to go. After all, Microsoft just updated DAO from version 3.50 that was bundled with Visual Basic 5.0 to version 3.51 that is bundled into Visual Basic 6.0. This DAO upgrade really just includes some optimizations and no really new functionality. However, it shows that DAO is far from gone and Microsoft's commitment to it suggests that it will be with us for years to come.

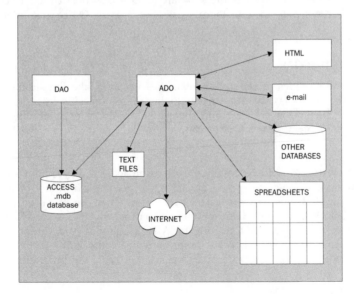

Some Pros and Cons of DAO and ADO

So there are some good reasons for sticking with DAO:

▶ If you are modifying an existing DAO application, stay with a proven winner.

▶ If you are deploying a small, desktop solution or one that runs on a local server, you can't go wrong with DAO.

▶ It's probably too early in the evolution of ADO to migrate most DAO to ADO right now, because ADO doesn't currently support users, groups and so on. If database security is an issue, stick with DAO for the time being.

▶ Microsoft Access itself uses the Jet engine and DAO, and Access is distributed with the hugely successful Microsoft Office Suite, so the market isn't going to disappear overnight.

The DAO **data control** (which links our VB programs quickly and easily to data in databases) is an intrinsic control - it's built into the language of Visual Basic 6.0.

Clearly, DAO is still alive and kicking and will be around for several years. The DAO tools have been included with VB 6.0 so they can continue to be used for desktop applications.

On the other hand, there are some situations where ADO would be your preferred route:

▶ If your project is just in the design-state and you will be deploying data over the Internet or using a data source other than Access, then you probably want to consider ADO.

▶ ADO is actually easier to user than DAO.

▶ ADO is more powerful than DAO and permits easy access to many more data sources.

▶ If you are developing using DAO for client-server applications and don't rely on the Jet database engine, then you can probably migrate to ADO now.

▶ Starting with VB 6.0, ADO is the standard data access object model across Microsoft tools - these not only include Visual Basic, but Access, Office and Internet Information Server.

Enjoying the Complexity

I know presenting both sides of the argument makes it sound like I'm sitting on the fence, but it reflects the way the world is. There are technologies co-existing side by side, there are existing applications whose lifetime is not over and there is a variety of programming solutions that are available for every problem. Our job is to choose the right solution and the best tools to implement it.

Confused? Don't worry! We will be covering both approaches and providing suggestions on which method is better for whatever you are trying to accomplish. Many of the examples in the book are desktop applications so we use DAO for those. Then we move on to developing Intra/ Internet applications. We will use ADO for these - that is why it was developed in the first place. When you have learned DAO, moving to ADO is simple. And I mean *simple*. Most of the methods are the same and you will feel at home moving to the ADO model, besides being comfortable with both approaches will make you a better database programmer.

Choosing Your Route and Reusability

Once you move to ADO, you will probably want to stick with it from then on. Developers tend to create modules of code and stick them in repositories for easy reuse as they move on to other projects. So using DAO and ADO in different projects would just make this reuse a bit more difficult.

The Good News Again

When you learn how to write programs that can communicate with the Access database, you will have the knowledge to talk with any type of data source; the knowledge gained will give you a firm foundation to build on.

Everything you learn to program with Access is directly applicable to the newer data access approach that uses ADO. With ADO, it is a straight shot to start programming user-friendly web applications using **Active Server Pages (ASP)** for use on your corporate Intranet or the Internet. Although we will stick with Access databases for the examples in this book (because everyone with Visual Basic 6.0 can get started immediately) the knowledge you gain here will let you start working with SQL Server, Oracle or just about any other data source once you complete this book. Read on!

Summary

We have covered a lot of ground in this chapter and I know that you didn't get your fingers on the keyboard too much. Relax. It was important to cover all this theoretical material; I wanted to give you an overview of databases and Jet. There is a saying that racecar drivers don't have to know how an engine works, but all the best drivers do. I think it's important to have a fundamental understanding of what's going on under the hood before we begin, and the material we've covered will give us a good background for the detailed work that we'll do later.

Here's a reminder of what we did in this chapter:

▶ We looked at what a database is, and at some of the principles of data storage and retrieval

▶ We learned the basics about **relational databases**

▶ We discussed the relationship between VB, the **database engine**, and the database

Take-Home Points

One more time, here is a list of the important terms we came across in this chapter:

▶ A database consists of one or more tables that hold related information

▶ A table consists of several records

▶ A record consists of fields of information

▶ A large table is broken down (normalized) into smaller tables to reduce replicated information

▶ Primary and foreign keys are used to relate the various tables

▶ Jet is the database engine that (transparently) handles our interaction with the database

▶ Jet can talk not only to databases, but spreadsheets and text files

▶ Visual Basic uses Data Access Objects (DAO) to program Jet

▶ ActiveX Data Objects (ADO) is the successor to DAO

The Next Step

So I guess you can't wait to start programming? I understand that, so in the next chapter we'll start looking at how we can use VB to hook up our user interface to the data store quickly and simply, using part of the new **ADO** technology. Let's go.

Exercises

1   In a relational database what are tables, records and fields?

2   What is a database engine? What is a data store?

3   What is a primary key? What is a foreign key? What is their relationship?

4   What is a database schema? Why is it useful?

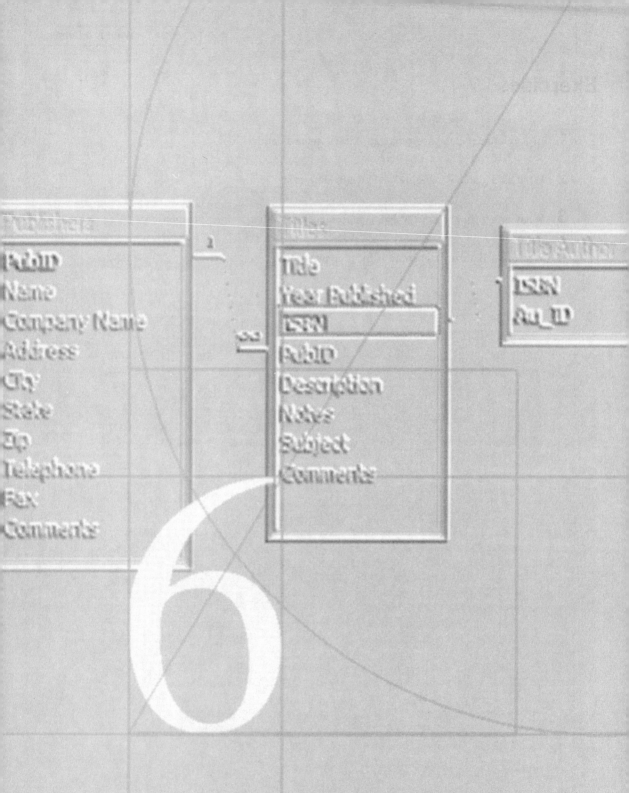

Meet the ActiveX Data Objects (ADO) Data Wizard

In this chapter we're going to give you a sneak preview of some of the things that you can do with ADO to display data from a database. We're doing this to give you a taste of how the data in **Biblio.mdb** looks, to demonstrate how easy data access can be, and to show off some of the formatting tools available in ADO. When we've looked at these, we're going to get our hands nice and oily by really getting under the hood of VB/database interactions for a few chapters. This way, we can return to ADO later in the book and set about using it in an informed and sophisticated way.

Here's what we'll cover in this chapter (we'll explain all the terms as we go along):

- Using the ADO **data control** to access data
- Generating **recordsets**
- Using the **Data Form Wizard** to build data access forms of different species
- Sorting data, and ASCII codes

We are going to hit the ground running by immediately creating a program that can access our **Biblio.mdb** database. The **ADO data control** provided with Visual Basic can automatically connect our program to a database. We can add this control to our VB forms, hook it up to database tables and show the user the data on a form. The quickest and easiest way to accomplish this is to use the **VB Data Form Wizard**. This handy little add-in tool will not only link a database to our program, but it will create a form, add labels, and text boxes to display the data. Best of all, we will do this *without* writing a single line of code.

Let's begin by getting to know the **data control**.

What is the ADO Data Control?

The **ADO data control** is a component that we can bolt on to our VB applications to quickly and easily connect our VB program to a database. We can add this control to our VB forms, hook it up to a database, and display the data on the form in a variety of ways by using other controls that we bind to the data control. One swift and simple way to do this is to use the VB **Data Form Wizard**. The ADO Data Control lies at the heart of the magic the wizard performs.

As database developers using VB 6.0, we suffer from an embarrassment of riches. By that I mean that we have several controls that are included with VB 6.0 that allow quick and painless access to just about any data source. The premier control is the ADO **data control**. With this tool you can perform most data access operations without writing any code at all. The data control provides access to data stored in databases that enables you to move from record to record as well as display and manipulate data.

The new ADO data control has the advantage of being a graphic control. It has VCR-like buttons, (First Record, Previous Record, Next Record and Last Record) and an easy-to-use interface that allows you to create database applications with no coding required.

The Recordset

Once the data control is connected to a database, one of the many data-aware controls (also known as **bound** controls) are used to display the information in a database. Based on the information we give to Jet about the data that we want to see, the database engine builds a **recordset** for us. The recordset is our working version of the underlying data in the tables. However, as a user, it appears that we are working directly with the data in the database and we can amend, delete or add data to the database through our interaction with the recordset.

In other words, a data-aware control provides access to a specific field or fields in a database record through the ADO data control. Then, when the user clicks one of the VCR-like buttons on the ADO data control, it moves from one record to the next. All of the bound controls connected to the ADO data control change to display data from fields in the current record. Not only that, but when the user changes data in a bound control and then moves to a different record using the VCR controls, the changes are saved in the data source - automatically and with no code required.

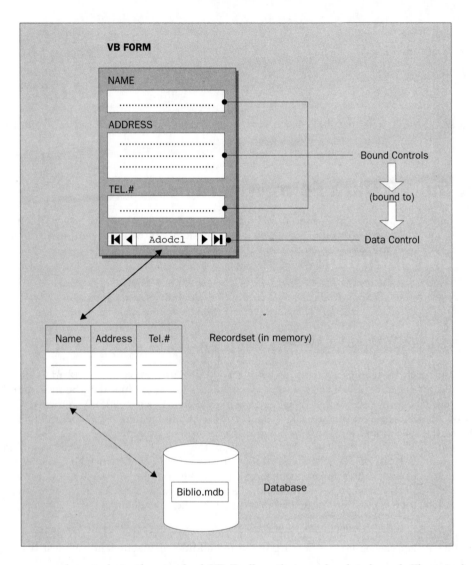

There are several controls in the standard VB Toolbox that can be data-bound. These include the TextBox, CheckBox, ComboBox, Image, Label, ListBox and PictureBox controls. Not only that, VB includes several additional data-bound ActiveX controls that can be data bound. The following data-bound ActiveX Controls are shipped with all versions of VB 6.0:

- DataList
- DataCombo
- DataGrid
- Microsoft FlexGrid
- Hierarchical FlexGrid
- Rich TextBox

> ◗ Microsoft Chart
>
> ◗ DateTimePicker
>
> ◗ ImageCombo
>
> ◗ MonthView

There are also hundreds of additional bound controls that can be purchased from third-party vendors.

Meet the VB Data Form Wizard

As promised, we will use the Data Form Wizard to set up everything we need to connect to a database and display the records. However, Visual Basic 6.0 provides several other Wizards that assist in the more mundane tasks of Visual Basic programming.

> *We have been using the term Wizard quite a bit. In general, Wizards provide easy-to-use wrappers for automating tasks, from the essentially simple but tedious to the sophisticated and complex. There are Wizards that automate everything from creating set-up programs for distributing our programs to constructing an entire application framework or skeleton program.*

The Data Wizard is used in conjunction with the ADO data control. The Wizard is designed to automatically generate Visual Basic forms as containers for individual data bound controls such as the text box. It is also used to manage information that is automatically retrieved from the database. Amazingly, you can use the Data Form Wizard to create single table query that manages the data from a single table on a single form. For example, we may wish to see all of the records in the Publishers table. We can instruct the wizard to open this table and simply select the fields to be displayed. If you need to display fields from two tables, the Wizard provides master/detail type forms to manage these more complex one-to-many data relationships. Alternatively, if you need to see several records at once, grid (datasheet) forms are used to manage data from a control. We will examine each of these in detail.

The Data Form Wizard is known as an **add-in**. This means that it is not part of the VB environment, but can be hooked in to provide the additional functionality we just discussed.

What is an Add-In?

The Visual Basic **Integrated Development Environment (IDE)** comes pre-packed with a set level of functionality. Add-ins are tools that extend the VB 6.0 IDE to make it even more powerful. As you have probably guessed, add-ins are *added-in* to the VB 6.0 IDE. In their most elementary form, add-ins can help the programmer with tedious or repetitive tasks. In more sophisticated incarnations, add-ins can provide assistance in generating forms or even entire application frameworks. For example, VB 6.0 even contains the Application Wizard that walks the user through creating an entire framework for a new program. When finished, a framework, or skeleton of the program is built. Microsoft and other party developers have created various add-ins you can use to help in the development of your software applications.

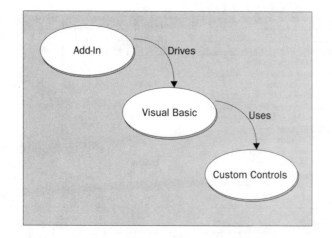

A **Wizard** is a special type of add-in. Typically the Wizard leads a programmer step-by-step through a task, such as building a data form. A Wizard consists of a number of forms, one for each step in the process of what the user is trying to accomplish. Each form contains an image in the upper-left corner and a label to the right of the image that typically contains instructions. While using the Data Form Wizard, we will be walked through the process of building a form that provides a connection to a database and bound controls that display the underlying records. The Data Form Wizard, included with the Professional and Enterprise Editions, operates within VB by creating forms to be used with databases. The Wizard will place custom controls on those forms and even write some rudimentary code to perform simple tasks.

Try It Out - Using the Add-In Manager

1 Let's fire up Visual Basic and start a new Standard EXE project to put the Data Form Wizard through its paces. Before the Wizard can be run, it must be added to our IDE. To link the Wizard to our IDE, click Add-Ins from the main VB menu and then select Add-In Manager.

2 Clicking Add-In Manager will bring up the Add-In Manager form, which displays all of the available add-ins. These were loaded on your hard drive when Visual Basic was installed. Make sure that the VB 6 Data Form Wizard is selected. Then check the Loaded/Unloaded check box. This will make the Wizard available from the drop-down list of add-ins available. If you wish this Wizard to be available always when you start up VB, then also check Load on Startup.

3 Click on OK; the Data Form Wizard will now show up as a menu choice on the drop-down menu when you choose Add-Ins from VB's main menu.

Now we're ready to create our first database program.

Try It Out - Using the Data Form Wizard

1 Before we start, create a new sub-directory in your **BegDB** folder called:

[*Drive letter*]:\BegDB\Chapter2

This way when we are asked to save our forms and project, we can just save the examples in this sub-directory. After you have created the directory, return to VB. Select Add-Ins from the toolbar and then choose Data Form Wizard. The Introduction screen is presented. Introduce yourself to the Wizard.

In order to use the Data Form Wizard, you must already have a project running or VB will let us know it's not happy:

2   Keep the (None) selection - in fact we have no choice if this is the first time you have run this Wizard. If you used the Wizard before and saved your choices, this option allows you to choose a wizard profile from the list of previously saved profiles. Since we have never run the Wizard before, there are no selections to choose from.

A wizard profile (`.rwp`) is a file that contains the settings you chose and saved when you previously ran the Data Form Wizard. Profiles can be useful if you decide to create multiple applications with the same overall look. This way you do not have to remember the settings you selected in the past and then select the same options every time you create an application. If you develop several programs that have data access, using saved profiles can really speed up your work.

Later, when you save your settings in profile files, you can choose from all previously run Wizard sessions that were saved. An example would look like this. Of course, you can give your named settings anything that makes sense.

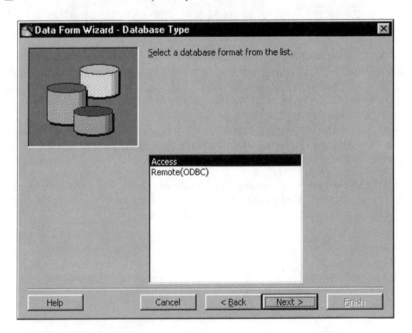

3 Press Next > to continue on our journey.

4 The data control, which is at the heart and soul of the Wizard, is capable of automatically connecting to the following databases:

▶ **Access** - You can connect to any version of the Microsoft Access **.mdb** (Jet) database.

▶ **Remote (ODBC)** - ODBC stands for **Open Database Connectivity**, which is an interface that lets Windows applications talk easily to a variety of database types. You can connect to any ODBC-compliant database driver. For example, if you need to connect to a SQL Server or Oracle database, you can use a driver file that will make the connection for you. We will be covering ODBC later on in the book. For now, just keep in mind that the Data Form Wizard can work with just about any database you might need to connect to.

We will be using Access 7.0 database files throughout the book. Access is the default choice and native to Visual Basic, so please select it. Then press Next > to move on.

FYI | While using the Wizard, you can click the < Back button to return to a previous screen if you need to make changes.

5 We are now presented with the Database options. Here we tell the Wizard which database file we will be using. We'll (surprise!) select the **Biblio.mdb** file in your **[*Drive letter*]:\BegDB** sub-directory.

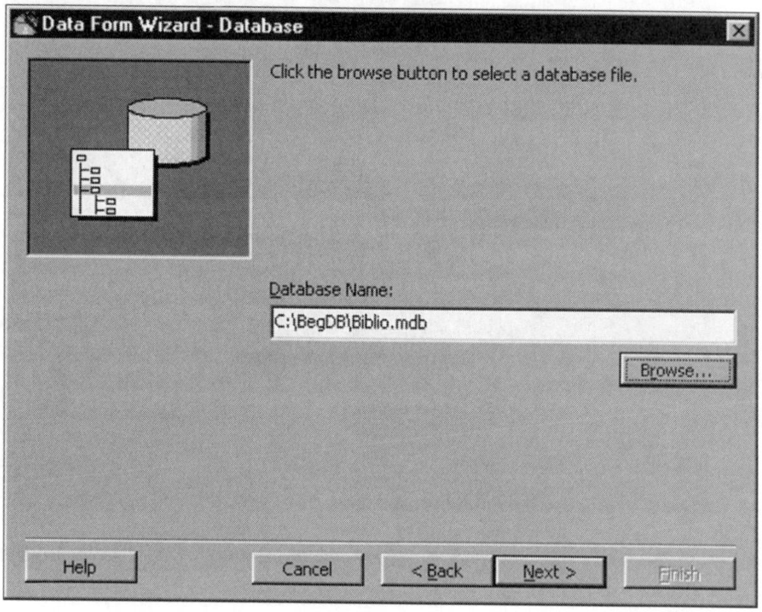

Data Form Wizard - Database

Click the browse button to select a database file.

Database Name:

C:\BegDB\Biblio.mdb

Browse...

| Help | | Cancel | < Back | Next > | Finish |

Just to make life a bit easier, clicking the B̲rowse button will permit you to navigate your hard drive and find the file you want. I prefer a few mouse clicks instead of typing. This approach ensures there will be no typos. Since we selected Access in the previous screen, click on the B̲rowse button and find the **Biblio.mdb** file from your **[Drive letter]:\BegDB** sub-directory. Double-click the database and then click N̲ext > to continue.

The next Wizard frame is displayed.

6 First, provide a name for the new form that the Wizard will create for us. Call the new form frmFirst.

Next, the Wizard provides us a list of Form Layout options on how we might wish the form to display our data:

▶ Single Record - Here the form will only display one record at a time. This is the default.

▶ Grid (Datasheet) - This option will insert the DataGrid control on our form to display selected fields in the Grid.

▶ Master/Detail - This option is a bit more sophisticated. The Wizard will display a **master** record source as well as linking a **detail** record source. For example, we may wish to show all titles published by each publisher. The master record would be each individual record from the Publishers table. When a publisher is selected, all of the titles published by this company would be displayed in as the detail records. As is typical in these layouts, the master record source will display a single record and the detail record source will show all child records in a Grid (Datasheet) format. When you change the master record source row, all of the data in the detail record source automatically changes. Of course, this will display all of the child records for the new master record.

▶ MS HFlexGrid - Here we tell the wizard to create a form that displays tabular data.

▶ MS Chart - The wizard will display a form that shows the data in a chart format.

The three Binding Type options allow you to choose from an ADO Data Control, ADO Code or data Class to access the specified data.

▶ ADO Data Control - The Wizard will use the ADO Data Control to access the specified data. We want the power of the control to manage the data for us.

▶ ADO Code - Here ADO code is used to access the specified data. The Wizard will write ADO code for us. While this is helpful when you understand how to write ADO code later on, we just want the Wizard to do it all for us.

▶ Class - This option uses data classes to access the specified data. The Wizard will use what is known as Object Oriented Programming. This selection takes the ADO code and places it in a special file called a class.

Don't worry if these choices look a bit like Klingon right now. We will walk through each of the options and see what they mean. For now, keep the default choices of Single Record and ADO Data Control.

7 Press <u>N</u>ext > to look at the Record Source screen. This tells the Wizard which field(s) to retrieve from the database name we selected two screens back.

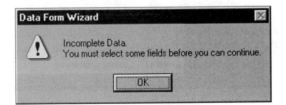

Since we selected the **Biblio.mdb** database, all of the tables in this database are available in the drop-down <u>R</u>ecord Source box. We are not concerned with any tables that begin with MSys - these are **Access system tables** (the system tables are used to store information about the structure of the various database attributes). We don't want to work with any of these.

Select Publishers as the <u>R</u>ecord Source.

When a table is selected into the <u>R</u>ecord Source list box, all of the fields in that table are listed in the <u>A</u>vailable Fields box. You can select any or all of these fields for the Wizard to display. If you attempt to press <u>N</u>ext > without selecting any fields, the Wizard will let you know that this is not a good idea.

Nobody likes seeing message with warning triangles on them - they make us all feel bad. So let's select some data fields.

8 This is an important screen. Notice how much information is provided to us in a single form. This form is a good example of graphically providing a lot of information to the user in a logical, obvious and well laid out manner. Notice that we have things like a dynamic graphic that visually shows us what is happening. This screen also shows all available fields as well as the ones we selected. They are mutually exclusive. Once we pick an available field, it jumps to the Selected Fields list box. If we happen to make a mistake in selecting the fields, the arrow keys permit us to modify our selection. Not only that, we can choose from the selected fields and determine which of those the results should be sorted on. Take a minute just to look at the screen and how it is laid out.

Let's select all of the fields by pressing ▶▶. Again, note how these four buttons convey a lot of information to the user graphically. If you choose ▶. Then the highlighted field is moved to the Selected Fields list box. Likewise, the ◀ removes the highlighted field from the Selected Fields to the Available Fields. Of course, ◀◀ removes all fields in the Selected Fields list box.

We can rearrange the order that the fields will ultimately be displayed in the finished form. Simply highlight any field in the Selected Fields list box then by pressing the up or down button to the right of the list box, the highlighted field will be moved up or down in the order it will be displayed on the finished form. The Wizard will add a bound text box and title to the finished form for each field we select here. The topmost field in the Selected Fields listbox will be the one displayed first.

> *When you look at a user interface on any commercial software program from now on, take a minute to reflect on its design and layout. While there are several books available on how to correctly display buttons and other controls, each individual application has a need for a different configuration of controls. So while standards manuals can tell us the correct sizes and captions, it is impossible to predict how to exactly lay out an interface for each specific program. It is by constantly examining interfaces of successful software that you can get a good sense of what works. This way you can take a best of breed solution and incorporate those ideas into your programs. Again, good-quality commercial software is the best learning ground for gathering ideas to apply.*

9   As we discussed earlier, each record in a table is a row and each field is a column. The Wizard will sort the data by any column (i.e. field) we want. Select the Company Name field in the Column to Sort By combo box. This will present the information sorted by the Company Name in alphabetical order. You may also have noticed that the Finish button is now enabled. In all Wizards, the Finish button is disabled until there is enough information for the Wizard to complete the task at hand. Since the Wizard has enough information, we could select Finish now. However, let's move on to see all the options the Wizard provides for us. Press Next > to see the controls that the Wizard can automatically add for us.

10   When our data is displayed, it would be nice to provide the user with buttons to easily manipulate the current record. Any of the buttons selected by checking the boxes will be displayed on the final product, not the Wizard. The default is to include all buttons:

▶   Add Button - places an Add button on the finished form with code to add new records to the database. Add clears all fields and adds a new record to the database.

▶   Update Button - places an Update button on the form with code to update data from the database. Update stores any changes made to the data entry fields in the database.

▶ <u>D</u>elete Button - places a Delete button on the form with code to delete records from the database. Delete deletes the current record.

▶ <u>R</u>efresh Button - places a Refresh button on the form with code to refresh data from the database. Refresh causes the query to re-execute. It is used primarily in multi-user applications.

▶ <u>C</u>lose Button - places a Close button on the form with code to close your form. Close will close the form and unload it.

Notice that the <u>S</u>how Data Control check box is both on and disabled. That is because the data control **must** be shown on our form so that we can navigate through the recordset. Therefore, we can't deselect it. Press <u>N</u>ext > to move on.

11 Remember when we were asked if we wanted to retrieve an existing profile when we started the Wizard? Well, here is where we save our work. If you select the ellipsis, a Save Profile dialog box is displayed. We can simply enter a name in the File <u>n</u>ame box and the profile will be saved with a **.rwp** extension.

Since we are just learning about the Wizard, we won't save our profile just now - so click Cancel on the Save Profile dialog box.

There will certainly be things we will do differently once we learn more about database programming. By not saving our work, the Wizard will not remember the settings and fields we just selected. It will just go ahead and create our form. When we save the profile, however, the Wizard remembers all of the selections make in the session. This way you can easily either recreate the form, or use the profile as a template and go back to tweak some portion of the Wizard's settings. For example, if we saved the profile and wanted to remove a field from the final product, we just reload the profile and step through the frames until we reach the Selected Fields list box. There we simply deselect the field we don't want. This saves us all of the steps up until that point and makes our life a bit easier.

12 That's it! Press Finish on the Finished! form. Let's see what the Wizard can do for us.

You will hear a flurry of disk activity while the Wizard does our bidding. The Wizard will follow our commands and automatically create a new data access form! Of course, the Wizard is doing quite a bit of work, so this process may take several seconds (or longer, depending on the specification of the machine). Take a look at the result.

The Final Product in Design Mode

Truly amazing! The Wizard created a form for us with a text box for each field and a command button for each function that we selected. Not only that, but the names for each of the fields we selected are placed in labels to serve as titles.

If we had changed the order of the fields a while ago on the Record Source screen, the Wizard would have presented the fields in the new order you selected. Since we didn't change the order, the Wizard placed the fields in the default order. You might wish to save the form now.

One of the things you might notice right away, is that while the Wizard did the hard work underneath, the user interface could use a bit of a touch up. For example, the field sizes are all the same size. Also, all of the fields are stacked on top of each other. We might want the State and Zip to be next to each other, for example. In addition, not only are the labels too big, but the Wizard takes the field name for the label. On a finished product, we would probably want Publisher's ID instead of PubID. However, these are just cosmetic changes and we can clean them up in a few minutes. Overall, the Wizard is a great time saver but - thank goodness - will never replace the programmer.

Whenever we start a new project, a default form is created and set as the startup form. VB always automatically adds a new form, called Form1, to a new project and sets it as the startup form. Since the Wizard created another form for us - frmFirst - be sure to set this as the Startup Object. We want our new, Data Wizard-generated form to be the one that starts up when our program is run. Here's how to do it:

From the main VB menu, select Project - Project1 Properties and select the General tab.

Make sure that frmFirst is entered in the Startup Object box, select OK and then press *F5* to run your newly created database program. If you create another form with the Wizard in the same project, you will have to change the startup object to this new form. Of course, VB knows all of the forms that are in your project, so you can just click the form you wish to run as startup from here.

The Final Product at Run-Time

Not too bad. I think you will agree that the Wizard does indeed have magical powers. Notice that the first record displayed is the first publisher in alphabetical order in the Publishers table of the **Biblio.mdb** database. Remember that we selected the recordset to be ordered by the Company Name field? The Wizard remembered and used this field to do our bidding. If you changed the order of any of the fields, the Wizard would have displayed them in the order you choose.

Let's take a quick tour of what is on the screen. We have a data control at the bottom of the screen. This ADO data control is connected to the **Biblio.mdb** database. Above that, we have four command buttons that permit the user to modify the underlying record in the database. Above that, we have we have ten labels and ten textboxes. The textboxes are bound to the ADO data control. Now when the program starts, the ADO data control connects to the database and grabs the first record. The data in the fields of that record are displayed in the bound text boxes.

> *VB has a great reputation as a prototyping tool. When a developer wishes to get something up and running quickly so a project can be visualized, the Wizard can really help out. Of course what the Wizard delivers needs to be modified as we discussed earlier, but we now have something to critique and so far, no code has been required.*

Take a look at the PubID number for the first record - 624. We will be looking at indexes and keys later on. If we had sorted by the PubID field, the A K PETERS entry would be at position 624 instead of 1. However, we asked the Wizard to sort by Company Name, so this is first alphabetically. Later in the book we will see how we can use SQL commands to sort the returned records in any way we might need them.

> *Caution: This is an active recordset. If you change or add anything in any of the fields and either press Update or move to another record with the VCR-like data control then your new changes will be committed to the database.*

Navigating the Recordset

As we mentioned, the ADO data control is the brains behind this program. We can use the VCR buttons to move between records.

When the ADO data control connects to a database, it retrieves a recordset. A recordset is quite simply, a set of records. Each recordset consists of one or more records. Each record consists of fields. So when we click on one of the navigation buttons, we move about the recordset record by record. Only one record can be current at any time.

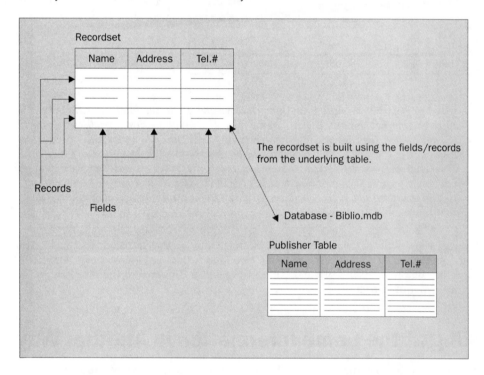

The control provides excellent visual cues for navigating the Publishers table. The |◀ brings us to the first record and the ▶| brings us to the last record in the recordset. Pressing the ◀ button moves us backwards a single record, while the ▶ moves us forward one record at a time. Go ahead and press the ▶| to go to the last record in the recordset. Almost instantly, we traverse over 700 records to arrive at the last one.

We can see that indeed, the Publishers table is sorted in alphabetical order by Company Name. The last publisher is ZILOG. Also, notice that the data control tells us how many records are in the Publishers table. Go ahead and spend a few minutes navigating through the Publishers table. Delete and add a record or two just to test out the program.

> *Caution! You will actually be making changes directly to the Publishers table through your new program. Think of the form as a window, through which we can see and change the contents of our underlying table. That is why we want to operate on a copy of the database. Go ahead and enter something in the Comments field. Then click the previous button to move to another record. This will save any changes made to a record. Then move back, using the next button. The comments you added to this record will be there. They were written to the database when you moved off that record.*

Now you know why we want to only work on a copy of the **Biblio.mdb** table. You will be modifying the tables as you test programs throughout the book. If you ever want to start with a fresh table, simply copy the original table from the **VB** directory to the **[Drive letter]:\BegDB** directory.

Looking at the Same Information in Another Way

When we were commanding the Wizard, we told it to create a Single Record form. There were several other choices available to us. The next choice was a Grid (Datasheet) format. Let's see what the result would be if we selected this. We'll rerun the Wizard and create a form that includes a Grid (Datasheet) format.

Try It Out - The Grid (Datasheet) Format

We are going to add another form to our project. This time, we will create a Grid form to permit the user to look at several records at once.

1 Repeat steps 1 through 6 of the previous Try It Out (**Using the Data Form Wizard**), this time name the form frmGrid (in step 6). In the same step, select Grid (Datasheet) as the form layout.

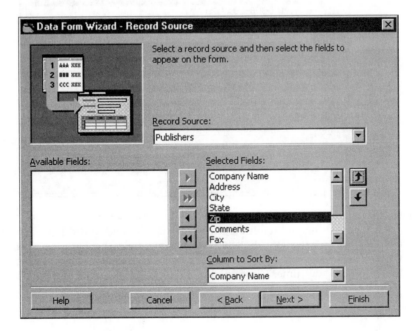

Click Next >.

2 Select the same record source, the Publishers table and select all of the fields. However, this time we want the fields ordered in a specific sequence. When the Grid is displayed, the Company Name should be first, then the Address, then City and State. Click on each of the fields and when it is highlighted, use the up/down arrows on the right of the Selected Fields list box to position the field in the correct order. As before, select the Company Name from the drop-down box to ensure the records are displayed in alphabetical order. Click Next > to move onto the next step in the Wizard.

3 This time, notice that the $\underline{S}$how Data Control text box is enabled. Why? Because a grid permits us an alternate method of navigating the recordset - it provides scroll bars for us to move about. Just so you can see what this form will look like without the data control, uncheck this box. Click $\underline{N}$ext >, then $\underline{F}$inish and allow the Wizard to perform its magic.

The new frmGrid will now be displayed in design mode. Although we don't want the data control displayed, there it is. That is because it will become invisible only during run-time.

4 We now want to run our new program. Remember to go to the Project Properties dialog box from the main menu in VB and change the $\underline{S}$tartup Object to frmGrid. Then press *F5* to run the program.

Notice that the ADO data control is not visible. Also notice that the fields are in the order we want them. Using the scroll bars (both horizontal and vertical) we can navigate the recordset. In this illustration, the top record is highlighted. This is because it is the current record. As we mentioned, even though we can see several records at once, only one record can be current at any time. Clicking another record makes that record the current record.

Try It Out - The Master/Detail Layout

The third method of displaying the data in a table is by selecting the Master/Detail option. This option is a bit different in that it requires us to select both the **master** record source as well as the **detail** record source. This is also known as a one-to-many relationship. For each record in the master table, there can be several related records in the detail table. When would you use something like this? Let's say that we wish to see all of the book titles published by each publisher. For each record in the Publishers (master) table, we will have several records in the Titles (detail) table. Let's run the Wizard and see how to do this.

1   Repeat steps 1 through 6 again (you can do this in your sleep now, I guess?). This time though, go ahead and select Master/Detail as the Form Layout and name the form frmMaster.

2   Click Next > to move on to the Master Record Source page.

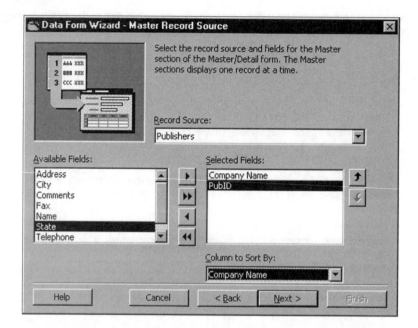

3   Since this is a Master/Detail form, we must define which is the master record source and
which is the detail record source. Notice that the title of this form is Master Record
Source. We want to find all of the titles published for each publisher, so the Publishers
table will be the Record Source for the master record. To make things simple, let's only
select the Company Name and the PubID as the Selected Fields. As before, sort the
recordset by the Company Name field. Click Next >.

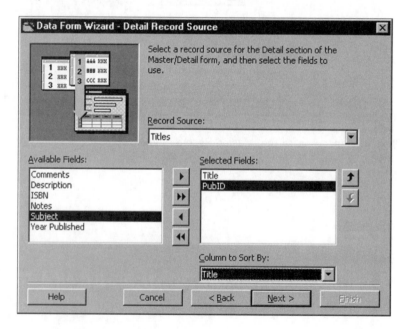

4 Now it's time to tell the Wizard which Detail Record Source to use. Select the Titles table from the drop-down Record Source box. Also just select the Title and PubID fields to display in the detail recordset. After you select the Title field as the Column to Sort By, click Next >.

5 Remember our discussion about relational databases in the last chapter? Here we can put that knowledge to work. In the Master list box, select the PubID field of the master (Publishers) table. Of course, this is the unique primary key for this table. Each publisher record has a unique value in this field. Next, select the PubID field in the Detail (Titles) table. This is the non-unique foreign key field for that table. That is because each unique publisher publishes many titles. So we use this key field in each table to relate them. This concept is known as a one-to-many relationship. Click Finish and let the Wizard to its work.

The Master/Detail Form in Design Mode

Notice that we not only have our text boxes, labels, command buttons and ADO data control, but a grid bound control as well. The grid control is perfect for displaying several records at once. Let's run the new **frmMaster**. Remember to change the Startup Object in the Project Properties dialog box to frmMaster.

The Master/Detail Form at Run-Time

Now we can clearly see the relational aspect of this database. Since we wanted the records in the master table (Publishers) to be sorted in alphabetic order, A K PETERS LTD comes up first. Underneath in the grid are all of the titles published by A K PETERS LTD. We also selected the PubID field of these records to be displayed to illustrate the primary/foreign key concept a bit more dramatically. Of course, we didn't need to have these fields displayed. We could have simply used them for the relationship and not shown them, but for this example it makes sense. Of course, we also requested the detail records to be sorted in alphabetical order as well.

If you are wondering how this magic takes place, it's really quite simple. When the control is initialized, it will always make the first record in the returned recordset current. The Wizard also wrote some ADO code to make this happen. While the Wizard was working away, it set some properties on the data control. We will examine properties in the next chapter, but essentially they tell the control how to behave. The properties were set to instruct the grid to display the values associated with the detail table.

Whenever the form is displayed for the first time or if the user resizes our form, the **Resize** event fires (or is executed). The Wizard added come code to ensure the grid control, which is named **grdDataGrid**, is as wide as the form. It also ensures that the text boxes and buttons can be seen.

End the program and double-click on the **frmGrid** form to bring up the code window and expose the code that the Wizard wrote. It's helpful to just take a look at what is there. Don't worry if it looks fairly strange, because it will if you have never seen it before. However, it's instructive to just get a sense of what is happening. As we progress through the book, we will be covering ADO code in detail. The nice thing about the Wizard-generated form is that we let it to the dirty work for us.

Now every time you navigate to the next record using the ADO data control, the next record in the master Publishers table is displayed. All of the records from the Titles table that are associated with that particular publisher are displayed. How? Well since the unique PubID of 624 is associated with the Publishers record for A K PETERS, behind the scenes each and every Titles record that has a PubID value of 624 is gathered up and placed in the grid. Pretty powerful stuff.

Here we can look at each publisher as the master - or **parent** record. We can see all of the associated detail - or **child** - records that contain books published by that publisher. Remember in the last chapter when we discussed unique primary keys and non-unique foreign keys? Well, take a look at this form. The primary key, PubID, from the publisher record is 624. One and only one publisher record contains this unique primary key. However, in the grid all of the child records that contain this same value for the PubID foreign key are displayed. The child grid selects *only* those records that match the value of the primary key in the parent record. This is the relationship we were discussing in the last chapter.

> *Now you can see how we can relate two (or more) tables using the primary and foreign key structure. This, in a nutshell, is the basis of a relational database.*

MS HFlexGrid Layout

The fourth method of presenting our data is by using the powerful MS HFlexGrid tool. Let's add yet another form to our project to see what this format looks like.

Try It Out - The MS HFlexGrid Layout

1 Follow the now familiar steps 1 - 5. You will notice that the Wizard will present us with a few more frames when we select the MS HFlexGrid layout. Since there is a lot of functionality built into this control, the Wizard needs a bit more information from us.

2 On the Form step of the Wizard, select MS HFlexGrid. Give the name frmFlex to our new form. Then click Next >.

3 On the Record Source frame of the Wizard, select Publishers as the Record Source. We want to show off the **merging** capabilities of this powerful MS HFlexGrid, so let's only select two fields, the State and Company Name. Since we will be merging all of the publishers that are located in a single state together, make the State the first field. Since each company has a unique name, we would not be able to see the merging capability of the form if we selected a field that only had unique values. However, as several publishers can reside in a single state, we want to make this first field so all publishers in a single state will be automatically merged together by the grid. Select the State field as the Column to Sort By and click Next >.

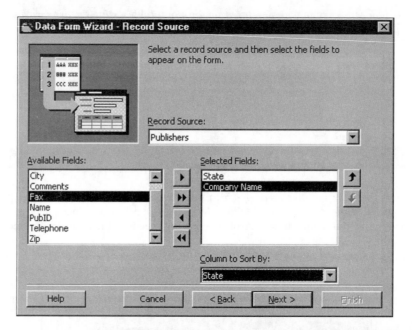

4 On the Select Grid Type frame, select the Outline option button. Of course, option buttons are mutually exclusive - you can only select one. By selecting the Outline grid type, we can easily see the powerful capabilities of this grid. Click Next >.

5   Here we can choose how we want the grid to look. Select Contemporary because this is the most sophisticated look. However, before you move on, try the other choices. The Wizard will dynamically change the format so you can see how each of the styles looks before you commit yourself. Be sure to finish with the Contemporary. Also notice that since the Wizard knows our data source, Publishers, it shows us actual data from the two fields we selected. This gives us a preview of how the finished product will look. Click Next to continue.

6   Now on the Set Column Settings frame, the Wizard gives us a change to resize the fields we have selected. You can even click on a field and drag it to another position if you wish to change the order. Resize the Company Name field so the entire name will be displayed, then click Next >.

7 On the Set Application UI (User Interface) Options frame be sure to click the **Allow** Column Dragging and Sorting check box. This will ensure that the user can move the fields. Don't worry if your mouse clicking finger is getting tired, we are almost finished! Click Next >.

8 The last frame is displayed. Click Finish and let the Wizard weave its familiar spell. When it completes building our form, it will be shown in design mode.

9 Let's run the program and see how it looks. Be sure to change the Startup Object to frmFlex in the Project Properties dialog box. Then press *F5* to run the program.

Many of the records near the top don't have a state associated with them, so they will be blank. So much for legacy databases! We can never be sure all of the data was entered correctly. Use the scroll bar on the right and scroll down towards the bottom. Notice how the grid automatically grouped the publishers that reside in Minnesota together. As you scroll up or down, the State field moves to show all of the publishers that reside in that state.

Notice that the ADO data control is **not** displayed. Here we navigate the recordset by using the scroll bars. **This particular grid is read only - we can't change any of the data**. We can only look at it. So keep this in mind when you use this control later on.

The MS Chart Layout

We will use the chart layout later on in the book. This option is only good when we have numeric data to display. Since we don't have any useful numeric data in the **Biblio.mdb** database, we will use the **Nwind.mdb** database for this example.

Try It Out - The MS Chart Layout

1 We are going to add yet another form to our project. This one will use the MS Chart option. Click on Add-Ins and select Data Form Wizard. Click on Next > until you get to the Database frame of the Wizard. Be sure to select the **Nwind.mdb** database. The Chart option requires numeric information in order to create a graph and this database has fields that we can use. Now click on Next >.

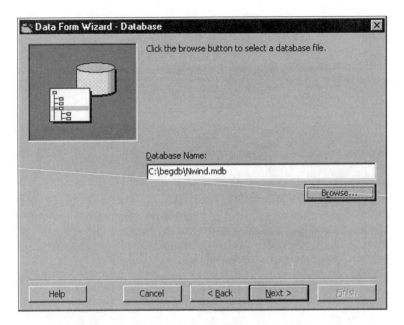

2 The next frame is the Form frame. Select MS Chart as the Form Layout. Give the name frmChart to our new form. Click Next > again.

3 In order to have something useful to graph, we might want to look at the relative sales of products based on the price point. In other words, what price point or points has the most sales? Select the Order Details table as the Record Source. Then select UnitPrice and Quantity as the two fields we wish to look at, and choose UnitPrice as the Column to Sort By. Click on Next >.

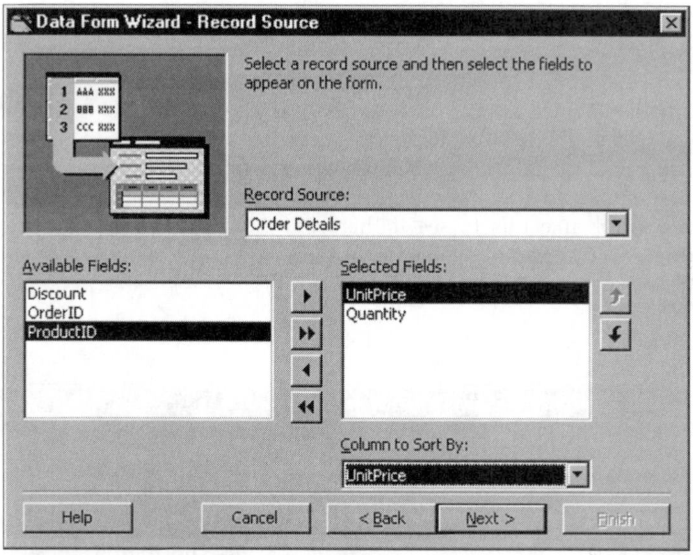

4 Next, the Wizard shows us the Select Chart Fields frame. We want the UnitPrice to be displayed on the X (horizontal) Axis. Since we sorted by UnitPrice in the last frame, the prices will be displayed in ascending order on the X axis. Select Quantity as the field to summarize on the Y (vertical) axis. In the Select the aggregate function to summarize the Y axis with. list box select Count.

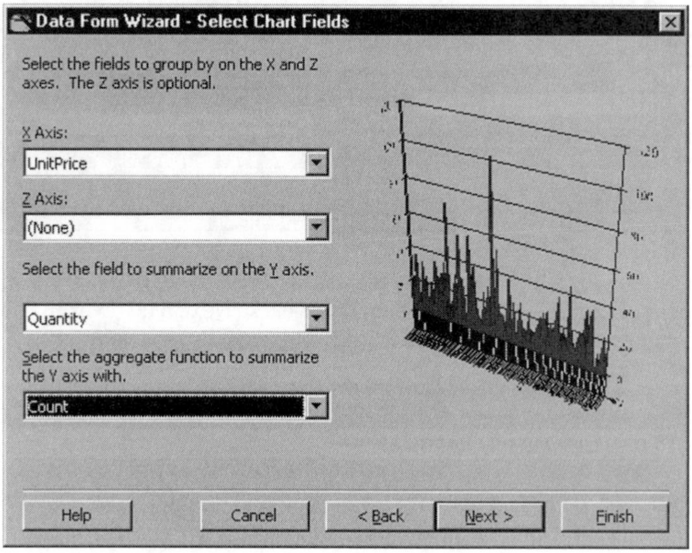

Notice how the Wizard dynamically displays the graph and how it will look. We can already tell that there is so much data that we can only see trends - not specific items. This is because the Wizard will provide a graph on all records in the table we selected - **Order Details**. Later on, we will learn how to select only specific records from the database. For now though, this will at least give us an indication of any spikes for certain price points.

Now click **Next >**.

5 The Wizard then brings up the **Select Chart Style** frame. Click on the various types and the Wizard will automatically display a preview of that type of graph. They all look fairly crowded, so select the **2D Line** - this shows the trends the best. Even the preview clearly shows a few spikes in price points that outsell the others. Many times, a product manager will want a graph like this to see if there is a 'magical' price point that they can use for a new product. So by examining historical data as we are here, the product manager gets a rough feel of what might be a good price.

Click **Next >**.

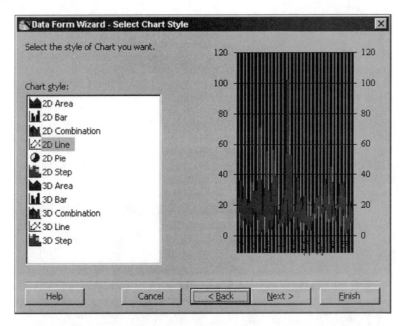

6 Next, the **Select Appearance Properties** frame is displayed. We won't make any selections here because of the sheer volume of data so click **Next**. However, if we were examining a recordset that was not so large, we could add legends and markers to assist reading the data points.

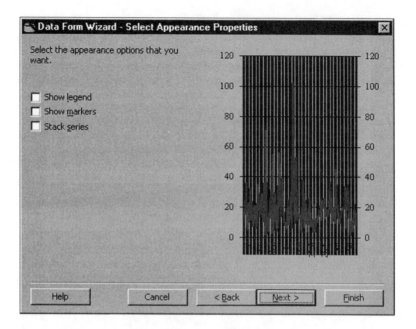

7 The Wizard now allows us to add captions to customize our graphs. Let's add a title here. In the Te<u>x</u>t box type Quantity to Price so that the product manager will know what is being shown. Notice that we can see the Y axis clearly, even in the preview. There is one price point that exceeds a hundred items sold. The price point with the next highest volume sold about seventy items. This will allow the product manager to evaluate the profit or contribution margin on each sold. However, it seems that the spike in items sold is almost in the middle of the price range of all of our products.

8 Click <u>N</u>ext > and <u>F</u>inish.

9 The Wizard now goes to work and builds our form, frmChart. Because we selected a 2D Line graph type, it displays a sample of this graph in design mode. Don't forget to change the <u>S</u>tartup Object to frmChart so we can run the graph and see how it looks.

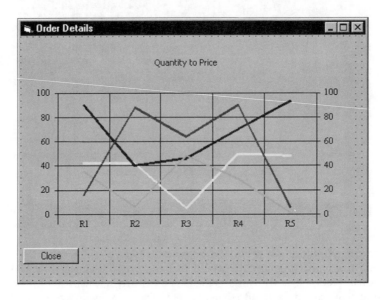

10 Press *F5* and run the form.

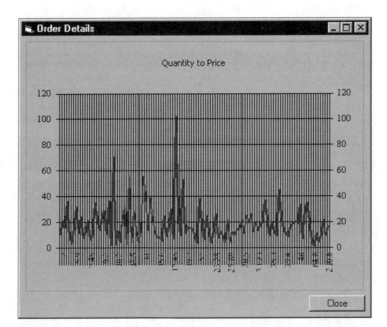

When we learn how to limit the data we want to retrieve from a database, we can easily send any information we wish to be graphed and we can summarize it in whatever way we want. For example, we may wish to group items in increments of $1.00 or so. So the first item on the X (horizontal) axis would include items <= $1.00, the next would be >= $1.01 and <= $2.00, and so on. This would make for a much clearer graph and possibly give some insight into the buying patterns of our customers. In any event, you can see how the Wizard walked us through a very complicated process with just a few mouse clicks.

11 End the program and double-click on the frmChart form to bring up the code window. You will be amazed at the amount of work the Wizard did to present the data.

Pay No Attention to the Man Behind the Curtain

Just like the great and powerful Wizard of Oz, there is actually a man behind the curtain or more specifically, there is really code behind the form. Although we didn't write it (see, I stuck to my promise) the Wizard did a bit of dabbling with some Visual Basic code. However, just like the Wizard of Oz, there is less than meets the eye. As we just saw in the previous example, using the Wizard there is no way to select specific records from the database. So we might get an approximation of what we want. The programmer will almost always have to go in and clean up after the Wizard.

The Dark Side of the Wizard

The Wizard actually performed a bit of sorcery and wrote some Visual Basic code behind the scenes to make our program work. While the Wizard can perform some simple repetitive tasks, it is certainly not all-powerful. Far from it, actually. In fact, the Wizard just creates a template for us to go in and fill in the rest of the code. The Wizard takes us through the first stage - often to create more powerful and flexible applications we will have to add to the base that the Wizard gives us.

The Wizard options that used the ADO data control can cause some problems under certain circumstances. For example, if we tried to open a table with no records in it the user would be staring at a blank record that was added. If the user tried to delete a record when none existed or there was trouble connecting to the database, an error message would pop up and stop our program cold. Oops! The Wizard forgot to add any error handling procedures other than a message box. This will tell us the error that occurred, but our program will still crash if something goes terribly wrong. Not a very good idea in a production environment.

Beyond those obvious difficulties, what if you show your new program to your users and one of them says they really don't like the small VCR-like buttons? What they really need are bigger buttons that have captions such as First, Previous, Next and Last. Another user might ask for some validation to ensure that only clean data is committed to the database. Another user might mention that the database field names that the Wizard used as titles should be a bit more descriptive. Someone else might mention that it's important to have the ability to select only titles that begin with the letter 'A' or 'D'. It can be time consuming to have to scroll through all of these records to get to the ones needed to work on. Users can be funny that way.

So you can see that the Wizard makes a great first statement, but to create robust and flexible database programs, we must really understand the data control and how it operates. Then we can use the Wizard to create our forms, but we will add our own code to make the program more flexible and bullet-proof.

I just wanted to show you the Wizard and how far it can go. While the Wizard might be useful for creating forms for us, in real life it is too limited to cater for all of our needs. So, in the next chapter we'll learn how to program the data control ourselves so that we can take more advantage of its flexibility and power. We will also identify areas where we will want to communicate directly with the database using ActiveX Data Objects.

A Word on Sorting

The underlying Titles table is not indexed. Even so, we really don't have to know where in the database a particular record is located. We can set up our SQL query so that a field's values are sorted in the returned recordset that the SQL query produces. We can then quickly retrieve all the records in ascending or descending order.

An index on a field in the database does not change the physical location of each record, but keeps a pointer to all records in the sorted sequence. This way Jet can peek at the index and quickly return the records in the correct sequence. We can add indexes to as many fields as we think are going to be requested in sorted order.

You must use indexes on database fields judiciously, however. Each index added to a field in our table does extract a slight performance penalty when the user is adding a record. This is because when the record is committed to the database, each field that has an index requires that the index be updated. This is done automatically for us once the index has been added. If the user is adding a single record at a time, they probably won't even notice; this very slight performance hit is well worth the benefit gained when returning sorted records from our tables. So just be sure to only add indexes to each field you will be sorting on.

ASCII Sort Order – A Primer

Still, even with an index, how does Jet *know* that an A comes before Z? After all, computers just understand numbers, don't they? Yes, that is true. The way items are sorted is by using **ASCII** codes. ASCII (American Standard Code for Information Interchange) is a code in which the numbers from 0 to 255 stand for letters, numbers, punctuation marks and other characters. ASCII code is standardized to not only facilitate transmitting text between computers or on a peripheral device, but so the computer 'knows' that A (ASCII 65) comes before Z (ASCII 90) when the database is sorting records for us. Since we will be doing a fair amount of retrieving records in various sorted orders, it is worth while taking a look at the ASCII table.

```
┌──────────────────────────────────────────────────────────┐
│ ? Visual Basic Reference                        _ □ X     │
├──────────────────────────────────────────────────────────┤
│ Help Topics │  Back  │  Options │                         │
├──────────────────────────────────────────────────────────┤
│  Character Set (0 – 127)                                  │
│  See Also      Specifics                                  │
│                                                           │
│    0    .      32  [space]   64   @      96   `           │
│    1    .      33  !         65   A      97   a           │
│    2    .      34  "         66   B      98   b           │
│    3    .      35  #         67   C      99   c           │
│    4    .      36  $         68   D     100   d           │
│    5    .      37  %         69   E     101   e           │
│    6    .      38  &         70   F     102   f           │
│    7    .      39  '         71   G     103   g           │
│    8   **      40  (         72   H     104   h           │
│    9   **      41  )         73   I     105   i           │
│   10   **      42  *         74   J     106   j           │
│   11    .      43  +         75   K     107   k           │
│   12    .      44  ,         76   L     108   l           │
│   13   **      45  -         77   M     109   m           │
│   14    .      46  .         78   N     110   n           │
│   15    .      47  /         79   O     111   o           │
│   16    .      48  0         80   P     112   p           │
└──────────────────────────────────────────────────────────┘
```

When you get a second, take a look at the ASCII table in the on-line help right in Visual Basic. Click on **Help-S**earch from the main VB menu and enter ASCII to find this table. Notice that symbols come before letters, followed by numbers. Next come uppercase letters and finally, lowercase letters. This is important to keep in mind for when we later want to get information from the database for our programs. If we are not comfortable with the ASCII sort order, we may be surprised at the results or we just might not retrieve all of the data we thought we would.

An interesting experiment is to actually convert the ASCII codes to the character and then back to the ASCII number.

Try It Out - Converting ASCII Codes

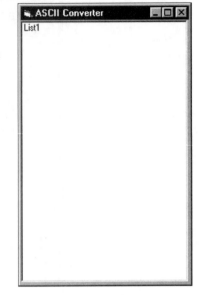

1 Start a new project and add a standard VB list box from your toolbox to the default form. Format the form and list box as shown:

In design view, click on the form to bring up the code window. In the **Form_Load** event procedure, add the following highlighted code:

```
Private Sub Form_Load()

Dim iAscii As Integer

For iAscii = 65 To 90
        List1.AddItem "Ascii Value: " & iAscii & " = " & Chr(iAscii) _
        & "   and  Character " & Chr(iAscii) & " = " & Asc(Chr(iAscii))
Next

End Sub
```

Here, we are simply taking the ASCII codes from 65 to 90 that list uppercase letters. VB has two helpful built-in functions to help us with ASCII codes:

- **Chr(*ASCII code*)** will take numeric ASCII values and convert them to the character in the ASCII table that equates to that number.
- **Asc(*character*)** will convert characters to ASCII numbers.

Here's the section of the code that does the work:

```
List1.AddItem "Ascii Value: " & iAscii & " = " & Chr(iAscii) _
& "   and  Character " & Chr(iAscii) & " = " & Asc(Chr(iAscii))
```

So for 65 to 90, we first take the number and get the ASCII character by using the **Chr()** function. Next, we take the character and convert it back to the ASCII numeric value.

ASCII Converter

```
Ascii Value: 65 = A   and Character A = 65
Ascii Value: 66 = B   and Character B = 66
Ascii Value: 67 = C   and Character C = 67
Ascii Value: 68 = D   and Character D = 68
Ascii Value: 69 = E   and Character E = 69
Ascii Value: 70 = F   and Character F = 70
Ascii Value: 71 = G   and Character G = 71
Ascii Value: 72 = H   and Character H = 72
Ascii Value: 73 = I   and Character I = 73
Ascii Value: 74 = J   and Character J = 74
Ascii Value: 75 = K   and Character K = 75
Ascii Value: 76 = L   and Character L = 76
Ascii Value: 77 = M   and Character M = 77
Ascii Value: 78 = N   and Character N = 78
Ascii Value: 79 = O   and Character O = 79
Ascii Value: 80 = P   and Character P = 80
Ascii Value: 81 = Q   and Character Q = 81
Ascii Value: 82 = R   and Character R = 82
Ascii Value: 83 = S   and Character S = 83
Ascii Value: 84 = T   and Character T = 84
Ascii Value: 85 = U   and Character U = 85
Ascii Value: 86 = V   and Character V = 86
Ascii Value: 87 = W   and Character W = 87
Ascii Value: 88 = X   and Character X = 88
Ascii Value: 89 = Y   and Character Y = 89
Ascii Value: 90 = Z   and Character Z = 90
```

2   Press *F5* and run the program.

So you can get a sense of how the computer knows the sequence of letters and numbers that makes sense to us humans. It converts everything to numbers. Computers are dumb - you've probably told your computer that it's dumb out loud once in a while. However, one thing they can do very well is determine if one number is less than or greater than another. This is the basis of sorting as our simple program demonstrates.

Summary

In this chapter we have had a quick look at the ADO data control and how we can use it in conjunction with the Data Form Wizard. We saw, amongst other things:

▶ It's easy to create a variety of good-looking user interfaces hooked up to a database

▶ The Wizard provides us with access to a range of data layout formats

▶ The underlying sorting principles of out database data are based on ASCII codes

What We Learned

This chapter got us started on working with the ADO data control, and we got some practice in linking data to our forms using the Data Form Wizard. Here are the take-home points for this chapter:

▶ The Data Form Wizard lets us quickly build forms that retrieve data from tables in databases

▶ The data control interacts with the database engine and the underlying database to produce a **recordset**

▶ We can pull information from several tables and display it in a single form – for example, by using the **Master/Detail** format

▶ The **primary key/foreign key** structure is used to link records from multiple tables in a relational database

▶ Multiple records can be displayed in **Grid** format

▶ ASCII codes determine how returned information is sorted

As we mentioned earlier, the Wizard provides us with a quick way of creating VB forms, giving us access to tables via the data control. Nevertheless, to create tailored, powerful, and flexible applications, we have to be able to weave a little magic of our own. This means stepping out from the Wizard's shadow and programming the data control ourselves. That's what we'll start doing in the next chapter.

Exercises

1   What is the major benefit of using a data control to build an application?

2   In what situation would you use a profile with the Data Form Wizard?

3   Describe the steps required by the user to add a new record to the Publishers table using the form `frmFirst` that we created in this chapter. What is good and bad about the required steps?

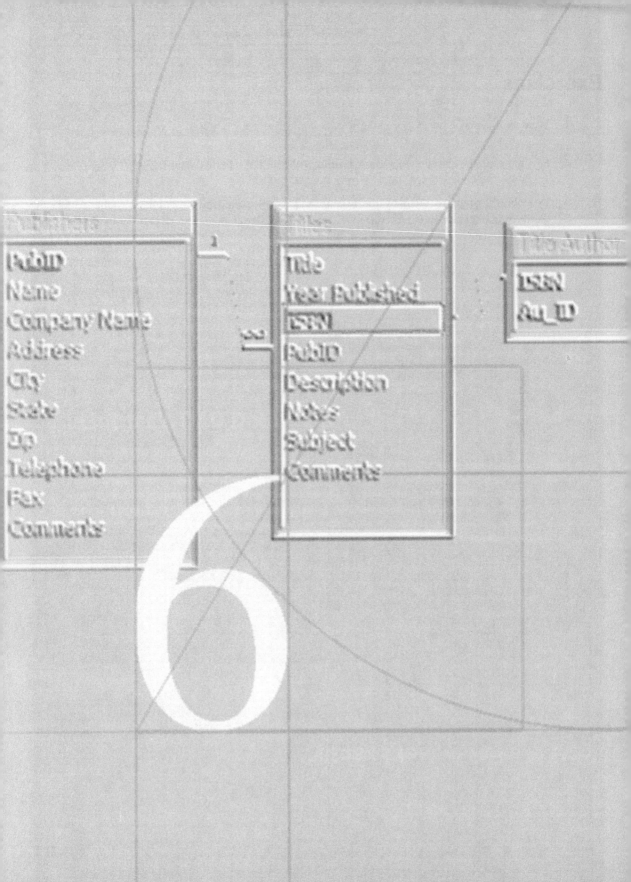

Programming the Data Control

In this chapter we get down to doing some programming of our own. As we saw in the last chapter, when we used the ADO data control and bound controls to display data, we can create a pretty good-looking interface using little or no code, and with the minimum of effort. Now, we're going to take on some of the Wizard's responsibilities and start programming these controls for ourselves.

Bound controls, controls that are bound to an underlying data field in a table, are one of the greatest advantages in programming with Visual Basic 6.0.

Why Not Just Let the Wizard Do It?

This book is about programming databases using VB, and we want to give you as thorough a grounding as we can, so that your knowledge base is as broad and as firm as possible. Here, we're going to start on the process of teaching you the VB programming techniques and database knowledge that will make you more knowledgeable, flexible, and sophisticated as a programmer.

Here's what we'll cover in this chapter:

- The data control and bound controls: how they relate to each other and interact
- Building forms around the established DAO data control
- Using the data control to retrieve data from related tables
- Using the ADO data control with ADO bound controls

As we saw in the last chapter, when we use the data control alongside bound controls with our database applications, we can create stunning visual interfaces for the database with little or no code. The data control and bound controls allow you to create sophisticated, visually appealing user interfaces quickly and with a minimum of effort. In this chapter we'll gain some more experience of doing this for ourselves.

The Data Control and Bound Controls

The data control is very eloquent in talking to a database and retrieving data. The data control retrieves the records we ask for and places them into memory for us to use. However, in order to *display* the records, we need visual tools that we can bind to the data control. We can use a family of bound controls to display our records. VB 6.0 provides us with a wide variety of bound controls so we can display our records in just about any way imaginable.

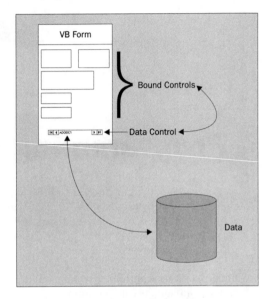

In the last chapter, we used the Wizard to create our user interface. The VB 6.0 Wizard only works with the ADO data control. Previous editions of VB (starting with version 3.0) used the DAO data control. The data control was a revolutionary concept, permitting the programmer to wire up a database without code. With successive releases of VB the DAO control has become more powerful. For desktop database systems, the DAO data control offers a bit more functionality because it is a more mature tool. So we're going to examine the DAO data control first before moving on to the ADO data control so that you can clearly see the differences between the two.

Intrinsic Controls

Each and every control has two common features: it has properties we can set and events that it knows how to respond to. In other words, when we draw a control on our form, it is born knowing how to do many things. More than that, each control is specialized so we can use it for a particular task. Here are the intrinsic (built-in) controls that are available to us through the standard tool palette:

The toolbox is a good example of how to use visual cues to convey lots of information to the user. As we progress through the book to build bigger and better programs, we will talk a lot about how to use the visual power of windows to convey information to the user. So while you are using VB, always make a mental note of how much information is provided by visual items - changing cursors, icons and grab bars, to name a few. We know exactly what VB is doing by these visual cues and tool tips that display the name of the control. That is the power of a sophisticated Windows program - using visuals so the user knows exactly what is happening and what is expected of them.

Later, when we add additional **non-intrinsic** controls to our project, such as the **ActiveX Data Control**, we must manually add this control to our tool palette. These controls, along with a multitude of others, are stored in **.ocx** (**ActiveX Control File**) format. As you know, when we add a new control to our palette, we can create multiple instances of the same control by drawing several on a form. However, our project only needs the single control available on our tool palette. We can use this single control as many times as we need. In other words, you only have a single text box control on the tool palette, but can draw ten of them on a form from this single control. Once a control is on our tool palette, it can be used as many times as necessary within our project. This is the magic of **.dll**s (**Dynamic Link Libraries**). One file can be used several times within our project.

What is a .DLL Again?

When you program in high-level programming languages such as C, Pascal and FORTRAN, all of the application's source code files are compiled and linked to various libraries. These files get bundled together to create an executable file. Various libraries are bundled in with the final single program file. These libraries are really files of pre-compiled functions and sub routines that are called to accomplish common tasks. For example, if our program needs math functions, we link in the math library that contains pre-compiled math functions such as square root, log, etc. When these library functions are linked to an application, all of that code becomes a **permanent** part of the application's executable file. When the program is compiled, all calls to the various functions are resolved at link time. This type of linking is given the name **static linking**.

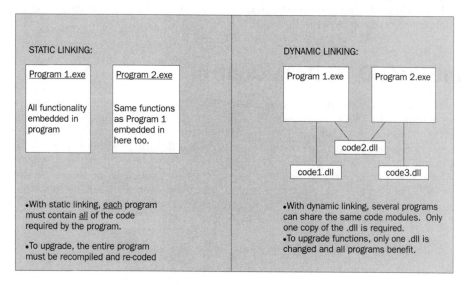

STATIC LINKING:

Program 1.exe

All functionality embedded in program

Program 2.exe

Same functions as Program 1 embedded in here too.

DYNAMIC LINKING:

Program 1.exe

Program 2.exe

code2.dll

code1.dll

code3.dll

•With static linking, <u>each</u> program must contain <u>all</u> of the code required by the program.

•To upgrade, the entire program must be recompiled and re-coded

•With dynamic linking, several programs can share the same code modules. Only one copy of the .dll is required.
•To upgrade functions, only one .dll is changed and all programs benefit.

Imagine if we wrote five programs, each of which had a file that included code to perform some function such as database access. Each of the five programs would include all of the code to perform this function. Although the five programs used the exact same functionally it would have to be stored in each of the programs. Talk about a waste of space! This 'bloat problem' is solved by **dynamic linking**.

Dynamic Linking

Windows introduced the concept of **dynamic linking**. This provides a mechanism to link applications to libraries, such as our data control, at run-time. These libraries reside in their own files. As such, they are not copied into applications' executable files, as they would be with static linking. These dynamic link libraries (DLLs) are named to emphasize that they are linked to an application when the program is loaded and executed, not when the program has its components linked in at design-time. So VB programmers don't need to manually link these files in at design-time. Windows links these files dynamically, at run-time.

When our program uses a `.dll` file (such as the ADO data control), the operating system loads the `.dll` file into memory. It then resolves references to functions in the `.dll` file so that they can be called by our application. When the functionality is no longer needed, it gets unloaded from memory. Now that's efficiency.

What does that mean to us? It means that as long as the `.dll` file is on the user's machine, our program can use it again and again (even within the same application). For example, we can draw ten ADO data controls on a form and use each of them. However, since it is a `.dll` file, only one copy of that file exists on the machine. Our program just creates additional **instances** of the control as we draw them on our form. When we run our program, it dynamically links to the file and we can take advantage of all of the built-in functionality. If the user is running another program at the same time that has an ADO data control, it also uses exactly the same `.dll` file.

When a control gets upgraded, possibly to add more functionality (or it just gets optimized), that single file gets replaced and all of the existing programs can use the new file. Pretty neat, eh? Oh, and we will be building our own `.dll` file later on in the book when we cover database programming over the Internet.

The Intrinsic DAO Data Control

As mentioned, VB 6.0 actually comes with both the ADO and DAO data controls. We will start off by examining the DAO control, which is more established. The DAO data control is one of the **intrinsic** controls of Visual Basic. When you start up a new VB project, the default tools are displayed on the tool palette. All of the controls on the default palette are intrinsic, meaning that they are built into the language itself. We don't have to do anything special to add them to the tool palette; the control is there whenever we start a new project. In addition, we don't pay a program-size penalty to use them - they are already there. Nor do we have to worry about distributing and registering additional files, because the DAO control is built into the language and is there whether we use it or not.

On our tool palette, the standard data control looks like this:

It shows us the familiar VCR-type scroll buttons and a schematic of some underlying data fields.

As we mentioned earlier, the DAO control has been around since VB 3.0 and it is now the most widespread data control on the planet, so it makes sense to get comfortable with this control first. It is simple to set up and use. Best of all though, it is very similar to the ADO data control. Both of these data controls have the ability to scoop up records from a table in the database and place them in memory, so that we can get at them and manipulate them. While in the memory, the records are held in a structure called a recordset.

What is a Recordset Exactly?

A **recordset** is a group of records that the data control retrieves from one or more tables in a database. In the last chapter, the Wizard used a data control to retrieve recordsets and display the results. The groups of records are placed into memory for us to use. When the data control creates the recordset, we can access the recordset just like any variable (in fact, a recordset is called an **object variable**). Just like an integer variable stores an integer value, a recordset stores the result of a query. The data control queries the database to ask for specific records; these records can be from one or more tables. The query can also ask for certain records, such as all books published only in 1998 from our Titles table in the **Biblio.mdb** database. Alternatively, a query result might contain parts of multiple tables that have been brought together in a relationship.

If we set the **RecordSource** property of a data control to contain this simple SQL query:

```
SELECT * FROM PUBLISHERS
```

The resultant recordset returned by Jet would contain **all** of the records in the **Publishers** table (the * is SQL's way of saying 'all'). When the form containing the data control is loaded, the recordset is created and stored in memory. A bound control, such as a text box, is then used to display the contents of this recordset to the user.

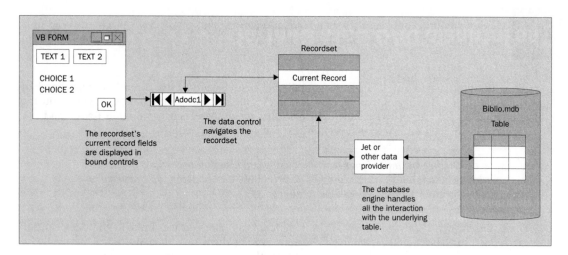

When we use the data control, we can't access the records in a database directly. The only way to view or change the data in the database is by using the recordset. A recordset has columns and rows, just like a table. The recordset is displayed visually in a data bound control drawn on the form.

What is a Data Bound Control?

Data bound controls (also known as **data aware controls**) are used to display the information in the recordset that was created using a data control. Recall in the last chapter that when the Wizard created our first data form, text boxes were placed on the form and information for each field in each record was displayed. Each of the text boxes was bound to the ADO data control by setting two text box properties telling it:

▶ Which data control to bind to

▶ Which field to display

So each text box was bound to the same data control, but each displayed a different field from the recordset that the data control held. Therefore, by simply setting two properties, the text boxes could display the information to the user. The datagrid is also a bound control - it was bound to the ADO data control and displayed the recordset in a grid format.

It is through bound controls such as the text box that we can visually present information stored in a database. When a data bound control is linked to a data control, Visual Basic essentially ties a field from the data control's recordset to the bound control. When the data control is initialized, the field value in the current record of the recordset is displayed in the bound control for the user to see and, depending on the type of control, this value can be modified. When the user clicks the data control button to move to the next record, the current record changes to the next record in the recordset and those new values are automatically displayed in the text boxes.

> **FYI**   Some bound controls, such as a label and MS HFlexGrid control (ADO): are read-only. So we can show the user the information in the recordset, but the data can't be modified.

When the user makes any changes to an **editable** bound control, the control accepts the changes and updates the underlying recordset (and thereby the database) automatically when you move to another record. All of the code to perform this magic has been pre-written for us and included in the control. Pretty simple, eh? So far, no code is required.

> *We can change the underlying recordset using code, so don't worry. We will be covering how to do that later on. For now though, we are going to review some of the bound controls that VB 6.0 has to offer.*

Visual Basic provides us with several intrinsic controls that you can bind to the data control. Of course, we can also use these controls without linking them to a database - they are called bound controls because they have the wiring so that if we wish to bind them, we just set the required properties. Consider the most frequently used control, the text box. We certainly don't always bind these to a data control. It is possible to say **Text1.Text = "Hello World"**. In this case, we have programmatically set the **Text** property. So as you can see, these controls are extremely flexible.

In addition to the data-aware controls provided with VB 6.0, many other powerful data-aware controls are available from third parties.

Types of Bound Controls Available to Us

When you start a new VB 6.0 project, there are, in addition to the intrinsic controls, several data-bound ActiveX (**.ocx**) controls that we can add to our project.

Intrinsic Controls

The standard built-in bound controls that you can use with the data control include the following:

- Check box
- Image
- Label
- Picture box
- Text box
- List box
- Combo box
- OLE container control

ActiveX Controls

In addition to the intrinsic bound controls, we are also provided with the following standard ActiveX controls:

- Data-bound list box
- Data-bound combo box
- MS HFlexGrid
- Apex Data-Bound Grid (DBGrid)
- Masked Edit

With VB 6.0, several new ActiveX controls have been added to our arsenal of bound controls. These controls are specifically designed to view and/or edit data:

- **DataGrid Control** - a new grid type control that can work with the ADO data control or ADO recordset objects.
- **DataList Control** - a control that functions exactly like the DBList control, but which is optimized for use with other ADO data sources.

- **DataCombo Control** - functions like the data-bound combo box control, but can be used with other ADO data sources.

- **Hierarchical FlexGrid Control** - this is capable of displaying hierarchical data.

- **DataRepeater Control** - this lets you use a user control to display data, and 'repeats' the control to view multiple records. We will build a project with the DataRepeater control later in the book.

- **MonthView Control** - displays dates graphically as a calendar. We use this tool in our Address Book project later on.

- **DateTimePicker Control** - similar to the MonthView control, displays dates in a text box; clicking the text box causes a graphic calendar to drop down for selection of a new date.

When you need a more complex data presentation interface, a few of these ActiveX controls can display whole groups of records, such as lists, tables or entire recordsets at one time, in a single control. These include the data-bound list box, the data-bound combo box and the MS HFlexGrid control (ADO): control. If you would like to add any of these controls to your project, move the mouse over the tool palette and right-click the mouse.

Select Components... and the Components dialog box appears. By simply checking the box to the left of the description, this control will be added to your project.

Notice that when the control is highlighted, the name of the `.ocx` file is displayed at the bottom of the dialog box. We will be referring to this a bit later in the chapter when we add additional controls. Several of the controls have similar names, such as 'Data Bound List Controls' and 'DataBound List Controls'. So many times it will be necessary to check the file name to ensure that the correct file is added.

> *If you find that you don't need a control, bring up the Components dialog box and de-select the choice. Be sure that you do this for all ActiveX controls that are in your tool palette but your program does not use. This is because the control will be included with your program when you use the Package and Deployment Wizard (formerly known as the Setup Wizard) set-up program to make disks to distribute. The Package and Deployment Wizard has no way of knowing that you are not using the controls. As long as any unneeded control is on your tool palette, VB will include the control and all the overhead that goes along with that.*

The good news is that Visual Basic 'knows' if we are really using a non-intrinsic control on our tool palette. If we try to deselect a control that we are using, VB will let us know and refuse to let go.

Working With Data Controls

Let's go ahead and bind three text box controls to a standard data control and walk through what is happening. Be sure to work with the copy of the **Biblio.mdb** database you made in **[Drive letter]:\BegDB**. We will be changing a few records in this chapter and we don't want to affect the original table.

While we're about it, create a new subdirectory in your **BegDB** directory and call it **Chapter3**. We'll store all our files and code from this chapter to this **[drive letter]:\BegDB\Chapter3** directory.

Here's our brief for the first exercise: we are asked to build a small VB form for a librarian who frequently needs to get the Title, Year Published and ISBN for books in the Titles table of the **Biblio.mdb** database. Let's see how we might go about doing that.

Try It Out - Fun with the Intrinsic Data Control

1 Create a new project and place the data control on the default form. Next, place three text boxes and three labels on the form. Set the labels' **Caption** properties as shown in the screenshot for each of the labels.

To set the properties of any control, click on the control with the mouse to give the control focus. Then press *F4* to bring up the Properties window (*F4* is quicker than selecting View-Properties Window from the main menu). Simply type in the new property. Here we enter the word Title in the Caption property.

2 Set the DatabaseName property of the data control to the copy of the **Biblio.mdb** database you have copied into the *[Drive letter]*:**\BegDB** sub directory. This is the first step in setting up the data control. By clicking the ellipsis, you can navigate the hard drive and simply click on the file.

3 The next step is to tell the data control the name of the table whose data we want to retrieve into our recordset. We will just select the Titles table for now (we will be covering how to use SQL to select subsets of records or combine records from multiple tables in Chapter 8). For now, just select Titles for the RecordSource property. This will retrieve the entire Titles table. The **DatabaseName** and **RecordSource** properties are the only two properties that must be set. Surprisingly, the data control is now ready to retrieve the records and create our recordset.

4 Bring up the Properties window for the Text1 text box control. In order to bind the text box to the data control, we must first specify the data control we wish to bind to. This is because we can have several data controls on the same form. Click on the down arrow next to DataSource and select the only choice - Data1.

5 Now that we have bound our text box to the data control, we must specify which field we want displayed. When you click on the DataField property, all of the fields in the recordset are displayed. Wow! Notice that VB checks out the recordset and shows us the appropriate choices. You don't even have to know ahead of time what the valid choices are - VB shows them to us.

Click on the Title field. Now the Title field of the current record in the recordset is bound to the text box. When we run the program, the entry in the underlying recordset in the Title field of the Titles table will be displayed.

6 Now set the **DataSource** property for text boxes two and three to **Data1**. Set the **DataField** property to **Year Published** for **Text2** and **ISBN** for **Text3**.

> **7** Save our project as **prjLibrarian.vbp** in the **BegDB\Chapter3** directory. Press *F5* and run the program.

How It Works

There, you have just written a database program without a single line of code! Pretty impressive. Go ahead and use the VCR buttons on **Data1** to navigate through the recordset. Every time you click a button, the underlying pointer to the current record is changed and the new current record is displayed in the bound controls.

> *First and foremost, you have just programmed! Yes, by simply drawing a control on a form, you are legitimately programming. We set some properties by clicking on the Properties window. Believe it or not, all of this clicking is considered programming - and we haven't actually written any VB code yet. That is the important part of Visual Basic that many beginners don't notice, but drawing the interface is an important part of visual programming.*

In summary, we must set the two most important properties of the data control:

▶ **DatabaseName** - tells the data control which database to open

▶ **RecordSource** - tells the data control which records to retrieve

Once that is set up, we must then set two properties on any bound control:

▶ **DataSource** - tells the bound control which data control to use

▶ **DataField** - tells the bound control which field in the recordset to display

That is the beauty of using bound controls. When you use the data control and its associated bound controls, the Microsoft Jet engine is invoked automatically. The Jet engine is then controlled programmatically when we manipulate the data control, such as moving to the next record. So the data control simply sends commands to Jet, and Jet returns the results to the data control. As you can see, using the data control and bound controls together can reduce your development time considerably. We just set a few properties in design mode. So far - no code!

FYI

When the form is loaded, a new instance of the data control is created (with the properties we just saw in the form) and it then initializes itself. Behind the scenes, the data control opens the database and creates a new recordset by creating an instance of the Jet 3.51 DAO object model.

One consideration you have to make is that each data control opens a new instance of the database. So, if you use three controls, there are three instances of the database open. This can be somewhat memory intensive. When we get into database programming using DAO and ADO, we can open a single instance of the database and then create multiple recordsets from this single instance. For now though, let's look at how easy the data control can make displaying records to our users.

Some hard-core database programmers refuse to use the data control because of the overhead it implies. Instead, they prefer to program using exclusively DAO or ADO commands. This might be a tad faster, but requires acres of code. For example, if our current example was done without the data control and the bound controls, all of the text boxes would need to be cleared and updated using code. The current position in the recordset also needs to be examined to ensure there is another record to move to. In addition, several other tasks need to be done that the data control performs for us automatically. Although this might be a bit faster because the overhead of the data control is not incurred, I think that you are beginning to see that there is just too much power here to ignore. Also, the data control is a great learning tool and efficient enough for smaller, simpler projects. Later on in the book we'll move on to the more powerful DAO and ADO tools.

Changing the Data

To really show that we are linked to the database, you can change the data in the database right from your bound control. Using the form we just created, for example, try changing the date in the first record to 1998.

As soon as we change a value in any bound control, the data control knows it. It has a **DataChanged** property that sets a value indicating that the data in the bound control has been changed. This property only gets set if the data is changed by some process other than that of retrieving data from the current record. The information hasn't yet been committed to the database. We must take an action to do that later. The new information - in this case the date we just changed - is stored in a memory buffer.

95

In order for us to have the change we just made written to the database with the data control, we must use the VCR buttons to move to another record. Just before the record moves, the data control checks the property **DataChanged** to see if any fields have been modified. If so, then it writes the changes to the recordset, which in turn writes them to the underlying database. When this process is complete, the record pointer is moved and the next record in the recordset is made current.

This process appears instantaneously and transparently to the user, but there is really a lot of work going on under the hood of the data control. When we start using DAO code, we will have to program all of the functionality that the data control now takes care of for us automatically. We can do everything we accomplished here in pure code; no data control is required.

Go ahead and give this a try. Change the date in the first record to 1998. Move forward one record. Now move back one record. The date field in the table has actually been changed to 1998! All without any code. As you are doing this, keep in mind all of the work that is really going on to make the change happen. Let's have a look at what's happening behind the scenes.

The Sequence of Events

Once your application begins, Visual Basic uses the **Data1** control's properties to open the **Biblio.mdb** database, create a database object and then create a recordset object containing the records we asked for. The **Data1** data control's **Database** and **Recordset** properties refer to the newly created database and recordset objects. Actually these may be manipulated independently of the data control - with or without bound controls. We will examine this technique a bit later in the book.

It's important to note that the data control is initialized **before** the initial **Form_Load** event for the host form on which it is located. If any errors occur during this initialization process, a non-trappable error results. This means that we can't create an error handler to trap (intercept) this error. Again, we will discuss error handling in detail later in the book. However, the moral of the story is to ensure that the database is available before using the data control in any production software.

How Does It Know That?

Right about now, you are probably asking yourself, "How does the text box know all of the fields available in the recordset?" That is a good question and is actually fundamental to each and every ActiveX tool you have in your tool palette. Although it doesn't seem like it, these controls are really running even when we are in design mode. When you draw a control, such as a text box on a form, a new instance of a text box is created and starts running. That's right, there is code actually running inside of the text box even though we are in design mode. This is so that we can properly set up the text box in design mode. Let's say we set the **Height** property of the text box in design mode. We certainly want that value remembered when the program is run! So the text box, since it is running in design mode, will save that property for us.

The text box (and every control for that matter) is always running code in design mode. When we linked the data control to the text box, its code checked out the data control's **RecordSource** property, which told it which fields were available. These fields were then displayed to us using the drop-down box.

In design mode, if any property of the text box is changed, that new value is saved in the 'host' of the control, which is the form. The form is really responsible for hosting the control and passing it information. Once the project is saved, the changes are written to the container of the control. If you were now to open the form in an editor, such as Notepad, you would see the following:

```
Begin VB.Form Form1
    Caption         =    "Form1"
    ClientHeight    =    3195
    ClientLeft      =    2145
    ClientTop       =    2775
    ClientWidth     =    4530
    LinkTopic       =    "Form1"
    ScaleHeight     =    3195
    ScaleWidth      =    4530
    Begin VB.TextBox Text1
        DataField       =    "Title"
        DataSource      =    "Data1"
        Height          =    375
        Left            =    1080
        TabIndex        =    0
        Text            =    "Text1"
        Top             =    720
        Width           =    1935
    End
    Begin VB.Data Data1
        Caption         =    "Data1"
        Connect         =    "Access"
        DatabaseName    =    "C:\BegDB\Biblio.mdb"
        DefaultCursorType=   0    'DefaultCursor
        DefaultType     =    2    'UseODBC
        Exclusive       =    0    'False
        Height          =    375
        Left            =    960
        Options         =    0
        ReadOnly        =    0    'False
        RecordsetType   =    1    'Dynaset
        RecordSource    =    "Titles"
        Top             =    2160
        Width           =    2175
    End
End
```

Since the form is hosting our controls, it is responsible for storing the properties each control needs to make them function the way we want. None of our controls can run by themselves - they need to be hosted by a form. For example, when we set the **RecordSource** property for the data control, it has to remember that setting. Imagine how annoying it would be if we had to reset the properties every time. It is the responsibility of the form to store any properties that are different from the defaults of the control.

Notice the various properties of the text box and the data control listed in the code snippet above. Everything that is needed to bring up the text box (**VB.TextBox Text1**) and data control (**VB.Data Data1**) happens to be stored in the **Form1.frm** file. Since the controls are really running in design mode, every time you make a change to a property, it gets written immediately to the **Form1.frm** file. So you can see that there is much more to our controls than meets the eye.

Parent/Child Data Control Relationship

There are many times when there is a **parent**/**child** relationship between database tables (i.e. a one-to-many relationship). For example, a single publisher publishes many titles. The **parent** is the publisher's record and the **child** records are the Titles records that are associated with that parent.

It would be nice to be able to show this relationship visually. Let's build a form that shows all of the titles associated with each publisher. The project will contain two data controls: the first will create a recordset of all of the publisher records and the second control will change dynamically to show only those titles associated with the publisher currently in the first data control.

Try It Out - Building a Parent/Child Form

1 Create a new project. Draw a text box, two labels, a MSFlexGrid and two data controls on the form. You must manually add the MSFlexGrid control to the tool palette. Bring up the Components dialog box and select Microsoft FlexGrid Control 6.0. (This control lives in file `Msflxgrd.ocx`.)

2 Set the **Caption** property of **Label1** to **Publisher**. Change the **Name** property of **Label2** to **lblTitles**. Leave the **Caption** property of the second label blank, we will be updating this as the program runs.

3 The **Data1** data control will create a recordset of all the publishers. This will be the parent. Set the **DatabaseName** property to the location of the copy of the **Biblio.mdb** database. Then, set the **RecordSource** property to **Publishers**. Set the **Caption** property of **Data1** to **Publishers**. This will remind the user that the control is used for navigating the Publishers table.

4 The **Data2** data control will create the recordset of titles associated with the publisher in the current record of the **Data1** data control. Set the **DatabaseName** property to the copy of the **Biblio.mdb** database file. Leave the **RecordSource** property of the **Data2** data control empty for now and set its **Visible** property to **False**. We will be controlling this with our code so there is no need for the user to see it. Set the **Caption** property of **Data2** to **Titles**. Although this will be invisible during run-time, we can see it during design-time and it will serve as a reminder to us which control is used for what purpose.

99

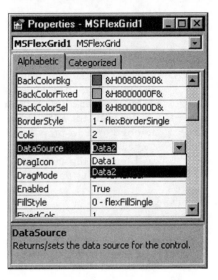

5 Set the **DataSource** property of **Text1** to **Data1** and the **DataField** property to **Name**. This will now display the name of the publisher in the current record of the recordset retrieved by **Data1**.

6 Set the **DataSource** property of the MSFlexGrid control to **Data2**. Remember that we want the grid to display titles associated with the publisher. As the program runs, it will automatically request titles for the publisher displayed from the **Data1** control.

7 Since the grid will size the fields to its liking, some of the information may be cut off in the display. So let's permit the user to resize the grid. Set the AllowUserResizing property to 3 - flexResizeBoth. This will allow the user to manually resize both row and column width with a mouse. Don't worry, later in the book we will show you how to programmatically resize the columns so that each will be the correct size depending on the width of the field it will be displaying.

8 OK, ready to get your hands dirty and write some code? Double-click on the **Data1** data control and select the **Reposition** event. Add the following code in the **Reposition** event procedure.

```
Private Sub Data1_Reposition()
Dim lPubID As Long
lPubID = Data1.Recordset!PubID
Data2.RecordSource = "SELECT * FROM TITLES WHERE PubID = " _
& lPubID
Data2.Refresh
End Sub
```

You might have guessed that the **"SELECT * FROM TITLES WHERE PubID = "** is a SQL statement. This one is fairly 'English-like'. We are asking for all fields in the **TITLES** table where the foreign key **PubID** is equal to the primary key **PubID** of the current record of the Publishers table. We will be covering SQL in detail in Chapter 8.

9 In the text box **Text1_Change** event procedure, add the following code:

```
Private Sub Text1_Change()
lblTitles.Caption = "Titles published by  " & Text1
End Sub
```

10 Save the project in your **BegDB\Chapter3** directory as **prjParentChild.vbp**. Press *F5* and run the program. Use the VCR buttons on the **Data1** data control to navigate through the Publishers recordset. Any titles associated with that publisher will be displayed in the grid.

How It Works

When the form gets initialized, the data controls that it hosts are also initialized. The first record in the Publishers table becomes the current record. As you navigate the **Publishers** recordset using the **Data1** data control, the name of the publisher in the current record is displayed in the bound text box. Notice that the **lblTitles** label changes to display the current publisher.

When the **Data1** data control is initialized and every time you move to another record, the **Reposition** event procedure is fired. Any code in the **Reposition** event gets run at this time. Therefore, this is the perfect place to put the code that retrieves any titles published by this publisher. We dynamically create an SQL query and use this query to define the **RecordSource** property of **Data2**. Then, by calling the **Refresh** method of the **Data2** control we execute the query. Since we set the **DataSource** of the MSFlexGrid to **Data2**, any records in the **Data2** recordset automatically get displayed in the grid.

When the **Data1_Reposition** event of the control becomes current, the contents of the text box change. When this changes, the **Text1_Change** event fires. At this point, we grab the contents of the text box, which is the new publisher's name, and display it in the **lblTitles** label.

> **FYI**
>
> Some of the publishers in the database do not have any titles associated with them. Scroll through the publishers' recordset with the data control until you find a publisher with several titles. Well, so much for legacy databases. You can never be sure of the data in them!

Let's take a look at the code in the reposition event of the **Data1** control again:

```
Dim lPubID As Long
lPubID = Data1.Recordset!PubID
Data2.RecordSource = "SELECT * FROM TITLES WHERE PubID = " _
& lPubID
Data2.Refresh
```

Remember when we discussed primary and foreign keys? Well, the **PubID** field has a unique value for each publisher record; it is the primary key for that table. Therefore, what we want to do is to take that value and find every record in the **Titles** table that is associated with that particular publisher. The **PubID** field in the **Titles** table is the foreign key. Every record in the **Titles** table has a **PubID** value for its publisher.

Every time the **Data1** data control repositions itself, we read the value of the **PubID** field into the variable **lPubID**. The **!** (known as **bang notation**) is used when we want to read or write a value to a particular field in a recordset. The **!** separates the recordset from the field. The syntax is **Recordset!*field*.** This notation is used for both DAO and ADO, so we will be learning about it in detail later on.

Once we have the value, we create a simple SQL statement that is passed to the **RecordSource** property of the **Data2** data control. We tell the **Data2** control to retrieve all records from the **Titles** table, where the **PubID** field in the **Titles** table equals the value of **lPubID** - the unique ID of that publisher derived from the **PubID** field in the recordset.

Then, we execute the **Refresh** method and create a new recordset based on the new **RecordSource** property we just set. We have essentially created a **dynamic SQL statement**. By that I mean that we are really constructing an SQL statement on the fly. Instead of hard-coding in a complete statement, we create it by adding the current publisher's **PubID** field. Therefore, depending on the current publisher, the unique **PubID** field of that particular publisher is built into the query.

If you wanted to get fancy, you could have accomplished the same thing by reading the value of the publisher's **PubID** field directly without using the **lPubID** variable. Since we are just storing the value of the current publisher record's **PubID**, we could have written this instead:

```
Data2.RecordSource = "SELECT * FROM TITLES WHERE PubID = " _
& Data1.Recordset!PubID
Data2.Refresh
```

Our dynamic SQL statement could be reduced to a single line of code. However, for debugging purposes, you might want to keep the first approach. When you get a bit more comfortable with VB, this latter approach is clearer and it saves you making a variable assignment.

Who Was That Masked Control?

Another useful bound control is the **masked edit control**. In the tool palette it looks like this:

The masked edit control does just what it says; we can supply a mask that will ensure that only data that conforms to the mask that we have defined can be displayed or input by the user. By using a mask, we can display the field in a very specific way or limit what the user enters - a mask is a format that we want the data to conform to. This control would come in handy, for example, if we wanted users to enter a social security number into the database. By setting up a mask such as **###-##-####** we can be sure the information is entered in the correct format. Likewise, if we need phone numbers, we might use a mask such as **(###)###-####** to ensure that the field is filled out correctly. Of course, we can't ensure the phone number was typed in correctly, but we can be sure that the format is correct and the correct number of digits was entered.

> *The masked edit control is only available in the Professional and Enterprise Editions of VB and from third-party vendors. However, it can come in very handy for production-quality data-entry screens so an example here makes sense.*

Try It Out - Using the Masked Edit Control

Let's say that we wanted to correctly display the ISBN number for all of the titles in the Titles table. We could set up a mask that correctly formats the field. Here's how:

1 Start a new project. Again, as with the MSFlexGrid in the previous example, the masked edit control will have to be added to your tool palette by right-clicking the mouse and selecting the **Microsoft Masked Edit Control 6.0.** from the list (it lives in the file **Msmask32.ocx**). Add the following controls to the form, laying them out as shown in the screenshot below:

> ▶ A label
> ▶ A masked edit control
> ▶ A data control

When you first draw the masked edit control on the form, it will look just like a text box. This screen shot shows what it looks like after we've added our mask:

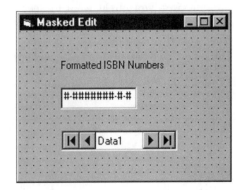

2 Set the data control's **DatabaseName** property to our **Biblio.mdb** database and the **RecordSource** property to **Titles**.

3 Type the following mask in the **Mask** property of the masked edit control:

#-#######-#-#

The **#** tells the mask to accept a number only in each position.

> *The mask must match the underlying data field otherwise you will just get the underline character in the edit control, but no mask. If you wish to show only the first 5 numbers of the ISBN number, set the PromptInclude property to False (the default is True).*

4 Set the masked edit control's **DataSource** property to **Data1** and the **DataField** property to **ISBN**.

5 Save the project as **prjMaskEdit.vbp** in the **BegDB\Chapter3** directory. Press *F5* and run your project. As you navigate the recordset you will see the first ten numbers in the **ISBN** field.

How It Works

When we want to ensure that the data in our database is squeaky clean, this control will enforce the format. When the user adds information, you can use the masked edit control to force the correct format for entering an ISBN number - or any data that fits a specific mask. Here I just wanted to show you that the control is available. We will be using this bound control when we build our address book later on in the book.

Introducing the New ADO ActiveX Data Control

In the last chapter, the Wizard created the forms for us using the brand-new **ADO data control**. Now we'll have a look at using the new-fangled ADO controls for ourselves. Let's add the ADO data control to your tool palette, as well as the new DataList controls.

Bring up the Components dialog in your tool palette and select the following two controls:

Microsoft ADO Data Control 6.0 (OLEDB)
Microsoft DataList Controls 6.0 (OLEDB)

Only controls that have OLEDB after their name can be used with the ADO data control. When you bring up the Components dialog box, you will see a Microsoft Data Bound List Controls 6.0 as an option. However, these controls work with the DAO data control - so be careful! It's easy to confuse these similar sounding controls. The Microsoft DataList Controls (the DataList and DataCombo) show a yellow cylinder on a blue grid background on the tool palette.

You will now have three extra icons in your tool palette:

▶ The ADO data control (Adodc)

▶ The DataList

▶ The DataCombo

When Microsoft DataList Controls 6.0 (OLEDB) is added, both the DataList and DataCombo controls are added. Why? Because they both reside in the same `.ocx` file. Whenever we wish to use one of these controls, they must both be added to our project. This is not a problem, but they do add a bit of bulk to our final file size. It is interesting to note that these are really Dynamic Link Library (`.dll`) files - they just happen to have a `.ocx` extension. (`.ocx` files are really `.dll` files, they just have a different extension. This is how we can only have a single instance of an ADO data control in our project, but use it as many times as needed.)

The DataList, DataCombo, DataGrid and MSFlexGrid controls all permit several records to be displayed or manipulated at once using an ADO data control. The other intrinsic controls (picture, label, text box, check box, image, OLE, list box and combo box) are also 'data-aware' and can be bound to a single field of a recordset managed by a DAO data control.

Confused yet? Just remember that any control that works with an ADO data control has (OLEDB) after its name in the Components dialog box.

Let's see how we can display several records at once using a few new ADO controls.

The ADO Data Control and the Bound DataList Control

Visual Basic 6.0 added a few neat data-bound controls. As mentioned, they only work correctly with the ADO data control, **not** with the DAO control. Never fear though, the ADO data control (Adodc) looks and feels like the intrinsic DAO control, so the transition from one to the other is easy to learn.

Wouldn't it be great if we could program a combo box to automatically update itself with the fields from some recordset? Typically when programmers needed to update a combo box, a recordset would be created and then code would have to be written to manually add the value of each field to the list box. The program would have to loop through the recordset and add each field using code. Here, we can let the ADO data control do the work for us. So in our next example, we will try out the new **bound list box** in conjunction with the ADO data control.

Try It Out - Using the DataCombo Control with the ADO Data Control

1   Start a new project. Add a DataCombo control and an ADO data control to the form. You will notice that the ADO data control bitmap on the tool palette looks like a smaller version of the standard data control except that it has a gold cylinder attached to the icon. This is the new visual cue that the control is **data-aware**. Data-aware controls bound to a data control automatically display data from one or more fields for the current record. The data control performs all operations on the current record. If you let the cursor linger over the control, the tool tip tells us that this control is the Adodc (ActiveX Data Object Data Control). Lay out the form as shown:

2   The first thing we must do is set up the properties on our ADO data control to tell it which recordset to create. ADO uses a different approach to open a data source. We will look at it now because we will be seeing quite a bit of it as we progress. Click on the ADO data control to give it focus and bring up the Properties box. Since ADO can connect to any type of data source, we must set up a **connection string**: this describes the data source that we want to access and tells the ADO data control how to get to it. However, like so many of the new VB 6.0 tools, the hard work is taken care of for us by following a few simple steps.

3   Click on the ConnectionString property and an ellipsis will magically appear. Click on this so that we can let VB create the connection string for us. As we have just discussed, the ConnectionString property of the ADO data control contains the information used to establish a connection to a data source.

The ADO data control requires a connection string to open our data source, **Biblio.mdb**. Remember above when we told the intrinsic data control about our database? Well, we also used the default connection type as Access. ADO does not know in advance these two pieces of information, so we must tell it **exactly** what to open. Clicking on the ConnectionString property of the ADO data control brings up a property page that will build the connection string for us.

4 The first step is to create the connection string. Click on B**u**ild to bring up the first form that will walk us through the process. Since we will be connecting to an Access database, select Microsoft Jet 3.51 OLE DB Provider (this opaque terminology refers to the generic database type that will be used – we'll cover this in detail later on, so don't worry about it for now). Press N**e**xt.

5 Here we select the databases to open. Click the ellipsis and select the familiar **Biblio.mdb** database. Since the database is not password protected, leave the defaults for the User Name and the check in the Blank Password box.

Since we are using an unsecured database, this entry is fine. The User name of Admin will permit us full access to our database. However, if this database **were** password protected, we would enter the User name and Password here. This information would be appended to our connection string.

One thing many programmers don't know is that Jet security is always enabled. Every time your program attempts to do something with a database, Jet first checks to ensure the user has sufficient permission to perform that action. Since there is no security-related screen or message displayed, users don't realize that security is enabled at all times. The default Admin user account has full permission for all objects in the database. We, by default, have full permission. Jet checks this and lets us do what we need to. This really makes sense because that means that there is no way to open a Jet database without security - there are no back doors to sneak into. If we don't implement security in our database, the security simply works transparently in the background.

6 Now that we've provided the name of our database, let's test the connection to ensure the ADO data control can connect. Press the Test Connection button. If everything was successful, we should see a friendly message telling us all is well.

7 Now click on the All tab of the Properties page. This will display all of the information the ADO data control needs to make the connection. Most of the items displayed are defaults. Advanced users can edit any of these values as needed.

Data Link Properties

| Provider | Connection | Advanced | All |

These are the initialization properties for this type of data. To edit a value, select a property, then choose Edit Value below.

Name	Value
Data Source	C:\begdb\Biblio.mdb
Extended Properties	;COUNTRY=0;CP=1252;LANGI
Jet OLEDB:Database Password	
Jet OLEDB:Global Partial Bulk...	2
Jet OLEDB:Registry Path	
Jet OLEDB:System database	
Locale Identifier	1033
Mode	Share Deny None
Password	
Persist Security Info	False
User ID	Admin

Edit Value...

OK   Cancel   Help

8 Now click OK to terminate the dialog box and the Property Pages. If you take a look at the ConnectionString property of the ADO data control, you can see the entry that was just created and inserted. Notice that the ConnectionString contains the Provider, security information and the Data Source, which is our database. So information that was set in several properties in the DAO control is all here in one place.

Properties - Adodc1

Adodc1 Adodc

| Alphabetic | Categorized |

⊟ **Behavior**	
DragIcon	(None)
DragMode	0 - vbManual
Visible	True
⊟ **Data**	
BOFAction	0 - adDoMoveFirst
CacheSize	50
CommandTimeout	30
CommandType	2 - adCmdTable
ConnectionString	Provider=Microsoft.Jet.OLEDB.3.51;Persist Security Info=False;Data So ...
ConnectionTimeout	15
CursorLocation	3 - adUseClient

ConnectionString
For OLEDB Providers that support connection strings

9 Now click on the RecordSource property of the ADO data control. Click on the ellipsis and a RecordSource Property page will be displayed. Since we are going to retrieve records from a table, select 2 - adCmdTable as the Command Type.

10 Later on, when we use SQL to create our queries, we will be selecting 1 - adCmdText. This permits us to place any SQL command in the Command Text (SQL) box directly below the Command Type box. Since we shall be selecting records from a table here, click the drop-down list box that now contains all of the tables in our **Biblio.mdb** database.

Select Titles as the table and then press OK to finish with the Property Pages.

11 We've now set up the connection between the ADO data control and the database - this connection is what will populate our recordset for us. Now we can turn our attention to setting up the control that will display the data for us - the **DataCombo control**.

Back on your form, bring up the **Properties** window for DataCombo control we added earlier. Since we want the ADO data control to do the dirty work of populating the DataCombo control for us, we need to provide the DataCombo with enough information so that it knows what to do. Click on the **Categorized** tab to group all of the **Data** related properties. Click on the **DataSource** drop-down box and select **Adodc1**, our ADO data control. This tells the DataCombo which specific data control to use (we might have forms that include several data controls).

12 Now we are ready to wire up our DataCombo control to the ADO data control. Set the **RowSource** property to **Adodc1**, the only choice available to us. Now click the drop-down listbox in the **ListField** property and select **Title**.

When you make a selection for the **ListField** property, VB automatically updates the **BoundColumn** property. (The **BoundColumn** field permits us to link two tables together with a single DataCombo control. We don't need to worry about this now, but it would permit us to update two tables simultaneously. We will discuss this shortly.) Set the Text property of the DataCombo control to "" (blank) so that the name of the control is not displayed.

13 Is your mouse finger tired from all of that clicking? Well, let's see the fruits of our labor. Press *F5* to run the program. Then click the drop-down box to reveal over 8,000 entries that have been added to the control for us.

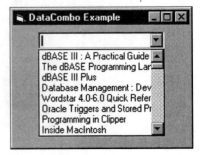

Ready for something wonderful? Type in a letter in the list box. If you type in a C for example, the first entry that begins with that letter is displayed. The control also does searching for us and with over 8,000 entries, this is a real help! Now if we wanted all of the entries displayed in alphabetical order, we would issue a SQL command that sorted in alphabetical order.

OK, you talked me into it. How do you do that? Well, I was going to wait until we got a bit further along, but now is as good a time as any to show you just how powerful this control can be. Bring up the Properties box for the ADO data control and select the RecordSource property. Click on the ellipsis.

```
Property Pages                                            [X]

General | Authentication | RecordSource | Color | Font

 ┌─ RecordSource ─────────────────────────────────────┐
 │  Command Type                                        │
 │  ┌────────────────────────────────────┐  ┌──┐       │
 │  │ 1 - adCmdText                      │  │▼ │       │
 │  └────────────────────────────────────┘  └──┘       │
 │                                                      │
 │  Table or Stored Procedure Name                      │
 │  ┌────────────────────────────────────┐  ┌──┐       │
 │  │ Titles                             │  │▼ │       │
 │  └────────────────────────────────────┘  └──┘       │
 │                                                      │
 │  Command Text (SQL)                                  │
 │  ┌─────────────────────────────────────┐ ┌─┐        │
 │  │ SELECT * FROM Titles ORDER BY Title│ │▲│        │
 │  │                                     │ │ │        │
 │  │                                     │ │▼│        │
 │  └─────────────────────────────────────┘ └─┘        │
 └──────────────────────────────────────────────────────┘

   ┌────────┐  ┌────────┐  ┌────────┐  ┌────────┐
   │   OK   │  │ Cancel │  │ Apply  │  │  Help  │
   └────────┘  └────────┘  └────────┘  └────────┘
```

14 Change the Command Type to 1 - adCmdText. This is the command used for SQL statements. Notice that the Table or Stored Procedure Name box is now disabled and the Command Text box is enabled. Type in the following SQL command:

```
SELECT * FROM Titles ORDER BY Title
```

15 Then click on OK. (Don't worry if SQL is new to you. We have an entire chapter on SQL later in this book, but note for the moment that this simple example shows how we can easily manipulate the recordset that is returned to the ADO data control.)

Save the project in your **BegDB\Chapter3** directory as **prjDataCombo.vbp**. Now press *F5* to run your program again.

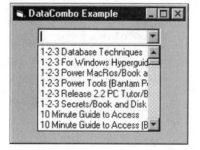

Cool! All of the entries are in alphabetical order. But wait! How come the titles that begin with 1-2-3 come before titles starting with the letter A? Well, good question. You might refer back to the last chapter when we discussed ASCII sorting; '1' is 49 in the ASCII table while 'A' is 65. So 1 comes before A and uppercase letters come before lowercase letters. See why we did that example in the last chapter? Understanding sorting is very useful when displaying information to our users.

The Mysterious BoundColumn Property.

OK, now as promised, we will discuss the **BoundColumn** property of the DataCombo box. Let's say we wish to add a new title to our Titles table. Well, remember that the PubID for each title relates back to the primary key of the Publishers table. Let's say that the user wishes to add a new title, but hasn't memorized the hundreds of PubID numbers. Sure, the user knows who published the book, but the PubID field is needed to relate the title to that publisher. This is where the **BoundColumn** property comes in.

Using the DataCombo box, we can display the names of the publishers. These would be shown in the drop-down DataCombo box. While this looks a bit complicated, it really solves this thorny problem. We would need two data controls to make this work. One data control, **Data1**, opens the Titles table while **Data2** opens the Publishers table. We set the **DataSource** property of our DataCombo to **Data1** and the **RowSource** property to **Data2**.

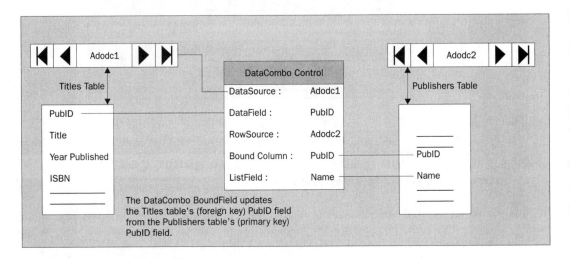

The **ListField** property determines which field is actually displayed to the user by our control. So we set that property to show the names of all of the publishers. Now the **BoundColumn** property goes to work. The **BoundColumn** determines which field in the Publishers table provides the PubID field to the Titles table. It is important to note that the PubID field in the Publishers table can't be edited - since it is the primary key for that table, **it should never be changed**. Instead, the value found in the PubID field of the Publishers table is written to the field specified by the **DataField** property - which is the foreign key of the Titles table, the PubID.

Remember that librarian we worked with earlier? Well, the library staff were so happy with our first program that they asked if there was an easy way for them to update the Titles table when they receive a new book. Of course, we couldn't say no.

Try It Out - The BoundColumn Property in Action

1 Start a new project. Add the following components to the form: a DataCombo, two ADO data controls, seven text boxes and seven labels directly above the text boxes. Lay the form out as shown below and set the **Text** property of the text boxes to the names of the fields that we will bind them to. This helps during design-time as we are sure which fields will display what data.

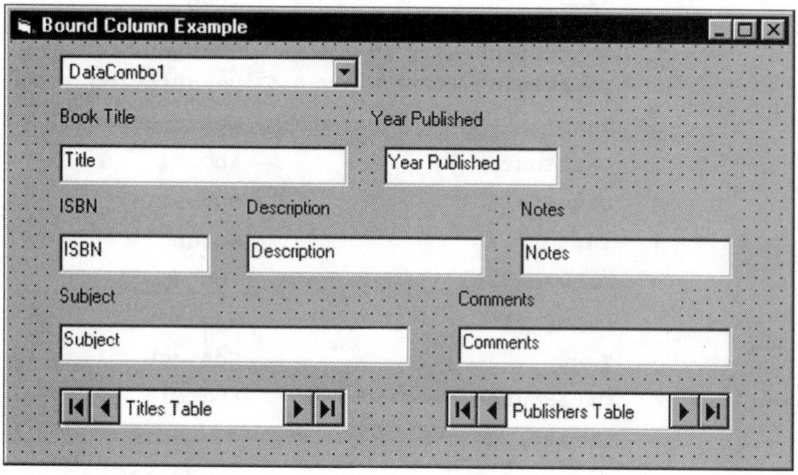

2 Use the reference table below to set the required properties:

Control	Property	Value
ADODC1	ConnectionString	Biblio.mdb
	CommandType	AdCmdTable
	RecordSource	Titles
	Caption	Titles Table
	EOFAction	adDoAddNew
ADODC2	ConnectionString	Biblio.mdb
	CommandType	adCmdTable
	RecordSource	Publishers
	Caption	Publishers Table
	Visible	False

Control	Property	Value
Text1	DataSource	ADODC1
	DataField	Title
	Text	Title
Text2	DataSource	ADODC1
	DataField	Year Published
	Text	Year Published
Text3	DataSource	ADODC1
	DataField	ISBN
	Text	ISBN
Text4	DataSource	ADODC1
	DataField	Description
	Text	Description
Text5	DataSource	ADODC1
	DataField	Notes
	Text	Notes
Text6	DataSource	ADODC1
	DataField	Subject
	Text	Subject
Text7	DataSource	ADODC1
	DataField	Comments
	Text	Comments
DataCombo1	DataSource	ADODC1
	DataField	PubID
	RowSource	ADODC2
	BoundColumn	PubID
	ListField	Name
Label1	Caption	Book Title
Label2	Caption	Year Published
Label3	Caption	ISBN
Label4	Caption	Description
Label5	Caption	Notes
Label6	Caption	Subject
Label7	Caption	Comments

Build the connection strings for the data controls as we did in our previous example, then bind the controls using the above matrix (refer back to the earlier examples if you want a refresher).

A few comments before we run the program. Notice that the **Adodc1.EOFAction** property is set to **adDoAddNew**. This is so that when we wish to add a new record, we move to the last record, then click the next record. This will open up a blank record for us to add our data. Normally, the default setting of **EOFAction** for the ADO data control is **adDoMoveLast** - this ensures that if the user attempts to go beyond the last record, they are prevented from doing so. By changing this property, we will permit the user to actually add a new record to the Titles table. Also notice that the **Visible** property of the Adodc2 data control is set to **False** - since we don't need to see this while the program operates, we hide it.

3 Save the project in your **BegDB\Chapter3** directory as **prjBoundCol.vbp**. Press *F5* to run the program.

4 Navigate through the recordset using the **Adodc1** data control that controls the Titles recordset. Notice that the publisher's name changes as we move and that the publisher's name is in the Publishers table, not the Titles table. So we can see how the data control is linking our two tables.

Now let's add a new title to the Titles table. We want to make sure this works perfectly before we turn it over to the librarian.

5 Click the 'last record' button on the right of the data control to bring you to the end of the recordset. Next, click the 'next record' button (the single right-pointing arrowhead) to bring up a new, blank record. We are now ready to add our new title.

Add some text in the blank fields, but do not click the DataCombo box. We want to test to be sure the PubID field will be added correctly. When the text is entered as shown, click the 'previous record' button to write the changes to the database.

6 As soon as we click the previous record button, VB gives us an error message. Since we have not selected a publisher from the drop-down list, there is no primary PubID key from the Publishers table to assign to our new record as a foreign key and since this value can't be NULL, the record will not be added.

7 Now go ahead and select a publisher from the DataCombo control. Once our DataCombo control has a valid publisher, it can now link the PubID field to the PubID field in the Titles table. Once you select a publisher, press the previous record button so that any changes are added to the database. In this case, we are adding a new record to the Titles table.

8 Now let's try a little experiment. Click the 'first record' button (the left-most VCR button) to take us all the way to the first record in the recordset. Now click the last record button again to take us to the end of the recordset. Our new record is added to the end of the recordset. As new records get added, they are always placed at the **end** of the recordset. Now, all of the discussion in the last chapter starts to make more sense. We might want to find all titles that start with the word "The". Since we indexed that field, a separate index file is updated whenever we add a new record. So when we want a specific Book Title, the index file is referenced by Jet. It knows the position of each record in the Titles table so can quickly retrieve all of the records we need. There is no need to look at each and every record - Jet knows the exact position of each record in the recordset.

The VB 6.0 Hierarchical FlexGrid Bound Control

The **Microsoft Hierarchical FlexGrid** affectionately called **MS HFlexGrid**, displays and operates on tabular data. It gives us the flexibility to sort, merge and format tables containing both string data and pictures. This merging and sorting is done at run-time, as we saw in the last chapter. Unfortunately, when it is bound to a data control, the MS HFlexGrid control (ADO) displays data in a read-only manner. However, even with the limitation of no editing, this is a great control for showing a lot of information professionally and easily. The Wizard used this control in the last chapter - now we'll have a go at it ourselves.

Try It Out - Using the Hierarchical FlexGrid Bound Control

1 Start a new project. Make sure you've got the ADO data control in your tool palette, then add a Hierarchical FlexGrid control (the Microsoft Hierarchical FlexGrid Control 6.0 (OLEDB) control in the Components dialog) to your tool palette as well.

2 Add an ADO data control and a MSFlexGrid control to your form as shown below.

3 Set the ConnectionString for the ADO data control as you normally would. Then set the RecordSource Command Type to 2 - adCmdTable and the Table to Titles. Now the data control is set up to retrieve all of the records from the Titles table. Also, set the **Visible** property to **False**. This will hide the ADO data control while the program is running. The user will have scroll bars on the MSFlexGrid control to navigate the recordset. (If you need a refresher on how to set these properties, refer to the previous examples.)

4   Set the **DataSource** property to **Adodc1**. Right-click on the grid to bring up the menu
and select Retrieve Structure. The grid will then actually display the structure of the
underlying table. Since we defined the table as Titles in the connection string of Adodc1,
that is what is displayed. There will be a bit of disk whirring and the structure will be
displayed right in the grid.

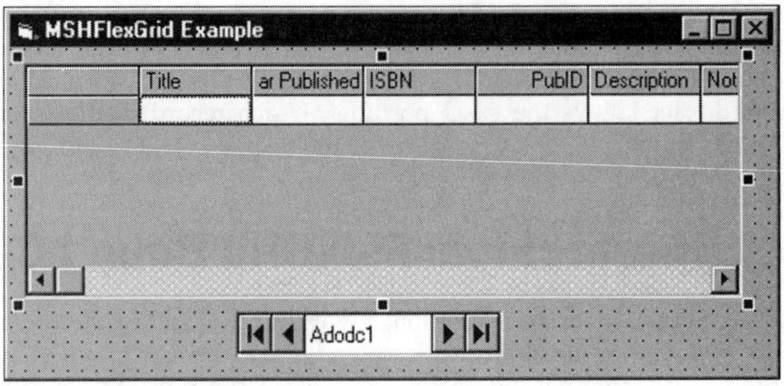

5   Right-click on the MS HFlexGrid control and select Properties to bring up the Property
Pages dialog box. On the General tab, set the Fixed Cols to 0. This will eliminate the
blank column on the rightmost of the grid as shown above. Next, change the
AllowUserResizing to 3 - Both. This will permit us to resize the columns during run-time.

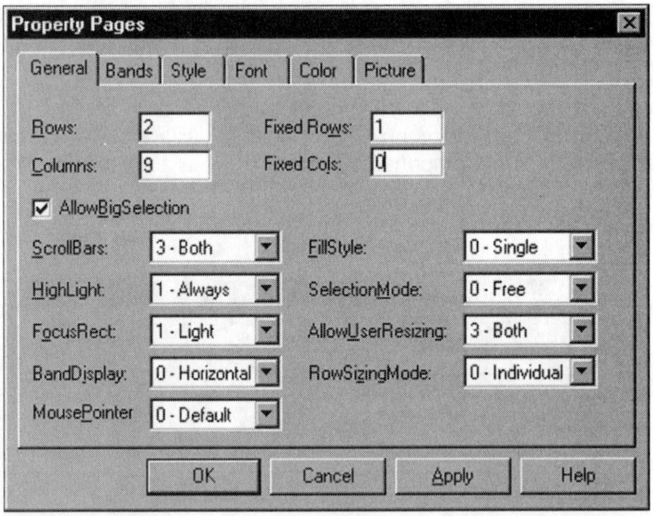

6   Next, click the Bands tab of the Property Page dialog box. We want to merge some fields,
so if we left the Title field as the first field displayed, none would be merged. Why?
Because each title is unique. We want to find a field that will merge the records with like
values in adjacent fields. Select the PubID in the Column Caption and use the 'up' arrow to
the right-hand side to move that field to the first position. To make our grid look slick,
change the Gridlines to 2 - Inset. Now click Apply to update the MSFlexGrid with our new
property settings.

Property Pages

| General | Bands | Style | Font | Color | Picture |

Band: `Band 0 ()`

Gridlines: `2 - Inset`   BandIndent `0`

TextStyle: `0 - Flat`   ☐ BandExpandable

TextStyleHeader: `0 - Flat`   ☐ ColumnHeaders

Column Caption	Column Name
☑ PubID	PubID
☑ Title	Title
☑ Year Published	Year Published
☑ ISBN	ISBN
☑ Description	Description
☑ Notes	Notes

| OK | Cancel | Apply | Help |

7 The grid should now look like this. Notice that the PubID is now the first field displayed, not the Title as before when we retrieved the structure of the table.

MSHFlexGrid Example

PubID	Title	ar Published	ISBN	Description	Notes	Sub

`|◀ ◀  Adodc1  ▶ ▶|`

8 In order to really show off the control, we are going to write a few lines of code to set some additional properties. In the **Form_Activate** event, add the following code:

```
Private Sub Form_Activate()
```

```
Dim iIndx As Integer

With MSHFlexGrid1
  . Row = 0
  For iIndx = 0 To .Cols - 1
     .Col = iIndx
     .CellAlignment = 4
     .MergeCol(iIndx) = True
 Next
.Col = 0
.ColSel = .Cols - 1
.Sort = flexSortGenericAscending
.MergeCells = flexMergeRestrictColumns
```

```
End With
```

```
End Sub
```

9   Don't worry if the syntax looks a bit strange. We will be covering the '.' dot notation in a later chapter. Here we are just setting the first row in the **For...Next loop**. The code starts at row 0 and then loops through each of the fields. It sets the alignment of the column to 4, which is 'right justify'. When the code exits the loop, we set the **Sort** to **flexSortGenAscend**, which means generic sorting. We then tell the control to merge with cells above if they have the same value.

Save the project as **prjHFGrid.vbp** in the **BegDB\Chapter3** directory. Press *F5* and run the program.

PubID	Title	Year Published
4	Theoretical Aspects of Object-Oriented Programming : T; Using Mpi : Portable Parallel Programming With the Mess	1994
5	Getting Graphic on the IBM Pc/Book and 64K Disk	1996
	3D Graphics Programming in Windows/Book and Disk	1994
9	3D Graphics Programming With Quickdraw 3D/Book an	1995
	A C User's Guide to ANSI C (Addison-Wesley Profession	1991

Not too bad for a mouse click or two and a handful of code - this is a pretty powerful control. When your data display requirements mean that you need to show several records at a time, the MSFlexGrid is the tool to use. You can see the power of the control for yourself in the above example. The merging and sorting properties that we set really provide an attractive and useful interface. Notice how all of the titles for PubID 4 are grouped together. Visually, the user can quickly see patterns in the data by the merging capabilities of this control. Essentially, we make it easy for the user to make sense of large amounts of data.

The data-bound MSFlexGrid control appears very similar to the standard grid control. However, with the MSFlexGrid you can set the **DataSource** property to a data control so that the control is automatically filled and the sorting/merging capabilities make it a professional tool for displaying several records. The column headers are set automatically from a data control's recordset field names. Under the hood, the MSFlexGrid control is really a fixed collection of columns, each with an undefined number of rows.

What Do All These Controls Have in Common?

Well, now that you have got some experience with a few of the data bound controls, you can see that there is a pattern; **they are all driven by a data control**. The data control is responsible for opening a connection to the database and getting the record source. Then we associate (bind) the control that will display the data to the data control. This relatively simple process, coupled with the armory of controls that VB 6.0 gives us, supplies us with a lot of power in processing and displaying our data.

Summary

In this chapter we have explored the data control some more and programmed it to retrieve data for us. We noted that there are two data controls: the well-established DAO data control built into VB, and the newer ADO data control, which is one of the key elements in the future VB data access strategy. We experimented with them both.

Here's our list of important points for this chapter:

What We Learned

▶ **Intrinsic** controls are built into the VB language and ActiveX Data Object (ADO) controls must be manually added to our tool palette

▶ ADO controls are really **DLLs**

▶ Bound controls work in concert with the data control

▶ Both the DAO and the ADO data control perform the same basic function: extracting recordsets from tables and linking the data to bound controls

▶ ADO bound controls are **hosted** by a form. The form is responsible for storing the control's properties

▶ We can display **parent/child** related data by programming our bound controls

▶ The **masked edit** control enforces a strict input format

▶ The ADO **DataCombo** control's **BoundColumn** property can be used to link tables and automatically update foreign key fields

Phew! We covered a raft-full of stuff in this chapter – but these were powerful techniques that require a minimum of coding on our part. In the next leg of our journey, in Chapter 4, we'll take a detailed look at designing a user interface that incorporates the ever-powerful data control.

Exercises

1 Explain the difference between an intrinsic control and an ActiveX control.

2 What two properties must be set prior to using the ADO data control? What do each of these properties accomplish?

3 How does a data aware, or bound control, know what information to display?

4 Explain the difference between the command types **adCmdText** and **adCmdTable** on an ADO data control.

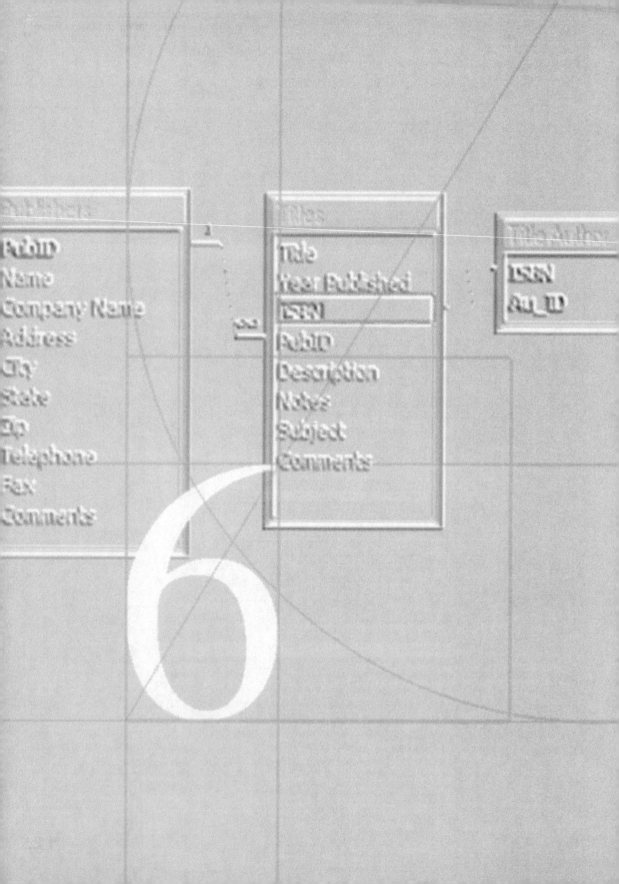

4

Designing a User Interface for the Data Control

Here our journey begins. We are now ready to get down to actually writing a Visual Basic program. Most Visual Basic programs have at least one **form** if they want to display something to the user. There are cases where you can have a non-visual program, such as a server that performs tasks in the background. However, we want to show the database information to the user, so we will be using a form as the foundation of our programs.

A form is the 'face' our program shows the world. A form is where the user interacts with our program - it is essentially the meeting point between our VB program and the user. The form is the foundation on which we draw our buttons, check boxes and other controls. Forms, and the controls we place on them, are the basic building blocks of a user interface. Fortunately, the concepts you learn about when working with the form are applicable for all visual parts of our program.

Designing the User Interface

The first step in writing a Visual Basic program is to draw up the user interface. That interface consists of, at the very minimum, a form. When we have that displayed, we can literally 'draw' our gizmos - such as buttons, boxes and labels - directly on the form. The form and all of the tools in your tool palette comprise the *visual portion* of our program, by which we mean everything that the user can see. This is different from the hidden, non-visible part of our program that will hold our code and make our program do useful things. For now though, it's important to become familiar with the visual part of our program.

Visual Basic is very strong at **prototyping**, or creating a quick non-working model of what a program will eventually look like.

You may have seen television programs about how car designers in Detroit will build a clay model of a proposed new car. It will be a full size model. It looks just like the finished product, but it's made out of clay! The designers do this so they can show engineers and prospective buyers how the finished car will look when it is actually built. One engineer may examine the model and say, "The wheel well is not deep enough for the oversized tires." A buyer might say, "I'm not crazy about the square tail lights." OK. No problem. The designer just goes back and changes the clay model until it's right. No real car is actually built until everyone agrees that the clay model is 'exactly' how the finished car should look.

Visual Basic programs work exactly the same way. When a company needs a new piece of software, they will ask a programmer to create a model of what a program should look like, without actually writing any code - a **prototype**. It is easy to create a visual representation of what our program will look like - usually without writing a single line of code. Once we have designed the program, the user may tell us to add another button here or move this check box over there. No problem. Only when we get the visual part of our program correct do we actually write any code.

Before Microsoft Windows came on the scene, programmers would write acres of code and then add a user interface almost as an afterthought. As such, the interface was often pretty klunky. Windows turns this approach on its head. Usually it is only when we get the visual part right - the user interface - that we start to write computer code. When we create a form (a form object) and draw controls (control objects) on it, we need to set various properties to achieve the 'right' user interface. For example, we might want to set a form's **Caption** property to 'Book Titles'. Since the form is the foundation of all of our visual programming, let's spend a minute looking at the form object and hit on a few important points that will serve us well as we proceed.

The Visual Basic Form

Let's look at a real form and see what it can do. Start a new **.exe** project. Each new **.exe** project adds a form to the project that is shown in the Visual Basic Project Explorer:

The Project Explorer displays a hierarchical list of the projects and all of the items contained in a project. A new **.exe** project only contains a single form when we start off. There are three icons on the menu bar of the Project Explorer.

> ▶ **View Code.** Clicking this displays the code window so you can write and edit code associated with the selected item. This will bring up the code window for our highlighted form.

> ▶ **View Object.** Clicking this displays the object window for the selected item. This will bring up our form.

▶ **Toggle Folders.** Clicking here shows the various object folders while showing or hiding the individual items. When we add code modules, we will have an additional folder called (surprise!) Modules. We can use this toggle switch to display/hide all items within our folders.

You can also bring up a form by double-clicking Form1 in the Project Explorer. Do that now.

One of the fantastic things about Visual Basic 6.0 is that everything is an object. This means that they have properties and methods. You will read about the printer object and we have set properties on the controls we have used so far - so that is a tip off that they are also objects. The form, the basis of our user interface is no exception. When you place a form on the screen by running your Visual Basic program, it is born knowing how to do several things. Take a moment to explore this concept by running Form1. Move your mouse to the edges of the form. Notice how the cursor changes from an arrow to a line with double arrowhead. This provides a visual cue that says the form can be resized. While the cursor is on the edge of the form and is displaying the double arrowhead, press and hold the left mouse button and move the mouse. You can resize the form!

Also, note the three little boxes in the upper right-hand corner of the form. The left box (the one with an underline) will minimize the form when clicked. The middle box (with either 1 or 2 stylized forms) will resize the form to its previous size. The rightmost box (with the X) will terminate (or close) the form. Now, click on the upper left-hand portion of the form, on the icon of a form next to the caption. A standard Windows drop-down menu appears. All of the choices are functional. The form also knows when it is clicked, resized, and more. So the form is an object that comes conveniently packaged with all of the standard Windows features we'd expect in a purchased application - resizing, minimizing, maximizing and so on. We didn't have to write a single line of code for all of this to happen.

> *Note: When programmers started to write the first software for Microsoft Windows back in 1991, they used a computer language called C. C is a so-called low level language. This means that the programmer had to do much of the work that Visual Basic does for us. To accomplish what we just did - simply displaying a form with a caption and three buttons - took 150 lines of code! With Visual Basic, we simply clicked a button and the form was ready-made.*

When we want to change the look or behavior of a form, we simply set a property. In fact, all objects (forms included) have properties that we can read or change. We will be talking quite a bit about properties in this book. So let's take a minute to take a look at some form properties to get a feel for what they are.

Properties Explained

Properties are attributes or characteristics of an object, such as our form. These attributes are things like **Caption**, **Size**, **BackColor** and so on. All of the visible parts of our program, such as forms and controls, will have a Properties window.

Properties - Form1	✕
Form1 Form	▾

Alphabetic | Categorized

(Name)	Form1
Appearance	1 - 3D
AutoRedraw	False
BackColor	☐ &H8000000F&
BorderStyle	2 - Sizable
Caption	Form1
ClipControls	True
ControlBox	True
DrawMode	13 - Copy Pen

Caption
Returns/sets the text displayed in an object's title bar or below an object's icon.

The Object drop-down combo box shows the currently selected object: in our case we are examining the properties for a form, Form1. If we have several forms in our project, only objects from the active form are visible in this drop-down Object box. However, if we have several controls and labels on that form, each of these will be displayed in the drop-down box.

The Properties window has two tabs - **Alphabetic** and **Categorized**. When the Alphabetic tab is selected, all of the properties for the selected object that can be changed at design time are presented to us in alphabetic order. Also any current default settings are displayed for these properties. To change any property setting, select the property name and type, or select the new setting if there are predefined choices.

The Categorized tab lists the same properties for the selected object by predefined categories. For example, the **Appearance** category contains the BackColor, Caption and ForeColor properties because they affect the appearance of the form.

Properties - Form1	✕
Form1 Form	▾

Alphabetic | Categorized

⊟ **Appearance**	
Appearance	1 - 3D
BackColor	☐ &H8000000F&
BorderStyle	2 - Sizable
Caption	Form1
FillColor	■ &H00000000&
FillStyle	1 - Transparent
FontTransparent	True
ForeColor	■ &H80000012&

Caption
Returns/sets the text displayed in an object's title bar or below an object's icon.

The Categorized tab allows you to either collapse the list to see just the category names or expand a category to see all the properties in that category. Just click on the plus (+) icon or minus (-) icon to the left of the category name to expand or collapse the list.

The description pane at the bottom of the box is very handy for beginners. This pane shows the property type and provides a short description of the property.

> *Tip: When you get more comfortable with the descriptions, you can hide the description pane by right-clicking the mouse on the pane. Uncheck description by clicking with the left mouse button. This will hide the Description panel. You can always display it again by checking the description. Give it a try now.*

In our form, we can change the **Form1.Caption** property by simply typing in a new caption in the property box. As you type it, you can see it change immediately on the form itself, but we will also be setting properties at run-time. You change the property of an object at run time by using the ***object.property*** syntax that we call **dot notation**. We have the object we want to address, like **Form1**, then a dot (**.**) and finally the property of that object we want to change. So if we wanted to change the caption of our form at run-time, we could add this line of code to our program:

```
Form1.Caption = "A new form caption"
```

Likewise, if we wanted to read the caption of the form at run-time we would store it in a variable with a line in our program such as:

```
sCurrentCaption = Form1.Caption
```

There are several types of properties for each object, depending on the task at hand. We just assigned and then read a string from the **Form1.Caption** property. Properties can also be **True** or **False** (**Boolean**), **numeric**, **Hex** for colors and **enumerated** such as the **Form1.Appearance** options of **0 - Flat**, **1 - 3D**, etc. Later on, we will actually be creating our own objects with properties of their own. We will further discuss properties at that point, but we need to be familiar with them as we write our first program.

If forms only had properties, they would not be nearly as useful as they actually are. Forms (and all visual tools) also know how to respond to events. This brings us to the second important concept in developing a database program. This is known as the **event-driven** model. What does this mean?

Event-Driven Programming Explained

When I started programming in Microsoft Windows in the early 1990's, I wondered aloud, "How does Windows know when I click a button? How can I select one program, then select an entirely different program with the click of a mouse? How does it do that?" It really seems almost magical until you understand **events**.

It is very important to have a clear 'mental model' of what is going on under the hood of Visual Basic. That is, what is an event and how does VB respond to events? Since event-driven programming is at the heart of Visual Basic and Windows, it's a good time for us to discover events.

Just think of our Wizard program example. **You** could click on the minimize box at the top of the form and the form will minimize itself. Or **you** could navigate through the recordset. Or **you** could click on the menu box in the upper left-hand form and select E<u>x</u>it. The form disappears. Do you notice a pattern here? Put on your thinking cap. In each case, you - the user - performed some action and Visual Basic **responded**. The program didn't take any action until you instructed it to. You navigated, you minimized and you exited the form. The moral of this story is that Windows (and Visual Basic) is passive in nature. You, the user, are in control. The user makes things happen - Visual Basic responds.

When you run your program, it just sits and waits… and waits… and waits for some user action. That action might be clicking a button, moving the mouse or pulling down a menu. When the action occurs, Visual Basic responds. Then it waits for the next action by the user.

Our events story starts with Microsoft Windows. Windows is an **Operating System** (**OS**). The OS does all of the low-level tasks like creating directories, handling files and managing computer memory. We never have to worry about those things. Windows also grabs every input from the user, from moving a mouse to clicking a button, to resizing a form. Windows takes all of these user actions and converts them to **messages**. These messages are placed in a **queue**, or holding pattern. Windows then examines each of these messages, one by one, and determines which program they belong to. If we click on a Visual Basic form, Windows knows that the message belongs to our Visual Basic program and sends the message to our form.

Likewise, if you are running a game, Windows passes that game the messages. Windows handles all of this processing in the background – it is invisible to us. We don't have to worry about how it is done. Our program just has to respond to the events when they occur.

> *There are several development programs that actually display Windows messages as they occur. Simply moving your mouse across the screen will generate hundreds of Windows messages. Likewise, pressing a key on the keyboard generates a key_down and key_up message, along with information such as which key was pressed, was the SHIFT key also pressed and so on.*

Mercifully, Visual Basic 6.0 protects us from all of these messages. Visual Basic bundles up various Window messages that are important to us and converts them into **events**. An **event** is something that happens to our program. For example, when a user clicks on our form with the mouse, a **Form_Click** event occurs in our form. When the user moves the mouse over our form, a **Form_MouseMove** event occurs. If you bring up the code window for **Form1**, you will see the Object drop-down combo on the left and the Event drop-down combo on the right.

Click the Event combo box and notice all of the events a newly minted form knows how to respond to. When the user clicks on the form with the mouse, the **Form_Click()** event procedure fires. Of course, if we don't have any code in this event procedure, nothing happens. If we want something to occur when the user clicks on the form, this is where we put the code. Makes sense, doesn't it? We will be adding code to various event procedures in our next project.

Don't worry about the details of all of the strange looking events that the form can to respond to. We will actually be using only a few of these event procedures in this book. As you get more proficient with Visual Basic, you will find yourself using more and more of them.

Did you notice that each of the events, such as **Form_Click**, has an underscore between the item we are working with (in this case the form) and the event? Each and every event procedure has three parts: the name of the object, an underscore _ and the name of the event. Together they make up the event procedure signature. This makes it very easy for us to spot an event procedure.

In every Visual Basic program, the following steps occur:

1 The user performs an action, such as clicking a button.

2 Windows grabs the action and converts it into a Windows Message.

3 Windows passes the messages to our Visual Basic program.

4 Visual Basic converts the messages into an event.

5 The appropriate event procedure in our form will fire.

6 If we put code in that event procedure, the code will run.

> *These steps are collectively known as event-driven programming. User actions cause events to happen in our program. We decide which events our program should respond to by placing code in that event procedure. In fact, each visual component of Visual Basic, such as buttons, has a set of event procedures that it will respond to.*

The Important Form Event Sequence

When our program starts, our form is loaded. To the user, it seems that our form just appears. However, there is actually a sequence of events that occur to display the form. When we run our program, these events take place:

1 `Form_Initialize` is the first event to be fired.

2 Next, the `Form_Load` event takes place. This event actually loads the form into the computer memory, preparing it to be shown.

3 `Form_Activate` fires after the form is actually displayed.

4 `Form_Paint` fires if anything needs to be painted on the form.

Back to Programming Databases

OK, ready to start our first database program? I bet you thought I forgot. Well, we will start by drawing a data control on our form to start the visual layout of our program. Now that we know about properties and event-driven programming, we are ready to delve into the powerful and fun world of database programming!

Into the Heart of the Data Control

Typically the data control is used in the parts of our program where user interaction with the information is required. That's because of the incredible power of binding data aware controls to show the data fields in the recordset of the data control.

In this chapter, we will be using the intrinsic **Data Access Objects (DAO)** data control. Why? Remember when we mentioned that if you are using an Access **.mdb** file that DAO is the way to fly? Well, we will again be using the intrinsic data control, and this time we will program it using DAO. Here's the good news. We could simply substitute the **ActiveX Data Objects (ADO)** control and the program would work exactly the same. The only difference is how we connect to the data source. The intrinsic control requires the same information as the ADO control, but its syntax is just a bit different, as we saw in the last chapter. However, once wired up, the code is the same.

Also, since there is such an army of DAO programmers, I thought we would start with the intrinsic control. Later on in the book, we will work exclusively with ADO, but I like to know all of my options, so in the book we will cover both methods. The next few chapters will deal with **.mdb** files (Microsoft Access) desktop applications, and DAO is the preferred way to access these data sources. However, when we move on to Internet programming, ADO is the preferred method.

> *Caveat: If you are using SQL 7.0 for your desktop database, then simply switch to the ADO control and follow along. Since VB 6.0 comes equipped with all of the tools necessary to write all of the applications in this book, including the ability to create .mdb files, let's stick with the intrinsic control for the time being.*

Duplicating the Functionality of the Wizard

It's actually easy to manually create a form just like the data-entry screen in our previous Wizard-based example. We simply set up the data control, bind some data-aware controls to it, and we are up and running. However, there are many situations where we don't require user interaction when accessing a database. Consider making a call to the database to retrieve information that is used to generate a report or graph. In these cases we will use other methods available to us, such as DAO and ADO. Both DAO and ADO are very powerful but are a bit more involved. Learning the data control inside and out will make the learning curve for these pretty flat.

For example, the DAO recordset object alone provides 24 methods and 26 properties. These are great for organizing, sorting, searching, updating, adding and deleting data in our database. Once we understand how the data control works, learning both DAO and ADO will be a snap. Keep in mind that the data control and DAO complement each other and can work closely together - depending on the task at hand. With VB 6.0, we also have an **ActiveX Data Object data control** that we will explore in a later chapter.

The data control handles data access by talking directly to the Microsoft Jet database engine. As mentioned, this is the same database engine that powers Microsoft Access and is native to Visual Basic. You can think of the data control as an interpreter between the programmer and Jet. We just set a few properties on the data control and it will talk to Jet for us. Remember when we discussed abstraction? Well, we are removed by several levels of abstraction from the mechanics of Jet by using the data control. We simply set its properties and put code in its methods and go. We don't have to concern ourselves with record locking, etc. Jet will do that for us.

By working with the data control, you are automatically provided with seamless access to many of the standard database formats. It also allows you to create data-aware applications with minimal coding. The data control permits you to move from record to record and even manipulate data in bound controls. Without a data control, our data-aware (bound) controls on a form can't automatically access data. Each and every bound control requires a data control to feed it records to display.

If you had your thinking caps on during the Wizard exercise, you might have noticed that we had to provide the critical information to make our program work. Specifically, we had to tell the Wizard what type of database we were connecting to (Access), the database file to use (**Biblio.mdb**), the table in that database to open up (Titles), and which fields to use in that table. All the Wizard was really doing was setting the data control properties. See, the Wizard is helpful but usually we can do a better job on our own. All the objects that we will be using (and later creating) have properties which we can manipulate through our VB code.

Let's Do it Ourselves this Time

To illustrate how powerful the data control is, let's create our own simple example. We don't need a Wizard. We will not only use the Wizard's magic, but we will far exceed it. This is the start of our project to create a working database program using all of the tools Visual Basic has to offer. Since the Publishers table is the main table, we will start with it. Remember that the Publishers table has a unique PubID field. We must have a publisher before we can have a book title. The unique PubID field will be read from that publisher's record and inserted into records about individual books (Titles). So it makes sense to start here.

Try It Out - Adding a Data Control to Our Form

1 Create a **Chapter4** sub-directory in your regular **BegDB** directory to save this chapter's files in. Start a new project and bring a new form up in the VB IDE.

2 Draw a data control on the form.

3 Click on the newly drawn data control to give it focus. Bring up the Properties window by pressing *F4*. We first want to set the **DatabaseName** property. Click on the ellipsis and the File Find dialog will pop up. You can use it to navigate your hard disk and find the file. Select the **Biblio.mdb** file from the **[Drive letter]:\BegDB** directory.

> *Note: If you haven't done so already, please make a sub-directory called **BegDB** and copy the **Biblio.mdb** file into it. We will be modifying the file so we always want to work on a copy. Select the file **Biblio.mdb** and it will be placed in the **DatabaseName** property field.*

4 Since that data control now knows which database we will be using, we can now set the **RecordSource** property. Click the down arrow of RecordSource in the properties window and all of the tables in the **Biblio.mdb** database are shown. Select the Publishers table.

5 Just to make our control align itself with the bottom of our form, click the drop-down box for the Align property and select 2 - Align Bottom. This will place the data control neatly at the bottom of our form.

6 Your form should now look something like this:

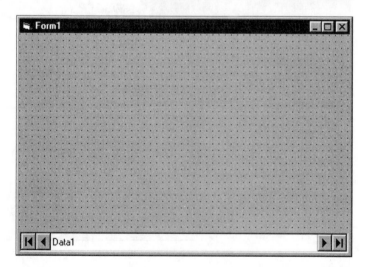

How It Works

There! By setting just two properties, the **DatabaseName** and the **RecordSource**, we have set up the data control to access a specific table in a specific database. We then set the **Align** property to align the data control visually on the bottom of our form. Since we will be using all of the default properties for the control, we are ready to move on. Later on, we will be examining the other properties of the data control, but most times, the default settings are perfect. Easier than falling off a log, don't you think?

Now that we have the data control all set up, we need to bind a few data-aware controls to it. While the data control can retrieve a recordset for us, it has no way of displaying the results. The data control is essentially the intermediary between the database and the **GUI (Graphical User Interface)** - our form. We use a data-aware control, such as a text box, to actually view the records in the recordset that are retrieved from the data control. We will now bind (i.e. connect) data-aware text boxes to the data control. Visual Basic has several data-aware controls that we will cover shortly. However, we will start out with the most frequently used control in our arsenal - the text box.

Try It Out - Adding Bound Text Boxes to Our Project

1 Draw a text box control on the form. We will bind the text box to the newly created **Data1** data control by setting the text box's DataSource property. Click the down arrow and select Data1. Since it is the only data control on our form, there is only a single choice. Normally we would next assign the DataField property to the field in the Publishers table we want to display. If we only had a single text box on our form, this would be the next step. However, since we have several fields we wish to show on our form, we will create a **control array** of text box data-aware controls. So just leave the DataField blank for a moment.

2   We are now ready to create a control array of bound text boxes. Essentially, a control array is just what the name implies - an array of controls. We draw a control on the form and then make copies of it. This way, while each individual control has its own visual part, they all share the same code. We will discuss why this is important in just a bit. Highlight the text box, **Text1**. This gives the text box the focus. Press *Ctrl* and *C* to copy it to the clip board. Now click on the form to give it focus. Press *Ctrl* and *V* to paste the text box back to the form. You will get a dialog asking if you wish to create a control array. Answer Y̲es. A copy of **Text1** is then placed in the upper left-hand corner of the form. Drag it down under the first text box. There are ten fields in the Publishers table, and we want to display all of them. Since we need ten text boxes and we already have two, repeat this step (of clicking on the form to give it focus and pressing *Ctrl* and *V*) to copy/paste eight more times. Drag each copy of the text box from the upper-left corner of the form and roughly group them in two columns of five.

Be sure that the text boxes are aligned so that Text1(0) through Text1(4) are in the left column and Text1(5) through Text1(9) are in the right column. Your form should look something like this:

3   Since we created a control array of ten text box controls, each has its own index number. This unique index number is how we will refer to each of the ten text boxes. We can now access each of the individual text boxes by its array number. Let's see how this works. Bring up the Properties box for the first text box. Notice that the Name of the text box is still Text1, but it is now referred to as Text1(0). That is because this text box is the first item (0) in the array of ten text boxes. In a standard, stand-alone text box the index (0) is not present. When we create a control array, all of the properties of the original are copied to the others. That is why we did not set the DataField property. Since each of the copies will be bound to a different field in the Publishers table, it is easier to set this property on each box when it is copied to the form. In other words, we set the properties that will be common to all copies of the original text box. Then, when we cut/paste, those properties are already set for us. We just need to set the specific ones for each text box.

Properties - Text1(0)

Text1(0) TextBox	

Alphabetic | Categorized

(Name)	Text1
Alignment	0 - Left Justify
Appearance	1 - 3D
BackColor	□ &H80000005&
BorderStyle	1 - Fixed Single
DataField	
DataSource	*Data1
DragIcon	(None)
DragMode	0 - Manual

(Name)
Returns the name used in code to identify an object.

Form1

	Text1		Text1
			Text1
	Text1		
			Text1
	Text1		
			Text1
	Text1		
Text1			
			Text1

Data1

4 Don't worry about making the text boxes nice and neat. Visual Basic has a very handy tool for doing this. Click on an empty portion of the form and, while holding down the left mouse button, draw a selection box around the top two text boxes. Notice that VB provides a sort of lasso to round up the text boxes. We want to align the top two boxes first and then we can perfectly align each of the columns.

Since the boxes are inside of the text boxes (grab handles for resizing a control are on the outside), we know that these boxes can be aligned together. Also note that the left-hand text box has solid align boxes while the right hand text box has just outlines - this is consistent with focus. The left-hand text box should have the focus. If the left-hand text box does *not* have the focus, click it with the mouse.

5 From VB's main menu, select F**o**rmat-**A**lign-**T**ops. This will ensure that the two text boxes are both vertically spaced from the top of the form. Next select F**o**rmat-**C**enter in Form-Horizontally. This will ensure that the two text boxes are evenly spaced horizontally. Now lasso the bottom text boxes in each column. Select F**o**rmat-**A**lign-**T**ops. This will ensure that both of these have the same top coordinates. We need to set the top-most and bottom-most text boxes of each column, so that we can evenly space the middle boxes.

Now lasso the first column, ensuring that the top box has the focus.

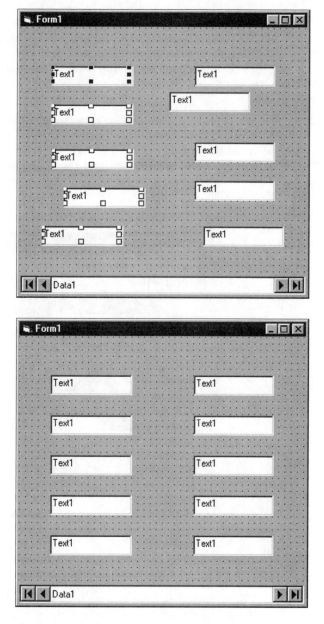

Select Format-Align-Lefts, then Format-Vertical Spacing-Make Equal. This will make a nicely spaced first column. Repeat the same steps for the second, right-hand column. Lasso the five text boxes and make the lefts equal, then set the vertical spacing. Since we already aligned the bottom boxes, the equal spacing aligns the middle boxes with the same vertical coordinates as the first column.

This seems like quite a bit of work and can be a bit tricky at first. However, the results are well worth it. Our program could have the tightest code and be blazing fast, but what will the user notice? "Hey, that text box doesn't line up, see that there," and then point to the screen. However if the user interface looks crisp and well aligned, the user will immediately have a positive feeling about our program.

> *If you ever need to tweak the position of a control, click it to give the control focus. Then hold down the Ctrl button and press one of the arrows on the number pad. So if you wish to move a text box to the right ever so slightly, click it, hold Ctrl and press →. This will move the control to the next grid line on the form. This is good for fine detail work.*

6 Just to make our program a bit more professional, take a minute and add labels above each of the text boxes. Use a control array for the labels. On the label we want to use to create the array from, set the label **Alignment** property to 2 - **Center**. Now set the **ForeColor** property to blue from the color palette, which is **&H00FF0000&**. Remember to do this for the first label. Then when you make a copy, these properties will already be set. When all the labels are in place, set the **Caption** property on each of them as shown below.

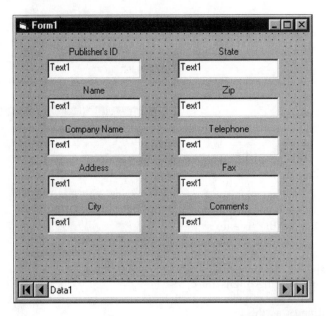

7 OK, now we just have to bind (connect) the text boxes to the data control. Starting at the upper left-hand text box (Text1(0)), bring up the Properties box and select PubID for the DataField. By selecting this field, we have just bound the PubID field of the recordset to the text box Text1(0). From this text box we can view, modify and add records to our Publishers table.

8 Now, for the remainder of the nine text boxes, going down the column, add the next available titles to the DataField for each of the text boxes.

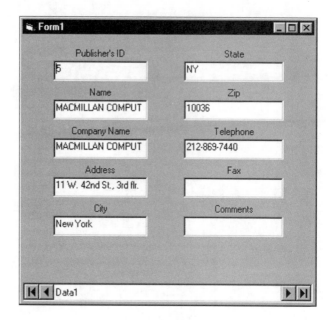

9 We are now ready to run our program! First though, save your project in the **BegDB\Chapter4** directory as **prjDataCtl** and press *F5* to run it.

How It Works

Not too bad for not having written a single line of code but not what we could call professional yet. The text box widths don't match the underlying fields. Look at the Name and Company Name fields. The truncation looks a bit shabby. Don't worry, that is easy to fix. Nevertheless, we have accessed a database table without writing any code, and the good news is that we can make our program much more powerful and flexible with minimal coding effort. Be sure to save your project as **prjDataCtl**. We will be enhancing it shortly, but for now, please take a minute and navigate through the recordset. Remember that we didn't request that the recordset be sorted in any way. So the order of the records you see will be the order they are in the database. This is probably not the order your users will need to retrieve them. We will be looking at rectifying this shortly.

Bound Controls Revisited

We just added 10 text boxes to our form. Since we set the **DataSource** and **DataField** properties of each text box, they have each been bound to a field in a data table. Bound controls provide access to specific data in your database. Bound controls that manage a single field, like the text box, typically display the value of a specific field in the current record. The **DataSource** property of a bound control specifies a valid data control name, and the **DataField** property specifies a valid field name in the recordset object created by the data control. Together, these two properties specify what data appears in the bound control. Pretty easy, wouldn't you say?

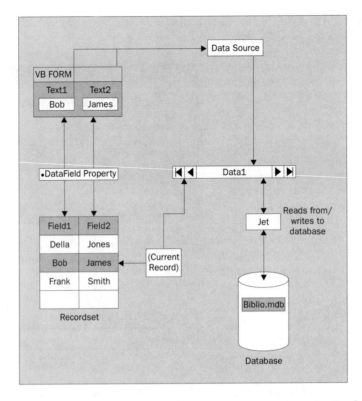

Take a moment to look at the figure. Although we just set two properties in the bound text boxes, there is quite a bit going on under the hood. The data control requests the fields to retrieve from Jet, which finds the appropriate data and passes it back to the control. The recordset, which is stored in memory, is managed from now on by the data control. The two bound text boxes have their **DataSource** properties set to the data control and their **DataField** properties set to the respective fields in the recordset. When the data control is initialized, it points to the first record in the recordset and makes it the current record. The text boxes then reflect the data from the appropriate field in the current record of the recordset. When the user navigates to another record via the data control, the text boxes are updated to reflect the new field values. If the user changes any information in one of the text boxes, when the user attempts to navigate to another record, the data control first passes the new data to Jet, which writes it to the database.

What Really Happened Here When We Ran Our Program?

The data control is automatically initialized when your application starts. The initialization actually occurs before the initial **Form_Load** procedure. If we have valid **DatabaseName** and **RecordSource** properties set, the Jet database engine attempts to create a new recordset object based on those properties. However, if one or more of these properties are set incorrectly at design time, an untrappable error occurs. The error will occur when Visual Basic attempts to use those properties to open the specified database and create the recordset object. We will discuss handling errors in our database programs a bit later on.

When everything works as advertised, the first record in the returned recordset becomes the current record. If the recordset is empty, then a blank record is tentatively added. It's called tentatively because really a buffer is opened to hold the data, but the record is not committed yet. The user will have to move to another record for the contents of the buffer to be written to the database as a new record. If they don't enter any data or quit the program, the record isn't added.

When a blank record is tentatively added, the data control empties the bound control(s). It then waits patiently for data entry from the user.

If you couldn't fight the urge to change the information in a field or two, here is what happens. When information in a bound control is changed and you then move to a different record, all of the bound controls automatically pass any changes to the data control. The data control automatically saves the changes to the database. Of course, the data control passes the information back to the Jet engine, which does all of the heavy lifting for database manipulation. Once the data is safely written to the database, the data control moves to the requested record. The data control then updates the bound controls with the data from the new current record.

Recordsets Revisited

We have been talking about a recordset that is created by the data control; a recordset object represents the records in the database table returned from a query. The recordset is an object because it has properties and methods. We will be manipulating these with code shortly.

We set the data control's **RecordSource** property to **Publishers**. This is really an **SQL** (**Structured Query Language**) query to the database that requests all records from the Publishers table. So the **RecordSource** property just takes our SQL request about which records to retrieve to create the recordset.

However, we can programmatically set the **RecordSource** property instead of setting the property manually as we have done so far. Our query to the data control may request records from several tables. We can create sophisticated queries using SQL. We will be covering SQL in depth in Chapter 8.

A recordset only exists as a temporary object in memory. A query retrieves the selected records from the database table(s) and creates a temporary recordset object in memory. This is the object that our data control creates and works with. All recordset objects are constructed using records (rows) and fields (columns) from the underlying database table(s). So conceptually, a recordset is just like a table in memory. It can consist of an entire table, or a subset of that table, or a subset of multiple tables. The recordset is essentially a reference back to a set of records in one or more underlying tables.

We might want to get a single field from a multi-field table; alternatively we might want a few fields from one table and one from another table. A recordset only contains the records we ask for. For example if our Titles table has 8,000 records and we only need records of books that begin with the letter A, our recordset might only contain 100 records. A SQL statement makes the request for the desired records to the data control. The data control then places the fields in a recordset in memory for us to work with.

When we edit a database field in our form through a bound control, the recordset is modified and the change gets written back to the underlying database table(s). Of course, the data control hands the changes back to Jet that really updates the database table(s) and any index(es).

We can create three different types of recordsets, depending on our requirements of the moment.

The three recordset object types are:

▶ **Table** - this a representation of an actual database table that you can use to add, change or delete records from. If you are only working on a single table and need to modify the records, this is the fastest type of recordset to use. A table type recordset can only operate on a single table at a time. In a table recordset, any changes are written directly back to the underlying table.

▶ **Dynaset** - this is the result of a query that can have updateable records. This is a dynamic set (dynaset) of records that you can use to add, change, or delete records from an underlying database table or tables. A dynaset type recordset can contain fields from one or more tables in a database. When we modify a field in the recordset, it is written back to the underlying table(s). This is the **default** setting of a data control. A dynaset is the most flexible and powerful type of recordset. However, it usually is not as fast in searches and data manipulation as the table type recordset.

▶ **Snapshot** - this is a static copy of a set of records that you can use to find data, or generate graphs or reports. A snapshot type recordset can contain fields from one or more tables in a database, however it can't be updated. If you don't need to modify the recordset, a snapshot type recordset is very fast. This type of recordset takes less processing overhead than either the table or dynaset type of recordset. So if you don't need to modify the records, but need to provide a read-only recordset, this is the way to go. A snapshot typically returns data and executes queries faster when working with ODBC data sources.

> *Note: If the number of records returned in a snapshot type recordset is large, it may actually perform slower than a dynaset. This is because unlike a dynaset, a snapshot stores a complete copy of all requested records in memory. A dynaset, on the other hand, only loads a group of references in memory and retrieves others as needed. On critical applications with a large number of records returned, you can open a recordset as both a snapshot and dynaset to determine which is faster. Don't forget that a snapshot is read-only.*

The data control uses the concept of a **current** record. This determines which record in the recordset is currently accessible. At any given time only one record is the current record. It is this record that is displayed in any controls that are bound to the data control. As you work with recordsets in code, you will need to ensure that the current record is always a valid record. It's possible, for example, to position the current record on a deleted record or to position it beyond either end of the recordset, thus making it invalid. More on this when we discuss the `BOFAction` and `EOFAction` properties of the data control.

The Strange and Terrible Saga of Control Arrays

We used control arrays for both our text boxes and labels in the above program. Many new Visual Basic programmers are afraid of control arrays. They really don't see why they are important and prefer to just ignore them. However, using control arrays not only makes programming easier, but can optimize our program as well. Some programmers prefer to write a program, get it running and then return at a later time to optimize it. This is exactly the wrong approach. By understanding how Visual Basic works, we start by writing optimized programs. When someone says they will go back and optimize, you can be pretty sure they are not very familiar with the language. As we progress thorough the book, I will note each area where writing code one way is better than another. The use of control arrays for our text boxes is one of these times.

A good candidate for a control array is when we have several of the same types of controls that must be added to a form. In our example, we added ten text boxes and ten labels. We decided to make two control arrays - one for the text boxes and another for the labels. Adding controls with control arrays uses fewer resources than simply adding multiple controls of the same type to a form. Control arrays are also useful if you want several controls to share code. For example, with the ten text boxes created as a control array, the same code is executed regardless of which button was clicked. The strength of a control array is that its components share the same code. While each control has its own visual component, the underlying event procedures are common to all controls in the array. In our text box array, you can tell which text box was chosen by looking at the **Index** parameter. With a control array, each new text box we add inherits the common event procedures of the array. This way we are not duplicating all of the code required as if we had ten individual text boxes.

> *Note: When working with a form, always keep in mind that every control and all of the code in the form must be loaded when the form is loaded. This is a bunch of '0's and '1's that must be loaded into memory. So the more we can reduce what is stored in a form (both controls and code), the better. Later, when we understand how the code behind the data control works, we will move most of it to a code module. Remember that the smaller the memory footprint your form has, the snappier it will load. This tickles the hearts of users.*

When we make a control array, VB adds the **Index** parameter for us. We can check its value to determine which text box is effected - since each of the text boxes share the same event procedures. Don't worry if this does not make perfect sense just yet. We will be adding code in a bit to show exactly how this will work. For now, take a look at how VB adds the **Index** parameter. Whenever the contents of any of the text boxes in our array change, this event fires. If we had two separate text boxes, each would have its own **Change** event procedure. Instead the ten share this one and we can tell which text box changed by checking the index.

```
Project1 - Form1 (Code)                        _ □ ×
Text1                    ▼    Change                  ▼

    Option Explicit

    Private Sub Text1_Change(Index As Integer)

    End Sub
```

Another benefit of control arrays is that they permit you to add controls at run-time.

> *If you want to create a new control item at run-time, that control must be a member of a control array.*

Without the control array structure, creating new controls at run-time is not possible. This is because a completely new control would not have any event procedures. Control arrays come to the rescue and solve this problem. Each new control inherits the common event procedures already written for the array. For example, if your form has several text boxes that each receives a date value, a control array can be set up so that all of the text boxes share the same validation code.

Under the Hood of the Data Control

In our previous sample program, we set the `Align`, `DatabaseName` and `RecordSource` properties of the data control. We set them in the Properties window, but they can just as easily be set in code.

When a recordset is created by the data control, it is a temporary structure that is stored in memory. We have access to this group of records either by linking bound controls, such as text boxes, or getting them directly from the data control through code. Through code, we can access any field, property or method of the recordset object. In any case, we usually think of the beginning of the recordset as the first record and the end of the recordset as the last record. As logical as this sounds, it's not exactly true. When the recordset reaches the **beginning of the file (BOF)**, the pointer in the recordset is actually set **prior** to the first record. Likewise, when the pointer reaches the **end of the file (EOF)**, it is pointing **past** the last record in the recordset. As you can guess, this can cause havoc if there is no current record when you reach the beginning or end of the recordset. The controls empty out and the user wonders what the heck is going on. If we move off the beginning of the recordset, VB gives us an error to boot. If we move off the end of the recordset, a tentative record is appended and the user stares at the screen wondering what happened. It is not apparent that they are expected to add data.

Luckily, the data control has two properties that can handle this for us. By default, the data control will set the pointer to the first record when the BOF is reached and the last record when the EOF is reached.

The BOFAction Property

The **BOFAction** property tells the data control what to do when the beginning of the recordset is reached.

The location of the current record pointer in the recordset determines the BOF and the EOF values. The data control uses the **BOF** and **EOF** properties of the recordset to determine whether it contains records or whether it's gone beyond the limits of the recordset when the user moves from record to record.

We can tell the data control how to handle these cases by setting the BOFAction property. If we go with the default setting (0 - Move First) then when we execute the **MoveFirst** method the record pointer is set to the first record. Any attempts to **MovePrevious** won't be allowed. Setting this is like a safety net - the control won't permit the user to drop off the edge of the recordset.

In other words, if either the **BOF** or **EOF** property is **True**, there is no current record. If you ask for a recordset that is empty (i.e. select all authors whose first name is Zeke), the recordset's **BOF** and **EOF** properties are set to **True**. The recordset also has a **RecordCount** property that we can use to find out how many records were returned. The property will be 0 if there are no records.

Let's say we want to find all authors whose first name is Jake and one record is returned. When our recordset contains at least one record, the first and only record is the current record. In this case, the recordset's **BOF** and **EOF** properties are **False**. These properties will remain **False** until the user moves beyond the beginning or end of the recordset by attempting a **MovePrevious** or **MoveNext**. When the user moves beyond the beginning or end of the recordset, there is no current record.

Let's say that you delete the single record in the recordset that contained Jake. In this case, the **BOF** and **EOF** properties will remain **False** until you attempt to reposition to another record.

The user might move to the last record in a recordset. The last record now becomes the current record. If the user then attempts to use a **MoveNext** the current record becomes invalid and the **EOF** property is set to **True**. Likewise, if the user is on the first record and attempts a **MovePrevious**, there is no current record and the **BOF** property is set to **True**. So if you wish to look at all records in a recordset, your code will typically loop through the records by using the **MoveNext** method until the **EOF** property is set to **True**. If you then try to use the **MoveNext** method while the **EOF** property is set to **True**, an error occurs.

The EOFAction Property

The **EOFAction** property tells the data control what to do when the end of the recordset has been reached. In this case, we have three possible options:

Again, the best bet is to leave the default setting of (0 - Move Last). In this case, the last record is pointed to when the end of the recordset is reached. The EOF flag is set to false. The second option (1 - EOF) will set the EOF flag to true when the end of the recordset is reached. The last option (2 - Add New) will automatically create and append a new record when the user moves past the last record in the recordset. This can be disorienting to the user if they don't know that they are supposed to add a new record. This is not intuitive to the user. All of the fields are cleared as the data control sets up an empty record. Since we are concentrating on writing production-level code here, we will NEVER permit the user to add a record by accident. It is much better to have the user request to add another record through an Add New button.

> *Note: The* **BOFAction** *and* **EOFAction** *properties only kick in if the user navigates the recordset using the data control* **VCR** *navigation buttons. They do not take effect if you use code to navigate the recordset using the data control. This is because we hijacked control of the recordset by using code. The data control does not update these properties internally if it is not used to navigate the recordset.*

The Connect Property

For the most part, we will be using the default **Connect** property of **Access**. However, when we want to connect to another data source, we can set the option directly through the Properties window. We could also set this property using code. Notice the Connect options available to us through the data control's drop-down box:

We've already noticed that the ADO data control **Connect** string gets a bit more complex; within that single string we need to include which driver we will be using and the location and name of the database/data source. However, the standard data control just requires us to click on a drop-down choice.

We will be covering other important properties of the data control as we use them in our program. In addition to the various properties available to program the data control, there are also several useful methods. Let's add a bit of code to see exactly how they work.

Just Add Code!

Let's start out with a quick touch that will add a professional touch to our program. It would be nice to show the user just where they are in the recordset. As the user navigates, we can display the absolute current position within the recordset. Now the user will see where they are as they in the database.

Each time the user navigates to another record by pressing the VCR buttons, the `Data1_Reposition()` event procedure fires. This is the perfect place to place code that will read the `AbsolutePosition` property of the `Data1.Recordset` and display it to the user. Again, since this event procedure will fire for each click, we can read the property and retrieve the position of the current record in the recordset. We will also place some code in the `Form_Activate()` event procedure. This is because when the `Activate` event fires, any controls on the form have been fully initialized.

> Note: The `AbsolutePosition` property is the position of the current record relative to 0. If the current record moves off the recordset (either before or behind), the `AbsolutePosition` property returns '-1'. When the `AbsolutePosition` returns a negative number, we no longer have a current record. You really can't think of this property as a record number as you have in some other databases. This number will change with each recordset, depending on how many records were returned and how they are ordered. It makes sense only in the context of an individual recordset, but this is great to determine the position of the current record in a specific recordset. Since you can get the `RecordCount` property to determine just how many records are in a recordset, you can use the `AbsolutePosition` to determine where the current record is in that particular recordset.

To show the current position in the recordset to the user, start off by adding a variable, `1TotalRecords` of type **Long**, in the General Declarations section of the form. We will store the total number of records in the recordset in this variable. Since we put **1TotalRecords** in the **General Declarations**, the visibility of the variable (i.e. **scope** of the variable) is form-wide. This means that any procedure in the form can read or write to this variable. Contrast this with a variable dimensioned (**Dim**'ed) in a sub routine. This is a **local** variable (local scope) and can only be seen from within that sub routine. Not only that, the variable only comes to life when the code in that sub is running and gets destroyed when the code exits the sub.

FYI

Prior to VB 5.0, we had to write code that looks like that below. We would have placed the code in the `Data1_Reposition()` and the `Form_Activate()` event procedures that looks like this. Don't add this code, but take a look at it. It makes sense and does what we want, but it is not the most efficient means of accessing several properties at once from a single object (in this case the data control).

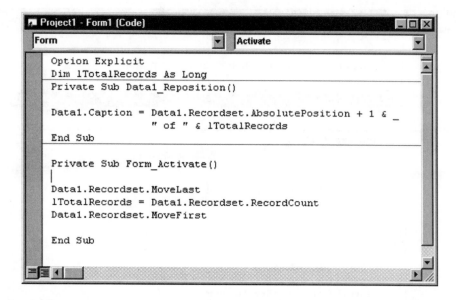

Notice that in the **Form_Activate()** event procedure we are referencing the **Data1.Recordset** four separate times. Each time, we are using a fully qualified reference such as **Data1.Recordset.MoveLast** or **Data1.Recordset.MoveFirst**. In other words, we must fully describe to VB the data control, then the recordset, then the method. Notice that there are two dots in **Data1.RecordSet.RecordCount**. Each dot is another level of resolution for Visual Basic to go through. Whenever there is a dot, Visual Basic must resolve it - and this takes time. Although a dot takes up very little space in code, it is costly to VB in execution speed. Why? Look at **Data1.Recordset.RecordCount**, each time VB must find the **Data1** control, then find the **Recordset** object and then find the **RecordCount** property. If we are referencing several recordset properties at once, this can be costly in terms of time.

Reduce the Dots - Efficient Object Reference

Starting with Visual Basic 5.0, we now have the **With...End With** construct. This construct permits us to access the data control and recordset only once. Visual Basic holds onto this reference and we can just access the properties and methods of the recordset.

> *A rule of thumb is to minimize or eliminate the dots wherever possible.*

1   Now take a look at this code and enter it in your program.

```
Project1 - Form1 (Code)                               _ □ X
Form                   ▼   Activate              ▼

    Option Explicit
    Dim lTotalRecords As Long
    Private Sub Data1_Reposition()

    Data1.Caption = Data1.Recordset.AbsolutePosition + 1 & _
                    " of " & lTotalRecords
    End Sub

    Private Sub Form_Activate()

    With Data1.Recordset
       .MoveLast
       lTotalRecords = .RecordCount
       .MoveFirst
    End With

    End Sub
```

How It Works

Notice that in the **Form_Activate()** event procedure we access the **Data1.Recordset** only once in the **With** statement.

```
With Data1.Recordset
   .MoveLast
   lTotalRecords = .RecordCount
   .MoveFirst
End With
```

VB holds onto that reference of the **Data1.Recordset** until the **End With** statement is reached. Within this construct, we can do anything with the **Data1.Recordset** by simply addressing the methods or properties. Notice that we are doing something strange-looking by moving to the last record in the recordset using the **MoveLast** property of the recordset. Then we get the value of the **RecordCount** property and assign it to the **lTotalRecords** variable. Finally, we immediately move back to the first record by calling the **MoveFirst** method of the recordset.

Why is this necessary? Because the number of records returned by the recordset can only be determined if Jet, via the data control, 'touches' all of the records. If we were to examine the recordset's **RecordCount** property before we moved to the last record, it would only show us the number of rows processed by the Jet engine. Namely, one. So by moving to the end of the recordset then immediately back, Jet has the opportunity to see all of the records and the **RecordCount** property contains the correct value.

This jumping back and forth to get the RecordCount is not required with the ADO data control.

So, these lines of code are for initializing the **RecordCount** property of the data control. Once we have done that, we can assign the current value to our form level variable **lTotalRecords**.

> *It's always faster to access a variable than it is to access the property of a control.*

We will need to reference the **RecordCount** each time the user moves to another record (we are displaying it in the **Data1.Caption**), it is much quicker to do this assignment and just read the variable. We wouldn't need to access the **Data1.Recordset.RecordCount** again unless the user adds or deletes a record. Also remember that Visual Basic must jump through more hoops for each dot. So here we only read the property once, assign it to our variable **lTotalRecords** and we are done with it.

Since the **Form_Activate()** event is only fired when the form is loaded (or it regains focus after another form has had focus), this process only happens once. We place the value of **RecordCount** in our form-level variable and can now access it from anywhere in the form.

The **Data1.Recordset** is implied from the **With** statement. Not only is this faster, it makes for less typing for the noble programmer. If we did not have this format we would have to write the following:

```
Data1.Recordset.MoveLast
lTotalRecords = Data1.Recordset.RecordCount
Data1.Recordset.MoveFirst
```

This is what is meant by a **fully qualified reference** - we must spell out the entire line. Notice that the approach above requires six dots while the **With...End With** only requires four dots. If we are setting several properties on the data control itself, we can really save on dots using the **With Data1...End With**. A rule of thumb to follow is that when setting more than two properties on an object, use the **With...End With** construct.

FYI

If you have to address an individual 'dot' property of an object more than twice in a procedure, it is more efficient to declare a local variable, transfer the value to the variable and reference the variable instead of the 'dot'. Of course, you only want to do this with static properties such as **Caption**. Properties such as **RecordCount** or **AbsolutePosition** can change on you and your variable could hold stale data.

The IntelliSense Feature

In order to make the lives of VB programmers more productive, Microsoft added the **IntelliSense** feature to VB 5.0 (and later versions). When this feature is turned on, VB provides instant syntax reference and object model assistance right in the code window. If it is turned on, VB will track the object you are working with and provide every possible method or property of the object. You just start typing and the drop-down list box jumps to the first entry that matched what has been typed. When the correct entry is found, just hit the *Tab* key and the rest of the work is filled in for you.

```
Project1 - Form1 (Code)                          _ □ X

Form                    ▼   Activate                  ▼

    Private Sub Form_Activate()

    With Data1.Recordset
      .MoveLast
      lTotalRecords = .re
      .MoveFirst          ┌─────────────────────┐
    End With              │ ☞ RecordCount      ▲│
                          │ ☞ RecordStatus     ░│
    End Sub               │ ⇴ Requery          ░│
                          │ ☞ Restartable      ░│
                          │ ⇴ Seek             ░│
                          │ ☞ Sort             ░│
                          │ ☞ StillExecuting   ▼│
                          └─────────────────────┘
```

To have this feature activated, select
Tools-Options and check the Auto
List Members check box. Then click
the OK button to save the choice.

```
Options                                                X

  Editor │ Editor Format │ General │ Docking │ Environment │ Advanced

  ┌─ Code Settings ─────────────────────────────────────────┐
  │  ☑ Auto Syntax Check          ☑ Auto Indent            │
  │  ☑ Require Variable Declaration                          │
  │                               Tab Width:  4             │
  │  ☑ Auto List Members                                    │
  │  ☑ Auto Quick Info                                      │
  │  ☑ Auto Data Tips                                       │
  └─────────────────────────────────────────────────────────┘

  ┌─ Window Settings ───────────────────────────────────────┐
  │  ☑ Drag-and-Drop Text Editing                           │
  │  ☑ Default to Full Module View                          │
  │  ☑ Procedure Separator                                  │
  └─────────────────────────────────────────────────────────┘

                        OK        Cancel        Help
```

This is a very handy feature. However, there are certain cases when the IntelliSense options may
not work as you expect:

▶ **There is a code error above the cursor.** If there is a code error or an incomplete function
   above the cursor, the IntelliSense feature will be unable to detect it.

▶ **You are inside a code comment.** If the insertion point is within a comment in your source
   file, the IntelliSense feature will not work.

▶ **You are inside a string literal.** If the insertion point is inside the quotation marks around
   a string literal, as in: **MsgBox("Data1.Recordset.|")** the IntelliSense option will not
   be available.

▶ **The automatic option is turned off.** IntelliSense works automatically by default, but as we mentioned, it can be disabled. If it does not work, ensure the Auto List Members check box is checked as shown above.

Why is the Code Placed in Form_Activate()?

When a form is loaded into memory, it actually goes through a series of events that we must understand. This sequence was described in the section 'The Important Form Event Sequence' in this chapter.

The first form event to fire is the **Form_Initialize()**. This can be used to initialize any variables that are private to the form. The next form event to fire (or **execute**) is the **Form_Load()**. Here all of the visual components, such as our text boxes, are drawn on the form. All of the properties of the visual components are also set here. If you attempt to access the **Data1** properties before the visual component is fully initialized (or **sited** as the experts say), you will get the extremely friendly and descriptive Run-time error '91' as shown below:

This error occurs because not all of the visual components have been initialized yet. Some programmers try to thwart this message box by forcing the form to be visible by calling **Me.Show** in the **Load** event and then accessing properties of the visual components later in the **Form_Load()** event procedure. This will work, but we are really changing the sequence of VB events by forcing the form to be shown before its time. The best place to access any visual components when loading a form is to do so in the **Form_Activate()** event. This event fires after the form is fully loaded, initialized and displayed. At this point you are sure that all visual components are ready to go.

> *The* **Form_Activate()** *event is fired each time the form becomes the active form. So if our form was a child form and was displayed with other forms, this event would fire each time the user selected our form. We might only want the code in the* **Form_Activate()** *event to fire only once, when the form is loaded. You could put a Boolean static variable in the event to be toggled when the form was loaded. Any additional times this event was fired, the static variable would be set and you could exit without processing the code. We will have examples of this later in the book.*

157

The Data Control Reposition Event

Remember what we said about the **Form_Activate()** event procedure; it will fire only once when the form is loaded (or if it later becomes inactive and then active again). But remember: we need a place to update the **Data1.Caption** each and every time the user navigates through the recordset. The perfect place to do that is in the **Data1_Reposition()** event procedure, which is why our code looks like this:

```
Private Sub Data1_Reposition()

Data1.Caption = Data1.Recordset.AbsolutePosition + 1 & _
                " of " & lTotalRecords

End Sub
```

We are simply getting the **AbsolutePosition** property of the **Data1.Recordset** and adding 1 to it. This is because this property starts at 0 and ends at 'the total number of records -1'. By adding 1, we can give the user an **absolute** position guide. Users love this sort of thing because it keeps them informed and makes them feel important – which they are of course, as it's the user who ultimately pays our wages!

When a data control is loaded, we mentioned that the first record in the recordset object becomes the current record. This causes the **Reposition** event to fire. Then, whenever a user navigates through the recordset whether using the VCR buttons, one of the **Move** methods (such as **MoveNext**), one of the **Find** methods (such as **FindFirst**) or any other property or method that changes the current record, the **Reposition** event fires. This event fires **after** each record becomes current. When we want to do any validation before moving to another record, we can use the **Data1_Validate** event procedure. This event fires *before* another record becomes current.

You might be asking yourself that since the **Data1_Reposition()** event fires when it is first loaded, why do we also need code in the **Form_Activate()** event procedure? Well, remember we need to get the total number of records once and assign it to **lTotalRecords**. If we only placed code in the **Data1_Reposition** event, then we would have to get the **RecordCount** each and every time the user navigated to the next record.

Eye Candy for the User

One of the things I like to do is give the user as much visual feedback as possible. This not only includes things such as setting the cursor to an hourglass during long processing, but also giving them any feedback that makes sense in the context of what they are working on. We will add another gadget to our form that you might find useful in other programs. Not only does the **Data1.Recordset** have an **AbsolutePosition** property, but a **PercentPosition** property as well. We will read this property and update a **progress bar** control as the user navigates the recordset.

In the life of every user interface, you need to make modifications. Now is such a time. You have probably noticed that many of the book titles were truncated. Other fields, such as the Year Published, took up too much real estate on the form. Please take a moment to make some modifications. This is one of the advantages of Visual Basic. To make any changes to the visual part of your program, you simply click and drag. The reason we need to change the user interface is that the text box positions don't match the underlying field lengths - and the layout is a bit clunky.

The underlying physical Publishers table consists of the following fields, types and lengths. We want to match the actual field lengths in the database more closely with how they are displayed on the user interface.

Field Name	Data Type	Length of Field
PubID	AutoNumber	Long
Name	Text	50
Company Name	Text	255
Address	Text	50
City	Text	20
State	Text	10
Zip	Text	15
Telephone	Text	15
Fax	Text	15
Comments	Memo	N/A

Now if we were designing a database, this would probably not be ideal. For example, it's doubtful that any company's name would be 255 characters long. Since there is no provision for country, we can 'assume' that these are only domestic publishers. The nice thing about Access is that it automatically provides **variable length** records. So if an entry in the Company Name field is blank, we don't have to worry about taking up 255 blank spaces. It is set to NULL until there is an entry. Therefore, if a company name is 10 characters long, only 10 characters are saved. Older databases used to commit the full 255 spaces, even if there was no entry for the field. This plagued database designers because of all of the disk real estate that would need to be taken up 'just in case' one field was much longer than the others were. Should you provide extra space to accommodate that odd entry that was longer than the others? If so, each field would be required to be as long as the longest possible. Or do we truncate the long entries and lose some information?

With Access, since no unnecessary hard drive real estate is taken up with the large field, I guess we can't complain too much. However, we will cover these issues when we design our own database in chapter 9.

Make Some Enhancements

Remember when we discussed prototyping? Well, now is our chance to experience it first hand.

1   We're going to rearrange your field lengths and positions so your form looks like this. Notice that there is a progress bar right above the data control. We will add this now too.

To add a ProgressBar control to your form you'll need to use the Toolbox's Components dialog to add Microsoft Windows Common Controls 6.0 – then add the control to your form.

Set the **Align** property to 2 - vbAlignBottom. This will automatically place the control just above the data control at the bottom of the form for us.

Typically, a progress bar control is used to show the progress of some lengthy operation or other by filling a rectangle with chunks from left to right. We will be using it for just such purposes later on. This control is perfect for showing the user a going relative position in the recordset.

2 Rearrange the field sizes and positions to better reflect the sizes of the fields displayed. You are probably asking yourself about all of those 'X's in various fields, right? We will get to that in a minute. But for now, add them to the **Text** property of each text box. Then size the fields so all of the X's are displayed. Since it's easy to get confused with setting up these text boxes, please follow this table.

Text Box Array Number	Field it is bound to	Number of X's to insert
Text1(0)	PubID	6
Text1(1)	Name	50
Text1(2)	Company Name	64
Text1(3)	Address	38
Text1(4)	City	20
Text1(5)	State	10
Text1(6)	Zip	15
Text1(7)	Phone	15
Text1(8)	Fax	15
Text1(9)	Comments	N/A

3 Extend the bound text box used for displaying the comments field, **Text1(9)**. Set the **MultiLine** property to true. This permits fields that go beyond the length of the text box to automatically be wrapped. Next set the ScrollBars property to 2 - Vertical. Then if an entry in the Comments field is wrapped and extends beyond the visible portion of the text box, we can simply scroll down. This makes very efficient use of our available going screen real estate.

4   Add the appropriate labels above the text boxes. Set the **Alignment** property of each label to 2 - Center. This makes it easy to size the label to the same size as the text box it is above. Doing this will ensure the caption of each label is horizontally centered above the text box.

5   Change the **Caption** property of the form from **Form1** to **Publishers** and the **Name** to **frmPublishers**.

6   Add the following lines of code to your program's **Data1_Reposition** event program to update the progress bar control during initialization and as the user navigates the recordset.

```
Private Sub Data1_Reposition()
With Data1.Recordset
  Data1.Caption = "Publisher " & (.AbsolutePosition + 1) & _
                           " of " & lTotalRecords
  ProgressBar1.Value = .PercentPosition
End With
End Sub
```

We changed the **Reposition** event procedure code to use the **With...End With** construct because now we are accessing the **Data1.Recordset** object twice.

Now as the user navigates through the recordset, they can see both the absolute position (the record number in the data control) as well as the relative percent position (the progress bar). You may choose one or the other, but I prefer to give users more information rather than less. It makes for a professional and solid program when users can see this type of information. And best of all, it only took five lines of code. Many times, it is the easiest things to accomplish that look to the user as the most difficult. Run your program and notice how the progress bar shows the relative position of the current record in the underlying recordset. Also notice that the text box sizes are closer fields of data they display.

> *Note: The* **PercentPosition** *is only an approximation of the location of the current record in the recordset. It should not be used for any critical measurements. However for our purpose, it's perfect. And remember to use the* **MoveLast** *method so Jet knows about all of the records. Otherwise the* **PercentPosition** *will give a faulty reading.*

7   Go ahead and save the project in your **BegDB\Chapter4** directory as **prjPublishers**. We will be enhancing this project in the next chapter.

Where Do We Go From Here?...

We covered a lot in this chapter, but actually, we are just getting our feet wet with the data control. To make our program ready for prime time, we must get down and do some real coding. For example, there is no way for a user to delete or add a record. There is no way to find a specific record. Nor is there a way to quickly scroll through the recordset. Also, if a user changes any data by accident, it will be automatically committed to the database. In the next chapter we will add these enhancements to our project. And even though we only wrote eight lines of code (count 'em) in this chapter, we have a form that displays records, displays the absolute and percent position in the recordset to the user and sets a multi-line scrollable text box to display comments. In the process, we also learned quite a bit about control arrays.

Take a moment to compare what we did to what the Wizard gave us in the last chapter. While the Wizard set up the text boxes for us and provided some default labels, it left out some pretty important components. The user could add more data to a field than the underlying database could accept. The fields were all the same size on the form and they were placed vertically - not very stylish. So already we have surpassed the Wizard in these respects. In the next chapter we will make a bulletproof production-quality program out of our project.

What We Learned

▶ Event-driven programming is passive in nature. VB waits for a user event and responds to it.

▶ Setting properties visually is actually considered as programming.

▶ The data control is used primarily on our visual interfaces by binding data aware controls to it, such as a text box.

▶ The data control has methods and properties that permit us to tailor functionality.

▶ The data control **Reposition** event procedure fires **after** each record becomes current while the **Validate** event procedure fires **before** another record becomes current.

▶ Adding design-time field length validation.

Onward!

We've started creating the front-end that our users will see. In the next chapter we'll move along and build up our user interface.

Exercises

1 Explain the difference between the properties and methods of an object.

2 Explain the steps that occur between the user clicking the mouse on a command button and your application performing some processing as a result.

3 Create a new **Standard EXE** project and place code to print a message in the immediate window in each of the following event handlers:

```
Form_Activate
Form_Initialize
Form_Load
Form_Paint
```

In what order do these events fire?

4 Why does the **RecordCount** property of a **Recordset** sometimes give an incorrect count of the records that are included in the **Recordset**?

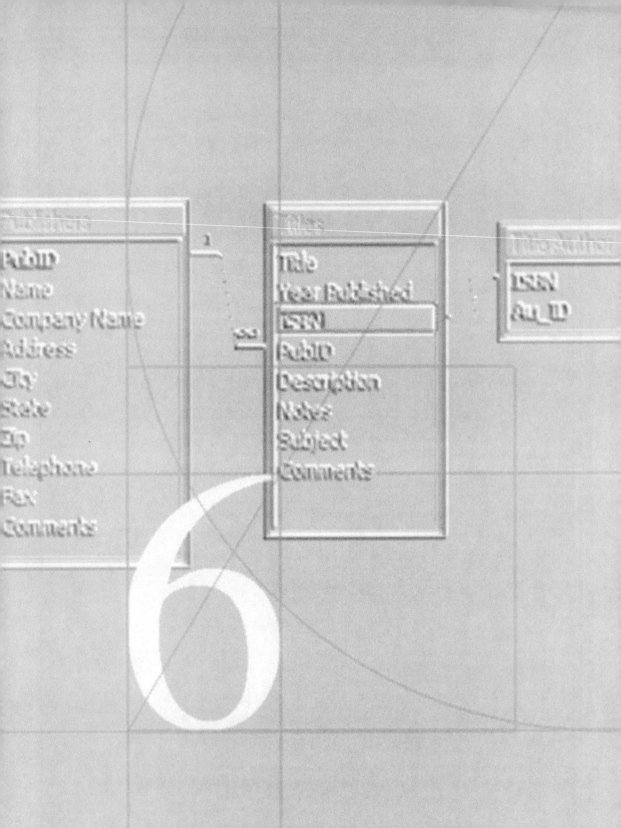

Programming a Bulletproof User Interface

Now we're going to continue the theme of the last chapter by enhancing the way our data control operates with our bound controls and - through the recordset - with the underlying database. We will be building a more robust and efficient interface, and preparing to encapsulate all the code that we'll build so that we can reuse it in other applications. Our form will become a great vehicle for data entry and manipulation.

The Data Control - Right or Wrong?

The data control has several methods associated with it, and we'll use these to operate the data control from code.

Some database programmers stay away from the data control – they feel that it is too slow and takes up too many resources. And it's true that once you get beyond smaller scale desktop applications these reservations have some force – Jet and Access are not designed for larger-scale operations. However, there are good reasons for us to use the data control in our examples here:

> It's ideal for small-scale applications

> When you consider what we did with just a few lines of code in the last chapter, the data control is just too powerful to ignore

> In terms of functionality, there are only a few things that we *can't* do compared to other DAO or ADO controls when working with recordsets

Most importantly, we're using the data control and Access as **learning tools**; we're exploring VB programming techniques and concepts that will add understanding, power and flexibility to your programming – whichever data access technology you are using to mediate between your VB program and the underlying data

So, instead of discarding the data control, we're going to move on and *enhance* it. Once we have made our user interface mean and lean, we are going to encapsulate its functionality in a **class** that will allow us to reuse all of our code – I think you'll find this a very useful approach.

Here's how we'll progress through this chapter:

> ▶ We'll look briefly at **classes** and **reusability**
>
> ▶ We'll examine the **properties** and **methods** of the **data control** – in detail
>
> ▶ We'll look closely at the **properties** and **methods** of the **recordset**
>
> ▶ We'll examine **the state-machine concept**, which 'monitors' what our application is doing and decides what the user should be allowed to do next
>
> ▶ We'll add code to our user interface to make the user and the controls work better together

Let's begin by thinking about what we'll do to enhance our user interface.

Building an Enhanced User Interface

As mentioned previously, if we want to add, delete or scroll through records quickly, or if we want to find records, validate entries and perform all of the tasks that a professional data-entry screen uses, we must program the data control. The best way to show you how to do this is to enhance the program we have been working on. How? We will put some buttons on the form and permit the user to update and navigate using these. Then we'll significantly enhance the default processes for navigation, and for adding, editing and deleting records. We'll add the successive enhancements bit by bit, explaining what each of them does as we go. At the end of the chapter we'll run all of the code that we've built into our application and see the results. However, before we go any further, let's take a close look at the important properties and methods of the data control. In this chapter, we will be programming the data control, so let's see its built-in functionality.

The Class System

Once we've got our user interface form up and running, if we wanted to add data access to our existing project or to a separate project, we could copy our original VB form so that we could use it as a base to build on. There would be minor differences between the two data access forms, but the bulk of the code would be the same. Of course, we want to eliminate any duplicate code wherever possible. One way to eliminate code redundancy is to encapsulate common code into a **class module**. Using a class module, we can hide all of the details of how the code works. We will demonstrate how to do that shortly - and when we complete the next exercise, we will have a solid example of code reuse to take forward with us when we start using classes in detail in chapter 7.

Back to the Data Control...

Remember that we initialized the data control by setting its **DatabaseName** and **RecordSource** properties. The data control then has enough information to return a recordset object, which in turn has its own methods and properties. We customize the data control object by referring to its properties using the syntax **Data1.*property*** and to the returned recordset object by using **Data1.Recordset.*property***.

In order to get a good understanding of this relationship between the data control and the recordset it manages, let's look at a few of the more important properties of the data control. We have already touched on a few of these, but here we'll get a broader picture of these properties.

Properties of the Data Control

Data Control Property	Description
`DatabaseName`	This is the fully qualified path to the database that you want the data control to open. For example, we use `C:\BeGDB\Biblio.mdb` for our examples. While running your program, if you change the `DatabaseName` property after you open the database object, the `Refresh` method is required to open the new database.
`Connect`	This string tells the data control what *type* of data store (e.g. Access, Paradox, etc.) is being used. The default is Access.
`RecordSource`	This defines the recordset that will be returned by the data control. This can be the name of a single table or the result of a complicated SQL statement.
`Recordset`	This is the virtual set of records returned by the data control based on the `DatabaseName` and the `RecordSource` properties
`RecordsetType`	This is a flag that determines if the returned recordset is of type `vbRSTypeTable`, `vbRSTypeDynaset` or `vbRSTypeSnapShot`. The default is a dynaset.
`EOFAction`	Determines what happens at the end of a recordset - move last or tentative append as discussed in the last chapter.
`BOFAction`	Determines what happens at the beginning of a recordset, move first or set a flag.
`Exclusive`	A flag of data type integer that determines the read/write rights to the database. The default is `False` for shared access. We'll see more on this when we discuss DAO.
`ReadOnly`	A flag of data type integer that determines if you can update the returned recordset. The default is `False` as we saw in our earlier example program.

Methods of the Data Control

Data Control Method	What it's Used for
`Refresh`	This method is called when we wish to open a new database, add/delete a record and wish the changes to immediately be written to the database, or change the `RecordSource` property of the data control.
`UpdateControls`	This method is used when the user wishes to cancel any changes made to the current record via the bound controls on the form. The bound controls are then refreshed with the values of the current record. We will call this method when the user presses the Cancel button on our program. Of course, it can only be used before any changes are committed to the database.
`UpdateRecord`	This is called when we want to save all of the values from the bound controls to the database. We will call this method in code when the user presses the Save button on our program.

Properties of the Recordset

The recordset can be a bit more complicated and has various restrictions depending upon the type returned: table, dynaset or snapshot. Most of these properties are in the province of DAO and ADO. So rather than confuse things right now, here is a very partial list of the recordset properties that we will be using with our data control when we enhance the program from the last chapter.

Recordset Properties	Description
`AbsolutePosition`	This is a data type long that either sets or gets the position of the current record. The first record is 0, so we must always add 1 to this number.
`BOF`	This true returns when the record pointer is **before** the first record.
`BookMark`	This sets or returns a bookmark that uniquely identifies the current record in the returned recordset object. Later, we will use this as a place marker when adding records.
`EditMode`	This returns a value that indicates the state of editing for the current record. We will use this when performing editing on our data.
`EOF`	This returns true when the record pointer is **after** the last record.
`PercentPosition`	This is a data type single that either sets or gets the position of the record as a percentage of total records. The value will always be between 0.00 and 100.00.
`RecordCount`	This is the total number of records in the returned recordset.

Likewise, the `Recordset` object has several methods. As with the properties, there are various restrictions based on the type of recordset returned. Here are a few that we will need for our purposes.

Methods of the Recordset

Recordset Method	What it's Used for
Close	This closes a returned recordset.
Edit	Using this method places the current record in the recordset into **edit** mode. This permits the user to edit any fields in bound controls.
AddNew	Adds a new record to a recordset of type table or dynaset. This causes all of the bound control fields to be emptied and made ready for a new record.
Delete	Deletes the current record from either a table or dynaset recordset type.
Update	Causes any changes made to the data in bound controls to be written to the database.
MoveFirst	Moves the current record pointer to the first record in the recordset.
MoveNext	Moves the current record pointer to the next record in the recordset.
MovePrevious	Moves the current record pointer to the previous record.
MoveLast	Moves the current record pointer to the last record in the recordset.
FindFirst	Locates the first record that matches a search criterion. The search starts at the first record in the recordset.
FindNext	Locates the next matching record, after the one found with **FindFirst**.
FindPrevious	Locates the first previous matching record, before the one found with **FindFirst**.
FindLast	Locates the last record that matches a search criterion. The search starts at the last record in the recordset.

Phew! I know this seems like a lot to digest, but don't worry. Essentially, all these methods and properties help us manipulate our data efficiently and accurately. We will explain each property and method in detail as we use them. We will also discuss when and where to use the proper methods and properties. Pretty soon, they will seem like old friends, but for now, take a minute to review and think about the above lists in the context of the data control, bound controls and the recordset, all of which we talked about in detail in previous chapters. By looking at these methods and properties you can get a sense that Visual Basic 6.0 provides a rich and robust toolset for working with databases. In fact, you will be able to do almost anything you want with these tools, from creating our own desktop database program, accessing a database over a Local Area Network or a Wide Area Network, connecting to legacy systems and even using a database over the Internet. That is because the ActiveX Data Objects (ADO) use most of these same methods and properties.

Why do we need to learn all of these methods and properties anyway? Well I'm glad you asked. Let's start at the beginning.

The State-Machine Concept

The first thing we are going to do is learn how to program the data control. We will be placing buttons on our form to permit navigation and editing for the user to easily read and write to a database. The reason we are designing the interface using buttons is because it permits us to ruthlessly enforce the concept of **state**. By creating a **state-machine**, we can know exactly what the user is doing at any time.

As the name implies, a software state-machine must be in a known 'state' at all times. For example, the program might be in an "add state" or an "edit state" or an "idle state". Not only that, when the program is in a certain state, it can only move to a new state if that new state is legal.

Let me explain some more. If the user adds a new record, it puts our program in an **add-state**. Since we know the user is adding, we will only permit either the **save-state** or the **cancel-state** to occur next. We will not permit the user to attempt to add another record, move to another record or dismiss the form while an 'add' is taking place. So when the Add New button is pressed, the user can only either save the record or cancel the 'add'. Nothing else – we must be ruthlessly efficient to ensure proper function and data integrity. If we know what the software is doing at all times, we can ensure that the next state the user moves to is a correct one, hence the name state-machine. While it might seem a bit authoritarian to totally control what the user does, in reality we are protecting the users from themselves. They will thank you for it - trust me on this one.

> *One of the hallmarks of a good program is that the software does not permit the user to make a wrong move.*

Designing a Robust User Interface

One of the most difficult parts of programming professional software is the human/machine interface. Users – and that often includes us - will do the wackiest things. If you have a numeric only field, a new user might accidentally enter something like 'HB88'. As professional programmers, we must be ever vigilant for any opportunity for the user to make a wrong move. If we find one, we must stamp it out immediately. The best and easiest bits of software to work with are those programs that gently guide the user through only correct steps. We must strive to design our program in such a way that it does not permit the user to make a mistake. We will accomplish our aims through guile and stealth. The user will not know what we are doing - they will only realize that our program is pretty easy to use. Don't worry, this is not subversive or underhand, just good programming practice.

We must always keep in mind that the user of our program has a job to do. They don't want to work with our program, they want to enter or retrieve some data. Our job is to make their task as simple and efficient as possible. As you become more adept at writing professional Visual Basic programs, you will begin to anticipate where a user could make a mistake - and correct it. This is the difference between a good programmer and a great programmer.

> *There is a saying in computer science that says the difference between a good programmer and a great programmer is that the great programmer has made more mistakes. Our goal is to find the mistakes that can be made and learn from them.*

OK, now let's put our new knowledge to work for us.

Try It Out - Enhancing the User Interface

1 Using the program from the last chapter, **prjPublishers.vbp**, add a new command button to your form. Name the control **cmdButton**. Remember our control arrays? We are going to make a control array of eleven **cmdButton**s.

2 Highlight the **cmdButton** and copy the button to the clipboard. Highlight the form and paste a copy of the button on the form. You will be asked if you want to create a control array. Answer Yes. Do this until you have eleven buttons on the form. They will have indexes from **cmdButton(0)** through **cmdButton(10)**.

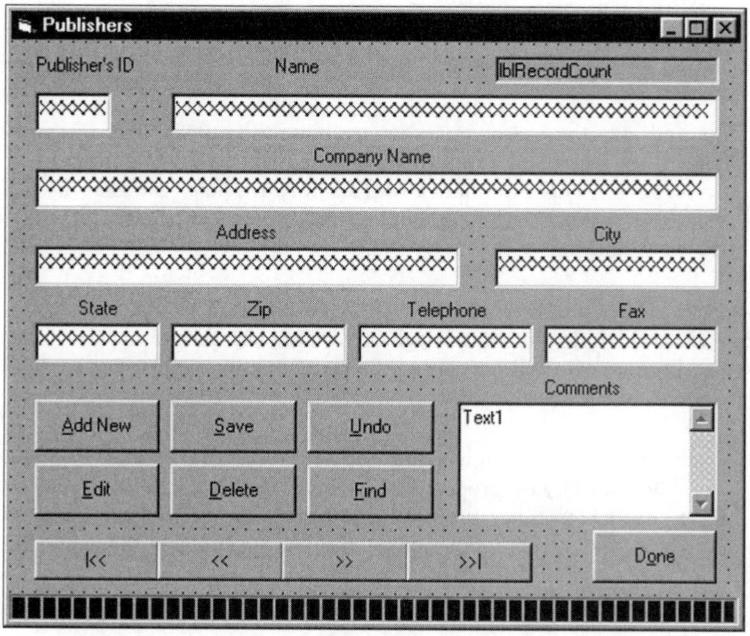

While placing the buttons on the form, it is critical that you associate the correct caption with the appropriate index. Please order them as shown below:

Caption	Command Button Control
|<<	cmdButton(0)
<<	cmdButton(1)
>>	cmdButton(2)
>>|	cmdButton(3)
&Add New	cmdButton(4)
&Edit	cmdButton(5)

Caption	Command Button Control
&Save	`cmdButton(6)`
&Delete	`cmdButton(7)`
&Undo	`cmdButton(8)`
&Find	`cmdButton(9)`
D&one	`cmdButton(10)`

Remember that in a control array, each control shares the same code. So when the user presses the |<< button, the index value of 0 will be passed into our **cmdButton_Click** event procedure. The index value of the button tells us which button was pressed.

When you have the buttons arranged in the above sequence, you might want to use the Format option on the VB menu that we worked with in the last chapter. This is great for easily making buttons the same size.

3 Arrange and size the buttons as shown above. Be sure to use the ampersand (**&**) before the character in the **Caption** property that you want to be underscored. VB will make these accelerator keys for us automatically. This way the user can use the *Alt* and underscored key instead of using the mouse. For example, pressing *Alt* and *A* will fire the code in click the <u>A</u>dd New button.

4 Set the **Visible** property of the data control to **False** and the **Align** property to **0 - None**. This will hide the control when we run our program. We don't want it visible anymore because we will be using our **cmdButton** control array to navigate. We will be programmatically controlling the data control from these buttons.

5 Add a label to the upper right-hand corner of the form. Name it **lblRecordCount**. Set the label's **BorderStyle** property to **1 - Fixed Single**, and its **Alignment** property to **0 - Left Justify**. Since we are hiding the data control, it would still be nice to show the user the current record position in the recordset - this label will do the job nicely. Since labels are read only and are very lightweight, this is a better choice than a text box.

FYI

Lightweight controls (labels, images, lines, and shapes) use fewer system resources than other controls - which of course improves the performance on your application. This is because these controls are known as windowless. Lightweight controls do not have a window handle (hWnd property). If you have a form with two text boxes, Windows sees this as three 'windows'. Each has a hWnd (handle to a Window) property. This way Windows tracks each and every 'window' internally and this takes resources. The downside to lightweight controls is that they cannot receive focus at runtime, they can't serve as containers for other controls, and they can't appear on top of other controls unless they are inside a container such as a picture box.

Modify the two lines of code in the **Data1_Reposition** event where we assigned the current record to the data control. Since the data control is now hidden, let's display the current record in the **lblRecordCount** label.

```
Private Sub Data1_Reposition()
```

```
With Data1.Recordset
 lblRecordCount.Caption = "Publisher " & _
        (.AbsolutePosition + 1) & " of " & lTotalRecords
 ProgressBar1.Value = .PercentPosition
End With
```

```
End Sub
```

6 Next, make sure you've got the following bit of code to the **Form_Activate** event:

```
Private Sub Form_Activate()
```

```
With Data1.Recordset
 .MoveLast
 lTotalRecords = .RecordCount
 .MoveFirst
End With
```

```
End Sub
```

7 In the **cmdButton_Click** event, if the **Index** parameter has a value of 0, then we know the user clicked the **|<<** button. We know the **|<<** button is in position 0 of the control array of command buttons. However, 'index 0' might not immediately make sense to someone trying to maintain our code.

A very handy feature added back in VB 5.0 comes to the rescue. That feature is called **enumerated constants**. We can essentially create our own constants that can be used in our code to make things clearer. The assigned values can't be modified at run-time and can include both positive and negative numbers. For example, we can create a set of constants that are associated with our control array of buttons. Then in our code, we can simply test for the constant **cmdMoveFirst** instead of 0. Go to the General Declarations section of the form and add the following highlighted code after the **Option Explicit** statement:

```
Private Enum cmdButtons
  cmdMoveFirst = 0
  cmdMovePrevious = 1
  cmdMoveNext = 2
  cmdMoveLast = 3
  cmdAddNew = 4
  cmdEdit = 5
  cmdSave = 6
  cmdDelete = 7
  cmdUndo = 8
  cmdFind = 9
  cmdDone = 10
End Enum
```

8 Now in our code, we can just look to see if the index is equal to a more readable enumerated constant, such as **cmdMoveFirst** instead of 0. Our code has taken a giant leap towards becoming self-documenting.

We can use the **Select Case** statement so our code is much more readable than if we used nested **If…Then** statements. Here, our **Select Case** statement will take the value of the index and test it against our constants. Add the following code to our **cmdButton**'s **Click** event procedure.

```
Private Sub cmdButton_Click(Index As Integer)
```

```
Select Case Index                'what is the value of the key pressed?
   Case cmdMoveFirst
      Data1.Recordset.MoveFirst
   Case cmdMovePrevious
      Data1.Recordset.MovePrevious
   Case cmdMoveNext
      Data1.Recordset.MoveNext
   Case cmdMoveLast
     Data1.Recordset.MoveLast
   Case cmdAddNew      '-- add a new record
   Case cmdEdit        '-- edit the current record
   Case cmdSave        '-- save the current record
   Case cmdDelete      '-- delete the current record
   Case cmdUndo        '-- undo changes to the current record
   Case cmdFind        '-- find a specific record
   Case cmdDone        '-- exit the form
End Select
```

```
End Sub
```

Since each of our ten buttons shares the same code (because they are all members of a control array) we can simply look at the **Index** parameter that Visual Basic passes as a parameter into the **cmdButton Click** event procedure. By interrogating the index variable, we know which button the user clicked. Moreover, with our enumerated constants, our code becomes self-documenting.

That is one of the benefits of a control array. All of the buttons do something similar, so we can group everything in one place. No matter which of the ten buttons the user clicks, this single **cmdButton_Click** event procedure fires. Another benefit is that control arrays use less system resources than the same number of individual controls.

We've added a **Case** statement for each of our buttons, but have only added code to the first four - the navigation buttons. The remainder of the cases are skeletons at this point. If the user clicks on buttons five through eleven at this point, nothing will happen. The code will just fall through the **Case** statement and exit the sub. However, this is where we will soon place our code to perform the other tasks on the recordset. I just wanted to show you what the **Select** statement looks like for now.

The **cmdButton_Click** event procedure uses various move methods of the **RecordSet**. We used the **MoveFirst, MovePrevious, MoveNext** and **MoveLast** methods. We know that there can only be one current record - these methods move the 'current record' pointer in the recordset. These methods permit us to programmatically navigate through the recordset - this is a lot of power.

With power comes responsibility. Since it is possible to move the record pointer either before or after the current recordset when we use code - unlike when we navigate using the VCR buttons on the data control - we must make sure that we don't allow the user to move the record pointer past the recordset. So we will have to put in safeguards in our program to ensure the user can't move off the recordset.

Notice that we are really using **Recordset** methods here. We access them through the **Data1** data control, which is holding on to the recordset for us.

There are currently eleven buttons with an index value from 0 though 10. If the user clicks any of the four navigation buttons (0 through 3), we will instruct the recordset object to move in some way. Although we have hidden the data control, it is still very much alive and kicking in the background. In fact, it is an integral part of our program. We have just hidden it from the user to make it easier and more powerful to use. This is because we are going to add additional capability to the control, such as finding and deleting records. Rather than have the user navigate using the control and then use buttons to perform other tasks, it makes more sense to provide a single, common interface - the **cmdButton** control array. So we hide the control and provide all of the recordset's functionality via the command buttons. This approach provides a cleaner, more consistent interface to our project.

9   Ready? Let's run our program and check out the navigation buttons. Of course, the other buttons aren't hooked up yet. Please press *F5* to run and then use **cmdButton**s 0 - 3 to navigate through the recordset. Of course each time the user clicks one of the navigation buttons, the hidden data control is really doing all of the work via our **cmdButton** control array.

Pretty easy, no? Well, you might be saying to yourself right this instant, "So what?" We could do the same thing with the VCR-like buttons on the data control itself. What is the big deal? Well, we are on our way to learning how to make a bulletproof data access form.

Houston, We Have a Problem

We do have a slight problem. Try this: press *F5* to run your program. Now, immediately click the **cmdMovePrevious** button (**<<**). Oops! A single mouse click and we crashed the program! We get the dreaded and infamous No current record error.

```
Microsoft Visual Basic

Run-time error '3021':

No current record.

  Continue        End         Debug         Help
```

This is not good. I can see the panicked look on the user's face already. We have just experienced 'programmatically moving off the recordset'. This is not something we want to encourage people to do.

Can you guess why this happened? When your form is loaded and the data control is initialized, the first record in the recordset becomes current. Then we immediately press the **cmdMovePrevious** button (**<<**). However, there is no previous record. Why? Because we were already at the first record when we pressed the **cmdMovePrevious** button. There is simply nowhere to go, so VB generates an error message. If we used the VCR buttons on the data control, this would not happen. We set the **BOF** property of the data control to **0 - Move First**. So the data control would simply stay at the first record, preventing the user from unceremoniously moving off the end of the recordset as we just did.

However, we are now using Visual Basic code to program the recordset. Recall that when the user presses the **cmdMovePrevious** button (**<<**), the code in our **cmdButton_Click** event procedure fires. Since the index for the **cmdMoveNext** button is 1, the code **Data1.Recordset.MovePrevious** is executed. VB assumes that we know what we are doing and so proceeds to carry out our command. Even though there is not a previous record (we are on the first record), the **.MovePrevious** is dutifully carried out.

I wanted to show you this because the DAO commands for the recordset we just used (**.RecordSet.MoveNext**) do exactly what we tell them to do. The code assumes we know what we are doing! When programming either the data control or DAO, we must always make sure that these errors don't happen. The best way to reinforce this is by experiencing the errors first hand. This example highlights the programmer's acronym DWIM - or 'Do What I Mean'. Of course, VB doesn't have particularly strong psychic powers, so it can't read our minds to see what we mean - instead it does exactly what we tell it to do. Seeing the errors helps provide us with a solid understanding of how the data control and DAO work. Once we understand that, the rest is much easier. Let's go ahead and clean up that pesky error.

Enhancing Record Navigation

Earlier we spoke about the state-machine concept. If we think about record navigation, it would be nice to disable the first two buttons when we got to the beginning of the recordset. After all, when we are at the first record, we can't go backwards any more. We certainly don't want to move off the beginning of the recordset. So we want to provide the user with a visual cue that the beginning of the recordset has been reached. We want to set up our state-machine that when it is in the state 'first record', it can only navigate forward in the recordset. In this state, 'go backwards' is an illegal command and so we want our program to disallow it. Likewise, when the recordset's current record is the last record, we only want the user to be able to navigate to previous records and of course, when there are no records, we don't want them to navigate at all. This is where the power of a state-machine comes into play. We won't permit the user to make a navigation mistake.

How will we accomplish this? To get a clear understanding of what we are going to so, let's look at the sequence of events. When the user presses any of the buttons in the **cmdButton** control array, some action will take place. The action might be navigation, adding, editing, etc. Depending on the action taken, our machine changes state. So whenever an action takes place, we will call a routine **updateButtons**. **updateButtons** will check to see what state our machine is in. Are we at the last record? Are we adding or deleting and so forth. **updateButtons** will be the brains of the state-machine operation. Calling **updateButtons** will execute something like the following code snippet (don't write any code yet – for the moment we just want to get an overview of what will happen).

```
Select case index          'what is the value of the key pressed?
    Case cmdMoveFirst
        Data1.Recordset.MoveFirst
        Call updateButtons
```

The **updateButtons** sub will do the following:

▶ Determine what state the machine is in

▶ Construct a string of 0s and 1s that will either enable or disable a specific **cmdButton**

For example, if the recordset is at the first record, the string built by **updateButtons** will look like this: '00111101011'. Notice that the first and second positions are 0. These correspond to the first and second command buttons. Recall that **cmdButton(0)** is Move First and **cmdButton(1)** is Move Previous. Both of these buttons are illegal for the user to press when we are at the first record in the recordset. So **updateButtons** builds a string with the first two positions set to a 0, which means 'disable these buttons'. We will explain the meaning of the other buttons later, but it's important to see the strategy here.

Once updateButtons builds the correct string for the current machine state, it calls a helper function, **navigateButtons**. The work of actually enabling or disabling the buttons is delegated to this sub-routine. **updateButtons** would call the sub, passing it the 0s and 1s that described the desired condition of the buttons with something like this:

```
navigateButtons ("00111101011")
```

Once all of the buttons in the **cmdButton** array have been set by **navigateButtons**, then control returns back to the calling routine - **updateButtons**. There is one more helper routine that **updateButtons** can call - **locktheControls**. This routine will **unlock** the text boxes to permit editing if the user wishes to edit or add. Otherwise, it will **lock** the text boxes. We will only allow the user to add or modify a record when they click the correct button. Adding or editing is a conscious task performed by the user. All other times, the bound text boxes are locked to ensure that no accidental changing of data can take place.

While this might seem like a lot to take on programmatically, it is actually very straightforward to accomplish. We also modularize the various tasks to isolate specific functionality. We can minimize on debugging by segregating them on the basis of their functionality, rather than placing all the subtasks in one giant subroutine. We can call each of the routines as needed from *anywhere* in the form. As we walk though each of these routines, we will cover why we did what. For now though, we'll focus on the important issue of how we are going to go about enforcing our state-machine concept.

A Level of Indirection

There is a well-known axiom in Computer Science that states: **Adding another level of indirection can solve anything**. This just means that a problem can always be solved by having a routine call another specialized routine and if that does not solve the problem, that routine can call another – and so on. We will apply this axiom to our program now. We will first write a sub-routine called **updateButtons**. Then we will write **navigateButtons**, which is called by **updateButtons**. This will set up which buttons can be pressed to navigate or edit the recordset. Finally we will write **locktheControls** that will either lock or unlock the bound text boxes.

Reusing the Code

Of course, we could call these subs from the **cmdButton_Click()** event procedure each time the user pressed any of the buttons - we would have to figure out which buttons to enable or disable, and either lock and unlock the controls. However, this approach would have several disadvantages: cramming all of this code in one spot would make our **Select Case** statement in the **cmdButton_Click()** event pretty cluttered; it also leaves the code in the form, which will slow down the loading; and it would prevent us from calling any of the routines independently. Finally, you could imagine how difficult it might be for someone maintaining our code to figure out what is going on. By isolating the code for specific tasks in individual procedures we aid coding clarity, improve performance and make maintenance much easier.

One of the most compelling reasons for the modular approach is to isolate this code from the user interface. This will make it general enough to be used in any of our programs in other applications. After all, who wants to write this more than once? So for now we will isolate the code in subroutines. Later, when we build our own class for programming a data control, we will totally remove the subroutine from our form and let it run free and independent. At the moment we are just getting it to work - in the next chapter we will do some cutting and pasting to place all of the code we create here in a reusable class module. I know you will like this.

OK, back to indirection. We don't want to be bothered with having to call both of our new helper routines each time the user presses a button. So we can create a level. We will first write **updateButtons**, which will manage the navigation buttons as well as locking and unlocking the controls for us. This way, we simply make a call to **updateButtons** in our **Select Case** construct. This routine will indirectly call both **locktheControls** and **navigateButtons** for us. All of the nitty-gritty details are taken care of for us. I think you will like the way we both encapsulate the functionality while simplifying things from the user interface standpoint. We will call **updateButtons** that in turn will call both **navigateButtons** and **locktheControls** for us - indirectly of course!

Building the Navigation Code for the User Interface

In the next few sections of this chapter we'll build up the code that will make our user interface more intuitive, more robust and more efficient. We'll start with the subroutine that determines the state of our application and sets up the buttons on the form to only allow legitimate navigation and actions.

Try It Out - The updateButtons Helper Routine

The **updateButtons** routine will interrogate the state of the recordset by checking out its **EditMode** property. We don't need to store any variables - just check the **EditMode** property. If there is currently no editing going on, we simply need to update the navigation buttons. However, if there is either an add or edit in progress, we want to disable the navigation buttons completely and manipulate the editing buttons.

1   Add a new subroutine to your form and name it **updateButtons** by opening the code window and selecting <u>T</u>ools-Add <u>P</u>rocedure from the main VB menu.

> *Note: The code window must be open to have the Add Procedure menu choice enabled.*

All subroutines and functions are automatically placed in the General section of the form. The Procedure dialog will provide us with a template for the type of routine. So we want a <u>S</u>ub and will go with the default Pu<u>b</u>lic. If we created a type of routine (Sub, Function, Property or Event) and wanted it to only be seen within the form or module, we would select Pri<u>v</u>ate as the scope. Local variables (those dim'ed within a procedure) go out of scope when the code in the procedure exits - no values can be retained locally. However, if we dim a local variable as static, its value is remembered. Essentially, it becomes the same as a form/module level variable in this way because its value persists as long as the form is running. Checking A̲ll Local variables as Statics makes each local variable's value persist for the life of the form - don't select this check box for this sub procedure though.

> *Note: Both subroutines and functions are separate procedures that can take arguments, perform a series of code statements and even change the value of its arguments. The difference between a subroutine and a function is that a subroutine can not return a value or be used in expressions.*
>
> *The* updateButtons *sub simply performs an action. On the other hand, a function has the ability to return a value to the caller. For example, you might write a* SquareIt *function that is passed in a number and the function then returns the squared value of that number.*

When we use the Add Procedure dialog box, a template is put in for the subroutine.

```
Public Sub updateButtons()

End Sub
```

The **updateButtons** sub will check out the **EditMode** of the **RecordSource** property. This will tell us the **state** of the recordset and we can then ensure only the correct buttons are enabled.

We will have to add the parameters to the subroutine 'signature'. Use the optional key word for the parameter **bLockEm**. Go ahead and add this code.

```
Public Sub updateButtons(Optional bLockEm As Variant)

'-----------------------------------------------------------------
'— The position of the 0 or 1 in the string represents
'— a specific button in our cmdButton control array.
'-----------------------------------------------------------------
'Position    Button
'   0         move first
'   1         move previous
'   2         move next
'   3         move last
'   4         add a new record
'   5         edit the current record
'   6         save the current record
'   7         delete the current record
'   8         undo any current changes
'   9         find a specific record
'   10        done. Unload the form
'------------------------------------------------

Select Case Data1.Recordset.EditMode

    Case dbEditNone    '—no editing taking place, just handle navigation
        If (lTotalRecords > 1) Then
            If (Data1.Recordset.BOF) Or _
```

```
                    (Data1.Recordset.AbsolutePosition = 0) Then
                        navigateButtons ("00111101011")
            ElseIf (Data1.Recordset.EOF) Or _
                    (Data1.Recordset.AbsolutePosition = lTotalRecords - 1) Then
                        navigateButtons ("11001101011")
            Else
                        navigateButtons ("11111101011")
            End If
        ElseIf (lTotalRecords > 0) Then
            navigateButtons ("00001101001")
        Else
            navigateButtons ("00001000001")
        End If
        If (Not IsMissing(bLockEm)) Then
            lockTheControls (bLockEm)
        End If
    Case dbEditInProgress    'we are editing a current record
        Call lockTheControls(False)
        Text1(1).SetFocus
        navigateButtons ("00000010100")
    Case dbEditAdd                'we are adding a new record
        Call lockTheControls(False)
        navigateButtons ("00000010100")
        Text1(1).SetFocus
    End Select

End Sub
```

How It Works

Yikes! This looks complicated, with all of the nested `If` statements - but when we break it down into pieces and understand each of those, we find it's pretty simple. Let's start at the beginning.

```
    Public Sub updateButtons(Optional bLockEm As Variant)
```

Notice the VB key word **Optional** in the 'signature' of the subroutine. **Optional** was brand new with VB 5.0. Unfortunately, any optional argument *has* to be a variant. Even though we only need a **True** or **False** value, we must declare **bLockEm** as a variant.

Because we used the **Optional** keyword, the variable **bLockEm** may or may not be there. Heck, it's optional! To easily test to see if an argument was passed into **updateButtons**, use the built-in function **IsMissing()**. This VB function returns a Boolean value indicating whether an optional variant argument has been passed to our procedure. Later on in the code we will need to take some action if indeed the variable *was* passed in.

What we want to do in the **updateButtons** sub is to determine the status of the recordset. Did the user try to navigate or edit the recordset? Recall that when a button in our **cmdButton** control array is pressed, a recordset **method** is invoked. For example, when the user clicks the **cmdButton(0)** button, which is **cmdMoveFirst**, the **MoveFirst** method of the recordset is invoked. As soon as the **MoveFirst** method is invoked, there is a call to **updateButtons** to enforce our state-machine concept.

```
    Select case index          'what is the value of the key pressed?
        Case cmdMoveFirst
            Data1.Recordset.MoveFirst
            Call updateButtons
```

183

When the code jumps to **updateButtons**, the first thing that is done is to check the **EditMode** property of the recordset. Based on the **EditMode**, we will enable or disable certain **cmdButtons** in our control array.

```
Select Case Data1.Recordset.EditMode
```

Here we are using a **Recordset** property to assist us in determining the state of the data control. **EditMode** will return a value that tells us the current state of the **Data1.Recordset**. We want to take specific actions if our program is just moving from record to record, editing a current record, or adding a new record. This is very easy to do; the **Data1.Recordset.EditMode** property will return one of three states. We can just check the state of the **EditMode** property and see which of the three built-in constants it is equal to:

Built-in Constant	What it Tells Us
DbEditNone	No editing operation is currently in progress with the recordset.
DbEditInProgress	The **Edit** method of the recordset has been invoked and the current record is in the copy buffer.
DbEditAdd	The **AddNew** method of the recordset has been invoked and the current record is in the copy buffer. It is a new record that hasn't yet been saved in the database.

The **EditMode** property is very useful in several ways. For example, say the editing process is interrupted by an error during validation. We can use the value of the **EditMode** property to determine whether it makes sense to use either the **Update** or **CancelUpdate** methods in response to the error. Alternatively, we might just want to return focus to the text box that caused the error and give the user another chance to get it right. In any event, it is a flag that we can check at any time to determine the state of the recordset that is held on to by the data control. Very handy - it does the work for us of determining the state of the recordset.

Case DbEditNone - We Are Not Editing or Adding a Record

Let's examine the first case statement in the **updateButtons** subroutine. If the data control recordset is not editing or adding, then this case will be true. In other words, **Data1.Recordset.Editmode = dbEditNone**. The most involved portion of the **If** statement is when there is more than one record in the recordset. If there is more than one record, then the user needs to be able to navigate to each of them. However, we must test to see if we are at the beginning or end of the recordset.

We know that when our form first gets initialized, the first record becomes current. The user might also navigate to the first record. In either case, when the current record is the first record, we must disable the first two navigation buttons, **cmdMoveFirst** and **cmdMovePrevious**. This automatically prevents the user from navigating off the front of the recordset. Likewise, when the end of the recordset is reached we want to disable the last two navigation buttons, **cmdMoveNext** and **cmdMoveLast**. When we are checking out the navigation buttons, we only have to be concerned with the first four string positions.

Build a String

We can see now that **updateButtons** actually determines which buttons should be enabled/disabled. **updateButtons** needs a fast and elegant way to pass that information on to the **navigateButtons** sub. A simple way to do this is to build a string of 0's and 1's. The position of the 0 or 1 in the string represents a command button in that position of the control array. The first four positions in our string represent **cmdMoveFirst**, **cmdMovePrevious**, **cmdMoveNext** and **cmdMoveLast**. Since we are not editing or adding (when **Data1.Recordset.Editmode = dbEditNone**), the last seven positions of the string will always be the same - **1101011**. This string part enables the Add, Edit, Delete, Find and Done buttons while disabling the Save and Undo buttons. That enforces our state-machine concept - only legitimate buttons are available for the user to press. Here's the relevant bit of code:

```
Case dbEditNone
    If (lTotalRecords > 1) Then
    If (Data1.Recordset.BOF) Or _
       (Data1.Recordset.AbsolutePosition = 0) Then
            navigateButtons ("00111101011")
       ElseIf (Data1.Recordset.EOF) Or _
          (Data1.Recordset.AbsolutePosition = lTotalRecords - 1) Then
            navigateButtons ("11001101011")
       Else
            navigateButtons ("11111101011")
       End If
    ElseIf (lTotalRecords > 0) Then
        navigateButtons ("00001101001")
    Else
        navigateButtons ("00001000001")
    End If
    If (Not IsMissing(bLockEm)) Then
        lockTheControls (bLockEm)
    End If
```

We first want to check to see if the recordset contains more than one record. We put this first because this will be the case that occurs most often. We put the most used test first so we don't waste CPU cycles on tests that occur infrequently.

> *In a Select statement, always put the Case that will occur most frequently as the first case, the one that will be the second most popular next, etc. By ranking the Case statements like this, we limit the number of tests that VB must make. Each test costs CPU cycles, so in an extended Select statement, a well thought out structure can speed up our program.*

```
If (lTotalRecords > 1) Then
```

If there is indeed more than one record in the recordset, we take a look to see if the recordset is at the beginning. We certainly don't want the user to navigate off the beginning of the recordset:

```
If (Data1.Recordset.BOF) Or _
        (Data1.Recordset.AbsolutePosition = 0) Then
```

So the routine checked to see if the recordset is at the beginning. This is done by examining both the **BOF** property and the **AbsolutePosition** property. If either is true, we know we are at the first record. If we are indeed at the beginning of the recordset, we simply disable the first two navigation buttons - **cmdMoveFirst** and **cmdMovePrevious** by putting '0's in the first two positions of our string.

```
navigateButtons ("00111101011")
```

If we are not at the beginning, our routine then takes a look to see if the user is at the end of the recordset. If so, the last two navigation buttons - **cmdMoveNext** and **cmdMoveLast** - are disabled.

```
navigateButtons ("11001101011")
```

If there are more than two records in the recordset and the current record is neither at the beginning or the end of the recordset, then we permit navigation both forward and backwards.

```
navigateButtons ("11111101011")
```

OK, great, but what if there is only a single record in the recordset? Then the next **ElseIf** statement is true and we disable all of the navigation buttons because there is nowhere else for the user to go.

```
ElseIf (lTotalRecords > 0) Then
        navigateButtons ("00001101001")
```

The final test performed when we are not editing or adding is true when there are no records in the recordset. This will happen when the user opens an empty recordset or deletes the last record. In either case, we want to disable **all** of the navigation buttons. In fact, we disable all of the buttons except the A̲dd New and D̲one buttons. These are the only two actions allowed in this special case.

```
Else
    navigateButtons ("00001000001")
End If
```

Finally, as promised, here is the **IsMissing** function. Normally when the user is not editing, all of the bound text boxes are locked and the background is white. However, when an edit operation is taking place, we will unlock the text boxes and set the background color to **vbYellow**. This provides the user with a visual cue to show an edit is taking place. Then when we either S̲ave or U̲ndo an A̲dd or E̲dit operation, we want to return the controls back to normal. That is, we want them to be locked and the background to be set to **vbWhite** again.

```
If (Not IsMissing(bLockEm)) Then
        lockTheControls (bLockEm)
End If
```

We decided to make **bLockEm** optional because if we don't need to take any locking/unlocking action, we just don't pass the value of **bLockEm** to the **updateButtons** procedure. If we want the controls locked, we pass in a **True** value, and if we want to be unlocked, we pass in a **False**.

186

So by using this optional value, we can create a tri-state condition:

▶ Do nothing
▶ Lock the controls
▶ Unlock the controls

Remember that we must call **updateButtons** on each movement through the recordset. Each time a user clicks the >> button, for example, this procedure is called. We surely don't want to lock the controls each time we move to a new record. That would be a needless waste of processing. So if the optional parameter - **bLockEm** - is not passed when **updateButtons** is called, we can bypass this step. That is because the controls are already locked and the background is already set to white.

We want to call **lockTheControls** whenever the user performs a **Save** or **Undo** operation. However, when the operation is completed, just before **updateButtons** is called, the **EditMode** is already set to **dbEditNone**. That is because the operation has already been completed by the time our code is reached. So to our code the situation looks just like when we navigate the recordset. Our routine has no way of knowing that we had the controls unlocked, but we want them locked again.

The **Optional** parameter is just perfect for a situation like this. When we complete either a **Save** or **Undo** operation, we can call **updateButtons** and pass it the true parameter. This way when the user simply navigates the recordset, we don't re-lock the already locked controls, but in the special **Save** or **Undo** situations, passing in **True** will ensure they get locked.

```
If (Not IsMissing(bLockEm)) Then
        lockTheControls (bLockEm)
End If
```

Case dbEditInProgress - We Are Editing a Record

The next case statement is true when the user is currently editing a record. Since we are programming the recordset we explicitly invoke the **Edit** method. Now the recordset knows it is being edited.

```
Case dbEditInProgress    'we are editing a current record
     Call lockTheControls(False)
     navigateButtons ("00000010100")
     Text1(1).SetFocus
```

The recordset is currently in edit mode, so we want to unlock all of the bound text boxes first. Our call to **lockTheControls(False)** will unlock each control. Remember when we added this a bit earlier? We will soon see how it will be used. Once each of the appropriate controls is unlocked, we disable each of the navigation buttons by setting the first four positions of the string to 0000. The rest of the string, 0010100, disables the Add New, Edit, Delete, Find and Done buttons while enabling the Save and Undo buttons.

So while editing, the user can only select Save to commit the changed record to the database or Undo which will restore the previous contents of the original record.

We then set focus to the first text box that can accept focus - the Name field. This little technique makes our program appear more solid to the user. Rather than have the focus remain on the button that was pressed, we set it to the first text box. Why? Because this is where the user must be to start editing. So rather than have them click the text box to give it focus, we place the focus there. Now the user knows exactly where they should be because we placed them there!

Case DbEditAdd - We Are Adding a New Record

If the user clicks the Add New button, the following code will be executed:

```
Case dbEditAdd                'we are adding a new record
    Call lockTheControls(False)
    navigateButtons ("00000010100")
    Text1(1).SetFocus
```

If you have your thinking caps on, you might notice that the code is identical to the **dbEditInProgress** code. Yes, we could have written

```
Case dbEditInProgress, dbEditAdd
```

and saved a line of code. This case statement would evaluate to **True** if the user was either adding or editing. Since the code is identical, that would work fine. Nevertheless, I think you will agree that our way is a bit more readable. There is no doubt in anyone's mind what is happening when we are reading the code. It is just another opportunity to make our code self-documenting.

We've now built the code that determines the state of our application and builds a string that encodes which of the buttons should be active in that state. Now we'll build the next chunk of code in our application – this will set up the buttons that the user can press in this state.

The navigateButtons Sub-Routine

Now that we have our string of buttons all dressed up; they need a place to go. The place they will go to is the **navigateButtons** subroutine. We will pass the string created in **updateButtons** as a parameter to this sub. **navigateButtons** will read the string and either enable or disable each of our **cmdButtons**. Depending on the presence of a 1 or not, the appropriate button will either be enabled or disabled. Passing a string is the easiest and cleanest way to quickly change the **Enabled** property on our buttons.

FYI

It is a bit ironic that with all of the progress we have made in software technology over the past 20 years, we still rely on 'bit fiddling' techniques to so some efficient programming. Technically, a 1 or a 0 is a character consisting of 8 bits. If we were really bit fiddling, we would be examining each of the bits in a single character, not the characters themselves. While we could certainly do this with VB, it would add another level of unneeded complexity to our program. We can simply simulate bit fiddling to make our program efficient and much easier to maintain than 'real' bit manipulation.

We will pass in the string consisting of the eleven 0s and 1s to this sub. The first 0 or 1 will tell the sub to either disable or enable the first control in the **cmdButton** control array. The second 0 or 1 will instruct the code on how to handle the second control, and so forth. This way we can efficiently pass in a string telling the sub how to show the navigation buttons. Of course, the purpose is to enforce our state-machine. We will only allow buttons to be enabled if they can legitimately be pressed in the current state.

Try It Out - Adding the navigateButtons Sub-Routine

1   Add a new sub routine to your form and name it **navigateButtons**. Add the following code to your sub routine.

```
Public Sub navigateButtons(sButtonString As String)

'----------------------------------------------------
'-- This routine handles setting the enabled  --
'-- property to true/false on the buttons.    --
'----------------------------------------------------
'-- A string of 0101 passed. If 0, disabled   --
'----------------------------------------------------

Dim iIndx As Integer
Dim iButtonLength As Integer

sButtonString = Trim$(sButtonString)
iButtonLength = Len(sButtonString)

For iIndx = 1 To iButtonLength
  If (Mid$(sButtonString, iIndx, 1) = "1") Then
    cmdButton(iIndx - 1).Enabled = True
  Else
    cmdButton(iIndx - 1).Enabled = False
  End If
Next

DoEvents

End Sub
```

*The string variable begins with **'s'** as in **sButtonString** and the integer variable **iIndx** begins with **'i'**. This way you will know what type of variable you are dealing with. Many people use the Hungarian notation convention for variable naming. This is a naming convention developed by Charles Simonyi, who happened to be born in Hungary. This is a widespread convention, but just be sure to use some convention you are comfortable with and be consistent. Also try to name your variables with names that tell what they are used for. This will save you a lot of debugging time. Trust me on this one – I've been there.*

How It Works

When we pass a string of 0s and 1s, each position in the string represents a **cmdButton**. The sub trims off any blanks just to be safe. Then it loops through each of the characters and determines if it is a 1, which means that we want to set that particular **cmdButton**'s **Enabled** property to **True**. Otherwise, we want to set the **Enabled** property for that button to **False**. When the particular button's **Enabled** property is **True**, the user can click it. When it's **False**, it is still visible, but grayed out and the user can't click it.

For example, when the user presses the Add New button, we will pass a string that disables all navigation and editing buttons except the Save and Undo buttons. They can't make a wrong choice. Ruthless.

```
iButtonLength = Len(sButtonString)

For iIndx = 1 To iButtonLength
```

There are a few points worth mentioning here. First, notice that we are storing the length of the string in the variable **iButtonLength**. The other option would have been to do something like:

```
For iIndx = 1 To Len(sButtonString)
```

Yes, we would have saved a line of code, but consider that for each time through the loop we would have to call the function **Len()**, on a value that we know won't change. Calling any function can be expensive in terms of processing time. So it's much faster to call the function once and store the value in a variable, **iButtonLength**. Please keep this approach in mind for every loop you write. While it might not make too much difference if we are only looping four times, if you are looping 100 or more times it could be noticeable. We want to do everything in our power to make our program snappy and responsive. It's attention to details like this that make a good program. Remember what we said earlier about 'going back to optimize'? Well here we are optimizing **while we are coding**. This is a sure sign that the programmer has thought about what they are doing.

Another thing worth mentioning is the loop itself. Strings begin at position 1 but control arrays start at position 0. Remember that our **cmdButton** array starts at index 0. The first time through the loop the **iIndx** will be at 1 but we want this to apply to our first **cmdButton**, which is **cmdButton(0)**. To make the first character in the string apply to the first button, we simply make the assignment to **cmdButton(iIndx - 1)**. Therefore an **iIndx** value of 1 will set the first button.

```
For iIndx = 1 To iButtonLength
  If (Mid$(sButtonString, iIndx, 1) = "1") Then
    cmdButton(iIndx - 1).Enabled = True
  Else
    cmdButton(iIndx - 1).Enabled = False
  End If
Next
```

Here we loop through the string of 0s and 1s passed in, examining each in turn. The **Mid$()** VB function takes the string as the first parameter, the current value of **iIndx** as the second, and 1 as the length. So the first time through the loop, the first character is stripped off and examined. If the first character in the 11-character string is a 1, we know that the first control should be enabled. The next line of code enables that particular control.

```
    cmdButton(iIndx - 1).Enabled = True
```

Wait! You might be wondering what that **(iIndx - 1)** is all about. Couldn't we have just set **iButtonLength** using something like:

```
    iButtonLength = Len(sButtonString) - 1

    For iIndx = 0 To iButtonLength
      If (Mid$(sButtonString, iIndx, 1) = "1") Then
        cmdButton(iIndx).Enabled = True
```

This way we don't have to do any subtraction and things look a bit clearer. So why can't we do that? Good question. Remember that we are doing string manipulation here on the string **sButtonString** that is passed in. We need to look at each character from the first to the last. And if we started at position 0? Well, a string *has* no position 0. Strings **always** begin at 1. VB would greet us with this warm and fuzzy, not to mention descriptive error message.

So we must loop through the string from 1 to the length of the string. The first position in the string sets the first **cmdButton** in our array, which starts at 0. So we subtract 1 from the current value of **iIndx** which gives us the corresponding button. Not a big deal, but it's important to know why we are doing it this way.

DoEvents is put in for good measure. It ensures that the enabled/disabled buttons are immediately set. **DoEvents** yields execution of the program to the operating system so it can process other events. You always want to put a **DoEvents** in areas that provide a visual face to the user to ensure they get redrawn - pronto. A little known fact is that **DoEvents** actually returns an integer value that tells you how many forms are currently loaded. Here we just choose to ignore the returned value. We don't need it.

> *Microsoft mention that DoEvents is not required for 32-bit Visual Basic programs running under Windows95/98/NT. Windows 3.1 was a cooperative multitasking system. This essentially meant that each program had to be a good Windows system and periodically relinquish control to the operating system. If not, a single program could hog the CPU essentially preventing other tasks from taking place. Windows95/98/NT, however are preemptive multitasking operating systems. This means that the OS will assign a time-slice of CPU to each task in a round robin fashion - so each task will eventually get a CPU slice.*

191

> *However, I have found that depending on what tasks are running, you might not get the CPU slice soon enough. You have probably seen programs that display a half-drawn screen while the OS does its job. This looks tacky. By liberally using a DoEvents command, we can force the redrawing of any visual part of our program. Again, this makes for a snappy interface so everything takes place instantaneously from the users' perspective. One thing users cannot tolerate is a slow program.*

So now we have added our second block of code – the bit that will (once we've hooked it up later on) actually update the user interface to show the correct availability of buttons dependent on the state of the application. We'll now further enhance the usability of our interface by building a sub-routine that enforces correct editing of records.

Preventing Accidental Record Editing - the LockFields Subroutine

We are now going to look at another helper subroutine that will prevent accidental editing of our bound fields. In the context of our concept, you may have noticed that a user can still really edit *any* of the records displayed. We want to set up our screen so the user has to make a conscious attempt to edit any records. In other words, he or she has to press the Edit button. This step ensures that there is no accidental saving of bad information. So now is the perfect time to write another helper subroutine that will assist us in either locking or unlocking the text boxes. First, try out the following exercise:

Try It Out - Locking and Unlocking Specific Records

1 Bring up the Properties box for the Publisher's ID text box, which is at index 0 of our control array of text boxes. Set the Locked property to True.

2 Prior to VB 4.0, programmers had to use various **API** commands to prevent editing of text boxes. Starting with VB 4.0 we got some help in this department. By simply setting the **Locked** property of a text box we will prevent the user from changing it's contents. We want to be able to call a routine that will either lock or unlock specific controls on our form. In the default mode, all of the data entry fields will be locked. When the user wishes to either edit or add a new record, we will unlock all of the fields. Now go to each of the other text boxes and set the **Locked** property to **True**. The quickest way to do this is to hold down the shift key and click on all the textboxes so that they're all highlighted – then you can set the Locked property just once and all of the text boxes will be locked.

3 When you have locked all of the text boxes, press *F5* to run your program and try to edit a text box. Notice that the information is still visible, but the text box is locked to prevent any editing. The strict enforcement of our state machine concept strikes again. A record can't be edited until we say it can.

4 Now I want to show you another incredibly handy property available on most controls, the **Tag** property. This time, open the Properties window of the second text box, which displays the **Name** field and scroll down to the Tag property. Add the number 1 to it.

Properties - Text1(1)	_ □ ×
Text1(1) TextBox	▼

Alphabetic	Categorized
OLEDragMode	0 - Manual
OLEDropMode	0 - None
PasswordChar	
RightToLeft	False
ScrollBars	0 - None
TabIndex	1
TabStop	True
Tag	**1**
Text	XXXXXXXXXXXXXXXXXXXXXX
ToolTipText	

Tag
Stores any extra data needed for your program.

The **Tag** property simply holds any information that our program might want to tuck away. Prior to VB 5.0, there was no **ToolTipText** property. The **ToolTipText** property allows us to put in a string that will be displayed when the cursor is held over the text box. Many programmers would place the ToolTip string in the **Tag** property. This was fine, but it meant that the **Tag** couldn't be used for any other purpose. Unlike other properties, the value that we store in the **Tag** property isn't used by Visual Basic. That means we can use this property to store any value we want. However, the **Tag** property only holds a string data type. No problem - we can simply convert the value to anything we need it to be.

The value we place in the **Tag** property does not affect any other property settings or cause side effects. We have ten bound text boxes on our form. For each of them, with the exception of **Text1(0)** (which displays the PubID field), we'll set the **Tag** property to 1.

5 For each of the text boxes on our screen, bring up the Properties window and add the number 1 in each of the **Tag** properties for the text boxes **except the PubID text box**. We will be using this property to identify those text boxes we wish to lock and unlock. (Since the PubID field is automatically generated by the system, we don't want the user to modify that field. By leaving the 1 out of the **Tag** property for the PubID field, it will never become unlocked.)

Locking and Unlocking Our Data Entry Fields Automatically

Now we are going to write a small subroutine that will lock and unlock our text boxes for us. We will call it whenever we need to add or edit a record. Remember when we discussed using the graphical nature of Windows to our advantage? In the sub we will not only lock and unlock the controls, but set the background color of the text boxes as well.

When not in add mode, the text boxes are locked and have a white background. However, when the users either add or edit a record, we will not only unlock the controls but also change their **BackColor** property to yellow. In this way, there will be no question in the users' minds that they are in a 'record modification' mode. Our program provides them with another visual cue - the background colors of the text boxes that are available to edit as well as the various disabled buttons. Here we can use the graphical nature of Windows to our advantage.

Remember that we didn't set the **Tag** property of the PubID field? This means that it will stay locked and the background will always remain white. The user now knows that this field can't be edited. If we keep this strategy throughout our program, on all of our data entry forms, the user will find it intuitive and simple to understand. That, after all, is our goal.

Remember when we just put the number 1 in the **Tag** property of the text boxes we wanted to lock and unlock? Well, now we can look at each of the controls' **Tag** property, determine if it contains a '1' and take the appropriate action.

Try It Out - Automatically Locking the Controls

1 Take a moment now and add a new subroutine to your form called **lockTheControls**. It will take a **True** or **False** parameter. This way we can use a single routine to either lock or unlock the controls by simply passing it a **True** or **False** parameter.

```
Public Sub lockTheControls(bLocked As Boolean)

Dim iIndx As Integer

With Screen.ActiveForm
For iIndx = 0 To .Controls.Count - 1
  If (.Controls(iIndx).Tag = "1") Then
    If (TypeOf .Controls(iIndx) Is TextBox) Then
      If (bLocked) Then
        .Controls(iIndx).locked = True
        .Controls(iIndx).BackColor = vbWhite
      Else
        .Controls(iIndx).locked = False
        .Controls(iIndx).BackColor = vbYellow
```

```
            End If
          End If
        End If
      Next
      End With
      End Sub
```

How It Works

This looks scary, but it's really straightforward if we take a minute to examine it. Let's see what **lockTheControls** does. Two things are important here. The first is the **Screen.ActiveForm**.

```
With Screen.ActiveForm
```

The **Screen** object is **global** in Visual Basic. It is built into the language and can be referenced anywhere in our project. **Screen** references the entire Windows desktop. You can use the **Screen** object to set the mouse pointer, determine which is the active form - or the active control for that matter. So we are grabbing a reference to the currently active form, which is, of course, our data-entry form. When a control on a form has focus, that form is the currently active form on the screen and we can get to it using **Screen.ActiveForm**.

Each form has a built-in **controls collection** listing the form's attached controls. This collection's index values start at position 0 – so the reference to the first control on the form would be **Controls(0)**. Like all collections, there is a **Count** property that tells how many controls are in this collection. Since the collection starts at 0, we want to subtract 1 from the count. This way, if there were 15 controls in the collection, we would correctly loop through 0 through 14, accessing each of the 15 controls.

We could just as easily have got the count by using the fully qualified statement:

```
For iIndx = 0 To Screen.ActiveForm.Controls.Count - 1
```

If we did that, each time through the loop, VB would have to 'resolve 3 dots'. For each of the controls, it would have to get the **Screen** object, then find the **ActiveForm**, then locate the **Controls** collection of the form and finally grab the **Count** property of that collection. Too much work. If you have quite a few controls on the form, this can be time consuming.

We discussed eliminating the dots already, but this is a point worth remembering. Using the **With** construct, VB grabs the **Screen.ActiveForm** value and remembers it until the **End With** is reached. Now we can simply access the properties of the **ActiveForm** without having to retrieve it again and again. So, back to our proper code:

```
With Screen.ActiveForm
   For iIndx = 0 To .Controls.Count - 1
     If (.Controls(iIndx).Tag = "1") Then
```

The **For** loop will iterate through all of the controls on the active form using the built-in collection that not only includes our text boxes, but the labels and command buttons. The collection essentially contains everything we placed on the form. The loop examines each of the form controls by using its index value in the built-in collection.

195

So the first time through the **For...Next** loop we look at the control at the first position, which is position 0 in the built-in form controls collection. Since every control on the form is in the controls collection, there are some we are not interested in. We only want the ones that have a **1** in the **Tag** property. Once we find a control that matches, we determine if that particular control is a text box.

You might be wondering why we need this line of code. After all, aren't we only using text boxes on our form? That's true, for now, but later we will make this routine a bit more extensible. For example, what if we are binding a grid to a data control? Or what if we bind a combo box? Each of the controls has a slightly different way of displaying, locking, etc. So by checking to see if the control is a text box, we can be sure that we only set properties **specific to that type of control**. We will be adding provisions for other controls later in the book as we enhance the subroutine.

```
If (TypeOf .Controls(iIndx) Is TextBox) Then
```

We can determine the type of control by using the VB keyword **TypeOf**. When we need to take a specific action on controls of various types, (for example, some objects may not support a particular property or method), we can use the **TypeOf** method.

The above line of code will evaluate to **True** if the particular control in position **iIndx** of the **ActiveForm** happens to be a textbox.

TypeOf can only be used in **If...Then...Else** statements. You must include the class name directly in your code. For example:

```
If TypeOf MyControl Is CheckBox Then
```

FYI

A very handy, related function is **TypeName()**. If you ever need to know the type of an object, just pass in the name and **TypeName()** will tell you. This is a bit more flexible because it does not have to be embedded in an If statement. For example if you passed in **Text1(0)**, **TypeName()** would tell you this is a text box.

For example, **MsgBox TypeName(Text1(0))** would provide the following:

Back to our real form.

Our code looks at each control on our form in the VB **ActiveForm** controls collection and determines if that control is a text box. If the control has a **1** in the **Tag** property and if it is a text box, we want to take action:

```
If (bLocked) Then
    .Controls(iIndx).locked = True
    .Controls(iIndx).BackColor = vbWhite
Else
```

196

```
        .Controls(iIndx).locked = False
        .Controls(iIndx).BackColor = vbYellow
    End If
```

Of course, **bLocked** is the Boolean parameter we passed into the subroutine when it was called. If the variable **bLocked** is **True**, then we just set the text box's **Locked** property to **True** and set the **BackColor** property of that text box to **vbWhite**. Likewise, if the variable passed is **False**, then we unlock the control and set its background color to **vbYellow**. Pretty straightforward now that we look at it. Visual Basic has the following color constants built right into the language:

- **vbBlack**
- **vbRed**
- **vbGreen**
- **vbYellow**
- **vbBlue**
- **vbMagenta**
- **vbCyan**
- **vbWhite**

So using these constants, we don't have to bother with hex values. In addition, since these constants (as all VB constants) are part of the language itself, we don't make our programs any larger by using them. The main point of this exercise is that we are rigorously enforcing when a user can edit or add. At the same time our program is providing a visual cue - changing the background color - so the users know they are about to do something important.

> *I first named this subroutine* **lockControls** *instead of* **lockTheControls** *and Visual Basic provided me with an error message stating there was a Type Mismatch. Nothing else. The program would not even run. It took me a few minutes to figure out what went so terribly wrong. As soon as I changed the name, everything was fine. There is no keyword with the name* **lockControls**, *so it must be an intrinsic property. This is known in technical circles as a 'gotcha'.*

All of the 'Smarts' Have Been Added to Our Buttons

That's it. This routine's bark was definitely worse than its bite. By using a level of indirection, we now need only call **updateButtons** where necessary - with no parameters. We let that routine call both **navigateButtons** and **lockTheControls** indirectly. We simply encapsulated all of the messiness of having to know which parameters to pass to what in this single routine.

> *Note: We do not call* **lockTheControls (True)** *when the user navigates the recordset. Remember why? We don't want to include this overhead each and every time the user moves to another record. That means that we must add the line* **lockTheControls (True)** *after any adding or editing. In most cases the user will probably be navigating the recordset more than adding. This way we don't incur the overhead when moving to each record.*

Adding the Interface Enhancements to our Program

The next stage in the process is to think about how we're going to incorporate our subroutines into the larger context of our application.

Incorporating the updateButtons Subroutine

Having built some usable code, we now must first add calls to the new **updateButtons** subroutine in a few strategic places within our program. Let's do it!

Try It Out - Updating Our Program with Calls to updateButtons

1   First, add the call to the **Form_Activate()** event procedure by appending the highlighted code:

```
Private Sub Form_Activate()

With Data1.Recordset
  .MoveLast
   lTotalRecords = .RecordCount
  .MoveFirst
End With
```

```
updateButtons True
```

```
End Sub
```

How It Works

What happens when our Publishers form is loaded and displayed? Well, when the form is first loaded, the recordset pointed to by the data control might have 0, 1 or more records - we have no way of knowing. So after we initialize the **RecordCount** of the recordset in the **Form_Activate()** event procedure, we place that value in the variable, **lTotalRecords**.

By calling **updateButtons** with the **True** (optional) parameter, we simply ensure the controls are locked. Yes, we did lock them in design mode, but this is just my own manic need to thwart any possible error. The extra processing time is negligible and since the form is loading, the user will never notice. It is possible that someone was working on the form in design mode and forgot to lock a control. This could be a tough bug to track down. However, a simple call ensures they are locked each and every time the form gets loaded. Belt and braces? No, just thorough!

When the data control is initialized our program checks to see how many records (if any) were returned in the recordset. If zero or one, our code disables all of the navigation buttons and manipulates the editing buttons. If there is more than one record, only the **cmdMoveFirst** and **cmdMovePrevious** buttons are disabled.

If there are no records in the recordset, the only buttons enabled are Add New and Done. Otherwise, if there is at least 1 record in the recordset, the user can Add New, Edit, Delete, Find or quit using Done. So instead of having to handle all of this logic in multiple places in the program, we isolated it. Now a simple call to **updateButtons** handles all of the various cases for us. Neat, eh?

Try It Out - The Navigation Buttons

Now, let's finish up the **Select** statement for our **cmdButton** control array.

1   Go back to the **cmdButton_Click()** event procedure and add the following highlighted sections of code:

```
Private Sub cmdButton_Click(Index As Integer)

Static vMyBookMark As Variant 'used to bookmark the current record

Select case index          'what is the value of the key pressed?
    Case cmdMoveFirst
        Data1.Recordset.MoveFirst
        Call updateButtons
    Case cmdMovePrevious
        Data1.Recordset.MovePrevious
        Call updateButtons
    Case cmdMoveNext
        Data1.Recordset.MoveNext
        Call updateButtons
    Case cmdMoveLast
        Data1.Recordset.MoveLast
        Call updateButtons
    Case cmdAddNew       '—add a new record
    Case cmdEdit         '-- edit the current record
    Case cmdSave         '-- save the current record
    Case cmdDelete       '-- delete the current record
    Case cmdUndo         '-- undo changes to the current record
    Case cmdFind         '-- find a specific record
    Case cmdDone         '-- Done. Unload the form
End Select
End Sub
```

How It Works

Here you can see how easy the **updateButtons** subroutine made our job. After the user clicks one of the navigation buttons, a simple call to **updateButtons** ensures everything is well in data land. By that I mean all of our buttons are enabled or disabled, reflecting the current state of our program. We don't pass the (optional) **True** parameter because we know the controls are locked already - remember that we just locked them in the **Form_Activate** event procedure. A call to **updateButtons** works just fine. Now are you ready to fill in the other case statements in the **cmdButton_Click()** event procedure?

BookMarking a Record

There is a great property that we are going to use to bookmark our current record. The **BookMark** property of a recordset can hold the position of a record for us. Why might we want to use this? Well, let's say that the user is on record 450 of a 2,000 record recordset. Then they want to add a record so they click **A**dd New. After thinking better about it, the user decides to forget it and so clicks the **U**ndo button. Wouldn't it be nice to return the user back to record 450 - right where they left off? Well, it's a snap with the **BookMark** property. First, we need a variable to store the bookmark of the record we want to remember. You just did this by adding following code snippet to the **cmdButton_Click()** event procedure:

```
Static vMyBookMark As Variant
```

It is important to declare the variable as **Static** so the value will be remembered when the event procedure is exited. Static variables are used at procedure level to declare variables and allocate storage space. Variables declared with the **Static** statement retain their values as long as the code is running. So unlike other local variables that are destroyed when the subroutine looses scope, those declared as **Static** remember their value. Now, just before we either add or edit a record, we will save the current record. This way, if the user cancels the operation, we can promptly return to the record the user was on just prior to the operation - and all by simply setting a property.

Enhancing Data Manipulation Via the User Interface

We're now going to turn our attention to making sure that the way that we allow users to add, update and delete data is made more robust and dependable.

Adding Records

We'll start by adding some code that utilizes the **BookMark** property to help make adding records more intuitive.

Try It Out - Enhancing How Records are Added to Our Recordset

1 Go to the **cmdButton_Click** event procedure of your form and add the following highlighted code. This will hold the bookmark for us. Place this code under the **Case cmdAddNew** statement in the **cmdButton_Click** event procedure.

```
Case cmdAddNew   '-- add a new record
      With Data1.Recordset
          If (.EditMode = dbEditNone) Then
              If (lTotalRecords > 0) Then
                  vMyBookMark = .BookMark
              Else
                  vMyBookMark = ""
              End If
              .AddNew
```

```
            Call updateButtons
            lblRecordCount = "Adding New Record"
        End If
    End With
```

How It Works

Here we check to see if the data control recordset is currently not in edit mode. It should never be because the user couldn't press the A̲dd New button if it was, but that's just my paranoia showing again. Next, we bookmark the current record by assigning the **BookMark** property to our variable **vMyBookMark**. This means that if we need to return to the current record, we know its location. Once the bookmark is safely stored away, the **Data1.Recordset.AddNew** method is called to insert a new record into the recordset.

However, we have to keep our eyes peeled for an empty recordset. If the recordset is empty, there is no current record to return to. In this case, we want to assign a **""** to the **vMyBookMark** variable so we can test it later. If we have at least one record, we store the value. Otherwise, we store a **""**.

.AddNew

On receiving an **AddNew command**, Jet prepares a fresh, clean, shiny new record for us. Jet then makes this new record the current record. All of the bound fields on the screen are cleared out and the form awaits input from the user. The new record's position in the current recordset depends on the type of recordset we are currently using.

For example, in a dynaset type like the one that we're using with our form and data control, the new record is **always** placed at the end of the recordset. The record will not be added to the recordset (and hence to the underlying data table(s)) until we tell it to by using the **Update** method. Any time before the user commits the record with **Update** the operation can be undone.

The **AddNew** statement also puts the **EditMode** of the **Recordset** into **dbEditAdd**. The next call to **updateButtons** will set up the buttons for us. Since **dbEditAdd** is now 'true', the appropriate buttons will be enabled/disabled. The bound controls will be unlocked and the background of the editable fields will be set to yellow. All with a single call to **updateButtons**.

See, our hard work is now paying off. We will be able to use all of this code in each form that requires data entry. Write once, use often. When we put the code in a class, we can start to achieve the Holy Grail of object programming - reusability.

Finally, in our never-ending effort to provide the user with informative feedback, we place the string **"Adding New Record"** in the **lblRecordCount**.

lblRecordCount = "Adding New Record"

This notification, plus the yellow background will leave the user in no doubt about what they are doing.

Editing Records

Next, let's add some code that will enhance the editing process.

1 Please add the highlighted sections of code to the **cmdButton_Click** event procedure for **Case cmdEdit**.

```
Case cmdEdit   '-- edit the current record
    With Data1.Recordset
        If (.EditMode = dbEditNone) Then
            vMyBookMark = .BookMark
            .Edit
            Call updateButtons
            lblRecordCount = "Editing"
        End If
    End With
```

How It Works

When the user clicks the Edit button, the **cmdButton_Click** event procedure will be fired with an index value of 5. Of course, this equates to our **cmdEdit** enumerated constant. The code in the **Case cmdEdit** construct will then execute.

The user can only select the Edit button when there is a record present. Also, the Edit button is only enabled when the recordset is currently not adding a new record or editing the current record. Again, for good measure we tuck away the location of the current record before we do anything. Since there is a current record we are editing, we know that there will be a valid value for the **BookMark** property.

The **Edit** method will now place the **Recordset** in edit mode and set the **EditMode** to **dbEditInProgress**. The **Edit** method will copy the contents of the current record to the copy buffer, in case the user needs to restore it for some reason. It is not committed to the recordset until the user presses Save. This way, we can still undo any changes if needed. Next, the call to **updateButtons** will set up our form for editing. We also update the **lblRecordCount** label with **"Editing"**.

Saving Records

Next, we'll enhance the code for the record-saving process.

1 Now add the following highlighted code snippet to the **Case cmdSave** section in the **cmdButton_Click** event procedure:

```
Case cmdSave  '-- save the current record
       Dim bMoveLast As Boolean
       With Data1.Recordset
         If (.EditMode <> dbEditNone) Then
             If .EditMode = dbEditAdd Then
               bMoveLast = True
             Else
               bMoveLast = False
             End If
             .Update
             lTotalRecords = .RecordCount
             If (bMoveLast = True) Then
                 .MoveLast
             Else
                 .Move 0
             End If
             updateButtons True
         Else
             .Move 0
         End If
       End With
```

How It Works

When the user clicks the Save button, the **cmdButton_Click** event procedure will be fired with an index value of 6, which equates to **cmdSave**. The Save button is only enabled during an Add New or an Edit. All other times it is disabled, thanks to the **updateButtons** subroutine that runs each time we move in the recordset.

If the user is either adding or editing a record, the Save button is enabled and can be pressed. Save calls the **Update** method of the recordset. The **Update** method saves the contents of the copy buffer to the **Recordset** object. The record has now been saved - committed to the database.

Remember when we mentioned that an added record is placed at the end of the recordset? Well if the user is editing a current record, we want to save that record and then remain on that record. Otherwise, the user will become disoriented if we save the record and move somewhere else. If the user adds a new record, we want to make that one the current record. It's pretty simple to detect and handle either case in our code:

```
Dim bMoveLast As Boolean
    With Data1.Recordset
       If (.EditMode <> dbEditNone) Then
           If .EditMode = dbEditAdd Then
             bMoveLast = True
           Else
             bMoveLast = False
           End If
```

Right before we save the record, we determine if the user is adding a new record or editing an existing record. If the **EditMode** of the recordset equals **dbEditAdd**, then we know that a new record has been added and we are preparing to save it. If that is the case, we set the **bMoveLast** variable to **True** - since all new records are saved at the end of the recordset, we want to move there after it has been saved. However, if **EditMode** is **not** equal to **dbEditAdd**, we know that **dbEditInProgress** is true - telling us that the user is editing a current record. In that case, we want to stay on the current record when the changes have been committed to the database.

Armed with this information, we invoke the **Update** method and save the record:

```
.Update
lTotalRecords = .RecordCount
If (bMoveLast = True) Then
    .MoveLast
Else
    .Move 0
End If
updateButtons True
```

The **lTotalRecords** variable is updated. If the user added a record, the count is incremented by one. If an edit took place, the record count stays the same. Our variable **lTotalRecords** will now reflect the correct number of records in the recordset.

If **bMoveLast = True**, we know that the user added a new record. We then move to the end of the recordset to make the newly minted record current. Otherwise, the user was editing a current record and we keep that current. The buttons on the user interface are then updated. We call **updateButtons** with the **True** optional parameter to ensure the bound fields get locked correctly after the operation.

Deleting Records

We've looked at the editing interface, now let's make the deleting process a bit tighter.

Try It Out - Enhancing Record Deletion

1 Add this highlighted code to the **cmdButton_Click** event procedure.

```
Case  cmdDelete  '-- delete the current record
    Dim iResponse As Integer
    Dim sAskUser As String
    sAskUser = "Are you sure you want to delete this record?"
    iResponse = MsgBox(sAskUser, vbQuestion + vbYesNo + _
                vbDefaultButton2,  "Publishers Table")
    If (iResponse = vbYes) Then
        With Data1.Recordset
            .Delete
            lTotalRecords = .RecordCount
            If (lTotalRecords > 0) Then
                If lTotalRecords = 1 Then
                    .MoveFirst
                ElseIf .BOF Then
                    .MovePrevious
                End If
            End If
        End With
    End If
    Call updateButtons
```

How It Works

When the user clicks the <u>D</u>elete button, the **cmdButton_Click** event procedure will be fired with an index value of 7, which equates to **cmdDelete**. The <u>D</u>elete button is only enabled when there is not an add or edit operation taking place. Of course, if the recordset is empty, it is also disabled.

Deleting a record is serious business. Even though the user must press the <u>D</u>elete button, we still want to prevent any accidental deletions from the database. So before anything is deleted, we present the user with a message that gives them the chance to change their mind:

```
iResponse = MsgBox(sAskUser, vbQuestion + vbYesNo + _
              vbDefaultButton2, "Publishers Table")
```

Since we absolutely want to prevent the user from accidentally deleting a record, we even made the default button the <u>N</u>o button. By adding the constant **vbDefaultButton2**, we make the second button the default. Notice the subtle dotted line rectangle inside the <u>N</u>o button? Now if the user presses *Enter*, the <u>N</u>o button is pressed. OK, call me paranoid, but setting default properties to the boxes with an eye towards the safety of the user's data is really solid programming and enforces our state-machine concept.

If the user clicks <u>N</u>o, then nothing happens. If they answer <u>Y</u>es, however, then the code deletes the record and updates the **lTotalRecords** variable to reflect the new current record count. If there are more than 0 records left, we move to the previous record. If the user deleted the first record, we go to the new beginning of the recordset. It could so happen that the user deletes the very last record in the recordset. If the user deleted the last remaining record, we don't move the current record pointer because there is nowhere to go.

Finally, the buttons are updated in **updateButtons**.

```
Call updateButtons
```

All cases are handled, including if the user deleted the last record. But we already covered that ground. On the call to **updateButtons**, if the recordset is empty, the only options available to the user will be <u>A</u>dd New and D<u>o</u>ne We have everything covered!

> *Note: Later we will discuss relationships. For example if we deleted a publisher, we would also delete all titles and authors uniquely related to this publisher. We would want to perform a nested delete. If we deleted a publisher but did not delete all the associated titles, those Titles records would be orphaned. We would have no way to retrieve them. For now, we are only dealing with a single table. Stay tuned for nested deletes when we get to DAO.*

Undoing Changes to Records

For our final bit of interface enhancement, let's add some code that gets called when the user wants to undo changes.

Try It Out - Undoing Any Changes

1 As ever, add this highlighted code to the **cmdButton_Click** event procedure, in the **Case cmdUndo** section:

```
Case cmdUndo    '-- undo changes to the current record

    With Data1.Recordset
        If (.EditMode <> dbEditNone) Then
            .CancelUpdate
            If (Len(vMyBookMark)) Then
                .BookMark = vMyBookMark
            End If
            updateButtons True
        Else
            .Move 0
        End If
    End With
```

There will be times that the user will abort a change to a record. No problem, we provide an escape hatch in the form of an <u>U</u>ndo button. Clicking the <u>U</u>ndo button will automatically call the **cmdButton_Click** event procedure with an index of 8, which is really **cmdUndo**.

How It Works

If the user aborts the edit or add process, pressing this button invokes the **CancelUpdate** method of the recordset. This cancels any pending updates for a **Recordset** object. The original data is copied back from the buffer to the bound fields. No harm done. Then we check the length of our bookmark variable to ensure it holds a bookmark value. If the length is > 0 we know there is a record to return to.

```
.BookMark = vMyBookMark
```

Simply setting the **BookMark** property whisks the user back to the record prior to either the <u>A</u>dd New or <u>E</u>dit operation.

Ready to run your program? Well you earned it. Press *F5* and put the program through its paces.

Notice the first two navigation buttons. Disabling the buttons just grays them out. It's a subtle change, but the user gets a visual cue that they can't press them. They know immediately - without reading anything - that they can't go backwards. They also know that they can't **S**ave or **U**ndo - because they are not editing or adding. We want to use the graphical nature of Windows to our advantage. This is one of those times.

Move up a few records and press **A**dd **New**. The bound controls will unlock themselves and their background will change from white to yellow. Notice the text in the `lblTotalRecords` label. Also notice the command buttons. In an add mode, the user can now only save or undo. Finally, the cursor is in the first field that permits data entry, the Name field. This is the power of using the state machine concept. The user has absolutely no idea that we are so rigorously controlling everything behind the scenes. We don't give the user the opportunity to make a mistake.

Now click the Undo button. Notice how the bookmark immediately places us back on the record we were on prior to the Add New? Users love this.

> *Be sure to save your project. We will be enhancing it some more in the next chapter.*

Now let's take a brief excursion into the wonderful world of **references**. Seeing how references work will provide us with a solid understanding of how our VB code can use everything from DAO to Excel to Word to the Microsoft Internet Explorer.

Adding a Reference

We have been using several of the **RecordSet** properties and methods when we used code to add, delete and edit records. We also needed to determine if the data control is currently in an edit or add mode. In order for our code to know how to do this, it looks at a **reference**. Luckily, VB6 is smart enough to add a reference to the Microsoft DAO 3.51 Object Library. If a **type library** has already been registered, like our DAO 3.51, you'll see it in the References dialog box. Take a moment now to look at this. From the main VB menu, select Project-References to display all available references. Notice that VB has already added the DAO 3.51 reference for us. It does this as soon as we add an intrinsic DAO data control to our form. We will now have the ability to reference the various DAO commands. Remember that the **RecordSet** properties and methods are really DAO commands.

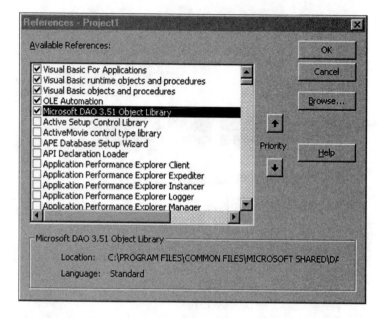

Before you can use an object's properties, methods and events in your application, you must first declare an object variable, then assign an object reference to the variable. Since we need to use the DAO properties and methods, the reference must be registered in our project. A reference is really a 'reference to a type library'. These binary files contain references to various objects we want to use in our project. Here in the screenshot, you can see all of the references available to your VB program. Later on in the book, when we send database data to Excel, we will add a reference to an Excel library. This way, VB does not have to hold every single method and property for every conceivable object. And as objects are updated or added, we simply add a reference to the type library and can program the object with VB. The type library provides all of the references VB needs to communicate with that object. In fact, later on in the book we will write our own Dynamic Link Library that accesses a database. We will have to add a reference to this `.dll` when we want to actually use it in our program.

Fun with the Object Browser

As we saw in the References dialog box, Visual Basic provides us with all kinds of type libraries. If you wish to sneak a peek at the DAO type library that has been added to our project, press *F2* to bring up the Object Browser.

The Project/Library box allows you to select a single
library or project, or to view all libraries and projects.

The Search Text box lets you find objects and members.

The Members list shows the properties,
methods, and events (members) that
belong to the class selected in the Classes
list.

Object Browser

<All Libraries>

Classes	Members of '<globals>'
<globals>	Abs
AlignConstants	App
AlignmentConstants	AppActivate
AmbientProperties	Asc
App	AscB
ApplicationStartCons	AscW
AsyncProperty	Atn
AsyncTypeConstants	Beep
BorderStyleConstant	Calendar
ButtonConstants	CBool

<All Libraries>

The <globals> entry in the Classes list is a placeholder
that lets you view the global objects, collections,
functions, and statements in the selected project or
library.

Click on the topmost drop-down box and select the DAO library that was added in the References. In the Classes list box, we can see all of the global objects, collections, functions and statements that are included in the DAO type library. Let's say we want to find the **MoveFirst** method. Type in movefirst in the second drop-down box and either press return or click the 'binoculars' button:

Here we can see the search results. The Library, Class and Member – MoveFirst - are listed. We can tell that this is a method because of the green flying brick. Note that at the bottom of the Object Browser we can see the file name and location of the DAO 3.51 library.

Object Browser

DAO

movefirst

Search Results

Library	Class	Member
DAO	Recordset	MoveFirst

Classes	Members of 'Recordset'
Property	Index
QueryDef	LastModified
QueryDefs	LastUpdated
QueryDefStateEnum	LockEdits
QueryDefTypeEnum	Move
Recordset	MoveFirst

Library **DAO**
   C:\PROGRAM FILES\COMMON FILES\MICROSOFT SHARED\DAO
\DAO350.DLL
   Microsoft DAO 3.51 Object Library

Take a few minutes to explore the Object Browser. Type in recordset in the second drop-down box. The results will show every instance of a recordset in the library:

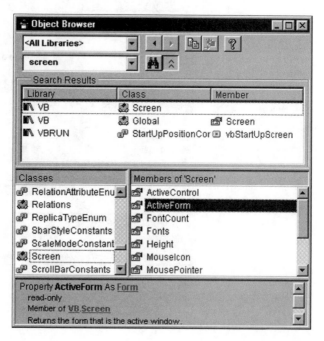

Select Recordset from the Classes list box. Now scroll through the various members of the recordset in the Members list box. Find the Fields property. Since this has a little blue ball hovering above the icon, this tells us that this is the default property. As mentioned, the green flying bricks are methods. When we start building our own classes, we will cover all this in detail. Now that the DAO 3.51 type library has been added to our project for us, we have access to all of these properties and methods listed. Best of all, you don't pay a resource penalty for any type library elements you don't use.

Remember earlier when we were discussing the **screen** object? Select <All Libraries> from the first drop-down box. Enter screen in the second drop-down box and press *Enter*. Here you can quickly see all of the properties and methods available to you. You can now get a sense of its power.

Time snooping around the Object Browser is time well spent. You just need to add a reference to the type library you wish to add to your project. Then all of the members of that object are shown. Notice that in the gray box at the bottom of the example, we can see a lot of information about the ActiveForm:

▶ It's a Property

▶ It's a Form

▶ It's read-only

▶ Reading the property into a variable will give us the name of the form that is the active window

This is jam packed with helpful information. And when we add a new reference to our project, it makes sense to browse to see what is available.

> *Often there will be undocumented methods or properties for an object. Right-click on the Object Browser to bring up the pop-up menu. Click Show Hidden Members to see all of the properties and methods. We will find out later on in the book how we can display our objects that we create right in the Object Browser. We also have the ability to hide any property or method we don't wish to be displayed. However, the Show Hidden Members will display everything. This is a good tool to find out everything about the object we are looking at.*

Summary

Here are the key things we did in this chapter:

▶ We created a bulletproof data entry screen by building navigation procedures to help the user to 'do the right thing'

▶ We isolated a lot of code used to help us create our 'state-machine'

The best part is yet to come. After the next chapter, when we get all our code down and working, we will be in a position to encapsulate all of the functionality in a class module that will make the code reusable on most any data entry screen we ever make. This 'black box' will hold all of the navigation and validation routines that we will write – and more. These routines will be made universal enough to use on any user interface that requires data entry.

What We Learned

▶ How to create and use a **control array** of command buttons and text boxes

▶ How to use the **state-machine concept** to control our interface

▶ How to set controls' properties using VB code

▶ How to use VB code to navigate and edit a recordset

▶ How the **Recordset.EditMode** tells us if we are adding or editing records – or neither

In the next chapter we'll put the finishing touches to our interface and build a **Find** function so that the user can easily search for specific records. This will prepare us for building our class module in Chapter 7.

Exercises

1 What is the purpose of the **BOFAction** property of the data control? What are the allowable values and what do they do?

2 When using DAO, with bound controls, to program a user interface which methods of the recordset object must be called to add a new record? Which methods must be called to edit an existing record?

3 What property of the recordset object allows the developer to "mark" a record and provides a way to quickly and easily return to that record? Write a line of code showing how to set this property. Write a line of code showing how to return to the marked record.

4 Write the code that will allow the developer to cancel the changes, which have been made to the current record. Place this code in the event procedure that handles the **Click** event of a command button named **cmdCancel**.

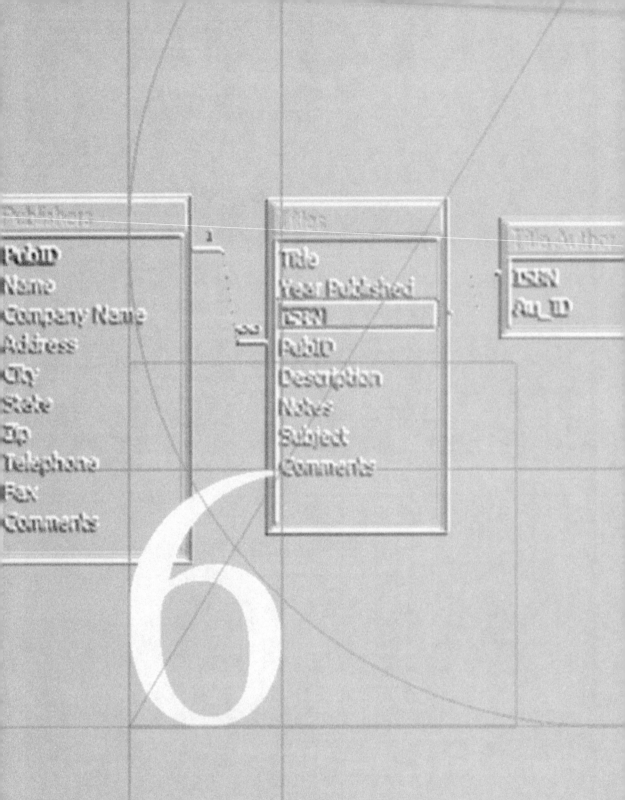

6

Completing the User Interface

This chapter plays out the final variations in our user interface creation theme: we continue to add the code that will help make our interface robust, easy to use, and universal. Here are the bases we'll cover in the chapter:

▶ Adding functionality to the command buttons

▶ Using **Focus** and **Tab Order** to make using the interface more efficient and intuitive

▶ Adding a **Find** form using a self-contained code module

▶ Implementing **data validation** so that the user enters appropriate information only

How's It Look?

The user interface is looking pretty good, and we have created some of the fundamental features of the interface:

We are now going to look at data validation and add a few professional touches to our user interface - for example by adding code for the rest of our buttons in the control array of command buttons. One of these - the Find button - will invoke a secondary (or **child**) form of the parent form that we have been working with up until now. The **Find** form will help users search for the particular records they're after.

First then, let's consider how to add some code that will make sure our form closes down cleanly.

Unloading our Form - a Few Concerns

We've added a fair bit of code that ensures that our user interface has some 'fail-safe' navigation procedures built into it, but you might have wondered about some other functionality that we need to add. For example, one thing that probably occurred to you is, "Hey, how on earth do we quit our form?" Well, that's a good question.

Bring up your project **prjPublishers** from the last chapter. We'll be developing the foundation we've created. You should create a new directory called **[Drive]:\BegDB\Chapter6** and save this project away there - we'll be enhancing the code and carrying it forward into the next chapter.

The first enhancement will be to improve the functionality of the Done button.

Try It Out - Adding Code to the Done Button

1 Place the following line of code in the **cmdButton _Click** event procedure for **Case cmdDone**. This code is called when the user clicks the 10th button in our control array, the Done button.

```
Case  cmdDone    '-- Done. Unload the form
        Unload Me
```

How It Works

This is a command telling the form (**Me** is implicit) to unload itself. It seems pretty straightforward, doesn't it? However, what if the user is currently adding or editing a record? We certainly don't want them to be able to unload the form under these circumstances now, do we?

As we know from our **updateButtons** subroutine in the last chapter, the Done button is disabled automatically during an Add New or Edit operation, but users can do terrible things if we don't make life easy for them. Take a look at the three buttons in the upper right-hand corner of the form:

Notice the rightmost **X** button. Pressing this will also permit the user to exit the form. So what do we do? What if they bypass our fancy control array and just click the **X**? What if they click the upper left-hand corner of our form to display the menu and then click <u>C</u>lose, as in the following screenshot?

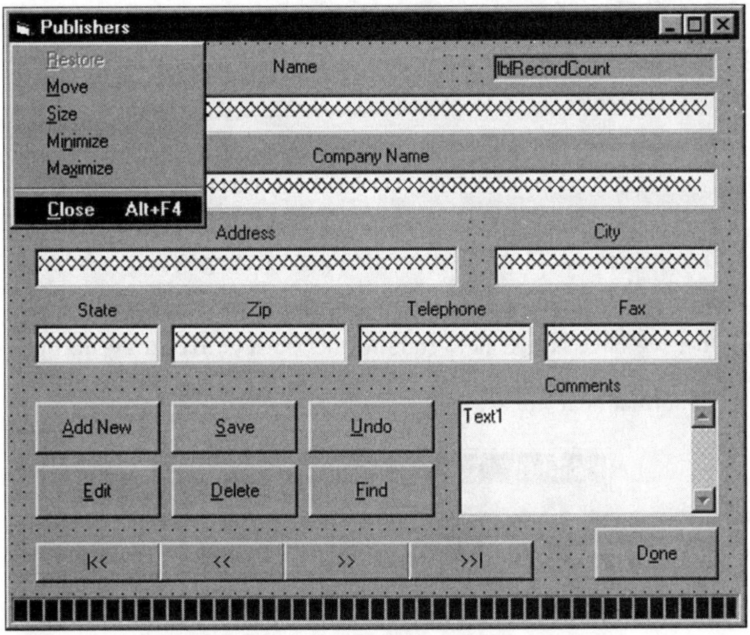

Another alternative scenario is that the person using our interface is a power user who knows that the key combination *Alt* and *F4* will close the form. Or what if the user just decides to close down Windows altogether during an edit? Yikes! How can we prevent the user from making an end run around our carefully constructed state machine?

Ensuring Uniform Unloading of Our Form

Luckily the form object provides us with a **central location** to check for unloading - whether we issue an **Unload** command, the **X** is pressed, the <u>C</u>lose menu option is selected or even if *Alt* and *F4* are pressed. The form event procedure that allows us to intercept any call to close the form is called **QueryUnload**. Let's add some code to the **QueryUnload** event and protect the users from themselves.

Try It Out - Adding Code to the QueryUnload Event

1 Open the form's code window and find the **QueryUnload** event procedure of the **Form** object. Add the following highlighted code:

```
Private Sub Form_QueryUnload(Cancel As Integer, UnloadMode As Integer)

  Dim iMessage As Integer

  If (Data1.Recordset.EditMode <> dbEditNone) Then
    iMessage = MsgBox("You must complete editing the current record", _
                      vbInformation, "Publishers")
    Cancel = True
  End If

End Sub
```

How It Works

QueryUnload is the central location to perform a last minute check to determine if we really *will* allow the form to unload. If the user is adding or editing, we certainly don't want the program to quit until they have entered some data. Our state-machine already ensures that the Done button is disabled, of course - our existing code disables it when an add or edit is in progress. Now that we have added new code to the **QueryUnload** event, the form is even safer: if the user now tries to exit by any other method without entering data in the add or edit, they will receive this informational message:

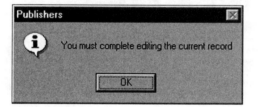

So, in order to exit the form, the user *has* to use the available command buttons that our state-machine manages for us. The **QueryUnload** event will fire on *any* attempt to unload the form programmatically - or any other way for that matter. One of most powerful features of this event procedure is that it tells you how the impending unload was caused. In fact, if you need to find out exactly how this or any form was closed, you can check the value of the **UnloadMode** that VB passes as a parameter to the form's **QueryUnload** event procedure.

Unload Mode has these values	How the form is being closed
VbFormControlMenu	The user clicked the close command from the control menu on the form.
VbFormCode	The **Unload** statement is invoked from the code, as we are doing.
VbAppWindows	Windows is shutting down.
VbAppTaskManager	The Task Manager is closing the application.
VbFormMDIForm	A child form of an MDI form is closing because the MDI is closing.

> *Tip: If you ever need to determine how the form is being unloaded, you could write code that checks for each of the possible UnloadModes in the QueryUnload event procedure. Look at the following example:*

```
Select Case UnloadMode
   Case vbFormControlMenu
      MsgBox "Unloading from the menu"
   Case vbFormCode
      MsgBox "Unloading from code"
   Case vbAppWindows
      MsgBox "Windows is unloading"
   Case vbAppTaskManager
      MsgBox "Unloading from the Task Manager"
   Case vbFormMDIForm
      MsgBox "Unloading MDI form"
End Select
```

So if the **Done** button is enabled, and pressed by the user, we would be unloading the form from code. The **Unload Me** command instructs the form to unload. If you had the code above to test, the **UnloadMode** would equal **vbFormCode** and you would see this.

> *Note: Under certain circumstances, a form will not fire the QueryUnload event. If you use the End statement to terminate your program or if you click the End button (or select End from the Run menu) in the development environment, this event does not fire.*

OK, let's get back to the code we really *did* add to the **QueryUnload** event. Suppose we are ready to unload our form. Before we decide to unload the form, we want to take a peek at the **EditMode** of the data control recordset.

```
If (Data1.Recordset.EditMode <> dbEditNone) Then
```

If the **EditMode** is not **dbEditNone** then we know the user is currently editing or adding a record, and we display an informative message:

```
iMessage = MsgBox("You must complete editing the current record", _
                  vbInformation, "Publishers")
```

The Lowly MsgBox Function

It's helpful to take advantage of the various capabilities of this powerful little gem called **MsgBox**. I have seen countless production programs that just use the default values, but it's easy to go beyond using the defaults. By some simple crafting, we can customize the message box to our program. The syntax looks like this:

```
iReturnValue  =  MsgBox(prompt[, buttons] [, title] [, helpfile, context])
```

While it is easy to use, so many programmers simply don't bother to use the *buttons* option or insert a customized title. Take a moment to look at MsgBox Function in the VB 6.0 on-line help. All of the button constants and return values are shown. When the user presses a button on the **MsgBox**, the value is placed in **iReturnValue** for us to test. At a minimum, always place a value for the message box's *title*. In our example, we used **Publishers** to customize the box.

Using App.EXEName

If you have several message boxes used in your program and *always* want to display the title, you could type in the title for each message box. But if we wanted to display Publishers as the title in 10 message boxes that we use in various parts of our program it would take up unneeded space if we had to store the title 10 times. The word Publishers has 10 letters. If we typed this in for 10 message boxes, this would take up 100 characters.

A better alternative would to simply place **App.EXEName** in the *title* position. This way we grab the title of the application from the global **App** object instead of repeating it several times throughout our code. This costs us nothing in memory because the **App.EXEName** already holds the title. When you get a second, take a look at the **App** object in the Object Browser and scan the other information available to you.

If you wish to present another name in the message boxes, instead of the name of the application, you should dim a constant in the General section of the form, like this:

```
Const myApp = "The Plutonic Nebulizer Program"
```

This way, the title is typed in only once, not 10 or 20 times. So when a message box is displayed, the title will always be the same. What's more, you don't have to worry about typos in any of them.

```
iReturnValue = MsgBox("You are about to destroy the earth.", _
                      vbExclamation + vbOKCancel, myApp)
```

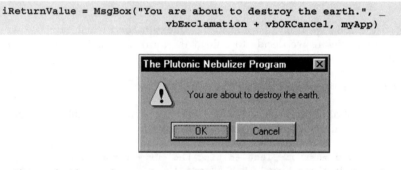

Later, if you decide to change the text that you want displayed as the title, just change the constant. There is no need to do a global find/replace to change all instances of the title in each and every message box. Since all message boxes use the same constant, they are instantly changed. Another step to improve our quality of life.

OK, let's get back to the explanation of our **Form_QueryUnload** event procedure.

Canceling the Form Unload

So, if we decide that the program *can't* be canceled now, we just set **Cancel** to **True**. This effectively cancels the **Form_Unload** event of the form.

```
Cancel = True
```

This is how word processor programs know when to ask you to save a changed document. They have a global Boolean variable, bDirty. On loading a document, bDirty is set to False. Any change to the document sets bDirty to True. Any time you save the document bDirty is reset to False. Then when you attempt to exit without saving, the QueryUnload event checks the status of this variable. If bDirty is True, it knows you modified the document but have not yet saved it, so you get prompted.

In our program, if the user is not in edit mode, we want to simply unload the form correctly and free up system resources. Let's look at how we can code for this.

Try It Out - Adding Code to the Form_Unload Event

1 The **Form_Unload** event is fired after **QueryUnload** if the unload is not cancelled. Add the following line to the **Form_Unload** event procedure. This terminates the form *and* frees up memory.

```
Private Sub Form_Unload(Cancel As Integer)
    Set frmPublishers = Nothing
End Sub
```

When you unload a form using the **Unload** method, only a portion of the memory occupied by the form is released. To free all memory, we want to eliminate the reference to the form by using the keyword **Nothing**. For any and all forms that you create, be sure to set them to **Nothing** in the **Unload** event procedure. This effectively releases any references to them.

Note: VB has a small quirk when forms are unloaded. If you do not set the form to Nothing it will retain the values of form-level variables in memory. This can cause some bugs that are very difficult to track down when the form is reloaded. If you have any form-level variables, they will retain the values they had when the form was last run. Not what you might expect. By setting it to Nothing we eliminate this problem and free up memory to boot.

2 While we are on the topic of form behavior, we really don't want the user to resize our Publishers form. After all, we did create it to present all of the fields in a clean, structured way, so it will serve no good purpose if the user shrinks the form or stretches it - other than to make it look ugly. So take a minute and set the form's BorderStyle property to 3-Fixed Dialog:

This style will not allow the user to resize the form or minimize it - so the buttons for these functions no longer appear on the form. However, the user can still dismiss the form - a single **X** button is displayed in the upper right-hand corner.

3 Press *F5* and run your program to test this out. Try as they might, the user cannot change the dimensions of the form by trying to resize the form.

So, we have now done our best to make sure that our form always closes down as cleanly as it can. Let's now turn our attention to making sure that the user of the form can input data into the form in as painless a way as possible.

Some Data-Entry Considerations

If you have ever seen a really good data-entry operator, you were probably pretty impressed. These operators can enter data like lightning - hands flash across the keyboard in a heads down, no messing, data-entry way. This is only possible if the data-entry screen is logically laid out and makes it very easy to move from field to field in a consistent sequence. In order to understand how we accomplish this in the Visual Basic programming world, it's important to understand the concept of **focus**.

What Exactly is Focus?

Focus is Windows' indication of where you are in a program. Controlling and understanding focus is a fundamental part of graphical programming. When you load a VB form, like our Publishers form, the cursor is somewhere on the active form. That 'somewhere' is a control that can receive focus, like a text box or command button. However, as we noted earlier, a label *can't* receive the focus.

When Windows processes a message, such as a mouse click, it sends it to VB, which in turn sends it to the object that currently has focus.

> *The control that currently has focus is the recipient of Windows messages from the user.*

Of course, messages can get sent *programmatically* to controls that don't have focus. However, for user input - a mouse click or a keystroke – the messages will always be sent to the control with focus.

Try It Out - Highlighting the Current Text Box - Hocus Focus

1 Why all the fuss about focus? Well, let's add a small routine to the General section of our form that will illustrate the point nicely. Call the subroutine **highLight** and add the following code:

```
Public Sub highLight()

With Screen.ActiveForm
    If (TypeOf .ActiveControl Is TextBox) Then
      .ActiveControl.SelStart = 0
      .ActiveControl.SelLength = Len(.ActiveControl)
    End If
End With

End Sub
```

2 Since we added all of the text boxes to our form in a control array, we know each text box shares the same code. So we can implement our new routine and with one subroutine call in the **Text1_GotFocus()** event procedure. Go to the **Text1_GotFocus** event and add the code below:

```
Private Sub Text1_GotFocus(Index As Integer)
    highLight
End Sub
```

3 Press *F5* to run your program. Notice that as you move around the text boxes using the tab key (or click with the mouse) the text in the control is highlighted, clearly showing which control has focus.

Another benefit of using a control array for the bound textboxes is also evident. Since each of the text boxes in the control array share the same code, we only need to add this single line to the **GotFocus** event procedure. No matter which of the text boxes gets focus, this same code will fire. Instead of writing the call to **highLight** in each of 10 individual textboxes, we only need to do it once. We don't really care which of the textboxes got focus here so we can ignore the **Index** parameter. Our **highLight** subroutine simply finds the currently active textbox and highlights the contents.

How It Works

When a control gets focus, we make a call to **highLight**. The **highLight** routine is a generalized routine that takes the screen's active text box control and checks to ensure that the control is indeed a text box. If so, the contents of the text box are highlighted. This is done by setting the length of selected text to the length of text in the box. Now the user can easily see which text box has focus, which makes for easy editing. If the field happens to be empty, they see only the yellow background. You have probably seen this technique used frequently in professional software programs.

We know that all of the text boxes in our control array share this code, right? So whenever the focus shifts from one text box to the next, the same code is fired and the **highLight** subroutine is called, effectively highlighting the contents of the text box that currently has the focus.

What we want to do in the code of the **highLight** routine is make the text in the text box the selected text - we want it to appear as it does when a user highlights text with a mouse. Here's the relevant section of code we use to do this:

```
With Screen.ActiveForm
    If (TypeOf .ActiveControl Is TextBox) Then
       .ActiveControl.SelStart = 0
       .ActiveControl.SelLength = Len(.ActiveControl)
    End If
End With
```

In the **highLight** subroutine we take the active control of the active form and check to see if it is indeed a text box. If it is (and we know it will be for now), we set the **SelStart** property to **0**. **SelStart** specifies the starting position of the selected block of text. A setting of **0** indicates the position just before the first character in the text box. **SelLength** specifies the number of characters selected. We take the length of the field contents and make the selected text exactly that long.

You may have noticed that when you tabbed around the form, the order that controls were selected in seemed pretty arbitrary. We'll fix this aspect of the interface now so that it works more professionally.

Highlighting the Right Field

To maintain consistency of our interface, we want to ensure that, no matter what field the user had highlighted before, when they navigate to the next record, the *first* field in the next record gets highlighted. The data control's **Reposition** event procedure is the natural place to make sure that this happens - so let's create the code to do it:

Try It Out - Updating the Data1_Reposition Event

1 Add this highlighted line of code to the **Data1_Reposition** event procedure.

```
Private Sub Data1_Reposition()

With Data1.Recordset
   lblRecordCount.Caption = "Publisher " & (.AbsolutePosition + 1) & _
                  " of " & lTotalRecords
   ProgressBar1.Value = .PercentPosition
   If (Text1(1).Visible) Then Text1(1).SetFocus
End With

End Sub
```

Since the **Reposition** event fires during the data control's initialization - which is before the graphical pieces are fully in place - we must test to see if the Name text box (**Text1(1)**) is currently visible. If we did not perform this check and tried to set the focus before everything was ready, VB would gladly provide us with the extremely unhelpful error '5':

Our simple check will ensure that focus is not shifted to the Name text box unless it is fully ready to accept it. So each time the user navigates to another record, the focus will be sent to the Name text box. This also means there's less chance of generating an error message - another potential land mine avoided.

We *could* have stored a form-level variable called **bIsVisibleYet** and set it to **True** in the **Form_Activate()** event procedure. Then we could test for the value before setting the focus. However, since we are dealing with time on a human scale, the extra millisecond required checking a property instead of a variable will never be noticed, and we have also saved ourselves some memory space since the **Visible** property does not take up any extra memory. So now, whenever the user moves to a new record, the focus will be shifted to the Name field. And whenever the Name (or any field) gets focus, **highLight** is called.

2   Press *F5* to run your program. See how much better our form looks with this simple, yet elegant touch?

There is no question in the user's mind that the **Name** field is now current. While programming Visual Basic 6.0 to work with databases, our main concern is to make the user interface as bulletproof as possible. All of our work behind the scenes pays huge dividends in the 'ease of use' department, and this simple routine goes a long way towards that end.

Some More About Focus

One potential problem we must keep in mind is that of trying to call **SetFocus** on a control *before* the controls are completely initialized. If we try to set focus in the form's **Load** event procedure, the visual components are not yet initialized. Attempting this will again bring up the oh-so-friendly error message '5' telling us (in)exactly where we went wrong!

This error message looks pretty scary. Most programmers interpret this error to mean something much more serious than simply calling **SetFocus** when the control is not yet initialized. This problem has caused countless hours of debugging because many programmers think the **Load** event is the natural place to address visual controls. It isn't. When loading a form, any calls to a visual method (anything that is visual and shown on the form - like **SetFocus**) should be placed in the form's **Activate** event procedure.

A *form* can only receive focus when there is no control on it that has the ability to receive focus. So if you create a new project with one form and no controls, that form will get focus by default. If you place a label on the form, the label can't receive focus, so the form still gets it. If you draw a text box on the form and start the project, that text box automatically gets focus - you can tell by the I-Beam cursor in the text box. If you draw three text boxes on the form, the first one that is drawn on the form gets the focus - regardless of where it is located on the form.

Take a look at this screenshot:

Notice that the first text box drawn, Text1, has the I-Beam cursor in it. If the user starts typing, all input will go directly to Text1. But what if we want the user to start out with Text3? **We need to change the focus programmatically**. We do this by using the specific control's **SetFocus** method to control focus absolutely. Remember, we want the focus to be where we *need* it to be, not necessarily where Windows' default behaviors *want* it to be. By using the **SetFocus** method, we can place the focus on a particular field or control so that the user input is directed to this object.

Also, focus can't be moved to a form or control if the **Enabled** property is set to **False**. When the **Enabled** property has been set to **False** during design-time, it must be set to **True** programmatically before it can receive the focus. So when we want to use the **SetFocus** method, the control always has to be enabled. If you attempt to **SetFocus** to a control that has had its **Enabled** property set to **False**, we get our now familiar and helpful Run-time error '5'.

I know what you thought was a simple topic turned out to be a bit involved. However, once we understand focus, we can use it in an expert fashion to make our user interface very intuitive. There is a method to this madness.

> *To summarize, it's important to note that focus can only be moved to a visible control or form. A form and the controls on it are not visible until the form's Load event has finished. When the Activate event procedure is fired, we are sure that all visual components are completely initialized, and it is now safe to call SetFocus.*

So now let's look at how we can be sure that the focus always moves where we want it to.

Setting the Tab Order

When the user 'tabs' from field to field, we want to ensure that the *Tab* key moves the focus to the next field on the form. When data-entry operators work, they enter data, then press the *Tab* key, enter data, press *Tab*, and so on. They expect the *Tab* to move them to the next field on the form. However, when you draw the first control on a form, the **TabIndex** property of the control is set to **0**. Now, when the form loads, that control automatically gets focus. When a second control is drawn, the **TabIndex** property is incremented, and set to **1** for that control. As each new control is drawn, the **TabIndex** gets incremented for that control.

The order in which the controls receive focus when the *Tab* key is hit is the order in which the controls were drawn on the form. Well, it practically never happens that we will draw each control on a form in the exact sequence that we wish the user to *Tab* in. During our prototyping phase, those pesky users (I jest obviously!) will almost always want this or that text box or button in a different place on the form.

Keeping Tabs on the Tabs

By default, the first control drawn on a form has a **TabIndex** value of **0**. The second has a **TabIndex** of **1** and so on. Luckily, the control's tab order position can be changed to meet our needs. By simply setting each control's **TabIndex** property to the sequence we wish the controls to be tabbed to, VB handles the re-sequencing for us. When we change the **TabIndex** property on a control, VB automatically re-numbers the tab order positions of the other controls to reflect insertions and deletions.

Bring up the Properties window for the first text box we drew on our form, the bound text box for the **PubID** field:

Notice that it has a TabIndex value of 0. The TabIndex setting on the last control drawn is always one less than the number of controls in the tab order - this is because the TabIndex numbering starts at 0. Even if you were to set the TabIndex property to a number higher than the number of controls on the form, Visual Basic would automatically convert that value back to the number of controls minus 1. If, however, you set the TabIndex property to a negative number, Visual Basic barks at us by generating an error message:

Any controls that cannot get the focus, as well as those that are disabled or invisible, are still included in the tab order but simply get skipped. As a user presses the *Tab* key, these controls get leap-frogged. When the user clicks the Add New button, the Add New, Edit, Delete, Find, Done and all navigation buttons are disabled. So, as the user presses the *Tab* key to move from field to field, these controls are passed over. We're going to take a minute now and set the TabIndex for the controls on the form in the order we wish the user to tab in.

> *If you set the tab order starting from 0, VB will not remember the earlier order. By that I mean when you get to control 5, there is no guarantee that controls with TabIndex properties of 0 through 4 will still be in that order.*

Try It Out - Changing the Tab Order

1 To accomplish what we want, go into the form in design view and change the TabIndex properties of all the controls. Start at the **last** control - the Done button - and set its TabIndex property to 0. Now, go to the second to last - the Move Last button - and set its TabIndex property to 0. Work through our sequence from the bottom of the list shown below to the top and give each TabIndex a value of 0. By the time you reach the PubID field, all of the preceding controls will now have the correct tab order.

Control	TabIndex Value
Publisher's ID text box	0
Name text box	1
Company Name text box	2
Address text box	3
City text box	4
State text box	5
Zip text box	6
Telephone text box	7
Fax text box	8
Comments text box	9
Add New command button	10
Save command button	11
Undo command button	12
Edit command button	13
Delete command button	14
Find command button	15
Move First command button	16
Move Previous command button	17
Move Next command button	18
Move Last command button	19
Done command button	20

How It Works

OK, working backwards now gives us the correct order listed above. Although it might seem a bit weird, we started at the D̲o̲ne button and make this **TabIndex 0**. Then we moved to the Move Last button and made this **TabIndex 0**. Then we went to Move Next and so forth. By the time you reach the PubID field, each **TabIndex** property will be re-sequenced correctly.

Of course each of the labels also have **TabIndex** values, but we are not concerned about them. Since a label can never receive focus, when a label's turn comes up in the tab sequence, focus is automatically shifted to the next control that *can* receive it.

Now when you run the program, the focus automatically goes to the Name field. That is because in the **Data1_Reposition** event we force focus to this text box. However, we don't want the focus to end up on the text box for the PubID field and since that has **TabIndex 0**, it would be the first control to get focus. One way to prevent this text box from getting focus is to set the **TabStop** property of the **PubID** field's text box to **False**. This provides the user with another visual cue that this field is 'off limits'.

The TabStop Property

In Windows applications, we know that we can move between controls and data entry fields using a tab key - this is a shortcut to efficiency. However, there will be times we don't *want* a control to be tabbed to.

Each control that can receive focus has a handy property that will prevent the cursor from moving to that field by tabbing to it. That property is called **TabStop** and accepts a Boolean value of **True** or **False**.

> *If the TabStop property is set to False, the user can't access the field with the Tab key.*

Try It Out - Testing the Tab Order and Tab Stop

1 Take a moment to bring up the Properties box of the bound text box Text1(0) that holds the **PubID** field. Set the TabStop property to False:

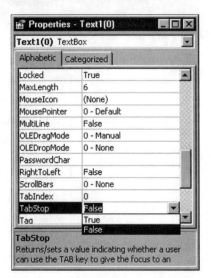

Remember that the **PubID** field is automatically generated by Jet. We don't want the user to fiddle with it.

2   Press *F5* to run your program. Now use the *Tab* key to move from field to field. Notice that no matter how hard you try, you cannot enter the text box labeled Publisher's ID with the tab key:

A byproduct of this maneuver is that when the form is loaded, the focus will automatically go to the first control in the tab sequence where the **TabStop** is **True**. However, we have already assumed authority through our code and forced focus to the text box that displays the **Name** field using **SetFocus** whenever the **Data1** control is repositioned.

You might be wondering why we just don't stick with the default and let the first control in the **TabIndex** sequence which has the **TabStop** property set to **True** (the **Name** field) get focus. Well, there are two reasons for this:

First, if the user tabbed to the third field on our form, then navigated to the next record, the focus will be on the Move Next button, not a data field. Why? Because that control was the last to receive user input - a mouse click. The user would then have to either tab to the **Name** field or click it with the mouse. Users hate extra steps. We want to anticipate how the user will use our form and accommodate their needs.

The second reason we use the **SetFocus** method instead of relying on the tab order is that since focus wouldn't be set to our text box, our highlight routine would not work properly. The navigation button would now have focus since it was the last control that received input from the user. This means, of course, that our text box does not get focus. And since we placed the highlight in the **GotFocus** event of the text box control array, it would not fire. So by forcing the focus, we accommodate the user and ensure that the **Name** field is highlighted. Then the user can tab through the fields in the correct sequence.

Ensuring the User Does Not Change the PubID

Notice that the **TabIndex** property is **0** for the **PubID** text box. That control is still in the tab sequence (all controls are) regardless of the **TabStop** property. However, this control just gets bypassed when the user tabs to the next field and the focus moves to the next control.

This little trick *only* prevents the user from accessing the **PubID** field with the *Tab* key. They can easily click on the field with the mouse. If the **PubID** field's **Enabled** property is **True** and the **Locked** property is **False**, the user can still access the field and accidentally change the value. The **TabStop = False** only prevents the user from tabbing to the control.

What we want to do is both ensure the user is *always* locked out of the **PubID** field and provide the user with a visual cue that the field is inaccessible.

Try It Out - Changing the Properties of the PubID Text Box

1   Bring up the Properties window for the Publisher's ID text box and click the down arrow in the BackColor property field.

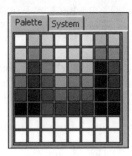

Properties - Text1(0)	
Text1(0) TextBox	
Alphabetic	Categorized

(Name)	Text1
Alignment	0 - Left Justify
Appearance	1 - 3D
BackColor	☐ &H80000005&
BorderStyle	1 - Fixed Single
DataField	PubID
DataSource	Data1
DragIcon	(None)
DragMode	0 - Manual
Enabled	True

BackColor
Returns/sets the background color used to display text and graphics in an object.

2   This will bring up a tabbed box that permits us to visually set the background color of that text box. Click on Palette to actually see the colors. Click on the first color in the third row. This will set the color to the same color as the form.

3 Now ensure that the text box labeled Publisher's ID has its Locked property set to True.

Also, set the text box's Enabled property to False. Together, these settings will ensure the Text1(0) bound text box can't be edited or even clicked on with the mouse.

Since this text box is not included in our procedures to lock and unlock controls (because we did not put a **1** in the **Tag** property), **we must be sure this is done at design-time**.

4 Press *F5* to run your program. The focus is still automatically in the **Name** field. Now press the *Tab* key and notice how the focus traverses our bound text boxes in order, then goes to only the enabled command buttons. Now try to click in the text box with the mouse. Notice that no matter what the user does, they can't get at the Publisher's ID text box.

We've now locked the user out from clicking or tabbing to this field - just what we wanted to do. Not only that, the field is now the same color as the form which *visually* tells the user that it is 'off limits'.

235

Using the Enter Key to Tab to the Next Control

Back in the dim and distant past, shrouded in darkness and mystery, DOS roamed the earth. All interfaces required the user to press the *Enter* key to move to another field. We modern types, however, have become used to the Windows way of using the *Tab* key to move to another field. Enlightened as that might be, many of our users have come from either DOS programs or 3270 mainframe applications. They like the *Enter* key. It has become second nature to them, and they just can't get used to all of this *Tab* key business. So let's anticipate that as we continue to give our user interface a more mature data entry capability.

Try It Out - Making Enter Behave Like Tab

1 In the **Text1_Keypress()** event procedure, enter the following code. Since we are using a control array, the code need only be entered once. Are you getting to like control arrays? They sure make some things easy for us.

```
Private Sub Text1_KeyPress(Index As Integer, KeyAscii As Integer)
    If KeyAscii = vbKeyReturn Then      ' The ENTER key.
        SendKeys "{tab}"                ' Send the focus to next control.
        KeyAscii = 0                    ' Throw this key away
    End If
End Sub
```

2 Press *F5* to run the code. Notice that now when you press the *Enter* key, you automatically tab to the next text box.

How It Works

If the user presses the *Enter* key in any one of our bound text boxes in the control array, our code takes action. We can detect the *Enter* key by comparing each key pressed with the built-in constant **vbKeyReturn** (Ascii value of 13). If the *Enter* key was pressed, **SendKeys** executes a **tab** command for us. (The **{}** is needed to execute the command.) Essentially **SendKeys** sends one (or more if we need it) keystrokes to the active window just as if we typed them in at the keyboard. So the user can hit *Enter* and not need to know that we converted their *Enter* to a *Tab*. Our new program will immediately feel comfortable to the DOS or mainframe user.

Since we are thinking about our friends who might have moved over from mainframe applications, here's another little olive branch we can extend to make their transition easier. Most mainframe applications automatically move to the next field when the maximum length of the current field is reached. To accomplish this in VB 6.0 is a snap. Here's how.

Try It Out - Automatically Tabbing to a New Field

1 Enter the following code into the **Text1_KeyUp** event procedure:

```
Private Sub Text1_KeyUp(Index As Integer, KeyCode As Integer, Shift As Integer)

  With Screen.ActiveForm
    If (Len(.ActiveControl.Text) = .ActiveControl.MaxLength) Then
      SendKeys "{Tab}"
    End If
  End With

End Sub
```

How It Works

The interesting lines here are contained in our **If…End If** loop; let's have a look at what this does:

When a character is entered into our text box, for every **KeyDown** event there is a corresponding **KeyUp** event. Here we simply place code in the **KeyUp** event procedure of **Text1** and see if the most recent character filled the text box. Remember when we set the **MaxLength** property of each of our text boxes? Well, here it really comes in handy. When the key on the keyboard is on its way back up after the user pressed it, this **Text1_KeyUp** code fires. If the length of the text in the current text box is equal to the **MaxLength** property of that text box, we simply send a **Tab** to move focus to the next field. Neat, eh? Best of all, we place it in the **KeyUp** event once and it will work for all of our text boxes.

Finding a Specific Record

We are almost finished with the visual part of the user interface. There is now a clean, well-structured and organized mechanism for data to be entered. But imagine if we have hundreds, thousands or tens of thousands of records in the table and our user needs to find a specific one. If a user has to scroll through the recordset with the navigation buttons for more than 10 seconds looking for it, we will make an enemy pretty fast. The user will be clicking the Next button while giving us the evil eye.

So let's anticipate that and put in a simple way for the user to quickly find any record in the database. Luckily for us, the data control has a **FindFirst** method that we can pull out and dust off. We just tell it which record to find and it does the dirty work for us. The user now has the desired record.

How Do We Find It?

The first question you probably have about finding a specific record is, "How exactly do we allow the user to select any record?" We *could* take the easy way out and display an input box that allows the user to type the name. That way, we just grab the name and fetch it. But what if the user doesn't know how to spell it? Is it Smith or Smyth or was it Smitty? They can't remember. They might know it starts with 'Sm', but aren't sure of the rest. They would know it if they saw it, however.

FYI We could write a Soundex routine that could locate records that are similar, such as Smith and Smyth. This is an algorithm that converts words to numbers. Like-sounding words have the same numbers. Its interesting that this routine was written in the early 1900s before computers!

Another approach would be to write a **pattern matching** routine (more on this later in the chapter) that would find records such as 'Sm*' - but that implies the user knows a bit about what to look for. It doesn't help if the user wants to scan records and select one. Hmm. We want to think of a way to elegantly display all of the publishers currently in the database. Then a user could scroll and simply click on the desired publisher. That sounds much better - it's a much more general solution that we can apply elsewhere.

The most obvious way to do this would be to place a bound list box on our form that would list all of the records in the field we specified. we only need to wire it up and we are done. The only difficulty with this approach is that on every recordset we need to search, we would have to add another data control and wire it up again by specifying the field. Also, that new list box control will take up valuable real estate on our form. After all, it has to be wide enough to display the full name of the publisher and high enough to show several choices at once. The final problem with this approach is that the bound list box is not an intrinsic control - it lives in its own `.ocx` file in the `Windows\System` directory. This means that when we distribute our application, we would have to be sure to ship the file and register it in the registry. Not a really difficult problem to solve, but one more thing for us to think about.

Smart programmers are basically lazy. They only want to do things once and be done with it. I'm guessing you might be a bit lazy like I am. You are? Great. Let's take another approach. We will develop a generalized Find form. This form can then be called from the Publishers form - **or any form that requires record searching**. We just set a few properties and it works. Interested? Good - let's get started.

What we want to do here is place the code that will search for a specific record in **a code module**. By segregating the code from the user interface (i.e. our form), we can build something that can be reused. If we are smart, we can build a code module that can be added to any new program we write that needs a Find form.

Adding a Code Module to Our Project

Code modules are files in our project that do not have a visual interface. They store code. There are two reasons why we might want to add a code module to our project.

First, whenever we can separate code out of our forms, such as procedures that don't effect the user interface, we want to place them in code modules. The less 0's and 1's our form has to load (in the guise of VB code in the event procedures), the more quickly the form appears on the user's screen. The second reason is **variable scope**. When we need function declarations for things such as Windows **Application Programmer's Interface** calls (fondly known as **API**) to be visible to our entire project, the code module is the place to put them.

So let's quit talking and start keying.

Try It Out - Adding a Code Module

1   Adding a code module to our project is a snap. Simply select Project from the main VB menu and select Add Module. Double-click on Module in the dialog box. A new code module is added to our project for us. A code module has precisely one property - its **Name**. Bring up the Properties window and name our newly minted code module Globals. Save it away as **Globals** too.

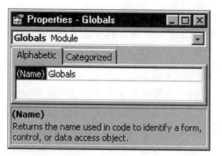

Creating a Generalized Find Form

Well, if we have a separate form that will list, say, all of the publishers in the table, how can we tell this form what to look for? If we can accomplish that, how do we return that value of the record to search for in our Publishers form? Essentially, we want to set some properties on the Find form that tells it what to retrieve. Then, once the Find form is loaded the user works with that Find form and either selects a publisher or cancels the operation.

It would really be handy to let the user start typing in the first letters of the desired publisher, like 'Sm'. Our Find form will then bring up all of the Smiths and Smyths automatically. This way we do in fact get the benefits of a Soundex routine, but without the limitations. Best of all, this approach is very easy to accomplish using the Windows **API**.

How We'll Make This Work

We will display a Find form that shows all of the publishers in the **Publishers** table. Once the user selects the desired publisher, the Find form is dismissed and our Publishers form automatically displays the desired record. In addition, if we build it right, we can use this Find form for any searching needs we may have later on. Again, our generalized approach to coding will pay big returns in the reuse department. Sometimes it pays off to be lazy.

Try It Out - An API Call to the Rescue

1 In order to gain access to the Win32 API call that simplifies our Find Record form, add the following declaration in the General Declarations section of the **Globals** code module. **Be sure to type in the Function declaration exactly as shown.**

```
Public Declare Function sendMessageByString& Lib "user32" _
    Alias "SendMessageA" (ByVal hwnd As Long, _
    ByVal wMsg As Long, ByVal wParam As Long, _
    ByVal lParam As String)

Public Const LB_SELECTSTRING = &H18C
Public gFindString As String
Public Const gDataBaseName = "C:\BegDB\Biblio.mdb"
```

How It Works

So what's happening here? The first line is a **function declaration** for an API function. Our Find form will use this function. Whenever the user types in a letter, we will make a call to this function to search a list box of all the publishers. It works like lightning. This function needs a magic number so it knows the exact task to perform. That is the `LB_SELECTSTRING` constant. This is one of hundreds of constants that Windows knows about. The `LB` means list box and the `SELECTSTRING` means 'search for the string we pass in'. We will look at how this works when we write code for the Find form.

By declaring our API function declaration in the General Declaration section of the code module, we can call this function from anywhere in our program. It works just as if it is a built-in function of VB. This API call sends a message to a control (which is just another window to the Windows OS):

```
Public Declare Function sendMessageByString& Lib "user32" _
    Alias "SendMessageA" (ByVal hwnd As Long, _
    ByVal wMsg As Long, ByVal wParam As Long, _
    ByVal lParam As String)
```

When we call this function, we will pass it four parameters. Remember earlier when we noted that every control that has a **hWnd** (handle to a Window) property is treated like any other window - such as a form - by Windows? When we call this function, we will pass in the **hWnd** of the control. Now the OS knows precisely which window, on which form, on which currently running program, it must send the message to. We will discuss the other parameters when we write the code in the Find form that uses this API call.

If you have never seen an API call before, it probably looks more like Klingon. It's like this: Windows has tucked away in its own **.dll** files a cornucopia of handy functions like this one, and we can use just about every one of them with VB 6.0. You must be wary when using the API, though. It can provide you with incredible functionality, but if you provide the wrong parameters, you're guaranteed a visit to General Protection Fault city. In this respect, the API is unforgiving.

Many programmers liken using the API to a legal agreement between VB and Windows. On one hand, the API provides a set of functions for us to use if we abide by the contract. The contract is that we call each function exactly. However, the APIs are written in something other than VB - usually C. The API calls are the same as those that VB itself uses 'under the hood'. Except that now we get access to them for our own programs. So what we are doing here is really extending the VB language itself by using DLLs.

> *Note: The VB designers had to make several trade-offs. Should they include every possible function and feature in the language? Or should they make the language slimmer but allow the programmer to access additional functionality using the API? Well, they wisely choose to permit programmers access to almost every API call. A few calls just can't be made with VB (for technical reasons) but over 95% can. Since API functions live in DLLs, whenever a new DLL is supplied, our program can take advantage of it automatically.*

Look Ma, No Typing!

Since API calls can be so useful, VB 6.0 provides us with a handy add-in that will provide the correct spelling and parameters of a declaration for us. From the main VB menu, select Add-Ins - Add-In Manager shown below. Click on VB 6 API Viewer and check the Loaded/Unloaded check box. When you click on OK this will load the API Viewer and make it available on the Add-Ins drop-down menu.

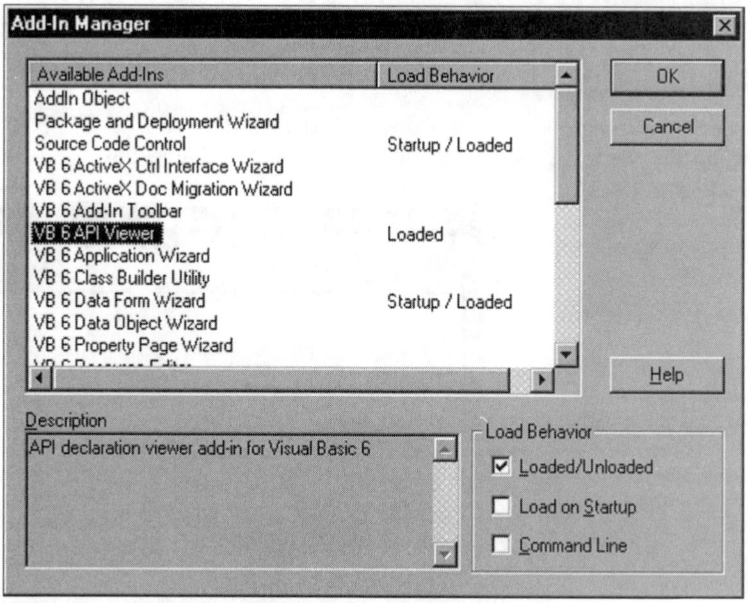

This handy utility will provide us with all of the function declarations for the available API calls. Let's bring up the API Viewer. Click Add-Ins | API Viewer from the menu. Since we just loaded it, the API Viewer is now a menu choice. From the API Viewer, click File | Load Text File to display the three text files on your machine.

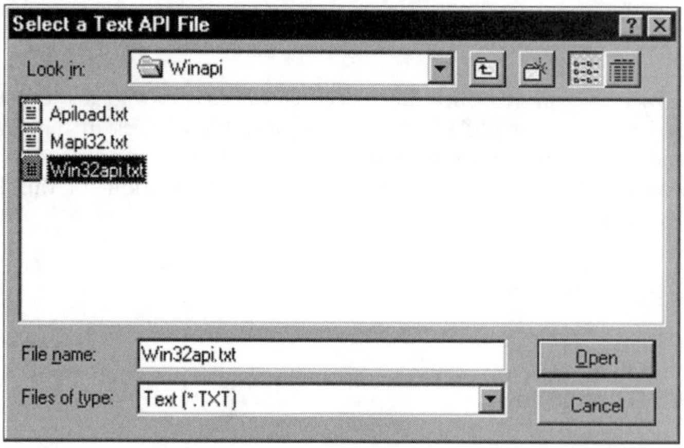

Select the Win32api.txt file and click Open. The process will take a few seconds to load the API Viewer with the entries from the text file. Once loaded, VB will ask you if you would like the file converted to a database for quicker loading. Click Yes.

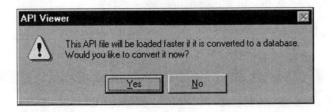

If you don't see this message box, select Convert Text to Database from the API Viewer's File menu to bring up the Select a Name for the New Database dialog box.

Keep the default name of Win32api.MDB and click Save.

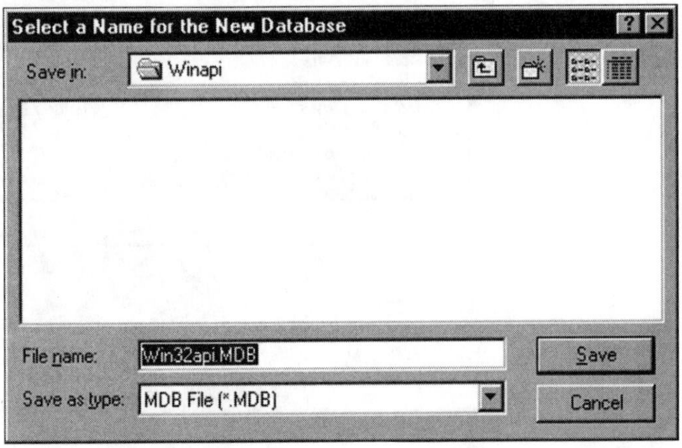

This process will also take several seconds to complete. Now the next time you bring up the API viewer, select Load Database File instead of Load Text File. This speeds up the loading of the viewer.

Test Out the API Viewer

In the top drop-down box, shown opposite, select Declares. Now to test out the API Viewer, start typing in the letters for SendMessage. Notice how the choices in the Available Items list box jump to the next entry that matches what you have typed in. Once you find it, double-click on SendMessage in the Available Items list box and the declaration for this function is displayed in the Selected Items list box.

If your code window is open, pressing Insert will place this right in the code for you. However, I prefer to use the Copy button instead. This places the declaration in the clipboard. Then you can locate exactly where you would like this to go in the VB code window and select Edit-Paste from the VB main menu. In larger programs where you may have several API calls, you can select several items into the Selected Items box and either insert or copy them all at once.

> *Note: One thing the API viewer does not give us is information on how to use the various API functions. However, if you know which one(s) you need, this technique not only saves time, but also ensures there will be no typos in your code.*

A Few Words on Global Variables

Remember that our Find form will be a separate form. Once it is displayed and the user selects a legitimate publisher from the Find form, how do we get the result back to our Publishers form? Well, we could set a form-level property with the name of the Publishers form - we can easily add our own properties to forms, and later in the book we will explore that. But adding our own property to the Publishers form would assume the Find form knows the *name* of the Publishers form. It would need to know the name of the calling form in order to set a property on that form. When we want to use our Find form on another, say Titles form, we would have to rewire our code in the Find form to set the property on the Titles form.

Since we want the Find form to be generalized, we need it to be able to return a value to any form that calls it. So the best way is to create a **global variable**. However, as a rule of thumb, we try to stay away from global variables as much as possible.

Why Not Use Globals?

Global variables have long been seen as a shoddy quick fix for short-term programming. Why? They are easy to define and use initially. You just make a variable global and you can access it anywhere in the project. However, they **almost always** create more problems than they solve in the long term. Here's why:

First and foremost on the laundry list for not using globals is that they increase the likelihood of bugs in your program. Each and every time you read or set a global's value, you can never be sure that the value was not modified somewhere in a distant part of the program. The value that you think you are getting might not be the same at all. This means that if you attempt to modify the value, you might break some code that is currently working somewhere else. Global variables therefore make code difficult to maintain. You can never be 100% sure that the modifications won't effect some small, infrequently used sub routine that relied on this variable. Since globals by definition are visible system-wide, you must constantly use the Find of the code editor to track down each use. Then you must determine on a case by case basis if your change will negatively affect each use. Not only is this review time-consuming, but can be error prone as well. Talk about needless work.

Then there are the memory concerns. If a variable is global, it is always in memory. More space, bigger program footprint. Ugh.

Always limit the scope of variables wherever possible. Use a form-level instead of global if possible and use a local instead of a form-level variable where possible. It makes debugging much easier and makes your code run faster.

OK, now after getting off my soapbox about not using global variables, there will be times when you just *can't* get around it. When you must use them though, be absolutely sure there is a justifiable reason. In our program, there is one time it makes sense to make this exception. Remember that in the code module's General section the variable **gFindString** is **Public**, so it has program-wide scope:

```
Public gFindString As String
```

It can be seen anywhere in our program as long as the program is running. It can also be modified from anywhere in our program. However, we will assign **gFindString** a value in the Find form and then read it in the Publishers form (or any other form at all). Since **gFindSting** is **Public** and in a code module, it is a global variable.

FYI As mentioned, most professional programmers strive to severely limit global variables. I was recently reading some code written by a programmer who bragged that he never used global (public) variables. He said he could always find a way around using a global. However, in this piece of code, he could not find a way out and had to resort to a few globals. He annotated the code with the words 'Yes, I am a sinner'.

We also have to initialize the data control on the Find form (as in all forms that use a data control). For now, we will hard code the location of the database. We place the location of our database here in the General section of the code module, like this:

```
Public Const gDataBaseName = "C:\BegDB\Biblio.mdb"
```

> *It is a major no-no to hard code in the location of a database. Later in the book we will cover how to dynamically set the database location. For now though, just place the location of your Biblio.mdb database in the gDataBaseName constant. (Yes, I am a sinner...)*

There is a better than 60% chance that the user will install your application in a directory other than the one you hard code. Let's say the user installs the application in `D:\Publishers\`. Our code, however, would be looking for the database in `C:\BegDB\`. This creates an error instantly. The user of your program will immediately be greeted with this friendly message from Visual Basic:

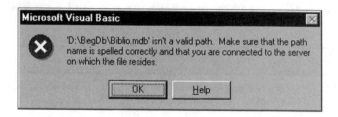

In the next chapter I will show you how to make our data controls (and DAO/ADO commands) work *no matter where* the user installs your application. Until then, set the global variable `gDataBaseName` to the location on your machine of the `Biblio.mdb` database. When we convert all of our hard work to a class, we will include a routine that will reset the data control `DatabaseName` to wherever the user installed the `.mdb` file.

Creating the Find Form

Here is the finished version of what we will create. This is our generalized Find form in action:

In this case, we are calling the Find form from the Publishers form. We instruct the Find form to display all valid publishers. When they are displayed, the user either scrolls through the list of entries or starts to type the name of the desired publisher.

Now comes the clever bit. With the help of the API call that we declared above, the list box automatically jumps to the first matching entry. When the user finds the desired publisher, the global variable **gFindString** is set with the highlighted entry and the Find form is dismissed. Then our Publishers form can read the global variable and do the search for the full record.

Try It Out - Creating the Find Form

1 Add another form to your project using <u>P</u>roject-Add <u>F</u>orm from the VB main menu. Name the form **frmFind**. Next, add the appropriate controls. Add three labels named **lblWhichTable**, **lblCaption** and **lblCount**.

Label Control	Property	Value
lblWhichTable	Caption	lblWhichTable
lblCaption	Caption	Double-click to select.
	ForeColor	&H00FF0000&, which is blue
	Alignment	2-Center
lblCount	Caption	lblCount
	Alignment	2-Center
	BorderStyle	1-Fixed Single

Add a text box and name it **txtFind**, making sure that you set its Text property to " " (blank). Now add a list box **List1**. Also, Include a command button with the caption <u>C</u>ancel and name it **cmdCancel**. Finally, add a data control with the name **dtaFind**. Set its **Visible** property to **False**. Lay out the form like this screenshot:

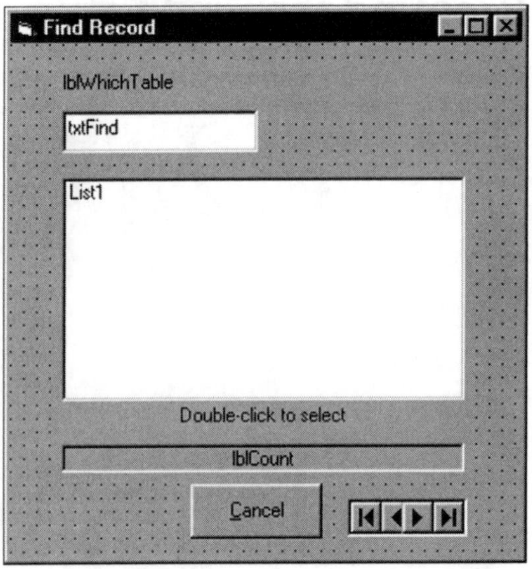

Once you have the form laid out, set its **Caption** to Find Record and the **BorderStyle** to **3-Fixed Dialog**. This will prevent the user from resizing our form.

2 We are now ready to add two properties to the Find form. With the code window open select Tools-Add Procedure. Enter the name recordSource and choose the Property option button:

Click OK.

3 A new property will be added to your form. When VB adds properties, it will add both a **Let** and a **Get** for the property name. This permits writing and reading of the property. However, we only want to set a value for the property from the calling form - we don't need to read the value. So simply delete the **Get** template for the **recordSource** property. This effectively makes our new property write-only, because we now only have a **Let**. Add one more property called **addCaption** and again make it write-only by deleting the **Get** template.

The **Get** property templates will automatically make the parameter **vNewValue As Variant**. Change the names to **sNewValue** (so we know it is a string) and the data type to **String** in both the **Let recordSource** and **Let addCaption** properties. Their code will now look like this:

```
Public Property Let recordSource(ByVal sNewValue As String)

End Property
```

```
Public Property Let addCaption(ByVal sNewValue As String)

End Property
```

This will ensure that we really pass in a string and nothing else - another safety precaution.

4 Add the following highlighted new code to the property templates in the Find form.

```
Public Property Let recordSource(ByVal sNewValue As String)
    dtaFind.recordSource = sNewValue
End Property

Public Property Let addCaption(ByVal sNewValue As String)
    lblWhichTable = sNewValue
End Property
```

247

How It Works

With these properties set up, we can now pass them values from the calling form before we even load the Find form. Actually, all we need to do is set these two properties from any calling form and we can use this handy Find utility. So from our calling form, we can set the properties by saying:

```
frmFind.recordSource = [Drive]:\BegDB\BIBLIO.MDB
frmFind.addCaption = "All Records"
```

Our Find form is now self-contained. We just set the **addCaption** property to place a custom caption on the form and the **recordSource** property instructs the data control on the Find form how to construct the recordset that will be displayed to the user. That's it. Now if we want to use this in a Titles table for example, we could add a caption that says, "Select a Title" and pass a record source to read the Titles table. Remember that we have a global variable, **gDataBaseName** that holds the location of our database? Well, the Find form just reads this. There is no need for us to worry about it.

One of the nice things in VB, starting with VB 4.0, is that we can add our own properties to a form. Best of all, the form does not have to be loaded for us to do so. Prior to VB 4.0, if we wanted forms to share information, we had to resort to stealth and guile. VB used to try to thwart our efforts and generally make it pretty difficult. But now, with our ability to add our own properties to forms, it couldn't be easier.

The Find form has its own data control we named **dtaFind**. As you can probably guess, before the Find form is loaded, we set the **DatabaseName** property, which effectively sets the data control's **DatabaseName** property for us. Likewise, the record source for the data control is set from the parameter we pass to the **recordSource** property we just wrote. Our Find form sets the **dtaFind.RecordSource** property. Finally, we can set the Find form's **addCaption** property. Depending on the table that we are opening, we can place any caption on the form we want.

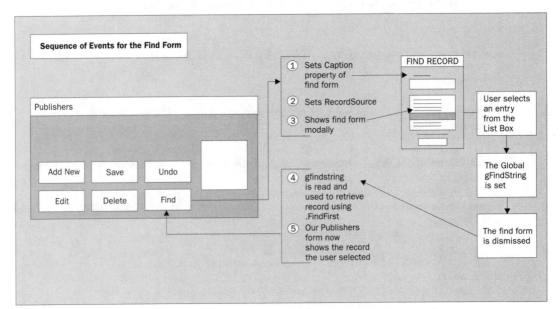

Now we need to add the code that will fire when the user calls the Find form when they want to search for a record.

Try It Out - Adding Code to the Find Form's Activate Event

1   After the properties are set from the calling form, the Find form is loaded. When our Find form is fully displayed its **Activate** event procedure fires. Place this code in the Find form's **Activate** event procedure:

```
Private Sub Form_Activate()
List1.Enabled = False
dtaFind.DatabaseName = gDataBaseName
dtaFind.Refresh
If (dtaFind.Recordset.RecordCount > 0) Then
  Screen.MousePointer = vbHourglass
  dtaFind.Recordset.MoveFirst
  While Not dtaFind.Recordset.EOF
      List1.AddItem dtaFind.Recordset.Fields(0) & ""
        dtaFind.Recordset.MoveNext
  Wend
  List1.Enabled = True
  DoEvents
End If

lblCount = "There are " & dtaFind.Recordset.RecordCount & " records"
Screen.MousePointer = vbDefault
End Sub
```

How It Works

This is the workhorse of the Find form. Let's take a look at what it is doing for us.

By setting the **Enabled** property of the list box to **False**, VB will not redraw the screen with each entry. This will eliminate any annoying flicker and permit the list to populate quickly:

```
List1.Enabled = False
```

The advantage of a global variable for the location of the database is that we don't need to set a customized property for it. In the next chapter, when we find out how to ensure the database is found by our program, we will set the global **gDataBaseName** so it can be read by any data control or database object variable that needs it. In our example here, setting it once in a global ensures that every control or variable that needs the location can go to a central source.

In this next line of code, we simply read the global **gDataBaseName** and set the **DatabaseName** of our data control. The **RecordSource** property of the **dtaFind** data control was set when we set our custom property **recordSource** from the calling form.

```
dtaFind.DatabaseName = gDataBaseName
```

Now that the **DatabaseName** and **RecordSource** properties of the **dtaFind** data control are set, we tell the control to retrieve the recordset. The **Refresh** method of the data control will create and return the recordset. You can use the **Refresh** method on a data control to open, or reopen, the database:

```
dtaFind.Refresh
```

If there are indeed records returned in a recordset based on the **RecordSource** property, we want to set the **MousePointer** to an hourglass. This is a visual cue to the user that the system is working away. Then we invoke the **MoveFirst** method of the recordset to ensure that we are at the first record. Of course, moving to the first record when a recordset is opened the default, but I prefer not to rely on default behavior. By explicitly moving to the first record, we know exactly what is happening. If you are going to distribute this to customers, it pays off to eliminate any chance of an error that we could have otherwise avoided:

```
If (dtaFind.Recordset.RecordCount > 0) Then
   Screen.MousePointer = vbHourglass
   dtaFind.Recordset.MoveFirst
```

Now we will loop through the recordset and add the first field of each record to the **List1** list box:

```
While Not dtaFind.Recordset.EOF
```

Here's the next interesting piece of code:

```
List1.AddItem dtaFind.Recordset.Fields(0) & ""
```

Notice the item that we are adding to our list box, **List1**. This bears special mention. We are accessing the recordset by the **ordinal** (sequential) position of the field in the recordset's **Fields** collection. After all, we will only request a recordset with one field - the field that we want displayed. Any more fields requested would not be used and would be a waste of time and space. But remember - we don't know the name of the field in advance. Our form could be used to find an entry in *any* field in *any* table. So we will take the value in position **0** of the recordset's **Fields** collection.

We happen to be requesting the **Name** field in the **Publishers** table in this example. What if we want to ask for the **Title** field from the **Titles** table to be displayed or any other field from any other table for that matter? After all, we want to generalize this handy form so that we can use it elsewhere. Therefore, we are looping through the recordset, adding the field that is in ordinal position 0 - i.e. the first (and only) field in the recordset. This way we don't have to provide a name for the field in our routine because we won't know it in advance anyway. Finally, we add an empty string to each entry.

Why Are We Adding a "" to Each Field Anyway?

Why are we appending the **""** to the end of the field? You might well ask – and it's a good question. Well, databases have a special value called **NULL**. It's special because it doesn't mean 'empty string' or 0. NULL means that the field contains no data. Nothing. Zilch. NULL. If we are looping through the recordset and one of the values in **Fields(0)** contains a NULL, we can't add it to the list box. If we try, Visual Basic barks at us with the following message:

```
Microsoft Visual Basic

Run-time error '94':

Invalid use of Null

        Continue        End        Debug        Help
```

So appending a **""** to the end of each field ensures that if we *do* encounter a NULL, a valid string will safely be added to the list box. If you want to eliminate any records from being displayed in the list box that have a NULL value, you could modify the code so it looks like this:

```
While Not dtaFind.Recordset.EOF
   If (Not IsNull(dtaFind.Recordset.Fields(0))) Then
      List1.AddItem dtaFind.Recordset.Fields(0)
   End If
   dtaFind.Recordset.MoveNext
Wend
```

This will only add records to our list box that do not contain NULL. However, the user will **never** be able to retrieve any records with a NULL value in this field. We might *want* them to be displayed – the NULL may well have been the result of an error in data entry. Any records with a NULL value will be displayed at the beginning of our list. The user may want to retrieve this record with a NULL value so it can be fixed.

Also, performing this **IsNull** check for each and every record added to the list is time-consuming. When we cover data validation later, we will ensure that a NULL never occurs in a required field in our databases. Unfortunately, if you work with legacy databases, there is no guarantee each and every record was entered correctly. Microsoft added a few NULL fields on purpose, so we can determine how to handle them. So this simply boils down to a design decision on your part. My suggestion is to add all records and let the user decide how to handle the NULL value. (OK, I'm off my soapbox.)

What Happens Next?

Back to our code:

```
   dtaFind.Recordset.MoveNext
   Wend
   List1.Enabled = True
   DoEvents
End If

lblCount = "There are " & dtaFind.Recordset.RecordCount & " records"
Screen.MousePointer = vbDefault
```

251

Next, the **MoveNext** method sets the current record pointer to the next record and then it is also added to the list box. This looping/adding continues until the end of the recordset is reached. When the list box has been fully populated with the entries from the recordset, we display the number of records to the user and then set the cursor back to normal, signaling that all is well. The user is now ready to search for the desired entry.

Now our **frmFind** is initialized and ready for action. Remember when we mentioned that we get the user to type in a letter in the text box, and that we then want to jump to that entry? To accomplish this, a simple API call is made each time the user types in a character in the text box **txtFind**. We'll now add some code to accomplish that.

Try It Out - Adding an API Call to the txtFind Text Box

1 Add the following code to the **Change** event of the **txtFind** text box on the **frmFind** form.

```
Private Sub txtFind_Change()
Dim entryNum As Long
Dim txtToFind As String
txtToFind = txtFind.Text

entryNum = sendMessageByString(List1.hwnd, _
        LB_SELECTSTRING, 0, txtToFind)
End Sub
```

How It Works

Each time the user types in a character in the **txtFind** textbox, the **Change** event procedure fires. We assign the contents of whatever is currently in the **txtFind** text box to our local variable, **txtToFind**:

```
txtToFind = txtFind.Text
```

Next, we make an API call to **sendMessageByString**, passing in a few parameters to the API function. First, we pass in the handle of the list box (**List1.hwnd**). The next parameter is the command we want executed. **sendMessageByString** can send any number of messages to the specific window - **List1** in this case. Remember when we defined the constant **LB_SELECTSTRING** in the General Declarations section of the code module?

```
Public Const LB_SELECTSTRING = &H18C
```

The first parameter tells the **sendMessage** API which window (control in our case) to send the message to and the **LB_SELECTSTRING** is the specific message. The prefix **LB** lets us know that this message is for a list box. **LB_SELECTSTRING** will find an entry in a list box that matches the partial string that we will pass in. This constant will find the first entry that matches, regardless of case.

The next parameter we pass in is a **0**. This value depends on the message being sent. The final parameter to the API call is the text we are looking for which is in the variable **txtToFind**. This call will work with a single character, and the first entry that matches will be highlighted. So if the user enters the letter D for example, the list box jumps to the first entry that starts with a D. Users love this. They will bring you roses when you show the Find box to them.

Since this is a function, we need to declare a return value. We won't use it, but the API call *requires* us to accept it. If the function call to the API returns a -1, then the search was unsuccessful and nothing happens. If a partial or full match was found, the list box index is automatically set to that entry. When the user finds the correct entry in the list box, they simply double-click on the one they want to find and the Find form is dismissed.

A Handle? What's a Handle?

We just did a bit of hand waving and said, "Well we just pass the handle of the list box to the API call." We briefly touched on handles earlier, but we need to fully understand them for using API calls. Here goes.

As mentioned, the interesting thing about Windows is that just about every visible object is really a window. Yes, it's true. A text box and a list box are just special types of windows. Windows identifies each of these objects with an integer value - a **handle**. Every window has a handle to that window, or **hwnd** property. The handle to the window (**hwnd**) is an integer value that uniquely identifies the object to the operating system.

Programmers sometimes refer to handles as 'magic cookies'. That's because Windows assigns the integer value dynamically - the handle is different each time you run the program. In fact, Windows sometimes even changes the handle value of an object as it rearranges memory behind the scenes. Clever old Windows, eh?

A handle is a moving target. So you don't hard code them, just refer to the **hwnd** property of the object you are using. So by referring to the **hwnd** property of the object, such as **List1.hwnd**, we are assured of getting the correct ID. We pass this 'magic cookie' to the API function so Windows knows which object we are referring to in the call. Now Windows knows we want to find a string in **List1** and not any other list box or control. We will be using the **hwnd** property extensively when using API calls.

Now let's continue by adding the code that will actually *return* the record we're after.

Try It Out - Returning the Record to Find

1 Add this code to the **DblClick** event procedure of the **List1** list box on our **frmFind** form.

```
Private Sub List1_DblClick()
'get the item the user clicks on and assign it
gFindString = List1
Unload frmFind
End Sub
```

Here, when the user double-clicks on the name displayed in the list box to retrieve, we set the global variable, **gFindString**, to the entry in the list box. Now the calling form can just read this value and find the record.

2 If the user decides to cancel the find operation, they can simply click the **cmdCancel** button. To let them do this, put this code in the **cmdCancel_Click** event.

```
Private Sub cmdCancel_Click()
Unload Me
End Sub
```

3 After setting the global variable, the Find form is immediately unloaded. When unloading any and every form in Visual Basic, don't forget the all-important setting to **Nothing**. So, let's implement this by adding the following code into the **Form_Unload** event:

```
Private Sub Form_Unload(Cancel As Integer)
Set frmFind = Nothing
End Sub
```

How It All Works

That's it – there's really nothing to it. All that needs to be done to see it in action is to call the Find form from our Publishers form. Remember that the **frmFind** is a self-contained, stand alone form. It can only be called from another form. The calling form will actually set the **frmFind**'s customized properties, and away it goes. Let's add the code on our calling form, **frmFind**, to make this happen.

Try It Out – Linking the Find Form to the Publishers Form

1 Return to the **frmPublishers** form and open the code window for the **cmdButton_Click** event.

2 In the **cmdButton_Click** event procedure of the Publishers form fill in the Find button's code:

```
Case cmdFind  '-- find a specific record
  Dim iReturn As Integer
  gFindString = ""

  With frmFind
   .addCaption = "Type Publisher Name to find"
   .recordSource = "SELECT Name FROM Publishers ORDER BY Name"
   .Show vbModal
  End With

  If (Len(gFindString) > 0) Then
   With Data1.Recordset
    .FindFirst "Name = '" & gFindString & "' "
     If (.NoMatch) Then
       iReturn = MsgBox("Publisher Name " & gFindString & _
          " was not found.", vbCritical, "Publisher")
     Else
```

```
               iReturn = MsgBox("Publisher Name " & gFindString & _
                   " was retrieved.", vbInformation, "Publisher")
        End If
   End With
   End If
   updateButtons
```

How It Works

Let's take a look at what's happening here. The first thing we want to do is set the global variable **gFindString** to an empty string. This is so it won't hold any old values from a previous **Find** request from this or any other form that uses it. (What if a previous **Find** placed a value in this field and the then user tried to find another record, but subsequently cancelled the operation? If the old value *were* still in **gFindString**, our code would have no way of knowing that the contents were from a previous search. By initializing the variable to **""**, we know it is empty:

```
   gFindString = ""
```

Before we call our Find form, **frmFind**, we simply set the two custom properties we added to the form before it is actually loaded. We put in a custom caption that permits us to show the name of the table we are going to display. Next, we pass the record source we want the data control in the Find form to retrieve. Notice that here we are programmatically setting **recordSource**. This is a SQL statement (we will be covering SQL in detail when we get to Chapter 8). As you can probably guess, this SQL statement simply instructs the data control to retrieve the name field from the Publishers table and, while it's at it, order it alphabetically:

```
   With frmFind
     .addCaption = "Type Publisher Name to find"
     .recordSource = "SELECT Name FROM Publishers ORDER BY Name"
     .Show vbModal
   End With
```

Remember a bit earlier when we were musing about the various ways to find a specific record, we discussed **pattern matching**? Well, guess what? We actually still have that option. Since we are passing an SQL command to the Find form's data control, we can send a pattern if it is ever needed. We will cover this in detail when we cover SQL, but it is very easy to send a command such as:

```
   "SELECT Name FROM Publishers WHERE Name LIKE 'Sm*' & _
       ORDER BY Name"
```

Then if you wanted to perform a search on Smith, Smyth or any other publisher that begins with 'Sm', the Find form will only retrieve records in the table that meet that criterion. Alternatively, if you need multiple criteria, you can get anything you need by using SQL. See - we did make the right choice after all! The Find form is truly flexible and will be able to meet all of your needs in any of your programs. You can pass any sort of pattern matching and the Find form will follow your commands.

> *Remember that we didn't set the Sorted property to True for the list box on our Find form. We did this because it is faster to return a sorted recordset than to have the list box sort all of the records itself. Also, there may be times when we don't want the records sorted, or we may want the recordset displayed in descending instead of ascending order. So we just use the SQL statement to determine if we want the records sorted or not. This approach makes our Find form that much more flexible and generalized.*

The properties have now been set on our Find form, so we load it:

```
.Show vbModal
```

Visual Basic 6.0 lets you specify whether you want to display a form modally or non-modally. We call the **Show** method of the Find form and pass it the parameter of **vbModal**. A form that is shown modally is placed *on top* of all other forms. When a form is shown as **vbModal**, the form is known as **task-modal**. This means the form locks out all user input from the rest of the application. The form has to be dismissed before the user can do anything else within our program. The user must either select a publisher to find from the list or click the Cancel button. In either case, the Find form will be dismissed.

> *Showing any form modally makes it just like a message box; it takes center stage and must be answered.*

Of course only one form at a time can be shown modally. Once the user makes a selection, the form unloads itself if an entry was selected from the list box - but not before it sets the global variable, **gFindString**. If the user cancels the **Find** operation (by pressing the Cancel button), **gFindString** will still be set to an empty string. We know this because we set it to **""** to begin with.

Searching the Recordset to Find Our Record

In the next key bit of code we examine the global variable that holds the name of the publisher the user is looking for. If it is empty, nothing happens. If there is an entry, we instruct our data control in the Publishers form to find it:

```
If (Len(gFindString) > 0) Then
  With Data1.Recordset
    .FindFirst "Name = '" & gFindString & "' "
    If (.NoMatch) Then
      iReturn = MsgBox("Publisher Name " & gFindString & _
        " was not found.", vbCritical, "Publisher")
    Else
      iReturn = MsgBox("Publisher Name " & gFindString & _
        " was retrieved.", vbInformation, "Publisher")
    End If
  End With
```

The first thing that is done is to determine if the user did indeed make a selection. Checking the length of the global variable does this. If the length is **> 0**, the user made a selection. And yes, we could have said something like **If gFindString = ""** in order to do this and see if the user made a selection, but the built-in length function is faster (this has to do with the way VB stores and compares strings).

If there *was* a selection made, the variable **gFindString** is passed to the **FindFirst** method of the recordset. This line tells the data control to find the first entry in the **Name** field that equals the value of our global variable that was set in the Find form. Since the variable is a string, Jet expects it to be surrounded by quotation marks. That is why we concatenate quotation marks to surround **gFindString**. So the format used for the **FindFirst** method is **Field = 'criteria'**. What could be easier? Since we are searching for a string value, we must embed the criteria, **gFindString** in this case, with single quotes. If we were searching of a date field, we would surround the criteria with **#**'s. And finally, if we were searching on a numeric field, no surrounding characters would be required:

```
.FindFirst "Name = '" & gFindString & "' "
```

In order to tell if a match was found in the database, the **NoMatch** property is checked. **NoMatch** will be **True** if the record was not found. If **NoMatch** is **True**, then we tell the user we are sorry but the record could not be found. If **NoMatch** is **False** (i.e. there was a match), the data control automatically and instantly moves to the desired record:

```
If (.NoMatch) Then
```

The good news is that the record will **always** be found. Why? Well, we are only searching on values that we **know** are there. Only valid entries are displayed in the Find form, so any return value must be in the table - therefore it will be found. One caveat is that we must be diligent that the recordset we display to the user is the same one that we are working with. In other words, if we are working with only a subset of the **Publishers** table in our Publishers form, we must only display that exact same subset in the Find form. If we do that, the record clicked will always be found. Then finally, we display a friendly, reassuring message to the user that the desired record was indeed retrieved successfully.

Go Ahead and Run Your Program

Click on the <u>F</u>ind button to display all of the entries. When the **Find** form loads, double-click on an entry. The **FindFirst** method will immediately display the publisher and the message box will be displayed:

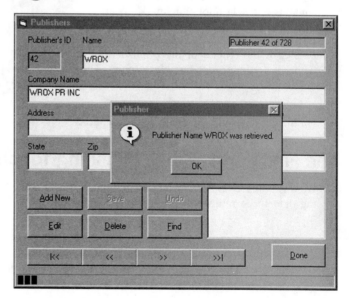

Well, as good as this looks; we are not quite done. There is a subtle error that can easily show up after we release our program if we are not aware of it. We think everything is working fine, then we get a call from our user and they are not happy. Let's anticipate this error and handle it.

Run the 'find' again and scroll down to O'REILLY & ASSOC. Notice something different about this record? It has an **embedded quotation** in it:

Go ahead and select O'REILLY & ASSOC, by double clicking on it. Because there is an embedded quotation, the number of quotes is not symmetrical. The name contains a single quotation mark, so an extra quote was added. When our program executes the **FindFirst** method, passing it the criteria of the publisher's name, something goes terribly wrong:

Hmm. Let's see what we can do about this.

The Find Form - Some Finishing Touches

We are going to put in a data scrubbing routine that will fix any embedded quotation marks in the data to be returned.

Try It Out - Checking and Fixing Records with Apostrophes

1   Open the code window on the **frmFind** form. Update the code in the **DblClick** event procedure of the **List1** list box with the following highlighted sections:

```
Private Sub List1_DblClick()

'get the item the user clicks on and assign it
If (InStr(List1, "'")) Then
gFindString = SrchReplace(List1)
Else
gFindString = List1
End If

Unload frmFind

End Sub
```

What we want to do here is test the value of what we are going to return to see if it has an embedded quotation mark. This is easy. We use the built-in **InStr** function to see if the is a ' in our **List1** entry. If the function returns back any number other than **0**, we know there is at least one quotation mark in the result:

```
If (InStr(List1, "'")) Then
```

If indeed there is an embedded quotation mark, the built-in **InStr** function will return a value > 0. If the return value is > 0, we will call a new function, **SrchReplace** and pass it the contents of **List1** for fixing up. As you know, a function will return a value. So we will simply assign the return value of the **SrchReplace** function to the global **gFindString**:

```
gFindString = SrchReplace(List1)
```

If there is no ' in the result, we will set **gFindString** to the contents of **List1** as before:

```
gFindString = List1
```

2   Now add the following **SrchReplace** function to the **frmFind** form. This will clean up any embedded quotes and return the refurbished entry so we can set **gFindString**. We want to write our routine so it will find any single ' and replace it with '' (two single quotes):

```
Function SrchReplace(ByVal sStringToFix As String) As String

Dim iPosition As Integer          'where is the offending char?
Dim sCharToReplace As String    'which char do we want to replace?
Dim sReplaceWith As String       'what should it be replaced with?
Dim sTempString As String        'build the correct returned string

sCharToReplace = "'"
sReplaceWith = "''"
```

```
iPosition = InStr(sStringToFix, sCharToReplace)

Do While iPosition
   sTempString = ""
   sTempString = sTempString & Left$(sStringToFix, iPosition - 1)
   sTempString = sTempString & sReplaceWith
   sTempString = sTempString & _
     Mid$(sStringToFix, iPosition + 1, Len(sStringToFix))
   iPosition = InStr(iPosition + 2, sStringToFix, sCharToReplace)
Loop

SrchReplace = sTempString

End Function
```

How It Works

To make our code easy to read, we simply dim two string variables, **sCharToReplace** and **sReplaceWith**. We then assign them with the appropriate characters. Of course we want to look for every occurrence of a single ' and replace it with two single quotes, but since both the ' and the ' ' are character literals, we must enclose them in quotation marks:

```
sCharToReplace = "'"
sReplaceWith = "''"
```

We start out by determining the location of the first ' in the string. The location will be placed into our local variable **iPosition**. The **sTempString** that we will use to build the scrubbed string is initialized.

Probably the clearest way to walk through this code is the use the example of O'REILLY & ASSOC. So the variable **sStringToFix** that was passed into the function now contains O'REILLY & ASSOC. Since the ' is in the second position, the variable **iPosition** = 2:

```
iPosition = InStr(sStringToFix, sCharToReplace)
```

Now we will iterate through the string **sStringToFix** as long as there is a ' remaining. Since **iPosition** = 2, we will loop through at least once:

```
Do While iPosition
sTempString = ""
```

Since we initialized **sTempString**, the first time through the loop it equals "". Now we take everything to the left of the ', which is in position 2 in this case. By subtracting 1 from the current position, the built-in **Left$** function returns everything up to the '. In this case, **sTempString** is now equal to O (the O from O'REILLY):

```
sTempString = sTempString & Left$(sStringToFix, iPosition - 1)
```

We wish to replace every occurrence of a single ' with a two single quotation marks ('') in order to make the result have symmetrical quotation marks. So the next line takes whatever was in **sTempString** and concatenates the variable **sReplaceWith**, which of course contains a ''. So **sTempString** now is equal to O'':

```
sTempString = sTempString & sReplaceWith
```

Next, we want to add the rest of the line back to the **sTempString**. The **Mid$** function is perfect for this. We tell it to take the original string, **sStringToFix**, start at 1 position past the location of the ' and add the remainder of the original string. So now **sTempString** will be equal to O''REILLY & ASSOC.

```
sTempString = sTempString & _
Mid$(sStringToFix, iPosition + 1, Len(sStringToFix))
```

At the bottom of the loop our code checks for the presence of another ' anywhere past the first one. Of course, the position of the current ' is at **iPosition**. By adding 2 to **iPosition**, we instruct **InStr** to start searching there. Of course there are no more apostrophes in this string so **iPosition** is now equal to 0. If there was another ' somewhere in the string, **InStr** would return a positive number and the loop would handle that occurrence just as the first one - replacing the ' with a ''.

```
iPosition = InStr(iPosition + 2, sStringToFix, sCharToReplace)
```

The loop terminates and we assign the newly formatted string, **sTempString** to the name of the function. Setting the return value to the name of the function is how we can pass it to the calling sub.

```
Loop

SrchReplace = sTempString
```

Go back to your **Publishers** form and retry the find. This time, if you select O'REILLY, the find will complete successfully and return the relevant record.

OK, now that we have cleaned up any possible errors in retrieving data from our database, we still have to ensure any data going into the database is clean.

Data Validation - the Programmer's Bane

One thing we still must do is to validate any data that the user wants to enter in to the database. We provided a clean, well-structured and organized mechanism for data to be entered, but if we permit bad or incomplete data to be entered, this exercise has been pointless, in other words. So the next logical step is to put in some validation code that will ensure the data entered is of the correct type.

It goes without saying that we only want clean data in our database. Luckily our program can easily enforce any business rules you might have for data entry. The first question is, "Where is the best place to put the validation events?" Well, since we are using data control, there is a handy built-in event called surprisingly, **Validate**.

Remember that earlier we placed code that updates the current record in a label in the data control's **Reposition** event. The progress bar is also updated there. The **Reposition** event of the data control is perfect for this because it is fired whenever the pointer to the current record changes. When the data control is first initialized or we use any of the **Move** methods, the **Reposition** event is fired. However, we want to validate our data fields **before** they are committed to the database. When the **Reposition** event fires, it's too late - the data has been committed. The **Validate** event solves our problem.

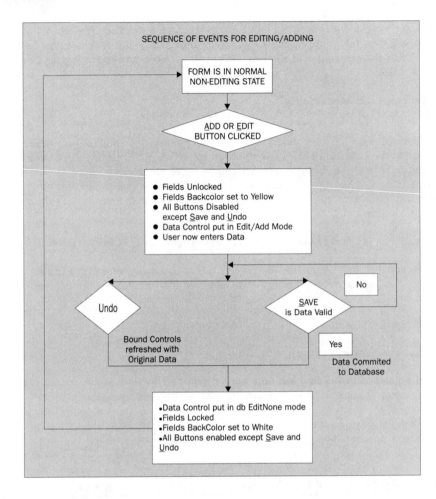

The Validate Event

Many programmers like to place any validation code in the **Validate** event of the data control. The **Validate** event is fired **before** the current record pointer moves to a new record. This means that **Validate** is fired before the **Update** method is invoked. It is also fired before a **Delete** or an **Unload** or **Close** command. So we can test any business rules here. If any fields don't pass muster, the commit process can be canceled. Note that **Validate** is not fired when data is saved with the **UpdateRecord** method.

We're going to add a simple rule in the **Validate** event of the data control so you can see how powerful it really is. The signature of the **Validate** event looks like this:

```
Private Sub Data1_Validate(Action As Integer, Save As Integer)
```

There are two parameters that are passed into the event by VB 6.0: the **Action** argument and the **Save** argument.

The Action Argument

Examining this argument will tell us what action actually triggered the event. Based on the action that caused the event, we can take appropriate action. Here is a list of the various events that might have caused the **Validate** event to be fired in the first place:

Visual Basic Constant	Description of the Action
vbDataActionCancel	This cancels the action that triggered the event
VbDataActionMoveFirst	**MoveFirst** method was called
VbDataActionMovePrevious	**MovePrevious** method was called
VbDataActionMoveNext	**MoveNext** method was called
vbDataActionMoveLast	**MoveLast** method was called
vbDataActionAddNew	**AddNew** method was called
vbDataActionUpdate	**Update** method was called
vbDataActionDelete	**Delete** method was called
vbDataActionFind	**Find** method was called
vbDataActionBookMark	**BookMark** property was set
vbDataActionClose	**Close** method was called
vbDataActionUnload	The form is unloaded

So when the **Validate** event is triggered, the **Action** argument will be set to one of these 12 constants. These are **enumerated constants** with values from 0 to 11. So you could check to see if **Action = 0**, which means the action was **vbDataActionCancel**. But this approach of using numbers instead of the names of the constants is incredibly difficult to debug and is definitely non-intuitive to someone trying to maintain your code. By using the built-in constants such as **vbDataActionFind**, the code becomes self-documenting because the name of the constant tells us exactly what is going on. When you get a minute, go to the on-line VB help and search for Data control, constants to see the entire list.

While in the **Validate** event, we can intercept an action and **even change it**. For example, say the user clicked the Move Next button on our form. The **Validate** event would fire and the **Action** argument would equal **vbDataActionMoveNext**. After our validation code checked out the fields, we might actually wish to reposition the record pointer to the first record instead of the next record. All we need to do is to set the **Action** argument to **vbDataActionMoveFirst** right inside the **Validate** event. So when the code exits the **Validate** event, the record pointer would be automatically set to the first record in the recordset. However, this interception only works on any of the Moves or the **AddNew** method. If you attempt to change the **Action** argument on any of the other values, VB simply ignores you and proceeds with the original action.

Another great feature of the **Action** argument is that it will allow us to simply ignore any movement of the record pointer. If, for example, our validation code decides not to move the record pointer, we simply set the **Action** argument to **0**. This will prevent the data control from moving to another record.

Note that setting **Action** to **0** has absolutely no effect on saving data to the database. It merely prevents the record pointer from moving to another record. So if no repositioning of the record pointer takes place, the values in the bound controls and the position of the current record stay the same.

The Save Argument

Let's say that the user was adding a record and one or more of the fields are incomplete. We might have certain business rules which state that all of the fields on this form **must** be filled out. Well, the user presses the <u>S</u>ave button, but of course we don't want to commit the entry to the database while it is incomplete. The **Save** argument is our handy tool for preventing 'incomplete' records from being saved. **Save** is set to **True** if the contents of any of the bound controls have been modified. If they have, we can check each of the bound controls to ensure that they meet our business rules.

When the **Validate** event is fired, VB checks all of the bound controls for us to see if the contents have changed since the last database action took place. If any controls have been changed, the **Save** argument is set to **True** for us.

If **Save** is **True**, the changes made to the bound controls will be saved to the database unless, of course, we decide that we really don't want to save the changes. Simply setting **Save** to **False** won't update the database.

Let's see how all this is accomplished.

Creating Some Validation Code

Let's give the **Validate** event a try. Remember that we are programming the data control ourselves so we can cancel a save action if our validation code disapproves of what's been entered in one or more of the fields. For example, let's assume that the **Name** field is a **required field**. This makes perfect sense - we certainly don't want to add and save a new publisher record without a name. It would be tough to find 'the publisher with no name' (unless they were wearing a poncho, smoking a cigar, and clutching a fistful of dollars).

Try It Out - The Validate Event in Action

Please take a minute and add the following code to the **Data1_Validate** event:

```
Private Sub Data1_Validate(Action As Integer, Save As Integer)

Dim iResponse As Integer

If (Action = vbDataActionUpdate) Then
   If (Len(Text1(1)) = 0) Then
      iResponse = MsgBox("Please enter a Company name.", _
                    vbInformation + vbOKOnly, "Publisher's Table")
      Text1(1).SetFocus
      Save = 0
      Action = 0
   End If
End If

End Sub
```

There, we have just added our own validation routine!

How It Works

When the **Validate** event is fired, a check is made to see if the cause of the event was from the **Update** method being called. If it was, the length of the bound text box that displays the **Name** field in our **Publishers** table is checked. That text box is in position 1 of our control array, so we must specify the location in the array by saying **Text1(1)**. We essentially put in a business rule that says the contents of the **Name** field can not be empty. If the length of the field contents is **0**, that means it's empty. The first thing we do in order to be friendly is to tell the user exactly what went wrong. There should be no question in the user's mind as to what happened:

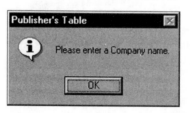

After the user clicks OK to dismiss the modal message box, we then take our validation correction action:

```
Text1(1).SetFocus
Save = 0
Action = 0
```

By calling the **SetFocus** method of the text box in question, we force the focus back to the text box that caused the error. So the user gets a message explaining the error and is now transported directly to the offending field. We then set the **Save** argument to **0**, which will prevent the record from being saved to the database. We also set the **Action** argument to **0** to ensure the record being edited stays current. This is just a precaution. OK, call me paranoid again. I'm used to it – they're all saying it about me.

We can put in any business rule we might need right in the **Validate** event procedure. If **Save** is **True**, we know that the user modified at least one field and that - if we don't prevent it - the changes will be saved to the database. So we can test the field(s) that require validation. If any of them don't stack up, you can:

▶ Place a message box informing the user what they must do

▶ Set the focus to the offending text box

▶ Cancel the **Save** by setting it to 0

We have just modularized our validation code by placing it all in a single routine.

Now - in the case where the record was not saved - we have to notify our **cmdButton** event procedure. Remember, the user clicked Save, but our code decided that the record was not ready to be saved. So the record was not committed to the database. Let's build the code to help out the **cmdButton**.

Try It Out - cmdButton Code for Unsaved Records

Since we are actually programming the data control, we have to ensure that our save code in the **cmdButton_Click** event is notified that the record has not really been saved. Remember, our code in the **Validate** event of the data control set **Save = 0** because a field was incomplete. So the save was canceled.

1 The good news is that it only requires two lines of code. Go back to the **cmdButton_Click** event procedure and take a look at **Case cmdSave** - saving the current record. Add the highlighted code below:

```
Case cmdSave   '-- save the current record
      Dim bMoveLast As Boolean
      With Data1.Recordset
        If (.EditMode <> dbEditNone) Then
            If .EditMode = dbEditAdd Then
              bMoveLast = True
            Else
              bMoveLast = False
            End If
            .Update
            If (.EditMode = dbEditNone) Then
               lTotalRecords = .RecordCount
               If (bMoveLast = True) Then
                  .MoveLast
               Else
                  .Move 0
               End If
               updateButtons True
            End If
        Else
            .Move 0
        End If
      End With
```

2 Now, run the Publishers form again and select the Add New option. If you try and save the record without entering a Publisher name, you will receive the informative message and be taken back to the edit to either amend your entry or undo the add. Just what we wanted.

3 Now make sure that you've saved your project in your **[Drive]:\BegDB\Chapter6** directory – we'll be using it all again later to build our class module.

How It Works

When we call the **Update** method on the recordset, the data control **Validate** method is invoked. If the update was successful, the **EditMode** property is set to **dbEditNone** and we go ahead and perform the record repositioning as well as update the buttons.

However, if we cancel the **Update** action in the **Validate** event procedure - like we just did by setting the **Save** to **0**, the **EditMode** of the data control is still set to editing. We haven't committed or canceled the edit process – we've just suspended it. Why? So we can permit the user to either fix the record and try again, or simply cancel the operation altogether.

We can find out if the record was saved with no problem by checking the **EditMode** of the data control. It should equal **dbEditNone**, indicating that the record was saved and we are no longer in an edit mode. However, if the **EditMode** still equals either **dbEditInProgress** or **dbEditAddNew** immediately after the **Update** method was invoked, we know we were attempting to add a new record but had a validation problem.

```
If (.EditMode = dbEditNone) Then
```

In the line of code we added, we now check to see if the **EditMode** equals **dbEditNone**. If so, all is well and we proceed with the record movement and reset our navigation buttons. Otherwise we know there was a validation problem. In this case, we simply bypass resetting our form and keep our form in the edit state so the user can either correct the error or cancel the operation. Pretty slick, eh?

Reflecting On the Data Control

OK, we finished programming our data control. I think you will agree that the data control has just too much power for us not to use it - at least for the visual portions of our program. We *definitely* want to use DAO for all of the non-visible parts of our program that have to do with database access for **.mdb** databases.

FYI

For a more advanced and complicated program, you could create an in-process .DLL with Visual Basic 6.0 that could contain your validation code and business rules. Let's say that you were selling a product and had to maintain tax rates for various states. You could put this information in a .DLL. Then when the tax rates changed, simply update the .DLL and distribute that. There would be no need to change and redistribute your program. Or if you are working on a network, you could place the business rules and validation in an out-of-process .EXE server. Then everything for validation would be stored in a central location. We will actually build a database access .DLL later in the book. Stay tuned.

Summary

Using the data control and a handful of code, we have made a bulletproof, user friendly data-entry screen. Not bad for starters, but there is much more. In the next chapter we will incorporate all of our hard work into a class. This class can then be used on any data-entry form you may come up with. I think you will be pleased with the results.

We covered a fair bit of territory in this chapter:

- We noted that whenever a form is about to become unloaded, we could intercept the command in the **QueryUnload** event of the form and decide to cancel the operation if we wish.

- **Focus** was covered in some detail. Focus is central to graphical programming, and you will now have a good feel for how it operates. Using focus, we examined the form's **ActiveControl** when setting a highlight routine.

- For ensuring the sequence of fields the user will tab to, we set the **TabIndex** and the **TabStop** properties of the bound text boxes.

- To ensure that the **PubID** field can absolutely never be changed, the **Locked** property was set to **True**.

- We added a code module and an API call to assist in finding a specific entry in a list box. The API Viewer was added to our project to eliminate some tedious typing of function declarations. The API call required us to pass in the handle of the list box so Windows knew which control to act on.

- We also dealt with adding custom properties to the Find form and displaying it modally.

- Finally, we discussed cleaning up data, both when retrieving entries from the database and by validating entries before we write them to the database.

What We Learned

This was an important chapter. We finished programming our data control and we covered some important concepts:

- The **QueryUnload** event of the form permits us to trap any attempt to unload it and cancel the operation if needed

- A control with **focus** is where the entry from the user will be directed

- **SetFocus** permits us to control where to direct the focus

- Using the **TypeOf** function we can determine any type of control on our form

- The **Reposition** event permits us to update labels and progress bars

- The **Validate** event permits us to add business rules to our form.

- We want to place any manipulation of visual components in the **Activate** event procedure of the form when loading

- Setting the **TabIndex** and **TabStop** properties of a field permits control of field navigation

◗ We added an **API** function call to assist in locating an entry in a list box

◗ The recordset method **FindFirst** and property **NoMatch** can easily be used to find a specific record

Now let's set about making sure that all of our hard work can be reused in the future, by building a **Data Control Class Module** that encapsulates all of our code. That's the subject of Chapter 7.

Exercises

1 Create a new standard project and add an event procedure for the **QueryUnload** event of **Form1**. Use a **Select** statement and display a message box for each of the possible values of the **UnloadMode** parameter. Build and run the application to test what causes each value to be sent to the event.

2 Explain when it would be useful to place code in an application that would allow the *Enter* key to act as a tab or to automatically move from one field to the next once all allowed characters have been entered. Explain when you might want to not program these features into an application.

3 Why should a programmer not hard code a handle into a program? What is the most common reason that a Visual Basic programmer requires access to a handle?

4 What purpose does the **NoMatch** property of the **Recordset** serve?

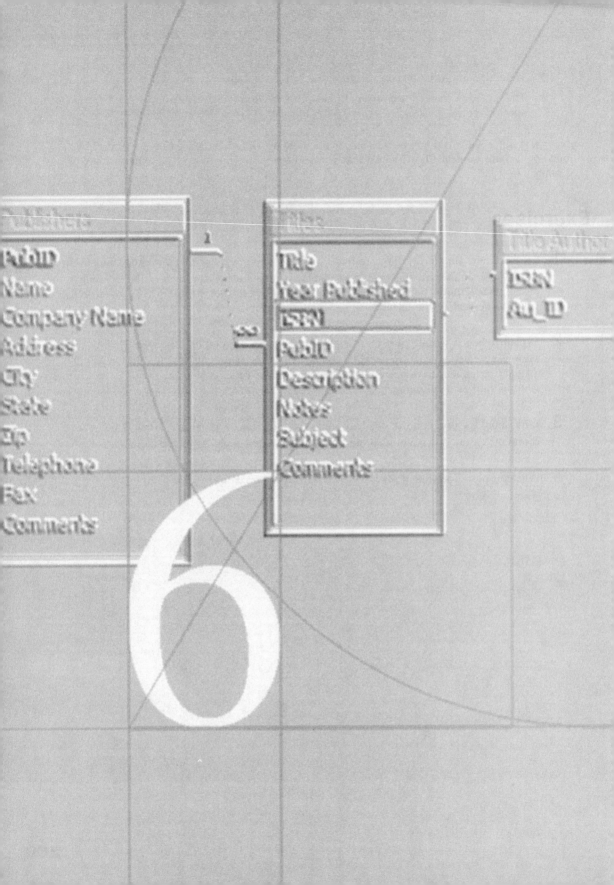

Building a Data Control Class Module

This chapter is all about making sure that we don't have to sweat so hard in the future. We're going to take all of the code that we've built into our data access user interface and encapsulate it in a reusable **class module**. We can then use the class module to create data entry forms for our future projects. Our class module will build on the code and functionality that we have assembled in the last few chapters, utilizing the data control for data access and entry.

As well as making our life as a programmer a bit less onerous, these techniques will help us integrate a sound design model into everything that we do.

What We'll Cover in This Chapter

Here's the sequence of events for this chapter:

- Principles of **classes** and **reusability**
- Building a **class module** that makes a **universal template** from the user interface code we've already constructed
- Tailoring the methods and properties of the class to meet our needs
- Customizing the **Find** form to make it universal
- Making the class module available to all our projects through VB menus
- Using the class to build a new data entry form from scratch

Let's get started!

The Joys of Repetitive Programming

It seems like a long, long time since I started programming the data control when it was released in Visual Basic 3.0. Back then, it would always take quite a while to make it solid enough for professional use. This involved, firstly, placing most of the code in a data-entry form. Then I would code and test, code and test, until it was right.

Then, on the next form, I would go through the exact same thing. Sure, there was a lot of cut and paste from one form to the next, but the process required me to code, tweak and test each form over and over. It got to be a fairly time-consuming process and - frankly - it was also pretty boring. Rather than concentrating on the application, I had to spend precious time ensuring the data control would be robust and not crash at a client's shop.

With a program that could have several data access forms, each performing a specific task, getting them all right took quite a while. Being lazy, I sat back and thought how I could get away from this tedium; it was no fun at all. I wanted to get on with programming the application.

Class Modules to the Rescue

Then, with the advent of Class Modules in VB 4.0, it hit me like a ton of bricks. Hey, why not just encapsulate the management of the data control - and its entire interaction with the user - into a class module? After all, isn't that the reason for classes to begin with? Code reuse? Sure. It was so obvious that if it was a snake it would have bit me.

So, that's just what I did. In fact, this particular code and approach is now in a financial program, which is currently in use by some of the largest companies in the U.S. So this code is not just an academic example, it is actual working production code that I hope you might find useful.

Using the data class module, overnight it went from taking me about 1 full day to create a fully bulletproof data-entry screen to about 15 or 30 minutes. Talk about reengineering. It was great. So I'd like to share this technique with you. The good news is that you can use the code you just wrote and cut and paste most of into the class module.

We will now build a class that manages all of the tedious, repetitive tasks required to have a professional, bulletproof data-entry form. Once our class is built, you can reuse the class with any form, with just a few lines of code to create the class and set a few properties. In fact, that is **the** key concept of this chapter - getting you to think of classes in terms of code reusability. After you review this chapter, you will probably discover several tasks where it makes sense to encapsulate code in VB class modules.

Reusable Components

Since version 1.0, Visual Basic has been concerned with the idea of **reusable components**. Just think of the text box control. You draw it on a form and it is born knowing how to do all kinds of things. No code is needed to tell it how to respond to a click or how to limit the number of characters allowed - all we have to do is set a few properties. If we need another text box on the form, we just draw another one - all the text box code and behavior is encapsulated in the text box control. In fact, the **.vbx** (now 32 bit ActiveX **.ocx**) controls available for Visual Basic have been the powerhouse that propelled Visual Basic to be one of the world's most popular programming languages. It is *the* most popular language for programming Windows applications.

There is a huge third-party market that develops controls to do just about anything you can think of. If you need to do *anything* - from voice recognition to map making, from graphing to communicating over the Internet - there are several ready-made controls to choose from. So now, instead of spending months writing a routine that handles low-level communication, simply plop the **Microsoft Comm Control 6.0** on a form and start communicating. Now that's power. The controls on the tool palette permit the programmer to get straight to work on the programming task at hand - the programmer doesn't have to build the tools required to get the job started. As a special bonus, with VB 6.0, you can now even create your own ActiveX controls, just like the big players.

Classes allow us mere mortals to achieve the same end - reusability. By encapsulating our code in a class, we can then simply **instantiate** that class (create an instance of the class) and we have all of the built-in functionality at our fingertips. We can set properties and even raise our own events. Let's step back and take a moment to define our terms. Then, it's off to create our own data control management class. I know you will like this chapter - because it's going to make your programming life so much easier!

What Exactly is a Class?

I'm sure you know or have read about **object-oriented programming** (OOP). In the purest sense, VB is not a true object-oriented language. However, it does have the necessary ingredients to create reusable objects.

So what is a class? A class is a **template** for something that we want to build. You can think of a blueprint for building a house as a class. It has the instructions for building the house, but it is not a house in itself. A blueprint is the instructions for how to build a house; if we take the blueprints and actually build a house from them, the completed house is an **object**. We have **instantiated** an **object** (house) from the **class** (blueprint). We can then build a second house (another object) from the same blueprint (class). We have just instantiated another object (house) from the same class (blueprint).

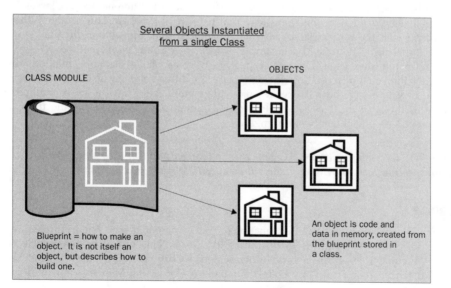

Don't worry if this sounds a bit abstract. It is. I remember when I was learning C++. I would read all of the books, go to seminars and eat the ice cream. It just didn't click. Then one day, wham! The light finally went on and I understood. At that instant my response was: "Is that all there is to it?" OOP - like most arcane processes - has its own jargon to mask some pretty simple concepts.

We will spend this chapter building a class. While we are at it, we will explain each and every concept mentioned above. Hopefully, by the end of this chapter you will be comfortable with the idea of classes and with using them. In fact, I'm confident that you will start to find uses for classes in many aspects of your programming. They are just too powerful to ignore. Remember the following: **Classes are templates. Objects are instances**.

OOP Buzzwords Revealed

While this is not an OOP book, we *will* be using the concept of classes, which is the cornerstone of the OOP technology. So we need to be sure we all understand the terminology. In a true OOP language, such as C++ or JAVA, there are three key elements the class concept must embody. They are:

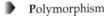 Polymorphism

 Inheritance

> Encapsulation

Just think of PIE and you can remember the big three. OOP is as easy as PIE, sort of. Well, what do these mystical sounding terms really mean?

Polymorphism

Polymorphism is from the Greek for 'having many forms'. Essentially, it means that different types of object can perform the same *kind* of action, but in different ways. Classes have **properties** that hold data, in the same way that a form has a **Caption** property that holds the text to display on the form. Classes also have **methods** that allow them do things, in the same way that forms have methods. For example, a form has a **Refresh** method. We call this method and the form refreshes itself. Different types of object can have the same methods, but the precise way that methods perform their actions can differ between object types. For example, if we had a **Bicycle** object and a **Corvette** object, they could both have a **move** method. However, the move method for the Bicycle would require human power to pedal while the Corvette move method would require a combustion engine.

> *In OOP terms, polymorphism means that we can call a method or a property irrespective of the particular ways that a specific object implements them.*

Inheritance

A new (child) object can **inherit** the functionality of a parent object. For example, we might have a **Vehicle** object that knows how to do things like 'turn'. This would be the Vehicle object's **Turn** method. We could then create a Bicycle object and a Corvette object based on the Vehicle object. We wouldn't need to recreate any code that made a Corvette a Vehicle - it would inherit it automatically. Both of the child objects, Bicycle and Corvette, would share methods common to all vehicles e.g. Turn. They would also have some different methods specific to their own type (class) e.g. Balance for a bicycle and Start Engine for a Corvette.

> *Inheritance means you can create a parent object and then use it (and its properties and methods) as the basis for a new object.*

Encapsulation

Think of the text box, we don't know or care how it limits the number of characters that can be placed in it. We just set the **MaxLength** property and the text box does the rest. The detailed, 'mechanical' implementation of how the length is limited is hidden from us; this is what encapsulation is.

> *Encapsulation means that all of the information about the implementation of an object is hidden within the class. The details of how it works are hidden from the outside world.*

VB and PIE

The classes we can create in VB support the concepts of polymorphism and encapsulation, but not inheritance. That's just fine. While inheritance can be useful when structuring collections of classes, it can be a major source of bugs and its implementation requires the use of code that is difficult to understand. So VB takes the best bits of the PIE and leaves behind the difficult to digest stuff. Again, don't worry if it still doesn't sound too clear or intuitive - all will be revealed as we progress through the chapter. I'm going to ask you to trust me again.

Copying Your Program

We are going to create a class that will handle all of the code to manage our data control. Take a minute and create a new sub directory on your PC and call it
[*drive letter*]:\BegDB\Chapter7. Then copy over all of the files that you built in the last chapter from **[*drive letter*]:\BegDB\Chapter6**. We want to work on a copy as when we have completed this chapter, we will remove almost all of the code from the original form. I don't want you to lose all of your hard work and this way you will have a copy to go back to. When you have copied all of the files for the last project into **\Chapter7**, open the **prjPublishers** project in the **\Chapter7** sub directory. Save it as **prjDataControl**. We will work on this copy for the rest of the chapter.

What We are Going to Accomplish

We are going to build a class module that will manage all of the functionality of a data control - how we use it to browse, edit and delete records, amongst other things. All of the code we wrote in the **frmPublishers** form to manage the control will now be placed in a **code module**. This way, we can simply add the code module to any new project we are working on that requires a user interface for a database; we will instantly have all the code we pre-wrote at our disposal. Just about the only items on the form will be the data control we will manage and a few properties we will set in our class. To make life easy, VB 6.0 has a **Class Builder** that takes much of the drudgery out of creating classes: we will use this to help in constructing our data control management class.

Building a Class in Visual Basic 6.0

Let's start right away by building our own class. Using the Class Builder will give us a template that will have data variables defined, a set of special **Let** and **Get** properties for each attribute, as well as any special methods we wish to add. Like the Data Form Wizard we examined earlier, it simply takes much of the tedium out of building a class module. The programmer still has to add the code to make the class do something useful.

Try It Out - Building a Class Module

1 With your new **prjDataControl** project open, go into the main VB menu and select Project-Add Class Module. You will be presented with the following screen:

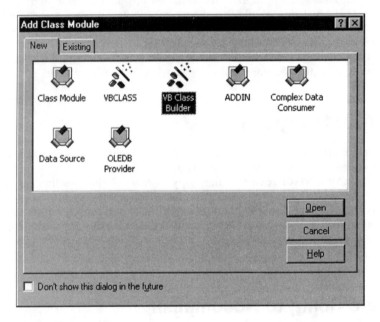

2 Select the VB Class Builder icon.

The Class Builder will be displayed. While this handy little feature does little more than add stubs (in other words the heading and footer, between which the code we write will be placed) to properties and methods for us, it *does* save much of the grunt work. Since we have not yet added a class to our project, only the Add New Class and Add New Collection buttons (the two left-most ones) on the Class Builder tool bar are enabled:

3 Notice that our project, **prjDataControl**, is the only item in the Classes box. We must now actually add a class to our project. Click the first button on the tool bar - Add New Class - and a dialog box is displayed asking what this new class should be called. Give it the name dataClass.

4 Click on the Attributes tab of the Class Module Builder. As we mentioned earlier in the book, one of the very handy tools available to us as we do object-oriented type programming is the Object Browser. The browser permits us to see all of the properties, methods and events that the class contains. Here, in the Class Module Builder, we can add some descriptive text that will show up in the Object Browser. It's always a good idea to add text that describes your class. You might want to supply the class to another developer that has never seen it before. This handy feature can describe the class and what it is used for.

5 Click OK. Notice that a new class module - dataClass - has automatically been added to our project in the Class Builder:

The new class module won't actually be added to our project until we are finished constructing it. But for now, it shows up in the Classes box. Now that we have added a class, dataClass shows up under our project heading. Since there is now an active class (but remember, it still hasn't been committed to the project), the rest of the tool bar items are enabled. When we have finished building the class, we will instruct the Class Builder to update our project with the new class, complete with the stubs for the properties and methods that we will define.

6 We must now start specifying what the **properties** (attributes) and **methods** (functions) are for our particular class - we need to add some properties to our class to make it useful. Since this class is intended solely to manage the functionality of a data control, the first property will specify to our class what data control is being used.

Click the **Add New Property to Current Class** button, which is the third button from the left on the tool bar (the pointing finger). This will bring up the **Property Builder** window:

In the **Name** box, call the new property dataCtl. Set the **Data** Type to Object. This property will permit us to reference the data control in the class.

7 Add a brief description of each property so that any programmer can easily see what it is used for. Click on the **Attributes** tab of the Property Builder dialog box and add the following **Description**:

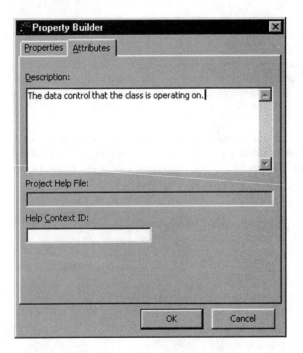

After you've added a description of the property, click OK to dismiss the dialog box.

8 Now add each of the following seven properties to the Class Builder for our class dataClass just as we did with dataCtl. Using the table, add the property's Name and Data Type on the Properties tab, and enter the Description in the Attributes tab of the Property Builder dialog box. We don't have to add the templates for the properties as the Class Builder utility will do it for us.

Property Name	Data Type	Description
Buttons	String	The string to handle the buttons in the array
dbName	String	The name of the database used
FormName	Object	The form that hosts the data control
LabelToUpdate	String	The label on the form to put status information
ProgressBar	Object	Will manage the progress bar
RecordSource	String	The SQL command to retrieve the recordset
Tag	String	The ID number of the bound controls

After adding
the eight
properties, your
Class Builder
should now
look like this:

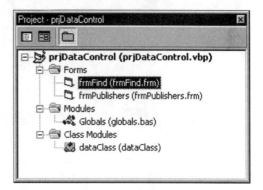

9 When you have added the eight properties
above, the project needs to be updated to add
the new class module we have just created.
Click File-Update Project from the main menu
of the Class Builder. Your project window
should now look like this:

We have now created our **dataClass** class module. Later in this chapter we will add code to
this class within the stubs we have just created using the Class Builder. Remember that a class
forms a template for creating a new object. Since our class needs a form to operate with, we
will build a generic data-entry form. The form that we will now build can be used - along with
its associated class - in any data-entry project we may come across. Talk about code reuse!

Try It Out - Create a Generic Data-Entry Form Template

1 Add a new form to your **prjDataControl** project with the name **frmDataClass**. This
form will be used to link to our **dataClass** class module.

2 We know that all good programmers are lazy, right? Well, we want to add a control array
of command buttons to our new (but currently blank) **frmDataClass** form. We also want
to add a progress bar and since we really don't feel like recreating the control array of
command buttons that we built for the **frmPublishers** form, let's just reuse that work.

281

Now that the new **frmDataClass** form has been added to your project, bring up the fruits of the previous chapters' labors - **frmPublishers**. Lasso the command buttons and the progress bar. You will also get the Comments label and Text1 textbox, but don't worry. Once the controls are lassoed as shown below, press good old *Ctrl-C* to copy them to the clipboard.

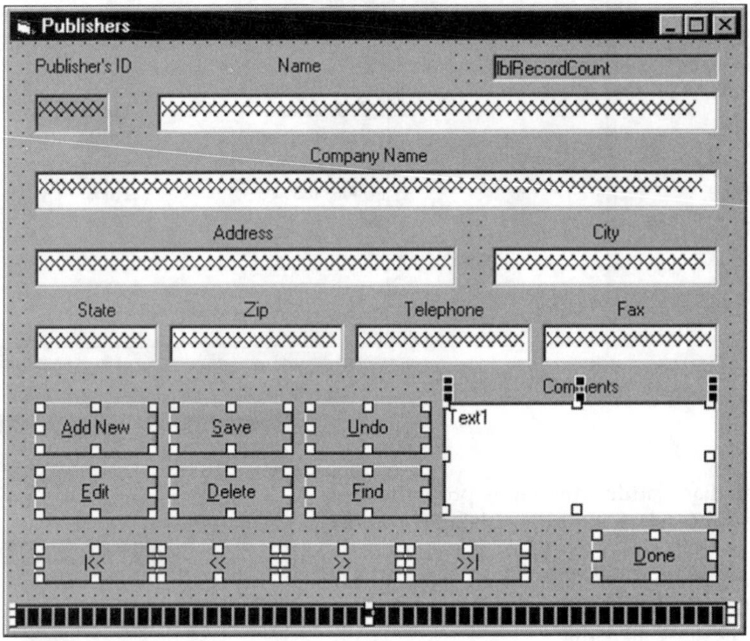

3 OK, now bring up the new, empty **frmDataClass** form. Click the mouse in the upper left-hand side of the form to ensure it is the active form and set the position for copying the controls. Now press *Ctrl-V* to copy the controls that are now in the clipboard to the form. Delete the Comments label and the Text1 text box. Set the **Caption** of the form to Template form for our dataClass. The new **frmDataClass** form should look like this after you have deleted the text box and the label:

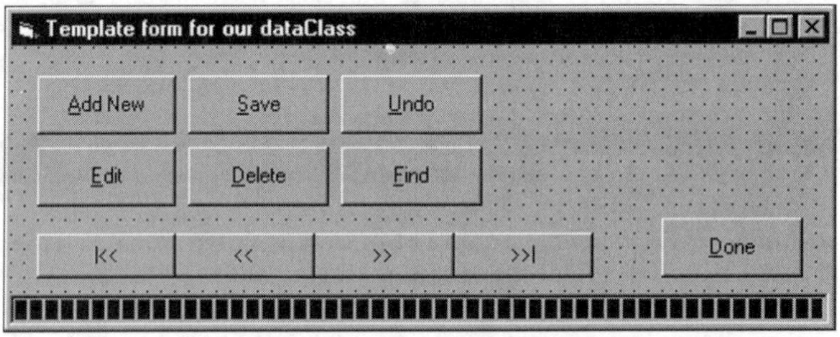

4 Now take a moment to rearrange the controls. Add a data control to the form and set its **Visible** property to **False**. Next add a label called **lblRecordCount** as shown in the next screenshot. Set the **Caption** property of this label to **lblRecordCount** as well. Set the **BorderStyle** of the label to **1 - Fixed Single**. This form can be the basis of the data-entry form template that you can use for any project you may ever develop. Your form should now look like this:

5 OK, let's wire up our new data-entry template to our **dataClass** class module. (Of course, nothing useful will happen yet because we haven't written any code in the class module, but we can test our class to ensure it can be successfully instantiated.) Once we know that we can create an object from our class, we can use this form as a test-bed while we work out any kinks in the class module.

In the **General Declarations** section of our new **frmDataClass** form add the following line:

```
Dim myDataClass As dataClass
```

This is an **object variable declaration**. The variable we declare here, **myDataClass**, will be used whenever we need to refer to our object. As with any other variable declaration, we begin the declaration of our new object with **Dim**, then specify the name for our new object (**myDataClass**) and finally tell VB that the object is to be declared as type **dataClass**.

6 In the **Form_Activate** event procedure of our **frmDataClass** form, add the following highlighted line of code.

```
Private Sub Form_Activate()
Set myDataClass = New dataClass
End Sub
```

This line of code creates an instance of the object from our class. As we are referring to our object we must use the object variable that we have just declared. When the **Activate** event procedure of the form fires, we set **myDataClass** to be a new instance of the **dataClass** class; hence the self-explanatory **Set** and **New** keywords. Now we can talk to our new object using **myDataClass**, it is officially an object!

We can reference the new object with the object variable **myDataClass**, but at this point our new object has no way to signal to us that it is alive. Let's add a simple message box to our **dataClass** class module that will alert us to when it becomes initialized.

283

7 Open the code window for the **dataClass** class module. You will see some strange and alien variables in the General Declarations section of the **dataClass** class module. Don't worry, we will get to those in a second. For now, click on the left drop-down box and select **Class**.

Each class module has exactly two built-in events - an **Initialize** and a **Terminate** event. The **Initialize** event is the first event that fires when an instance of the class is created.

8 Add the code in the screenshot below to the **Initialize** event. This event will fire when we create an instance of the class in our form. Now our object will have a way of telling us it's alive and well.

```
prjDataControl - dataClass (Code)

Class                        Initialize

    Private Sub Class_Initialize()
      MsgBox ("I've been Initialized!")
    End Sub
```

9 Click the right drop-down box and you will see the other event, **Terminate**. This is the last event that fires when the object variable that holds a reference to the object gets set to **Nothing** or goes out of scope. We will delete these messages when we wrap up, but we'll leave them for now as they demonstrate nicely that our object has 'life' inherited from the class module.

Add the following highlighted line of code to the class **Terminate** event.

```
Private Sub Class_Terminate()
MsgBox ("I've been Terminated!")
End Sub
```

10 Now we want to change the startup object of our project to the new **frmDataClass** form. Select Project-prjDataControl Properties from the menu and choose frmDataClass as the Startup Object for the project. Your Project Explorer should now look like this:

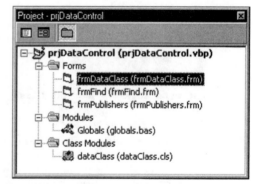

11 Press *F5* to run the project. When the **Activate** event in our **frmDataClass** fires, it sets the reference to a new instance of our class, **dataClass**. When the class comes to life (i.e. becomes a full-fledged object), the **Initialize** event in the class module fires. The message box tells us that our new class is alive and kicking! Of course it is not doing anything useful yet. We need to write some code to make it earn its keep. But we know that the class is now wired to our **frmDataClass** form.

How It Works

In our **frmDataClass** form we dim'ed an object **myDataClass** as type **dataClass**. This told VB that - at some time in the future - we would instantiate an object of type **dataClass**. Then when the **Form_Activate** event of **frmDataClass** was fired, the following code was executed:

```
Set myDataClass = New dataClass
```

This line set a reference to our object variable - **myDataClass** and created a new instance of **dataClass** in the computer's memory. The class template (**dataClass**) was loaded into memory to become an object (**myDataClass**). Now when we want to communicate with our object, we will use **myDataClass** to get hold of it.

Adding Code to Our Class

Of course, the class does not do anything useful yet. For now, it just becomes instantiated as an object. We need to add some code for it to really do anything. We now know that we can create an instance of our class to make an object, so let's press on and make our class do some work by adding some code to it.

Try It Out - Placing Code in Our Class Module

1 Now take a look at the **dataClass** class you just created by double-clicking on the dataClass icon in the Project Explorer window. The General Declarations section of the **dataClass** class module now has the private variables that were automatically added by the Class Builder. Notice that there are some strange and alien-looking variables dimensioned for us by the Class Builder. There are eight of them, one for each of the eight properties we just added:

```
Option Explicit

'local variable(s) to hold property value(s)
Private mvardataCtl As Object 'local copy
Private mvarButtons As String 'local copy
Private mvardbName As String 'local copy
Private mvarFormName As Object 'local copy
Private mvarLabelToUpdate As String 'local copy
Private mvarProgressBar As Object 'local copy
Private mvarRecordSource As String 'local copy
Private mvarTag As String 'local copy
```

Wow! Looks scary, but again, all the Class Builder utility did was to add a variable declaration in the **General Declarations** area of the code to hold a value for each of the properties we added earlier. Why do they look so strange and terrifying? VB took the name of the property and appended a **mvar** to the front of it; **mvar** stands for **member variable**.

So our property **Buttons** will update a private member variable **mvarButtons** with a string value. Pretty straightforward, really. Since the variable is **Private**, the value can't be changed from outside of our class. That is what is meant by **data encapsulation** - the only way a value can be set or read is by using the **Property Let** (to set to) or **Property Get** (to read from our class property **Buttons**).

2 We will be using a **Private** variable in our class to hold the total number of records in the current recordset. Since we will be displaying the record count each time the user navigates between records, we want to read this value from a variable instead of the data control. It's much faster to access a variable in memory than to read an object's property.

Add this declaration to the **General Declarations** section of **dataClass**.

```
Private mvarTotalRecords As Long
```

We will only be reading and writing to **mvarTotalRecords** from within our class. So it does not have a property associated with it.

3 While you are in the **General** section of the class module, add the enumerated constants used for determining which button was pressed in our command array on the calling form. A cut and paste from the **frmPublishers** form will do just fine here. Ensure the enumerated constants are **Private** - we don't want these referenced outside of our class module.

```
Private Enum cmdButtons
  cmdMoveFirst = 0
  cmdMovePrevious = 1
  cmdMoveNext = 2
  cmdMoveLast = 3
  cmdAddNew = 4
  cmdEdit = 5
  cmdSave = 6
  cmdDelete = 7
```

```
      cmdUndo = 8
      cmdFind = 9
      cmdDone = 10
End Enum
```

Data Encapsulation

Remember when we were discussing encapsulation? Well, this is what it means in our context:

> *We only permit access to our private mvar variables by using our properties. If you think of a room in a house, people can get in through the various windows and doors. However, we only want people to enter a room through the front door, so we lock the windows and back door to force everyone to use the front door.*

Now that we've built the foundations of our class, let's move on and look at how we can get at the class's associated properties, and how we can assign values to them.

Our Class's Properties

The really useful feature about the Class Builder is its template-building facilities. Not only did the Class Builder add our private **mvar** variables in the **General Declarations** section, it was also kind enough to add the properties we need to let us read and write to these variables.

Take a look at each of the properties that were added automatically by the Class Builder. In the code window of the **dataClass** class module, select General in the left-hand drop down box and then click the right drop-down box. Notice that the Class Builder furnished us with both a PropertyGet and a PropertyLet for each of the properties we added.

Also, when we added the property **Buttons**, the private member variable **mvarButtons** was added to the **General Declarations** section of the code, in order to hold the value.

```
Private mvarButtons As String  'local copy
```

The Class Builder then added both a **Property Let** to write the contents from the outside *into* **mvarButtons** and a **Property Get** property to retrieve the value of **mvarButtons** *from* the class.

Assigning Values to Our Class's Properties

For example, let's suppose that we have created an instance of **dataClass** in our program and that it is now an object. For now, assume we instantiated the class with the name **myDataClass**. If we wanted to set the property **LabelToUpdate**, we would use the following syntax:

```
myDataClass.LabelToUpdate = "Hokey Smokes"
```

The class property is on the left side of the equal sign; therefore the **Let** code is automatically fired for the **LabelToUpdate** property. Since we defined the data type as **String**, the signature of the **Property Let** for **LabelToUpdate** is expecting a string variable for a parameter value. Look at the code below, which was generated for us by the Class Builder. The value passed into the **vData** parameter of **Public Property Let LabelToUpdate** is **Hokey Smokes**. Our procedure now sets the private member variable, **mvarLabelToUpdate** equal to the string **Hokey Smokes**. The only way to set this *private* variable is through the *public* property. Since we are assigning a value from the outside of the class, VB knows to invoke the **Property Let**. We don't have to worry about that part - VB always gets it right.

```
Public Property Let LabelToUpdate(ByVal vData As String)
'used when assigning a value to the property, on the left side of an assignment.
'Syntax: X.LabelToUpdate = 5
    mvarLabelToUpdate = vData
End Property
```

Reading Our Class's Properties

Likewise, if we want to read the value of our private member variable **mvarLabelToUpdate**, VB will invoke the **Property Get**. For example, to read the value of this variable from the outside of our class, we could do something like this:

```
sMyStringVariable = myDataClass.LabelToUpdate
```

Since the class property is on the right side of the equal sign, VB knows this is a read of the value, and the **Property Get** of **LabelToUpdate** (shown below) is automatically fired. The **Get** takes the value of **mvarLabelToUpdate** and passes it back to the caller. Notice that the return value of **LabelToUpdate** is a string. The Class Builder ensures that the values are consistent in both the **Let** and **Get** properties.

```
Public Property Get LabelToUpdate() As String
'used when retrieving value of a property, on the right side of an assignment.
'Syntax: Debug.Print X.LabelToUpdate
    LabelToUpdate = mvarLabelToUpdate
End Property
```

If you had your thinking caps on, you might have noticed that a **Let** property is just a glorified sub routine and a **Get** property is a glorified function (because it returns a value). Conceptually, that's how they work. And now you know how our private variables can get assigned or read - **via their properties**.

Setting Objects in Our dataClass

You may recall that three of our eight properties we created were of type **Object**. We defined the **dataCtl**, **FormName** and **ProgressBar** as data type **Object**. Since these are objects, we must treat them just a bit differently than the other data types. If we want to pass an object, we must set a reference to it. Let's take a look at the **dataCtl** property to see just what this means. The Class Builder gave us the following variable for the **dataCtl**:

```
Private mvardataCtl As Object 'local copy
```

Since this is an object (a data control object), we must set a reference to it. However, instead of providing a **Property Let**, the Class Builder has added a **Set**:

```
Public Property Set dataCtl(ByVal vData As Object)
'used when assigning an Object to the property, on the left side of a Set
statement.
'Syntax: Set x.dataCtl = Form1
    Set mvardataCtl = vData
End Property
```

Notice that inside the **Property Set**, the Class Builder used the **Set** keyword to assign the value of **vData** to the private variable **mvardataCtl**.

```
Set mvardataCtl = vData
```

VB knows that **mvardataCtl** is an object, so it was good enough to provide the **Set** for us. Behind the scenes, our class takes the reference to **dataCtl** and places it in the variable **vData**, which is of type **Object**.

Making a Property Read-Only or Write-Only

We need to make the properties in our class write-only. So what do we do?

> *Deleting the **Property Get** of **dataCtl** effectively makes the property write-only. If we want a property to be read-only, just delete the **Property Let**.*

We want to delete a few of the templates that the Class Builder so nicely put in for us. It just so happens that in this class, we want all of our eight properties to be write-only. Do you remember the dark side of the Data Wizard we discovered? Well the Class Builder also has a dark side. It does not give us the option to create read- or write-only properties - it always gives us both as by default. Fortunately, the benefits outweigh these small inefficiencies. So let's get rid of the property templates we don't need.

Try It Out - Making Our Properties Write-Only

1 Please take a minute and clean up our class by deleting each of the **Get** templates from the eight properties in our class **dataClass**.

Property	Read/Write	Delete Template
Buttons	Write Only	Get Buttons
dataCtl	Write Only	Get dataCtl
dbName	Write Only	Get dbName
FormName	Write Only	Get FormName
LabelToUpdate	Write Only	Get LabelToUpdate
ProgressBar	Write Only	Get ProgressBar
RecordSource	Write Only	Get RecordSource
Tag	Write Only	Get Tag

2 There! If you take a look at your class module now, you will see the following properties. Be sure you have deleted the unnecessary ones.

```
Public Property Let Buttons(ByVal vData As String)
    mvarButtons = vData
End Property

Public Property Set dataCtl(ByVal vData As Object)
    Set mvardataCtl = vData
End Property

Public Property Let dbName(ByVal vData As String)
    mvardbName = vData
End Property

Public Property Set FormName(ByVal vData As Object)
    Set mvarFormName = vData
End Property

Public Property Let LabelToUpdate(ByVal vData As String)
    mvarLabelToUpdate = vData
End Property

Public Property Set ProgressBar(ByVal vData As Object)
    Set mvarProgressBar = vData
End Property

Public Property Let RecordSource(ByVal vData As String)
    mvarRecordSource = vData
End Property

Public Property Let Tag(ByVal vData As String)
    mvarTag = vData
End Property
```

3 There should be five **Property Let**s and three **Property Set**s. For clarity, I have also deleted the remark statements that the Class Builder put in for us. Please remove these as well - this way we can concentrate on the code.

Let's Take a Closer Look at the Properties

OK, we have cleaned up the structure of our **dataClass** class module and it is now starting to look a bit more manageable. However, the class still does not really do anything useful yet. That part is up to us. Let's tweak a few properties to make them useful to the class.

The Let Buttons Property

We use this property to pass in the name of the control array of our buttons from the calling form. Once our class knows the name of the control array, it can manage all of the enabling/ disabling that our form requires. We don't have to make any changes to this property.

```
Public Property Let Buttons(ByVal vData As String)
   mvarButtons = vData
End Property
```

The Set dataCtl Property

When the **dataClass** is being initialized, it needs to know which data control it will be operating on. We may, for example, have two data controls on a form when we need a parent/ child relationship. In this case, our form would create two separate **dataClass** objects - one to manage each data control. The data control is linked to and referenced by, the **dataCtl** property. Since the **dataCtl** is an object, we need to use the **Set** command to set a reference to the control.

```
Set mvardataCtl = vData
```

Try It Out - Property Set dataCtl

1 Please change **Property Set dataCtl** so it looks like this:

```
Public Property Set dataCtl(ByVal vData As Object)
    Set mvardataCtl = vData
    mvardataCtl.RecordsetType = 1   'ensure a dynaset for absposition
End Property
```

We force the recordset type to **dynaset** so we can take advantage of the absolute position feature. By setting the **RecordsetType** to **1**, the code is telling the class to set the recordset to type dynaset.

> *The handy VB IntelliSense feature that usually displays all of the properties and methods of an object will not operate here. Why? Because we have not instantiated the class and it is not yet an object. At this time, VB does not know if* **mvardataCtl** *is a data control or a cucumber.*

The Let dbName Property

We also want to tell the **dataClass** where the database is located. This permits the class to work on the database no matter where the user might have installed it. The name is just a string, so we use this property to assign the name of the database to our private property variable **mvardbName**. No changes are required to this property.

```
Public Property Let dbName(ByVal vData As String)
    mvardbName = vData
End Property
```

The Set FormName Property

Our class needs to know the name of the form the data control lives on. By knowing the form name, we can lock/unlock the controls with the correct ID in the **Tag** property. We will also use the name of the form when we need to update a label to notify the user that the form is in add or edit mode.

```
Public Property Set FormName(ByVal vData As Object)
    Set mvarFormName = vData
End Property
```

The Let LabelToUpdate Property

When we want to display information on the form that is using our **dataClass**, we can simply take a look at the **mvarlabeltoUpdate** variable. This way, no matter what the name of the label on the form is called, our class knows the correct name. We don't need to make any changes here.

```
Public Property Let LabelToUpdate(ByVal vData As String)
    mvarLabelToUpdate = vData
End Property
```

The Set ProgressBar Property

As the user navigates through the recordset, we want our class to update the progress bar on the calling form automatically. Since this is an object, we can reference it and set the current position from within our class module. Again, nothing to change here.

```
Public Property Set ProgressBar(ByVal vData As Object)
    Set mvarProgressBar = vData
End Property
```

The Let RecordSource Property

Just like using a data control normally, we need to tell it which records to retrieve from the database.

Try It Out - The Property Let RecordSource

1 Please take a minute and add this highlighted code to the **Let RecordSource** property.

```
Public Property Let RecordSource(ByVal vData As String)
    mvarRecordSource = vData

        If (mvardataCtl Is Nothing) Then
           Exit Property
        End If

        mvardataCtl.DatabaseName = mvardbName
        mvardataCtl.RecordSource = mvarRecordSource
        mvardataCtl.Refresh

     '-- Are there any records? --
        If (mvardataCtl.Recordset.RecordCount < 1) Then
          mvarTotalRecords = 0
          Exit Property
        End If

     '-- There is at least 1 record --
        Screen.MousePointer = vbHourglass
        mvardataCtl.Recordset.MoveLast
        mvarTotalRecords = mvardataCtl.Recordset.RecordCount
        mvardataCtl.Recordset.MoveFirst
        Screen.MousePointer = vbDefault

End Property
```

How It Works

Let's walk through what we are doing here. When the user sets the **RecordSource** of our class from the outside, it will set our private variable **mvarRecordSource**. The **RecordSource** might be something like **SELECT * FROM Publishers**. Now that we have this, we can go ahead and have the data control we are referencing in our class create the recordset. However, we must be sure that the reference to the data control was actually set. We do this by checking if the private variable that references the data control (**mvardataCtl**) is equal to **Nothing**. If it is, we exit the property because VB would generate an error if we attempt to create a recordset with a non-existent data control.

```
mvarRecordSource = vData

If (mvardataCtl Is Nothing) Then
   Exit Property
End If
```

If indeed the referenced data control is stored in **mvardataCtl**, we can go ahead and set its **RecordSource**. We must first tell the data control which database to reference. Next we set the **RecordSource** of the referenced data control. We do that by passing in the (private) **mvarRecordSource** that was set from outside our class. Finally, a **Refresh** method to the referenced data control will create the recordset.

```
        mvardataCt1.DatabaseName = mvardbName
        mvardataCt1.RecordSource = mvarRecordSource
        mvardataCt1.Refresh
```

Once the data control creates the recordset, it could be that there are no records returned. If that is the case, we set our private variable, **mvarTotalRecords** to **0** and exit the property.

```
'-- Are there any records? --
If (mvardataCt1.Recordset.RecordCount < 1) Then
  mvarTotalRecords = 0
  Exit Property
End If
```

If there are records in the recordset returned by the referenced data control, we set the **MousePointer** to an hourglass to show the user a task is taking place. We then move to the last record to ensure we get a correct count. The private variable **mvarTotalRecords** is then set to the **RecordCount** of the recordset. Next, we jump back to the first record and set the **MousePointer** back to the default.

```
'-- There is at least 1 record --
Screen.MousePointer = vbHourglass
mvardataCt1.Recordset.MoveLast
mvarTotalRecords = mvardataCt1.Recordset.RecordCount
mvardataCt1.Recordset.MoveFirst
Screen.MousePointer = vbDefault
```

The Let Tag Property

Remember how we identified the controls on the form that the data control will manage? We used the **Tag** property of the control. When the **dataClass** is set up, we will tell it the ID to use for controls to lock and unlock. The ID is a string (such as "1") and it will be stored in the private variable **mvarTag**. We don't make any changes to the code here.

```
Public Property Let Tag (ByVal vData As String)
    mvarTag = vData
End Property
```

That's it for our properties. It wasn't too bad now, was it? Consider that you only need to add this code once to the class. It will now work each and every time you need a data-entry form. Best of all, we can leave in place most of the defaults that the Class Builder put in for us.

Back to the Class Builder

Open the Class Builder again. We are going to use it to add a few methods to our **dataClass**. Methods are used to actually make the class do something. We've fiddled a bit with the default properties that the Class Builder put in; we deleted all of the **Get** properties and added a few lines of code to the **Set dataCt1** and **Let RecordSource** properties. Well, that all got the Builder a bit confused - it now thinks that the properties of type string are now variants. See, the Class Builder isn't that smart after all. Don't worry, you just have to look at the actual class module to see that everything is in order.

A nice feature of the Class Builder is that you can rerun it and offset its slight confusion by adding new properties that you might have forgotten or missed. You can also use the Class Builder to add methods.

What we'll do next is look at the **methods** of the class that we've created.

Methods of Our dataClass

Now that the properties are in place and we have deleted the templates that are not needed, we will add a few methods to make things happen.

Try It Out - Adding Methods to the dataClass

1 Open up the Class Builder again and click the Add New Method to Current Class button on the Class Builder tool bar. It is the fourth button from the left - the one with the flying green brick. We will now add a method called **ProcessCMD**. This is simply shorthand for 'process Command Button'. We will pass the command button's control array index to this procedure. This occurs when the user presses the command button on the host form which is using our new data class.

2 We want to add an argument (i.e. a parameter) to our method. Remember that we want to pass in the index of the button that was pressed in the control array. Press the **+** sign to right of the Arguments list box. This will display the Add Argument dialog box. Add index for the Name and Integer as the Data Type.

Add Argument

Name:

`index`

OK

☐ ByVal

Cancel

Data Type:

`Integer`

☐ Array

☐ Optional

Default Value: (quote strings as needed)

3 Click on OK on both the Add Argument and Method Builder dialog boxes.

4 Now please use the following table and the procedure we've just gone through to add these additional methods to our class.

Method Name	Argument Name	Data Type
`lockTheControls`	`bLocked`	Boolean
`navigateButtons`	`sButtonString`	String
`updateButtons`	`vLockEm`	Variant (Check the Optional box)
`updateLabel`	`sLabelString`	String

5 After you have added the five methods to your class, click on the Methods tab of the Class Builder. You can see the names and arguments of the methods you just added. Neat.

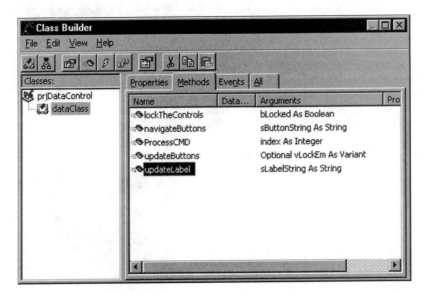

Class Builder

File Edit View Help

Classes:

prjDataControl
dataClass

Properties | Methods | Events | All

Name	Data...	Arguments	Pro
lockTheControls		bLocked As Boolean	
navigateButtons		sButtonString As String	
ProcessCMD		index As Integer	
updateButtons		Optional vLockEm As Variant	
updateLabel		sLabelString As String	

6 Click on File-Update Project to save these changes.

Next, we will go on and add the code to these methods that will make the class more useful and powerful for us.

Adding Code to Our Class's Methods

Well, the Class Builder added the templates for us, but we must now put in some code so the methods will actually do something. Remember that we kept a copy of the **frmPublishers** form hanging around in our project? We hijacked the controls from the form earlier by cutting and pasting them to our new **frmDataClass**. Well, we are not done with the **frmPublishers** form just yet - we are going to cannibalize it some more now. We will add the code to the **ProcessCMD** method in our **dataClass** module by cutting and pasting some code from the **frmPublishers** form.

Just Add Code

Go to the **frmPublishers** form and copy the code from the **cmdButton_Click** event procedure. Paste the **body of the code** from this event procedure in the new subroutine **ProcessCMD** that we have just built into the **dataClass** class module. By that I mean **do not** copy the first line **Private Sub cmdButton_Click(Index as Integer)** or the last line **Exit Sub**. Just everything in between.

Now we can set to work tailoring and enhancing the code for our various methods.

The ProcessCMD Method

Remember all of the code in our command button array that did special things, depending on which button was pressed? Well, now this new **ProcessCMD** method will manage all of that complexity for us. When the user clicks on a button, we will now simply call **myDataClass.ProcessCMD(Index)** and pass the index value, the one which VB sends to the **Click** event procedure, to the method. Cool.

Try It Out - Using the ProcessCMD Method

1 Now that you have pasted the code from the **cmdButton_Click** event procedure into the **ProcessCMD** method, we need to tweak it just a bit. Please take a minute and look at the highlighted lines below. These are the lines you will need to change. Most of the changes are trivial. For example, all instances of **Data1** now get replaced with **mvardataCtl**. This is because that private variable now holds the data control the class is operating on. **lTotalRecords** gets changed to **mvarTotalRecords** for the same reason. The only addition is **updateLabel**. That's because when we set a label on the calling form, we must iterate through each of the controls and find the label control to update. It makes sense to put this code to do this in a private sub. As such, **updateLabel** can only be called from within our class.

Since we want to replace each occurrence of **Data1** in the **ProcessCMD** method with **mvardataCtl**, you might want to use the Replace function of the VB Editor. Open the code window of the **dataClass** and be sure your cursor is in the **ProcessCMD** method. Next, click Edit-Replace from the VB main menu. Make sure the Search is set to Current Procedure.

I prefer to review each change, so selecting Replace allows you to either accept the change or not. Clicking Replace All is Kamikaze mode - all occurrences of **Data1** will get changed with **mvardataCtl** - whether you wanted them to or not. Banzai!

2 Now, go ahead and amend the code by interpolating the highlighted code lines below into the **ProcessCMD** subroutine:

```
Public Sub ProcessCMD(ByVal index As Integer)

Static vMyBookMark As Variant
On Error Resume Next

Select Case Index

  Case cmdMoveFirst              '--- move first ---
     mvardataCtl.Recordset.MoveFirst
     Call updateButtons

  Case cmdMovePrevious           '--- move previous ---
     mvardataCtl.Recordset.MovePrevious
     Call updateButtons

  Case cmdMoveNext               '--- move next ---
     mvardataCtl.Recordset.MoveNext
     Call updateButtons

  Case cmdMoveLast    '-- move last ---
     mvardataCtl.Recordset.MoveLast
     Call updateButtons

  '-- Now we are modifying the database --
  Case cmdAddNew  '-- add a new record
     With mvardataCtl.Recordset
         If (.EditMode = dbEditNone) Then
             If (mvarTotalRecords > 0) Then
                 vMyBookMark = .Bookmark
             Else
```

```
                    vMyBookMark = ""
                End If
                .AddNew
                Call updateButtons
                updateLabel("Adding New Record")
            End If
        End With

    Case cmdEdit '-- edit the current record
        With mvardataCtl.Recordset
            If (.EditMode = dbEditNone) Then
                vMyBookMark = .Bookmark
                .Edit
                Call updateButtons
                updateLabel("Editing")
            End If
        End With

    Case cmdSave '-- save the current record
        Dim bMoveLast As Boolean
        With mvardataCtl.Recordset
            If (.EditMode <> dbEditNone) Then
                If .EditMode = dbEditAdd Then
                    bMoveLast = True
                Else
                    bMoveLast = False
                End If
                .Update
                If (.EditMode = dbEditNone) Then
                    mvarTotalRecords = .RecordCount
                    If (bMoveLast = True) Then
                        .MoveLast
                    Else
                        .Move 0
                    End If
                    updateButtons True
                End If
            Else
                .Move 0
            End If
        End With

    Case cmdDelete  '-- delete the current record
        Dim iResponse As Integer
        Dim sAskUser As String
        sAskUser = "Are you sure you want to delete this record?"
        iResponse = MsgBox(sAskUser, vbQuestion + vbYesNo + _
                    vbDefaultButton2, "Publishers Table")
        If (iResponse = vbYes) Then
            With mvardataCtl.Recordset
                .Delete
                mvarTotalRecords = .RecordCount
                If (mvarTotalRecords > 0) Then
                    If .BOF Then
                        .MoveFirst
                    Else
                        .MovePrevious
                    End If
```

```
                End If
            End With
        End If
        Call updateButtons

    Case cmdUndo '-- undo changes to the current record
        With mvardataCtl.Recordset
            If (.EditMode <> dbEditNone) Then
                .CancelUpdate
                If (Len(vMyBookMark)) Then
                    .Bookmark = vMyBookMark
                End If
                updateButtons True
            Else
                .Move 0
            End If
        End With
        updateButtons True

    Case cmdFind '-- find a specific record
        Dim iReturn As Integer
        gFindString = ""

        With frmFind
            .addCaption = "Type Publisher Name to find"
            .RecordSource = "SELECT Name FROM Publishers ORDER BY name"
            .Show vbModal
        End With

        If (Len(gFindString) > 0) Then
            With mvardataCtl.Recordset
                .FindFirst "Name = '" & gFindString & "'"
                If (.NoMatch) Then
                    iReturn = MsgBox("Publisher Name " & gFindString & _
                        " was not found.", vbCritical, "Publisher")
                Else
                    iReturn = MsgBox("Publisher Name " & gFindString & _
                        " was retrieved.", vbInformation, "Publisher")
                End If
            End With
        End If
        updateButtons

    Case cmdDone    '-- Done. Unload the form
        Unload mvarFormName
End Select

End Sub
```

How It Works

Well, there is no magic here - we covered all of the code in the last chapter. So it was nice to have to do very little work in this method. Notice that we left the structure of the code completely intact. However, every instance of **Data1** was switched to **mvardataCtl**. That's because we are now managing the data control on the calling form with the reference to it in the private variable **mvardataCtl**.

We also changed each instance of **lTotalRecords** to **mvarTotalRecords** because we are storing the value in our private variable of that name.

Also, we can no longer update a form's label caption directly as we can when the code is in the same form. So we had to change the two places where we update the label (when we add or edit) to call our method **updateLabel()**.

One new entry is the error statement. This will force VB to the next line of code after an error has occurred. We want to add this line because when the **dataClass** is used in parent/child forms, any validation that interrupts saving a record - for example, if a primary key is left empty - will generate an error in our class. This statement will essentially ignore that error:

```
On Error Resume Next
```

Finally, when the user pressed **cmdDone**, we originally had **Unload Me**. We had to change that to **Unload mvarFormName** so we could explicitly tell VB which form to unload. After all, the form could be named anything. We don't know the name of the form in advance, so we just grab it from our private variable.

The updateButtons Method

We will take the same approach with the **updateButtons** method of our **dataClass**. We will copy the code we wrote in the last chapter and tweak it a bit so it works with our private variables.

Try It Out - Using the updateButtons Method

1 Just cut the code from the **updateButtons** in the **frmPublishers** form and paste it in the **updateButtons** method template. The code is almost identical to that in the form. Change the **Public** in the first line to **Private**. This will ensure the code can only be run from within our class.

2 Make the changes indicated by the highlighted code lines below. The changes required are to change **Data1** to **mvardataCtl**, **lTotalRecords** to **mvarTotalRecords** and **bLockEm** to **vLockEm**. A quick find/replace will take care of these changes.

```
Private Sub updateButtons(Optional vLockem As Variant)

Dim sLabelString As String

Select Case mvardataCtl.Recordset.EditMode

    Case dbEditNone
        If (mvarTotalRecords > 2) Then
            If (mvardataCtl.Recordset.BOF) Or _
               (mvardataCtl.Recordset.AbsolutePosition = 0) Then
                    navigateButtons ("00111101011")
            ElseIf (mvardataCtl.Recordset.EOF) Or _
                   (mvardataCtl.Recordset.AbsolutePosition = mvarTotalRecords - 1) Then
                    navigateButtons ("11001101011")
            Else
                    navigateButtons ("11111101011")
```

```
            End If
        ElseIf (mvartotalRecords > 0) Then
            navigateButtons ("00001101001")
        Else
            navigateButtons ("00001000001")
        End If
        If (Not IsMissing(vLockem)) Then
            lockTheControls (vLockem)
        End If
    Case dbEditInProgress     'we are editing a current record
        Call lockTheControls(False)
        navigateButtons ("00000010100")
    Case dbEditAdd            'we are adding a new record
        Call lockTheControls(False)
        navigateButtons ("00000010100")
    End Select
```

```
    mvarProgressBar.Value = mvardataCtl.Recordset.PercentPosition

    sLabelString = mvardataCtl.Recordset.AbsolutePosition + 1
    sLabelString = sLabelString & " of " & mvarTotalRecords
    Call updateLabel(sLabelString)
```

```
    End Sub
```

3 Remove the two lines of code from the **Case dbEditInProgress** and **Case dbEditAdd** sections that read:

```
Text1(1).SetFocus
```

How It Works

Again, we covered most of this ground in the last chapter. In our class module, **ProcessCMD** will intercept the index of the button the user presses in the **cmdButton** control array. It will do its work and then call the **updateButtons** method of our class.

There are a few new lines at the end of the sub procedure. **PercentPosition** returns a value indicating the location of the current record in **mvardataCtl.Recordset**. **mvardataCtl.Recordset.PercentPosition** is then assigned to the **Value** property of **mvarProgressBar**.

```
    mvarProgressBar.Value = mvardataCtl.Recordset.PercentPosition
```

The **AbsolutePosition** property of **mvardataCtl.RecordSet** is added to **1** and the value returned is assigned to the string **sLabelString**. **AbsolutePosition** can return a value from 0 to one less than the total number of records in the recordset. Therefore the value of the actual record is the **AbsolutePosition + 1**.

```
    sLabelString = mvardataCtl.Recordset.AbsolutePosition + 1
```

The value of the actual record, now held in **sLabelString**, is concatenated to **" of "** and the total number of records, held in **mvarTotalRecords**. This string is then assigned to **sLabelString**.

```
    sLabelString = sLabelString & " of " & mvarTotalRecords
```

Finally, we call the **updateLabel** method, passing our **sLabelString** string.

```
Call updateLabel(sLabelString)
```

The navigateButtons Helper Subroutine

Just like last chapter, the **navigateButtons** subroutine is called from **updateButtons**. This routine will actually enable or disable specific buttons, depending on the state of the application. Luckily we can swipe most of the code from the last chapter and tweak it just a bit.

Try It Out - Modifying the navigateButtons Subroutine

1 Again, please take a second to cut the **navigateButtons** code from the **frmPublishers** form and paste it to our class method of the same name. Also make this sub **Private** since it will only be available within our class module.

2 Remove the lines that read:

```
cmdButton(iIndx - 1).Enabled = True
```

and

```
cmdButton(iIndx - 1).Enabled = False
```

Replace these lines with the following highlighted ones.

```
Private Sub navigateButtons(sButtonString As String)

Dim iIndx As Integer
Dim iButtonLength As Integer

sButtonString = Trim$(sButtonString)
iButtonLength = Len(sButtonString)

For iIndx = 1 To iButtonLength
  If (Mid$(sButtonString, iIndx, 1) =  "1") Then
    mvarFormName.Controls(mvarButtons)(iIndx - 1).Enabled = True
  Else
    mvarFormName.Controls(mvarButtons)(iIndx - 1).Enabled = False
  End If
Next

DoEvents

End Sub
```

How It Works

We are taking the **sButtonString** from the **updateButtons** method and enforcing our state machine by either enabling or disabling specific buttons for the task at hand.

However, remember that we are setting properties of a control array of buttons on a form somewhere in the current project. So we must use this somewhat strange syntax to ensure we can access the buttons from outside the form.

```
mvarFormName.Controls(mvarButtons)(iIndx - 1).Enabled = True
```

While this looks complicated, it's really straightforward. Let's examine each part of this statement. Once we look at the pieces, you'll see that it really does make sense.

First, we fully qualify the command by providing the name of the form we are interested in, **mvarFormName**. Remember that a sophisticated VB program can have 50 or more forms. So our class must tell VB which one we are interested in specifically. Then we look at the **Controls** collection of that specific form. Of all of the controls on the form, we are interested in the one with the name we will store in **mvarButtons**. Since this control happens to be a control array, we must also pass in the index number. Like any complex VB statement, once we break it down into its parts, you can see it really isn't rocket science.

Try It Out - Modifying the lockTheControls Subroutine

1 Return to the **frmPublishers** form and copy the code from the **lockTheControls** routine, paste it in the **lockTheControls** method template. Then amend the highlighted lines of code:

```
Private Sub lockTheControls(bLocked As Boolean)

On Error Resume Next

Dim iIndx As Integer

With mvarFormName
    For iIndx = 0 To .Controls.Count - 1
      If (.Controls(iIndx).Tag = mvarTag) Then
        If (TypeOf .Controls(iIndx) Is TextBox) Then
          If (bLocked) Then
            .Controls(iIndx).Locked = True
            .Controls(iIndx).BackColor = vbWhite
          Else
            .Controls(iIndx).Locked = False
            .Controls(iIndx).BackColor = vbYellow
          End If
        End If
      End If
    Next
End With

End Sub
```

How It Works

Notice that this sub is also **Private**, so be sure to change this. Again, here we substitute the hard coded name of the form with that stored in the private procedure variable **mvarFormName**. Also notice that instead of checking for a tag value of "1", we will instead look at **mvarTag**. This is because we might have several data controls on a single form; each will require the controls that it manages to have a unique ID, so to speak. When our class in initialized, one of the properties the programmer will set is the **Tag**. This will identify the specific controls that this particular class will manage.

Really, this code is the same as the last chapter. If we need the controls to be locked, we pass in a value of **True**. This sub/then looks at each and every control on the form stored in **mvarFormName**. If the tag on the control matches the **mvarTag** private variable, then the routine knows it is interested in this particular control. We then lock this control and set its **BackColor** property to white. If we call **lockTheControls** with a value of **False**, the controls with a tag value of **mvarTag** get unlocked and the **BackColor** property gets set to yellow.

Now let's look at our next sub - the **updateLabel** subroutine.

We want to be able to set the caption on the calling form to show things such as the current record, or to notify the user when we are adding or editing. Like before, we must tell VB exactly which label on which form we are interested in. This will take just a bit of sleight of hand. Unlike the other subroutines, we will actually have to get our hands dirty and write this one from scratch! Oh well, at least we only need to write it once.

This subroutine gets passed a string of text to place in a label on the calling form. However, in order to do that from a class module, we have to loop through each of the controls on the form and look at the name of each control. If the control we are currently looking at has the same name as **mvarLabelToUpdate** - bingo! We found it. So this routine just loops through the controls collection on the form **mvarformName**. It then compares the name of each control with the name of the label that is stored in **mvarLabelToUpdate**. When the label is found, the new caption is set.

Try It Out - Writing the updateLabel Subroutine

1   Find the **updateLabel** subroutine and add the following code to it:

```
Private Sub updateLabel(sLabelString As String)
```

```
Dim iIndx As Integer

With mvarFormName
  For iIndx = 0 To .Controls.Count - 1
    If (.Controls(iIndx).Name = mvarLabelToUpdate) Then
       .Controls(iIndx).Caption = sLabelString
       Exit Sub
    End If
  Next
End With
```

```
End Sub
```

There. Are your fingers tired yet from the cutting and pasting? Well, trust me - it will be worth it. Your class is now ready for action.

OK, if you haven't already, save your work now. It's been a long road, but we are just about ready to reap the fruits of your labor.

Alright, we are now finally ready to take our **dataClass** our for a spin. Kick the tires. That sort of thing.

1 Add a text box to the **frmDataClass** form. We will just test the class, so a single text box will do fine for now. Set the **Tag** property of the **Text1** text box to **1** and the **DataSource** property to **Data1**.

Template form for our dataClass					_ □ X
|◄ ◄ Data1 ► ►|		Text1			
Add New	Save	Undo	Edit	Delete	Find
|<<	<<	>>	>>|	lblRecordCount	Done

2 Earlier we added a line in **frmDataClass**'s **Activate** event that instantiated the class and made it an object. Open the code window in the **Activate** event and add the following highlighted code now. We will set our **dataClass** properties before we use the class. This will make our new class fully functional.

```
Private Sub Form_Activate()

Static bInIsOld As Boolean 'the default value of a Boolean is False

If blnIsOld = False Then

Set myDataClass = New dataClass

With myDataClass
    Set .FormName = Me      'pass in the current form
    Set .dataCtl = Data1    'the data control to manage
    Set .ProgressBar = ProgressBar1
    .dbName = gDataBaseName
    .Buttons = "cmdButton"
    .RecordSource = "SELECT * FROM Publishers"
    .LabelToUpdate = lblRecordCount
    .Tag = "1"              'identifies the controls
    .ProcessCMD 0           'default to the 1st record
End With

bInIsOld = True

End If

Text1.DataField = "Name"

End Sub
```

3 Now that we have the class, we can greatly simplify the coding of much of the rest of the form! Remember all of the code in the **cmdButton_Click** event procedure? Of course, we moved all of the code that handled what to do when a user pressed a specific button into our class module. So in order to have our **frmDataClass** form respond to the array of command buttons on it, we must add a single line of code to its **cmdButton_Click** event. This line will pass the index of the button clicked to our object and it will now manage the interface for us. Add the highlighted code below to the **cmdButton_Click** event:

```
Private Sub cmdButton_Click(Index As Integer)
```

```
myDataClass.ProcessCMD (Index)
```

```
End Sub
```

4 When the user is editing or adding a record on our form, the Done button is disabled. So the user gets a visual cue that they cannot exit the form. However, remember in the last chapter when we covered all of the alternate methods for exiting a form? Well, they still apply. Add the following code to the **QueryUnload** event in the **frmDataClass** form. This will make sure that the user can't exit the form during an edit operation.

```
Private Sub Form_QueryUnload(Cancel As Integer, UnloadMode As Integer)
```

```
Dim iMessage As Integer

If (Data1.Recordset.EditMode <> dbEditNone) Then
  iMessage = MsgBox("You must complete editing the current record", _
                    vbInformation, App.EXEName)
  Cancel = True
End If
```

```
End Sub
```

5 Now copy the **highLight** sub routine from the **frmPublishers** form to the **Globals** module. Your **Globals** code module should now look like this.

```
Public Sub highLight()

With Screen.ActiveForm
   If (TypeOf .ActiveControl Is TextBox) Then
     .ActiveControl.SelStart = 0
     .ActiveControl.SelLength = Len(.ActiveControl)
   End If
End With

End Sub
```

6 Without further delay, press *F5* to run the form. It will operate just as if we had all of the code in the form itself.

Go ahead and navigate the recordset. Click the Edit key to ensure the text box unlocks and the **BackColor** property changes to yellow. Cancel the edit and press Find. The Find form will now display the publishers. When you get more comfortable with the class, you could add another property that would permit the programmer to set the **RecordSource** property for the Find form. Recall that the **RecordSource** property for the Find form is set in the **cmdFind** option of the **ProcessCMD** method of the class. I wanted to keep this as streamlined as possible at first. However once you see how flexible this approach is, you will probably come up with all sorts of enhancements.

7   Finally, press the Done button. Notice that the form will close and the I've been Terminated! message box gets displayed. This gives you a good sense of the duration of your class. By now, you are probably a bit sick of seeing these messages. Please take a minute and delete both messages in the **dataClass**'s **Initialize** and **Terminate** events.

How It Works

Let's go back a while and work our way through the code we've just added.

As we already know, the following line actually creates the object in memory and permits us to set its properties and call its methods:

```
Set myDataClass = New dataClass
```

Once the class is instantiated and in memory as a result of us using the **New** keyword in the assignment statement, we can set its properties to get it fixed up properly.

The first thing we do is assign the name of the form by passing in the keyword **Me**:

```
Set .FormName = Me
```

FormName was declared as type **Object**, so we need to instantiate it by using **Set**. The **Me** keyword behaves like an implicitly declared variable. Using **Me** is particularly useful for passing information about the currently executing form to a procedure in another module or class. Also, if we later change the name of the form - no problem. **Me** passes in the current form no matter what its name is.

We must now tell the class which data control to manipulate. When we set this property, the class code sets it to the private variable **mvardataCtl** that is referenced throughout our class. Note also that as **dataCtl** was declared as an **Object** we need to use the **Set** keyword.

```
Set .dataCtl = Data1   'the data control to manage
```

Next, we pass a reference to our progress bar. Remember that we defined this as data type **Object**, this way we can reference this control from our class.

```
Set .ProgressBar = ProgressBar1
```

Next, we tell the class the database to use. We have to set this property so our class can set up the managed data control. Remember that we are storing the name and location of the database name in our **Globals.bas** code module.

```
.dbName = gDataBaseName
```

In order for our class to know about the control array of buttons, we must set the **Buttons** property. Notice that the name of the control is in quotes; we are passing the name of the control array:

```
.Buttons = "cmdButton"
```

Next, we must tell the class which **RecordSource** to use. So here we just set the property of the class:

```
.RecordSource = "SELECT * FROM Publishers"
```

We have placed a label on the form to display the current record. We also want to alert the user when we are adding or editing. By telling our class the name of the label, it can do that for us:

```
.LabelToUpdate = lblRecordCount
```

Remember when we placed a value in the **Tag** property of the controls that were tied to the data control? We are just telling the class which controls to lock and unlock during editing. And if we want two classes - one to manage the parent records and a second to manage the child records, we simply give the class the **Tag** ID of the controls it needs to worry about:

```
.Tag = "1"                'identifies the controls
```

The last thing we do while initializing our object is to default to the first record. This way, it simulates pressing the "First Record" button in the control array. Doing this will ensure the correct buttons are enabled/disabled.

```
.ProcessCMD 0             'default to the 1st record
```

We will now tell the bound text box, **Text1**, which field it should display. Remember we are just testing now. Later we will add additional fields.

```
Text1.DataField = "Name"
```

What We've Accomplished

We now have a generic data entry form template. This can be used for each and every new data entry project you might come up against. Now all of the 0's and 1's that we had in our original form have been moved into our class module and only a few lines of code are required in our host form. To give you a sense of the power of the new **dataClass**, let's look at the steps required to use it on a brand new project:

- ▶ Load our **frmDataClass** form to use as the new form
- ▶ Add any bound controls for the specific task, such as text boxes, and bind them to the data control
- ▶ Place an ID in the **Tag** property of the bound controls
- ▶ Set the properties for the class

That's it. Instead of rewriting the code to handle adding, editing, navigating, deleting and finding records for each and every data entry form you will ever create, we have encapsulated that functionality in a class. We also have a **frmDataClass** form that will be the raw material for every new data entry form. Now each data entry form will not only be simple to set up, but they will all have the same look and feel. This consistency brings a sense of security to your users.

To make the **frmDataClass** and **frmFind** forms and the **dataClass** class module available for each of your new projects, we will soon make them VB templates. This means that you can select them right from the VB menu when starting a new project!

Since we want to make these three items a permanent feature of your VB tool box, let's take just a minute and make some final updates to ensure we can use them under any circumstances. When we feel that our class is robust enough, we will save it as a VB template.

Polishing the dataClass Class Module

We want to now fix up the Find capabilities of our **dataClass**. Remember that we hardcoded the **addCaption** and **RecordSource** properties in the **cmdFind** section of the **ProcessCMD** method in our **dataClass**. What a mouthful! Take a look at the code we currently have.

```
Case cmdFind '-- find a specific record
     Dim iReturn As Integer
     gFindString = ""

     With frmFind
         .addCaption = "Type Publisher Name to find"
         .RecordSource = "SELECT Name FROM Publishers ORDER BY Name"
         .Show vbModal
     End With

     If (Len(gFindString) > 0) Then
         With mvardataCtl.Recordset
             .FindFirst "Name = '" & gFindString & "'"
```

Take a moment to review the highlighted lines of code. Here we hardcoded in the caption to display on the **frmFind** form as well as the recordset. Then, we hardcoded in the **Name** as the field to match on. If we want to search for anything other than a publisher's name, we will be out of luck. What if we were looking at the **Titles** table and wanted to match on **Title**? Or wanted to match on any other field in any other database?

To make our work genuinely useful, we want to be able to use our generalized **frmFind** form for **any table** we might come up against.

Luckily, the changes are pretty simple. Let's make them now.

Try It Out - Making Our dataClass More Sophisticated

We can call on the VB Class Builder again to help us out. We want to add three additional properties to our class. One will take the customized caption we want to place on the **frmFind** form. The second property will permit the programmer to assign the recordset to retrieve and display in the **frmFind**. The third will be the field we want to match on.

1 Open up the VB Class Builder. Add the following three properties to our class.

dataClass Property to Add	Data Type
FindCaption	String
FindRecordSource	String
FindMatchField	String

2 Now add another method to our **dataClass**. The programmer might not only wish to find a record on a text field, such as the name of a publisher - there might be a need to search on a numeric field, such as the **PubID**. Another requirement might be to find a record based on a certain date criterion. When we retrieve records from our recordset, these three data types - string, numeric and data must all be formatted just a bit differently when using the **FindFirst** method of the recordset. So we will add another method to our class module:

dataClass Method to Add	Return Data Type
BuildCriteria	String

3 After you have added these new properties and the new method, select File-Update Project from the Class Builder main menu. This step will actually add these new properties and method to your **dataClass** class module. Now close the Class Builder.

4 Open the code window for the **dataClass** class module. We want to make these properties write-only, so delete the **Get** templates for the three new properties, i.e. delete the **Get FindCaption**, **Get FindRecordSource** and **Get FindMatchField** templates. There, we have now made these three new properties write-only.

5 Take a look at the General Declarations section of the **dataClass** class module. You will notice that the Class Builder dutifully added three new private member variables for us:

```
'local variable(s) to hold property value(s)
Private mvarFindCaption As String 'local copy
Private mvarFindRecordSource As String 'local copy
Private mvarFindMatchField As String 'local copy
```

6 Now we want to construct the **BuildCriteria** function. This handy little routine will determine the type of field the programmer wants to use in the **FindMatchField** property and format it so it can be found correctly. Yes, we could have had the programmer using our **dataClass** specify the type of field, but why? We can easily determine the type of field ourselves. The programmer might think the type of field is numeric when it is really text. So to eliminate any 'operator error', we will determine the field type ourselves and build the correct criteria string to pass to the **FindFirst** method of the recordset. Please add the following code to the **BuildCriteria** method. Also make it **Private** instead of the default **Public**.

```
Private Function BuildCriteria() As String

  Dim sCriteria As String
  Dim fField As Field
  Dim sMessage As String
  Dim iIndx As Integer

  Set fField = mvardataCtl.Recordset.Fields(mvarFindMatchField)

  Select Case fField.Type
    Case dbInteger, dbLong, dbCurrency, dbSingle, dbDouble
      BuildCriteria = "" & mvarFindMatchField & " = " & gFindString
    Case dbDate
      BuildCriteria = "" & mvarFindMatchField & " = #" & gFindString & "#"
    Case dbText
      BuildCriteria = "" & mvarFindMatchField & " = '" & gFindString & "'"
    Case Else
      sMessage = "Sorry, you can't use the find feature on fields"
      sMessage = sMessage & " of type: " & fField.Type
      iIndx = MsgBox(sMessage, vbCritical, App.EXEName)
  End Select

End Function
```

Notice that behind the scenes, a method is really a function! Since we are making this **Private**, it can only be used within our **dataClass**. In addition, since all of our methods, except the **ProcessCMD**, are **Private**, they can't be seen in the Class Builder. Using the **Private** keyword hides them from the outside world.

How It Works

The first thing we do is to **Dim** a variable of type **Field**. Do you remember in the last chapter, when we looked at the DAO 3.51 type library that was added in the References dialog box? Well, now VB knows what a **Field** data type is by referring to the DAO type library.

```
Set fField = mvardataCtl.Recordset.Fields(mvarFindMatchField)
```

What we want to do is determine the data type of the field. It's pretty easy, really. First we set the **fField** variable to the **Field** of the recordset. Since the private member variable **mvarFindMatchField** contains the name of the field we want to match on, we simply retrieve it from the **Fields** collection by passing in the name. This line will set the **fField** variable to whichever field the programmer wants to match on. Now that we have that field tucked away in the **fField** variable, we can look at its attributes.

Remember when we mentioned that the Jet database engine is really doing the work behind the scenes? Well, Jet requires different types of variables used in the **FindFirst** method of the recordset to be formatted in specific ways. We will handle this with a simple **Select Case** statement.

```
Select Case fField.Type
```

One of the handy attributes of a field object is its **Type**. This will tell us what kind of data this field is holding. I have seen several database tables that store numbers in text fields. So if the user wants to find a number that is really stored as text, our handy routine will figure this out for us, an intrinsic constant will be returned such as **dbInteger**, **dbLong** or **dbDate**. Field types never lie. They have x-ray vision that tells us what data type the field really holds.

```
Case dbInteger, dbLong, dbCurrency, dbSingle, dbDouble
    BuildCriteria = "" & mvarFindMatchField & " = " & gFindString
```

If the field type we want to match on is numeric, we don't want to put any surrounding quotation marks around it. Why? Because it is not a string literal - it's a number, darn it! You may recall that we return values from functions by setting the name of the function to the return value. We are doing just that here. Let's say that the programmer wanted to search on the **PubID** field for the publisher with **PubID** number 42. Then **PubID** would be stored in the **mvarFindMatchField** and 42 would be stored in the global variable **gFindString**. The **BuildCriteria** function would return the value **PubID = 42**.

If the field type is a date, Jet requires the field we're trying to match on to be surrounded with **#**s. So our next **Case** statement will handle the return value if it is a date:

```
Case dbDate
    BuildCriteria = "" & mvarFindMatchField & " = #" & gFindString & "#"
```

The most frequently used type of search will be on a text field. Since we are searching for a string literal (a literal is a string enclosed in quotes), we want to format the criteria correctly. So this **Case** statement simply encloses the string that we want to find in single quotation marks. This way Jet can find it for us:

```
Case dbText
    BuildCriteria = "" & mvarFindMatchField & " = '" & gFindString & "'"
```

If the programmer set the properties of our **dataClass** to search on the **Name** field of the **Publishers** table, this routine would return **Name = 'APRESS'** when the user selected this publisher from the **frmFind** form.

Finally, we want to display a message to the programmer if they try to search on an invalid field type, such as a **Boolean** or **Memo** field. This way, the first time they test the find capability they will see the error of their ways:

```
Case Else
    sMessage = "Sorry, you can't use the find feature on fields"
    sMessage = sMessage & " of type: " & fField.Type
    iIndx = MsgBox(sMessage, vbCritical, App.EXEName)
```

Try It Out - Updating Our cmdFind Routine

1 In order to take advantage of our new generalized **BuildCriteria** function, we will
simply change three lines of code. Open the **dataClass** class code module and go to the
ProcessCMD method.

Locate the **cmdFind** section and modify these seven highlighted lines of code:

```
Case cmdFind '-- find a specific record
    Dim iReturn As Integer
    gFindString = ""

    With frmFind
       .addCaption = mvarFindCaption
       .RecordSource = mvarFindRecordSource
       .Show vbModal
    End With
    If (Len(gFindString) > 0) Then
      Dim sResullt As String
       With mvardataCtl.Recordset
        sResult = BuildCriteria()
        If Len(sResult) >0 Then
         .FindFirst sResult
       If (.NoMatch) Then
          iReturn = MsgBox(mvarFindMatchField & " " & gFindString & _
                 " was not found.", vbCritical, App.EXEName)
       Else
          iReturn = MsgBox(mvarFindMatchField & " " & gFindString & _
               " was retrieved.", vbInformation, App.EXEName)
     End If
     end If
    End With
   End If
   updateButtons
```

How It Works

Recall how we had these two custom properties of the **frmFind** form (**addCaption** and
RecordSource) hard coded in this **ProcessCMD** method. Now we are permitting the
programmer to set the caption that will show up on the Find form, and the **RecordSource** that
will display whatever is desired. The programmer will set these using the **FindCaption** and
FindRecordSource properties we just added.

```
.addCaption = mvarFindCaption
.RecordSource = mvarFindRecordSource
```

Of course, the **FindMatchField** property we also just added will tell our **BuildCriteria**
method which field to match on in the recordset, so we no longer need the hard coded
statement **"Name = '" & gFindString & "'"**.

We also replace the lines:

```
iReturn = MsgBox("Publisher Name " & gFindString & _
   " was not found.", vbCritical, "Publisher")
Else
```

314

```
    iReturn = MsgBox("Publisher Name " & gFindString & _
        " was retrieved.", vbInformation, "Publisher")
```

with:

```
    iReturn = MsgBox(mvarFindMatchField & " " & gFindString & _
        " was not found.", vbCritical, App.EXEName)
Else
    iReturn = MsgBox(mvarFindMatchField & " " & gFindString & _
        " was retrieved.", vbInformation, App.EXEName)
```

Here we've just replaced the hard coded **"Publisher Name"** with the variable **mvarFindMatchField**, in which we can place the name of the field to search in. We've also replaced **"Publisher"** with **App.EXEName** (which holds the name of the currently running application) for the message box's caption.

Let's take these changes for a test drive. We want to ensure that our new and improved find routine will work on numbers as well as text.

Try It Out - Testing our Find Form

1 Bring up the **frmDataClass** form.

2 We now want to add values to the three new properties we just added for finding specific records. Add the following three lines of code to the **frmDataClass** form's **Activate** event procedure.

```
Private Sub Form_Activate()

Set myDataClass = New dataClass

With myDataClass
Set     .FormName = Me      'pass in the current form
Set     .dataCtl = Data1    'the data control to manage
Set     .ProgressBar = ProgressBar1
        .dbName = gDataBaseName
        .Buttons = "cmdButton"
        .RecordSource = "SELECT * FROM Publishers"
        .LabelToUpdate = lblRecordCount
        .FindCaption = "Select a Publisher's ID"
```

```
        .FindRecordSource = "SELECT PubID FROM Publishers"
        .FindMatchField = "PubID"
     .Tag = "1"          'identifies the controls
     .ProcessCMD 0       'default to the 1st record
End With

Text1.DataField = "Name"
End Sub
```

3 Let's give it a try. Press *F5* to run the program. Press Find to display the **frmFind** form. Notice that our custom title is prominently displayed. Now the user knows exactly what all of these numbers are. Select PubID 42 by double-clicking.

How It Works

Here we just set the **FindCaption** property of our **dataClass** class module to display a customized message on the **frmFind** form. Next, we provide the SQL string requesting the **frmFind** to retrieve and display all of the values from the **PubID** field in the **Publishers** table. Finally, when the user selects an option from the **frmFind** form, we instruct our class module which field (in the recordset currently being managed) should be matched. In this case, we want to match the **PubID** field.

As soon as the Find form is dismissed, our code in the **cmdFind** area of the **dataClass**'s ProcessCMD section went to work. The **BuildCriteria** method was called to determine what field type we were searching on. It determined that the field was numeric, so formatted the search string correctly and passed it to the **FindFirst** method of the recordset managed by our class. As you can see, everything worked as advertised.

Making Our Templates Available to All Our VB Projects

Now that we have done all of this hard work building our **frmDataClass** and **frmFind** forms as well as the **dataClass** class, we want to have them available for any new project. This is a snap. We will create what VB calls **templates**. We will now save these three items so they can be selected right from VB as choices for additions in any new project.

Try It Out - Creating Our Own DataClass Template

1 Select the **frmDataClass** form so it has the focus. Now from the main VB menu select File-Save frmDataClass.frm As... The Save File As dialog box is displayed. What we want to do is store this form in the VB template directory for forms. This is the special directory that VB 6.0 uses to display the various form choices available to us when we add a form to our project. My VB form template directory is here:

[*Drive letter*]:\Program Files\Microsoft\VB\Template\Form

Find your directory now. Once you locate the VB form template directory, save the form as **DataClass.frm**. By changing the name in the File name box, we will make this form a template. When you have located the directory and renamed the file, press Save.

2 Now do the same thing for the **frmFind**. Save this form as **FindForm.frm** in the same directory as the last form.

Now the next time you have an important project that requires data entry, you can simply add a new form to your project. However, instead of selecting a standard form, choose the DataClass form. Add another form and choose the FindForm. You would simply need to add a few text boxes and the dataClass class module and you'd be done!

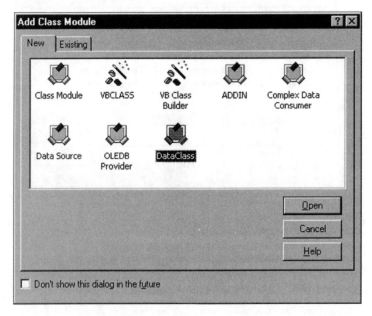

3 Now we want to save our **dataClass** class module. Highlight dataClass in the Project Explorer. Save the class as **DataClass.cls** in the following directory:

[*Drive letter*]:\Program Files\Microsoft\VB\Template\Classes

Now when you wish to use the new **DataClass** class, just add it to your project via the VB menu.

The nice thing about the **DataClass** is that you only need to add it once to any new project and you can use it as many times as required within the project. We simply dim an object variable as type **DataClass** each time we want to use the functionality of the class.

4 We want to save the **Globals.bas** module as well. Remember, this module holds the API function declaration, the location of the database, the **highLight** routine, and the global string that we use to pass information to and from the Find form. Before we save it, open the **Globals.bas** file and make this small update by appending the highlighted code:

```
Public Sub highLight()

If (Not Screen.ActiveForm Is Nothing) Then
 With Screen.ActiveForm
    If (TypeOf .ActiveControl Is TextBox) Then
     .ActiveControl.SelStart = 0
     .ActiveControl.SelLength = Len(.ActiveControl)
    End If
 End With
End If
End Sub
```

We want to add this code because this routine will be placed in bound text boxes. Why? Because when we are designing our form later, we want to temporarily set up the data control so that we can take advantage of the drop-down list box of fields in the **DataField** property. In other words, we don't want to type in - say - "Titles" in a text box bound to the **Titles** field - we just want to click on the choice. While testing our form, the **GotFocus** event, which triggers **highLight** gets fired before the controls (and even the form) are fully initialized. If we didn't take this precaution, we would get an error from VB because the **GotFocus** event will fire and, when the **Screen.ActiveForm** is referenced, it is not yet a fully initialized. VB can't find the reference, so it generates an error. This simple fix will permit us to work with the data control at design time.

5 When you have made the change, create a new directory called **Modules** in your **Template** directory. Save the **Globals.bas** code module as **DataGlobals.Bas** in the **Modules** directory.

When we select Add Module for our new project, we now have a new option - DataGlobals:

OK, we've set up all of our templates -

let's create something using these new facilities.

The figure below illustrates what were going to do:

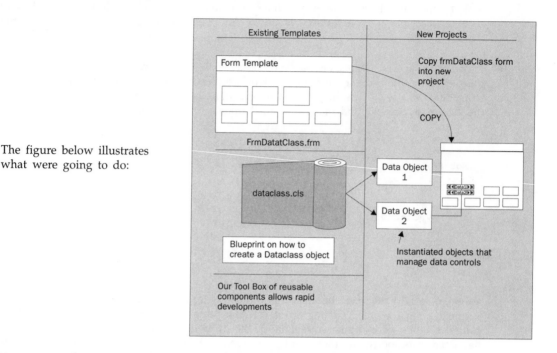

You can see that we're going to take our existing **dataClass** class module and instantiate it as two objects that manage data controls on a form. These will be combined with a form.

Try It Out - Create a Data-Entry Form Using Templates

We'll now see just how easy it is to create a fully functioning data-entry form with our new forms and class.

1 Start a new VB project. A default form will be added to our project. Right-click on the default form, Form1, in the Project Explorer. Select Remove Form1 to eliminate it from our project. Now select Project-Add Form from the VB menu. Select DataClass. Repeat the steps and add a form of type FindForm.

2 From the VB menu, select Project-Add Class Module and select DataClass. Now select Project-Add Module and select DataGlobals. Now select File-Save Project As... and save all of the files in \Chapter7\NewDataClass.

> *Important: If you don't specify where to save the new files, they will overwrite the originals in the template directories. By instructing VB to save them in a new directory, copies of the forms and modules will be placed in the new directory. We want to work on copies, not the originals! So please ensure these files are saved in another directory before moving on.*

Your Project Explorer should look like this now:

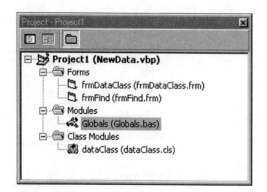

3   Let's say we want a data-entry form for the **Titles** table. We will use an entirely different table to what we have been using (i.e. **Publishers**) to show you just how powerful our class approach is. Set the data control's **DatabaseName** property to **[Drive]:\BegDB\Biblio.mdb** and the **RecordSource** property to **Titles**. This way we can get drop-down boxes in the Properties window when we need to define the **DataField** property of each of our text boxes. Add four text boxes according to the following table:

Control	Property	Value
Text1	DataSource	Data1
	DataField	Title
	Tag	1
	Text	Title
Text2	DataSource	Data1
	DataField	Year Published
	Tag	1
	Text	Year Published
Text3	DataSource	Data1
	DataField	ISBN
	Tag	1
	Text	ISBN
Text4	DataSource	Data1
	DataField	PubID
	Locked	True
	Text	PubID

4 Lay out the bound text boxes so they look like this. Then add four labels as shown:

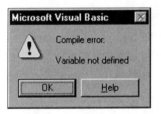

5 Select Project-References from the main VB menu and add Microsoft DAO 3.51 Object Library. Since we did not draw a data control on a form, it was already embedded on the **frmDataClass** form, the reference is not automatically added for us. If you forget to add the reference, the first time VB comes across a DAO constant, such as **dbEditNone**, it will generate a Variable not defined error.

6 Open the **Activate** event procedure on the **frmDataClass** and make the following changes:

```
Private Sub Form_Activate()

Set myDataClass = New dataClass

With myDataClass
Set .FormName = Me      'pass in the current form
Set .dataCtl = Data1    'the data control to manage
Set .ProgressBar = ProgressBar1
    .dbName = gDataBaseName
    .Buttons = "cmdButton"
    .RecordSource = "SELECT * FROM Titles"
    .LabelToUpdate = lblRecordCount
    .FindCaption = "Select a Book Title"
    .FindRecordSource = "SELECT Title FROM Titles ORDER BY Title"
    .FindMatchField = "Title"
```

```
    .Tag = "1"          'identifies the controls
    .ProcessCMD 0       'default to the 1st record
End With
```

```
Text3.SetFocus
```

```
End Sub
```

We are setting the **RecordSource** property of the data control managed by our instance of **dataClass**. The only other thing we must do is set up the customized search criteria. We pass in the SQL statement for the **FindRecordSource** property that is sent to the Find form from our class. Notice that we are using the SQL structure **ORDER BY Title**. This will return the recordset in sorted order. Finally, we set the **FindMatchField** property to **"Title"**. This is so that when the user selects a title from the Find form, we want to match the choice with the field **Title** in the **Titles** table. That property is used by our **BuildCriteria** method, which constructs the search criteria string that is passed to the **FindFirst** method in **dataClass**.

We then add the line **Text3.SetFocus**. This simply ensures that the **ISBN** field gets focus when the form is initialized. We don't want the focus to be in some random location.

7 In the **GotFocus** event procedures of each of the four text boxes, add this line:

```
Private Sub Text1_GotFocus()
  highLight
End Sub
```

> *Of course, if you choose to use a control array of text boxes, then this only needs to be added in the common **GotFocus()** event.*

8 Remember when we set the data control's **DatabaseName** property to **[Drive]:\BegDB\Biblio.mdb** and the **RecordSource** property to **Titles**? That was so we could take advantage of the drop-down list of choices for the text boxes' **DataField** property. Now go back to the Properties window for the data control and delete the **DatabaseName** property and the **RecordSource** property. Remember that we can't be sure where the database will be when our program is installed on the users' machine. So for now, we are keeping a reference to the database in the **Globals.bas** file. Later in the book, we will cover how to locate the database no matter where it might be located.

9 Finally, we must process any commands from the array of command buttons on the **frmDataClass** form. Yes, you must place two lines of code here.

The first just sets the focus to the **ISBN** text box whenever the user makes any selection from the buttons. It simply sets the focus in the same place no matter what the user does. There is a saying that consistency is the hobgoblin of small minds, but when it comes to user interfaces, it is a virtue. Users will look at you with awe and admiration. Previously we did this in the **Reposition** event of the data control. Now though, since our class does not know which field you may want to get the focus, we just add it here.

Then in the second line, we pass in the **Index** of the **cmdButton** pressed to the **ProcessCMD** method of our class. Now our class does all of the dirty work that we once had in the **cmdButton_Click** event procedure.

```
Private Sub cmdButton_Click(Index As Integer)
Text3.SetFocus
myDataClass.ProcessCMD Index
End Sub
```

10 Select Project-Project1 Properties... and select frmDataClass as the Startup Object. Press *F5* to run your project. Go ahead and test out all of the navigation and edit keys. They will all work as advertised. Now press the Find button. Our customized Find form is displayed. Notice that the custom title is displayed over the text box and the book titles are displayed in alphabetical order. It may take a few seconds to fill the list box. There are over 8,000 entries that must be loaded.

11 Type beg in the text box. Remember that we used an API call to jump to the first entry that partially matches what is typed in. Double-click the Beginners Guide to Visual Basic. The name is stashed in the **gFindString** global variable in the **Globals.bas** code module and the form gets dismissed. Control returns to our class module, which then reads the length of **gFindString** in the **Case cmdFind** section of the **ProcessCMD** method. If the length is > 0, we know a selection has been made. Next, our method **BuildCriteria** determines the type of field and formats the find criteria string appropriately. The result is passed to the **FindFirst** method of the data control managed by our class. Voila!

12 If you wish to edit an entry, the command buttons get disabled, except for Save and Undo. Go ahead and press Edit to test our class out. The caption Editing gets placed in the **lblCaption** label to inform the user what we are doing. The fields get unlocked and the background color changes to yellow. Then the first field gets focus; the **highLight** routine is called to make this happen. Not a bad example of code reuse!

How It Works

Let's take a moment to consider what we just did. We created a brand new project. We added the **DataClass.frm** and the **FindForm.frm** from the VB template choices. We then selected the **DataClass.cls** class module and the **DataGlobals.bas** code module, also from VB template choices. By way of a few mouse clicks, we added the basis for our new data-entry project.

We added four bound text boxes, as this project allows data-entry. So really all we had to do was to clean up a few details, such as calling **highLight** and the **ProcessCMD** method from our array of control buttons. That's it!

Remember earlier on when I said it was possible to develop a fully functional data-entry screen in about 15 minutes? Well, here it is. We selected an arbitrary table and some arbitrary fields, rearranged a few things to make our form look nice, and we're done. Hopefully, you will find this code we just wrote helpful in future projects.

> *Note: If you need a data-entry form, but don't want to provide a Find feature, simply set the* **Visible** *property of that button to* **False***. This way, the user does not even know it is there, but there is no need to change the underlying template.*

Data Validation...Again

Of course, we will still need data validation for production code. The one thing about validation rules is that they are usually specific to each form. Our class can't know in advance what the specific rules might be. Some fields might be mandatory. Others might require numeric values only. Those are the types of things that will vary from form to form. So just add any validation you might need in the **Validate** event of the data control. If you were building a **Publishers** table data-entry screen, the code might look something like this:

```
Private Sub Data1_Validate(Action As Integer, Save As Integer)

    Dim iResponse As Integer

    If (Action = vbDataActionUpdate) Then
      If (Len(Text1(1)) = 0) Then
        iResponse = MsgBox("Please enter a Company name.", _
                    vbInformation + vbOKOnly, "Publisher's Table")
        Text1(1).SetFocus
        Save = 0
        Action = 0
      End If
    End If

End Sub
```

Do you get the idea? With each specific data-entry screen you design, there will be some fields that are required. Other fields might require numeric values only. However, each particular data-entry form will have it's own special needs.

The **dataClass** class distilled all of the common elements of data entry - field navigation, setting the buttons to reflect the state, editing, adding, finding records, etc. By using the class, we can concentrate on the application itself. We can now zero in on adding the specific items, such as data validation. All of the common tasks have been encapsulated in the class for us and in my experience, 80% of all code is either common tasks or error handling.

Each time you use the template for data entry, you get all of the functionality in the class, as well as a common look and feel. You have just cut down development time orders of magnitude. You will probably find ways to enhance the **dataClass**. In fact, we will be tweaking the class in just a moment. Please feel free to add any additional properties, methods, or validation routines you may need to make the **dataClass** even more powerful.

The Object Browser - Revisited

Press *F2* to bring up the Object Browser. Take a look at your class **dataClass**. Examining a class that you build with the browser is the best way to become friends with the capabilities of this tool. You now know 'exactly' what the properties and methods mean because you wrote them. It's now easy to take this knowledge and apply it to any other object you may browse.

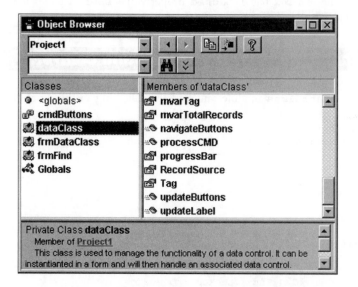

*If you want to add or change a description of a property, no problem. You can do so without the Class Builder. Bring up the code window of the **dataClass**, select Tools from the VB menu and click Procedure Attributes. Here you can select the procedure you wish to modify, enter a description and click OK. The new description will now show up in the Object Browser.*

Refining Our dataClass Class

When we were building our class module, we were only concerned about text boxes. However, if you are going to use this in business solutions, there will be times you want to display data in a grid format. Consider the **DBGrid** control. We could use our **dataClass** to manage a grid control. Remember our **lockTheControls** method? It's just fine for locking/unlocking text boxes. But where the text box has a **Locked** property, the **DBGrid** has a few more properties we must be concerned with.

Try It Out - What if We Want to Use a DBGrid Control?

1 Bring up the **dataClass** module and add the following to the **lockTheControls** subroutine.

```
Private Sub lockTheControls(bLocked As Boolean)

On Error Resume Next

Dim iIndx As Integer

With mvarFormName
For iIndx = 0 To .Controls.Count - 1
    If (.Controls(iIndx).Tag = mvarTag) Then
        If (TypeOf .Controls(iIndx) Is TextBox) Then
            If (bLocked) Then
                .Controls(iIndx).Locked = True
                .Controls(iIndx).BackColor = vbWhite
            Else
                .Controls(iIndx).Locked = False
                .Controls(iIndx).BackColor = vbYellow
            End If
        ElseIf (TypeOf .Controls(iIndx) Is DBGrid) Then
            If (bLocked) Then
                .Controls(iIndx).AllowAddNew = False
                .Controls(iIndx).AllowDelete = False
                .Controls(iIndx).AllowUpdate = False
                .Controls(iIndx).BackColor = vbWhite
            Else
                .Controls(iIndx).AllowAddNew = True
                .Controls(iIndx).AllowDelete = True
                .Controls(iIndx).AllowUpdate = True
                .Controls(iIndx).BackColor = vbYellow
            End If
        End If
    End If
Next
End With
End Sub
```

As you can see, a few more properties need to be set before using the **DBGrid** control. When the control is locked, we want to set the **AllowAddNew**, **AllowDelete** and **AllowUpdate** properties to **False** as well as resetting the background color to white. When unlocked, we set these properties to **True** and set the background color to yellow to ensure we have a consistent user interface. As you add more controls to your interfaces, simply update this code to handle them. For example, your projects might include spin buttons or list boxes. Just add a check for them and set the appropriate properties.

2 While we are in the **dataClass** module sprucing things up a bit, we must add one line of code in the **Let RecordSource** property. We will soon be demonstrating how our new class can be used for parent/child forms. Well, whenever the class that manages the parent recordset moves to another record, the **dataClass** managing the child record source must gather up all associated records. Therefore, we must make a call to **updateButtons** after each **Refresh** to the data control managed by our class. This will ensure that if our class is used to manage a child recordset, the buttons will be updated correctly each time the user navigates to a new parent record.

When a new parent record is made current, the data control managing the child records must be updated to show each child record associated with the new parent. As such, the buttons for the child **dataClass** must then be updated. So by placing this single line of code below, we ensure that our **dataClass** can easily manage the display of child records.

```
Public Property Let RecordSource(ByVal vData As String)
    mvarRecordSource = vData

    If (mvardataCtl Is Nothing) Then
        Exit Property
    End If

    mvardataCtl.DatabaseName = mvardbName
    mvardataCtl.RecordSource = mvarRecordSource
    mvardataCtl.Refresh

    If (mvardataCtl.Recordset.RecordCount < 1) Then
        mvarTotalRecords = 0
        Exit Property
    End If

    Screen.MousePointer = vbHourglass
    mvardataCtl.Recordset.MoveLast
    mvarTotalRecords = mvardataCtl.Recordset.RecordCount
    mvardataCtl.Recordset.MoveFirst
    updateButtons  'added for child
    Screen.MousePointer = vbDefault

End Property
```

3 Now save our improved class in your **\Template\Classes** directory as **DataClass.cls**.

In order to show how flexible this class really is; let's create a parent/child form using our improved **dataClass** data control class. This will really show off the power of classes and objects.

A Parent/Child Form - the Data Control Class in Action

Many times we need to show both a parent record with its associated child records. For example, we might want to show a publisher with its associated titles records. By using our new **dataClass** class, we can do so with a minimum of coding on our part. We will have two data controls working in concert (a parent and a child) so we have to take a few extra precautions. Don't worry though, we will walk through everything in detail so you will be comfortable on how to do this with any parent/child relationships you may encounter.

We will place two data controls on our form. **Data1** will manage the **Publishers** table and **Data2** will handle the **Titles** table. When the user selects a publisher, all of the related titles will be displayed in a grid control. We will create two objects from our **dataClass** class module, one for each data control. So we will only have a single class module in our project, but we will instantiate two objects from it.

Try It Out - Building a Parent/Child Form

1 Create a new project and add the template files we created earlier, i.e. the DataClass and FindForm forms, the improved DataClass class and the DataGlobals module. Rearrange the command array of buttons as shown. It looks a bit strange because we are going to actually hide a few of the controls when we resize the form. **We can't delete any unneeded buttons!** Remember that our class looks at each of them. So they don't need to be visible - but they must be there. If there are any buttons you do not wish to use, just move them out of view. Move the Add New, Save, Undo, Edit, Delete and Done buttons to the bottom of the form. We will hide these in a bit. Now add two text boxes and a second data control, **Data2**.

The controls, properties and values of the command buttons are specified in the table below:

Control	Property	Value
Data1	DatabaseName	Biblio.mdb
	RecordSource	Publishers
	Caption	Publishers
	Enabled	False
Data2	DatabaseName	Biblio.mdb
	RecordSource	Titles
	Caption	Titles
	Enabled	False
Text1	DataSource	Data1
	DataField	PubID
	Text	PubID
	Tag	1
	BackColor	&H00C0C0C0& - gray
Text2	DataSource	Data1
	DataField	Name
	Text	Name

2 Right click on the tools palette and select Components. Choose the Microsoft Data Bound Grid Control 5.0 (SP3) and add it to your tool palette.

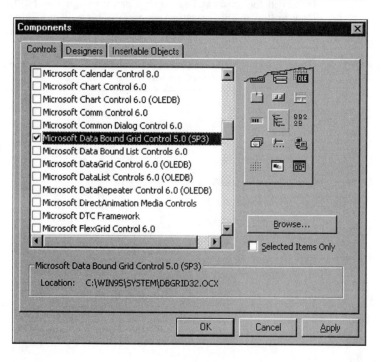

3 Add a grid control to your **frmDataClass** form as shown below:

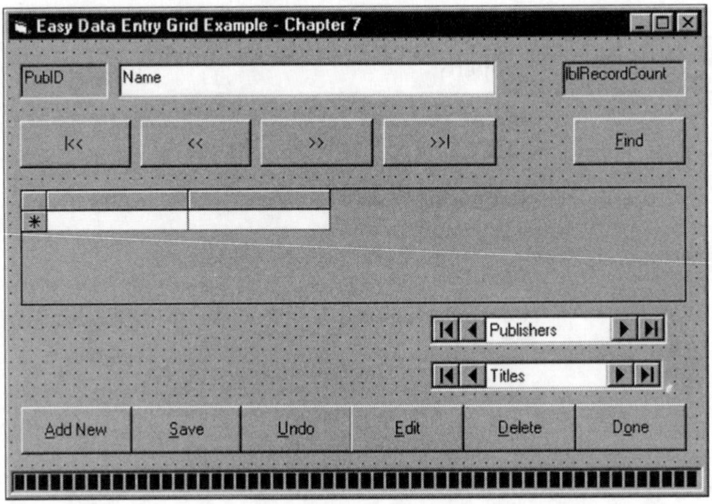

4 **Data1** will be handling the **Publishers** table and **Data2** will take care of the **Titles** table. We must now create a new control array of buttons for the **Data2** data control. The built-in control array, **cmdButton**, just manages the **Publishers** table via **Data1**.

Now create a new control array of eleven buttons to manage the **Titles** table. The new control array should be placed below the grid control and above the editing buttons of the **cmdButton** control array. Name the new control array **cmdTitles**. We will use each button in the **cmdTitles** control array except the Find button, so move it below the Add New button in the **cmdTitles** array. This will be hidden. It is critical that you get the **Index** properties correct in the **cmdTitles** control array. The **Index** properties should be as follows:

Button Caption	Index
|<<	0
<<	1
>>	2
>>|	3
&Add New	4
&Edit	5
&Save	6
&Delete	7
&Undo	8
&Find (this will be hidden, but create it)	9
D&one	10

The buttons in the **cmdTitles** control array should be arranged as shown below. Make sure the Find button, **cmdTitles(9)**, is positioned beneath the other buttons in the **cmdTitles** control array and above the editing buttons of the **cmdButton** array. When we resize the form, this Find button, as well as the data controls and the editing buttons from **cmdButtons** will be hidden.

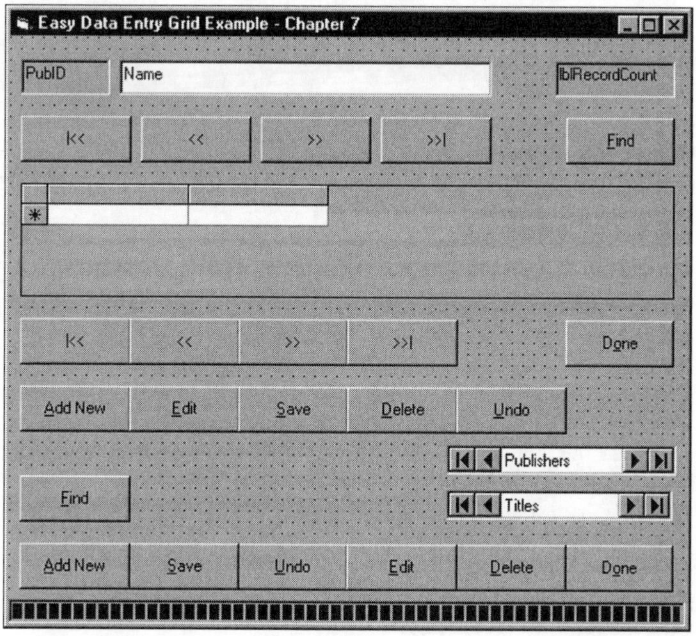

Remember that our class looks at the **Index** number of the control array button pressed. So we must be sure that they are created in the correct position. Since we are hiding the Find button (control array position 9), the user can't see it. However, as our class loops through each button to enable/disable them, the button is there on the form so our class works fine. The class does not know or care that we have hidden the button. It can find it so the code works. In other projects, you may choose to set the **Visible** property of some of the control array buttons to **False**. No problem. As long as the buttons exist on the form in the correct order, your code will work.

5 Set the **DataSource** of the DBgrid to **Data2** and the **Tag** to **2**. Add a new label called **lblTitles** below the grid control, and set its **BorderStyle** property to **1 - Fixed Single** and its **Caption** to **lblTitles**. Now resize the form as shown. We keep all of the control array buttons we don't need - they just get hidden when we resize the form.

6 Now that we have laid out the form, we need to add a bit of code. In the General Declarations section of the **frmDataClass** form, delete the following line:

```
Dim myDataClass As dataClass
```

Now add these two lines:

```
Option Explicit
    Dim publishersClass As dataClass
    Dim titlesClass As dataClass
```

7 Now move on to the **Activate** event of the **frmDataClass** form. Amend the code so that it looks like this:

```
Private Sub Form_Activate()

    Set publishersClass = New dataClass
    Set titlesClass = New dataClass

With publishersClass
    Set .FormName = Me      'pass in the current form
    Set .dataCtl = Data1    'the data control to manage
    Set .ProgressBar = ProgressBar1
    .dbName = gDataBaseName
    .Buttons = "cmdButton"
    .RecordSource = "SELECT * FROM Publishers"
    .LabelToUpdate = lblRecordCount
    .FindCaption = "Select a Publisher"
    .FindRecordSource = "SELECT Name FROM Publishers ORDER BY Name"
    .FindMatchField = "Name"
    .Tag = "1"              'identifies the controls
    .ProcessCMD 0           'default to the 1st record
End With
```

```
    With titlesClass
        Set .FormName = Me
        Set .dataCtl = Data2
        Set .ProgressBar = ProgressBar1
        .dbName = gDataBaseName
        .Buttons = "cmdTitles"
        .RecordSource = "SELECT * FROM Titles WHERE PubID = " _
                        & Data1.Recordset!PubID
        .LabelToUpdate = lblTitles
        .Tag = "2"
        .ProcessCMD 0
    End With
End Sub
```

Notice that we are creating two separate objects from our single class. One will manage our **Publishers** table and the other the **Titles** table.

```
Set publishersClass = New dataClass
Set titlesClass = New dataClass
```

Other than that, we have covered setting these properties already. The only point that bears reviewing is the **RecordSource** property for displaying the child records in the grid. Here we are building an SQL statement requesting all titles that have the same **PubID** value as the current record in the **Publishers** table.

```
.RecordSource = "SELECT * FROM TITLES WHERE PubID = " _
                & Data1.Recordset!PubID
```

We also set the **Tag** property to **2**. This way our **dataClass** can find the grid control for locking and unlocking. That is the bound control that will be managed by the **titlesClass** object.

8 We have to call the **ProcessCMD** method, of course. Add this code to the **cmdButton_Click** event procedure. We want to set the focus to the Name text box whenever the user clicks a navigation or Find button. Remember that these are the only ones we are showing our user. We can then go and pass the **Index** value to our class method - add these two lines:

```
Private Sub cmdButton_Click(Index As Integer)
```

```
Text2.SetFocus
publishersClass.ProcessCMD Index
```

```
End Sub
```

Likewise, when the user clicks one of the **cmdTitles** buttons, we want to inform our **titlesClass**. There is one thing we must be aware of with this particular table. The **PubID** field is required. If we don't provide a value for this field, we get an error message. This is one of those form specific instances we need to concern ourselves about. Know your tables and your indexes and required fields. This will allow you to handle the specifics for the underlying table.

Whenever the user adds a new record, we place the primary key of the current **Publishers** record (located in **Data1.Recordset!PubID**) into the foreign key field of the new record just added (located in **Data2.Recordset!PubID**). The new **Titles** record hasn't been saved yet, we are simply placing the correct value in this field in case it is saved. If we didn't place a correct value in this field, VB would remind us with error '3314' because this is defined as a required field in the database.

9   Since this is a required field, let's just go ahead and add the value to the recordset for the user. We inform the **titlesClass** of the **Index** of the button pressed as expected. However, if the button was Add New - index position 4 - we want to take the value of the **PubID** from the parent **Publishers** record and update the **PubID** of the new **Titles** record. The record is not added yet - it is tentative until the user presses Save, then it gets committed to the database. Of course, the user could select Undo, which cancels the operation, but here we ensure that the correct value gets added automatically. And why don't we use **cmdAddNew** instead of **Index = 4**? Good question. We have not defined these enumerated constants in our form and they are private to our class. Since we only need to interrogate this one button in our form, let's just stick with using the array index. It's cleaner and faster. However, we'll make a notation that we are adding in the code.

```
Private Sub cmdTitles_Click(Index As Integer)
```

```
titlesClass.ProcessCMD Index

If (Index = 4) Then            ' we know it is an add
  Data2.Recordset!PubID = Data1.Recordset!PubID
End If
```

```
End Sub
```

The Various Gotchas in a Parent/Child Data-Entry Form Revealed

We have two data controls on a single form working in concert with each other, so we need to cover a few subtle things that will crop up and plague the unprepared.

When the user navigates the parent **Publishers** table, we want to refresh the grid to show each of the titles associated with that publisher. We have to be careful that when the form is initializing, the **Reposition** event will fire. As mentioned, when we load the form, the **Data1** data control gets initialized. The **Reposition** event will fire then. In addition, when we are creating the object for the **Data1** data control, this event will fire again. The

Data1_Reposition event will fire a few times before we actually create the object **titlesClass**. If we attempted to set any of the properties for the **titlesClass** object before we have instantiated it, we would receive the following friendly reminder that our object variable has not been set.

Try It Out - Checking that titlesClass has been Instantiated

1   So let's just check to see if our class has been instantiated yet. If it has, then we know it is safe to pass a value to our **RecordSource** property.

```
Private Sub Data1_Reposition()
```
```
If (TypeName(titlesClass) <> "Nothing") Then
titlesClass.RecordSource = _
        "SELECT * FROM Titles WHERE PubID = " _
        & Data1.Recordset!PubID
End If
End Sub
```

How It Works

This line of code will ensure that we don't attempt to set any properties of the **titlesClass** until it is instantiated.

```
If (TypeName(titlesClass) <> "Nothing") Then
```

Once we are assured that the object has been created, we can go ahead and set the **RecordSource** property of our object.

```
titlesClass.RecordSource = _
"SELECT * FROM Titles WHERE PubID = " _
& Data1.Recordset!PubID
```

The **SELECT** is a SQL statement. We will be covering SQL in detail in the next chapter. However, you can probably guess what the statement is saying. We are creating a recordset of all of the **Titles** records where the foreign key **PubID** in the **Titles** table is equal to the primary key in the current **Publishers** table. Any titles for this publisher will be added to the recordset for the **Data2** data control and displayed in the **DBGrid** control.

Try It Out - Adding New Titles Records...

1   We are only permitting record navigation and a <u>F</u>ind operation on the **Publishers** table.
However, we will permit the user to add new **Titles** records. Before we permit the user
to save a new or modified record to the database, we pass it through our business rules.
The best place to put these rules is in the **Validate** event procedure of the **Data2** data
control. Here we just check the **ISBN**, **Title** and **Year Published** fields, but you can
add any additional business rules you require. When a rule is not met, we cancel the
action that would move the current record and set **Save** to **False** to ensure that the
record is not saved until the validation criteria are met. However, the user can still choose
to undo the change.

```
Private Sub Data2_Validate(Action As Integer, Save As Integer)
'=========================================================
'== Place Business rules for the Titles records here ==
'=========================================================
If (Action = vbDataActionUpdate) Then
  If (Len(DBGrid1.Columns("ISBN").Text) < 5) Then
    DBGrid1.Col = 3
    MsgBox ("Please enter a valid ISBN number.")
    Action = 0
    Save = False
    Exit Sub
  ElseIf (Len(DBGrid1.Columns("Title").Text) < 3) Then
    MsgBox ("Please enter a valid Title.")
    Action = 0
    Save = False
    Exit Sub
  ElseIf (Len(DBGrid1.Columns("Year Published").Text) < 4) Then
    MsgBox ("Please enter a valid Year Published.")
    Action = 0
    Save = False
    Exit Sub
  End If
End If
End Sub
```

Now if the user attempts to save a record without entering a
valid ISBN, VB will display a message informing them of the
error of their ways.

2 From the VB menu, select Project-Project1 Properties. Specify frmDataClass as the Startup Object. Finally, press *F5* and run the program. You've earned it.

Summary

I hope you appreciate the data control class module and find uses for it in your everyday database applications. I have used it in software systems that are currently in use across the United States. Just think, without the class, we would have had to code all of the functionality we encapsulated for each of the two data controls. This is a perfect example of why we should use classes for any code that is reusable.

The data control is perfect for user interfaces, but not for behind the scenes database access. When we investigate DAO, you will see how we can program Jet directly. You will also see when it makes sense to use the data control and when it's better to use DAO. At this point though, you have mastered the data control and will have noticed its strengths and weaknesses.

What We Learned

- Classes enable us to achieve **code reusability**. Classes manage tedious, repetitive tasks. The class can then be reused with any form.

- A **class** is a **template** for something we want to build. An **object** is the manifestation, or **instance**, of that class.

- Whenever we need to refer to an object we use its **object variable**.

- The **Class Builder** can assist in the mundane tasks of setting up property and method templates.

- For every property that we define, the Class Builder adds a **member variable** (**mvar**) to hold the value of that property.

- Our private mvar variables can only be accessed via our properties - this is known as **data encapsulation**.

▶ We can make a property **write-only** by deleting the **Property Get**. To make a property **read-only** we need to delete the **Property Set** or **Let**.

▶ Public subroutines within our class are seen as methods to the outside world.

▶ We can instantiate as many objects from our class as we need. We created two objects from our **dataClass** class and used them to display parent and child records on a form.

Exercises

1 What is the relationship between a class and an object?

2 What is the difference between a **Private** and **Public** member of a class?

3 What do **Property Let**, **Property Set** and **Property Get** procedures do? Why would you use these procedures rather than a **Public** variable?

4 What code must you add to a procedure in your form that allows you to create and setup an object from a class named **dtaClass**?

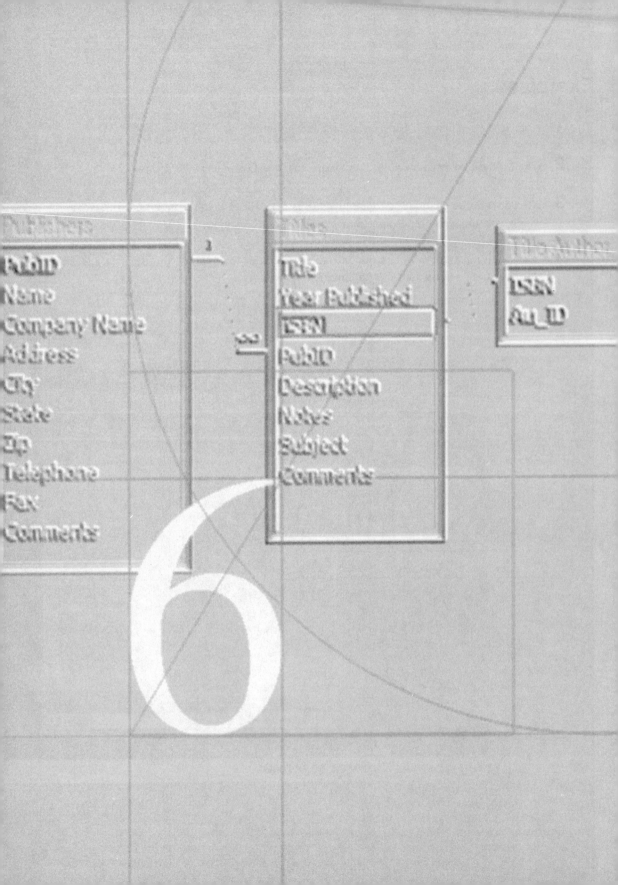

Getting the Data You Want from the Database

In this chapter we'll take our first steps into the world of SQL. We'll see that SQL is one of the key bits of grammar that we use with the languages that allow us to communicate with relational databases. The great thing about learning about SQL here is that this knowledge is applicable to whichever relational database access technology we use - DAO, ADO, SQL Server, or whatever. As an industry standard, SQL is an important tool for us to learn about and use.

Here's how we'll go about discovering SQL:

- The **background** to SQL
- Getting at the data we need - **SQL syntax** and **keywords**
- Building a SQL query-tester
- Using SQL to retrieve specific data from databases
- Retrieving only data that matches specified criteria - **filtering** the recordset
- **Grouping** the results of queries
- Retrieving data from multiple tables - **joining** data
- Generating **dynamic SQL** based on choices selected on the user interface

We'll start by looking at the background to the development of SQL.

SQL - What's the Story?

SQL - Where do we start? Well, the beginning is usually a good place. This book is about Visual Basic 6.0 and databases. A database is a powerful tool, but if we can't retrieve the data we need, it's worse than useless. We would quickly become frustrated if we couldn't easily and quickly retrieve all of the valuable information stored inside.

Luckily there is a standardized way of asking our database to give us the specific information we need: **Structured Query Language**, or **SQL**. SQL is really a database programming language. It is closely associated with the invention of the relational database by Dr. E. F. Codd in the footloose and care-free days of the early 1970s.

Over the years, SQL has evolved into a widely used standard. To ensure consistency of the language, it is defined by an **ANSI** (American National Standards Institute) standard. However, even with the standardization, there are still minor variations of the language in different database implementations and Jet is no exception. The variations are minor and generally a superset of (or addition to) the ANSI SQL. So when we vary from the standard, this will be pointed out to you. You may or may not want to use the Jet specific variations. Although they are powerful, if you include them in a query requesting information from another database management system - Oracle, for example - they won't work. However, if you are using Jet with Access, then by all means take advantage of the extra power and ease of use that these database-specific implementations provide. As I said - they are powerful and easy to use.

> *If want to learn more about the differences between Jet SQL and the versions used by large-scale enterprise databases, in particular SQL Server, then please refer to Appendix A - One Standard, Many Flavors.*

Is It a Language, Is It a Technology? No, It's SQL!

OK, even though SQL is called a language, that term can be just a bit misleading. You see SQL is not a complete programming language like Visual Basic. For example, it does not have an **If...Then...Else** construct for testing conditions. Nor does it have **Do** or **For** statements.

In reality, SQL is more like a sub-language consisting of about 30 or so specialized statements for database management tasks. These statements are then embedded into another real programming language, like Visual Basic. SQL is not a stand-alone product; it can't be used by itself. You can't go to your favorite computer store and say, "I want to purchase SQL". Instead, SQL is an important part of a database management system - a language for communicating with Jet, or most database engines for that matter. What you learn in this chapter will help you communicate with just about any database on the market.

We have actually been using simple SQL statements when we programmed the data control. For example, the "**SELECT * FROM TITLES**" string is really an SQL statement. The Microsoft Jet engine will accept SQL statements like the one above. Jet takes the SQL query - which is just text - and **parses** (breaks apart), analyzes and optimizes it. Then the action requested by the query is carried out and a recordset is returned.

SQL - Your Co-operative and Flexible Co-worker

With SQL, we can not only retrieve records, but perform other tasks as well, such as updating or deleting records in a database - directly, on one or more tables. For example, say we want to update the price of all green widgets by 10%. A simple SQL statement can update these records for us in one fell swoop. Alternatively, we might wish to permit the user to delete all records that have a date less than, say, January 1, 1998, for a clean-up process. A simple one-line SQL statement will take care of that for us as well. So you see, SQL is a two-edged sword. It will do our bidding, but it expects us to know what we are doing. We have to be on our toes always because it is so easy to delete hundreds or thousands of records with a single line of code. You may recall that in our class module, we always prompt the user when deleting a single record. Well, using SQL, we can delete all records with a single command! So we must use this power with caution. However, we will see that SQL can permit us to do a lot of work with a single command.

Another neat feature is that we can also create **dynamic SQL queries**. These are SQL queries that we actually build as the program is running. For example, you might have a form with several choices for the user. Once the choices are made, we can dynamically embed the variables that store these choices in a SQL statement that will retrieve only the records the user needs - all on the fly. This approach is incredibly useful when we want the user to select parameters for a report or graph. The user might want to see all widgets purchased between March and April of 1998. We can have a pre-structured SQL query that retrieves widgets; the only thing it needs us to do is prompt the user to insert a date range.

Getting the Data We Need

Essentially, SQL has a simple basic grammar. To get a database engine to process some SQL, we construct a SQL **statement**. In SQL terms, a **statement** is the whole string of SQL keywords and supplementary information (such as table and field names) that we ask the database engine to process for us. The statement tells the database engine (Jet, in our case), what data we want to access, and what we want to do with it. A statement is broken up into **clauses**, each of which contains a specific SQL keyword and the additional information that belongs with that keyword. In this chapter we will build SQL **statements** using the **clauses** as building blocks.

Some SQL statements just read (**query**) the database, but others can update or delete records. In this chapter, although we will perform updating and deleting, we will concentrate on queries that retrieve data. These data retrieval queries are embodied in **SELECT** statements.

Introducing the SELECT Statement

When we look at SQL from 50,000 feet, we notice that there are just six fundamental parts (four of them optional) of a SQL **SELECT** statement.

We use these six basic **SELECT** statement components and add detailed information to them to fill out the specifics of the query. The combination of SQL keywords and the information that we provide tells SQL (and thereby Jet) which fields from which tables we want to retrieve, and in what form we want to see them.

The table below shows us summary of the basic components - or keywords - of a SQL **SELECT** query:

SQL Keyword		Specific Information/Data We Provide
SELECT		The columns (i.e. fields) to be selected
FROM		The table name(s)
JOIN	Optional	If we are using multiple tables, we define how they are joined
GROUP BY	Optional	Columns used for grouping aggregate functions
HAVING	Optional	Criteria set for aggregate functions
ORDER BY	Optional	Defines how the recordset should be sorted

The general format for SQL commands is:

```
KEYWORD <data> KEYWORD <data>...
```

Now don't worry if this looks complicated. It really is straightforward once you get the hang of it. Please trust me on this one. We will go over everything in detail, as it is critical that you learn your way around SQL to become a truly proficient database programmer. So we will take our time, and have fun as well.

The entire SQL language consists of about 30 statements. Each statement requests a specific action from the database. We might want to retrieve records or delete records - the keywords tell the database exactly what to do.

The Simplest SQL Statement - Revealed!

The **SELECT** statement is the most commonly used SQL command. The **SELECT** clause defines the data items to be retrieved by the **SELECT** statement. The items might be fields (usually known as **columns** in SQL-speak) from a database table.

The **SELECT** clause is fundamental to setting up a command that will retrieve data for us. Starting with the simplest possible SQL query, we can say:

```
SELECT * FROM Tablename
```

The * means 'all the records in all the columns'. So there it is, the simplest SQL statement of all - 'select all the records in all the columns from the named table'.

Let's elaborate on this a little. For example, the following **SELECT** query will return all columns of all records in the **Publishers** table:

```
SELECT * FROM Publishers
```

The **SELECT** clause lists the columns (i.e. fields) to be retrieved for the **SELECT** statement. The asterisk, or **wildcard** character, indicates that all columns (fields) of the named table are to be retrieved. Later on, you will see how you could specify that only certain columns are to be retrieved. After all, most times when we query a database we only want to see certain fields that meet our user's criteria.

The **FROM** clause lists the table(s) that contain the fields to be retrieved in the **SELECT** clause. So our statement in English simply says, "**SELECT** all of the fields **FROM** the **Publishers** table."

The real power of SQL will be revealed when you want to limit or filter the records that are returned from the database. We might only want to retrieve the records from the **Publishers** table that show publishers that reside in New York City. If the **Publishers** table has a field that identifies the city the publisher resided in, we can easily construct a query that will make the database engine perform this task.

Build the SQL Query Tester

I hope you are like me in that I need to actually see what is happening when talking about SQL. It's all fine and good to talk in abstraction about SQL queries, but I like to actually see the results of my query. So let's build a simple SQL Query Tester program. This will permit us to try the queries as we read about them and see the results for ourselves. This is the best and easiest way for you to master SQL.

Try It Out - The SQL Query Tester Program

1 Create a new subdirectory in your **BegDB** directory and call it **Chapter8**. Start a new project called **prjSQL**. Add a DBGrid, six labels, a text box, a command button and a data control as shown:

Control	Property	Value
DbGrid1	Caption	SQL Results
	DataSource	Data1
Label1	Caption	Record Count
Label2	Caption	Current Record
Label3	Caption	Updatable
lblRecordCount	BorderStyle	1 - Fixed Single
	Caption	No caption
lblCurrentRecord	BorderStyle	1 - Fixed Single
	Caption	No caption
lblUpdatable	Borderstyle	1 - Fixed Single
	Caption	No caption

Control	Property	Value
Text1	Multiline	True
	ScrollBars	2 - Vertical
	Text	Blank
cmdRun	Caption	&Execute
	Default	False
Data1	DatabaseName	C:\BegDB\Biblio.mdb

Take care to make sure that the **Default** property of the **cmdRun** button is set to **False**. If you don't do this, then each time you press the *Enter* key while editing in the text box (for example, when you get to the end of a line in a long SQL statement) the **cmdRun** button will execute - we don't want this to happen.

> *When* **Default** *is* **True**, *any time you press the Enter key anywhere on the form, the* **cmdRun** *button is clicked.*

While this **Default** = **True** behavior is great for a message box, it is a real problem for our SQL Query Tester.

2 When the user interface is defined, add the following code in the **cmdRun** command button:

```
Private Sub cmdRun_Click()

On Error GoTo SQLError:

Data1.RecordSource = Text1
Data1.Refresh

If Data1.RecordSource <> "" Then
  If (Data1.Recordset.RecordCount > 0) Then
    With Data1.Recordset
      .MoveLast
      .MoveFirst
      lblRecordCount = .RecordCount
      lblUpdatable = IIf(.Updatable, "Yes", "No")
    End With
  Else
    lblRecordCount = "Records Returned: 0"
    lblCurrentRecord = "No records"
    lblUpdatable = ""
  End If
Else
  MsgBox ("Please enter a SQL statement")
End If
```

```
  Exit Sub
  SQLError:
    Dim sError As String
    sError = "Error Number: " & Err.Number & vbCrLf
    sError = sError & Err.Description
    MsgBox (sError)
    Exit Sub
```

```
End Sub
```

When learning SQL, or trying new statements, you will find that SQL can be a temperamental beast. I don't mean by this that SQL is capricious, but rather that it is very unforgiving of error - everything must be **exactly** right. If we type in an SQL command that is not perfect, VB will let us know with the incredibly friendly error '3141' - and believe me, this is likely to happen a lot as you are learning your way around SQL:

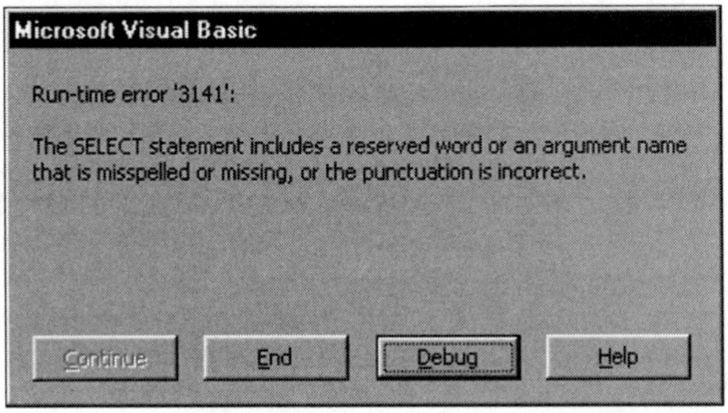

So to prevent a premature headache, or worse - giving up on SQL altogether - we have put the following handy line in our event procedure:

```
  On Error GoTo SQLError:
```

This **On Error** statement instructs VB that if an error does occur, instead of crashing our program as seen above, **GoTo** the label **SQLError**.

At the very end of our event procedure, we place the label **SQLError**. This is known as an **error handler**:

```
  Exit Sub
  SQLError:
    Dim sError As String
    sError = "Error Number: " & Err.Number & vbCrLf
    sError = sError & Err.Description
    MsgBox (sError)
    Exit Sub
```

Notice that right before our handler we place an **Exit Sub**. This is very important because if you omit this statement the code will always enter the error handler even when there is no error. This has a tendency to confuse the user. So if there is no error, our code simply exits the procedure.

However, if our SQL statement *does* cause an error, VB transfers control to our error handler. Inside the handler, we just display the error to the user and exit the procedure. No harm done. We can get the error but our program is not crashed. Now if we mistype or create an invalid SQL command, we get a message like this:

Notice the **vbCrLf**. This is a built-in VB constant for Carriage Return/Line Feed and tells VB to start a new line. Therefore Error Number: 3141 and its accompanying description appear on separate lines in the following message box.

Notice that it is the same error VB gave us above. This time, however, the program does not crash. After the message is displayed, the procedure is exited and the program lives to fight another day - or at least to process another SQL command. Believe me, when you see all of the errors that do occur when you're learning SQL, you will be glad you put in the error handler.

Note that we are using a **GoTo** statement to define where VB should jump to on an error. We have all heard about the bad reputation of **GoTo**s and spaghetti code. But don't worry here. This is just the way that VB implements error handlers. It is the one and only way to do it, so this is a perfectly legitimate technique to use for our error handlers.

OK, back to the **cmdRun** button. When you click the **cmdRun** button, whatever SQL statement (i.e. string) is in the text box is then assigned to the **RecordSource** property of the **Data1** data control. The data control is then refreshed and (assuming it is a correctly structured query) any resulting records will be displayed on the bound DBGrid ActiveX control:

```
Data1.RecordSource = Text1
Data1.Refresh
```

If we forget to type anything in the text box before the **cmdRun** button is pressed, an error will occur. We need to check to be sure that a **RecordSource** has indeed been entered in the text box and assigned to the data control. If we didn't take this preventative step, we would get our old friend error '91':

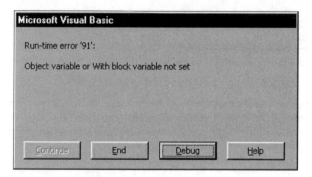

The following simple precaution prevents us from crashing our program and having to restart:

```
If Data1.RecordSource <> "" Then
  If (Data1.Recordset.RecordCount > 0) Then
    With Data1.Recordset
      .MoveLast
      .MoveFirst
      lblRecordCount = .RecordCount
      lblUpdatable = IIf(.Updatable, "Yes", "No")
    End With
  Else
    lblRecordCount = "Records Returned: 0"
    lblCurrentRecord = "No records"
    lblUpdatable = ""
  End If
Else
  MsgBox ("Please enter a SQL statement")
End If
```

This code checks to see if the **Data1.RecordSource** derived from the contents of the text box is empty. If it is, then the program will issue the message box prompting us to **"Please enter a SQL statement"**. Otherwise, the engine-room code of the program is executed.

When we *do* provide a valid SQL command in the text box, the following lines of code will display information about the returned recordset for us:

```
      .MoveLast
      .MoveFirst
      lblRecordCount = .RecordCount
      lblUpdatable = IIf(.Updatable, "Yes", "No")
```

Recall that Jet has to touch every record to give us an accurate count of the total records in the recordset. So by moving to the last record and then immediately to the first, we can display an accurate count on our form.

> *Remember the* **Updatable** *property of the recordset when you are working on projects of your own. VB will provide an error message if you try to add or delete records. The code might look correct and you can't figure out what is wrong. There is a good chance that the recordset you created is not updatable.*

You might be wondering about the strange and enigmatic **IIf** statement. This infrequently used VB function is perfect for returning one of two parts, depending on the evaluation of an expression. In this example the **IIf** function returns **"Yes"** if the expression **.Updatable** is true and **"No"** if **.Updatable** is false. If you wish to use this handy little function elsewhere, the syntax is:

```
IIf(expr, truepart, falsepart)
```

IIf always evaluates both the truepart and the falsepart. This happens even though it returns only one of them. Herein lies a potential problem with unintended side effects. For example, if evaluating the falsepart of the function results in a division by zero error, an error occurs. This error even occurs if *expr* is true. So just be careful.

OK, back to our *Try It Out* for the SQL Query Tester.

3 In the **Reposition** event procedure of the **Data1** data control, place the following line of code. This will show us the current record when you click on various records in the DBDataGrid. Yep. It's just a bit of eye candy. But since it's so simple, let's add it:

```
Private Sub Data1_Reposition()

    lblCurrentRecord = Data1.Recordset.AbsolutePosition + 1

End Sub
```

That's it. We just add code to the two event procedures and we have a full-fledged SQL Query tester.

4 OK, now save your project as **BegDB\Chapter8\prjSQL**.

5 Press *F5* and run your new program. Then type SELECT * FROM Titles into the text box and click the <u>E</u>xecute button. You'll see something like this:

There, our SQL Query tester in action. Notice that SELECT and FROM are capitalized. SQL is case insensitive, but the SQL keywords are capitalized by convention. This is a good habit to get into because we can visually separate the keywords from the variables we want to retrieve.

Also, any extra white space is not important in an SQL statement. Jet parses the SQL statement and throws away any extra spaces. This is handy when we start to format more advanced SQL statements. It permits us to format the statements just like we would with an **If...Then...Else** statement. We can neatly indent the statements to make them easy to read. In the above, for example, we could just have written the SQL statement as:

```
SELECT
    *
FROM Titles
```

Also, as SQL is case insensitive, we could have written the query like this:

```
SeLeCt * FrOm TiTlEs
```

The query will work as advertised, but it doesn't do much for your eyes trying to read it. So by convention, the SQL keywords are capitalized. This assists in having a good, common approach to coding. This is far more than the "Neatness counts" we all heard in grammar school. It shows a precision in *thinking* as well. If we code neatly, we find it helps us to think neatly - and vice versa. So be sure to indent your queries if they are more than a single line long. Capitalize the SQL keywords to visually separate the components of the query.

> *Reminder: When a recordset is returned by executing an SQL query, it's really creating its own (temporary) table with rows and columns. No matter whether you are using one table or multiple tables in the SQL query string, you are returned a unique table, not the exact underlying table from the database. The recordset is in memory only.*

Selecting Specific Fields from a Single Table

In the example above, we selected all of the fields from a single table by using the wildcard '*'. Now we will start being more 'selective' and begin to see some of the power of SQL.

We now want to select just three fields from the **Publishers** table. Here's how - type the SQL statement below into the Query Tester's text box:

```
SELECT
  PubID,
  Name,
  [Company Name]
FROM Publishers
```

When you insert the names of the fields you want to retrieve here, be sure to separate the first two fields with commas. There is **no** comma after the last field, **Company Name** (this simple requirement has caused countless hours in SQL debugging).

Now click on <u>E</u>xecute. Here's the result:

So the statement SELECT PubID, Name, [Company Name] FROM Publishers produces the displayed recordset. When a field has a space in it, such as Company Name, it must be enclosed in brackets [ ] as shown. And I'll say it once again:

> *Don't add a comma after the last field, Company Name. If you do, VB will be glad to provide you with an error message.*

At this point, you may be wondering why you would want to limit the fields you bring back. You might be wondering, "If a * gets me everything, why would I want to mess with specifying individual field names?" Actually, that is a very good question.

> *The only time you should be using a SELECT * is when you actually need access to all the fields. This all boils down to a performance issue.*

You can dramatically impact performance by including fields in your query that you don't really need, particularly if you have any memo fields in your table. Additionally, when we start sending recordsets over a Local Area Network or the Internet, trimming them to only the fields we need yields massive performance benefits.

Filtering the Returned Recordset - the Good Stuff

As I mentioned earlier, the real power of SQL becomes apparent when we see how we can limit the records that are returned to us. We probably only want a subset of all records in the table(s) we are querying. Best of all, SQL gives us several alternatives for limiting the records returned. By using the correct combination of SQL keywords, we can retrieve just about any combination of data that will ever be required. As we go through the chapter, we will look at all of the filtering options available to us.

Here's the first filtering option - the **WHERE** clause.

The WHERE Clause

The **WHERE** clause allows us to say "I only want to see the records that satisfy certain conditions". Whereas the **SELECT** clause determines the **columns** (fields) of the original table to be returned, we use the **WHERE** clause to precisely determine the **rows** (records) that are returned (that is, the subset of records whose values satisfy the **WHERE** conditions that we've specified).

Let's say that you only want to display the records for publishers that have a PubID greater than 200. Simple! The **WHERE** clause is used to specify the rows in the table that we wish to be returned to us in the recordset. To do this, simply put your filtering **criteria** (or conditions) after the **WHERE** keyword as shown below. Essentially, the structure of a SQL query including a **WHERE** clause will be:

```
SELECT field(s) FROM table WHERE condition
```

So our example query looks like this:

```
SELECT
    *
FROM Publishers
WHERE PubID > 200
```

Only publishers with a **PubID** starting at **201** and above will be returned. Or if you only want to retrieve the single publisher with the **PubID** of **200**, just change the **>** sign to a **=** sign. Go ahead and give this a try:

```
SELECT
    *
FROM Publishers
WHERE PubID = 200
```

In English, the above statement tells the database to '**SELECT** all fields **FROM** the **Publishers** table for records **WHERE** the **PubID** field is equal to **200**'. Starting to make sense? I think like anything, once you start using SQL you will begin to see how it is really very logical in it's structure. We can use any of the following operators (or combinations of them, using the **AND** operator) in the **WHERE** clause:

Comparison Operator	What it means
<	The field contents are less than the value
<=	The field contents are less than or equal to the value
>	The field contents are greater than the value
>=	The field contents are greater than or equal to the value
=	The field contents are equal to the value
<>	The field contents do not equal the value
BETWEEN	The field contents fall within a range
LIKE	The field contents match a pattern
IN	The field contents match one of a number of criteria

We'll look at how to combine these operators later in the chapter. For the moment, let's concentrate on the individual operators themselves.

Partial String Matching - the Like Clause

Let's say that we want to retrieve all the publishers whose name begins with the letters 'Sp'. Suppose you can't remember if the publisher you are looking for was Springer or Sport? A simple comparison test can be used to retrieve rows where the contents of a field match a specified text pattern. The **LIKE** clause checks to see if the contents of the field match the criteria. Again, we use the wildcard (*) symbol:

```
SELECT
    *
FROM Publishers
WHERE Name LIKE "sp*"
```

Notice that we are retrieving a text field. Be sure to surround text values to be retrieved with quotes. This example will return all fields of all records where the entry in the **Name** field begins with **Sp**.

This query would return the following:

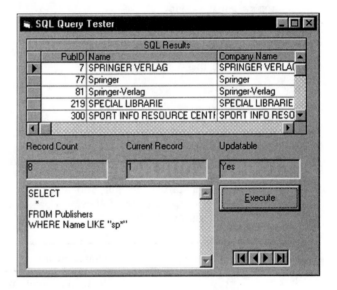

Jet permits us to use the wildcard character * with the **LIKE** operator. This is one of those cases I warned you about where Jet uses a different character. The ANSI SQL equivalent of * is %, which is used as the default wildcard by both Microsoft SQL Server and Oracle as well as legacy databases. So whenever we discuss Jet specific characters like this one, you must keep in mind that if you are going to use another database, these characters might not be permissible. In fact, Jet doesn't like the ANSI character %. If you exchange the * for the %, Jet returns exactly zero records. It interprets the % as a character, *not* as the ASCII wildcard. So this is one of the 'gotchas' I mentioned earlier.

Records Within a Range - the Between Clause

Many times you will need to retrieve records where field values lie within a certain **range** of values. We can use the **BETWEEN** keyword for this. Say you want to retrieve all publisher records that have a **PubID** value between 200 and 300. This SQL query will return all records between 200 and 300 inclusive (i.e. including 200 and 300):

```
SELECT
    *
FROM Publishers
WHERE PubID BETWEEN 200 AND 300
```

We could also use the **BETWEEN** clause on alpha fields. If we need to find all publishers with names that start with letters between D and I, we can simply use the following SQL statement:

```
SELECT
    *
FROM Publishers
WHERE Name BETWEEN "D" AND "I"
```

Retrieving Records Using the IN Clause

This handy clause permits us to select records that match one of a number of discrete values that we specify. If we wanted to select publishers that are based in New York, Carmel or Cambridge only, the **IN** clause does the trick:

```
SELECT
    *
FROM Publishers
WHERE City IN ("New York", "Carmel", "Cambridge")
```

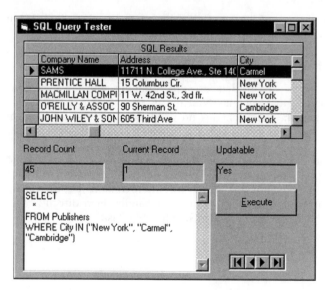

Conversely, if you want to view the publishers that are *not* located in any of these three cities, just insert a **NOT** before the **IN**. This will return all publisher records where the publisher is not based in any of these three cities:

```
SELECT
  *
FROM Publishers
WHERE City NOT IN ("New York", "Carmel", "Cambridge")
```

Nested Conditions

There will be times when you need to apply several constraints to return the correct recordset. Let's say that you wanted publishers not in the above three cities, but of those, only records where the **Comments** field is not Null. The format for nested conditions is:

```
SELECT field(s) FROM table WHERE condition1 AND condition2
```

Here the **AND** operator connects both conditions to ensure they are both true. If both are true, the record satisfies the request and is returned. Other Boolean operators are also valid when linking conditions:

AND - both conditions must be true

OR - one of the conditions must be true

NOT - the condition(s) must be false

For example:

```
SELECT
  *
FROM Publishers
WHERE City NOT IN ("New York", "Carmel", "Cambridge") AND Comments IS NOT NULL
```

This example of the **WHERE** clause may not read real well in English but it specifies exactly what the programmer wants to see!

Null Fields and You

Null is a special term used in database programming and has a tendency to be misunderstood by beginners. A field that contains Null means that there is no data stored in the field. A Null value indicates that the field contains no valid data. Null is not the same as a zero for a numeric field, nor a zero-length string (""), which is sometimes referred to as a null string.

Null values create what is known as **three-valued logic** for our SQL conditions. For any given record, the search condition may be True or False. Alternatively, it may be Null because one of the fields used in evaluation the search condition contains a Null value. So, many times it is useful to explicitly check for Null values and handle them directly. SQL provides us with a special test for Null (**IS NULL**) which handles this task.

> *VB also provides us with a built-in function to determine if a field value or variable is Null. Use the* `IsNull` *function to determine whether an expression contains a Null value. Expressions that you might expect to evaluate to* `True` *under some circumstances, such as* `If Var = Null` *and* `If Var <> Null`*, will ALWAYS return* `False`*. This is because any expression containing a Null is itself* `Null` *and, therefore,* `False`*. So using* `IsNull(myVar)` *will always return* `True` *or* `False`*.*

The Delete Query

The **DELETE** query is a powerful but dangerous query. The **DELETE** query uses the same join and selection syntax as the **SELECT** statement. However, instead of retrieving records that meet the criteria, it **deletes** the selected records. Records can be deleted from one or more tables in a single query. The simplest form of a delete query would delete all records from a single table following (please don't test out any of these **DELETE** queries just yet! Trust me that they work as advertised, otherwise your **Biblio.mdb** database will shrink alarmingly):

```
DELETE * FROM Publishers
```

You can select any specific records to delete by simply substituting the **DELETE** keyword for the **SELECT** keyword in the examples that we've already looked at. For instance, to delete all records where the publishers reside in any city except New York, Carmel or Cambridge, you would do the:

```
DELETE
    *
FROM Publishers
WHERE City NOT IN ("New York", "Carmel", "Cambridge")
```

Unique or Non-Unique Fields?

Up till now, we have been requesting several fields. However, many times a specific field will contain the same entry for several records. For example, the **City** field contains New York for several of the publisher records. In other words, several publishers reside in New York.

If you need to show only unique cities where the various publishers are based, just use the **DISTINCT** keyword after the **SELECT** keyword and before any field that you want to be made unique. Let's say that we want to see all of the cities where publishers are located, but we don't want any duplicates of the various cities. The result of the following query will provide only unique cities - no duplicates allowed:

```
SELECT DISTINCT
    City
FROM Publishers
```

In other words, only a single entry for each city is retrieved. So even if we had 20 publishers that reside in New York, that city name would only show up once in the resulting recordset.

So the **DISTINCT** keyword will limit the returned records to one per unique entry for the field. If we use the **DISTINCT** keyword at the beginning of the **SELECT** clause, as above, this will eliminate duplicate rows of query results. So if we needed to see the records for each city that has a publisher in it, we could accomplish this pretty easily:

> *If you select a field with a primary key, each record will have a unique value in this field. Therefore, all records will be returned even if you use **DISTINCT**.*

Ordering the Returned Recordset

Remember back when we were building our generic Find form? Back then we discussed that SQL could be used to return the records in the order you wanted. We didn't set the **Sorted** property of the list box because we wanted to rely on SQL to sort the data. We might want the result returned in descending order, for example. SQL is the only way to do that. Well, here's how it's done - you will find this very useful and painless:

```
SELECT
    *
FROM Publishers
ORDER BY [Company Name]
```

Notice that the field **Company Name** has a space in it, so don't forget to include the brackets.

Here's the result of this query:

I thought you'd like this one. If you want the records in descending order, just add the qualifier **DESC** at the end:

```
SELECT
    *
FROM Publishers
ORDER BY [Company Name] DESC
```

If you want to combine a **WHERE** clause along with an **ORDER BY**, no problem:

```
SELECT
    *
FROM Publishers
WHERE City = "New York"
ORDER BY [Company Name] DESC
```

Now let's take a look at some 'summarizing' features that SQL provides us with - the **aggregate functions**.

Aggregate Functions

The Jet engine supports the standard SQL **aggregate functions** COUNT, SUM, AVG, MAX and MIN. I don't know why, but I really like the aggregate functions. It must be some sort of personality quirk. It is fairly magical the way aggregate SQL functions can get summary information in the blink of an eye. Enter the following SQL query statement on the **Authors** table to get a sense of the age of the various authors:

```
SELECT
    COUNT(Author) AS NumEntries,
    SUM([Year Born]) AS SumYear,
    AVG([Year Born]) AS AvgYear,
```

```
     MIN([Year Born]) AS OldestAuth,
     MAX([Year Born]) AS YoungAuth
   FROM Authors
```

The **COUNT()** function can be used on any field type, including text, as it returns the number of records in a field. The others must be used only on numeric fields since they perform math functions. Makes sense, right? For example, if you try to perform a **SUM** on the **Author** field which is text, as in **SUM(Author)**, VB gives us the following error:

Project1

Error Number: 3169
The Microsoft Jet database engine could not execute the SQL statement because it contains a field that has an invalid data type.

OK

Enter the SQL statement above to check out the years the authors were born. Be sure to include a comma after each of the functions except the last. When you run the query you'll get something like this:

SQL Query Tester

SQL Results

	NumEntries	SumYear	AvgYear	OldestAuth	YoungAuth
▶	6246	38953	1947.65	1936	1963

Record Count   Current Record   Updatable

1   1   No

```
SELECT
  COUNT(Author) AS NumEntries,
  SUM([Year Born]) AS SumYear,
  AVG([Year Born]) AS AvgYear,
  MIN([Year Born]) AS OldestAuth,
  MAX([Year Born]) AS YoungAuth
FROM Authors
```

Execute

We use an aggregate function and then tell Jet how to label the results column in the returned record set (that's what the **AS fieldname** part does). The outline of an aggregate function is:

AggregateFunction(FieldInTable) AS NameToReturn

In this syntax, we define a **NameToReturn** - this is called **aliasing**.

Aliasing the Column Names

When we create a recordset object using the **SELECT** statement, the table's column names become the field object names in the recordset. However, often we don't want the cryptic table names to be shown to a user. Whenever you want different column names displayed, use the **AS** clause. In our example, the count of all entries is in a column that we called **NumEntries**. We are simply giving an alias to the field name as it is returned in the recordset. It has not been changed in the underlying table.

In the example above, notice that we want the count of the authors, so we pass the **Author** field as the parameter to the aggregate function **COUNT**. We tell it to alias the name of the field to **NumEntries** by using the **AS** clause. Jet dutifully carries out our command before you can say "SQL". We will use these handy functions when we start to analyze data later on in the book, but you can see how easy they are to use. Also, the aggregate functions only return a *single* record - the **summary** record.

Often, you will need to return fields from different tables that have the same field name. Whenever queries are structured that could return ambiguous or duplicate field names, the **AS** clause must be used to provide a different name for the field. We might perform a join operation on several tables. Two of the tables might have the same field name, such as "Discount". We might wish to alias one of the discount fields as "Special Discount" to distinguish the fields.

Another use of aliasing fields is when you are doing arithmetic on fields. We might want to calculate a total price by multiplying a price by a tax field. Since we don't have these fields, let's just multiply two numeric fields form the **Titles** table. Of course, the result makes absolutely no sense, but it does illustrate aliasing. Let's go ahead and multiply the **PubID** field by the **[Year Published]**. We will alias this field as **FunnyNumber**:

```
SELECT
  Title,
  PubID * [Year Published] AS FunnyNumber
FROM
  Titles
```

Here's the result of the query:

You've probably noticed that we used the ***** symbol again here, even though we're not selecting all the columns in the table. Because of the *****'s position in the SQL statement, SQL interprets it in this case as the arithmetic operator 'multiply by'. So SQL is intelligent enough to pick up on the context and interpret the syntax accordingly. This is one of the benefits of having a **structured** query language.

Null Values Revisited

One thing to keep in mind is that if there are records that have a Null value in the field we are trying to aggregate, that field is ignored in the summary. So the results may be skewed because we are looking at 100 records but only 20 of them have valid data in the field we are examining. The output will be the result of only those 20 fields.

> *When you use the* **COUNT()** *function, a tally of all non-Null fields will be returned. If you want to count all records, Null or not, use the special* **COUNT(*)** *function. In fact, Microsoft recommends that you use the* **COUNT(*)** *function whenever possible because this is highly optimized.*

Like all analysis, we must look at the data closely. As we alluded to earlier, many records may have missing data in certain fields. In fact, most of the **Authors** records don't even have a **Year Born** entry. So you can see that if the field is Null, the data is not included in the summary information. If we want to see how many authors actually had a date for the **Year Born**, simply request all of the **Year Born** field entries where the field contains a value that **IS NOT NULL**:

```
SELECT
    [Year Born]
FROM Authors
WHERE [Year Born] IS NOT NULL
```

This will produce:

Surprise! Out of over 6,000 author records, only 20 of them gave a year born. I guess we can deduce that we authors are a vain lot. However, of the records where dates are provided, the SQL statement gives us the information we asked for. The results are based on 20 records, not 6,000.

You can easily combine the aggregate functions with **WHERE** to restrict the statistics to a select subset of records. Below, we only want to see the stats on authors that have a name that begins with the letter 'A':

```
SELECT
   COUNT(Author) AS NumEntries,
   SUM([Year Born]) AS SumYear,
   AVG([Year Born]) AS AvgYear,
   MIN([Year Born]) AS OldestAuth,
   MAX([Year Born]) AS YoungAuth
FROM Authors
WHERE Author LIKE "A*"
```

A Statistical Aside

Here's some manna for the statistics buffs among you (please bear with me for a moment if you're not statistically minded). Jet has a few specific statistical functions that you can easily use:

▶ **STDEV** (standard deviation)

▶ **STDEVP** (standard deviation of the population)

▶ **VAR** (variance)

▶ **VARP** (variance of the population)

Try this SQL statement:

```
SELECT
   STDEV([Year Born]) AS StandDev,
   STDEVP([Year Born]) AS StandDevP,
   VAR([Year Born]) AS Variance,
   VARP([Year Born]) AS VarianceP
FROM Authors
```

This provides us with the following result:

Please keep in mind that these statistical functions are Jet specific - they probably won't work if you are using another database management system. But if you are using Access, they can come in mighty handy when you need to do analysis. The **STDEVP** function evaluates the standard deviation on an entire population while the **STDEV** function evaluates a population sample.

If the underlying recordset created from the SQL contains fewer than two records (or no records, for the **STDEVP** function), both of these functions return a **Null** value. This simply tells us that a standard deviation can't be calculated on those records.

Like the **STDEVP** function, the **VARP** function evaluates a variance on a population. The **VAR** function evaluates a variance on a population sample.

Like their standard deviation cousins, the **VAR** and **VARP** functions will return **Null** if the underlying query contains fewer than two records.

The GROUP BY Clause - Summarizing Values

When you need to combine records that have identical values in a specified field into a single record, the **GROUP BY** clause does the trick. Look at the following example. The data from the **Publishers** table can be 'grouped by' the **City** field:

```
SELECT
   City,
   COUNT (City) AS Tally
FROM Publishers
GROUP BY City
```

Each publisher belongs to one and only one city. We've also created a summary value for each record (the Tally of how many publishers there are in each city) by including the aggregate function, **COUNT**. Like all aggregate functions, any fields that contain Null aren't included:

So you can see that although our **Publishers** table contains over 700 entries, these publishers are concentrated in only 36 cities.

Grouping With the HAVING Clause

When you need to **GROUP** items, as in the above example, you can select only those that meet a set of criteria. This is where the **HAVING** clause comes in. For example, if we wanted to group all cities that start with the letter A, we would do the following:

```
SELECT
  City,
  COUNT (City) AS Tally
FROM Publishers
GROUP BY City
HAVING City LIKE "A*"
```

This would return:

Again, if you had your thinking cap on, you'd be saying "Hey! Isn't the **HAVING** clause just like the **WHERE** clause we just learned about?" Yes it is, but **HAVING** is used only in conjunction with the **GROUP BY** clause.

Joining Tables

The real power of using a relational database becomes apparent when we start to group information from several tables. Let's say we wanted to see all of the book titles published by each publisher. To show this we need to **join** two tables, **Publishers** and **Titles**, using the common field value, **PubID**. We would use the **WHERE** clause in the following SQL statement.

```
SELECT
 Publishers.Name,
 Titles.Title
FROM Publishers, Titles
WHERE Publishers.PubID = Titles.PubID
```

Since we are retrieving a column from each of two tables, we first fully qualify the column by using the *table.field* approach. A fully qualified column name specifies the name of the table *and* the name of the column to be retrieved in that table, using a period (.) to separate them. Technically this is only required if the field name exists in more than one of the tables addressed by the query, but it's good practice and you should try to use this approach consistently.

So we want the **Name** field from the **Publishers** table and the **Title** field from the **Titles** table. We want to fully qualify the fields, such as **Publishers.Name**, so Jet knows precisely which fields we want. Next, the **FROM** statement tells Jet which tables to look at to retrieve the fields. Finally, the **WHERE** clause says match up the **Name** and **Title** records where the **PubID** field is the same in each.

Here's the result of running this query:

Remember when we were discussing keys? Well, this is where they come into play.

The **Publishers.PubID** is unique for each publisher record and each **Titles** record contains a **PubID** value relating to a certain publisher. So in the above example we can see that a single publisher is responsible for several titles.

The INNER JOIN

If we attempted to perform the above query using Microsoft Access, it would generate an **INNER JOIN** clause. An **INNER JOIN** retrieves only those records that have a match on both sides of the **JOIN**. Have a look at this query:

```
SELECT
    Publishers.Name,
    Titles.Title
FROM Publishers
INNER JOIN Titles
ON Publishers.PubID = Titles.PubID
```

Here's the result:

Using this clause would return the exact same recordset as the **WHERE** clause we previously covered.

When joining tables, try to use the **INNER JOIN** approach. This is because Jet requires the **INNER JOIN** for the recordset to be updatable. Take a look at the Updatable label on both examples. The **WHERE** clause is not updatable while the **INNER JOIN** is. The **INNER JOIN** is a bit more programmatically correct as well. The **WHERE** implies the **JOIN** while the **INNER JOIN** actually spells it out to Jet. Plus it spells it out to the programmer - it's self-documenting.

The OUTER JOIN

As we said, an **INNER JOIN** retrieves only those records that have a match on both sides. So if there was a **Publishers** record without any Titles records associated with it, that record would not show up in the recordset using an **INNER JOIN**. If you want to show *all* of the records in the **Publishers** table - even though there might not be any **Titles** associated with it - use the **RIGHT OUTER JOIN**:

```
SELECT
    Publishers.Name,
    Titles.Title
FROM Titles
RIGHT OUTER JOIN Publishers
ON Publishers.PubID = Titles.PubID
```

And here's the result:

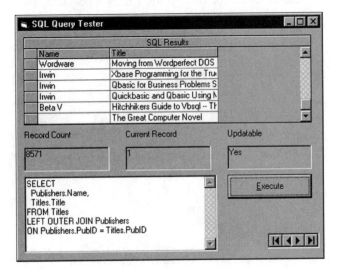

Notice that the first record does not have any titles associated with it.

On the other hand, if we wanted to show all the records from the **Titles** table - even though there might not be any **Publishers** associated with it - use the **LEFT OUTER JOIN**:

```
SELECT
    Publishers.Name,
    Titles.Title
FROM Titles
LEFT OUTER JOIN Publishers
ON Publishers.PubID = Titles.PubID
```

This would give us:

(I had to add the record for The Great Computer Novel to my **Biblio.mdb**, as all the titles in the **Titles** table were associated with publishers.)

At first, this **JOIN** business seems a bit complex, but let's look a bit closer. The syntax for **OUTER** and **INNER JOIN**s is as follows:

```
Tablename1 RIGHT/LEFT OUTER JOIN Tablename2
```

RIGHT OUTER JOINs include all of the records from the second-named (rightmost in the **JOIN** clause) table, even if there are no matching values for records in the first (leftmost) table. **LEFT OUTER JOIN**s include all of the records from the first-named (leftmost) of two tables, even if there are no matching values for records in the second (rightmost) table.

Remember the **INNER JOIN** clause only retrieves records if there is a corresponding match in *both* tables. However, the **LEFT** and **RIGHT OUTER** joins link the records from tables even if there are no corresponding records in the other table. It's that simple.

The SQL Update Statement

SQL provides an easy to way to perform bulk updates. Let's say that we wanted to update a group of selected records in the **Publishers** table. The city of Ipswitch in the state of New York has started giving tax breaks to publishers. All of the publishers that currently reside in New York have moved to Ipswitch. So we want to change the record of each publisher that currently resides in New York to reflect their new domicile in Ipswitch.

Well, first let's take a look at how many publishers currently reside in New York City. It's easy to build a SQL query to find out all of the publishers that fit this criterion:

```
SELECT
  *
FROM Publishers
WHERE City = "New York"
```

This would give us:

Notice that we have 28 publishers that reside in New York City.

If we wanted to update all of the records of publishers that reside in New York and change their current city entries to Ipswitch, we could write a simple VB program that would do it. In fact, we will! We'll just use the data control and the code below will accomplish what we need.

Try It Out - Update the Database Using SQL - the Brute Force Method

1 Add a new form to your project and name it **frmUpdate**. Add a single data control and two command buttons. Name the buttons **cmdIpswitch** and **cmdNewYork**, and set their captions as shown in the screenshot below. Set the **DatabaseName** property of the data control to **[drive letter]:\BegDB\Biblio.mdb**.

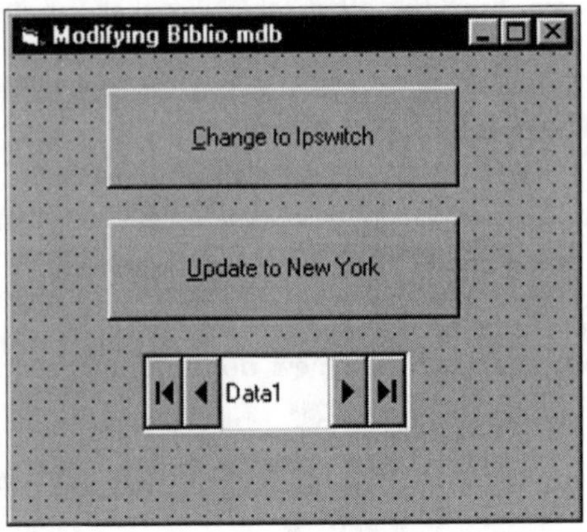

```
  Modifying Biblio.mdb          _ □ X

       ┌─────────────────────────┐
       │   Change to Ipswitch     │
       └─────────────────────────┘

       ┌─────────────────────────┐
       │   Update to New York     │
       └─────────────────────────┘

          |◄ ◄ Data1    ► ►|
```

2 Add the following code to the **cmdIpswitch** command button's **Click** event:

```
Private Sub cmdIpswitch_Click()

With Data1
  .RecordSource = "SELECT * FROM Publishers WHERE City = 'New York'"
  .Refresh
  .Recordset.MoveFirst
  While (Not .Recordset.EOF)
     .Recordset.Edit
     .Recordset!City = "Ipswitch"
     .Recordset.Update
     .Recordset.MoveNext
  Wend
End With

End Sub
```

The first thing we have to do is create a recordset consisting of all records where the publishers reside in New York City:

```
RecordSource = "SELECT * FROM Publishers WHERE City = 'New York'"
.Refresh
.Recordset.MoveFirst
```

We refresh the data control to create the recordset and then move to the first record. We happen to know that there are 28 publishers that fit this criterion. We then loop through the recordset and change each record one by one:

```
While (Not .Recordset.EOF)
    .Recordset.Edit
    .Recordset!City = "Ipswitch"
    .Recordset.Update
    .Recordset.MoveNext
Wend
```

The **Edit** method puts the current record into edit mode. We then change the value of the **City** field to **Ipswitch**. Finally, we update the change and move on to the next record. The process continues until the updating is complete.

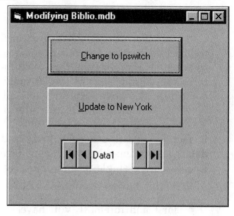

3 Now run the **frmUpdate** form. Be sure to set the project property **Startup Object** to **frmUpdate**. Then click the Change to Ipswitch button.

This is a brute force method. We handle each record individually. While we only have 28 records, it's not a big deal, but if we have 28,000, this process can take a while. Let's run our query and ensure that the **City** field has been changed in the appropriate records:

```
SELECT
    *
FROM Publishers
WHERE City = "Ipswitch"
```

The records will now look like this:

OK, great. Each of the 28 records has been changed (we didn't update the Address field, but we'll let that pass). We can run a query to check by finding all publishers that reside in Ipswitch. The problem is that once the publishers all rushed there, Ipswitch soon decides to triple the tax rate! All of the 28 publishers now rush back to New York City. Of course we could use the above code to select all records where the city is 'Ipswitch' and change then to 'New York'. However, SQL provides a better way.

In fact, if you are using the **Edit** and **Update** methods to update several records in your database, you may be writing inefficient code. Why? Consider what happens when you have to update only a single record: there are several steps that must be taken.

▶ First and foremost, you have to locate the record(s) as we did by issuing the SQL query to our data control. This found all of the relevant records and placed them in a recordset.

▶ We then had to call the **Edit** method to get at the records data (the record is actually locked when we use **Edit**).

▶ Next, we changed to data - 'New York' was changed to 'Ipswitch'.

▶ Once changed, we updated the record using the **Update** method.

▶ The current record pointer was moved to the next record and we went back to step 2 until all of the records were changed.

That is just too much work! If there are many records, your application can slow to a crawl.

Luckily there is an easier way. The SQL **UPDATE** requires a single statement to accomplish the same thing. To use this command, you are required to only use a single method, the **Execute** database method. We will be using this command often later in the book, but let's see how we can use it with our SQL **UPDATE** statement. To accomplish the same thing as we did above, we only need three lines of code - and if the database is already open, a *single* line is all that is required.

Try It Out - Updating the Database Using SQL - the Simple Way

1 Now add the following code to the **cmdNewYork** command button's **Click** event:

```
Private Sub cmdNewYork_Click()

Dim dbBiblio As Database

Set dbBiblio = OpenDatabase("C:\BegDB\Biblio.mdb")
dbBiblio.Execute "UPDATE Publishers SET City = _
                          'New York' WHERE City = 'Ipswitch'"

End Sub
```

2 Switch back to the **frmUpdate** form in your project. Press *F5* and click the Update to New York button. All of the records will be changed back to their original value.

How It Works

First, we dim a database object – **dbBiblio**. After our database object is open, we use its **Execute** method and issue the following SQL **UPDATE** statement.

```
dbBiblio.Execute "UPDATE Publishers SET City = 'New York'
   WHERE City = 'Ipswitch'"
```

The format of the **UPDATE** query looks like this:

```
UPDATE TableName SET Field = value2 WHERE Field = value1
```

Every **UPDATE** query begins with the **UPDATE** command. This is then followed by the table name in the database you want to update. Next comes the **SET** keyword, which is followed by a list of field(s) that should be modified and the values they should be changed to. In our example, we simply set the **City** field, but you can change as many fields as is required in a single **UPDATE**.

Finally, the optional **WHERE** keyword can be used to limit the scope of the changes. In our example, we only wished to modify the records **WHERE City = Ipswitch**.

"Pay no attention to the man behind the curtain"

That is my favorite line from The Wizard of Oz and applies to what we are going to do next. If you have a copy of Microsoft Access, open it up. We're going to build a SQL query.

Try It Out - Using SQL with Access

1 Open our **Biblio.mdb** database. Click the Queries tab and select New. Select Design View, then click OK:

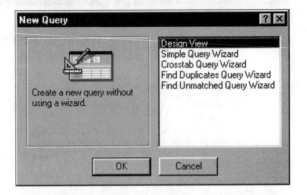

2 Next, the tables in the **Biblio.mdb** file will be displayed. First Add the Publishers table, then the Titles table. When they are selected, click Close.

3 Notice how Access automatically linked the two tables:

The Publishers table contains the PubID field that holds a unique value for each publisher. This is the primary key. Notice the 1 to the right of the table. The PubID field is the foreign key in the Titles table. Each publisher can publish several books; therefore the PubID field in the Titles table does not contain unique values. Also notice the ∞ character on the left side of the Titles table. This annotation tells us that the relationship is a one-to-many. One (1) Publishers.PubID field is related to many (∞) Titles.PubID fields.

4 Now in the first Field column in the bottom pane of the window, click the drop-down box and select Publishers.Name. In the second field column, click the drop-down arrow and select Titles.Title. Now on the main Access tool bar, click on the '!' exclamation button to execute the query. Voila, the result appears:

5 Now you might be thinking, "Interesting but how is this useful?" OK, here's why. Click on View from the main Access menu and then select SQL View. The SQL statement that was used to generate the output is displayed in all its glory:

We can now simply cut and paste the query to the VB code window and use the SQL code that Access generated for us in our VB programs.

Using Access-generated SQL in VB

You might be thinking that this is not a big deal for this simple example. However, when you start joining several tables, being able to see what you are doing graphically is a tremendous help. Then you can run the queries right in Access. Doing this makes it simple to check the results of the recordset to be sure that the query does what you want. Then when you are sure the query is correct, simply cut and paste. Now that you understand the fundamentals of SQL, you can actually read the statements and know how to modify them.

Notice that the Access-built SQL is a long string:

```
SELECT Publishers.Name, Titles.Title
FROM Publishers INNER JOIN Titles ON
Publishers.PubID = Titles.PubID;
```

A straight cut and paste of this into your code window would cause VB to give you an error. So, We must tailor the string so it can be used by VB. Here's how to do it:

```
Dim sSQL As String

sSQL = "SELECT Publishers.Name, Titles.Title "
sSQL = sSQL & " FROM Publishers "
sSQL = sSQL & " INNER JOIN Titles ON Publishers.PubID = Titles.PubID"
```

Be sure to leave a space on the end of each line except the last, otherwise VB bunches the last word on one line with the first word on the next - which causes major havoc with the SQL parser.

Remember that white space is ignored (it isn't included in the parsed query), but it must be there for VB to see the separate words. Also, each assignment to **sSQL** should be on a single line. This makes it easier to read and doesn't require the line continuation character. You could now just assign **sSQL** to the data control's **RecordSource** property.

If the truth be told, I always use this Access/test/cut/paste sequence. It's simply too powerful to ignore and you are assured of a syntactically correct SQL statement. Saves on headache medication, for sure.

Now let's move on and think about how we can incorporate choices that the user makes on our visual interface into our SQL statements. In doing this we will be learning how to create **dynamic SQL statements** - SQL built in-flight while our application is running.

Enough Theory - Let's Build a Dynamic SQL Generator!

Let's start with a simple example of creating a **dynamic SQL statement**. This will come in handy when the user wants to make a choice to retrieve specific information from the database.

Let's say you wanted to let the user display all of the publishers that reside in a single city. We will create a dynamic SQL statement that is actually built 'on the fly'. Our program has no way of knowing in advance what the user will select. We will insert a user-selected variable or variables to complete a pre-prepared skeleton SQL statement and then execute it.

Try It Out - The Dynamic SQL Generator

1 Start a new project. Draw a DBGrid, a list box and two data controls on the form, like this:

2 Now set the controls' properties to match this table:

Control	Property	Value
Data1	DatabaseName	C:\BegDB\Biblio.mdb
	Visible	False
Data2	DatabaseName	C:\BegDB\Biblio.mdb
	Visible	False
DBGrid1	DataSource	Data2

3 Now bring up the code window and add the following to the **Form_Load** event procedure:

```
Private Sub Form_Load()

Dim mySQL As String

mySQL = "SELECT City FROM Publishers GROUP BY City"

Data1.RecordSource = mySQL
Data1.Refresh
```

```
'Loop through all of the records returned.
While Not Data1.Recordset.EOF
  With Data1.Recordset
      If (Not IsNull(!city)) Then     'Ensure that the field is not null.
          List1.AddItem !city 'If the field is not null, add it.
      End If
      .MoveNext
  End With
Wend
```

```
End Sub
```

First, we want to construct a SQL statement that will return a recordset with each of the unique cities in the **Publishers** table. Using the **GROUP BY** clause will provide one record for each city:

```
mySQL = "SELECT City FROM Publishers GROUP By City"
```

We then assign the variable **mySQL** to the **RecordSource** property of the **Data1** data control and refresh it:

```
Data1.RecordSource = mySQL
Data1.Refresh
```

Then if there are any records returned (and we know there will be), we place them in the list box:

```
If (Not IsNull(!city)) Then     'Ensure that the field is not null.
      List1.AddItem !city                'If the field is not null, add it.
End If
```

Notice that we check each field to ensure that it is not **Null**. This is because if a **Null** is returned, VB will give us an error:

The database in fact, does have a few **Null** values, so we need to cater for this. You could use the trick we used before, which is to append a "" to the field to ensure that we are at least adding an empty string, such as:

```
List1.AddItem "" & !city
```

VB will not now give us an error, but we would have a blank entry for **Null** values in our list box where the city entry should be. This could be a bit confusing to the user. So our approach will only display valid cities in the list box. Remember that even though we would never permit a **Null** value in a critical field, legacy systems are not always that watertight. Always plan for the worst. It does take a toll to do a test on each and every field. The **IsNull()** is fast, but it is called for each entry in the list box. So when you are designing databases, be sure to validate all data entry. Then you can be sure that there are no **Null** values and can skip this test.

> *In a production system, we would never use a data control to simply update a list box. When we discuss ADO, we will see a much more elegant and quicker way to update a list box or data grid. For now though, let's stick to what we already know.*

So now when the form is loaded, the **Data1** data control will automatically populate the list box with each of the unique cities in the **Publishers** table. The data grid will be empty because it is connected to data control **Data2**, which we haven't set yet.

4 Now place the following code in the list box's **Click** event. This is what will actually fill in the data grid:

```
Private Sub List1_Click()

Data2.RecordSource = "SELECT * FROM Publishers WHERE City = '" & _
                            List1 & "' ORDER BY Name"
Data2.Refresh

End Sub
```

You can see what we are doing here. When the form is loaded, the list box contains all of the cities that the publishers reside in. When the user clicks on one of the cities displayed in the list box, the **Click** event of the list box gets fired. At this point the **Data2** data control gets set up: the **RecordSource** property is assigned the SQL statement to select all of the publishers in the city that the user clicked on.

```
Data2.RecordSource = "SELECT * FROM Publishers WHERE City = '" & _
                            List1 & "' ORDER BY Name"
```

The value of **List1** will contain the value of the list box entry that the user clicks on. As you may already know, the list box has a **ListIndex** property that is set to the item in a list box that the user clicks on. Say the user clicks on the city of Carmel. Since we are concatenating the string to the value of **List1**, or list box, the above string is equivalent to:

```
Data2.RecordSource = "SELECT * FROM Publishers WHERE City = 'Carmel'
ORDER BY Name"
```

So we are just substituting the variable for the name of the city (which was left blank in our skeletal SQL statement). The user has entered their choice and we have used this to generate a dynamic SQL statement.

> *When we are matching in a string, it's important to remember that it must be enclosed in single quotes.*

So you can see how powerful this approach can be. Rather than hard code any match criteria, we simply place a variable as a placeholder. Then we assign the value dynamically and execute the SQL query. We are doing this with a single variable, but if we needed to match on several criteria, we can add as many variables as required for the query.

5   OK. Press *F5* and run your program. Click on a few cities to view all of the publishers that reside in those cities.

It's worth making a note about the user interface. You may recall me standing on my soapbox a while back and preaching about designing an interface that prevents the user from making a mistake. Well, this is a good example. Here the user is only presented with a list of valid cities. They simply click on a list of cities that we know are in the database. An alternative approach would have been to present a dialog box and have the user enter a city, grab the value and stuff it in our SQL statement. Sure, this would work, but what if the user typed in a non-existent city? Or what if in our above example the user typed in "Camrel" instead of "Carmel" by mistake? And finally, our approach requires a single mouse click instead of clicking to display a dialog box and then six keystrokes to enter the city. User entry lite.

So you can see that it's always good to think about how to present the user with predefined choices where possible. The human/computer interface can be the most challenging part of designing a system. Limit or eliminate the requirement for the user to enter data wherever possible. In our example, it is impossible for the user to make a mistake.

What Else Can We Do With SQL?

There are two additional features of SQL to discuss here. The first are **parameter driven SQL statements**. This feature is similar to our example where we inserted a variable in the SQL string, but we simply define a parameter to hold a value and then set it in our code.

Secondly, earlier we touched on the fact that we can actually **manipulate** data in a database using SQL - changing or deleting records, for instance. For example, we can delete all of the records in a table with a single line of code. Or, we might want to find all Managers in an employee database and give each of them a 10% raise. Well, even though there might be 10,000 records in the database, we can accomplish this daunting task with a single line of code! Since you are now familiar with the structure of SQL queries, you will have no difficulty creating queries that can actually modify data in one or more tables in a single line of code. This is powerful stuff, especially when used in conjunction with the visual interface where we can prompt the user to enter or choose data

In advanced uses of SQL, you can even create and delete tables on the fly. And you can easily do bulk changes on selected records. For example, using SQL you could easily do things like find all records where the employee title is Manager and give their salary a 5% boost.

Summary

In this chapter we have provided an outline some important features of SQL - and the **SELECT** statement in particular. To cover all of SQL's features would require a small forest of paper: SQL has a publishing industry all to itself. While it's true that we have only scratched the surface of this vast and involved subject, we *have* given you sufficient information to get started with SQL in the context of this book.

What We Learned

- SQL is a sub-language that permits us to retrieve and package fields from any grouping of records from tables in a database.

- There are six fundamental parts of an SQL **SELECT** statement, but four of the parts are optional.

- Aggregate functions allow us to summarize fields from a database.

- NULL is unique to databases. It means that there is no valid data in the field.

- When we want to update a recordset that contains two or more tables, we must use the **JOIN** clause, instead of **WHERE** to ensure the recordset is updatable.

- By concatenating variables in our SQL string, we can dynamically create unique SQL queries.

In the next chapter we're going to start preparing to put together all the things that we have learned so far. We're going to design and build a database, and in the chapter *after* next we'll put together an application that will use that database.

Exercises

1 Write an SQL select statement to return the title and year published for all of the books in the Titles table sorted by their title.

2 Explain the difference between an **INNER** and **OUTER JOIN**.

3 Write an SQL **SELECT** statement to return the publisher name and the number of titles published by them. Include only those publishers that have one or more titles published.

4 Why is the **IsNull** function important when creating database applications?

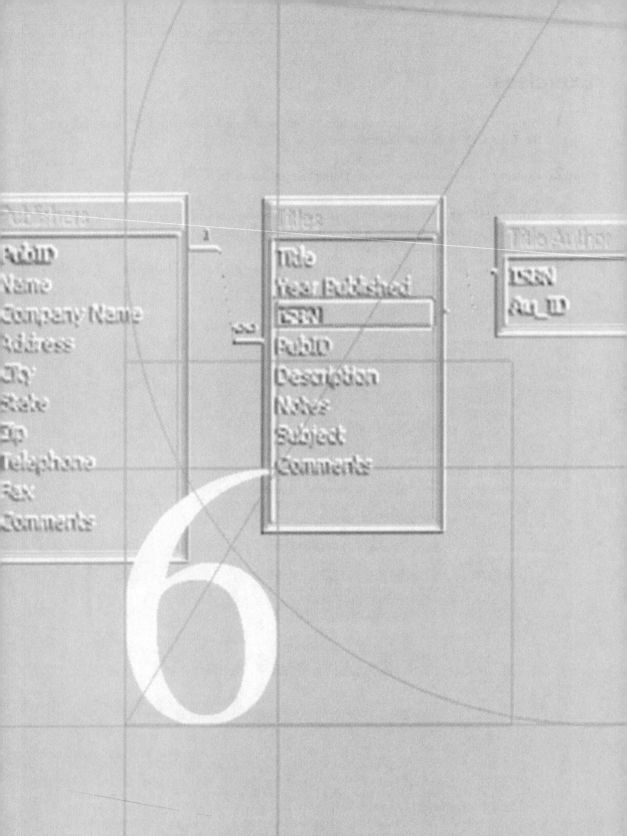

Database Design, Construction and Analysis

In this chapter we're going to design and build a database that we can use with the Address Book application we'll develop in the subsequent chapter. This small-scale application is a working program that you'll be able to use every day on your PC, and which you can distribute to your friends and colleagues.

This project is important because it will teach us about the basic principles of database design. Once we have gone through the design theory, we'll implement the theory using Data Access Objects (DAO). We're using DAO because it is perfect for projects of this scale and provides us with good opportunities to reinforce the design theory by creating the database directly from code. We get to see the nuts and bolts that hold the thing together.

But once again, all of the stuff that we'll learn here will stand us in good stead for the future, since - beyond the specifics of syntax and technique - there is a common foundation to all our applications:

> VB as the front-end (including data controls and bound controls we manipulate programmatically). This will use a data access technology such as DAO or ADO to communicate with:

> A database engine layer (eg Jet/SQL Server) which in turn give us access to:

> A data store (in this case, a database)

In any system, irrespective of the specific tools and techniques of its particular technology, we can apply the design and coding principles we'll use in this chapter and the next.

Here's how we'll progress through *this* chapter:

> When to use DAO/ADO

> Building the **Contacts** database that will underlie our Address Book application

> Making sure our data is stored efficiently in the database – **Normalization**

> Database creation

> ► Key and Index creation
>
> ► Looking at the **DAO object model** - objects and collections
>
> ► **Analyzing the database**: using DAO to trawl our database for information about how its tables are structured - properties, relationships, fields etc.

We'll start by clarifying exactly why we're using DAO for this project.

When to use DAO and ADO - A Rule of Thumb

Since we are building a desktop application, a combination of Jet and DAO is the method of choice. In fact, in Visual Basic 6.0, all file server and desktop applications should use Jet and DAO. They are proven, solid, and have many tools available to them. Microsoft has taken pains to optimize Jet 3.51 with this release of VB.

Jet has built-in optimizations for smaller databases. So if you are developing desktop applications, or those deployed on a small Local Area Network, Microsoft recommends using Jet/DAO.

However, if you are using SQL Server, then it makes sense to develop any new applications using ADO. Although some might argue that SQL Server 7.0 is indeed a desktop database, my guess is that most readers would not consider it the case today. Why? Well, the memory footprint is about 7MB whereas Jet's weighs in at just about 3MB. While it is true that SQL Server will run under Windows 95/98, it requires almost 128MB of RAM and a Pentium II processor. As you're still fairly new to database programming, I'm going to assume that you are developing desktop or file server applications.

> *For these desktop/file server applications, it still makes sense to use Jet/DAO, but if you are developing systems using SQL Server or Oracle for enterprise-wide solutions, then it makes sense to move to ADO now. In either case though, everything you learn in this chapter using Jet/DAO will be immediately available when you eventually make the move to ADO. Ultimately though, we'll all make the move to ADO.*

These versions of Jet and DAO will be the last. Microsoft has stated that Jet/DAO will be supported because it is by far the most popular method of accessing databases on the planet. With such a large installed base and pool of programming talent, it will take a while for everyone to move up to ADO. It will certainly happen, but not overnight. So we are really on the cusp here of a new and exciting method of data access. The good news is that what you learn here will permit you to use ADO almost immediately. Of course, we will jump into ADO in depth in the next few chapters, so fasten your seat belts.

Giving VB 6.0 the Reference to DAO

Since we will be using DAO, and it is not an intrinsic part of the language, we must tell VB everything it needs to know about how to reference the DAO objects. This is simple, but a critical step in working with DAO. From the main VB menu, select Project_|_References... Click on Microsoft DAO 3.51 Object Library. This will add all of the necessary information required to use DAO in our project.

In this chapter we will be referencing things like databases. A database is a DAO reference. While VB does not know what a database is, DAO does. Remember when we discussed the limits of the VB language? The language can't know all the specific details of databases, Excel, Word, or any of the specific linkages it can use. If all of these thousands of references were built into the language two things would happen. First, the language would be incredibly bloated. Second, whenever enhancements came out (like an upgrade to DAO 3.51), the entire VB language would need to be updated to take advantage of the upgrade. So **type libraries** permit VB to reference the specifics about, say, DAO programming. By adding these references, we have essentially extended the language itself. VB now knows what a database is and how to operate with one.

If you attempted to dimension a database, prior to adding the DAO reference above, VB would have no idea of what you were talking about. When you attempted to run your program with a reference to a database, a friendly Compile error would be handed to us:

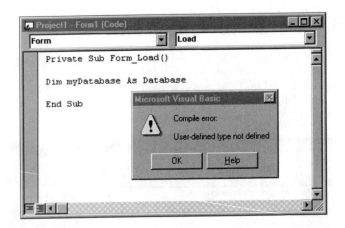

However, as soon as the DAO reference is added, VB now knows what a **Database** is, and you can now see the DAO references, such as a Database, when you try to dimension a new database object. We've provided VB with everything it needs for us to do our database design. In fact, the IntelliSense drop-down box now provides Database as a choice for us:

> *If you don't see Database in the drop-down list, you have not added the reference to DAO 3.51 in your project yet.*

The Personal Address Book

Once we have built our database and are satisfied with it, we will then build a program that you will hopefully find to be truly useful - the Address Book. I think you will like this one. We will save the actual coding for the Address Book until the next chapter. The coding for all of the database access will be done using DAO exclusively - no intrinsic data controls!

However, in this chapter we will be learning how to design and normalize a database first. Once we have the design complete, I'll show you how to build it using both **VisData** and DAO. VisData is a handy, graphical program that ships with VB 6.0. It provides us with a user interface to build an Access database. So if you don't have Microsoft Access installed on your PC, VisData will give you much, but not all, of Access's functionality.

An alternative to using VisData, is to actually creating a database the hard way - using straight DAO VB code. In fact, you may choose to use both methods, as there are a few things that VisData just can't do. So you may choose to use VisData for the bulk of your database development, and fine-tune it with a few DAO commands.

Once we have all of the design under out belts, we will build the Address Book in the next chapter using DAO.

In case you were wondering what the finished product will look like and can't wait till the next chapter, here it is:

We all need a handy tool for storing friends' and associates' telephone numbers. Many times we have a bound paper telephone book where we can scribble down names and phone numbers. This is fine, but it doesn't provide a handy way to sort or search. With modern society, many of our friends not only have a home and business phone number but a cell phone number as well. With the advent of the Internet, most of our friends also have an e-mail address. Several have both a work and personal e-mail address. Many also have a business and possibly a personal fax number. Finally, our friends have a home and business street address we need to store. Phew! You get the idea. Well, our handy little program will be able to store and organize all of the personal information about our contacts. If you feel ambitious, it is simple to expand the program to store any other tidbits of information on your friends and business contacts that you may find useful. Possibly you want to store the birthday of a spouse, or have a tickler file that pops up each day with a list of people you need to call that day. We will build the foundation, but feel free to expand the program in any way you see fit.

The program contains a comments box that can remind us of topics of conversation, a meeting date and so on. We want to create a database that can store every shred of information we might need for all of our friends and business associates.

Before we start, let's define an important database term - **normalization**.

Normalization

Database table normalization is the process of organizing data in a database. The process of normalization includes both creating tables and establishing relationships between those tables using rules designed to protect the data and to make the database more flexible. These twin goals are achieved by eliminating both **redundancy** in the data fields as well as the **inconsistent dependency** between various fields.

If our database has redundant data, this wastes hard disk real estate. Not only that, it can cause a maintenance nightmare. For example, if data exists in more than one place and it has to be updated, the data must be changed in exactly the same way in all locations. In our address book, a friend's address change is much easier to implement if the address is stored only in a table that holds our contacts and nowhere else in the database.

We also mentioned **inconsistent dependency**. While it makes sense for a user to look in the Contacts table for the address of a particular friend or business associate, it may not make sense to look there for a log of all of the phone calls we have had with this person. The call log is related to, or dependent on, the person, or contact, and should therefore be moved to a Phonelog table. If a database has inconsistent dependencies, it can be difficult to access the data. It might be that the path to find the data may be missing or even broken.

So let's take a look at how we might start thinking about what fields we want to put into our Address Book project. By definition, these fields will be **unnormalized**. Once we figure out what fields (columns) we want in our database tables, we can then move on to the process of normalization.

Unnormalized Data Elements for the Address Book

Field Name	Data Type	Number of Characters
LastName	Text	20
FirstName	Text	15
MiddleInitial	Text	1
BirthDay	Date	
HomeStreet	Text	20
HomeCity	Text	10
HomeZip	Text	10
HomePhone	Text	15
HomeFax	Text	15

Field Name	Data Type	Number of Characters
HomeEmail	Text	30
CellPhone	Text	15
NotesOnPhoneCall	Memo	
CallDescription	Text	20

Our knee-jerk reaction might be just to create a database with a single monolithic table where each record looks like the above. What would be wrong with that? Well, let's say that we called a friend twice in the same day to discuss two separate projects we are working on. We would have to duplicate the entire record to simply add another NotesOnPhoneCall (what we discussed in this phone conversation) and CallDescription (what classification was the call: Business, Personal, etc.) field. Each of the other fields in our monolithic table would be duplicated except the NotesOnPhoneCall and CallDescription fields that held the topics of our conversations. If we have several CallDescription fields, such as Business, Programming, Stained Glass, etc., these fields would be repeated for many of the records.

You get the idea. The fields that are repeated over and over again without changing, such as CallDescription, are known as **repeating groups**. This is very wasteful on space and can cause our database to grow quickly. Not only that, there are other subtle problems that can crop up when we try to update our table. We will talk about these in a minute.

Before we write the first line of code for a database program, we must think long and hard about how the tables will be laid out. **The best database programs are designed - not built.** By that I mean that a good database design can mean the difference between a well-behaved and easily maintainable system and a monster that is constantly giving us problems. What we must do first is take a look at the fields we want in the database and then apply an approach that will eliminate all of the repeating groups. As a byproduct, our program will be faster and won't be susceptible to subtle bugs.

This approach is known by computer science types as **normalization**. We must think about our database and determine how we can actually break our single large table into several smaller but related tables. The process of looking at the fields we need and determining the fields that will be placed in each table is called **data modeling**. By going through the exercise of normalizing the data, we not only eliminate duplicated data in the tables, but accommodate any future changes as well. In a production database, we want to strive for what is known as the **3rd normal form**. That sounds a bit esoteric, but it's straightforward really.

> *Almost without exception, the difference between an effective and ineffective database program can be traced back to how the database itself is laid out.*

Of course, this is dependent on the skill and knowledge of the developer that designed the database. Because tools like Access make it so easy to create a database, some developers never take the time to learn about normalization. However, this will be the most important step in creating a truly professional database program. Let's see how we get there.

1st Normal Form - Eliminate Any Repeating Groups

First we want to take a look at all of the related fields in our single table. Then we want to give each logical group a separate table and provide a primary key in each.

> *To get to the 1st normal form, we look at our table and eliminate any repeating groups.*

Let's say in our single table approach that we wanted to review all of the NotesOnPhoneCall data items for our business associate Michael Hammer. First, we must find the Michael Hammer records. Once we have rounded up all of the Michael Hammer records, we scan all of the NotesOnPhoneCall fields associated with these records. Not only is this awkward, but it's also very inefficient and sloppy. If we have 100 records of conversations with Mr. Hammer, we will have his name, address and all of the rest of the information (that does not change) duplicated 100 times - once in each new record. This is not good.

So we first want to move the NotesOnPhoneCall to its own table. Why? Because there will be many of these records associated with a single contact. By moving repeating groups from the main monolithic table into its own table will result in the 1st normal form. We still need to relate these two tables in some manner so we can associate all of the notes for each contact. This is very easy. We can add a field to each of the two tables called ContactID. This will be the field that we use to relate the tables.

Contact Table	Notes Table
ContactID - Primary Key (unique)	ContactID - Primary Key (duplicates allowed)
LastName	DateofCall
FirstName	TypeofCall
	NotesOnPhoneCall

The primary key (ContactID) in the Contact table matches the primary key (also called ContactID) in the Notes table. This provides the foreign key in the Notes table, which can relate the two tables in a join operation. The primary advantage of a relational database is that there are no pointers. We will link the tables by defining relations between them. A **relation** consists of the link between records of two tables that have identical field values.

Earlier we discussed the one-to-many relationship between a single publisher and the titles that it publishes. The publisher information is stored once and has a unique PubID. Each of the titles published by this publisher has the same value in its **PubID** foreign key field. The publisher is stored once, but we can easily round up all of the titles associated with this publisher by grabbing all of the **Titles** records that have the same **PubID** as the publisher.

In our example above, we can see that a contact, Michael Hammer, will have a single ContactID. Say the value happens to be 5 (although the value is not important). The only thing that is important is that this value is unique in the Contact table. Now there might be 100s of calls logged for Mr. Hammer. Each of the 100s of calls will have the same ContactID value (5), in the Notes table. So we can relate the Notes table records that apply to Mr. Hammer by simply using an SQL statement that retrieves all of the Notes records that have a ContactID of 5. We do not have to replicate each and every field in the Contact table when we log a new call.

2nd Normal Form - Splitting Tables

If a field in a table is not fully dependent on the key, take it out and place it in a separate table. Take a look at the Contact table. The ContactID identifies each contact. Each of the fields we placed in this table is dependent on the key. The table essentially defines the contact. The contact name, address, and phone numbers are unique to that contact. So we did a good job on the Contact table. Each field is dependent on the primary key, ContactID.

Now look at the Notes table. The TypeOfCall might be either business or personal. This way we can associate notes with both business and personal activities. For example, one note might be items to discuss in an upcoming business meeting. Another note for the same person might be of a personal nature, for example, to meet for lunch next week. We might want to add another TypeOfCall for another group of calls. We might need a professional TypeOfCall, where we note a meeting next week to talk about databases or certification. Alternatively, we might belong to a hobby group that makes stained glass. We could then have a hobby designation for TypeOfCall. You get the idea - since we want this to be an extensible and very useable system, we must try to anticipate every eventuality.

Let's say that you have a business that distributes software. Several of your customers might have more than one of your products. You could easily make the TypeOfCall relate to a call on a specific software product. So you could bring up the record and see which product the person called about. Since this is personal in nature, we will stick with our classifications. However it's easy to see how something like this could easily be used in business.

If you have hundreds or thousands of records to modify, it's possible you might miss a few. For example, you might what to change all records listed as Professional in the TypeOfCall field to Business. If you forget to update a record, that record would have an incorrect TypeOfCall. Do you remember when I mentioned a few subtle bugs that can creep into your program? Well, this is one known as an **update anomaly**.

What happens when the last person in your database that had a Hobby classification call gets deleted? In this case, since the Hobby TypeOfCall is not stored anywhere except in the Contact record, it is now gone for good. This is referred to as a **delete anomaly**.

If we were to take a look at some possible entries in the Notes table, they might look something like this:

ContactID	DateOfCall	TypeOfCall	NotesOnPhoneCall
34	3/9/98 9:10am	Business	xxxxxxxxxx
34	3/9/98 11:01am	Professional	xxxxxxxxxx
51	3/9/98 12:04pm	Personal	xxxxxxxxxx
64	3/9/98 12:33pm	Business	xxxxxxxxxx
23	3/9/98 14:33pm	Professional	xxxxxxxxxx
43	3/9/98 15:33pm	Hobby	xxxxxxxxxx
43	3/9/98 17:33pm	Professional	xxxxxxxxxx

Notice that the TypeOfCall appears redundantly for various entries in the Notes table. In the above table, Business is repeated twice, Professional three times, etc. There is one of those pesky repeating groups again.

To remove the possibility of an update or delete anomaly, we will convert the tables to 2nd normal form. We do this by separating the fields that depend on the key (ContactID) from those depending only on the CallTypeID. This results in two separate tables. The first is the CallType, which gives our CallTypeID and CallDescription. The second is the Notes table, which holds the information about who we talked to as well as the time and contents of the particular call.

OK, you might be thinking that this is quite a bit of work, right? But consider that the type of call now only depends on the CallTypeID field. Suppose you wanted to reclassify a type of call in the old table – say, if you decided later that the Professional calls should really be Business. In that case you would have to go through each and every record that has "Professional" in the TypeOfCall field and change it to "Business". Do you remember our software business example? If we change the name of our product from DOS WidgetMaster to Win WidgetMaster 1.0, we would have to go through each and every record in the Notes table.

The beauty of the normalized approach is that if we want to reclassify a type of call, we simply make the change in a single record in the CallType table. By changing the contents of the field CallDescription, it becomes instantly available throughout the application. Since the CallTypeID is the same (and that is how we relate the tables) the new CallDescription is associated with all of the records that had the old name.

3rd Normal Form - Eliminate Columns Not Dependent on Key

The 3rd normal form is the Holy Grail of database design. We determine that if a field does not contribute to a description of the key, we must remove that field to a separate table. So each field in a table must be dependent on the key and independent of one another. In the 2nd normal form, we normalized the tables to assure dependency on the primary key.

> *In the 3rd normal form we scrutinize all non-key fields to ensure there is no interdependency. By that I mean that a change in one field does not force a change in another.*

As you can see, the process of normalization is simply breaking down our initial table into smaller, related tables. We know that the ContactID of our contact in our address book is the anchor, so that table becomes our base table. We want to examine all fields in this table and ensure that there are no fields that don't contribute to the contact.

In other words, the name and address will be in our Contact table. So will all of the static pieces of information that further identify the contact, like phone numbers, etc. For the sake of brevity, we will not break down the home fields into additional tables. A contact might have a primary home and a summer home in the Rockies. However, for our program, we will assume a single residence. However, feel free to normalize these if you wish.

Take another look at the Contact table. This will contain the static information on our contact. We inserted the ContactID field that uniquely identifies each contact in our database. This is because we could have two John Smiths as contacts. By using a numeric, unique ID field, we don't have to worry about collisions. This is recommended (by me) when there is the slightest possibility of a redundant entry in the key field. By using a unique number, you are assured that there will never, ever be a collision. If your contact gets married and changes her name, you simply change the name in the Contact table - but the ContactID remains the same. So all of the call logs to this person remain intact. They just now show up under Jamie Smith instead of Jamie Conners. Below is our normalized Contact table. Notice that each of the fields is unique to the key (the ContactID) and identifies the contact.

The Contact table satisfies the 1st normal form. It does not contain any repeating groups. In addition, since the table doesn't contain a multi-valued key (a key based on more than one field), the 2nd normal form is satisfied. We are using the ContactID as the primary key for this table. Finally, each of the fields contributes to the identification of the contact. Therefore, we have satisfied the 3rd normal form. It looks good, so let's build our database.

This is a screen in Access. The database we are going to build will look like this. Notice the one-to-many relationship between the Contact and the Notes table using the ContactID field.

> *I have seen several production databases that totally ignore normalization. I find this amazing, but it's true. By spending time on the front-end, laying out our tables properly and going through the normalization process, we will save hours of coding and debugging later on. We also eliminate the anomalies mentioned earlier. Many times these don't show up until the software is in operation for some time and then you really have a headache!*

As mentioned, we always want to adhere to 3rd normal form wherever possible. While it is desirable for all of the reasons mentioned above, there are some instances where it is just not practical. Take a look at the Contact table. If we really, really wanted to eliminate all possible inter-field dependencies as discussed, you would have to create separate tables for the Cities, ZIP codes and States. After all, we can (and probably will) have several contacts that live in the same city, let alone the same state. These fields will be duplicated for each contact that lives in the same city or state as another. In theory, we always want to pursue 3rd normal form. However, if we create many small tables, this may degrade our application's performance. It might even exceed the open file and memory capacities of your PC if taken to the extreme. So you, as the database designer, are now faced with the **design decision**. You must decide where to draw the line. However, knowing the normalization process and the task at hand usually makes this task manageable. Notice above how we made a design decision and didn't make these smaller tables.

One last point on normalization. After we've gone through all of the trouble to normalize our data, there might come a time when we want to de-normalize it again. Yikes! Why would we want to do that? Well, there is a relatively new branch of database analysis called **data warehousing**. (We will touch on this and something called **data mining** in a later chapter.) Many times the management of an organization wants to see trends in data. For example, the marketing types might want to scrutinize the demographics of the people that purchase our products. Is there a slow migration to the sunny clime of Florida for a large number of people that purchase our products? If so, there might be talk about moving the warehouse or distribution center closer to the largest concentration of people that buy our products. This could certainly cut down on shipping costs.

To build a data warehouse, we would have to de-normalize a lot of our data. This is because we might store orders from customers in an Orders table. If we wanted to see orders from a specific part of the country, we would find all clients in the Clients table that reside in the southeastern United States. We would then have to round up all orders placed by these customers from the orders table. Next, these pieces would be **re-aggregated**, or put together, in a single table for further analysis. Don't worry though, we won't destroy what we have so carefully constructed. We will simply aggregate data from several normalized tables into one massive table to perform the analysis.

There might be other times when you might want to de-normalize your database for performance reasons. In a multi-user environment for example, there are times when some higher traffic tables are de-normalized to reduce the number of joins required to get at the data. Funny, it seems that we have come full circle with this normalization business.

Creating our Database

If you have Microsoft Access 8.0, it is by far the easiest way to create your database. If fact, it does not get any easier. For the serious developers among you, that is the method of database creation that I suggest - use Access for all serious database development. However, if you don't have Access or just want to learn something new, I am going to show you two additional methods at your disposal for creating a database. VB 6.0 comes equipped with a handy little tool called **VisData**. This little gem will easily and painlessly create a database for you. It does have its limitations, but don't worry; I'll show you how to get around them with some trickery and guile. After all, this is a database book.

For the adventurous among you, stay tuned and we will also use DAO to create our database. This is by far the more powerful of the two methods and permits you to do anything that Access does as it relates to building databases. Please take the time to read both approaches to building the database, using DAO and using VisData, and then choose for yourself which method you want to use.

How do Access, VisData, the Data Control, Jet and DAO Relate to Each Other?

Microsoft Access is a stand-alone relational database product. Access includes two features that can be used by Visual Basic programmers - **Data Access Objects (DAO)** and **Microsoft Jet**. The Jet database engine is the **data manager** on which Microsoft Access is built. Jet can be manipulated by DAO using VB code or with the intrinsic data control using no code.

The Visual Basic 6.0 intrinsic **data control** takes advantage of DAO to provide even simpler data access using bound controls. As we have already seen, the **DBList**, **DBGrid** and **DBCombo** controls, when bound to an intrinsic data control, can provide nearly all of the DAO functionality without even having to write any code.

VisData (which happens to be written in Visual Basic) is a program that provides a graphical front end to create and manipulate Access databases. So VisData is a limited front-end to Access tables. VisData communicates with the database by using DAO and Jet.

Try It Out - Creating a Database with VisData

1 VisData is accessible right from the main menu of VB 6.0. Click Add-Ins and select Visual Data Manager.

> *Tip: If you ever need to locate the program itself, VisData is usually installed in the same directory as Visual Basic. You can do a quick file find on VISDATA.EXE to locate this gem. When you locate the file, double-click to start it up.*

2 Click on File | New | Microsoft Access | Version 7.0 MDB.

3 When the Select Microsoft Access Database to Create file save dialog box comes up, be sure to navigate to the **\BegDB** directory in the Save in drop-down box. Give your new database the name **Contacts.mdb** and click Save. This will create an empty database. The empty **.mdb** file will take up about 40Kb of disk space. Remember that we haven't added any tables yet. This is just the overhead of the database. So you should always make sure that you really need a database for your application before you create one. If you are just storing a few pieces of information, you might not want the large footprint of a database and a simple file will do.

4 Again, be sure to place the newly minted database in the **[Drive Letter]:\BegDB** sub directory that we created a while back. When the database is created, VisData will provide us with the interface shown below:

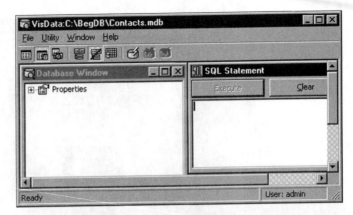

5 We just mentioned that an **.mdb** table has a large footprint, even when it's empty. Click on the + sign next to Properties and take a look at the default properties for our new **Contacts.mdb** database. You can see that even before we add a single field to a single table, the database already has some default properties:

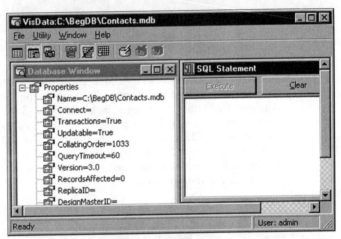

6 Click on the - sign to collapse the database properties. We want to add our first table. Right-click on the Properties in the Database Window. Click on New Table:

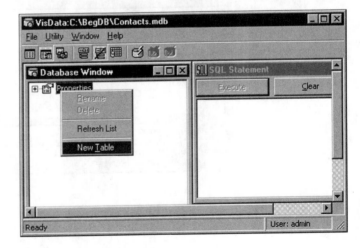

7 Now we will design our Contacts table for the Contacts database. Enter the name as shown below:

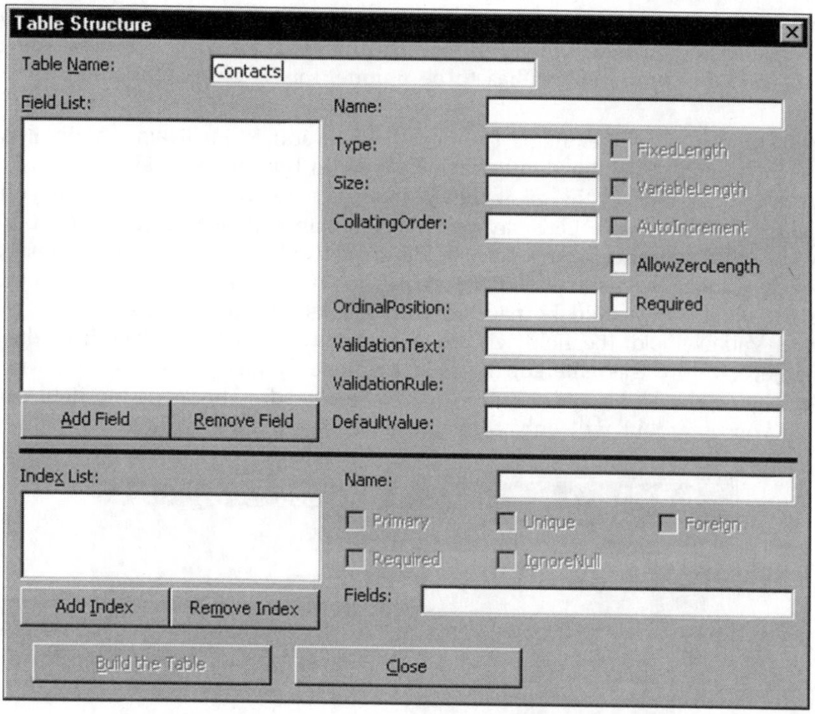

8 We now want to add our fields to the new table. The table will not actually be built until we press the Build the Table button in the lower left-hand side of the dialog box. Notice that it is now disabled. This is because we have not yet added any fields. Click on the Add Field button under the Field List box:

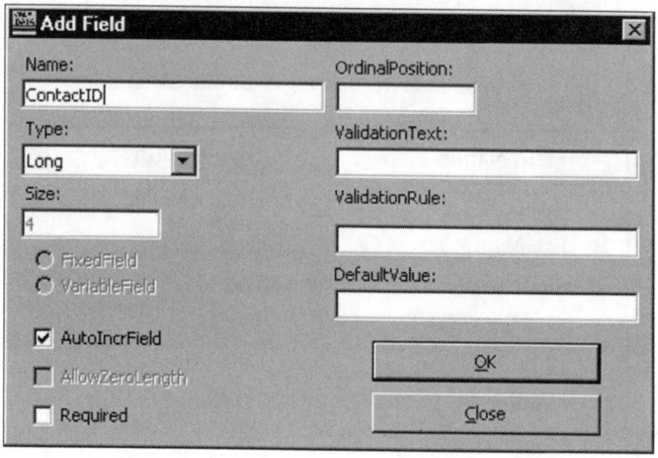

9 Add the field ContactID as shown. Make it type Long and select the AutoIncrField check box. One of the things beefed up in the VB 6.0 release of VisData is the ability to make a field of type AutoIncrField. In earlier versions of VisData I have used, this option was always grayed out. An AutoIncrField type of a field is incredibly handy because it automatically adds a new, unique number to the field. So when we need things like a primary key, that by definition has to be unique, this is perfect for that task.

10 Click OK and add another field. The next field to add is LastName. Make it type Text with a Size of 20. Click on the VariableField radio button and check the box AllowZeroLength. One of the great things about Access .mdb tables is that you can make the fields variable length. Let's say that the last name of one of your friends is Chow. Many databases require fixed length fields. In a fixed length field, since this name is only 4 characters long, the field wastes 16 characters. 20% of the field would contain the name while the other 80% would be padded with blanks. Not a good use of disk real estate. By selecting VariableField, the field will be dynamically sized to the length of the entry. If the last name of Chow was entered, the field would only take up 4 characters, not the entire 20. Be sure to check this radio button for all text fields. This way, the field can grow up to the size you enter, but will only consume what is necessary to hold the value entered:

11 Proceed to add the following fields to our new Contacts table:

Field Name	Type/Length
ContactID	Long
LastName	Text 20
FirstName	Text 15
MiddleInitial	Text 1
BirthDay	Date/Time
HomeStreet	Text 20
HomeCity	Text 10
HomeState	Text 2
HomeZip	Text 10

Field Name	Type/Length
HomePhone	Text 15
HomeFax	Text 15
HomeEmail	Text 30
HomeCellPhone	Text 15

12 OK, that's a bit tedious. However, since we thought about our structure on the front end, we only have to do this once. See, planning even helps here. After you have added each of the fields, click <u>C</u>lose on the **Add Field** dialog box. Now take a look at the table structure:

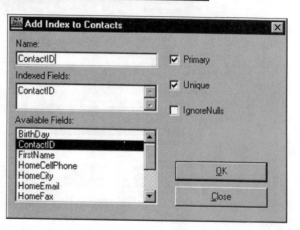

13 Before we actually build our table, we want to add a primary key to our **Contacts** table. Click on the **Add** <u>I</u>**ndex** button. This will display the **Add Index** dialog box:

14 Click the ContactID from the Available Fields list box. We want to make this the primary index so check the Primary check box. Remember that we made this field type AutoIncrField? This will ensure the field has a unique value. Check the Unique check box here.

15 When an index is created, it must have a name. Any name will do, let's name this index ContactID so we can keep things straight. All indexes must have a name so we can refer to the index when we use DAO. Now click OK to create the primary key.

16 Let's add another index here. We want to select two fields, the LastName and the FirstName to be included in the new index. Give the new index the name contactName. Do **not** select Primary, we already defined the ContactID field as our primary index for the Contacts table. **Don't** check Unique either. We could have more than one entry with the name John Smith:

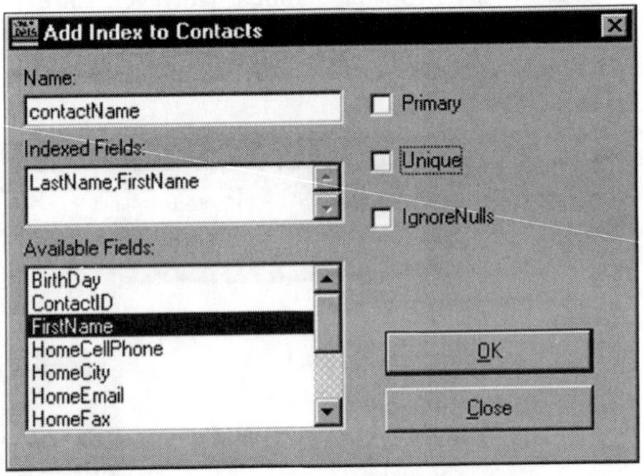

17 Click OK to add the new index, then click Close to dismiss the Add Index dialog box. There, we have created our table. All of the fields are displayed in the Field List and both indexes are in the Index List. If everything is in order, click Build the Table. Up to now, we have been creating a definition of a table. Clicking the Build button actually constructs the table with the fields and indexes we have just defined:

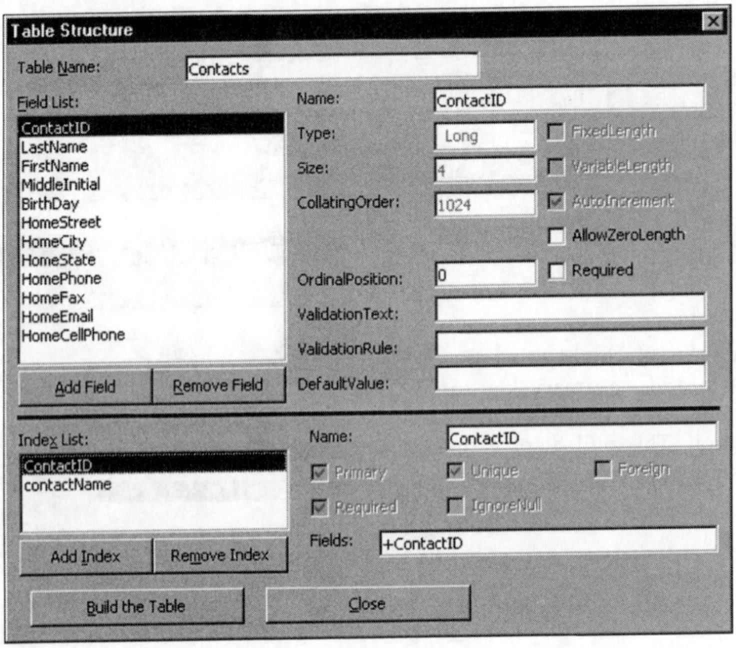

Guidelines for Creating Indexes

Because they are easy to create, some beginners add more indexes than are needed. First, it is not a good idea to index fields that have duplicated data, such as Boolean fields that will only be true or false. This also goes for gender fields, such as male/female. Stay away from indexing state codes that can have a maximum of 50 different types. As for concurrency issues, this will come up during multi-user applications. One index can represent several data pages. Simply put, this means that modifying an index on a specific record can lock other users in a totally different part of the database from updating an indexed field on their screen. So the moral of the story is to use indexes when you need them, but use them judiciously because there is a performance hit.

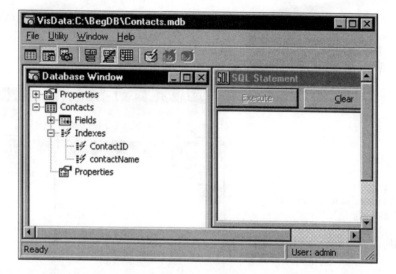

Try It Out - Now Build the Other Two Tables

1 OK, following the same procedure, let's build two additional two tables. Name the first table Notes and build it according to this table:

Field	Data Type
ContactID	Long
DateOfCall	Date/Time
CallTypeID	Long
NotesOnPhoneCall	Memo
CallCounter	Long (AutoInc)

When you add the CallCounter field to the Notes table, make sure you check the AutoIncrField check box.

There is no need to add an index to the Notes table. Press <u>B</u>uild the Table button after you have finished. This step actually constructs the table in the database.

2 Build the second table and call it CallType. Add fields to CallType according to the following table:

Field	Data Type
CallTypeID	Long(index this field)
CallDescription	Text 20

Add an index to the CallTypeID field in the CallType table. Check the Primary and Unique check boxes.

Again, click on the <u>B</u>uild the Table button when you have finished.

3 When you are finished, your VisData screen should look like this:

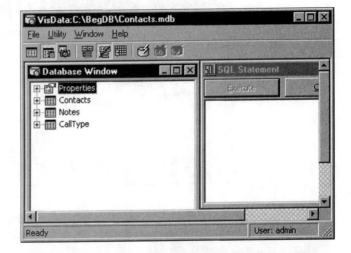

4 If you need to modify any of the tables, simply right-click on the table name and choose <u>D</u>esign. This will permit you to add or delete fields if you make a mistake:

There, that's all there is to it. We have just finished creating the database (**schema**) using VisData. In the next section we will do the same thing but with DAO and then use that model to build our address book application in the next chapter.

Creating a Database with DAO

DAO provides a framework for using Visual Basic 6.0 code to create and manipulate databases. DAO supplies a hierarchical set of objects that directly use the Microsoft Jet database engine to access data. Using DAO, you can access the following:

▶ Microsoft Jet (**.mdb**) databases

▶ ODBC data sources, using an ODBC driver

▶ Installable ISAM databases, such as dBASE®, Paradox™ and Microsoft FoxPro which the database engine can read directly. And remember, we could also read these with the data control.

Actually, we have been using DAO already for several examples in the book. DAO 3.50 is the first version to bring incredible power to developers who are developing not only file-server, but client-server database applications as well. In addition to providing programmatic access to the Microsoft Jet database engine and several other back ends as described above, DAO 3.51 now provides access to remote database servers like Microsoft SQL Server and Oracle databases. These are an important part of **client/server applications**.

Another path DAO 3.51 provides for accessing remote data is known as **ODBCDirect**. Before 3.50, if you wanted to access data through **Open Database Connectivity** (**ODBC**), DAO first passed your calls to the Jet database engine. Then Jet passed the calls along to the ODBC driver. Although this method got the job done, you can see that it is not always the most efficient way. Most developers using this approach quickly realized two weaknesses. The first, of course, was that it was necessary to load Jet, even though the database being accessed was not a Microsoft Jet database. Second, because of the relatively large memory footprint of Jet, the process could be slow. Now, with **ODBCDirect**, developers have a direct path to ODBC and their data. Today developers have two paths to data with a single DAO interface. With DAO, you can choose either ODBCDirect or Microsoft Jet.

Of course, one of the two paths will make more sense depending on what the application is doing. But there might be times you will need to use both paths in the same application, depending on the tasks you are working on.

Naturally, if your application is hitting a Microsoft Jet **.mdb** database as we have been doing in this book, you should definitely use the Microsoft Jet approach. This is because ODBCDirect was created specifically for accessing remote data. Another reason to use the power of Jet would be if you want to join data in tables stored in different back ends such as Oracle and Microsoft SQL Server. You will need to use Jet in this case because in its bag of tricks is the ability to provide **heterogeneous joins**. It is possible to join a table in a Microsoft Access database with another table in, say, a FoxPro database. Such a join between tables created in different **database management systems** (**DBMSs**) is called a heterogeneous join.

> *A back end server refers to the system that is the repository for the data. This is in contrast to the client, which presents data to the user. In a client/server system, the back end is the server. In an integrated database system, such as Microsoft Visual FoxPro or Microsoft Excel, the back end is the core database functionality of the specific product. Typically, the back end contains the code that handles not only data storage, but also indexes, any validation required, and any other database functions.*

So you might now be thinking that ODBCDirect doesn't provide much functionality at all. Well, actually most client/server developers simply want to read data in, probably modify it and write it back to the back end. Speed is of the essence. So in those cases, ODBCDirect is the way to fly.

As you can see from the drawing, we can use DAO 3.51 and access just about any type of data we need. In our book examples, we will be taking the path from VB 6.0 to DAO to Jet to various `.mdb` databases. But as you can see, DAO permits several paths to get at many data sources. ADO takes this concept much further, as we will see a bit later on:

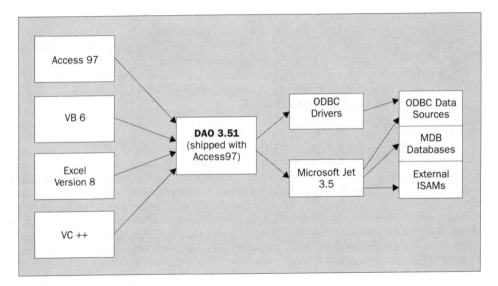

Jet is extremely flexible in its ability to transparently handle data from a variety of sources. External data falls into two categories. There is **Indexed Sequential Access Method (ISAM)** and **Open Database Connectivity (ODBC)**. The **ISAM** data sources are the traditionally PC-based databases such as Paradox and Microsoft Access.

ISAM File Server, and Relational Client Server

When we consider database application design, of course we must consider how the VB 6.0 application code interacts with the database at hand. Some applications treat the database simply as a storage place for a bunch of records. Here, the client application itself performs most of the operations on the data, such as filtering, aggregating, or matching records, and all of the other database tasks. This style of database access is common in desktop database programs - such as Access - that use an ISAM database.

The second style of database access, true **client server** style, is much more appropriate for a program interacting with a relational database like SQL Server. In this scenario, the server takes on most of the database operations. Let's take a look at both styles.

ISAM Data Access

Over the years, ODBC has matured to be the primary means of accessing remote data while Jet has become the native Jet and ISAM interface of choice for desktop solutions. Basically, DAO/Jet is primarily designed to communicate with databases because it supports most common ISAM data access techniques. Therefore DAO/Jet is *the* solution when it comes to using native Jet (**.mdb**, an ISAM data source) or other ISAM data sources such as Btrieve, FoxPro, Paradox and dBase.

The ISAM data sources are the traditional desktop PC-based database formats. These include Access itself, FoxPro, Paradox, and others. When we use Jet, it communicates to the data store using built-in ISAM files that manipulate the database. Jet manages ISAM indexes and locates rows based on those indexes. So, using **.mdb** files, we are working with a file-server as opposed to a client-server, which is what we use when our application's database is located on a network of some sort.

When using ISAM files, applications typically open an ISAM file and process each record one-by-one until the end of the file is reached. Because the ISAM engine performs only the most basic data access operations, your application must take on the role of creating and using internal recordset data structures on the local PC. What does this mean? Well, in a client-server database, such as SQL Server, all of the grunt work is done on the server. Using ISAM, even though the database is on the server, all of the data must be sent back to the application where it does the grunt work locally.

The strength of Jet is in its ability to join data from a variety of data sources and also permit updates against this disparate data - no small feat. When an application must leverage existing ISAM data, one of the most powerful tools available is the Microsoft Jet database engine.

The Relational Style Client-Server Data Access

In this style of data access all of the data operations are performed at the server. One of the capabilities of SQL Server and other relational style client/server databases is the capacity to filter data at the server and only send back the results - not the entire table. This means that only the minimum data required is returned to the client. Using a true client server facility minimizes expensive network traffic between the server and client.

Now let's move on to DAO. We will actually review how to build the exact same table we did using VisData, but the hard way - using DAO. You may be wondering why you would want to do things the hard way? Good question. Sometimes it's the only way. For example, you may run into a situation where you need to define a database table on the fly - using code. You may have a program that permits Help Desk operators to build a new custom database for new product offerings. This table may require special fields to hold specific comments. There is no way to know ahead of time what the database will look like. DAO makes this possible.

411

The DAO Object Model - what is it?

Look at the figure below: this is a diagram showing the **DAO object hierarchy**. At the top is the **DBEngine** object. This is the root that controls and contains all of the other objects in the hierarchy. The **DBEngine** contains an **Errors** collection and a **Workspaces** collection. A **collection** is just a set of related objects. A Workspace contains all open databases. It only exists for an active session. So the Workspaces collection contains all of the Workspaces that are currently active for a specific running instance of DAO. As you study the drawing, you will realize that DAO is really a collection of collections. DAO can be seen represented as the object model conceptually like this:

Yikes! What the heck is an object model anyway? Well, before your eyes glaze over, let's spend a minute on this hierarchy. It really does make sense once you spend a few minutes examining it. The diagram is just a quick way for DAO to organize its functionality and for us to access it.

Objects and Collections

Think of the diagram above as a visual model of DAO. The DBEngine object contains a collection of Workspaces. Each Workspace contains a collection of Databases. We know that each database contains tables, right? Take a look at the TableDef collection. This is simply a collection of table definitions (descriptions of each table) that are contained in each database. Next, we know that each table contains field objects, right? Well, under each TableDef we can see a collection of Field objects. This is just a collection of all of the fields for that specific table. Also, each table might have one or more indexes, so these would be contained in the Index collection. Each Index object has a collection of one or more Field objects that it uses for indexing. So you can see that DAO is really nothing more than a collection of objects.

For now, let's just look at the Database collection. A workspace can contain several open databases that you might be working on. For example, you might have a database open that has sales figures for your new software and another that contains summary information for marketing. The Databases collection would contain a collection of two databases. Each of those two databases has its own collection of tables, open recordsets, etc.

A **Database** object represents an open database.

Workspace
  └ Databases
      └ Database
          TableDefs
          Containers
          QueryDefs
          Recordsets
          Relations

Working with Collections

To use an object in Visual Basic, you must specify which object it is that you intend to use. With the DAO structure there are two types of objects with which we will work. They are objects that exist individually and those that belong to collections. Referring to the DAO object model above, we can see that the DBEngine is a stand-alone object. There is only one of those objects.

The other objects in the DAO object model belong to collections. We need to distinguish which object in the collection we want to work with, and of course which collection contains the object. For example, the DAO Database object has a TableDef collection. If you refer to a TableDef object, you need to specify the Database to which it belongs.

Getting and using Objects Contained in Collections

In DAO, each object in the object hierarchy maintains one or more collections of subordinate objects. For example, take a look at the DBEngine, the Jet database engine. The DBEngine object maintains a collection of open workspaces. Each workspace object then can maintain a collection of open databases.

Let's take a look at a Chevy Corvette Collection:

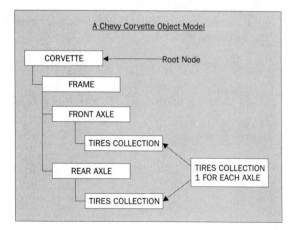

A Chevy Corvette Object Model

The Corvette object has a Frame property that could be accessed to receive a

413

reference to its Frame object. The Frame object has a FrontAxle and RealAxle property, each of which would return an Axle object. The Axle object would have a Tire property that would return a Tire collection object. The Tire collection contains Tire objects (left and right tire objects).

Database Objects

The Databases collection consists of all Database objects currently open within a Workspace object. You might open a Workspace and then open a Database object for an Access table and another for a Paradox table. Possibly you are converting the Paradox data to Access for a project. Both databases can be opened within the same Workspace. When we open a database in Visual Basic 6.0, we get a reference to the database. We might have something like this:

```
Dim myDatabase as Database
Dim sPathtoDB as String

sPathToDB = "C:\MYDATABASE.MDB"
myDataBase = OpenDatabase(sPathToDB)
```

myDataBase is now set to a reference to the database **MYDATABASE.MDB**. **myDataBase** is an **object variable**. Unlike other variables, they have no value in and of themselves. By that I mean that an object variable points to an object (like a database) in memory. So our variable **myDataBase** is our handle to the database and all of its hierarchy of objects.

Connect the Dots

In order to access something in the collection, we just keep appending the collection names with dots. For example, let's say we wanted to look at all of the tables that are contained in the **Biblio.mdb** database. We know that the TableDef objects collection is contained in each Database object. So to get at them, we just connect the dots. As an example, you could create a very simple VB project to list all of the tables in the **Biblio.mdb** database.

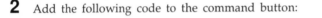

Try It Out - Listing the Biblio.mdb tables using DAO

1 Create a new project called **\Chapter9\prjTables**. Add a list box and a command button as shown:

2 Add the following code to the command button:

```
Private Sub Command1_Click()

    Dim myDatabase As Database
    Dim myTable As TableDef          'this will hold the tableDef(inition)

    Set myDatabase = OpenDatabase("C:\BegDB\BIBLIO.MDB")

    For Each myTable In myDatabase.TableDefs      'dots to get the tableDefs
        List1.AddItem myTable.Name                'dots to get the names
    Next

End Sub
```

3   Select <u>P</u>roject | Refere<u>n</u>ces and add the Microsoft DAO 3.51 Object Library reference to the project:

4   Press *F5* to run the program. Each and every table in the database is listed and displayed in the list box:

We can see that the program gives us the information we wanted. All of the tables that begin with **MSys** are maintained by the **.mdb** file for storing disparate information. We are not interested in them, but our little program lists all TableDefs for all of the tables.

How It Works

As explained earlier, in order to work with an object that belongs to a collection, we must refer to that specific object in its collection. Since objects are related to one another in an object hierarchy, you must also make clear where the object and the specific collection exists in the overall hierarchy. In other words, if the object you are looking for is a member of a collection, you must first qualify the object with the name of its collection. If that collection belongs to yet another object, you must qualify the object with the name of that collection, and so on. We do that by connecting the dots.

We refer to DAO objects in code in the same way that we refer to other objects. Because the DBEngine object doesn't have a collection, we can refer to it directly. It is implied, so we really don't have to specify the DBEngine. However, we must refer to other objects within their collections and according to their positions in the object hierarchy.

We can refer to an object within a collection in one of two ways. You can specify its **Name** property or you can refer to its index number, which tells you its position within the specific collection. In the following example, which refers to a Database object within the DAO Databases collection, we are referring to a database by its name.

The first thing we do is to **Dim** an object variable as type **Database**:

```
Dim myDatabase As Database
Dim myTable As TableDef          'this will hold the TableDef(inition)
```

We then **Dim** another object variable as type **TableDef**. In DAO, a **TableDef** is an object that defines the structure of a **base table** or an attached table. A base table is a table in a Microsoft Jet (**.mdb**) database.

We then call the **OpenDatabase** method of the DBEngine to open a specific database and set its reference to the object variable, **myDatabase**. We can now refer to the open database, **Biblio.mdb**, via this object variable:

```
Set myDatabase = OpenDatabase("C:\BegDB\BIBLIO.MDB")
```

In order to print out all the tables in a database, the procedure must loop through, or **enumerate**, all the TableDef objects in the TableDef collection. We accomplished this by using the **For Each…Next** statement to perform the same operation on each member of the collection.

To use the **For Each…Next** statement, we first identified which objects we wanted to enumerate, and of course which collection they reside in. Therefore, we enumerate the **TableDefs** collection of the database referenced by **myDatabase**. Each item in the **TableDefs** collection is assigned to the variable **myTable**. By enumerating the collection this way, the first time through the loop, the first item in the collection is referenced by **myTable**. We then print out that object's name. Then the next time through the loop, the second object in the **TableDefs** collection is referenced by the **myTable** object variable and we print out its name. This process is continued until each item in the **TableDefs** collection is referenced:

```
For Each myTable In myDatabase.TableDefs    'dots to get the tableDefs
    List1.AddItem myTable.Name              'dots to get the names
Next
```

By using the variable, **myTable**, we can perform a method, or set or return a property on each object in the collection. In our case, we are just printing the name. The great thing about enumerating a collection is that we don't have to even know how many objects the collection contains.

You can traverse or iterate through a DAO (or any) collection in the following way:

```
For intCounter = 0 To object.collection.Count - 1
  ' do something with the object
Next intCounter
```

However, the preferred method is the one we used:

```
For Each object In collection
    ' do something with the object
Next object
```

Let's say we wanted to get the fields in each table. Well, just connect the **Fields** collection with a dot. To take it just a step further, if we simply wanted to find out how many fields are in each of the tables, we could write something like this:

```
Dim myDatabase As Database
Dim myTable As TableDef
Dim myFields As Fields
Dim myField As Field

Set myDatabase = OpenDatabase("C:\BegDb\BIBLIO.MDB")

For Each myTable In myDatabase.TableDefs
    List1.AddItem myTable.Name & " has " & myTable.Fields.Count _
                    & " fields"
Next
```

Notice how we have **myTable.Fields.Count**. We just connected the dots to get to the next level in the DAO object model.

Recordset Objects

Once we have our reference to a database, we can have access to the tables and fields the collections contain. We are no strangers to recordsets. We use them to manipulate record-level data in the database. Like the database, we use an object variable to gain access to the recordset:

```
Dim rsMyTable as Recordset
Set rsMyTable = myDataBase.OpenRecordset("Contacts")
```

If we don't specify a type of recordset to open, DAO defaults to opening a table.

Options for Opening a Recordset

We use the **OpenRecordset** method to open a recordset object. We can specify which type of recordset we want by using the following constants:

dbOpenTable	Opens a table-type recordset object. This can only work on a single table.
dbOpenDynamic	Opens a dynamic-type recordset object.
dbOpenDynaset	Opens a dynaset-type recordset object. This permits joining several tables.
dbOpenSnapshot	Opens a snapshot-type recordset object. This is a read-only recordset
dbOpenForwardOnly	Opens a forward-only-type recordset object. This can only scroll forward.

So if we wanted to open a dynaset, we simply place the type after the SQL query:

```
Dim mySQL as string
mySQL = "SELECT Customer.Type, Notes.Detail FROM Customer, Notes"
mySQL =  mySQL & " WHERE Customer.Type = 5"
```

```
Set rsMyTable = myDataBase.OpenRecordset(mySQL, dbOpenDynaset)
```

Now once we have a reference to the recordset, we can reference its fields using the **!** bang operator:

```
With rsMyTable
    .MoveFirst
    MsgBox(rsMyTable!Type)
End With
```

So we first get a reference variable to the database, **myDataBase**. That reference can now access the collection of tables contained in the database. We get the data in those tables by creating a recordset. The reference variable, **rsMyTable**, now references the recordset created from **mySQL** and with the recordset, we can get at the collection of fields. So it's pretty straightforward, really.

If you are like me, the easiest way to really understand something is to work with it. So if you have stayed with me this far, we are now ready to create our normalized database using straight DAO.

Try It Out - Creating the Database with DAO

1 Start a new project and create a form with a single button on it. Name the button **cmdCreateDB**. Since we will be using the non-visual DAO to create this database there is no need for anything fancy here. Please add the Microsoft DAO 3.51 Object Library reference to the project before we start writing any code.

2 In the general section of the form, enter the following definitions:

```
Option Explicit
Dim db As Database
Dim tblDef As TableDef
Dim fldDef As Field
Dim indx As Index
Dim dbName As String
```

3 Then in the **Click** event procedure of the **cmdCreateDB** button, enter the following:

```
Private Sub cmdCreateDB_Click()
```

```
dbName = "C:\BegDB\CONTACTS.MDB"
If (Len(Dir(dbName))) Then
  Kill dbName
End If

Set db = DBEngine.Workspaces(0).CreateDatabase(dbName, dbLangGeneral)

Call createContactTable

Call createNotesTable

Call createCallTypeTable

Call createRelationships

MsgBox("Database successfully created.")
```

```
End Sub
```

Here, we first give our database the name **Contacts.mdb** and create it in our **BegDB** sub-directory.

> *Note: If you have already created the database Contacts.mdb using VisData, this program will delete that table. If you wish to build the table with DAO, then you might wish to create another subdirectory for this project.*

The **If** statement simply checks to see if the database already exists. If it does, we delete it and start fresh. The reason for this is that you may not get all of the typing down correctly the first time or you may wish to modify the tables or attributes. This way you won't get a pesky error from Visual Basic telling you that the database already exists:

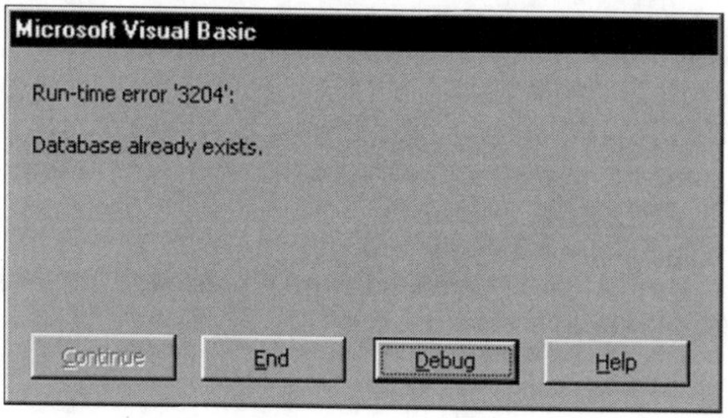

Then after we successfully create the database, we simply call four subroutines. The first three create each of our three normalized tables that we decided we needed for our address book. The fourth creates the relationships between two of the tables. Again, all of this is done with DAO and no part of it has a visual interface.

4 Add a subroutine called **createContactTable** and enter the following code:

```
Public Sub createContactTable()
```

```
'-- Create the Contact table here --
Set tblDef = db.CreateTableDef("Contact")

'--Create the fields in the contact table --
Set fldDef = tblDef.CreateField("ContactID", dbLong)
fldDef.Attributes = dbAutoIncrField
tblDef.Fields.Append fldDef
Set fldDef = tblDef.CreateField("LastName", dbText, 20)
tblDef.Fields.Append fldDef
Set fldDef = tblDef.CreateField("FirstName", dbText, 15)
tblDef.Fields.Append fldDef
Set fldDef = tblDef.CreateField("MiddleInitial", dbText, 1)
tblDef.Fields.Append fldDef
Set fldDef = tblDef.CreateField("Birthday", dbDate)
tblDef.Fields.Append fldDef
Set fldDef = tblDef.CreateField("HomeStreet", dbText, 20)
tblDef.Fields.Append fldDef
Set fldDef = tblDef.CreateField("HomeCity", dbText, 12)
tblDef.Fields.Append fldDef
Set fldDef = tblDef.CreateField("HomeState", dbText, 2)
tblDef.Fields.Append fldDef
Set fldDef = tblDef.CreateField("HomeZip", dbText, 10)
tblDef.Fields.Append fldDef
Set fldDef = tblDef.CreateField("HomePhone", dbText, 15)
tblDef.Fields.Append fldDef
Set fldDef = tblDef.CreateField("HomeFax", dbText, 15)
tblDef.Fields.Append fldDef
Set fldDef = tblDef.CreateField("HomeEmail", dbText, 30)
tblDef.Fields.Append fldDef
Set fldDef = tblDef.CreateField("HomeCellPhone", dbText, 15)
tblDef.Fields.Append fldDef
db.TableDefs.Append tblDef

'-- Add the Primary Key --
Set indx = tblDef.CreateIndex("PrimaryKey")
Set fldDef = indx.CreateField("ContactID")
indx.Fields.Append fldDef
indx.Primary = True
tblDef.Indexes.Append indx
```

```
End Sub
```

OK, let's review what is going on here. In this sub we are creating a table and then adding all of the fields we need. Then while we are at it, we will also add the primary key. We will need this key for searching out our contacts.

The first thing we want to do is create our table. Since we set our reference variable **db** to the new database we created in the **Click** event, we tell DAO that we want to create a new table in that database. By using the **CreateTableDef** method, we are creating the definition of a new table.

```
Set tblDef = db.CreateTableDef("Contact")
```

Now we have access to our reference variable **tblDef** that is pointing to the new table we have just created. However, our table isn't of much use to us unless we add some fields to it.

```
Set fldDef = tblDef.CreateField("ContactID", dbLong)
fldDef.Attributes = dbAutoIncrField
tblDef.Fields.Append fldDef
```

So again, we set our **fldDef** reference variable to a new field we call **"ContactID"**. The second parameter we pass is the type of field we need, in this case a **Long** integer.

Once we have successfully created the field, we make it auto-incrementing. We want this so that for each contact we add to the database, DAO will automatically add a unique number to this field. This way we can reference any other records that relate to this contact with this unique number. We simply set the attribute of this field to **dbAutoIncrField**. That's it! We now have a field that will do the work of adding a unique value to the field for us.

Once we have the field defined and its attribute set, we want to append that field to the **Fields** collection of the table definition. Now our field is part of our new table. We don't have to worry about setting any additional attributes of any fields for the rest of the table.

The rest of the fields we add are straightforward. The next will be a field called **"LastName"** of type **Text** with a length of **20**.

```
Set fldDef = tblDef.CreateField("LastName", dbText, 20)
```

See, it's pretty simple. Once all of the fields have been added to the table, we then want to append the newly minted table to the database collection of table definitions.

```
db.TableDefs.Append tblDef
```

As mentioned, we want to add a primary key index to our table. Let's do this with the **ContactID** field. We want to use this field because, since it is auto-incrementing, DAO will ensure it is unique. It is possible we could have two Smiths. Then we would want to include the first name to make the key multi-field. We could also have two John Smiths. Then we would need to consider the middle initial and so on. By using this approach we can create a single field key that is guaranteed to be unique.

```
Set indx = tblDef.CreateIndex("PrimaryKey")
Set fldDef = indx.CreateField("ContactID")
indx.Fields.Append fldDef
indx.Primary = True
tblDef.Indexes.Append indx
```

We now set our **indx** reference variable to be a new index of type **PrimaryKey**. Then we tell DAO that we want our **PrimaryKey** to be attached to the field **"ContactID"**. Once complete, we append the new indexed field, **fldDef**, to the collection of fields for the index of our table. We notify DAO that this field is the primary key for the table. There can be several indexes on several fields in our table. However, there can only be a single primary index per table. Finally, we append the new index, **indx**, to the collection of indexes of our new table. Again, our new table, **Contacts**, is referenced by the reference variable **tblDef**. That's all there is to it.

5 Add another subroutine called **createNotesTable** as follows:

```
Public Sub createNotesTable()
```

```
'-- Create the Notes table here --
Set tblDef = db.CreateTableDef("Notes")

'—Create the fields in the Notes table --
Set fldDef = tblDef.CreateField("ContactID", dbLong)
tblDef.Fields.Append fldDef
Set fldDef = tblDef.CreateField("DateOfCall", dbDate)
tblDef.Fields.Append fldDef
Set fldDef = tblDef.CreateField("CallTypeID", dbLong)
tblDef.Fields.Append fldDef
Set fldDef = tblDef.CreateField("NotesOnPhoneCall", dbMemo)
tblDef.Fields.Append fldDef
Set fldDef = tblDef.CreateField("CallCounter", dbLong)
fldDef.Attributes = dbAutoIncrField
tblDef.Fields.Append fldDef
db.TableDefs.Append tblDef
```

```
End Sub
```

This table is much simpler. We do not need to add an index, so we just add the fields and append them to the table, then append the table to the database. Notice that for the **NotesOnPhoneCall** field we use a type **dbMemo**. This will essentially permit us to create an unlimited amount of text in the field. You may decide that you want to make it a text field with 250 characters. Simply go back and change this field definition and rerun the program. A fresh new database will be created with the new field definition.

6 Add another subroutine to create the **CallType** table as follows:

```
Public Sub createCallTypeTable()
```

```
'-- Create the CallType table here --
Set tblDef = db.CreateTableDef("CallType")

'—Create the fields in the CallType table --
Set fldDef = tblDef.CreateField("CallTypeID", dbLong)
fldDef.Attributes = dbAutoIncrField
tblDef.Fields.Append fldDef
Set fldDef = tblDef.CreateField("CallDescription", dbText, 20)
tblDef.Fields.Append fldDef
db.TableDefs.Append tblDef
```

```
'-- Add the Primary Key --
Set indx = tblDef.CreateIndex("PrimaryKey")
Set fldDef = indx.CreateField("CallTypeID")
indx.Fields.Append fldDef
indx.Primary = True
tblDef.Indexes.Append indx
```

End Sub

The same logic applies here. There are no surprises. Notice that we are adding an auto-incrementing attribute to the **CallTypeID** field. This way we can uniquely identify each type of call. When a call is made, this ID will be stored in the **Notes.CallID** field. So if we want to change the value of the **CallDescription** field from say **Business** to **Projects**, the underlying relationship between the tables has not changed. The new description is instantly available throughout the program. There is no need to search all of the fields that contain **Business** and change them to **Projects**. That is the beauty of normalization.

7 Finally, add another subroutine that will hold the DAO code to add a relationship between the **Contact** and **Notes** tables:

```
Public Sub createRelationships()
```

```
Dim makeRelation As Relation
Dim fld As Field

Set makeRelation = db.CreateRelation("MyRelationship")
makeRelation.Table = "Contact"
makeRelation.ForeignTable = "Notes"

Set fld = makeRelation.CreateField("ContactID")
fld.ForeignName = "ContactID"
makeRelation.Fields.Append fld
makeRelation.Attributes = dbRelationDeleteCascade
db.Relations.Append makeRelation
```

End Sub

Referential integrity is used in table relationships to help ensure information in one table matches information in another. For example, each entry in the **Notes** table must be associated with a specific contact in the **Contact** table. A **Notes** record cannot be added to the database for a contact that does not exist in the database.

Traditionally, if we wanted to ensure referential integrity, tons of code was required. Let's say that we wanted to delete a contact, John Smith, from our database and that we had 200 contact calls logged in the **Notes** table for John Smith. The **ContactID** field in the **Notes** table relates all of the notes for John Smith to him. When we delete the John Smith record from our **Contact** table, we must ensure that we delete all of the **Notes** records for John Smith as well. If we failed to do this, there would be orphaned records in the **Notes** table that could never be accessed.

DAO permits us to automatically define a relationship in code. By doing this, we can ensure that if we delete a **Contact** record, each and every **Notes** record for that contact is also deleted. Being basically lazy, we can save some code and ensure that it is done right at the same time.

```
Set makeRelation = db.CreateRelation("MyRelationship")
makeRelation.Table = "Contact"
makeRelation.ForeignTable = "Notes"
```

Using the same approach as before, we set our reference variable, **makeRelation**, to a new relation using the DAO **CreateRelation** method. We must give it a name, in this case **MyRelationship**. The name is never used, but DAO expects one none the less. Once our reference variable is set, we tell it the base table and the foreign table. These are the two tables we are relating.

```
Set fld = makeRelation.CreateField ("ContactID")
fld.ForeignName = "ContactID"
```

The base table field, **ContactID**, is set to our **fld** reference variable. Then we specify the key we want to relate this field to in our foreign table. Of course, we named that field **ContactID** as well. Now the relationship is set between the unique primary key **ContactID** in the base table **Contact** and the non-unique foreign key, **ContactID**, in the related table **Notes**.

```
makeRelation.Fields.Append fld
makeRelation.Attributes = dbRelationDeleteCascade
db.Relations.Append makeRelation
```

The **fld** pointer to the relationship is then appended to the relation object. We then tell DAO what type of relationship we intend. In this case, we want cascading deletes. This simply means that when we delete a record in the base table **Contact**, all related records in the **Notes** table will be automatically deleted as well. If we omitted the **dbRelationDeleteCascade** attribute, DAO would not allow us to delete the record from the base table as long as there were records left in the related table.

Essentially what we are doing by defining the relationship is ensuring that the data in our tables remains logically consistent. You could find instances where you need to define a relationship with cascading updates. With the attribute set to cascading updates, changing a record in the primary table causes all related records in the related table to be changed as well.

8   OK, press *F5* to run your program. Then press the **cmdCreateDB** command button and your database will be created. Once complete, use VisData to view your new database. Of course, we now know that VisData can be used to not only create a database, but to view one as well:

Analyzing a .mdb File Using DAO

OK, now let's see what else we can do with DAO. We are now going to build a Database Analyzer that can take any **.mdb** file and, using DAO, show us every shred of information about that database. You will see that DAO really allows us to get down to the metal with **.mdb** files.

Try It Out - The Database Analyzer

1 Start a new project. Right-click on the tool palette and select Components... Then check Microsoft Windows Common Controls 6.0, which is in file **MSCOMCTL.OCX**. Also select MICROSOFT COMMON DIALOG CONTROL. Click OK to add these to your palette.

Now place two labels, a **tree view control**, a progress bar, a common dialog control and two command buttons on the form. Arrange them so that your form looks like this:

2 On the form, create the following:

Control	Property	Value	Comments
Form1	Caption	Microsoft Access Database Analyzer	
	Icon		I inserted a `.ico` file of an eye here. You could also insert a `.cur` file.
Label1	**Name**	**lblTitle**	Shows the database being scanned
TreeView1	**Name**	**dbTree**	
Label2	**Caption**	Scanning Tables in Database	
	Alignment	**2 - Center**	
ProgressBar1			Contained in the same `.ocx` as the tree view control
CommonDialog1			Used for selecting the database to analyze
Command1	**Name**	**cmdLocate**	
	Caption	&Select Database	
Command2	**Name**	**cmdAnalyze**	
	Caption	&Analyze Database	

3 Now let's get our hands dirty and write some code.

In the general area of the form, dimension the string that will hold the location of the database. Since it is at the form level, it has form level scope (visibility):

```
Dim dataBaseLocation As String
```

4   Open the code window for the **cmdLocate** command button and add the following code:

```
Private Sub cmdLocate_Click()

On Error GoTo ErrHandler

With CommonDialog1

    .CancelError = True
    ' Set flags
    .Flags = cdlOFNHideReadOnly
    ' Set filters
    .Filter = "MS Access Files (*.MDB)|*.MDB"
    ' Specify default filter
    .FilterIndex = 1
    .DialogTitle = "Select table to analyze"
    ' Display the Open dialog box
    .ShowOpen
    'Display name of selected file
    dataBaseLocation = .FileName

End With

lblTitle = "Table Selected: " & dataBaseLocation
cmdAnalyze.Enabled = True

Exit Sub

ErrHandler:
  'User pressed the Cancel button
  dataBaseLocation = ""
  lblTitle = "Selection Canceled"
  Exit Sub

End Sub
```

What we are doing here is presenting the File Open dialog box to the user when they click this button. This will permit the user to select any **.mdb** file on the machine and analyze it.

```
    .CancelError = True
    ' Set flags
    .Flags = cdlOFNHideReadOnly
    ' Set filters
    .Filter = "MS Access Files (*.MDB)|*.MDB"
    ' Specify default filter
    .FilterIndex = 1
    .DialogTitle = "Select table to analyze"
```

This bit of code simply preps our dialog box so we can customize it for our application. The common dialog control will be invisible at run-time. We are just setting properties to define how it will look when we invoke it.

By setting the **CancelError** property to **True**, we tell the common dialog to generate an error if the user cancels the dialog. This way if the user cancels the dialog, we can just jump to the error handler, **ErrHandler**, and exit the sub. One of the really neat features is the ability to set the filter, which tells the dialog which file types to display. We will only add one, for type **.mdb**. Setting the **FilterIndex** to **1** ensures that it is displayed in the Files of type: box as shown. Setting the **DialogTitle** property puts the final customization on the dialog.

```
.ShowOpen
    'Display name of selected file
    dataBaseLocation = .filename
```

ShowOpen invokes the box as a modal dialog. Now the user must either select an **.mdb** file or press Cancel. If Cancel is selected, we exit the routine. Otherwise, we assign the fully qualified name of the file returned by the dialog box to our form-level variable **dataBaseLocation**.

5   Now, open the code window for the **Click** event procedure of the **cmdAnalyze** command button. Add the following to the code window:

```
Private Sub cmdAnalyze_Click()

Dim dbase As Database
Dim tble As TableDef
Dim fld As Field
Dim prp As Property
Dim propString As String
Dim treeNode As Node
Dim currentFieldNumber As Integer
Dim currentFieldKey As String
Dim currentPropertyNumber As Integer
Dim currentPropertyKey As String
Dim currentTableName As String
Dim currentTableCount As Integer

Screen.MousePointer = vbHourglass

'--Don't permit the user to click when analyzing --
cmdAnalyze.Enabled = False
cmdLocate.Enabled = False
```

```vb
currentTableCount = 0
currentPropertyNumber = 1
currentFieldNumber = 1

'—Clear the TreeView control from any prior analysis --
dbTree.Nodes.Clear

'—Reasonability test ---
If (InStr(1, dataBaseLocation, ".MDB", 1) < 1) Then
  Screen.MousePointer = vbDefault
  MsgBox ("Please select an MDB file.")
  cmdAnalyze.Enabled = True
  cmdLocate.Enabled = True
  Exit Sub
End If

'—Set our reference variable to the selected database --
Set dbase = OpenDatabase(dataBaseLocation)

'—Reset the progress bar --
ProgressBar1.Value = 0
ProgressBar1.Max = dbase.TableDefs.Count

'-- The Root Node: The Name of the database --
Set treeNode = dbTree.Nodes.Add(, , "r", _
        "Database: " & dataBaseLocation)

'-- The next heirarchical structure is tables --
Set treeNode = dbTree.Nodes.Add("r", tvwChild, _
        "tble", "Tables")

'-- First, retrieve each table in the database --
For Each tble In dbase.TableDefs
    currentTableCount = currentTableCount + 1
    ProgressBar1.Value = currentTableCount
    currentTableName = "" & tble.Name & ""
    Set treeNode = dbTree.Nodes.Add("tble", _
        tvwChild, currentTableName, tble.Name)

'-- Now place the header 'Properties' under the table entry
    currentPropertyKey = "" & "Property" & _
        CStr(currentPropertyNumber) & ""
    currentPropertyNumber = currentPropertyNumber + 1
    Set treeNode = dbTree.Nodes.Add(currentTableName, tvwChild, _
        currentPropertyKey, "Properties")

    With tble
        For Each prp In tble.Properties
            propString = RetrieveProp(prp)
            Set treeNode = dbTree.Nodes.Add(currentPropertyKey, _
                tvwChild, , propString)
        Next

    currentFieldKey = "" & "Field " & CStr(currentFieldNumber) _
        & ""
    currentFieldNumber = currentFieldNumber + 1
    Set treeNode = dbTree.Nodes.Add(currentTableName, _
      tvwChild, currentFieldKey, "Fields")
```

```
        For Each fld In .Fields
            Set treeNode = dbTree.Nodes.Add(currentFieldKey, _
        tvwChild, , fld.Name)


        Next
    End With
Next

ProgressBar1.Value = 0
cmdAnalyze.Enabled = True
cmdLocate.Enabled = True
Screen.MousePointer = vbDefault
End Sub
```

As you can tell from the code density, this is where all of the work is done. We use DAO to iterate through the various collections in the database and place the output in a tree view control. This control fits our needs nicely because it displays hierarchical data at various levels in the tree. Since the database is really nothing more than a series of hierarchical collections, we can graphically display the data in a meaningful way to the user. Let's take a look at what this code is doing.

After we set up some variables and disable the command buttons so the user can't click them while our program is chugging away, we clear the tree view control we named **dbTree**. This control is also a collection of nodes. With each node we can set its level in the tree, its parent and how it looks. So now we clear out any previous information that might be in the tree view **Nodes** collection from a previous analysis.

```
dbTree.Nodes.Clear
```

We now need to ensure that the user didn't enter a file other than an **.mdb** file. By using the built-in **InStr** function, we can see if the string **".MDB"** is located somewhere in the file name string. If not, the function will return a 0. Then we simply inform the user of the error and permit him or her to try again:

```
'—Reasonability test ---
If (InStr(1, dataBaseLocation, ".MDB", 1) < 1) Then
    Screen.MousePointer = vbDefault
    MsgBox ("Please select an MDB file.")
    cmdAnalyze.Enabled = True
    cmdLocate.Enabled = True
    Exit Sub
End If
```

When we are sure that we have a valid database, we can use the DAO **OpenDataBase** method and pass it the fully qualified string with the **.mdb** location. Remember that we got this automatically from the common dialog control:

```
'—Set our reference variable to the selected database --
Set dbase = OpenDatabase(dataBaseLocation)
```

Once our reference variable **dBase** is pointing to a valid open database, we simply take a look at how many tables are inside. By interrogating the **Count** property of the **dbase.TableDefs** collection, we can tell our progress bar control what the maximum value of the bar will be. This way we can easily increment the progress bar as each table is being analyzed. As mentioned before, there is nothing like providing the user with some 'eye candy'. The progress bar not only lets the user know that something is happening, but it also provides a relative graphical indicator of how much time is remaining:

```
'—Reset the progress bar --
ProgressBar1.Value = 0
ProgressBar1.Max = dbase.TableDefs.Count
```

The name of the database will be put at the root of our tree view control. When adding items to this control, there are six parameters we must pass. All but one of them is optional.

A **tree** is comprised of cascading branches of **nodes**. Each node typically consists of an image (set with the **Image** property) and a label (set with the **Text** property). Images for a node is supplied by an **image list control** associated with the tree view control. A node can be expanded or collapsed, depending on whether or not the node has any child nodes which descend from it. At the topmost level of the tree is a **root** node or nodes. Each root node can have any number of child nodes. The total number of nodes is not limited except by your computer memory.

The syntax of adding a new node to the tree view control is:

myTreeView.Add(*relative, relationship, key, text, image, selectedImage***)**

The **Add** method has these parts:

Part	Description
Relative – Optional	This is the key of an existing node. We then can tell what the relationship is to that node (e.g. this is a child)
Relationship – Optional	This specifies the relative position of this node to the key in the relative position - see the settings below
Key – Optional	A unique string that can be used to retrieve this node
Text – Required	The string that appears in the node
Image – Optional	The index of an image in an associated image list control
SelectedImage – Optional	The index of an image in an associated image list control when this node is selected

The settings for the relationship of this node to that of the node in the relative position are:

Constant	Description
TvwFirst	This node is placed before all others at the same level as the node in the relative position
TvwLast	This node is placed after all others at the same level as the node in the relative position.
TvwNext	This node is placed after the node in the node named in the relative position
TvwPrevious	This node is placed before the node in the node named in the relative position.
TvwChild	This node becomes a child of the node named in the relative position.

431

Don't worry if this looks a little confusing to you now. As we examine the code in detail it will begin to make much more sense.

The **Add** method of the control returns a reference to the newly added node. So we place a string **"r"** in the key slot and enter the database name in the text position. This will show up as the root on our control:

```
'-- The Root Node: The Name of the database --
Set treeNode = dbTree.Nodes.Add(, , "r", "Database: " _
        & dataBaseLocation)
```

Now that the root is added, we want to add the text Tables under the root as a classification. This text is a child of the root node that now contains the fully qualified name of the database. When the user clicks on the name of the database, they will see Tables with a "+" designating that if this is clicked, the next level down will be a list of the tables. To accomplish this, we add another node. By placing the **"r"** of the root node in the relative position and the constant **tvwChild** in the relationship position, the control now knows this node comes under the root. We give this node the string key **"tble"** so we can place the list of tables under this node. Finally, we want to display the word **"Tables"** in this node:

```
'-- The next heirarchical structure is tables --
Set treeNode = dbTree.Nodes.Add("r", tvwChild, "tble", "Tables")
```

Now the word Tables is in our tree view control. So the next step is to iterate through the tables in the database and place them at the next level in our hierarchical tree. So the outer loop will process each table in our database. We don't have to worry about looping because the **For...Each** syntax handles that for us:

```
'-- First, retrieve each table in the database --
For Each tble In dbase.TableDefs
```

At the start of analyzing a new table, the **currentTableCount** is incremented. We can feed this to the progress bar. Since the **Max** property of this control has already been set, it will take care of figuring out how many blue blocks to display:

```
currentTableCount = currentTableCount + 1
ProgressBar1.Value = currentTableCount
```

For each table in the **TableDefs** collection, we want to display each of them directly under the **Tables** node. When the user clicks on Tables, the tree view will expand and show the table names underneath. Therefore, a new node must be added. The **"tble"** string is placed in the relative slot in the **Add** method. Next, we tell the control that this node will be a child of the node that contains **"tble"** in its key slot. Of course, that node is the **Tables** node. In addition, the tree view control needs a unique name for the key, so we simply take the current name of the table as the key because this will be unique. Finally, as the text to be displayed, we show the name of the table:

```
currentTableName = "" & tble.Name & ""
Set treeNode = dbTree.Nodes.Add("tble", _
tvwChild, currentTableName, tble.Name)
```

Now we do a bit of slight of hand. As mentioned, the key for each node must be both unique and a string. We simply take the integer **currentPropertyNumber**, convert it to a string (with the **CStr** function) and append it to the string **"Property"**. This is then assigned to the variable **currentPropertyKey**. We do this so that it is guaranteed to be unique and is also easy for us to read. Once we create the unique string to place in the **Properties** node, we increment the **currentPropertyNumber** so it will be unique when we add the next property. We will never see this, but we need it to ensure uniqueness. Then the node is added as a child under the **Table** node that was just added:

```
    currentPropertyKey = "" & "Property" & _
CStr(currentPropertyNumber) & ""
    currentPropertyNumber = currentPropertyNumber + 1
    Set treeNode = dbTree.Nodes.Add(currentTableName, tvwChild, _
currentPropertyKey, "Properties")
```

Now that the literal string **"Properties"** has been added under the table name, we iterate through each of the properties of that specific table and add them to the tree view control using the logic described above:

```
With tble
   For Each prp In tble.Properties
propString = RetrieveProp(prp)
Set treeNode = dbTree.Nodes.Add(currentPropertyKey, _
      tvwChild, , propString)
   Next
```

The only code left to write is a routine called **RetrieveProp**. We will get to that in a second.

We just added the properties of the table. Now we use the same logic and add the literal **"Fields"** under the table name. This is done by making the new node a child of the **currentTableName**:

```
    currentFieldKey = "" & "Field " & CStr(currentFieldNumber) & ""
    currentFieldNumber = currentFieldNumber + 1
    Set treeNode = dbTree.Nodes.Add(currentTableName, _
tvwChild, currentFieldKey, "Fields")
```

Finally, we now want to iterate through each of the fields in the table and display them under the literal **"Fields"** node. We do this by making each node a child of the node identified by the **currentFieldKey**:

```
   For Each fld In .Fields
     Set treeNode = dbTree.Nodes.Add(currentFieldKey, _
       tvwChild, , fld.Name)
   Next
End With
```

When the final field is displayed, the code drops down to the **End With** and jumps back to the top of the loop and does it all over again with the next table. So what we are doing is this:

The DatabaseName
> Tables
>> TheFirstTable
>>> Properties of TheFirstTable
>>>> properties...
>>> Fields of TheFirstTable
>>>> fields...
>> TheSecondTable
>>> Properties of TheSecondTable
>>>> properties...
>>> Fields of TheSecondTable
>>>> fields...

Hopefully you can see how the tree view control is perfect for showing the various DAO collections graphically. Finally, we need to add a helper function called **RetrieveProp**.

6 Add a function called **RetrieveProp** and type in the following code:

```
Public Function RetrieveProp(myProperty As Property) As String
```

```
Dim tempProperty As Variant

Err = 0

On Error Resume Next
tempProperty = myProperty.Value

If (Err = 0) Then
    RetrieveProp = myProperty.Name
    If Len(tempProperty) Then
        RetrieveProp = RetrieveProp & " - Value: " & tempProperty
    End If
Else
    RetrieveProp = myProperty.Name
End If
```

```
End Function
```

You may be wondering why we need a helper function to retrieve a property from each table and don't just read it directly. Well, some properties might not have a value. So this routine will check for us and handle any errors that might occur when reading a non-existent property:

```
Err = 0

On Error Resume Next
tempProperty = myProperty.Value
```

We first set the global **Err** object to **0**. This will clear out any error number that might be in the **Err.Number** property. Then, by instructing VB to resume the next statement in spite of an error, we can interrogate the **Err** object and see if an error occurred. This way our program keeps going and we can take evasive measures if an error did indeed occur. So we attempt to read the **Value** of the property passed into our function. If the **Err** object contains a **0** after reading the **myProperty.Value**, then no error occurred. Then we assign it to the name of the function if it's not blank. However, if there was an error, we just assign the name of the property, not its value, to the return value of our function:

```
If (Err = 0) Then
    RetrieveProp = myProperty.Name
    If Len(tempProperty) Then
        RetrieveProp = RetrieveProp & "  -  Value: " & tempProperty
    End If
Else
    RetrieveProp = myProperty.Name
End If
```

7 Phew! That was a lot of typing. Before you run the project, add a reference to the Microsoft DAO 3.51 Object Library. Now save the project as **prjDBAnalyzer.vbp**.

8 Now press *F5* to start the program running. Select the **Contacts.mdb** that we just created using DAO. When it is selected from the common dialog box, the title is placed in the label above the tree view control as shown. It will be the fully qualified name of the table - the name and the complete path. Then click the <u>A</u>nalyze Database command button. Notice that we are adhering to our user interface principles: we disable both command buttons so the user knows they are not available while our program is working. We also set the mouse to an hourglass to show that the program is chugging away. Finally, we display a progress bar to show the relative completion of the analysis. So for all of the work that is going on under the hood, the user has only two buttons to select and can't make a mistake. While exploiting the power of DAO, we maintain a good user interface to make the program simple for the user to operate.

> *Remember that the user doesn't know DAO from DOA. To them, your user interface IS the program.*

9 When the analysis is complete, double-click on the name of the database at the root of the tree view control. The name Tables will be displayed. Click on Tables and all of the tables will be displayed. Notice that there are more tables in our database than we inserted. The tables that start with MS are tables that Jet added when the database was created. These are system tables that manage queries, relationships and all of the other niceties we come to expect with an **.mdb** database:

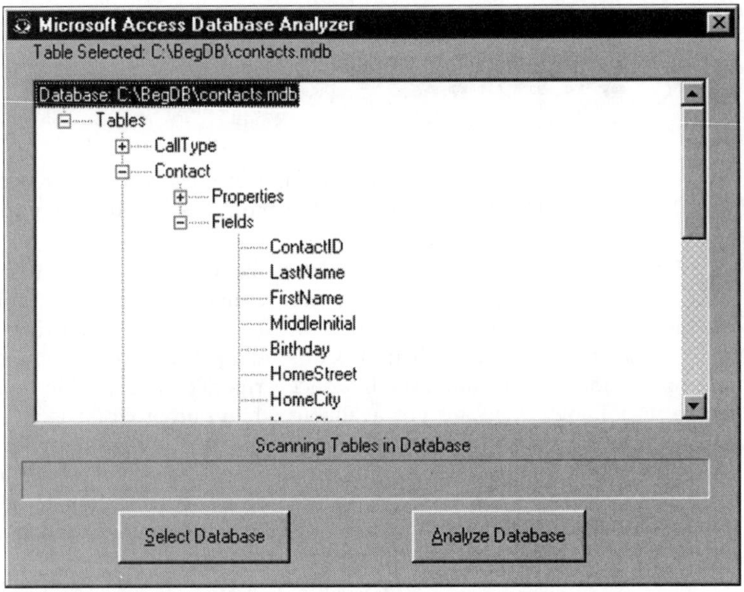

10 Click on a table and Properties and Fields are displayed. Click on Properties and view all of the DAO properties for that table:

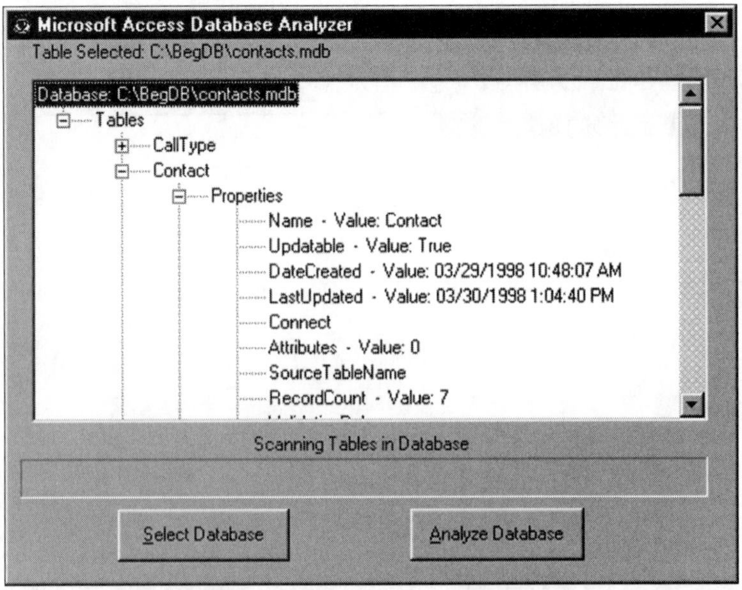

I hope you are convinced of the power of DAO, and how you can really get down to the nuts and bolts of an **.mdb** database when you need to.

Summary

In this chapter we have designed and constructed a database from scratch. We saw:

▶ How to use the **Normalization** process to make sure that our data is stored as simply and efficiently as possible

▶ How to use DAO to construct a database, create indexes, and add relationship-building keys

▶ The basis of the DAO **object model**, which abstracts the design of the database

▶ How to **analyze** our database

What We Learned

▶ We found out how to determine what fields of information we need for our table

▶ Using normalization, the table is successively broken down to smaller, discrete tables that relate to each other

▶ We learnt the structure of the DAO object model, and how it is made up of collections of related objects

▶ We learnt how to build the database using both VisData and DAO

▶ DAO was covered and we considered how to iterate programmatically through the various collections stored in the hierarchy

▶ Finally, we used DAO object model and VB 6.0 code to break a table apart and analyze the component pieces

In the next chapter we're going to create a VB application that will make use of the Contacts database that we built here.

Exercises

1 What are the first three levels of database normalization and what does each require?

2 When is it advantageous to open a recordset as a **Snapshot**? Or as **ForwardOnly**?

3 What is the advantage of creating an index on a table? What is the disadvantage?

4 What benefits are there for a programmer to create a relationship in an Access database?

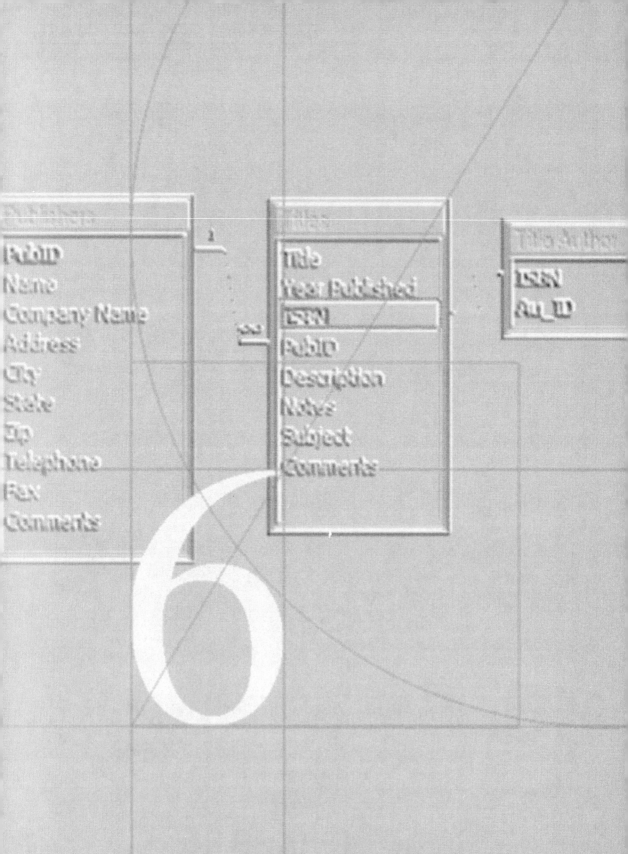

10

Programming The Address Book

Ready to working in this chapter? Good! We are going to build on everything we have learned so far and structure these things into an application. In addition, we are going to learn a little bit about some of the handy tools that are available in VB 6.0. Specifically, we will be looking at the following controls:

- Tool bar
- Tree view
- List view
- Status bar
- Calendar
- Tab strip
- Masked edit
- Image list

It is difficult to find any really good examples of how to use these powerful tools. Most VB books either just mention that they exist, or skip over them completely. For that reason many VB programmers don't use most of them in their programs. However, I'm sure that once you've learned about them you will see that they can be incorporated usefully into your future database projects. The more aware we are of all the VB tools available to us, the more flexible and adaptable we'll be in our approach to future programming challenges. Not only will we include these sophisticated controls, but we will also be learning how to create a pop-up menu. When the user right-clicks over a call description, a pop up menu permits the user to either add or delete another call.

In this chapter, I thought we would not only work hard but have some fun in the process. The Address Book program is something that you can use every day. When completed, this is certainly a program that you can also distribute to your friends.

So we will take the database concepts we have been learning and put it to use in a real application. Since the user interface 'is the program' to your user, we will make the program fun to use. More importantly, rather than just learning from a series of 'academic exercises', we will put everything together and build a working program. Just like what we must do in the real world.

Take a look at the finished product. Notice the toolbar across the top. Even though the **CoolBar** control (the button bar across the top of the Internet Explorer) is bundled with VB 6, there is an easier tool to use that looks identical - the tool bar control.

As you move the mouse over each button, the button rises - just begging to be clicked. As the mouse leaves the button, it sinks to the same level as the rest of the buttons. So by using this interface, our program will look very hip and up to date.

How It Works

We will be using the **Contacts** database we developed in the last chapter. The user interface will display each of the letters of the alphabet in the tree view control. Remember our brief discussion of nodes in the last chapter when we were discussing the DAO object model? The same concept applies to a tree view control. We will be adding parent and child nodes. Do you see a pattern here? Like the object model, the tree view is a collection of collections. That is one of the reasons we spend some time on how to iterate through items in a collection, VB 6.0 uses this concept everywhere.

If a contact with the last name beginning with that letter is present in the database, a "+" sign will provide a visual cue to the user. Remember when we discussed making it impossible for the user to make a mistake? Keeping with this approach, we will ensure all data is validated before we permit it to be saved to the database. Also, only the valid options available to the user will be enabled.

Thus, for each contact, we can add or delete telephone call notes. By right clicking on the ListView control with the right mouse button, a pop-up menu is displayed. If there are no calls logged, only the Add New option is enabled. Otherwise the user can either add a new call or delete an existing entry.

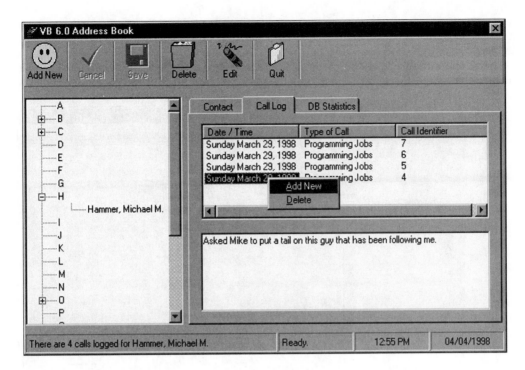

If the user adds a new call, the call entry screen is displayed modally. The calendar control will default to today's date, but the user can set it to whatever date is required. In addition, the user can define various categories for Call Types. Remember in the last chapter when we discussed business, programming, professional, etc. call classifications? Well, here the description is up to the user. If your program is used at a software help desk, for example, the Call Description might be the software product the client called on. You get the idea - the user can fully define how they want to use your program.

Finally, I'll show you a few undocumented Jet calls that will provide some good background on all of the work that is being performed behind the scenes. You can get a sense of how Jet uses a built-in cache to hold often-used information. This will really impress your friends. Take a look at the DB Statistics tab to see all of the work Jet is doing behind the scenes to manage our SQL queries, adds, deletes, and just about everything else we are doing with the database.

OK, let's get started. We'll start a new project and place the controls on the form - the GUI design phase of our project. Don't worry about the details of setting them up for the moment, we will go over that in more detail later.

Try It Out - Creating our Address Book

1 Start a new project and save it in a new **BegDB\Chapter10** subdirectory. Use the default form and call it **frmAddress**.

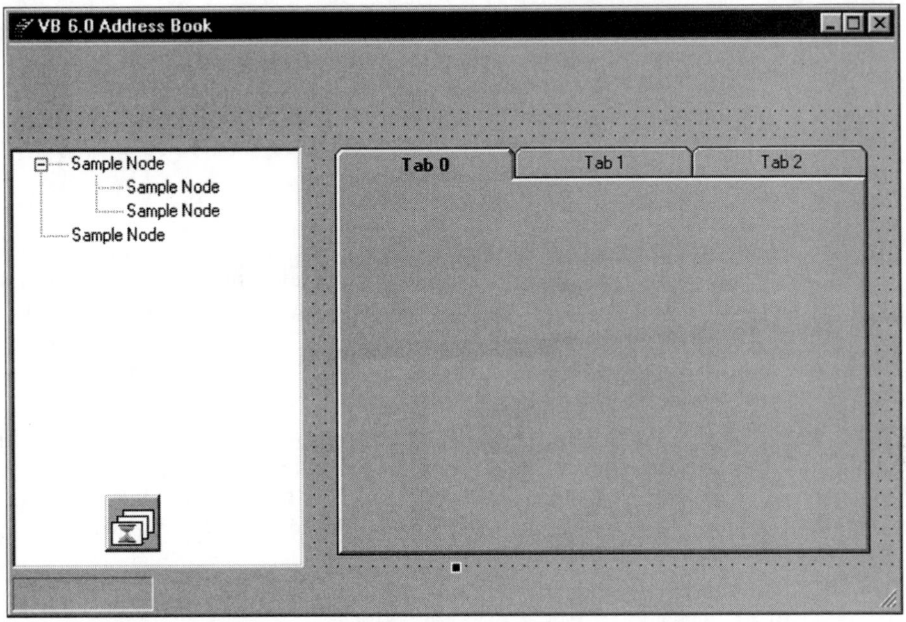

2 Next, add a toolbar to the top of your form. Be sure to add the Microsoft Windows Common Controls 6.0 to your tool palette. It can be found in the file **mscomctl.ocx**. By adding this file, the components for the status bar, the tree view, the list view and the image list control will also be added to your tool palette. The toolbar control will be blank at first. Don't worry! We have to add the buttons and pictures. Just draw it on the form so you will see how much form real estate it takes up.

Although the tab strip was added to your palette when you added the above file, it is fairly klunky to use. You need to maintain separate containers for each tab. In general, it is difficult and error prone. Instead we will use this little gem which is the Microsoft Tabbed Dialog Control 6.0 which can be found in **tabctl32.ocx**. This is much more friendly. Add the control to your tool palette and then draw it on the form.

Don't worry about laying it out yet. We will get to that. Leave about a third of the form available for when we draw on the tree view control to the left. And don't add anything to the control just yet. We will take care of that when we start coding.

3 Next, draw a tree view control on the form as shown above. This will ultimately display all of the letters in the alphabet and show all of our logged contacts.

4 Now draw a status bar control on the bottom of your form. Again, we will set up all of these controls in a minute. I just want you to get the general arrangement of the controls on your form first. This control will permit us a sophisticated method of providing the user textual feedback on their actions. When you draw the control, it will be blank and only have a single depressed box. Again, you can get a sense of how much space it will take up.

5 The image list control will hold the images that we want to display in our toolbar. Leave the default name **ImageList1**. Just draw this over the tree view control so that we can access it easily. Since it is invisible during run-time, the placement isn't important. We will add bitmaps to this control, then link it to our toolbar control.

6 Let's set up the tool bar control. An integral part of the tool bar is the image list control. Right-click on the image list control and select Properties... Then click the Images tab. We want to add 6 images. Place them in the order of Add New, Cancel, Save, Delete, Edit and Quit. By pressing Insert Picture you can browse the icons that come with VB 6.0. On my machine, the images were located in:

```
[Drive]:\Program Files\Microsoft Visual Studio\Common\Graphics\Icons
```

When you have located the icons that you want as the pictures in the tool bar, double-click on the file name and the picture will be added to your image list control. Notice that each picture has an Index value. When we link the pictures to the tool bar, we will use this index number to select the correct one.

7 When you have the pictures selected, click OK and we can move on to setting up the tool bar control.

8 Now right-click on the tool bar control at the top of your form to display the property pages. Click the drop-down combo next to ImageList. You will see ImageList1 there. This is the image list control we just added the icons to. This links the image list to our tool bar. In order to get the CoolBar look, select the Style type of 1 - tbrFlat.

Property Pages

General | Buttons | Picture

MousePointer: 0 - ccDefault

OLEDropMode: 0 - ccOLEDropNone

ImageList: ImageList1

DisabledImageList: <None>

HotImageList: <None>

HelpContextID: 0   HelpFile:

ButtonHeight: 959.81   ☑ AllowCustomize   ☑ Wrappable

ButtonWidth: 1395.21   ☑ ShowTips   ☑ Enabled

Appearance: 1 - cc3D   BorderStyle: 0 - ccNone

TextAlignment: 0 - tbrTextAlignBottom

Style: 1 - tbrFlat

OK   Cancel   Apply   Help

9 Now click the Buttons tab. Here is where the work gets done to customize our tool bar. We are going to add 12 buttons. The odd number buttons will be our actual buttons. The even number buttons will be separators that give us the recessed look. OK, for the first button, click on Insert Button. In the Caption box add Add New and type 1 in the Image box. This will link the first image in our image list control with button number 1.

Property Pages

General | Buttons | Picture

Index: 1   Insert Button   Remove Button

Caption: Add New   Description:

Key: Value: 0 - tbrUnpressed

Style: 0 - tbrDefault   Width: (Placeholder) 0.00

ToolTipText: Image: 1

Tag:

☑ Visible   ☑ Enabled   ☐ MixedState

ButtonMenus

Index: 0   Insert ButtonMenu   Remove ButtonMenu

Text: Key: Tag:

☑ Enabled   ☑ Visible

OK   Cancel   Apply   Help

10 That takes care of the first button. If you press Apply now, the image you selected to be in button 1 will be displayed in tool bar on our form. Now we are ready to add the next button. Press Insert Button and a new button is added to the tool bar for us. Since this is an even number, we want the Style to be 3 - tbrSeparator. This will give us the cool bar look. Now select Apply again.

11 Now add the remaining 10 buttons. Remember the next button will be Index number 3, a valid button. So leave the style as 0 - tbrDefault and add 2 to the Image box. Then add button 4 as a separator, and so on.

Button Number	Text	Style	Image Number
1	Add New	tbrDefault	1
2		tbrSeparator	
3	Cancel	tbrDefault	2
4		tbrSeparator	
5	Save	tbrDefault	3
6		tbrSeparator	
7	Delete	tbrDefault	4
8		tbrSeparator	
9	Edit	tbrDefault	5
10		tbrSeparator	
11	Quit	tbrDefault	6
12		tbrSeparator	

There, the toolbar is done. Pretty easy, yes? We can determine which button was pressed with the **Button.Index** property a little later on. The great thing about this control is the way it raises and lowers itself when the mouse passes over any of the active buttons. So we've just added images to the image list control, linked the image list to the tool bar, and then added text and images to the buttons.

12 Take a break now and run the program. This way you can take a look at the tool bar and how it operates. Of course, we don't have any code behind the buttons yet, but you can get a good idea of how it will operate.

The Microsoft Tab Control

Now let's tackle the tab control. For some reason, the Microsoft documentation just discusses the tab strip control. The documentation is cryptic and there are no examples to help out. Luckily with a little digging, we can discover and use the tab control that we added to our project. Most programmers are not aware of this second tab control, but it is well worth using because it is so intuitive to configure and use in our programs.

Try It Out - The Tab Control

1 Name the tab control **tbContact**.

2 Right-click on the control and bring up the Property Pages for the tab control. Select the Style as 1 - ssStylePropertyPage. This will show the control with the style of tabs that are seen on this property page - less rounded and more modern. A bit understated. For the TabCaption, add the word Contact. Then enter 3 in the Tab Count box. This will expand the control to show 3 tabs. Click the > button beneath Current Tab and replace Tab 1 with Call Log in the TabCaption text box. Click on the > again and type DB Statistics for the TabCaption. When you are finished, click OK.

449

The Status Bar Control

I like this control because it is simple and adds a touch of sophistication to our program.

Try It Out - The Status Bar Control

1 Name the control **sbStatus**.

2 Right-click on the **sbStatus** status bar control to bring up the properties box. Click the Panels tab. We are going to add four panels to our status bar at the bottom of our form.

Property Pages

General | Panels | Font | Picture

Index: 1 ◄ ►   Insert Panel   Remove Panel

Text:

ToolTipText:

Key: Minimum Width: 1440.00

Tag: Actual Width: 4529.76

Alignment: 0 - sbrLeft

Style: 0 - sbrText   Picture

Bevel: 1 - sbrInset   Browse...

AutoSize: 1 - sbrSpring   No Picture   ☑ Enabled   ☑ Visible

OK   Cancel   Apply   Help

3 The first panel is added for us, as we saw when we drew the control on the form. Our first panel will be the largest, so we set the AutoSize to 1 - sbrSpring. This will make the first panel spring to take up any additional space not used by the other panels. Now select Insert Panel and click on the forward arrow next to Index.

4 Add the additional panels according to this table:

Panel Number	Alignment	Style	AutoSize
1	0 - sbrLeft	0 - sbrText	1 - sbrSpring
2	0 - sbrLeft	0 - sbrText	0 - sbrNoAutoSize
3	1 - sbrCenter	5 - sbrTime	0 - sbrNoAutoSize
4	1 - sbrCenter	6 - sbrDate	0 - sbrNoAutoSize

That's it for setting up the status bar. One of the really neat features of this control is that the 3rd and 4th panels - the ones with the time and date - take care of themselves. They will poll the system clock and update themselves automatically. We now have the 1st and 2nd panels at our disposal to provide information to the user as our program goes through its paces.

Try It Out - The Tree View Control

1 Actually this is pretty simple to set up. First of all, name this control **tvContact**. We will get into the details of how to program the control in a few minutes.

2 Now, right-click on the tree view control to bring up the Property Pages.

There are only two properties that we need to change. For the Style select
6 - tvwTreelinesPlusMinusText and for the LineStyle select 1- tvwRootLines. This will handle the little + and - signs for us. Notice that there is the capability to add an ImageList for this control as well. This permits you to add custom graphics for the various levels of the hierarchy. If you wanted, it would be simple to just add additional images to our single image list control that is used for the tool bar. By using the **Index** property, we could use images at the end of the ones used for the tool bar. When you are finished, click OK.

> *You might remember back in the dim dark past of when you started this book we discussed visual programming. Even though we have been drawing controls and clicking boxes, we have been programming. We have been setting properties visually by clicking boxes in these controls. So please remember - you have been programming all along. Even before the first line of VB code has been written.*

The Masked Edit Control ##|

Many programmers shy away from this control because it can be a bit funky. However, once you know its idiosyncrasies it can be a powerful friend. We want to use the masked edit control for fields such as phone numbers and dates because it ensures restricted data input. We will define the mask at design-time so the user will see "( )   - " for a phone number. This provides a visual reminder that the number must be entered in a certain format. It generally behaves like a standard text box, but the programmer can add a mask to ensure the correct input from the user. When we add the mask (the entire reason we would want to use this to begin with), the control starts to act differently from a text box. When we add a literal, such as "(", the insertion point automatically skips over the literal as data is added. When you insert or delete data in the field, all of the non-literal characters to the right of the literal are shifted. This control is located in `msmask32.ocx`.

Try It Out - The Contact Tab

1 Add the following controls to the Contact tab of the tab control.

Control	Name	MaxLength	Tag
text box	txtFirstName	15	1
text box	txtMiddleInitial	1	1
text box	txtLastName	20	1
text box	txtHomeStreet	20	1
text box	txtHomeCity	12	1
text box	txtHomeState	2	1
masked edit	mskHomeZip	10	1
masked edit	mskHomePhone	13	1
masked edit	mskHomeFax	13	1
masked edit	mskHomeCellPhone	13	1
text box	txtHomeEmail	30	1
masked edit	mskBirthday	10	1
label	lblBirthday	N/A	1

2 Change the **BorderStyle** property of **lblBirthday** to **1 - Fixed Single** and delete its **Caption**.

Arrange these controls so that the Contact tab looks like this:

3 You can see that we are using our technique for identifying the controls that we wish to lock and unlock. Yes, the **Tag** property has a **1** entered in the controls we wish to manipulate through our code. When we go to add a new contact or edit an existing one, we will iterate through all of the controls on the form. Each one that has a **1** in the **Tag** property will be set up appropriately. Don't forget to add the "X"s to each of the controls so you can make them the correct length - no shorter or longer than necessary.

4 Now set the **Mask** property for each of the masked edit controls:

Masked Edit Control	Mask
mskHomeZip	#####-####
mskHomePhone	(###)###-####
mskHomeFax	(###)###-####
mskHomeCellPhone	(###)###-####
mskBirthday	##/##/####

Notice that each of the masks includes the '#' character. This tells the control to only accept numbers - no letters. If the user tries to enter a letter, nothing will happen. The "#" is a digit placeholder. This eliminates the need for us to write code to check for numbers only. It certainly can't prevent the user from entering a wrong telephone number, but it forces them to add the area code and prevents an entry such as 21A-334-45D3 by mistake.

453

5 Now add the labels as shown to describe the fields to the user. When you have finished that, click on the Call Log tab.

6 On the top half of the form, draw a list view control.

This control will display a summary of the controls. Name the control **lvCalls**. Right-click on the control to bring up the Property Pages. Make sure that the View is 2 - lvwList then click OK.

7 Add a text box under the list view control and call it **txtNotes**. Set its **Locked** property to **True** and delete the **Text** property.

8 Now click on the DB Statistics tab.

9 Add 3 labels, **lblDateCreated**, **lblLastUpdated** and **lblRecordCount**. Set the **BorderStyle** properties to **1 - Fixed Single** and clear the **Caption** properties for all the labels.

Below that add a frame and six more labels inside the frame. Name the labels **lblDiskReads**, **lblDiskWrites**, **lblReadCache**, **lblReadAhead**, **lblLocksPlaced** and **lblReleaseLocks**. Again, set the **BorderStyle** to **1 - Fixed Single** and clear the **Caption** property for each of these labels. These labels will be used to display the database statistics. Set the **Caption** property of the frame to **Database Stats**.

When you have finished, add the descriptive labels as shown to describe each field to the user.

Let's Write Some Code!!

OK, that's the GUI design phase out of the way. I know you are itching to write some database code. After all, that's why you have read this far. Well, OK. Drawing the controls is more fun.

Since this is a database program, we will start out with opening the database. Since both of our forms, the **frmAddress** and later the **frmCall** must access the database, let's place the reference to the database in a code module.

Try It Out - Using a Code Module to Reference the Database

1 Add a module to your project. Name it **modCode**. Add this declaration line to the General section of the module:

```
Public dbContact As Database
```

> *If you don't see* Database *show up on the list of choices as shown, it means that you have forgotten to add the Microsoft DAO 3.1 Object Library to your project. Please add that reference now.*

2 When the reference is added, please add the following code to the General section of the code module **modCode**.

```
Option Explicit

Public dbContact As Database

Public Const progname = "Address Book"

Public rsContactTable As Recordset

Public Enum currentState
  NOW_ADDING
  NOW_SAVING
  NOW_EDITING
  NOW_DELETING
  NOW_IDLE
End Enum

Public Enum bButton
  bAdd = 1
  bCancel = 3
  bSave = 5
  bDelete = 7
  bEdit = 9
  bQuit = 11
End Enum
```

Here we are declaring **dbContact** as a reference variable that will be set to the open database **Contacts.mdb**. We will use the constant **progname** whenever we need to display a message box to the user. By making it a **Const** here, we simply reference this whenever we need a title for our message box. This really saves space. Say we had to display a message box in 50 places in a program. That would mean creating 50 strings that say the same thing throughout our program. Here we declare it only once. Always try to get in the habit of doing this for static strings that are displayed throughout your program. Making it a **Const** simply means that the value can't be changed.

Notice we are also using our old friend, the **Enum** statement to define various states of our program. Here we see another application of the state-machine concept we discussed earlier in the book. We can enforce the current state of the application (Idle, Adding, etc.) This way we can be sure that our program knows the current state and will only permit the appropriate choices for that particular state. We can then set a variable to one of the **Enum** values so the program knows if it is editing, saving, etc.

We also are using **Enum** here to define the index numbers of the buttons on our tool bar control. Why? Well, when you go back to your code in two months to enhance it, which would you rather find?

```
Toolbar1.Buttons(9).Enabled = False
```

Or

```
Toolbar1.Buttons(bEdit).Enabled = False
```

You get the idea. Take advantage of the **Enum** statement for tasks like this. By using it wisely, you can really make your code self-documenting.

3 Next, add a function called **openTheDatabase** to our code module with a fully qualified return type of **Boolean**. This return value will signal to the caller if we were successful in opening our database.

```
Public Function openTheDatabase() As Boolean

Dim dbPath As String

On Error GoTo dbErrors

dbPath = App.Path & "\contacts.mdb"

Set dbContact = DBEngine.Workspaces(0).OpenDatabase(dbPath, False)

Set rsContactTable = dbContact.OpenRecordset("Contact", dbOpenTable)

openTheDatabase = True

Exit Function

dbErrors:

openTheDatabase = False
MsgBox (Err.Description)

End Function
```

How It Works

First and foremost, our program needs to know the location of our database. So we are using the built-in system wide object, **App**, that will tell us the current directory of our program. The **Path** property of the **App** object will return the location of the currently running VB6 program.

```
dbPath = App.Path & "\contacts.mdb"
```

Of course, if you place the database in another location, be sure to modify this string. However, if you always install the database in the same location as your program files, this line will ensure that the database is found, no matter where the wacky user installs your system. This command sets the location to the same location and drive as your application.

```
Set dbContact = DBEngine.Workspaces(0).OpenDatabase(dbPath, False)
```

As previously mentioned, the **DBEngine** object is the top-level object in the DAO object hierarchy. It contains all of the other DAO objects and collections. The **DBEngine** object is the default object in the object model. Since this is the case, we don't actually need to refer to it explicitly. We will illustrate the hierarchy now.

The **DBEngine** object contains two collections: the **Workspaces** collection and the **Errors** collection. The **Workspaces** collection is the default collection of the **DBEngine** object, so we don't need to refer to it explicitly either. But for consistency, we will show how it is used. You can return a reference to the first **Workspace** object in the **Workspaces** collection of the **DBEngine** object by getting its ordinal position, which is 0. If you don't specifically create a new **Workspace** object, DAO automatically creates a default workspace when you need it.

Since we are not using the intrinsic data control, we will be doing everything in DAO. We are starting to see why it is important to us as programmers to understand how to find our way around object models.

We pass the **OpenDatabase** method the location of the database and **False** as the second parameter. This means that we are not opening the database in exclusive mode. If you know you are going to be the only one using the database, you can pass **True** as the parameter. This little trick speeds up access because Jet does not have to worry about locking and taking various precautions in case others were to open the same database.

```
Set rsContactTable = dbContact.OpenRecordset("Contact", dbOpenTable)
```

After the database is successfully opened, we can now open a recordset. Since the **rsContactTable** will be used throughout the app, we open it here and make it global. Notice that we are opening this recordset as type **dbOpenTable**. Since this is a single table and not the result of a join operation, we can use this method. This is by far the fastest type of recordset. So when you are opening a straight single table, choose this method.

If everything goes as planned, we set the return value of the function to **True** and exit the function.

```
openTheDatabase = True
```

If there were any problems, our error handler will display the description of the error and the function will return **False** to the caller.

All right - on to our **frmAddress** form.

Try It Out - The frmAddress Form

1 In the General Declarations section of the **frmAddress** form, add the following code:

```
Option Explicit

Dim contactNode As Node
Dim rsNotesTable As Recordset
Dim rsCallType As Recordset

Dim iCurrentState As Integer
Dim lCurrentContactKey As Long
Dim sCurrentContactName As String
Dim bFieldsPopulated As Boolean   'flag to see if the fields have data
```

2 Now when our form loads, the first thing we want to do is ensure that the database was opened properly. We call the **openTheDatabase()** function defined above in our code module. If it returns **False**, then we display a message and take drastic measures by ending the program. However, the user will get the message in the code module that will tell us of the problem so we can fix it. Add the following code to perform this function. This code goes in the **Load** event of the **frmAddress** form.

```
Private Sub Form_Load()

If (Not openTheDatabase()) Then
   MsgBox "Sorry - the database could not be opened."
   END        'terminate the program unconditionally
End If

'-- Remove the Xs in our text boxes --
Call clearFields
bFieldsPopulated = False
iCurrentState = NOW_IDLE

End Sub
```

How It Works

In the General Declaration section we declared **contactNode** as type **Node**. The **contactNode** is used to populate our tree view control. This is a type of variable, just like an integer or string. Then we dim two form level reference variables, **rsNotesTable** s **rsCallType**. These will hold recordsets that we will open as the program operates. **iCurrentState** is used to inform the program what state it is in, such as adding, deleting, etc. We will set it with the enumerated values we just defined in our code module. The next two variables, **lCurrentContactKey** and **sCurrentContactName** will be set from the tree view control when the user selects a contact. The first holds the unique ID of the contact and the second holds the contact's name to display on our form. Finally, the semaphore variable, **bFieldsPopulated** is used to notify the program if the fields need to be cleared or not.

> *Always strive to keep your variables as local as possible. Never use a global variable when a form-level variable will do. Never use a form-level variable when a local variable will do. This helps in modularity and memory management. Local variables are destroyed when the current procedure is exited. If you* Dim *a variable at form level that is only used in a procedure it keeps hanging around taking up memory until the form closes.*

When the database is successfully opened, we call a routine that clears all fields of those X's we put in. This routine will also be used when we add another user. Why? Well, since the text boxes and the masked edit controls are not bound to a data control, there could be old data lurking in there. For example, say that one contact has a home email address entered and you select another contact that does not have an email address. If we do not take care to clear our all fields for each contact, the old value of the email address would still be there for the new contact.

```
bFieldsPopulated = False
```

We just loaded the program, so no contact was selected yet. We set our form-level semaphore variable, **bFieldsPopulated**, to **False**. This tells the program that there should be no data in the fields. Remember that since these controls are not bound to a data control, it is our responsibility to fill and clear them with data from the database.

Then we set the current state of the program to **NOW_IDLE**. So the program is ready for the user to take some action. Remember what we said way back about Windows being passive in nature? Well, this is a perfect example. The user could decide to add a new contact or delete an existing contact, or possibly edit a contact. Alternatively, the user just might want to quit. Our program has to be ready for each of these possibilities and respond accordingly.

While we are writing code for the various form event procedures, we'll update the **Activate** procedure too.

Try It Out - Coding the Activate Procedure

1 Add this code to the **Activate** procedure.

```
Private Sub Form_Activate()

Static bLoadedAlready As Boolean

sbStatus.Panels.Item(2).Text = "Loading...."

If (Not bLoadedAlready) Then
  Call initializeForm
  bLoadedAlready = True
End If

sbStatus.Panels.Item(2).Text = "Ready."

End Sub
```

How It Works

When we load up our program, the **Activate** event fires right after the **Load** event. You might have remembered that we should try to put all code that works with the visual component of the program here. When this event fires, we know that all of the controls are properly 'sited', or displayed and initialized.

```
Static bLoadedAlready As Boolean
```

The **Activate** event not only fires when our program is loaded, but also when the form gets focus. Later on when we display the **frmCall** form that permits the user to add call details, the form is shown modally. When **frmCall** is dismissed, our current form **frmAddress** receives focus and the **Activate** event is again fired. Well, we only want to call our procedure **initializeForm** in this event when the program loads. It does things like clears out fields. We don't want this happening when control returns to this form after the user adds some call details. So the best way to accomplish this is to define another semaphore type of variable named **bLoadedAlready**.

Notice that we defined this variable as type **Static**. When static is used at the procedure-level to declare variables, VB allocates storage space. Any variable declared with the **Static** statement retains its value as long as the code is running. So unlike normal local variables that only have a lifetime as long as that procedure is running, **Static** variables retain their value for the lifetime of the program. Just like other variables, if we don't give it a type such as **Boolean**, it will become a **Variant**. We don't need the overhead of 16 bytes to hold a true or false value. A **Boolean** will do just fine. When this event procedure is first entered, the value of **bLoadedAlready** defaults to **False**. So when we enter **Activate** when the program is loaded, we toggle the variable to **True**. Now the program knows it has already been initialized. When the user adds calls and then dismisses the **frmCall** form, this event fires. The semaphore **bAlreadyLoaded** retains its value so the program will not perform initialization again.

The bottom line is that the **initializeForm** routine is guaranteed to run once and only once for any session with our address book program. All of the static variables, **If** statements and semaphores are used to implement that capability.

A Bit More on the Status Bar Control

We will be updating the status bar control as our program goes through normal operations. You will place lines like the following in various procedures to provide textual feedback to the user:

```
sbStatus.Panels.Item(2).Text = "Loading...."
```

The status bar control permits up to 16 individual panels to be shown. Each of the panels is contained in the control's panels collection. The panel can hold either text or pictures. The status bar typically is used to display information about the object being viewed. We will use this to show information about the current contact being viewed. Both this control and the tree view control provide us with tools to make our interface economical in terms of form real estate, yet provide a rich source of information to the user. So in the above line, we are just adding the text **"Loading...."** to the text property of the second item of the panels collection. Of course, that is the second panel. Throughout the program, we will use the first panel to show information about the current contact and the second panel to display information about the working of the program. More eye-candy for the user and it's simple for us. A single line of code will update a panel to give feedback to the user.

All right, now we'll add a new subroutine to the **frmAddress** form called **initializeForm**.

Try It Out - Creating the initializeForm Subroutine

1 Create a new subroutine called **initializeForm** in the **frmAddress** form. Then add the following code to it:

```
Public Sub initializeForm()

    Screen.MousePointer = vbHourglass    '--show activity is occurring
    iCurrentState = NOW_IDLE             '--set the current state of the prog.
    sbStatus.Panels.Item(2).Text = "Loading..."
    tbContact.Tab = 0                    '-- make the 1st of the 3 tabs current
    DoEvents                             '-- ensure the visual components are updated
    Call clearFields
    Call lockFields(True)
    Call updateTree
    Call updateForm
    Call setUpListView
    tbContact.Enabled = False
    Screen.MousePointer = vbDefault
    sbStatus.Panels.Item(2).Text = "Ready."

End Sub
```

How It Works

Hopefully the names of the various routines provide enough description so that you know what is happening before even looking at the code, but let's discuss what is happening in this subroutine.

The first few lines are simply giving the user some visual cues that there is activity. We then set the tab control, **tbContact**, to show the first tab (tab 0). This ensures that when the program is loaded, the user interface is in a known state. We always want the first tab to be shown. If you were working on the program and had the third tab current when you saved the program, the third tab would be displayed when the program loaded. The tab control saves its state when it is saved. This line simply ensures the correct tab is displayed when loaded.

The **DoEvents** ensures that all visual changes are shown immediately. Use **DoEvents** to create a snappy looking user interface. If we omitted the **DoEvents**, the program could execute a few sub routines that take up precious CPU cycles. As such, it might take a few milliseconds to redraw the interface and the user might see a half-drawn window briefly. We don't want that in a professional application. So a liberal sprinkling of **DoEvents** right after issuing a command that effects the visual part of our program makes the program appear snappy.

```
    Call clearFields
    Call lockFields(True)
    Call updateTree
    Call updateForm
    Call setUpListView
```

As you can see, we again encapsulated several specific tasks into their own subroutines. This way we can simply call them when needed. For example, if we need to change anything to do with clearing fields, we just need to work on a single location in our program - the **clearFields** routine.

Now let's examine these five helper routines in detail, starting with **clearFields**.

The clearFields Subroutine

As we discussed, since the controls on the form are not data bound, we are responsible for clearing them when needed. This routine iterates through the **Controls** collection of the form. The **Tag** for each control is examined. If the **Tag** is the string **"1"**, then the program knows this field must be cleared of any data.

Try It Out - Coding the clearFields Subroutine

1 Add this code in the **frmAddress** form:

```
Public Sub clearFields()

Dim indx As Integer
Dim tempMask As String

With Me.Controls
   For indx = 0 To .Count - 1
      If Me.Controls(indx).Tag = "1" Then
         If (TypeOf Me.Controls(indx) Is TextBox) Then
            Me.Controls(indx).Text = ""
         ElseIf (TypeOf Me.Controls(indx) Is MaskEdBox) Then
            tempMask = Me.Controls(indx).Mask
            Me.Controls(indx).Mask = ""
            Me.Controls(indx).Text = ""
            Me.Controls(indx).Mask = tempMask
         Else
            Me.Controls(indx).Caption = ""
         End If
      End If
   Next
End With
DoEvents

End Sub
```

How It Works

This is the same technique we used earlier. **Me** represents the current form. So we access the **Controls** collection on the form. The collection of controls starts at 0, so we iterate through all of the controls from **0** to **.Count - 1**. For each control, which we access through the index in the **Controls** collection, we check the **Tag** property to see if we are interested in it.

```
With Me.Controls
  For indx = 0 To .Count - 1
    If Me.Controls(indx).Tag = "1" Then
```

By now it must be apparent that many controls in VB are collections. Once we understand how to access collections - as we were doing with the DAO hierarchy - things really start to make sense.

```
If (TypeOf Me.Controls(indx) Is TextBox) Then
    Me.Controls(indx).Text = ""
ElseIf (TypeOf Me.Controls(indx) Is MaskEdBox) Then
    tempMask = Me.Controls(indx).Mask
    Me.Controls(indx).Mask = ""
    Me.Controls(indx).Text = ""
    Me.Controls(indx).Mask = tempMask
Else
    Me.Controls(indx).Caption = ""
End If
```

Different controls are cleared in different ways. For a text box, we just set the **Text** property to **""**, but a masked edit control is a bit different. First, we must remove the mask before it can be cleared. Of course, we need to save the mask. This is because we are using various masks, such as one for zip code, one for phone numbers, and a third for dates. So before we clear the control, we save the specific mask in the string variable **tempMask**. Once the mask is safely tucked away, we can set the **Mask** property to **""** and clear the control by setting the **Text** property to **""**, just like a normal text box. Remember how we said that this control works like a text box when it does not have a mask? Then when it is cleared out, we reassign its mask to the **Mask** property. Finally, any additional controls, such as a label, are cleared by setting the **Caption** property to **""**.

So we have generalized the **clearFields** routine. We just call the routine and it takes care of clearing any type of control on the form. The task of clearing fields has been encapsulated. Down the road, if you wanted to add a combo box for example, you simply need to add that type of control to the loop and invoke its special way of being cleared.

The lockFields Subroutine

Normally, we want the fields to be locked. We certainly don't want the user to change any data in the fields if the program is not in an Add or Edit state. Since we will be locking/unlocking controls independently of clearing fields, it makes sense to separate this task into its own sub. Of course we will need to unlock the controls when editing or adding and then lock them when we are finished. Rather than write two subs - **lockFields** and **unLockFields**, we can simply pass a **Boolean** parameter that instructs this single sub what to do. If we were to write two separate routines, more than 90% of the code would be duplicated. So thinking about structuring subroutines for economy in this way really saves on space and our time.

Try It Out - Coding the lockFields Subroutine

1   Add the following code to the **frmAddress** form.

```
Public Sub lockFields(bDoLock As Boolean)

Dim indx As Integer

For indx = 0 To Me.Controls.Count - 1
  If Me.Controls(indx).Tag = "1" Then
    If (TypeOf Me.Controls(indx) Is TextBox) Then
      If (bDoLock = True) Then
        Me.Controls(indx).Locked = True
        Me.Controls(indx).BackColor = vbWhite
      Else
        Me.Controls(indx).Locked = False
        Me.Controls(indx).BackColor = vbYellow
      End If
    ElseIf (TypeOf Me.Controls(indx) Is MaskEdBox) Then
      If (bDoLock = True) Then
        Me.Controls(indx).Enabled = False
        Me.Controls(indx).BackColor = vbWhite
      Else
        Me.Controls(indx).Enabled = True
        Me.Controls(indx).BackColor = vbYellow
      End If
    End If
  End If
Next
DoEvents

End Sub
```

How It Works

We have used a routine similar to this earlier in the book, so it isn't necessary to spend much time on it. We are just checking the parameter to determine if the control should be locked or unlocked. If the control should be unlocked, the background is set to yellow and the **Locked** property is set to **False** (if it's a text box) or **Enabled** is set to **True** (if the control is a masked edit). The masked edit does not have a **Locked** property. We then do the opposite when the controls are to be locked. No magic here!

The updateTree Subroutine

OK, now for some fun. The tree view control that we named **tvContact**, will display all of the letters of the alphabet and the names of our contacts in the database. This routine populates the tree view control. We call it when the program is first loaded, of course. It is then called whenever a new contact is added, edited or deleted. This routine encapsulates reading all of our contacts in the database and refreshing the tree view when required.

1 Insert the following code in the **frmAddress** form:

```
Public Sub updateTree()

Dim indx As Integer
Dim rsAllNames As Recordset
Dim sqlNames As String
Dim sContactName As String
Dim currentAlpha As String

tvContact.Nodes.Clear

sqlNames = "SELECT ContactID, LastName, FirstName, MiddleInitial "
sqlNames = sqlNames &         "FROM Contact ORDER BY"
sqlNames = sqlNames & " LastName, FirstName, MiddleInitial "

Set rsAllNames = dbContact.OpenRecordset(sqlNames)

If (rsAllNames.RecordCount > 0) Then
    rsAllNames.MoveFirst
End If

For indx = Asc("A") To Asc("Z")
   currentAlpha = Chr(indx)

   Set contactNode = tvContact.Nodes.Add _
                  (, , currentAlpha, currentAlpha)

   If (Not rsAllNames.EOF) Then
      Do While UCase$(Left(rsAllNames!lastname, 1)) = currentAlpha
         With rsAllNames
            sContactName = !lastname & ", "
            sContactName = sContactName & !FirstName
            If (Not IsNull(!MiddleInitial)) Then
               sContactName = sContactName & " " & !MiddleInitial & "."
            End If
         End With

         DoEvents

         Set contactNode = tvContact.Nodes.Add(currentAlpha, _
                     tvwChild, "ID" & CStr(rsAllNames!ContactID), sContactName)
         rsAllNames.MoveNext
         If (rsAllNames.EOF) Then
            Exit Do
         End If
      Loop
   End If
Next

sbStatus.Panels.Item(1).Text = "There are " & _
                rsAllNames.RecordCount & " contacts in the database."
```

```
sbStatus.Panels.Item(1).Text = "There are " & _
                    rsAllNames.RecordCount & " contacts in the database."

rsAllNames.Close

DoEvents

End Sub
```

This code will update the tree view control and display the letters from A to Z.

How It Works

The first thing we want to do is clear the tree view control of any old data. Since we will call this after any editing or addition, we know there will be old data in the tree. So we clear any nodes in the control.

```
tvContact.Nodes.Clear
```

▶ A **Node** object is an item in a tree view control that can contain images and text

▶ A **Nodes** collection contains one or more **Node** objects

Node objects are manipulated by using standard collection methods (for example, the **Add** and **Remove** methods). We can access each element in the collection of **Nodes** by its index, or by a unique key that you store in the **Key** property of the **Node**. We will use our unique **ContactID** for each of our contacts in the database as this key.

A tree view control displays a hierarchical list of **Node** objects, each of which consists of a label and an optional bitmap. In our case, we will add letters of the alphabet to nodes on one level and any contacts with a last name that starts with that letter as a child node, on the next level. A tree view control is typically used to display any kind of information that might usefully be shown as a hierarchy. So this control is perfect for our requirements.

Before we can populate the tree, we must create a recordset from the database that contains the information about all of our contacts on file. Then we build a SQL statement that will retrieve all of our contacts' last names, first names and middle initial ordered by last name, first name and middle initial.

```
sqlNames = "SELECT ContactID, LastName, FirstName, MiddleInitial "
sqlNames = sqlNames & " FROM Contact ORDER BY"
sqlNames = sqlNames & " LastName, FirstName, MiddleInitial "
```

Since the key to our table is the unique **ContactID**, we want to ensure the returned recordset is ordered by names. This is because the **ContactID** is created whenever a new contact is added to the database. Since we don't add contacts in alphabetical order, it does not do us much good here, but we do need it to uniquely identify each and every contact. Remember when we discussed that we could have two "John M. Smiths" in the database? Well, by retrieving the **ContactID** with each contact, we can uniquely identify each contact.

We now create the recordset using the **OpenRecordset** method. We supply the SQL **SELECT** statement we just constructed above.

```
Set rsAllNames = dbContact.OpenRecordset(sqlNames)
```

We **Dim**'d a local reference variable, **rsAllNames** to hold the recordset. Since we don't need this except to update the tree, it goes out of scope when we exit this sub. This is another example of not keeping variables hanging around when they are not needed.

When the recordset is created, we check to see if there are any contacts. If so, we go to the first. The subroutine is not exited here because even if there are no contacts, we want to populate the tree view (minimally) with the letters of the alphabet.

The easiest way to get the letters A to Z is to grab them from the ASCII table. The ASCII codes 65 to 90 represent the capital letters A to Z. Take a look at the ASCII table in the on-line help in VB sometime. The ASCII 65 represents a capital "A". The **Asc()** VB function will return the ASCII integer code for the character we pass it. So we don't need to know that "A" is 65 and "Z" is 90. We just look from **Asc("A")** - which is 65 - through to **Asc("Z")** - which is 90.

```
For indx = Asc("A") To Asc("Z")
   currentAlpha = Chr(indx)
```

Now we want to add the character to the tree view control. So we need to add a node to the tree view control's **Nodes** collection. We do that with the following line.

```
Set contactNode = tvContact.Nodes.Add _
                (, , currentAlpha, currentAlpha)
```

We covered this a bit in the last chapter when we populated the tree view control when analyzing an **.mdb** database. So here we are only passing two of the parameters to the **Add** method. The first parameter is for the unique key that identifies this node and since the letter of the alphabet is unique, it works just fine. Incidentally, the key must be a string value. The next parameter is for the text that will be shown in the control. Again, we want to show the letter, so we just use the same variable. Talk about recycling! So **currentAlpha** is used for both the key and to display the letter in the tree view control.

OK, now we have the letter in the tree view control at the first, or root level. Let's say that this is the first time through the loop. In that case we added the letter "A" to the control. Now we want to scan the recordset of our contracts to see if we have any contacts whose last name begins with the letter "A".

```
If (Not rsAllNames.EOF) Then
  Do While UCase$(Left(rsAllNames!LastName, 1)) = currentAlpha
```

Remember that we ordered the recordset to be sorted on last names? Well, now we check the current record (which will be the first record since we are looking at how the loop operates the first time through). We simply take the leftmost character of the field **rsAllNames!LastName** to determine if it matches the **currentAlpha** character, which is of course "A". To bulletproof our program, we convert the leftmost character to uppercase using **UCase$**. We know that **currentAlpha** will be an uppercase "A", but what if the user entered a name like "Adam ant" by mistake? If we didn't convert the character to uppercase, we could miss this entry. Always try to anticipate situations like this. Now let's assume that there was an entry "Adam Ant" in the first record.

```
With rsAllNames
  sContactName = !LastName & ", "
  sContactName = sContactName & !FirstName
  If (Not IsNull(!MiddleInitial)) Then
    sContactName = sContactName & " " & !MiddleInitial & "."
  End If
End With
```

We now want to concatenate the string **sContactName** to show the contact in the form **LastName, FirstName** and **MiddleInitial** if available. We could check for **Null** for all of the fields, but in our validation routine for adding names, we put in a business rule that requires both a first and last name. The middle initial is optional. Now this could pose a problem if we wanted to enter "Sting" or "Prince" as a contact, but this is a design decision we made. So above we are just taking the current record, extracting the fields, and concatenating the string **sContactName** in the form **LastName FirstName, MiddleInitial**. So the first record would produce "Ant, Adam G."

The next step is to add the contact under the letter "A" in our tree view control.

```
Set contactNode = tvContact.Nodes.Add(currentAlpha, _
              tvwChild, "ID" & CStr(rsAllNames!ContactID), sContactName)
```

Remember that when we added the letter "A", we used **currentAlpha** (which happens to hold the string "A") as the key. Well, we want to add Adam Ant under the letter "A", so we use **currentAlpha** in the relative position of the **Add** method. Then we instruct the control that this new node is a child of the "A" node. Remember that the key position requires a string. For some reason, VB6 does not like strict numerics converted to a string. So we concatenate the string **"ID"** to the string of the **!ContactID**. So if Adam Ant had a **ContactID** of say 23, the key for this node would be "ID23". Finally we add the name of the contact in the text position of the **Add** method. So now contact "Adam G. Ant" is added under the "A" in our tree view control as "Ant, Adam G."

Then we move to the next record in the recordset.

```
rsAllNames.MoveNext
```

If we reached the end of the recordset, we exit the **Do While** loop. Otherwise, we return to the top of the **Do While** loop to see if we have another contact that has a last name that begins with "A".

```
    If (rsAllNames.EOF) Then
        Exit Do
    End If
Loop
```

Then the outer loop is invoked and we add the next letter, "B", to the tree and repeat the above sequence to add any contacts whose last name begins with "B".

After the entire tree view control is populated, we update the status bar to inform the user how many contacts are currently in the database.

```
sbStatus.Panels.Item(1).Text = "There are " & _
            rsAllNames.RecordCount & " contacts in the database."
```

Finally, before exiting the routine, we want to explicitly close the local recordset.

```
rsAllNames.Close
```

If we omitted this line, the recordset would close because the local reference variable **rsAllNames** goes out of scope. However, it is good programming form to get into the habit of explicitly closing recordsets whenever they are open and no longer needed. When the tree is populated, the **updateForm** routine is then called. Let's code that next.

The updateForm Subroutine

We call **updateForm** whenever a change in state of our program occurs. All this routine does is check the form-level variable **iCurrentState** to determine what state the program happens to be in. For example, it might be idle, in which case it informs the user via the status bar that it is ready. Next, the tool bar buttons are either enabled or disabled, depending on the state.

Try It Out - Coding the updateForm Subroutine

1 In the **frmAddress** form, key in the following code:

```
Public Sub updateForm()

Select Case iCurrentState
  Case NOW_ADDING, NOW_EDITING
    If (iCurrentState = NOW_ADDING) Then
      sbStatus.Panels.Item(2).Text = "Adding..."
      Call clearFields
    Else
      sbStatus.Panels.Item(2).Text = "Editing..."
    End If
    tbContact.Enabled = True
    tbContact.Tab = 0                    '-- make the 1st tab current
    tbContact.TabEnabled(1) = False   '--disable the 2nd and 3rd tabs
    tbContact.TabEnabled(2) = False
    tvContact.Enabled = False
    lockFields (False)                   '-- unlock fields and set background
    txtFirstName.SetFocus                '-- set focus to first name field
    Toolbar1.Buttons(bAdd).Enabled = False
    Toolbar1.Buttons(bCancel).Enabled = True
    Toolbar1.Buttons(bSave).Enabled = True
    Toolbar1.Buttons(bDelete).Enabled = False
    Toolbar1.Buttons(bEdit).Enabled = False
    Toolbar1.Buttons(bQuit).Enabled = False
  Case NOW_IDLE
    sbStatus.Panels.Item(2).Text = "Ready."
    Toolbar1.Buttons(bAdd).Enabled = True
    Toolbar1.Buttons(bCancel).Enabled = False
    Toolbar1.Buttons(bSave).Enabled = False
    Toolbar1.Buttons(bQuit).Enabled = True
    If (Len(txtLastName)) Then
      Toolbar1.Buttons(bDelete).Enabled = True
      Toolbar1.Buttons(bEdit).Enabled = True
    Else
      Toolbar1.Buttons(bDelete).Enabled = False
      Toolbar1.Buttons(bEdit).Enabled = False
    End If
    tvContact.Enabled = True
    tbContact.TabEnabled(1) = True
    tbContact.TabEnabled(2) = True
  Case NOW_DELETING
    sbStatus.Panels.Item(2).Text = "Deleting...."
    Toolbar1.Buttons(bAdd).Enabled = False
    Toolbar1.Buttons(bCancel).Enabled = False
    Toolbar1.Buttons(bSave).Enabled = False
    Toolbar1.Buttons(bDelete).Enabled = False
    Toolbar1.Buttons(bEdit).Enabled = False
    Toolbar1.Buttons(bQuit).Enabled = False
  Case NOW_SAVING
    sbStatus.Panels.Item(2).Text = "Saving...."
    tvContact.Enabled = True
    Toolbar1.Buttons(bAdd).Enabled = False
```

```
      Toolbar1.Buttons(bCancel).Enabled = False
      Toolbar1.Buttons(bSave).Enabled = False
      Toolbar1.Buttons(bDelete).Enabled = False
      Toolbar1.Buttons(bEdit).Enabled = False
      Toolbar1.Buttons(bQuit).Enabled = False
      If (Len(mskBirthday)) Then
       lblBirthday = Format$(mskBirthday, "mmmm dd, yyyy")
      End If
  End Select

  DoEvents

  End Sub
```

How It Works

Not much explanation is required here. We have seen this before in previous chapters. This approach isolates all of the messy details of setting up buttons and controls into a single routine. Once it is working, you can forget about it. Imagine if you had to handle enabling/disabling various buttons and controls under each of the tool bar buttons. In other words, I have seen programmers placing gobs of code in the Add New button `Click` event. Then more in the Edit `Click` event, etc. All of it is disconnected and leads to subtle bugs. By placing everything here and calling this helper routine from all those other places, we can logically see how they fit together and ensure everything functions in an integrated manner.

The only other piece of information to bring up is the `Enum` for the button numbers. See how easy it is to read `Toolbar1.Buttons(bAdd).Enabled = False`? We can now have real self-documenting code. Since our buttons are odd numbers, 1,3,5,7,9 and 11, this could be a struggle to remember when debugging. But the `Enum` makes this a snap. Please use it.

The setUpListView Subroutine

This routine is called once, upon loading the form. It is used to set up the list view control, `lvCalls`. The list view control is used to display all of the call notes for an individual contact in our database. The list view control contains `ListItem` and `ColumnHeader` objects in (surprise!) collections. A `ListItem` object defines the various characteristics of items in the list view control, such as:

▶ A brief description of the item

▶ Icons that may appear with the item, supplied by an image list control

▶ Additional pieces of text, called subitems, associated with a `ListItem` object that you can display in `Report` view

Let's set up our code now.

Try It Out - Coding the setUpListView Subroutine

```
Public Sub setUpListView()

Dim clmHdr As ColumnHeader
Static bBeenHereBefore As Boolean

If bBeenHereBefore = False Then

Set clmHdr = lvCalls.ColumnHeaders. _
             Add(, , "Date / Time", lvCalls.Width \ 3)
Set clmHdr = lvCalls.ColumnHeaders. _
             Add(, , "Type of Call", lvCalls.Width \ 3)
Set clmHdr = lvCalls.ColumnHeaders. _
             Add(, , "Call Identifier", lvCalls.Width \ 3)
bBeenHereBefore = True
End If

lvCalls.View = lvwReport

End Sub
```

How It Works

In **setUpListView** we are just adding the columns. Data - in the form of the **ListItems** - will be added later. We are passing just two of the five possible parameters into the **Add** method here - the text and the width. The text is just the header that will be shown for the column, such as **"Date / Time"**. The width is the width of the control divided by 3. So each of the columns will take up a third of the control real estate. Finally, we tell the list view control to show itself in a report format.

The Initialized Address Book Program

Whew! All of this to set up the form. However, for all of the code above, the program initializes in less than 1 second. Not too bad. Of course, if you have several hundred contacts in your database, it might take a tad longer.

Now let's take a look at the various capabilities of the program. For the user to do anything with the existing contacts, they must navigate the tree view control. The neat thing about this control is that it will handle expanding and collapsing the various hierarchical structures when the user clicks on the control with the mouse.

So let's take a look at what happens when the user clicks on a contact that is displayed in the tree.

1 Place this code in the **tvContact_NodeClick** event:

```
Private Sub tvContact_NodeClick(ByVal Node As MSComctlLib.Node)

If (Len(Node.Key) = 1) Then Exit Sub

'-- Here we retrieve the contact the user clicked on --
lCurrentContactKey = CLng(Mid$(Node.Key, 3, Len(Node.Key)))
With rsContactTable
    .Index = "PrimaryKey"
    .Seek "=", lCurrentContactKey
    If Not .NoMatch Then
      bFieldsPopulated = True
      sCurrentContactName = tvContact.SelectedItem
      Call populateFields
      Call populateListView
      tbContact.Enabled = True
    Else
      MsgBox ("Ohhhh Nooo")
    End If
End With

End Sub
```

How It Works

If the user just clicks on a letter such as "A" instead of a name, we don't want to take any action. To determine when this situation occurs, we just check the length of the **Key** property of the node that was clicked. If it is only one character long, like a letter of the alphabet, we simply exit the routine.

```
If (Len(Node.Key) = 1) Then Exit Sub
```

However, if the user clicked on a contact, the first thing we do is retrieve the **ContactID** of that contact, which we tucked in the **Key** property of the **Node**.

```
'-- Here we retrieve the contact the user clicked on --
lCurrentContactKey = CLng(Mid$(Node.Key, 3, Len(Node.Key)))
```

Remember when we populated the tree view control with our contacts? We took the unique **ContactID** of each contact and placed it in the **Key** of that **Node**. So now we will use that value to retrieve the information on that contact from our database. Remember we had to store it as a string and had to append **"ID"** to the front of it? Well, now using the **Mid$** function we take everything from the third character onwards. So if the **Node.Key** for this contact was **"ID34"**, the **Mid$** function starts at the third character and takes everything from there to the end of the key which would give us **"34"**. Since that is still a string, we cast it as a **Long** using the built-in function **CLng()** and the result is assigned to our form-level variable **lCurrentContactKey**.

```
With rsContactTable
  .Index = "PrimaryKey"
  .Seek "=", lCurrentContactKey
```

Once we have a key value to search for, we use DAO to set the **Index** of the
rsContactTable to **"PrimaryKey"**. You may recall that we set the primary key of the table to
ContactID. Since we opened this recordset as a table, we can use the **Seek** method. The **Seek**
member function lets you search for a record in a table-type recordset based on a table index.

The **Seek** method is much faster than the **FindFirst** method, but it can only be used on tables
where indexes have been defined. So we use that little trick to make our program lightning fast.
We use the **Seek** method of the recordset to find the value in the index that is equal to the
ContactID of the contact the user clicked on.

```
If Not .NoMatch Then
  bFieldsPopulated = True
  sCurrentContactName = tvContact.SelectedItem
  Call populateFields
  Call populateListView
  tbContact.Enabled = True
Else
  MsgBox ("Ohhhh Nooo")
End If
```

If the contact in the database is found (and we know they will be, because we only put in
known keys), we then grab the name of the contact name. The form-level variable
sCurrentContactName holds the name of the contact as it appears in the tree. We can now
access this variable in other parts of our program to display information to the user. Now the
record pointer is pointing to the contact the user selected as a result of the **Seek** method, so we
want to populate the fields on the form with information about that contact. Let's take a look at
the routine, **populateFields**, that does just that.

The populateFields Subroutine

Now that we have a valid record in **rsContactTable**, as identified by the
sCurrentContactName information, let's display the fields in our program to the user. Here's
the code to do it!

Try It Out - Coding the populateFields Subroutine

1 Add the following code to the **frmAddress** form:

```
Public Sub populateFields()

Dim sBirthday As String

'-- Here we retrieve the fields from the database and --
'-- populate the fields in the user interface.        --

Call clearFields
```

```
With rsContactTable
  If (Not IsNull(!LastName)) Then txtLastName = !LastName
  If (Not IsNull(!MiddleInitial)) Then
    txtMiddleInitial = !MiddleInitial
  End If
  If (Not IsNull(!FirstName)) Then txtFirstName = !FirstName
  If (Not IsNull(!HomeStreet)) Then
    txtHomeStreet = !HomeStreet
  End If
  If (Not IsNull(!HomeCity)) Then
    txtHomeCity = !HomeCity
  End If
  If (Not IsNull(!HomeState)) Then
    txtHomeState = !HomeState
  End If
  If (Not IsNull(!HomeZip)) Then
    mskHomeZip = !HomeZip
  End If
  If (Not IsNull(!HomePhone)) Then
    mskHomePhone = !HomePhone
  End If
  If (Not IsNull(!HomeFax)) Then
    mskHomeFax = !HomeFax
  End If
  If (Not IsNull(!HomeEmail)) Then
    txtHomeEmail = !HomeEmail
  End If
  If (Not IsNull(!HomeCellPhone)) Then
    mskHomeCellPhone = !HomeCellPhone
  End If
  If (Not IsNull(!Birthday)) Then
    sBirthday = !Birthday
    convertDate sBirthday
    mskBirthday = sBirthday
    lblBirthday = Format$(!Birthday, "dddd mmmm dd, yyyy")
  End If
  DoEvents

  Call updateForm

End With

End Sub
```

How It Works

The first thing we want to do is call our **clearFields** routine. Again, that will ensure that each of the fields will be cleared out of any old data from looking at records from prior contacts. Then we just update each field on the tab control with the appropriate fields from the current contact record.

```
With rsContactTable
  If (Not IsNull(!LastName)) Then txtLastName = !LastName
  If (Not IsNull(!MiddleInitial)) Then
txtMiddleInitial = !MiddleInitial
  End If
  If (Not IsNull(!FirstName)) Then txtFirstName = !FirstName
```

We check to ensure that the field is not null and, if not, we assign the record field to the appropriate control. Yes, I know that earlier I mentioned that the first and last name fields would never be null, but I told you I was paranoid! Then we just do the rest for the remaining fields. Any of them could indeed be null because we only check for the first and last names to be there before adding the contact. So this routine just correctly adds the data - if it is there - on the selected contact.

The interesting thing here is that if a birthday was added for a contact, we format the data and place the result in the label **lblBirthday**. This is actually harder to achieve than it might sound. First we take the value in the **Birthday** field and assign it to the string **sBirthday**. A subroutine **convertDate** is then called, which is passed the variable **sBirthday**. A value is returned and displayed in the **mskBirthday** masked edit box.

```
If (Not IsNull(!Birthday)) Then
    sBirthday = !Birthday
    convertDate sBirthday
    mskBirthday = sBirthday
    lblBirthday = Format$(!Birthday, "dddd mmmm dd, yyyy")
End If
```

Finally, when the fields have been populated, we call **updateForm**, which will update all of the buttons.

```
Call updateForm
```

Converting Dates

A curious bug can arise in the code if we do not format the date held in the **Birthday** field correctly. We have gone to great pains to ensure that our dates are entered correctly by using a masked edit box to force the user of our program to enter the year in four digit format. Microsoft Access stores data entered in **Date/Time** format with four digit years. However, the 97 version of Microsoft Access abbreviates the year format for dates between 1/1/1930 and 12/31/2029. So that 1/1/1930 through to 12/31/1999 becomes 1/1/30 through 12/31/99, and 1/1/2000 through to 12/31/2029 becomes 1/1/00 through 12/31/29.

This results in a breakdown in communication between Jet and our application for all dates between 1/1/1930 - 12/31/2029. When we retrieve the **Birthday** field from our **Contacts** database **mskBirthday** is expecting the year to be four digits long, but Jet is passing a two-digit year to **populateFields** so an error will result.

Therefore, we call a subroutine, **convertDate**, to format all dates correctly.

Try It Out - The convertDate Subroutine

1 Add the following code to the **frmAddress** form:

```
Public Sub convertDate(sBirthday As String)

Dim sYear As String

If Len(sBirthday) = 8 Then
    sYear = Mid$(sBirthday, 7, 2)
    If sYear >= 30 Then
        sBirthday = Mid$(sBirthday, 1, 6) & "19" & sYear
    Else
        sBirthday = Mid$(sBirthday, 1, 6) & "20" & sYear
    End If
End If

End Sub
```

How It Works

First of all we check to see how long the string **sBirthday** is. A date that is formatted correctly should be 10 digits long - 2 digits for the month, 2 digits for the day, 4 digits for the year, and 2 '/' to separate the month, day and year. An incorrectly formatted date will be 8 digits long.

Once we've determined that our date is 8 digits long, we strip off the last 2 numbers using the **Mid$** function and place them in the variable **sYear**. Then we test to see if **sYear** is greater than or equal to **30**.

Mid$(sBirthday, 1, 6) strips off the first 6 characters of our **sBirthday** string. We then concatenate the string to **"19"** and finally concatenate the **sYear** string.

If **sYear** is smaller than **30**, the process is exactly the same except that **"20"** is concatenated into our string instead of **"19"**.

The populateListView Subroutine

Once the data fields for our contact are successfully displayed, we want to see if there are any calls logged for that contact. Since we normalized our tables in the last chapter, we will now construct and invoke an SQL query to retrieve any call records.

Try It Out - Coding the populateListView Subroutine

1 Add this code to the **frmAddress** form:

```
Public Sub populateListView()

Dim itemToAdd As ListItem
Dim noteSQL As String

lvCalls.ListItems.Clear
txtNotes = ""
txtNotes.Locked = True

noteSQL = "SELECT DISTINCTROW Notes.DateOfCall,"
noteSQL =  noteSQL & "Notes.CallTypeID, Notes.NotesOnPhoneCall, "
noteSQL = noteSQL & " Notes.CallCounter, CallType.CallDescription,"
noteSQL = noteSQL & " Notes.ContactID "
noteSQL = noteSQL & " FROM Notes "
noteSQL = noteSQL & " INNER JOIN CallType ON Notes.CallTypeID ="
noteSQL = noteSQL & " CallType.CallTypeID "
noteSQL = noteSQL & " WHERE Notes.ContactID = " & _
          lCurrentContactKey
noteSQL = noteSQL & " ORDER BY Notes.DateOfCall DESC"

Set rsCallType = dbContact.OpenRecordset(noteSQL)

If (rsCallType.RecordCount > 0) Then
   rsCallType.MoveFirst
    While Not rsCallType.EOF
       Set itemToAdd = lvCalls.ListItems.Add(, , _
                      Format$(rsCallType!DateOfCall, "dddd mmmm dd, yyyy"))
       itemToAdd.SubItems(1) = rsCallType!CallDescription
       itemToAdd.SubItems(2) = CStr(rsCallType!CallCounter)
       rsCallType.MoveNext
    Wend
   sbStatus.Panels.Item(1).Text = "There are " & _
                   rsCallType.RecordCount &  " calls logged for " _
                   & sCurrentContactName
Else
   Set itemToAdd = lvCalls.ListItems.Add(, , "No calls logged")
   sbStatus.Panels.Item(1).Text = "No calls logged for " _
                                  & sCurrentContactName
End If

lvCalls.SelectedItem = lvCalls.ListItems(1)
Call lvCalls_ItemClick(lvCalls.SelectedItem)
DoEvents

End Sub
```

How It Works

We want to clear out any calls in the list view control from a previous contact. The **txtNotes** text box that holds the text of any previous call is also cleared out. For good measure, we ensure that the **txtNotes** control is locked so the user can't mistakenly overwrite any data.

479

```
lvCalls.ListItems.Clear
txtNotes = ""
txtNotes.Locked = True
```

Next, we construct the **noteSQL** string that will contain the SQL statement to retrieve any call records from the user. Notice that we want to retrieve several fields from the **Notes** table. We want to grab the **DateOfCall**, the **CallTypeID**, the **NotesOnPhoneCall**, the **CallCounter**, the **CallDescription** and the **ContactID** fields, where the **ContactID** is equal to the form-level variable **lCurrentContactKey**. You may recall that we set this variable when the user clicked on a contact's name from the tree view control. Of course, this unique key forms the relationship between the tables.

```
noteSQL = "SELECT DISTINCTROW Notes.DateOfCall,"
noteSQL =  noteSQL & "Notes.CallTypeID, Notes.NotesOnPhoneCall, "
noteSQL = noteSQL & " Notes.CallCounter, CallType.CallDescription,"
noteSQL = noteSQL & " Notes.ContactID "
noteSQL = noteSQL & " FROM Notes "
noteSQL = noteSQL & " INNER JOIN CallType ON Notes.CallTypeID ="
noteSQL = noteSQL & " CallType.CallTypeID "
noteSQL = noteSQL & " WHERE Notes.ContactID = " & _
          lCurrentContactKey
noteSQL = noteSQL & " ORDER BY Notes.DateOfCall DESC"
```

We want all of the records returned in descending order of the date of the call. This will place the most recent call at beginning of the recordset. We want to display the most current call first, so this simply speeds things up for us. Once the SQL statement is formed, we set the form-level variable **rsCallType** to point to the returned recordset.

```
Set rsCallType = dbContact.OpenRecordset(noteSQL)
```

If there are indeed calls logged for this contact, we want to add the date, the type of call, and the call counter number to our list view control. So the user is then given a summary of the calls in a sorted order.

```
If (rsCallType.RecordCount > 0) Then
   rsCallType.MoveFirst
    While Not rsCallType.EOF
      Set itemToAdd = lvCalls.ListItems.Add(, , _
                      Format$(rsCallType!DateOfCall, "dddd mmmm dd, yyyy"))
      itemToAdd.SubItems(1) = rsCallType!CallDescription
      itemToAdd.SubItems(2) = CStr(rsCallType!CallCounter)
      rsCallType.MoveNext
    Wend
    sbStatus.Panels.Item(1).Text = "There are " & _
                    rsCallType.RecordCount &  " calls logged for " & _
                    sCurrentContactName
```

Here the code moves to the first record in the recordset. Then as long as there are records, we call the **Add** method of the list view control to add a new **ListItem** node. Once the value of the recordset field **!DateOfCall** is formatted and added, we then add two additional **SubItems** to the **ListItem**. The **!CallDescription** and then the **!CallCounter** are both added to the **ListItem**. Then the **MoveNext** method of the recordset is invoked and the record pointer moves to the next call record. When all of the calls are displayed, we update the status bar to tell the user how many calls are logged for the current contact.

If there are no calls on file for this contact, we inform the user of this as well.

```
Else
    Set itemToAdd = lvCalls.ListItems.Add(, , "No calls logged")
    sbStatus.Panels.Item(1).Text = "No calls logged for " _
                                    & sCurrentContactName
End If
```

For a nice professional touch to our program, we select the first item in the list. If there are calls listed, the text will be displayed in the **txtNotes** box automatically. A nice detail.

```
lvCalls.SelectedItem = lvCalls.ListItems(1)
Call lvCalls_ItemClick(lvCalls.SelectedItem)
DoEvents
```

Now let's take a look at the **lvCalls_ItemClick** event of the list view control to see how the notes of the call are displayed.

The List View Control Code

We going to put code in the **ItemClick** event so that when an item is clicked, either programmatically as above, or by the user with a mouse, we update the **txtNotes** text box.

Try It Out - Coding the List View Control

1 Add the following code to the **lvCalls_ItemClick** event procedure:

```
Private Sub lvCalls_ItemClick(ByVal Item As ComctlLib.ListItem)

If (rsCallType.RecordCount > 0) Then
    rsCallType.MoveFirst
    '-- Find the record that has the ID --
    rsCallType.FindFirst "CallCounter = " & _
                    lvCalls.ListItems(Item.Index).SubItems(2)
    txtNotes = rsCallType!NotesOnPhoneCall
End If

End Sub
```

How It Works

When the user clicks on a call that is shown in the list view control, this little routine will find the record in the **rsCallType** recordset for that item. Remember that the **rsCallType** recordset is updated when a new contact is retrieved. Then we just grab the **CallCounter** that we placed in the **SubItem** of the **ListItem** in the list view control, **lvCalls**. Since that is a unique value, we just do a search for that value in the recordset. Also, because the recordset will only contain records of calls for that contact this is very fast.

Sorting the List View

Above, we showed how to retrieve a record by taking a value from the list view control. While we are on the list view control, let's put in another nice touch. When the user clicks on a column, such as the Date/Time, we will sort the contents. So if there are 20 calls logged, and the user wants to see the first call, simply clicking on the column will reverse sorts them. Each column can be sorted in this way.

Try It Out - Coding the List View Sort

1 Add this code to the **lvCalls_ColumnClick** event.

```
Private Sub lvCalls_ColumnClick(ByVal ColumnHeader As ComctlLib.ColumnHeader)

Dim nSortCol As Integer

' When a ColumnHeader object is clicked, the list view
' control is sorted by the SubItems of that column.
' Set the SortKey to the index of the ColumnHeader - 1

nSortCol = ColumnHeader.Index - 1

If (lvCalls.SortKey = nSortCol) Then
   lvCalls.SortOrder = 1 - lvCalls.SortOrder
Else
   lvCalls.SortKey = nSortCol
   lvCalls.SortOrder = lvwAscending
End If

'-- Do the sort now
lvCalls.Sorted = True

End Sub
```

This routine just takes the column the user clicked on and sorts in the opposite way the column is currently sorted. It will work for any of the three columns that are available for the user to click on.

2 Lastly with the list view control, we want to display a pop-up menu called **mnuPopup**. Go to the main menu of VB and create a new menu called **mnuPopup**. Provide two sub menus as shown with the names **mnuAddNew** and **mnuDelete**. Uncheck the <u>V</u>isible check box for **mnuPopup**. This will prevent the menu from showing up on the form but will be available to us as a pop-up.

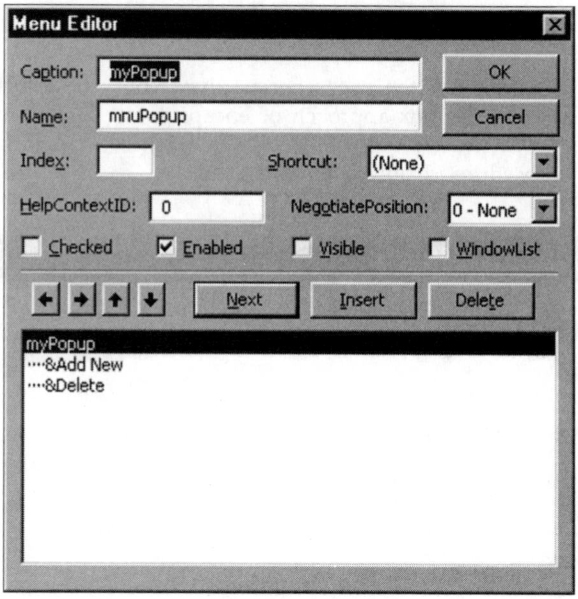

Now when the menu is built, we can invoke it from our list view control's **MouseDown** event procedure as shown below.

3 Add this code to the **lvCalls_MouseDown** event procedure

```
Private Sub lvCalls_MouseDown(Button As Integer, Shift As Integer, x As Single, y
As Single)
```

```
If Button = vbRightButton Then

    If (rsCallType.RecordCount < 1) Then
      mnuDelete.Enabled = False
    Else
      mnuDelete.Enabled = True
    End If
    PopupMenu mnuPopup
End If
```

```
End Sub
```

This handy little routine will check the button that the user pressed when the list view control is clicked. If it is the right button, then that means we want to invoke the menu. If there are no calls in the **rsCallType** recordset for the user, there is nothing for them to delete. This is in keeping with our philosophy of only providing the user with legitimate options. So if there are no records, we disable the **mnuDelete** menu option. We then display the **mnuPopup** using the VB command **PopupMenu** and passing it the name of the menu. We will defer how a call is added until we see how a new contact is added – let's do that now.

The Tool Bar of the Address Book

The button bar is where the action happens from the user's perspective. Notice how little code is required. That is because we adhered strictly to our approach of encapsulating logical functions in sub routines. Then we just invoke them when required. As an example, let's take a look at the code in the **ButtonClick** event procedure of our tool bar control.

Try It Out - Adding code to the Toolbar

1 Add the following code to the **Toolbar1_ButtonClick** event procedure:

```
Private Sub Toolbar1_ButtonClick(ByVal Button As ComctlLib.Button)

    Select Case Button.Index
    Case bAdd   '-- Add New

        iCurrentState = NOW_ADDING
        Call updateForm

    Case bCancel  '—Cancel

        If (bFieldsPopulated = True) Then
            Call populateFields
        End If
        Call lockFields(True)
        iCurrentState = NOW_IDLE
        Call updateForm

    Case bSave '—Saving

    '-- Here we are saving either a new or edited entry --
        If (Not validateEntry()) Then
            Exit Sub
        End If
        postContact

    Case bDelete   '—Deleting

        Dim indx As Integer
        Dim sMsg As String
        Dim sDeleteSQL As String
        sMsg = "Delete " & tvContact.SelectedItem & _
               " and all related call logs?"
        indx = MsgBox(sMsg, vbYesNo + vbCritical, progname)
        If (indx <> vbYes) Then Exit Sub
        sDeleteSQL = "DELETE * FROM Contact WHERE ContactID = " _
                     & lCurrentContactKey
        dbContact.Execute (sDeleteSQL)

        Call initializeForm

    Case bEdit   '-- Editing
```

```
        iCurrentState = NOW_EDITING
        updateForm

    Case bQuit   '-- Quitting

      rsContactTable.Close
      dbContact.Close
      Set rsContactTable = Nothing
      Set dbContact = Nothing
      Unload Me

    End Select

  End Sub
```

How It Works

When the user clicks the Add button (which we use enumerated values to detect), the state variable **iCurrentState** is set and we call **updateForm**. We examined that earlier. We saw that **updateForm** takes care of clearing the fields, unlocking the fields, and updating the enabled properties of the various buttons. Pretty neat, eh? Two lines.

```
    Case bAdd   '-- Add New

        iCurrentState = NOW_ADDING
        Call updateForm
```

If the user cancels, it could be that the user was either adding a new record or editing a current contact. This way, if the fields were previously populated, then the call to **populateFields** is made. We looked at this earlier. It simply takes the current record and populates all of the fields in our program. We then ensure that the fields get locked. The current state is set to **NOW_IDLE**. Then when the call to **updateForm** is made, all of the buttons and status messages are set.

```
    Case bCancel   '—Cancel

        If (bFieldsPopulated = True) Then
          Call populateFields
        End If
        Call lockFields(True)
        iCurrentState = NOW_IDLE
        Call updateForm
```

When the user saves, it could be that a new contact is being saved, or a change made to an existing contact is being saved. In either case, we want to ensure that our business rules are being met. The routine **validateEntry** tests the fields and will return a Boolean true or false value indicating passing or failing the validations. If the validation was successful, the call to **postContact** will update the database.

```
    Case bSave   '—Saving

        '-- Here we are saving either a new or edited entry
        If (Not validateEntry()) Then
          Exit Sub
        End If
        postContact
```

Validating the Data Entry

Notice above when we wish to save either a new contact, or a current record we just edited. Before we save just any data, we are calling a validate routine to ensure that there is at least a name for our contact. The **validateEntry** routine is pretty simple. We just perform three tests. Both the first and last name of a contact must be entered. The third test is that if the user did indeed enter a date for the birthday, it is a valid date in the form of mm/dd/yyyy. That's all. If any of these three tests fail, the user is notified of exactly what went wrong and the focus is automatically placed in that field. The user is happy. We'll code for that now.

Try It Out - Coding for Data Entry Validation

1 Add the following code to the **frmAddress** form:

```
Public Function validateEntry() As Boolean

Dim indx As Integer

validateEntry = True
sbStatus.Panels.Item(2).Text = "Validating..."
If (Len(txtFirstName) < 1) Then
  tbContact.Tab = 0
  indx = MsgBox("Please enter the first name of the contact.", _
        vbInformation + vbOKOnly, progname)
  txtFirstName.SetFocus
  validateEntry = False
  Exit Function
End If

If (Len(txtLastName) < 1) Then
  tbContact.Tab = 0
  indx = MsgBox("Please enter the last name of the contact.", _
        vbInformation + vbOKOnly, progname)
  txtLastName.SetFocus
  validateEntry = False
  Exit Function
End If

mskBirthday.PromptInclude = False
If (Len(mskBirthday.Text) > 0) Then
  mskBirthday.PromptInclude = True
  If (Not IsDate(mskBirthday)) Then
    tbContact.Tab = 0
    indx = MsgBox("Please enter a valid birthdate mm/dd/yyyy.", _
          vbInformation + vbOKOnly, progname)
    mskBirthday.SetFocus
    validateEntry = False
    Exit Function
  End If
End If
mskBirthday.PromptInclude = False

End Function
```

How It Works

There are just two things worth mentioning in this routine. Notice the three message boxes where we tell the user what the error is if the validation fails. Remember when we defined the constant **progname** in the code module? Well, this is where that technique pays off. Instead of having to define three literal strings for the three boxes, we simply use the constant.

The second thing has to do with one of the idiosyncrasies of the masked edit box. Before we test it, we must set the **PromptInclude** property to **False**. This is because even if the user did not enter anything in the field, it will always have a length of 10 because the prompt is 10 characters long (__/__/____). So we remove that. Then we can check the **Text** property, which will provide anything in the masked edit other than the prompt. If there is something there, it tells us the user entered a date. So we reassign the prompt and check to see if it is a valid date with the built-in function **IsDate()**. If all of the validations are successful, the program calls **postContact** to enter the new contact (or edited contact) into the database.

Posting the Contact to the Database

When the user wants to save the added or edited record, the above validation routine ensures that there is at least a name present. If indeed the record passed our validation code, then the **postContact** routine is called. This is the routine that updates the database with any new contacts or edits that the user makes on an existing contact. We first provide the user with feedback by changing the mouse icon to an hourglass and adding text to the status bar.

Try It Out - Posting the Contact

1 Add the following code to the **frmAddress** form:

```
Public Sub postContact()




Screen.MousePointer = vbHourglass
sbStatus.Panels.Item(2).Text = "Posting Contact...."

If (iCurrentState = NOW_ADDING) Then
      rsContactTable.AddNew
Else
   With rsContactTable
      .MoveFirst
      .Index = "PrimaryKey"
      .Seek "=", lCurrentContactKey
      If Not .NoMatch Then
         rsContactTable.Edit
      Else
         MsgBox ("Ohhhh Nooo")
      End If
   End With
End If
```

```
With rsContactTable
    If (Len(txtFirstName)) Then !FirstName = txtFirstName
    If (Len(txtMiddleInitial)) Then !MiddleInitial = txtMiddleInitial
    If (Len(txtLastName)) Then !LastName = txtLastName
    If (Len(txtHomeStreet)) Then !HomeStreet = txtHomeStreet
    If (Len(txtHomeCity)) Then !HomeCity = txtHomeCity
    If (Len(txtHomeState)) Then !HomeState = txtHomeState
    If (Len(mskHomeZip)) Then !HomeZip = mskHomeZip
    If (Len(mskHomePhone)) Then !HomePhone = mskHomePhone
    If (Len(mskHomeFax)) Then !HomeFax = mskHomeFax
    If (Len(mskHomeCellPhone)) Then !HomeCellPhone = mskHomeCellPhone
    If (Len(txtHomeEmail)) Then !HomeEmail = txtHomeEmail
    mskBirthday.PromptInclude = False
    If (Len(mskBirthday.Text) > 0) Then
      mskBirthday.PromptInclude = True
      !Birthday = mskBirthday
      lblBirthday = Format$(!Birthday, "dddd mmmm dd, yyyy")
    End If
    mskBirthday.PromptInclude = True
    .Update

End With

DoEvents

If (iCurrentState = NOW_ADDING) Then
  Call initializeForm
Else
  iCurrentState = NOW_IDLE
  Call lockFields(True)
  Call updateForm
End If

sbStatus.Panels.Item(2).Text = "Ready."
Screen.MousePointer = vbDefault

End Sub
```

How It Works

If **iCurrentState <> NOW_ADDING**, then we know that the user is editing an existing contact. So we want to save the changes to the database. We set the **Index** property of the **rsContactTable** and perform a **Seek** using the form-level **lCurrentContactKey** value. Recall that this variable is set when the user clicks on the tree view control for a contact. It is stored in the tree view node for that user and represents the **ContactID** for the current contact. A **Seek** is performed, the record is retrieved and the **Edit** method is invoked. We know the record will be found because the tree view nodes only contain valid keys of users that are already in the database.

```
Else
    With rsContactTable
        .MoveFirst
        .Index = "PrimaryKey"
        .Seek "=", lCurrentContactKey
        If Not .NoMatch Then
```

488

```
            rsContactTable.Edit
        Else
            MsgBox ("Ohhhh Nooo")
        End If
    End With
End If
```

At this point we have the current record - either a new one for a new contact or the existing record for editing. We then populate the fields in the record with the values in the form fields. Remember that to get to this stage, the information had to pass our validation routine. So we are sure that this is clean data being entered into the database. Once the data is entered into the database, the **Update** method is invoked to write the data to disk.

```
    .Update
```

When the data is successfully placed in the database, we update the user interface. If a new record was added, then we call **initializeForm**. You may recall that this is called when we load the program. It forces the tree view to be refreshed and sets up the form.

```
If (iCurrentState = NOW_ADDING) Then
   Call initializeForm
Else
   iCurrentState = NOW_IDLE
   Call lockFields(True)
   Call updateForm
End If
```

If the user was saving the result of an edit, we want to keep the current contact information on the screen. So the fields are locked and the form is updated. This routine simply sets up the tool bar buttons and posts status information to the user indicating that all is well.

```
sbStatus.Panels.Item(2).Text = "Ready."
Screen.MousePointer = vbDefault
```

Finally, just a bit more visual feedback for the user. We always try to err on the side of too much information.

Back to the Tool Bar

Deleting a record is serious business. We want to inform the user that the current contact and all related records will be gone forever. Look at the code we already have in the **Toolbar1_ButtonClick** event procedure:

```
Case bDelete  '--Deleting

    Dim indx As Integer
    Dim sMsg As String
    Dim sDeleteSQL As String
    sMsg = "Delete " & tvContact.SelectedItem & " and all related call logs?"
    indx = MsgBox(sMsg, vbYesNo + vbCritical, progname)
    If (indx <> vbYes) Then Exit Sub
    sDeleteSQL = "DELETE * FROM contact WHERE contactID = " & lCurrentContactKey
```

```
        dbContact.Execute (sDeleteSQL)

        Call initializeForm
```

If the user agrees and does indeed want to delete this contact, we construct an SQL statement that will delete the current contact record from the **Contact** table. Remember that when we built the table using DAO we added the relationship and provided the cascading delete attribute? Well, normally we would have to write code to also delete the records from the **Notes** table that equaled the **ContactID** of the user. However, since we have defined cascading deletes, and **Contact** is the base table, all associated **Notes** records for this contact will **automatically** be deleted. Pretty neat, eh? This not only saves us code, but ensures that the referential integrity of the related tables is maintained. Once the contact and related **Notes** records are deleted, a call to **initializeForm** ensures all of the controls and the form are refreshed.

If the user wants to edit an existing contact, we simply set the state of the program to **NOW_EDITING**. Then a call to **updateForm** ensures all of the controls are unlocked and the tool bar buttons are set correctly for that state.

```
    Case bEdit  '-- Editing

        iCurrentState = NOW_EDITING
        updateForm
```

For the **Case bQuit** we just do some memory management. When the user wishes to exit our program, we close the global references to both the **rsContactTable** and the **dbContact** database. Prior to DAO 3.5, if you attempted to close a recordset after the database was closed, a trappable error occurred. In any event, when they are closed, we set the references to **Nothing**. This ensures all memory is reclaimed from the objects.

```
    Case bQuit  '--Quitting

        rsContactTable.Close
        dbContact.Close
        Set rsContactTable = Nothing
        Set dbContact = Nothing
        Unload Me
```

Hopefully you're having no trouble following along with the code for the **frmAddress** form. Here's a 'roadmap' of what's going on inside our application to clarify things for you.

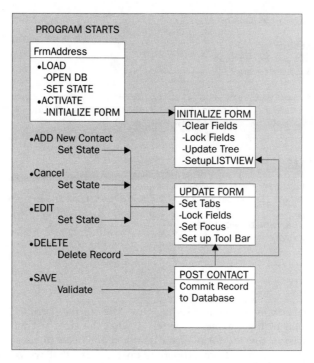

Adding Call Notes for the Current Contact

OK, ready to add a call log for the current user? Have you stayed with me so far? You have, well congratulations. OK, remember the menu that was added a while back. Menu items only have a single event procedure - namely **Click**.

Try It Out - Coding the Popup Menu

1 Add this code to the **Click** event of the **mnuAddNew** menu we built earlier:

```
Private Sub mnuAddNew_Click()

    frmCall.sContactName = sCurrentContactName
    frmCall.lContactNumber = lCurrentContactKey
    frmCall.Show vbModal
    Call populateListView

End Sub
```

2 Add this code to the **Click** event of the **mnuDelete** menu we built earlier:

```
Private Sub mnuDelete_Click()

    Dim indx As Integer
    Dim rsDeleteCall As Recordset
    Dim sDeleteCall As String

    indx = MsgBox("Are you sure you wish to delete this call from " & _
                lvCalls.ListItems(lvCalls.SelectedItem.Index) & "?", _
                vbYesNo + vbQuestion, progname)


    If (indx <> vbYes) Then Exit Sub

    sDeleteCall = "DELETE * FROM Notes WHERE CallCounter = " & _
                lvCalls.ListItems(lvCalls.SelectedItem.Index).SubItems(2)

    dbContact.Execute (sDeleteCall)
    Call populateListView

End Sub
```

How It Works

In the **mnuAddNew_Click** event we are setting properties in the **frmCall** form (we'll create this in the very next section of this chapter) that tell it what the current contact name and **ContactID** is. Then we show the form modally. When we need to pass information between forms, it is now easy to do - we have properties on the form that we can set, and these can be used to attach/pass information. So we can set the properties on the **frmCall** form even while that form is not loaded! Now that is powerful. Next, we need to create the form that this subroutine sets the properties of - the **frmCall** form.

The frmCall Form - Where to Log Calls

This form will not only permit the user to add call logs for any contact, but also to add new call description categories.

Try It Out - Creating the frmCall Form

1 Add another form to your project called **frmCall**. Lay the form out as shown - details on how to do this follow below.

The top part of the form permits the user to add, delete or modify call descriptions. This is where they will add descriptions such as 'Business', 'Personal', 'Hobby', etc. The bottom three-quarters is where the user selects the date of the call and then adds the specific notes of that call.

2 Add the Microsoft Calendar Control to your tool palette. It is located in file **mscal.ocx**.

3 On the top one-quarter of the form, for the call description, add the following controls.

Control	Name of Control	Caption
label	**lblDescription**	Call Description
combo box	**cboDescription**	N/A
frame	**Frame1**	Call Types
command button	**cmdAddType**	&Add
command button	**cmdDeleteType**	&Delete
command button	**cmdSaveType**	&Save
command button	**cmdCancelType**	&Cancel

4 Now, on the bottom three-quarters of the form, add these controls:

Control	Name of Control	Caption
label	`lblCaption`	N/A - set in code
text box	`txtNotesOnPhone`	N/A
calendar	`Calendar1`	N/A
command button	`cmdCallAdd`	Add Ca&ll
command button	`cmdCallCancel`	Canc&el

Be sure to set the `txtNotesOnPhone.MultiLine` property to `True`.

Just Add Code

This form will permit the user to log new calls for any contacts. So if Michael Hammer calls today with an update on the work I've asked him to do, it's easy to add a new call log. A brief description of the call can also be added. In fact, if you wish to add an entirely new category for calls, such as "Model Rail Road", this is where it would be done.

Try It Out - Building the frmCall Form

1 In the general section of the form, add the following code:

```
Option Explicit

Dim rsCallType As Recordset
Dim currentSelection As Long
Dim bDescriptionChanged As Boolean
Dim sCurrentDescription As String
Dim iCurrentState As Integer

Public sContactName As String
   'looks like a property from the outside
Public lContactNumber As Long
   'also looks like a property
```

How It Works

Notice that the last two items declared in `frmCall` are `Public`. That means that these two variables can be accessed from the outside. Remember that we set these properties from our `frmAddress` just before calling this form. **Public form-level variables look like properties from the outside.** So by setting properties on this form, we can easily pass values. We set these two properties before loading this form. Then we can read these variables within our form.

When the form is loaded, the `Activate` event fires after all of the visual components are sited. This means that we can now set them.

When the **frmCall** is called modally from the **frmAddress** form, we want to retrieve all valid call types so that we can show them to the user when they wish to categorize a call. We also set up the calendar to default to today. Focus is forced to the **txtNotesOnPhone** text box.

Try It Out - Adding Code to the frmCall Activate Event

1 Add this code to the **frmCall_Activate** event procedure:

```
Private Sub Form_Activate()

currentSelection = 0

'—open our form-level recordset using dbOpenTable
Set rsCallType = dbContact.OpenRecordset("CallType", dbOpenTable)

'—Set the focus to our Notes text box
txtNotesOnPhone.SetFocus

iCurrentState = NOW_IDLE

'—Load our combo box with all current call descriptions
Call updatedescriptionCombo

'—Initialize our calendar control to today
Calendar1.Day = Day(Now)
Calendar1.Month = Month(Now)
Calendar1.Year = Year(Now)

lblCaption = "Enter the notes on the call to " & sContactName

'—force all visual changes to the screen to look snappy
DoEvents

End Sub
```

How It Works

This code is standard procedure to you now. We make the form consistent when it loads by explicitly setting it up. The calendar is refreshed and we update the combo box with the valid call descriptions. Finally, a label instructs the user what to do. From a user's perspective, it looks very straightforward.

The updatedescriptionCombo Subroutine

Now let's take a quick look at the **updatedescriptionCombo** subroutine that is called from the form's **Activate** event procedure. Of course, this will populate our combo box with all of the current entries in the **rsCallType** we just opened in the **Activate** event. Again, **rsCallType** has form-level visibility.

1 Add this code to the **frmCall** form:

```
Public Sub updatedescriptionCombo()

Dim indx As Integer

cboDescription.Clear

If (rsCallType.RecordCount < 1) Then
  cboDescription.AddItem "<No Entries>"
  cboDescription.Locked = True
  cmdDeleteType.Enabled = False
  txtNotesOnPhone.Enabled = False
  cmdCallAdd.Enabled = False
Else
  rsCallType.MoveFirst
  While (Not rsCallType.EOF)
    cboDescription.AddItem rsCallType!CallDescription
    cboDescription.ItemData(cboDescription.NewIndex) = rsCallType!CallTypeID
    rsCallType.MoveNext
  Wend
  txtNotesOnPhone.Enabled = True
  cmdCallAdd.Enabled = True
End If

cmdSaveType.Enabled = False
cmdCancelType.Enabled = False

If iCurrentState = NOW_ADDING Then
  For indx = 0 To (cboDescription.ListCount - 1)
     cboDescription.ListIndex = indx
     If (cboDescription.ItemData(cboDescription.ListIndex) = _
          currentSelection) Then
         Exit For
     End If
   Next
Else
   cboDescription.ListIndex = 0
End If

bDescriptionChanged = False
sCurrentDescription = cboDescription.Text
iCurrentState = NOW_IDLE
Call updateButtons

End Sub
```

How It Works

OK, we first load the combo box with the **!CallDescription** of the current record. At the same time, we tuck the **!CallTypeID** field into the **ItemData** section of the combo box. This way we can have access to the **CallTypeID** value to use in our SQL queries. This way the

!CallDescription can be changed, but the underlying key, the **CallTypeID**, is the constant that the user never sees. Remember that if we want to change "Business" to "Programming", the **CallTypeID** is not changed. So the new call description is available throughout the program.

```
cboDescription.AddItem rsCallType!CallDescription
cboDescription.ItemData(cboDescription.NewIndex) = rsCallType!CallTypeID
```

We should mention that if the user is currently adding a record, we want to ensure that the correct **CallTypeID** is added to the call. So we loop through the combo box until we find the **CallTypeID** that is equal to the variable **currentSelection**.

```
If iCurrentState = NOW_ADDING Then
  For indx = 0 To (cboDescription.ListCount - 1)
      cboDescription.ListIndex = indx
      If (cboDescription.ItemData(cboDescription.ListIndex) = _
            currentSelection) Then
          Exit For
      End If
  Next
Else
```

Now we'll add code to both the **Change** and **Click** event procedures of the **cboDescription** combo box. If the user wishes to add a new description, they just type it right in the combo box. As soon as this happens, we set the state of the software and call **updateButtons**. This will permit the user to either add the new call description or to cancel the new entry.

Try It Out - Code to Add a New Call Description

1 Add the following code to the **cboDescription_Change** event:

```
Private Sub cboDescription_Change()

bDescriptionChanged = True     '--set our form-level Boolean
If (iCurrentState <> NOW_ADDING) Then
  iCurrentState = NOW_EDITING
End If
Call updateButtons              '--our centralised button handler

End Sub
```

2 Now add the following code to the **cboDescription_Click** event:

```
Private Sub cboDescription_Click()

sCurrentDescription = Trim$(Left$(cboDescription.Text, 20))
currentSelection = cboDescription.ItemData (cboDescription.ListIndex)

End Sub
```

3 Now add the following to the **cmdAddType_Click** event. **cmdAddType** is contained within the frame control.

```
Private Sub cmdAddType_Click()

    iCurrentState = NOW_ADDING
    Call updateButtons
    cboDescription.Locked = False
    cboDescription.Text = ""
    cboDescription.SetFocus

End Sub
```

How It Works

As mentioned, if the user enters information into the combo box, our program assumes they might wish to save the changes. The state is set and the buttons are updated to permit the user to save the changes if they so desire. However, if they press the **cmdAddType** button, we know the user wishes to add a new type. We set the state of the software and a call to **updateButtons** ensures the correct buttons are enabled and disabled. We then unlock the control, clear out the text portion and force focus to the combo box.

Deleting a Call Description

When the user wants to delete a call description, there are some implications. We first ensure that there is a correct entry to delete. Then we provide a message to ensure the user actually wants to delete the record.

Try It Out - Adding Code to Delete a Call Description

1 Add this code in the **cmdDeleteType_Click** event:

```
Private Sub cmdDeleteType_Click()

    Dim indx As Integer
    Dim sMessage As String

    iCurrentState = NOW_DELETING
    Call updateButtons

    If (Len(cboDescription.Text) < 1) Then
        indx = MsgBox("Please choose an entry to delete", _
            vbOKOnly + vbInformation, progname)
        iCurrentState = NOW_IDLE
        Call updateButtons
        Exit Sub
    ElseIf (cboDescription.ListCount < 1) Then
        indx = MsgBox("There are no entries to delete", _
            vbOKOnly + vbInformation, progname)
        iCurrentState = NOW_IDLE
        Call updateButtons
        Exit Sub
```

```
    Else
      sMessage = "Do you wish to delete the call " & vbCrLf
      sMessage = sMessage & "type " & cboDescription.Text & vbCrLf
      sMessage = sMessage & "and all associated calls in your"
      sMessage = sMessage & " database?" & vbCrLf
      indx = MsgBox(sMessage, vbYesNo + vbCritical, progname)

      If indx <> vbYes Then
        iCurrentState = NOW_IDLE
        Call updateButtons
        Exit Sub
      End If

  'OK, now we delete the record
      Dim lKeyToDelete As Long
      Dim sDeleteSQL
      lKeyToDelete = cboDescription.ItemData (cboDescription.ListIndex)
      sDeleteSQL = "DELETE * FROM CallType WHERE CallTypeID = " & lKeyToDelete
      dbContact.Execute (sDeleteSQL)

      iCurrentState = NOW_IDLE
      Call updatedescriptionCombo
      Call updateButtons

    End If

End Sub
```

How It Works

Let's look at some code snippets and examine what they do.

We build our SQL string and use the DAO method **Execute** to actually delete the record. We get the **CallTypeID** we wish to delete by grabbing it from the **ItemData** stash where we placed it. Then we instruct Jet to delete all records where the **ItemData** value is equal to the **CallTypeID** of the record. We know that there will be only one record that meets this criterion, but the DAO method is very fast.

```
    Dim lKeyToDelete As Long
      Dim sDeleteSQL As String
      lKeyToDelete = cboDescription.ItemData (cboDescription.ListIndex)
      sDeleteSQL = "DELETE * FROM CallType WHERE CallTypeID = " & lKeyToDelete
      dbContact.Execute (sDeleteSQL)
```

When the record is deleted, we now clear the combo box and reset it with the current records that are left, as we saw in the **updatedescriptionCombo** routine. Of course, the call description we just deleted will be gone.

```
      iCurrentState = NOW_IDLE
      Call updatedescriptionCombo
      Call updateButtons
```

Now we want to save either the new call description or the new name for an existing record...

499

Try It Out - Saving a Call Description

1 Add this code to the **cmdSaveType_Click** event:

```
Private Sub cmdSaveType_Click()

Dim indx As Integer
Dim sqlMaxID As String
Dim rsMaxIDNumber As Recordset
Dim lNewTypeID As Long
Dim sMessage As String

If (Len(cboDescription.Text) < 1) Then
  sMessage = "Please enter the Call Type Description in "
  sMessage = sMessage & "the combo box."
  indx = MsgBox(sMessage, vbOKOnly + vbInformation, progname)
  Exit Sub
End If

'--If the user is not adding a new description, we know that
'--the user wishes to edit a current entry. Checking the
'--iCurrentState tells us which mode

If (iCurrentState <> NOW_ADDING) Then
  indx = MsgBox("Change all entries for '" & _
        sCurrentDescription & "' to '" & cboDescription.Text & _
        "'?", vbYesNo + vbQuestion, progname)
Else
  indx = MsgBox("Add call type: " & cboDescription.Text, _
        vbYesNo + vbQuestion, progname)
End If

'--the user aborts the change. Restore the form
If (indx <> vbYes) Then
  iCurrentState = NOW_IDLE
  Call updatedescriptionCombo
  Exit Sub
End If

'--Otherwise update the table with either a new record or
'--change the description field if this is an edit.
Set rsCallType = dbContact.OpenRecordset ("CallType", dbOpenTable)

If (iCurrentState = NOW_ADDING) Then
  sqlMaxID = "SELECT Max(CallType.CallTypeID) AS LastType"
  sqlMaxID = sqlMaxID & " FROM CallType"
  Set rsMaxIDNumber = dbContact.OpenRecordset(sqlMaxID)

  rsCallType.AddNew
  lNewTypeID = rsCallType!CallTypeID
  rsCallType!CallDescription = Trim$ (Left$(cboDescription.Text, 20))
  currentSelection = lNewTypeID
Else
```

```
   rsCallType.Edit
   rsCallType!CallDescription = sCurrentDescription
   currentSelection = rsCallType!CallTypeID
End If
rsCallType.Update

cmdSaveType.Enabled = False

Call updatedescriptionCombo

iCurrentState = NOW_IDLE
```

End Sub

If the user canceled any changes to the description box, then the combo box must be reset.

2   Add this code to the **cmdCancelType_Click** event:

```
Private Sub cmdCancelType_Click()
```

```
iCurrentState = NOW_IDLE
Call updatedescriptionCombo
```

End Sub

Remember our **updateButtons** helper routine from before? We will use the same approach to centralize enabling/disabling our buttons. See how self-documenting the enums make our code? Even a non-programmer can understand what is happening here.

Try It Out - The Ever Popular updateButtons Subroutine

1   Add this code to the **frmCall** form:

```
Public Sub updateButtons()

Select Case iCurrentState
  Case NOW_ADDING
    cmdAddType.Enabled = False
    cmdDeleteType.Enabled = False
    cmdSaveType.Enabled = True
    cmdCancelType.Enabled = True
  Case NOW_DELETING
    cmdAddType.Enabled = False
    cmdDeleteType.Enabled = False
    cmdSaveType.Enabled = True
    cmdCancelType.Enabled = True
  Case NOW_EDITING
    cmdAddType.Enabled = False
    cmdDeleteType.Enabled = False
    cmdSaveType.Enabled = True
    cmdCancelType.Enabled = True
```

```
      Case NOW_IDLE
        cmdAddType.Enabled = True
        If (rsCallType.RecordCount < 1) Then
          cmdDeleteType.Enabled = False
        Else
          cmdDeleteType.Enabled = True
        End If
        cmdSaveType.Enabled = False
        cmdCancelType.Enabled = False
    End Select

    End Sub
```

There, we have just added the code that will permit the user to add, delete or edit call descriptions. This way, the user can group any number of calls from a single contact into any category - personal, business, etc.

Add a New Call or Cancel the Operation?

OK, now we are ready to add code to the two command buttons for either adding a new call to the database or canceling the operation completely.

Try It Out - Adding a New Call

1   Add the following code to the **cmdCallAdd_Click** event. When the user clicks this button, this code will first ensure that there is something in the **txtNotesOnPhone** text box to save. If there is, we add a new record to the **Notes** table and save the appropriate information.

```
Private Sub cmdCallAdd_Click()

Dim indx As Integer
Dim rsNotes As Recordset

'—Sanity check. Don't save a blank message
If (Len(txtNotesOnPhone) < 1) Then
  indx = MsgBox("Please enter the discussion in the text box", _
               vbOKOnly + vbInformation, progname)
  Exit Sub
End If

Screen.MousePointer = vbHourglass
DoEvents

'—Open the Notes table to accept our new entry
Set rsNotes = dbContact.OpenRecordset("Notes", dbOpenTable)
rsNotes.AddNew
rsNotes!ContactID = lContactNumber
rsNotes!DateOfCall = Calendar1.Value
rsNotes!CallTypeID = currentSelection
```

```
rsNotes!NotesOnPhoneCall = txtNotesOnPhone
rsNotes.Update

Me.Hide
DoEvents

Unload Me
Screen.MousePointer = vbDefault
```

End Sub

As mentioned, if there is something to save, we open a table type recordset on the **Notes** table. A new record is added. We then save the unique **lContactNumber** that identifies our contact. The **Calendar1.Value** that returns the date of the call (in a date type variable) is saved as well as the ID for the type of the call. Finally, the actual notes for the call are saved. The **Update** method of the recordset commits the new record to the database.

2 Now add this code to the **cmdCallCancel_Click** event:

```
Private Sub cmdCallCancel_Click()
```

```
Unload Me
```

End Sub

3 When the form is unloaded, be sure to set the form to **Nothing**. This totally removes all references to and memory used by the form. It's good to get in this habit for every form you unload. Here's the code to do this – enter it in the **Unload** event of the **frmCall** form.

```
Private Sub Form_Unload(Cancel As Integer)
```

```
Set frmCall = Nothing
```

End Sub

Again, to clarify the 'roadmap' of the code in **frmCall** here's a figure displaying how all our subroutines and functions are related.

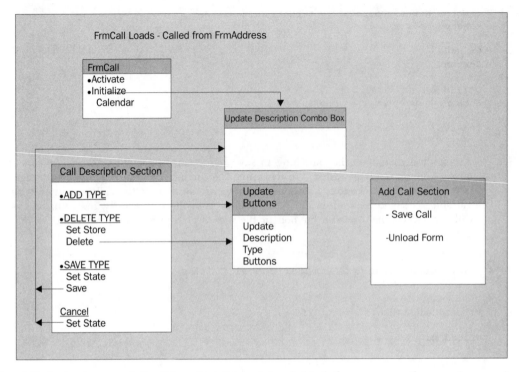

Now let's look at some of the things that Jet is doing behind the scenes as the user is accessing the database.

The DB Statistics Tab

We will now add a few statistics to the 3rd tab just so we can see how hard the Jet engine is working. We will interrogate the **ISAMStats** function, which just returns raw information about disk reads, writes, locks and caching. Usually, professionals use this information to tune a database. However, you might find it informative to see exactly how much work is really happening under the hood. We just call the **ISAMStats** function and pass a number (StatNum) from 0 through 5 as a parameter. Where StatNum is one of the following values:

> 0 - Number of disk reads
>
> 1 - Number of disk writes
>
> 2 - Number of reads from cache
>
> 3 - Number of reads from read-ahead cache
>
> 4 - Number of locks placed
>
> 5 - Number of release lock calls

1 Go to the **frmAddress** form and click on the tab control. Under the **Click** event, add the following code:

```
Private Sub tbContact_Click(PreviousTab As Integer)

If (tbContact.Tab = 2) Then
   lblDateCreated = Format$(rsContactTable.DateCreated, _
                    "dddd mmmm dd, yyyy hh:mm AMPM")
   lblLastUpdated = Format$(rsContactTable.LastUpdated, _
                    "dddd mmmm dd, yyyy hh:mm AMPM")
   lblRecordCount = "Contacts in Database: " & _
                    rsContactTable.RecordCount
   lblDiskReads = ISAMStats(0)
   lblDiskWrites = ISAMStats(1)
   lblReadCache = ISAMStats(2)
   lblReadAhead = ISAMStats(3)
   lblLocksPlaced = ISAMStats(4)
   lblReleaseLocks = ISAMStats(5)
End If

End Sub
```

How It Works

Here we are just using an undocumented Jet function, **ISAMStats()** that returns a value depending on the value we pass in. It is very instructive to look at this tab after you have added a few contacts. You will be surprised at all of the work Jet has been doing on your behalf.

We check the tab that user clicked. If it is **2**, we know it's the 3rd tab. Remember that collections start at 0. If we know they clicked the DB Statistics tab, we simply refresh the labels with the Jet statistics. So each time the user clicks this tab, fresh information on the working of the database is displayed; we dynamically update the fields on the **Click** event. This ensures that the very latest information is available to the user. Again, we just provided this as an illustration to show how much work is really going on.

How It All Works – A Global Recap

Well, it was a lot of work, but you have created a real-world working database program. This program shows many things. For example, even though this is a database program, much of the code was really written to manage the user interface. This is consistent with what we learned in the earlier chapters. When we write a Windows program, we first draw the interface, set properties and then write code. The interface drives every Windows program and this is no exception.

We used straight DAO to accomplish the database access. We modularized all of the code in logical modules so they could be reused within the program. For example, the **updateForm** sub sets the appropriate tab on the tab control, locks the fields, sets the focus, and updates the tool bar. We call this modularized code when the user wishes to add a new contact, cancel an add or edit, or decides to edit a current record. All of this code has to do with managing the interface. The DAO code for the entire program is a small percentage of code. This is typical of all Windows database programs.

Reflect back on the last chapter when we encapsulated much of the management of the data control into our **dataClass** class module. I hope that this chapter is a good advertisement on why we want to do just that. Now if you wrote another program that required user data-entry, you could cut/paste/tweak parts of this program. But it would still have to be customized for the specific job at hand. This was a lot of work! We only want to do something like this to learn. And we only want to do it once, right? So I can already see the lights going on. Why not encapsulate the DAO code in a class module as well? Good idea. As they say, this exercise is left to the reader.

OK, go ahead and save the project and press *F5* to run it.

Press the Add New button and add a new contact. Notice how the fields get cleared, unlocked and the background color changes to yellow. The tool bar updates to only provide the user with a Cancel or Save option. Notice the status bar informing the user we are Adding...

After you complete the entry, press the Save button. Save commits the record to the database and updates the form. Your new entry is now in the tree view control. Click on the new entry and the record will be displayed in the first tab. Notice the date - 1899. Since we are fully qualifying the century, the date issue is not a problem.

Click on the Call Log tab for the new contact. Notice that the list view control shows us that there are no calls logged for Mr. Mann. Right-clicking on the list view displays a pop up menu. Since there are no calls logged yet, only the Add New menu option is enabled. Click Add New.

The **frmCall** form is now displayed modally. Notice that the label above the box reminds us the contact name we are working with. The calendar defaults to today, but you can enter any date that is relevant. Also, you will want to add a new description. Click on Add in the Call Types frame and add one or more call descriptions. Then add some text into the description text box. When you are finished, click the Add Call button. This will commit this record to the **Notes** table.

Now the **frmCall** form is dismissed and the call we just added is shown in the list view control. Also you may remember that we placed code in the list view so that if the user clicks on the Date/Time or Type of Call header, the entries will be sorted in either ascending or descending order. Another nice touch for the user.

Finally, click on the DB Statistics tab to review the info on how Jet has been working behind the scenes.

What We Learned

We covered a lot of ground in this chapter. We learned about controls, multi-form programs, some new SQL commands and more. I hope you found it as much fun as I did. Some of the key things that we learned were:

▶ We programmed and used the following: the tool bar, tree view, list view, status bar, calendar, tab strip, masked edit, and image list controls

▶ A pop-up menu was built and used

▶ Enumerated variables were used throughout to ease programming and readability

▶ SQL commands along with the **Execute** method were used to delete records

▶ How to format our dates, so that a year abbreviated to two digits becomes four digits long

Exercises

1   Describe the steps required to add a tool bar with pictures to a Visual Basic form.

2   For what kind of data might you choose to use a tree view control to display the information to the user?

3   Describe how to create a pop-up menu. Also create the code for a **MouseDown** event on a form to display a pop-up menu if the right mouse button is clicked.

4   Write an SQL **DELETE** statement to delete a record from a table named **HotContacts** where the **FirstName** is **"Phred"** and the **LastName** is **"Friendly"**.

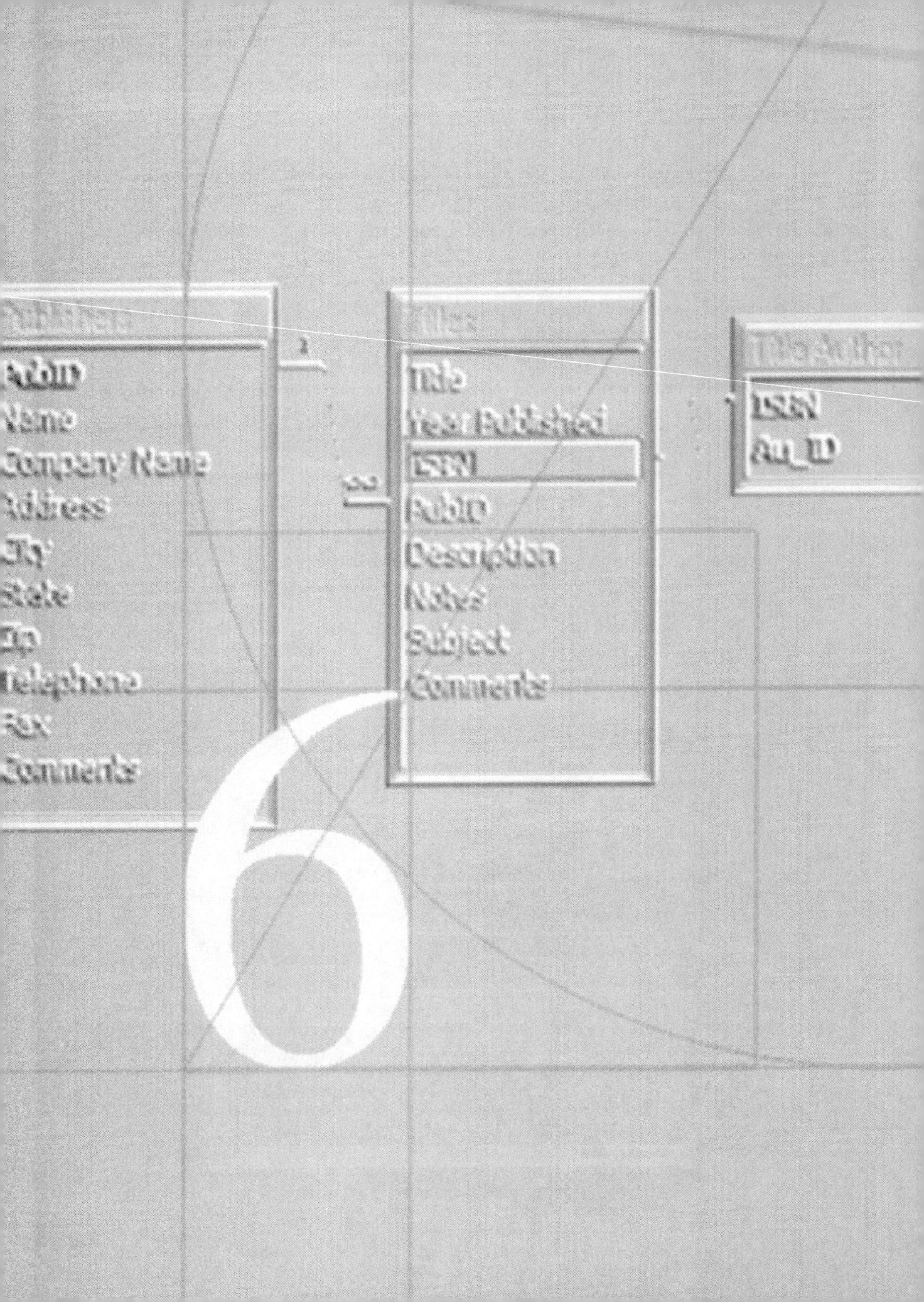

PubID
Name
Company Name
Address
City
State
Zip
Telephone
Fax
Comments
Title
Year Published
ISBN
PubID
Description
Notes
Subject
Comments
ISBN
Au_ID
6

11

Universal Data Access Using ADO

In this chapter we're going to start getting to grips with what will definitely be the database access technology of the future – ADO. We'll look quickly at the historical background to the development of ADO before moving on to discuss more recent developments in data access technologies. Then we will begin exploring the concepts and components of ADO itself before going on to create our first pieces of code that will program ADO for us. There's a lot of ground to cover – as always in this exciting field – so let's get going!

What's the Background to ADO?

In the early days of computing, dumb terminals were wired to powerful mainframe computers. The centralized Information Services (IS) department of a company ran the computing show. The mainframe gurus told us what we could and could not do. Then in August of 1981, the first IBM personal computer was released and the world changed. Control was eventually wrested from the centralized IS department at companies and flowed to the every individual with a personal computer.

Each personal computer had its own CPU and hard drive to run programs and store data. Centralized computing for many day to day activities disintegrated and each person with a personal computer took individual control of their data destiny. There was talk of big iron mainframes going the way of the dinosaur - who needed them? We had just as much processing power on our desktops. Life was good.

But there were problems too. For example, lots of individual computers sitting on people's desks, and all wanting to share information and common data. Out of the many desktop solutions to this need to access data by distributed computing stations was Data Access Objects (**DAO**). We've already learned about DAO and how easy it is to create desktop and file server database programs.

Now, with VB 6.0, a brand new Jet database engine 3.51 just made this solution stronger. In fact, Jet 3.51 is faster and more robust than Jet 3.5 that shipped with VB 5.0. Microsoft wanted to enhance a proven, strong database access solution and, when developing desktop database solutions using **.mdb** or ISAM files, Microsoft says the combination of Jet and DAO is definitely the way to go. Microsoft has upgraded DAO and will continue to support this approach for the foreseeable future. And don't forget, DAO is the most popular desktop database access method around! So the installed base of solid, robust applications using DAO is tremendous.

But DAO's days are numbered. It is a technology that will not be enhanced any further. So we programmers *must* learn ADO because that is the future for us. And while ADO is relatively new, VB 6.0 has provided us tools to hit the ground running.

The Limitations of DAO

We have seen two needs of modern business rapidly emerge that require a new and more sophisticated approach to gathering data. The first need is that of **accessing legacy data** - that is, information that is stored around the business enterprise in disparate forms in various types of computers. Companies like IBM and Oracle suggest that the solution is to move everything into a single database structure. Well, if the world stood still, this would *still* be problematical at best. The second need is that of accessing **non-relational** data. With the advent of businesses' use of the Internet and corporate Intranets, there is a need to get information from e-mail, HTML pages, and even video! Clearly DAO is not up to this job.

So while other companies talk about trying to marshal all of the information stored in disparate formats in to a single standardized database structure, Microsoft has approached this problem from the other end of the spectrum. Their strategy is to access the data exactly where it is. Using what is known as **Universal Data Access (UDA)**, there is no need to change or modify anything on the data side. Using a single data access model, the programmer can use the same code to access essentially any data, anywhere, at any time. If this sounds too good to be true, I think you will be pleasantly surprised at how easy VB 6.0 has made accessing data using the UDA strategy. Let's take a closer look.

The Quest for Data

While .mdb databases (native to the Access database system) are easy to access (no pun intended) there are times when programmers need to get data from other desktop sources. For example, we might need to read or write data from dBASE, Paradox, FoxPro, or other databases. We might also need to retrieve information from Excel or Lotus spreadsheets, or even text files. If you take a look at the intrinsic (built-in) data control in VB 6.0, you will notice that there are several additional data sources that the control can talk to in addition to its native Access:

The real benefit of connecting to one of the external **ISAM** (Indexed Sequential Access Method) file types listed in the connect property of the data control is that we can work on the data - as is - without changing its structure. We can leave the data where it is and use VB 6.0 to connect with the various data source types. So any applications that created these files can continue to operate unchanged. We just go in and read or write data to and from these sources.

For example, there might be cases where an ASCII file is downloaded from a legacy mainframe system that we need to retrieve. Or possibly, several departments create Excel spreadsheets that track customer orders. We can simply connect to them, extract the data, and consolidate the information in an Access table.

Another probable scenario is that we want to get all of the data in an older Paradox system into a newer Access table. In a single VB 6.0 application we can read the Paradox data and write it to an Access table in one fell swoop. I have done that several times and am still amazed at how easy the data control makes this. In many ways, it is transparent to the programmer that VB 6.0, in conjunction with the data control, is talking to both Access and Paradox at the same time.

Jet performs this seemingly magical task by using various **.dll** files called ISAM drivers. Indexed Sequential Access Method drivers are **.dll** files that contain the specific code to talk to the various data sources. Jet supports several data access connections:

Data Source	Version supported by Jet
Access	All versions
Paradox	3.x, 4.x, 5.x
DBASE	III, IV, 5.0
Excel	3,4,5, and 8
FoxPro	2, 2.5, 2.6 and 3.0
Lotus 1-2-3	wk1, wk3, and wk4
Text	Any fixed or delimited text file

All data access from the data control, including Access itself, is handled under the hood with installable ISAM drivers. We just program the data control, and it handles the translation to the other data sources. We didn't bother with setting the **DataSource** on the data control we have been using in our programs so far. If you don't specify a specific connection, the default connection is to Access.

We mentioned earlier in the book that there are not only different formats of data, but there are even variations in the way tables themselves are laid out. Access, for example, uses the notion of a container. There is a single **.mdb** database that contains all of the tables within it. Paradox, however, has a separate file for every table. So if a database in Access has 10 tables, there will be a single **.mdb** file that contains 10 tables. Paradox, on the other hand, will have 10 separate independent tables.

As we mentioned earlier, DAO is the interface to the Jet database engine. The DAO/Jet combination is primarily designed to access ISAM databases as it supports most of the common ISAM data access techniques.

> *DAO/Jet is still the solution to use when it comes to accessing native Jet (.mdb) or ISAM data sources such as Btrieve, FoxPro, Paradox, and dBase.*

In addition to the ISAM `.dll` files that contain the code to handle specific data sources, as listed above, there is another more generalized method available to you. Microsoft's standard for providing data access to various data sources is **Open Database Connectivity** (ODBC). Essentially, this is a SQL approach to retrieving data. ODBC is supported by all sorts of software applications from spreadsheets to word processors to databases. ODBC provides **database interoperability**, which really means that it gives us methods by which data can be exchanged among different databases. So if an ISAM driver is not available, it is possible to communicate with a data source if it understands ODBC. Starting with DAO 3.5, an important enhancement was added - **ODBCDirect**. Selecting this option completely bypasses Jet and can really speed things up.

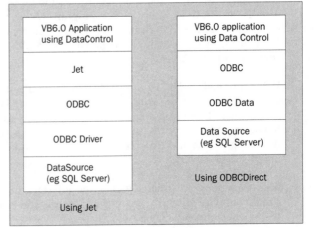

Using ODBCDirect allows you to deploy client/server applications using Microsoft Access without using Microsoft Jet as the middle layer. ODBCDirect is an interface directly to ODBC. So in most cases, it is faster.

If your application is hitting a Microsoft Jet **.mdb** or any other file-share databases it supports, you should use the Microsoft Jet path. This is because ODBCDirect was created specifically to access **remote** data. You should also use Jet if you want to join data in tables stored in different back-ends such as Oracle and SQL Server. You would need Jet in this case because it provides heterogeneous joins. You can create tables using ODBCDirect by executing SQL statements, but it's more convenient to use the Jet **TableDef** object we saw in the last chapter. So by now you are probably wondering why would you ever use ODBCDirect anyway? Good question. Most client/server developers simply need to quickly read data in, change it, and write it back to the back end. And if they need to do this quickly, then ODBCDirect is the way to go. It will make your code faster because it gives you direct access to the ODBC data source. It does not require loading the Jet engine, so this uses far fewer resources on the client side. This approach makes the ODBC server responsible for *all* query processing.

Change is the Only Constant

But the world does not stand still and the rate of change has only accelerated in the past 18 months, and it's the **Internet** that has been driving this change like no other technology ever seen before. With the advent of the Internet in everyone's lives, a mechanism was needed to easily send information across the Internet from host servers to browser-based clients. For example, companies are rushing to build database solutions to distribute information not only across the enterprise, but across the globe. A client in England needs to get product information on the new camping gear from a supplier in Washington State. The tyrant of geography is no more - the Internet is changing the way we live.

Consider the ubiquitous Web browser, such as the Microsoft Internet Explorer. The browser is of course a computer program. Not only that, but the web browser is the most widely distributed and used computer program in history. More computers of all stripes run a browser than any other type of application. Since the browser application is a client, it gets served data from a server computer somewhere in the world. And the browser client, since it is a computer program, can take the data it is served and do things with it.

For example, a simple text file formatted using Hyper Text Markup Language (HTML) tags can be rendered perfectly in **any** browser running on an IBM compatible, MAC, Sun, or any other type of computer. Since the browser can render HTML pages on any computer, the server simply serves the HTML file and it's the individual browser's responsibility to format and render the output. So the server doesn't know or care what type of browser is receiving the data - it just serves it up.

Back to the Future

The business world has discovered the Internet in a big way. The Internet was a 25-year overnight success. Even though it has been around since the late 1960s, it wasn't until the mid 90s, with the advent of the graphical web browser, that the Internet took off like a rocket. Since then, businesses started scrambling for ways to send database information around the globe from servers to browser clients. Wait a minute! A centralized server sending data to a client connected to it? This sounds like the 60s all over again, right? Centralized main frame computers talking to light clients. The world is migrating to mainframe servers serving client browsers connected to them. Information *centralized* on mainframe servers. Hmmm. Where have we heard this before?

So now programmers need to not only access relational data sources, but non-relational data as well. As we mentioned, Microsoft's approach is to provide a common method to get at data stored in various formats. They think it makes sense to focus on the access to the data rather than to the physical layout of the database itself. After all, what if we need to get at data in a relational database, a legacy system, an Excel spreadsheet, a web site, some text files, and email? And what if these are stored in various locations? Rather than change the world to conform to a single data structure, we want to change the way we retrieve data stored in various structures. It makes sense.

Universal Data Access

As programmers at the dawn of new millennium, our problem is one of data access. We have been using Data Access Objects (DAO) in the book both to program our database and to create new tables. But if there is a need to access data sources *other* than Microsoft Access, the enterprise edition of Visual Basic 6.0 provides **Remote Data Objects (RDO)**. RDO permits Visual Basic programmers to work with relational ODBC data sources. And DAO/Jet is used when we want to work with Jet and ISAM data sources. So traditionally, if we needed to work with remote ODBC data sources we would select RDO. However, when we need to access ISAM or Jet data sources, then DAO is the clear choice. But now Microsoft is offering us a new and much more efficient approach that permits us to use a **single high level, efficient programming paradigm to work with everything**. It's called **Universal Data Access** (UDA).

Universal Data Access is Microsoft's high-performance solution to access a variety of information sources, including relational and non-relational data sources. UDA is an easy to use programming interface – it is a tool *and* it is language independent. In other words, UDA is really a bundle of technologies that enable us to integrate diverse data sources, relational and otherwise. These tools permit companies to create easy-to-maintain solutions, and take their pick of best of breed tools and application programs.

Universal Data Access does not require the expensive and time-consuming (and many times impractical) shuttling of data from various databases into a single data store. Also, companies are not required to commit to a single vendor's products - pretty attractive for any IS department. Universal Data Access is based on **open industry specifications**: it enjoys broad industry support and currently works with all major established database platforms.

The way to employ UDA is by using ActiveX Data Objects. You can see that by using ADO, we can access any data either by using tried and true ODBC or an OLE DB provider:

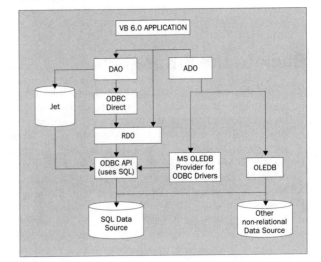

So you can see that our Visual Basic 6.0 application can use DAO as we have been doing up till now. DAO can access Jet directly as we have been doing. This gives us the interface into Access, Paradox, dBase, Excel, FoxPro, Lotus 1-2-3, and text files. We can also use ODBC to talk to any SQL compliant data source. This can be accomplished either through Jet, or ODBCDirect that bypasses the Jet engine. But consider the multitude of steps that must be gone through under the hood.

Now, by using ADO, we can simply use the OLE DB provider for the specific data source and voila! - we have connected. However, we can still employ the OLE DB provider for ODBC to use ADO for communicating with any ODBC sources. So using ADO, we get everything we got with DAO, and more. And, it is actually easier to use. Life *is* good.

Why ADO is the Cool New Way to Access Data

Universal Data Access is really an evolutionary step from today's standard data interfaces we have discussed. We know about the alphabet soup of ODBC, RDO, and DAO. UDA is a step to extend the functionality of these well-known and solid technologies. The bundle of technologies that make up UDA consist of **ActiveX Data Objects** (ADO), **Remote Data Services**, (RDS, formerly known as Advanced Database Connector or ADC), **OLE DB**, and **Open Database Connectivity** (ODBC). Together, these interfaces provide us the means to work with just about any data source. And together they are known as **Universal Data Access**.

So let's start looking in detail at ADO.

Say Hello to ActiveX Data Objects - ADO

Both RDO (which is used, remember, for sending data over a network) and DAO (for desktop solutions) are relatively robust and mature technologies. So Microsoft decided to create a universal method of accessing data that encompasses all of the functionality of both in a single interface.

With the Internet changing the way people handle data, not only do programmers need to access relational data sources, but also non-relational data such as hyper text markup language (HTML), mail, video, text, legacy system data, and just about anything else you can imagine. So over the next 18 months or so, Active Data Objects (ADO) will emerge as the *single, unified* alternative that will replace the current alphabet soup of data access choices. Programmers will write code that conforms to ADO and the rest of the data access will be handled under the hood. It sounds magical, doesn't it? Well, I think those people up in Redmond really *are* wizards.

The cool thing about ADO is that it not only provides us a consistent interface but also gives us high-performance access to just about any source of data. So whether you need to create a front end to a local database, or a middle tier that contains business objects, or even get data from an Internet browser, ADO is the single data interface you will need to use for your solution. Sounds almost too good to be true, don't you think? Well, stay tuned and let's see how it's done.

OLE DB is the Answer!

The latest technology that performs this magic is OLE DB. OLE DB is designed to provide universal access to several relational and non-relational data sources. We will communicate with OLE DB using Active Data Objects. By using ADO in conjunction with OLE DB, we can talk to Access, Oracle, SQL Server, or any other data source by simply using the ADO object model.

To the VB 6.0 database programmer, ADO is the interface we need to understand. Take a look at this figure:

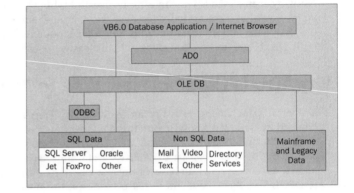

Notice that this model is much 'flatter' than the previous diagram. ADO and UDA are all about simplicity.

You can see that by using ADO from either a web browser or a Visual Basic 6.0 application, we can talk to just about any data source. OLE DB handles the grunt work out of our sight to make all of this magic work. And best of all, ADO is actually easier to work with than DAO! As we mentioned, Microsoft has indicated that DAO and RDO will eventually be replaced with ADO. So it does make sense to start learning it now. OLE DB will now handle working with the standard relational data and non-relational data from just about anywhere on the planet.

Let's take a closer look at ADO. We'll begin by making sure that VB knows all about ADO.

Try It Out – Telling VB About ADO

1 Start a new project called **\Chapter11\prjfirstADO**. Now go into the Project-References dialog and add the Microsoft ActiveX Data Objects 2.0 Library and ActiveX Data Objects Recordset 2.0 Library references to your project. Now VB 6.0 knows about the ADO components we want to use.

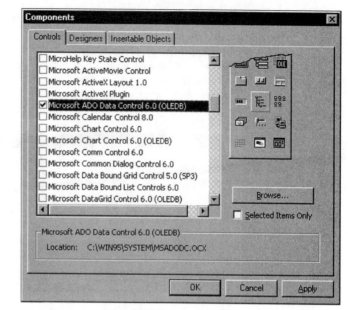

Then right click on your tool palette and select Components. Select the Microsoft ADO Data Control 6.0 (OLEDB):

Click OK. This will add an ADO data control to your palette.

2 Name the default form in the project **frmADO**. Draw an ADO Data Control (ADODC) on the form. Next, draw a textbox and label as shown on the form as well. We are going to create a simple bound text box program like our first data control program. And we will use the label to show where we are in the recordset.

In order to hook up the ADODC to our **Biblio.mdb** database, we must first set some properties. We did this a bit earlier in the book, remember?

Right click on the ADODC and select ADODC Properties. This will bring up a Property Page dialog box for the control. The first thing we must do is tell the control some important information. Unlike the singular DatabaseName property we need to set on the standard data control, the ADO data control requires a **connection string**. The connection string consists of the specific OLE DB provider to use, as well as the data source we want to access. The connection string is the critical piece of information the ADODC control needs to find the data source. Let's take just a minute to review the connection string, because we will be using them for the rest of the examples in this chapter, and throughout the rest of the book.

Review of Steps to Set Up the ADODC ConnectionString

If you haven't already done so, right click on the ADODC control and select ADODC Properties. We are presented with the property page for the ADODC control. Since setting up the ConnectionString must contain just about every piece of information required to connect to our data source, this comes in very handy indeed! Recall that the connection string needs to know things like the location and name of the database, any passwords that might be required, and the OLE DB data provider.

Property Pages

General | Authentication | RecordSource | Color | Font

Source of Connection

○ Use Data Link File

[   ] Browse...

○ Use ODBC Data Source Name

[▼] New...

● Use Connection String

[   ] Build...

Other Attributes: [   ]

OK   Cancel   Apply   Help

Click the Build button and let's step through the process.

Data Link Properties

Provider | Connection | Advanced | All

Select the data you want to connect to:

OLE DB Provider(s)
Microsoft Jet 3.51 OLE DB Provider
Microsoft OLE DB Provider for ODBC Drivers
Microsoft OLE DB Provider for Oracle
Microsoft OLE DB Provider for SQL Server
Microsoft OLE DB Simple Provider
MSDataShape

We are presented with another set of property pages for the Data Link. Notice the list of OLE DB Providers that are shipped with VB 6.0. If we wanted to connect to a generic ODBC source, we have a provider for ODBC Drivers. Notice that we have providers for Oracle and SQL Server. And as time goes on, all of the major database providers will ship their own OLE DB providers. This way, ADO can talk directly to the specific provider, just as DAO can now talk to ODBC.

Next >>

OK   Cancel   Help

Select the Microsoft Jet 3.51 OLE DB Provider.

Click the **Next>>** button. This brings up the Connection tab. Here is where we must tell VB the location and name of the database we will be using. Click the button with the ellipsis and locate the usual **\BegDB\Biblio.mdb** database. Since the database does not require a password, don't change the entries for logging on to the database. As you'll recall, Admin is the default user name for Access databases:

It always is a good idea to use the **Test Connection** option. This way, if there was something wrong with the location or name of the database, we would get an error advising us of this. Let's say that you entered the name of the database but forgot to add the **.mdb** extension. By testing the Data Link, we would know immediately:

523

We can then correct the error in the name and location of the database and press Test Connection once again.

There, that's better. Now click the **Advanced** tab just to see what options are available to us. Leave the default **Share Deny None** (if you needed to open the database in a read only, exclusive mode you would check the Read box):

Now click the **All** tab. Here you can see all of the information the Data Link property box garnered for us:

This is all of the information that will be used to create the connection string. If you need to modify any of the properties, simply click the Edit Value... button. This will give you a chance to modify any value in the connect string prior to clicking the OK button.

Edit Property Value

Property Description

Data Source

Property Value

C:\begdb\Biblio.mdb

Reset Value   OK   Cancel

After the connection string is built, click OK to dismiss the property pages for the Data Link. Now the control has the information it needs to connect to the data source. However, we still need to inform the data control which table(s) we wish to access. Right click on the ADODC data control again and select ADODC Properties. Notice that the connection string text box is now filled in:

Property Pages

General | Authentication | RecordSource | Color | Font

Source of Connection

○ Use Data Link File

Browse...

○ Use ODBC Data Source Name

New...

● Use Connection String

Provider=Microsoft.Jet.OLEDB.3.51;Persist Security   Build...

Other Attributes:

OK   Cancel   Apply   Help

Click on the RecordSource tab and click the drop down list box for the Command Type:

Select 2 - adCmdTable. Now the control knows we want to access records from a table directly. If the **DataSource** is not known in advance, then adCmdUnknown is selected. If we were going to issue a SQL command, then adCmdText would be selected, and the bottom text box, Command Text (SQL), would become enabled. Finally, if we have stored, pre-compiled procedures, we would choose adCmdStoredProc. This time, be sure to select choice 2 - adCmdTable.

Now the control knows that we want to access records from a table, and it knows the name of the database from when we set up the Data Link. Now, the Table or Stored Procedure Name listbox becomes enabled. Click the listbox and all of the tables in the database are shown:

Select the Publishers table and click OK.

The data control now has the connection string built, and will be able to retrieve a recordset for us from the data source. Double-click on the data control to bring up the code window. You might notice that the **Adodc1** data control has a few new event procedures. And many more parameters are passed in by VB so we can really know what is going on.

Try It Out - Back To Telling VB About ADO

1 Now that the ADODC data control has been set up, let's bind the **Text1** textbox. Bring up the property dialog box for **Text1**. Set the DataSource property to Adodc1.

2 Now click the drop down box for the **DataField**. Notice that just like the DAO data control, all of the valid fields are displayed:

Select the Name field.

3 Now double click on the ADODC data control to bring up the code window. In the **MoveComplete** event procedure of the control, add the following highlighted code:

```
Private Sub Adodc1_MoveComplete(ByVal adReason As ADODB.EventReasonEnum, ByVal
pError As ADODB.Error, adStatus As ADODB.EventStatusEnum, ByVal pRecordset As
ADODB.Recordset)
```

```
Label1 = "Record " & Adodc1.Recordset.AbsolutePosition _
         & " of " & Adodc1.Recordset.RecordCount
```

```
End Sub
```

The **MoveComplete** event of the ADODC control will fire when the control navigates to a new record. So this is the perfect place to update our label, **label1**, to show what record is the current record in the recordset managed by the ADODC control. Of course, we read the **.AbsolutePostion** property to tell us what record we are on and then read the **.RecordCount** to inform us how many records are in the recordset.

Remember way back when we noted that when the form's **Activate** event procedure is fired, we can be sure that all of the visible components (like the ADO data control) are fully initialized and displayed? Let's place a line of code that will display the current record when the form is fully loaded.

4 Add the following code to the **frmADO** form's **Form_Activate** event. When this event fires, we know the ADODC data control has been completely initialized so it is safe to read the properties:

```
Private Sub Form_Activate()

Label1 = "Record " & Adodc1.Recordset.AbsolutePosition _
        & " of " & Adodc1.Recordset.RecordCount

End Sub
```

5 Go ahead and run the program.

To the user, there is absolutely no difference between the intrinsic data control and our new ADO data control. See - I told you that the transition would be painless.

How It Works

Well, no magic here. We just used the same techniques we used earlier for the DAO data control. The only twist here was setting up the connection string. As you can see, this is a bit more involved. But the connection string provides **a generalized method to encapsulate all of the information** required to talk to the OLE DB provider, locate the database, and provide password information. But once the string was built, the rest of the code was pretty much the same. As the user navigates the recordset with the ADODC control, we update the label.

The ADO Data Control Properties

Let's take a quick look at the properties of an ADO data control and a standard data control. Bring up the property window for the ADODC data control:

Notice that with the ADO data control, we have the connection string that tells the control which OLE DB provider to use. This string contains the fully qualified name and location of the database to open. And then the `.RecordSource` property tells the control which table to open - in our case Publishers. And since we want to open a table, instead of a dynaset from a join, the `.CommandType` of adCmdTable is selected. Take another look at the ConnectionString - notice that the OLEDB 3.51 provider is listed.

The DAO and ADO Data Control Properties Compared

Let's have a look back at the DAO data control's properties by way of comparison with ADO:

The standard DAO data control shown here uses the `.DatabaseName` property to reference the fully qualified name and location of the database. The `.Connect` property tells the control to use the installable ISAM file for connecting with Access (remember that there are options here for Paradox, FoxPro, etc.) and the `.RecordSource` property is the same. We selected Publishers. Notice that the `.RecordsetType` is 0 - Table. So we include the exact same information to the control, but it is located in different properties. The ADO data control can do so much more with the same information.

The ADO Object Model

Remember when we examined the DAO Object model? It was quite a bit more involved than the ADO object model. We'll take a look at the ADO object model, then write a quick program that examines the various parts of the structure. Here's a graphic summarizing the model:

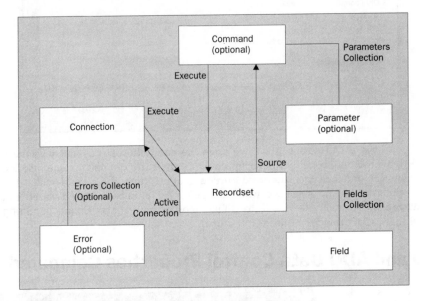

Here's how what we do with our code relates to the figure: Once we open a **Connection** to the database, we will then create a **Recordset** with that connection. From the **Recordset**, we will access the **Fields Collection** and, through it, the fields of the database.

We will write a simple program that shows each of these components of the ADO object model. But let's review the model first. This way, we can refer to the model as we write our program.

Step 1 - The Connection Object

The **Connection** object allows us to establish connection sessions with data sources. In other words, the connection represents a **physical** connection to a data source. The connection we set up provides a mechanism for initializing and establishing the connection. Once the connection object is created, we can use its methods and properties to access the data source (in this case the database) that we have connected to. We will also use the connection for executing queries and using transactions (we'll talk about these in detail later). The underlying OLE DB provider is used for connecting to the data source.

Let's briefly summarize the **methods** of the connection object:

Connection Object Methods	Description
Open	Opens a new connection to a data source
Close	Closes a connection as well as any dependant objects
Execute	Executes a query, typically a SQL statement
BeginTrans	Starts a new transaction
CommitTrans	Commits changes made during the transaction
RollBackTrans	Cancels any changes done during a transaction

And here are the connection object's **properties**:

Connection Object Properties	Description
ConnectionString	Contains the necessary information to establish a connection
ConnectionTimeOut	Determines how long to wait to establish a connection.
CommandTimeOut	Determines how long to wait while executing a command.
State	Indicates if a connection is open.
Provider	Indicates the name of the provider
Version	Indicates the ADO version.
CursorLocation	Sets/returns the location of the cursor engine.

As we mentioned, the connection object allows us to establish sessions with data sources. But remember, behind the scenes the underlying OLE DB provider is actually used for connecting to the data source. That is how the magic is accomplished.

We *program* the ADO interface. But remember when we selected the OLE DB provider when we selected "Build..." next to the Connection String option? It is the OLE DB provider that knows how to take commands from ADO and translate them into language that the specific data source will understand. Makes sense now, doesn't it? And as more and more suppliers create OLE DB providers for their data sources, ADO will take over the world.

Step 2 - Opening a Recordset

Once the connection is opened, we can then retrieve a recordset from it. We use the **Open** method of a recordset object to open a recordset. Using the **Open** method establishes the physical connection to a data source and opens a recordset that represents records from a base table or the results of a query. Once we have the recordset, we can access the Fields Collection, just as if we're operating with the DAO recordset. Let's see how these pieces fit together.

The **Connection** and **Recordset** objects are the key components we will use for manipulating data. A VB 6.0 application can use the connection object to establish connections with the database server. The **Command** object is used to issue commands, such as queries, updates, and so on to the database. And we use the Recordset object to view and manipulate the returned data, as we'll do when we update a listbox in a simple program we will write later.

The language used with the command object is dependent on the underlying provider for the database. But for our purposes, we will be using relational databases where the command language is generally SQL. You might want to refer back to Chapter 8 for an SQL refresher.

Programming with Active Data Objects

We are already familiar with programming DAO. But you can access more data sources with ADO, and I think you will be pleasantly surprised to find out that programming with ADO is actually simpler! You don't believe me? Let's give it a try. We'll start off with a simple ADO program that just fills a listbox with database data for us.

Try It Out – Programming ADO

In this exercise, we will open an ADODB **connection** and an ADO **recordset**. When these tasks have been completed, we will populate the listbox with the names in the **Publishers** table.

1 Add a new form to your project and name it **frmADOPublishers**. Be sure that you have selected <u>P</u>roject | Refere<u>n</u>ces and include the ActiveX Data Objects 2.0 Library in your project.

Then add a listbox and a command button as shown:

2 Add the following code to the command button's **Click** event:

```
Private Sub Command1_Click()

Dim adoConnection As ADODB.Connection
Dim adoRecordset As ADODB.Recordset
Dim connectString As String

'—Create a new connection --
Set adoConnection = New ADODB.Connection
'—Create a new recordset --
Set adoRecordset = New ADODB.Recordset
```

```
'—Build our connection string to use when we open the connection --
connectString = "Provider=Microsoft.Jet.OLEDB.3.51;" _
                & "Data Source=C:\Begdb\Biblio.mdb"

adoConnection.Open connectString
adoRecordset.Open "Publishers", adoConnection

Do Until adoRecordset.EOF
  List1.AddItem adoRecordset!Name
  adoRecordset.MoveNext
Loop

adoRecordset.Close
adoConnection.Close
Set adoRecordset = Nothing
Set adoConnection = Nothing
```

End Sub

3 Select Project-Project1 Prop<u>e</u>rties... and add **frmADOPublishers** as the Startup Object.

Run the program, and click the <u>F</u>ill List button.

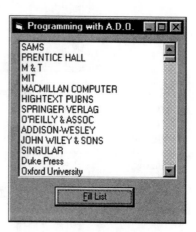

By pressing the <u>F</u>ill List button, we call upon ADO to open a data source and then use code to iterate through the recordset and fill up the listbox. Pretty straightforward, eh?

How It Works

Let's take a closer look at what we have just done.

Notice that we need to dim an **ADODB.Connection** object.

```
Dim adoConnection As ADODB.Connection
```

The connection object allows you to establish connection sessions with data sources, and this object provides a mechanism for initializing and establishing the connection to our data source. Remember the connection string we created with our ADO data control? We will pass the connection object the same kind of string.

Once our connection is open, we want to create a recordset. Just like our DAO counterpart, we dim an ADODB recordset.

```
Dim adoRecordset As ADODB.Recordset
```

First of all, since our VB 6.0 supports both DAO and ADO, we must be careful to fully qualify the type of recordset we need. If we forget to specify that the recordset is of type ADODB, the environment will gladly provide a recordset - except that it will be for DAO, not ADO. So take a look at what would happen if you tried to create a recordset:

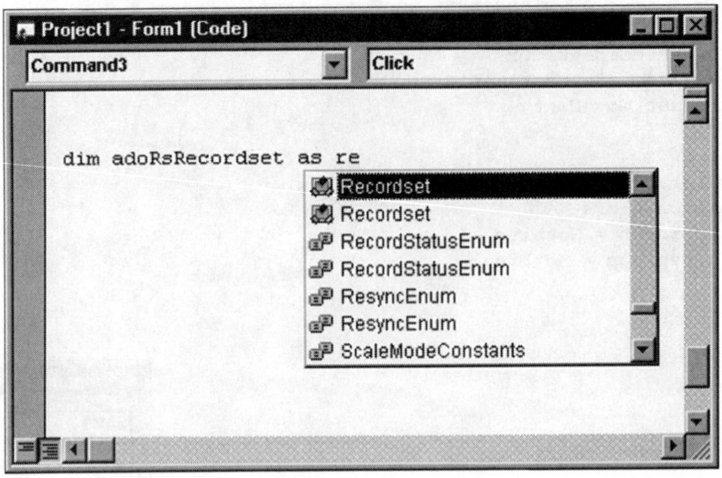

The problem is that the Recordset highlighted by IntelliSense here would be a DAO type recordset – not what we want. So please be careful to specify an ADO recordset. This is done by first specifying ADODB. As soon as you press the "." dot after ADODB, you will see the various methods, constants, and events that are available to an ADODB. Of course we want the recordset of the ADODB object. Be sure that you select the correct type of recordset as shown below:

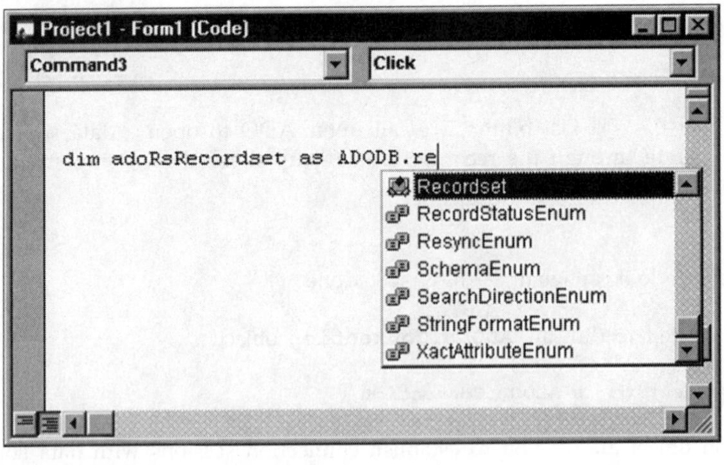

Since you remembered to add the ActiveX references to your project, VB 6.0 now is able to provide the Intelli-help choices in the drop down box.

After we dim our connection and recordset object variables, we want to set them to a **new** connection and a **new** recordset.

Remember that in DAO we would set an object variable to a database, then another to a recordset that was built on the database object variable. Opening the DAO database required that we pass in the fully qualified name *and* location of the database.

In ADO, however, we will pass that information in as part of the connection string when we actually *open* the connection.

Here we are creating a new connection and recordset object. By using the Set keyword, we set a reference to our object variables, **adoConnection** and **adoRecordset**:

```
'—Create a new connection --
Set adoConnection = New ADODB.Connection
```

```
'—Create a new recordset --
Set adoRecordset = New ADODB.Recordset
```

```
'—Build our connection string to use when we open the connection --
connectString = "Provider=Microsoft.Jet.OLEDB.3.51;" _
                & "Data Source=C:\BegDB\Biblio.mdb"
```

Of course, we could just as easily have added this last line directly to the **Open** method of the **adoConnection** object. But placing it in a string is a good way to get comfortable with the actual string of parameters.

Before establishing a connection, our application must set up a connection string, as well as connection time-out, default database, and connection attributes. The connection object also allows you to set up the **CommandTimeout** property for all the command objects associated with this particular connection. We will just use the default for now, which is 15 seconds.

We are ready to open the connection with the string we defined above. The string provides the connection object with enough information on the OLE DB provider and the database to establish the link.

The easiest way to open a connection is simply pass the connection string to the Open method of the connection object:

```
adoConnection.Open connectString
```

To see if the connection was successful, you could check out the **State** property of the connection object. State will return **adStateOpen** if the connection is open and (surprise!) **adStateClosed** if it isn't. If you wanted to test the connection, you could simply add something like:

```
'We can test to see if the attempt to connect worked.
If adoConnection.State = adStateOpen Then
    MsgBox "The Connection is now open!"
Else
    MsgBox "Sorry. The connection could not be opened."
End If
```

Once our connection object is linked to the database by using the open method, we can now use this connection to open a recordset or perform some action on the data source.

If there is an error in the connection string, VB will not know it until we try to open the connection object, **adoConnection**. By simply assigning the connect string to the **connectString** variable (or even directly to the connection object), any errors won't show up until we try to actually use the string by connecting. So if an error does crop up, you can be sure that the connection string is the culprit.

Now we are ready to open the recordset by using its **.Open** method. We are using only two parameters here - the table we want opened and the connection to use.

```
adoRecordset.Open "Publishers", adoConnection
```

There are several additional parameters we can pass to more granularly define the recordset we want opened. The syntax of the **.Open** method for a fully qualified recordset looks like this:

```
RecordSet.Open Source, ActiveConnection, CursorType, LockType, Options
```

As you can see, in our program we are only passing in the source of the data and the active connection. We will soon cover these additional parameters when we write some additional programs. But for now, we will simply rely on their default values.

Now that we have an open connection and a recordset, it is very straightforward to update our list box. Notice that the syntax is the same as we used for DAO: we use the same "**!**" 'bang' operator to access a specific field from the recordset:

```
Do Until adoRecordset.EOF
  List1.AddItem adoRecordset!Name
  adoRecordset.MoveNext
Loop
```

Finally, we close the recordset and the connection. Since these are object variables are dim'ed locally, they would go 'out of scope' as the code exited the procedure. But it is good programming practice to always close these items when they are no longer needed:

```
adoRecordset.Close
adoConnection.Close
Set adoRecordset = Nothing
Set adoConnection = Nothing
```

There, we have just opened an ADO connection, created a recordset, and accessed the Name field. Not too bad.

Creating a New Data Source

As you already know, the Open method of the Connection object is used to establish a connection. With the OLE DB - ODBC Provider, an ADO application can use the ODBC connection mechanism to connect to a database server. ODBC allows applications to establish a connection through various ODBC data sources, or by explicitly specifying the data source information. This is commonly referred to as **DSN-Less connection**. DSN stands for Data Source Name. To see the difference, take a look at these examples. First, the standard, DSN connection:

```
Dim myADOConnection As New ADODB.Connection

'A DSN Connection looks like this
myADOConnection.Open "myDSN", "sa"
```

Next, here's the DSN-Less example:

```
'A DSN-Less connection looks like this
myADOConnection.Open   "Provider=Microsoft.Jet.OLEDB.3.51;" _
                                        & "Data Source=C:\Begdb\Biblio.mdb"
myADOConnection.Close
Set myADOConnection = Nothing
```

The DSN example opens a connection using the myDSN ODBC data source that points to a **.mdb** database. In other words, the DSN connection has all of the required information stored in it. With a DSN-Less connection, we provide *all* of the information required to open the connection.

We can now find a wide variety of ODBC drivers that can be used with ADO to establish a connection to data. Soon, there will be OLE DB providers available to connect to most data sources. You can use a different provider by setting the **Provider** property of the Connection. But if you want to connect with an ODBC-compliant data source, you could use the following Try It Out as an example and create your own DSN. Let's take a look at how this works.

First, we will build the New Data Link by creating a new ODBC Data Source. Then we will use the SQL OLE DB data provider to talk to it. We will go through these steps so you can see how to connect to virtually any data source.

First then, we want to build a Data Source Name (DSN). This can be referenced, and it will contain all of the information required to access a data source.

Try It Out – Creating a New Data Source

1 From your Windows 95/98 Settings-Control panel, select the 32bit ODBC icon:

32bit ODBC

This will bring up the ODBC Data source Administrator dialog box. Any data sources already defined will be listed:

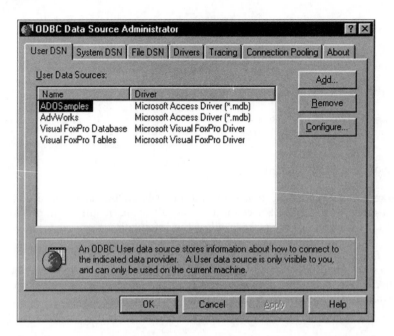

2 Click on A**dd** to create a new user data source. When you click A**dd**, the Create New Data Source dialog box appears with a list of drivers:

Choose the driver for which you are adding a user data source. Since we are using **.mdb** files, select the Microsoft Access Driver. Any drivers that are installed on your machine will show up. Notice that the Access driver is version 3.51 - new with Visual Basic 6.0.

3 Double click on the Microsoft Access Driver (*.mdb) to display the Setup dialog box:

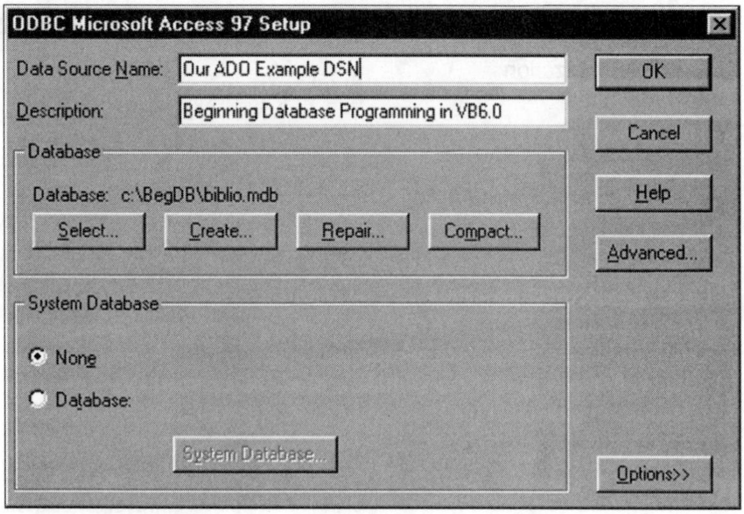

Provide the name of the data source as Our ADO Example DSN and the description as Beginning Database Programming in VB6.0. Now we need to set up the database. Within the Database frame, click the Select... button. Here you can navigate to our old friend, the **\BegDb\Biblio.mdb** database.

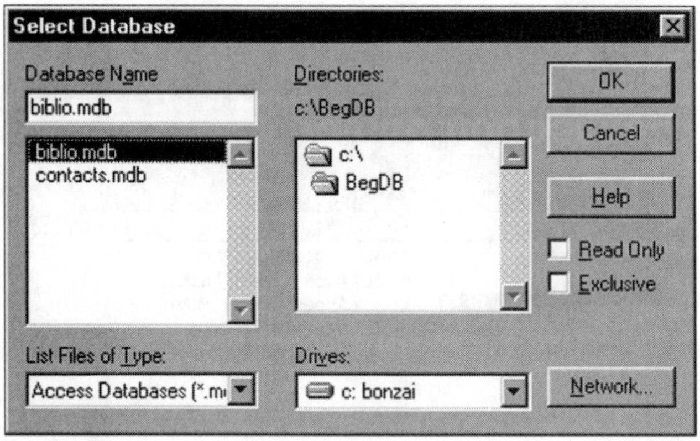

When you click OK, you will now see the database name and location defined on the Setup dialog box.

4 Next, click on the Advanced... button to display the Default Authorization.

5 Remember when we were discussing Access security (long ago, in Chapter 2)? Be sure to add Admin as the Login name. Then click OK. Now choose the User DSN tab and notice that our new DSN description is listed as a valid choice:

6 Make sure that Our ADO Example DSN has the Access driver file selected. Again, when you install new drivers on your machine, they will be listed as options here. Now we'll test new ODBC Data Source.

Try It Out - Testing our DSN

1   To ensure everything is working, let's go back to our form, **frmADO**, and right-click the **ADODC** control to bring up the properties page.

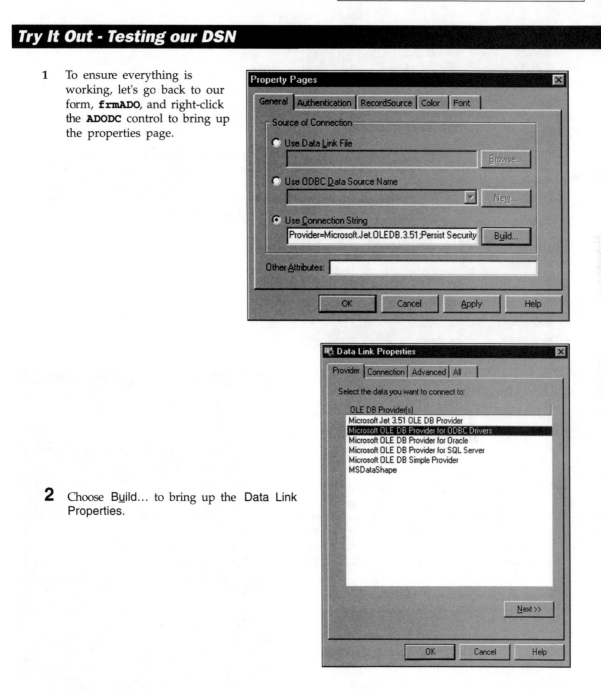

2   Choose Bu̱ild... to bring up the Data Link Properties.

Since we just defined a new ODBC DSN, on the Provider tab select the OLE DB Provider for ODBC Drivers entry. Then click N̲ext >>.

3   Now select our newly minted data source - Our ADO Example DSN - from the drop down box.

Be sure to add **Admin** for the User Name. However, it is already built into our DSN connection. If you needed to set this up for a specific user, it would be done here. Then click **Test Connection** to ensure everything is fine.

4 Click the Advanced tab and select the **Share Deny None** choice as shown. Again, you would do this if you wanted to change the defaults defined when the DSN setup was built. But we do it here just to show you how to accomplish this:

5 Click OK and run your program.

We have just created an ODBC data source that can be used with an Access database. If you needed another data source, you would follow the same steps with that driver. Now the OLE DB provider can take our commands from ADO and translate them to the new ADO ODBC data source. So the OLE DB acts as a universal translator from ADO to whichever ODBC driver we happen to be using.

In case you were wondering what the connection string looks like, here it is:

```
Provider=MSDASQL.1;Persist Security Info=False;User ID=Admin;Data Source=Our ADO
Example DSN;Mode=Share Deny None
```

As you can see, all of the required information is now built into the string. Notice that the provider is now **MSDASQL.1**. We are now accessing the **Biblio.mdb** database via the ADO data control using ODBC.

Let's take a look at using some VB code to access our data via our new DSN.

Try It Out - Testing our New DSN Connection in Code

1 Add a form to your project, and name it **frmDSN**. Add a single command button to the form and give it the name **cmdTestDSN**. Give it a caption as shown:

2 In the **Click** event of the command button, add the following code:

```
Private Sub cmdTestDSN_Click()
```

```
Dim myConnection As ADODB.Connection
Set myConnection = New ADODB.Connection

'If we wanted, we could set the provider property to the OLE
'DB Provider for ODBC. However we will set it in the connect 'string.

' Open a connection using an ODBC DSN. The MS OLE DB for
' SQL is MSDASQL. We gave our new data source the name "Our ADO Example DSN"
' so let's use it.

myConnection.ConnectionString = "Provider=MSDASQL.1;Persist Security
Info=False;User ID=Admin;Data Source=Our ADO Example DSN"

myConnection.Open

' Determine if we conected.
If myConnection.State = adStateOpen Then
   MsgBox "Welcome to the Biblio Database!"
Else
   MsgBox "The connection could not be made."
End If

' Close the connection.
myConnection.Close
```

```
End Sub
```

3 Let's give it a try. Run the program and press the command button. Success!

How It Works

Since we only want to test an ODBC connection, we only need to dim a new object variable as type **ADODB.Connection**. We then immediately initialize the object variable using the **Set** key word:

```
Dim myConnection As ADODB.Connection
Set myConnection = New ADODB.Connection
```

Next, we just lifted the connection string that was built from our DSN. If you wish to copy it, simply bring up the ADO data control and copy the connection string. Our DSN provider placed the full connection string there. Since this is a string, be sure that the entire string here is on a single line in the code window:

```
myConnection.ConnectionString = "Provider=MSDASQL.1;Persist Security
Info=False;User ID=Admin;Data Source=Our ADO Example DSN
```

Once we set the `.ConnectionString` property of the connection object, we simply invoke the `.Open` method to establish a connection to the data source:

```
myConnection.Open
```

We can then interrogate the `.State` property to see if the connection is open:

```
If myConnection.State = adStateOpen Then
   MsgBox "Welcome to the Biblio Database!"
Else
   MsgBox "The connection could not be made."
End If
```

If you need to find out the state of the connection, you can easily check the `.State` property against these constants:

Constant	Description
AdStateClosed	Default. Indicates that the object is closed.
AdStateOpen	Indicates that the object is open.
AdStateConnecting	Indicates that the **Recordset** object is connecting.
AdStateExecuting	Indicates that the **Recordset** object is executing a command.
AdStateFetching	Indicates that the rows of the **Recordset** object are being fetched.

And since in our program the state is equal to **adStateOpen**, we display our message box indicating success! We then close the connection.

Now that we've demonstrated how to open up our connection to the data source, let's consider how to run some SQL against the data in the data source. We send any processing commands via the **Execute** method of the connection object.

Using the Connection Object's Execute Method

We can use the **Execute** method to send a command (typically an SQL statement, but it might be other text) to the data source. If our SQL statement returns rows (instead of, say, updating some records) then a **Recordset** is created. The Execute method in reality *always* returns a Recordset. However, it is a **closed** Recordset if the command doesn't return results.

Let's see an example of the Execute method in action.

Try It Out - Testing the Execute Method

1 Add another button to the **frmDSN** form to test the execute method. Name the new command button **cmdExecute** and give it the caption Text Execute, as shown here:

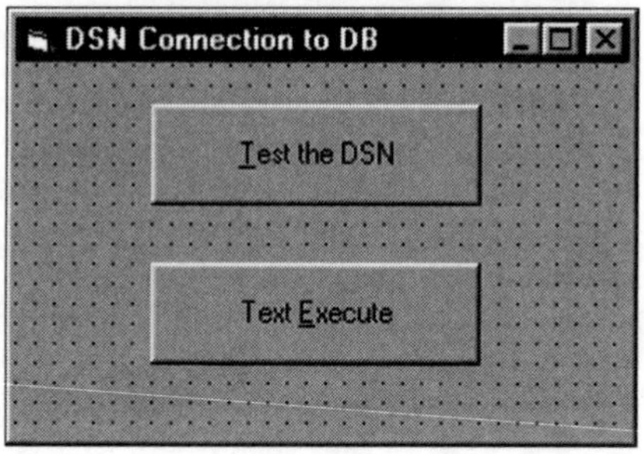

2 Add the following code to the **cmdExecute** button's **Click** event:

```
Private Sub cmdExecute_Click()
```

```
Dim myConnection As ADODB.Connection
Dim myRecordSet As ADODB.Recordset

Set myConnection = New ADODB.Connection

myConnection.ConnectionString = "Provider=Microsoft.Jet.OLEDB.3.51;" _
               & "Data Source=C:\BegDB\Biblio.mdb"

myConnection.Open

' Create a Recordset by executing a SQL statement
Set myRecordSet = myConnection.Execute("Select * From Titles")

' Show the first title in the recordset.
MsgBox myRecordSet("Title")

' Close the recordset and connection.
myRecordSet.Close
myConnection.Close
```

```
End Sub
```

3 Run the program and press the Text Execute button. You'll see this message box appear:

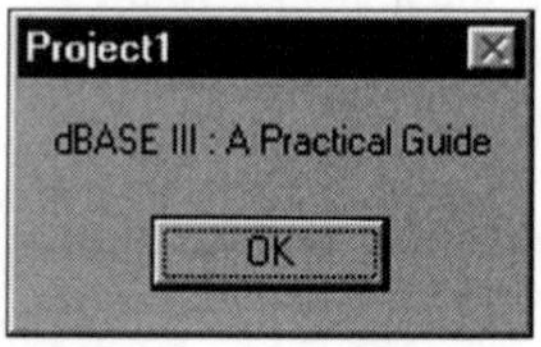

How It Works

We learned a few interesting things in this example. First, we added the connection string directly to the connection object. In prior examples we first assigned the connection string to a string variable, then passed in the string variable to the **connection.ConnectionString** property. This current example is a bare, minimalist approach to a connection string. We just pass the provider and the data source:

```
myConnection.ConnectionString = "Provider=Microsoft.Jet.OLEDB.3.51;" _
                 & "Data Source=C:\BegDB\Biblio.mdb"
```

Then, once the connection string property is set, we open the connection:

```
myConnection.Open
```

Once the connection is open, we now want to issue an SQL statement. We do this by using the **.Execute** method of the connection object. Here we are selecting all of the records from the **Titles** table:

```
' Create a Recordset by executing a SQL statement
Set myRecordSet = myConnection.Execute("Select * From Titles")
```

And finally, we simply display the contents of the **Title** field. Notice that we access the field by using the name of the field. Of course, we could have used the "!" bang operator or the ordinal position as we have done in the past:

```
MsgBox myRecordSet("Title")
```

And since the current record is the first record in the recordset, the title of the first book in the first record is displayed.

One thing to keep in mind is that the returned Recordset will always be a read-only, forward-only cursor. This means you can't edit or scroll backwards. If you need a Recordset object with a bit more functionality, then create a Recordset object with the desired property settings. After the settings are in place, use the Recordset object's **Open** method to execute the query that will return the desired cursor type. We'll talk some more about using cursors in conjunction with recordsets later in the chapter.

Now, let's discuss in more detail how we can interact with the recordset. The logical place to start is with how we open a recordset.

Opening Recordsets

To open a recordset, we use the **.Open** method of the recordset object and pass in the name of the table we want to be placed in the recordset (as well as the name of the open connection) as parameters. In this example, we can open a recordset with only two parameters as shown:

```
adoRecordset.Open "Publishers", adoConnection
```

Once the recordset is opened, we simply loop through like we did using DAO. In fact, the syntax to access a field is exactly the same using the **recordset!field** notation. So once we open the recordset, the programming is almost identical to DAO:

```
Do Until adoRecordset.EOF
  List1.AddItem adoRecordset!Name
  adoRecordset.MoveNext
Loop
```

Finally, when we want to close both the recordset and connection, just use the **Close** method of both objects:

```
adoRecordset.Close
adoConnection.Close
Set sdoRecordset = Nothing
Set adoConnection = Nothing
```

We certainly did dimension these object variables locally - they only exist in the click event procedure of the command button. As such, they go out of scope when the program leaves the procedure. So if we omitted the **.Close** methods, both would be closed by default when they go out of scope. But we have been talking consistently about not relying on the default behavior of Visual Basic. This has to do with both initializing variables as well as releasing them. So it is good form to explicitly close both of the object variables before exiting the procedure. We should also set both object variables to **Nothing** which effectively releases the pointers to them and frees up the memory they consume.

Fun with Schemas

Remember when we wrote the Database Analyzer using DAO a while back? This worked great, but on Access **.mdb** files only. However, what happens if we are using an OLE DB data provider and we don't know exactly what fields are available? Well, we can accomplish the same thing for any data source as we did using out DAO Table Analyzer, using ADO. Since ADO really talks to the OLE DB layer, **we can get any information on the underlying data source from the OLE DB provider**. This can easily be done by using the **OpenSchema** method of our connection object.

By using the **OpenSchema** method, we can spy on information about the particular data source we are connected to. We can easily get information about the data source, such as the tables on the server and the columns in those tables.

Take a look at the figure below:

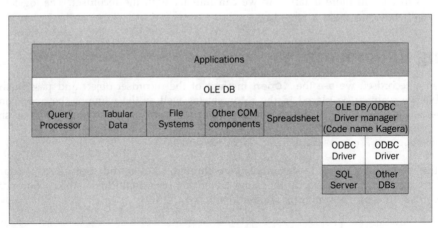

Our application uses ADO to talk to the OLE DB data provider. Our application probably does not have to know how to communicate with all of the various data stores. We just use ADO to talk to the OLE DB provider and it takes care of the nitty gritty of how to communicate with the various and sundry data stores. When we select a specific OLD DB data provider, we know that our application can just use ADO to talk to that OLE DB provider. And using this approach, we are removed from having to know about the details of each and every data source. We just leave that up to the OLE DB provider.

But, despite all this built-in invisibility, what if our program needs to know something about the data store we are accessing? For example, what if we need to find out things like field names? Or what if we need to know if certain variables will be supported? Well, this is a snap using ADO.

It is the responsibility of the OLE DB provider to give us this type of information. This way our application can quickly get information on the underlying data store that might range from a relational database such as Access to an email message or text file.

When reading about OLE DB, you will see the terms **Consumer** and **Provider**. A **consumer** is any application that uses - or consumes - OLE DB interfaces. For example, our programs have been using ADO to talk to OLE DB to connect to our Access database. Our ADO code and the data control are both consumers of OLE DB services.

An OLE DB provider uses OLE DB interfaces, such as our ODBC connection that we created. This means that an OLE DB **provider** (our ODBC connection) allows consumers of their services to access data in a uniform way via the OLE DB interface. Conceptually, an OLE DB provider is similar to an ODBC driver. That driver provides a uniform mechanism for accessing relational data - it understands SQL. But the cool thing about OLE DB providers is that they not only provide a mechanism for relational data, but they can talk to non-relational data sources as well.

OK, what if our program needs to find out information about the underlying data store? What we'll do next is create some code that will allow us to display information about how the data source that we want to access is laid out. We'll display the description of what's in the data source – its **schema**.

Try It Out - Getting the Schema of the Data Source using ADO

1 Add a new form to your project. Call the form **frmSchema**. Add a single command button named **cmdSchema** - nothing fancy:

We will use this single form for these next few examples - we will just add a few command buttons and print the results to VB's Immediate Window using the **Print** method of the **debug.object**. Rather than cloud the examples with a lot of formatting code, I want to focus on the ADO code. So just use a single form and add another button when asked. Thanks!

2 OK enough talk. Let's do some coding. Add the following code to the **Click** event procedure of the command button. This code will establish a connection with a data source. Then we will ask the data source which tables and fields are available. You will quickly notice that the ADO code is much easier to write than the equivalent DAO code.

```
Private Sub cmdSchema_Click()

Dim adoConnection As ADODB.Connection
Dim adoRsFields As ADODB.Recordset
Dim sConnection As String
Dim sCurrentTable As String
Dim sNewTable As String

Set adoConnection = New ADODB.Connection

sConnection = "Provider=Microsoft.Jet.OLEDB.3.51;Data Source=c:\BegDB\Biblio.mdb"

adoConnection.Open sConnection

Set adoRsFields = adoConnection.OpenSchema(adSchemaColumns)

sCurrentTable = ""
sNewTable = ""

Do Until adoRsFields.EOF
  sCurrentTable = adoRsFields!TABLE_NAME
  If (sCurrentTable <> sNewTable) Then
    sNewTable = adoRsFields!TABLE_NAME
    Debug.Print "Current Table: " & adoRsFields!TABLE_NAME
  End If
  Debug.Print "    Field: " & adoRsFields!COLUMN_NAME
  adoRsFields.MoveNext
Loop

adoRsFields.Close
Set adoRsFields = Nothing
adoConnection.Close
Set adoConnection = Nothing

End Sub
```

3 Run your **frmSchema** form and click on the Schema button. We will step through what the code is doing shortly, but first, take a look at the results that appear in the Immediate window:

```
Immediate                          _ □ ×
Current Table: Publishers           ▲
    Field: Address
    Field: City
    Field: Comments
    Field: Company Name
    Field: Fax
    Field: Name
    Field: PubID
    Field: State
    Field: Telephone
    Field: Zip
Current Table: Title Author
    Field: Au_ID
    Field: ISBN
Current Table: Titles
    Field: Comments
    Field: Description
    Field: ISBN
    Field: Notes
    Field: PubID
    Field: Subject
    Field: Title
    Field: Year Published          ▼
◄ ◄                              ► 
```

Since we are using the **debug.print** method, the output is just being sent to the Immediate window. Of course, if you wish, you can get fancy and place the output in a **TreeView** control as we did using DAO a few chapters back. But in this example we can see just how easy it is to interrogate the OLE DB provider to get this type of information.

You will see some tables that start with Msys such as MSysIMEXColumns. These tables are used by Jet to store various meta-information about the tables and database. Meta-information really means information about information. So you get to spy on the various tools that Jet uses to maintain an Access database. Of course, these would not be present if you used ADO to open a non-Access data source.

```
Immediate                          _ □ ×
Current Table: MSysIMEXColumns      ▲
    Field: DataType
    Field: FieldName
    Field: IndexType
    Field: SkipColumn
    Field: SpecID
    Field: Start
    Field: Width                    ▼
◄ ◄                              ► 
```

How It Works

We start out by dim'ing our local variables. We dim an ADODB connection and recordset object as usual:

```
Dim adoConnection As ADODB.Connection
Dim adoRsFields As ADODB.Recordset
Dim sConnection As String
Dim sCurrentTable As String
Dim sNewTable As String
```

Next, we set a reference to our (new) connection in preparation for opening it. Of course, that reference is in our object variable **adoConnection**. In order to open the connection, we must set the **.ConnectionString** property. So again, to illustrate the point, we just assign the connection string to a string variable, **sConnection**. Next, we invoke the **.Open** method of the connection object and pass in the **sConnection** variable that holds the connection string as a parameter:

```
Set adoConnection = New ADODB.Connection

sConnection = "Provider=Microsoft.Jet.OLEDB.3.51;Data Source=c:\BegDB\Biblio.mdb"

adoConnection.Open sConnection
```

We now have an open connection. Why not do something with it?

Our cunning plan is to retrieve a recordset of information about the data source. By using the **.OpenSchema** method, we can get returned to us information about the data source, such as information about the tables on the server and the columns in the tables. There are several constants that can be used to retrieve specific information about the underlying data source. Of these, we will use the **adSchemaColumns** constant – this will return the table name and the column name. This way we can find out about what tables are in the database, and what fields are in the tables (in our next example, we will find out the details about the individual fields in the tables):

```
Set adoRsFields = adoConnection.OpenSchema(adSchemaColumns)
```

At this point, we have a valid recordset containing the information about the table and field names. Now we will loop through the recordset and print the results in the debug (immediate) window. The two string variables, **sCurrentTable** and **sNewTable**, are used as placeholders. We will loop through the results and provide the table name as a header and then print the fields inside that table in an indented manner.

The returned recordset, **adoRsFields**, will have a combination of **Table Name** and **Field Name** in each record:

```
sCurrentTable = ""
sNewTable = ""

Do Until adoRsFields.EOF
  sCurrentTable = adoRsFields!TABLE_NAME
  If (sCurrentTable <> sNewTable) Then
    sNewTable = adoRsFields!TABLE_NAME
    Debug.Print "Current Table: " & adoRsFields!TABLE_NAME
```

```
    End If
    Debug.Print "    Field: " & adoRsFields!COLUMN_NAME
    adoRsFields.MoveNext
  Loop
```

The **Do** loop simply runs the code inside of it until the end of the recordset. The first time though the loop, we assign the value of the current table name to the variable **sCurrentTable**. Of course, there will be several fields for each table, so we want to only print the table name once.

The next line is used to determine if there is a new table name in the current record. However, we initialized the variable **sCurrentTable** to "", so the **sCurrentTable** value and the name of the table are not equal. Therefore, we first assign the name of the current table to **sNewTable** and then print the name of the table in the Immediate window.

The code then exits the **If...End If** and prints the name of the field in that same record. Recall that each record in the recordset will have both the current table and a field in that table. Then the current record pointer is incremented by using the **.MoveNext** method of the recordset.

The next time through the loop, we assign the name of the table in that record to **sCurrentTable**. If the name of that table is equal to the name of the table name that was just printed out, **If...End If** structure is bypassed and only the field is printed.

Trawling for Data Types

There will be times when we need to know the data types that are supported by the underlying data source. For example, we would not want to try to write a variable to an underlying field if that field could not support the data, right? For example, it would be embarrassing to write a variant to an integer field, only to be surprised by an error message.

It would be great if there were a simple way for us to find out what is supported by whatever data store we are connected to, right? Well, ADO provides an easy and painless way to find out.

As mentioned above, you can also use the **.OpenSchema** method to find out this important information. By passing in the constant **adSchemaProviderTypes** as a parameter, a recordset is returned that shows all of the types provided. Let's have a go at doing that now.

Try It Out – Determining Data Types of the Data Source using ADO

1   Add another button to your **frmSchema** form that was used in the proceeding example. Name it **cmdDataTypes and** caption it as shown:

2 Next, add this code to the click event of the **cmdDataTypes** button. If you are lazy like me, you can cut and paste from the **cmdSchema_Click** event and just change a few lines:

```
Private Sub cmdDataTypes_Click()
Dim adoConnection As ADODB.Connection
Dim adoRsFields As ADODB.Recordset
Dim sConnection As String
Set adoConnection = New ADODB.Connection
sConnection = "Provider=Microsoft.Jet.OLEDB.3.51;Data Source=c:\BegDB\Biblio.mdb"
adoConnection.Open sConnection
Set adoRsFields = adoConnection.OpenSchema(adSchemaProviderTypes)
Do Until adoRsFields.EOF
  Debug.Print "Data Type: " & adoRsFields!TYPE_NAME & vbTab _
                  & "Column Size: " & adoRsFields!COLUMN_SIZE
  adoRsFields.MoveNext
Loop
adoRsFields.Close
Set adoRsFields = Nothing
adoConnection.Close
Set adoConnection = Nothing
End Sub
```

3 Press *F5* to run the program. Press the <u>D</u>ata Types button. When you run the program, the following output is sent to the immediate window:

How It Works

Since the code is almost identical to our last program, we don't need to dwell on what is happening. But let's take a look at the output. Of course, the Data Type tells us all of the data types available in this particular data source. The Column Size tells us the length of a column or parameter. The length refers to either the maximum or the defined length for this type by the provider. For character data, this is the maximum or defined length in characters. For date/time data types, this is the length of the string representation (which assumes the maximum allowed precision of the fractional seconds component). If the data type is numeric, the column size is the upper bound on the maximum precision of the data type. Pretty cool.

Reacquaint Yourself With the Object Browser

Earlier in this book we touched on the Object Browser. Well, this is a very handy tool to use for becoming familiar with the various members of the ADODB model. Take a minute and select View | Object Browser from the main VB 6.0 IDE window. Select ADODB from the drop down window and take a look around. This will be time well spent in becoming familiar with all of the members of ADODB:

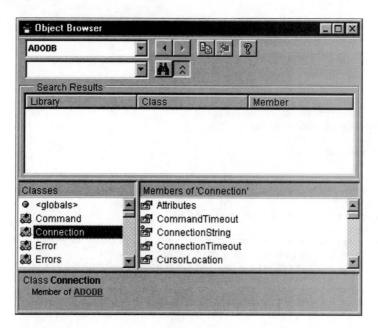

Let's walk through what some of the information displayed here is all about.

The ADO Errors Collection

One thing we need to learn about is the Errors collection. When an error is encountered by ADO, the Errors collection is filled with detail on the culprit. Depending on the source of the error, or even if there are bugs in the underlying OLE DB provider to ADO, the Errors collection may not be populated. But for the most part, VB will tell you the cause of the problem. The Errors collection is available *only* from the connection object.

Let's take a look at how we can access the information that's held in the Errors collection.

Try It Out – Harvesting Errors from the Errors Collection

1 Add another command button to your **frmSchema** form and name it **cmdErrors**. Add an Error Collection caption so that it looks like this:

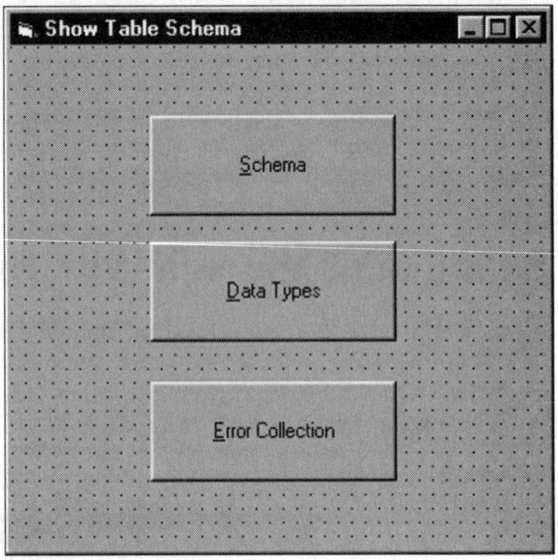

2 Add this code to the click event procedure of the **cmdErrors** button:

```
Private Sub cmdErrors_Click()

Dim adoConnection As ADODB.Connection
Dim adoErrors As ADODB.Errors

Dim i As Integer
Dim StrTmp

On Error GoTo AdoError

Set adoConnection = New ADODB.Connection

' Open connection to Bogus ODBC Data Source for BIBLIO.MDB
adoConnection.ConnectionString = "DBQ=BIBLIO.MDB;" & _
                 "DRIVER={Microsoft Access Driver (*.mdb)};" & _
                 "DefaultDir=C:\OhNooo\Directory\Path;"

adoConnection.Open

' Remaining code goes here, but of course our program
' will never reach it because the connection string
' will generate an error because of the bogus directory

' Close the open objects
adoConnection.Close

' Destroy anything not destroyed yet
Set adoConnection = Nothing

Exit Sub
```

```
AdoError:

    Dim errorCollection As Variant
    Dim errLoop As Error
    Dim strError As String
    Dim iCounter As Integer

    ' In case our adoConnection is not set or
    ' there were other initialization problems
    On Error Resume Next

    iCounter = 1

    ' Enumerate Errors collection and display properties of
    ' each Error object.
    strError = ""
    Set errorCollection = adoConnection.Errors
    For Each errLoop In errorCollection
        With errLoop
            strError = "Error #" & iCounter & vbCrLf
            strError = strError & " ADO Error #" & .Number & vbCrLf
            strError = strError & " Description  " & .Description & vbCrLf
            strError = strError & " Source       " & .Source & vbCrLf
            Debug.Print strError
            iCounter = iCounter + 1
        End With
    Next

End Sub
```

3 Press *F5* and run the program, then click on the Error Collection button.

The Errors Collection Output

We didn't place these in screen shots of the immediate window because the output is actually longer than the screen. The error messages have gone from being rather terse to chatty Cathy in nature. They now are almost conversational. Here is what you will see in the immediate window:

```
Error #1
 ADO Error #-2147467259
 Description   [Microsoft][ODBC Microsoft Access 97 Driver] '(unknown)' isn't
         a valid path.  Make sure that the path name is spelled correctly and
         that you are connected to the server on which the file resides.
 Source        Microsoft OLE DB Provider for ODBC Drivers

Error #2
 ADO Error #-2147467259
 Description   [Microsoft][ODBC Driver Manager] Driver's SQLSetConnectAttr
         failed
 Source        Microsoft OLE DB Provider for ODBC Drivers
```

Now that's handy. Instead of some strange number, the ADO errors are more 'wordy' - and they even look like English. This is more like it!

Let's have a look at how this all fits together.

How It Works

We first want to set up an error handler to trap and skin any errors that may occur in our program:

```
On Error GoTo AdoError
```

When the code hits this line, our local error handler, **AdoError**, becomes active. From this point forward, when an error occurs in our procedure, control *automatically* jumps to the label **AdoError** that contains our handler.

Our connection string is then defined.

```
adoConnection.ConnectionString = "DBQ=BIBLIO.MDB;" & _
              "DRIVER={Microsoft Access Driver (*.mdb)};" & _
              "DefaultDir=C:\OhNooo\Directory\Path;"
```

Of course, we don't have a directory called **C:\OhNooo\Directory\Path** so the connection object will not be able to communicate with the database.

Simply setting the bogus connection string does not cause the error. But when we invoke the **.Open** method with the faulty string, this *does* cause our problem and generates the error.

```
adoConnection.Open
```

When our program can't establish a connection with the database, an error is generated. And since we have an active error handler, the code jumps there immediately.

Once in our error handler, we can then loop through the error collection of our **adoConnection** object. And each error provides us with a Number, a Description of the error, and the source of the error. Very handy, and a lot of useful descriptive information:

```
Set errorCollection = adoConnection.Errors
    For Each errLoop In errorCollection
        With errLoop
            strError = "Error #" & iCounter & vbCrLf
            strError = strError & " ADO Error #" & .Number & vbCrLf
            strError = strError & " Description " & .Description & vbCrLf
            strError = strError & " Source       " & .Source & vbCrLf
            Debug.Print strError
            iCounter = iCounter + 1
        End With
    Next
```

We route each error to the immediate window using our trusty **debug.print**. This is the result of attempting to connect with a database that resides in a bogus path. Notice that the first error is smart enough to know that the problem is a bad path! It not only tells us the problem, but is polite enough to suggest what we should do about it:

Error #1
ADO Error #-2147467259
Description   [Microsoft][ODBC Microsoft Access 97 Driver] '(unknown)' isn't
              a valid path. Make sure that the path name is spelled correctly and
              that you are connected to the server on which the file resides.
Source   Microsoft OLE DB Provider for ODBC Drivers

Next, we'll see how we can have a look at how we can display some information about the
Data Provider itself.

Finding Out All About Our Data Provider

Well, while we are at spying on what data types and column sizes, why not find out about the
data provider? Well, it's easy. And you might notice that again, the connection object is the
workhorse of this operation.

Try It Out – Getting Information about the Data Provider

1 Keep the venerable form **frmSchema** used for the above exercises and add yet another
command button. Name this one **cmdProvider** and caption it Provider.

2 Add the following code to the **Click** event procedure of the new command button:

```
Private Sub cmdProvider_Click()
Dim adoConnection As ADODB.Connection
Dim sConnection As String
Set adoConnection = New ADODB.Connection
sConnection = "Provider=Microsoft.Jet.OLEDB.3.51;Data Source=c:\BegDB\Biblio.mdb"
adoConnection.Open sConnection
'Output all of the version information to the debug window.
Debug.Print "ADO Version: " & adoConnection.Version & vbCrLf
Debug.Print "Database Name: " & adoConnection.Properties("DBMS Name") & vbCrLf
Debug.Print "Database Version: " & _
                    adoConnection.Properties("DBMS Version") & vbCrLf
Debug.Print "OLE DB Version: " & _
                    adoConnection.Properties("OLE DB Version") & vbCrLf
Debug.Print "Provider Name: " & adoConnection.Properties("Provider Name") & vbCrLf
Debug.Print "Provider Version: " & _
                    adoConnection.Properties("Provider Version") & vbCrLf
End Sub
```

3 Your immediate window is probably getting a bit crowded just about now. You might wish
to highlight the contents and press delete to clear it out. Unfortunately the debug has only
two methods - print and assert. It would be very handy if it also had a **.Clear** method.
Ah well...

559

OK, run your program and press the Provider button. Take a look at the immediate window - it should look something like this:

```
ADO Version: 2.0

Database Name: MS Jet

Database Version: 03.51.0000

OLE DB Version: 02.00

Provider Name: MSJTOR35.DLL

Provider Version: 03.52.1321
```

How It Works

Most of the code is identical as the previous examples. But for this code we only open a connection. Then, by interrogating the `.Version` property of the connection object, we can get its value and send it to the debug window. We then print out values from the **Properties** collection of the connection object. The properties collection contains provider information that can be read-only or read/write:

```
Debug.Print  "ADO Version:  " & adoConnection.Version & vbCrLf
Debug.Print  "Database Name:  " & _
                     adoConnection.Properties("DBMS Name") & vbCrLf
```

A Word on Setting References

Some programmers prefer to save a line of code and dimension Object variables. For example, we dimensioned the connection object variable like so:

```
Dim adoConnection As ADODB.Connection
```

This tells VB that we will have a variable called **adoConnection** that will be of **ADODB.Connection** type. This is not unlike dimensioning a variable of type integer or string. Then in the next line, we actually create the variable:

```
Set adoConnection = New ADODB.Connection
```

At this point, we have an object variable, **adoConnection**, of type **ADODB.Connection**. Some programmers like to save a line of code and actually insert the **NEW** keyword directly in the declaration like this:

```
Dim adoConnection As NEW ADODB.Connection
```

Notice that the keyword **NEW** is *inside* the dimension statement. If we add the word **NEW** here, then we do not need the line of code that **Set**s the reference to a **NEW** connection. The **adoConnection** variable is set to **Nothing** and no memory is yet allocated for it. If we don't use it in our code, then it never really gets created. The only memory penalty is that of an unused object variable. But the first time we reference it, the variable springs to life.

Functionally it does not matter is we use the **NEW** keyword when we dimension the object variable or if we explicitly set the dimensioned variable to a **NEW ADODB.Connection** in a separate step. Either way, we get a reference variable that points to a separate object - in this case an **ADODB.Connection**.

Visual Basic 6.0 always initializes intrinsic variables to something. Typically the value is zero or empty. But object variables such as our **adoConnection** get initialized to **Nothing**.

As a rule of thumb, I recommend using an explicit **Set** statement, as we have done, when using object variables. There are several reasons for this, but of course you may not find them compelling.

If we declared the **adoConnection** using the **NEW** keyword, then the first time we touch the variable (i.e. use it), the object is created for us automatically. But you can never set a break point on a **DIM** statement because declarations are not executed at run time. If you use the **Set** statement, you can use the debugger to step on that line. So if there is an error setting the object variable, it will be clear to us what caused the error. If we used **NEW**, then the variable is created when me touch it, like making an assignment. If there is an error, it could be due to setting or due to the assignment itself.

But in any case, our object variables are declared *locally*, so they go out of scope as soon as the procedure is exited. If you declare a form level or global object variable using the **NEW** keyword, then it will be in your program until you set it to **Nothing**. But if you want to use it again, just reference it and it will be there for you. Again, I prefer to always have control of when an object variable is instantiated and destroyed. There are always exceptions to the rule, but for our purposes it just gives you finer granularity on control of what is happening, rather than permitting VB to be in control.

Using the **NEW** keyword in the declaration statement is known as **explicit** creation of the object, meaning that **Set** is not required. Again, when we use the **As New** syntax in the declaration, we lose control. But worse than that, we can't tell if the variable has already been created. In fact, when we test to see if it has been created by using something like "**If adoConnection is Nothing**", that might actually create the object! Why, because we are referencing it. Yikes!

When we use the **Set** statement, this *explicitly* assigns an object to an object variable. When we are done with it, we simply set **adoConnection = Nothing**. If we wish to use this again (within its scope, of course) we must use the **Set** statement again. If we declared it implicitly, we just reference the object variable and it is there to do our bidding. So this can look a bit confusing, but really makes sense when you realize what is going on under the hood.

The ADO Object Model - Revisited

Remember when we looked at the DAO object model back in Chapter 9? Well, you will be pleased to know that the ADO model is much flatter. There are fewer collections, but the model sports much more functionality.

Here is a slightly different slant on the ADO object model than we presented at the beginning of the chapter. It has the same information, but here it is presented a bit differently. The gray boxes represent **collections**. Remember when we iterated through each of the errors in the Errors Collection?

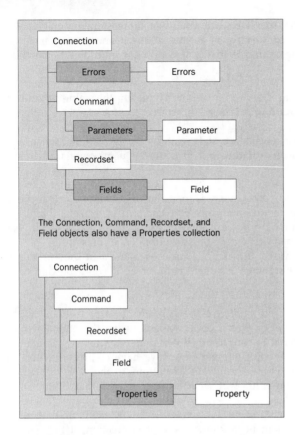

The Connection, Command, Recordset, and Field objects also have a Properties collection

There are some differences between the DAO and ADO object model. For example, all objects represented can be created independently. The exceptions are the **Error** and **Field** objects because they are dependent on the **Connection** and **Recordset** objects respectively. Otherwise, they make no sense!

Notice that the DAO hierarchy that all database programmers are used to has deliberately been de-emphasized in the ADO model. This will give you much more flexibility to reuse objects across various context boundaries. What does this mean exactly? Well, in ADO you can create a *single* **Command** object. Then you can use it with more than one **Connection** object.

Recall that the **Connection** object represents a connection to the underlying data source. In our previous examples, we illustrated the connection object talking to our Access **Biblio.mdb** data source. The Connection interface provides an **Execute** method. We used this to process a SQL command via the connection.

We also mentioned that if the command generates rows, a default Recordset object will be returned. However, if you need to use a more specialized or complex Recordset object with data returned from the Connection, you should create the new Recordset object (specifying the way you need it to behave), bind it to the Connection, and open the cursor (more about cursors in a moment).

The Parameter Object

Another cool feature of the Command object is the use of a **Parameter** object collection. This is used to hold command-specific parameters. The Parameter interface to the Command Object (now that's a mouthful!) represents a parameter of a command. So you can easily create Parameter objects, and then add them to the parameter collection. Why? Well, this really speeds things up.

What the Heck is a Cursor, Anyway?

No, this is not the little flashing mark that shows you where you are on the screen. You can think of a **cursor** - in ADO terms - as another way of referring to a recordset. All of the cursor information - what the underlying OLE DB/ODBC code retrieves from the data source - is contained in the Recordset. The Recordset object is referred to as your 'cursor of data'.

When we have been programming databases so far, we have tended to think of processing our data in terms of a logical sequence of records. For example, we have written an application that read through the records in the publishers table and displayed the name in a grid. The application read through all of the records in a recordset and displayed the name field from each record until it reached the end of the file (EOF).

When your database applications use queries to do data access, the "data" that is returned is a query result set based on the SQL query statements. When we consider the query result set, or recordset, we can't think of it in terms of a "next row" concept, as we can think about the rows in a spreadsheet. Nor is there any way to operate on the individual recordset rows.

This scenario tends to be a bit awkward because most developers understand sequential record-based retrieval - however they many times have no corresponding experience with query result sets, our recordsets. While your query-based database application knows typically what to expect in the recordset, it may need to do more processing. For example, it may need to evaluate certain columns in selected rows to reach some sort of conclusion.

What is meant by this? Well, consider our application that retrieved all of the records from the Publishers table but only displayed - say - 10 records at a time in the grid. Such applications need some sort of mechanism to map one row (or a small block of 10 rows simultaneously displayed in our grid) from the recordset set into the bound grid control. How can the grid know which records to display out of the over 700 when only 10 are shown at a single time? The user can scroll forwards, backwards, or jump to the end of the recordset using the scroll bar. How can the program know which records are to be displayed when it working on a recordset that has no concept of 'next row'?

Enter the cursor. Cursors are animals that expose the entire recordset so that your application can use rows in much the same way we would use records in a sequential file. The following shows how a cursor 'really' makes rows available to your application. Let's say that our application issued the following SQL Query:

```
SELECT * FROM Publishers WHERE City = "New York"
```

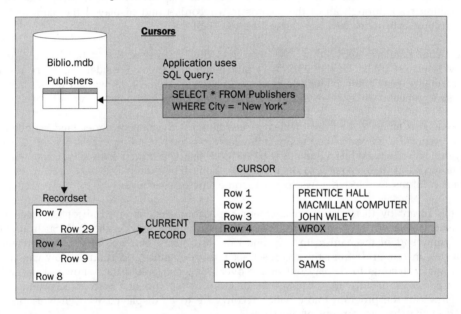

We can see our records as if they were indeed sequential. This permits us to iterate through the recordset and display the publisher's name in a grid. We have been blissfully unaware of the magic of cursors that makes this happen. Let's take a look at what is really going on beneath the smooth surface that is presented to us:

Notice that when our application issues the SQL query, the results are really returned **in no specific order**. The records returned reflect the arbitrary order in which they exist in the database - usually the order that they were entered in. However, they are presented to us in a nice, sequential order. This is what a cursor does for us - it manages the recordset. With our cursor, we can:

▶ Specify positioning at a specific row in the recordset

▶ Retrieve one row, or a block of rows to display in our grid, based on the current result set position

▶ Modify data in the row at the current position in the recordset

Notice that, as far as the user is concerned, the publisher records are appearing one at a time. However, behind the scenes the application is using a **scrollable cursor** to browse up and down through the recordset.

By using a **read-only** cursor, the user can browse through the recordset but not make updates. A **read/write** cursor can implement changes to individual rows. More complex cursors can be defined with **keysets**. These point back to base rows directly in a database table.

Some cursors are read-only in a forward direction, which makes them very fast. They don't have to bother with handling the mechanics of moving backwards as well. These are great for updating a read-only grid: we just loop through the recordset and display the data. Other cursors can move back and forth in the recordset and provide a dynamic refresh of the recordset based on changes other users happen to make to the database. Although each cursor "library" uses a slightly different syntax and usually has somewhat different approach to implement these things, they are all similar in most respects

But don't worry. Cursors aren't really as enigmatic as they might appear. We have actually been using them all along - albeit unwittingly - every time we have written a DAO or ADO program. These interfaces *all* use cursors in some form. Whenever our VB 6.0 database application requires data access, we request a recordset to be opened. We really received a type of cursor from the interface. These DAO or ADO interfaces can have their own cursor library. Or they might use the cursors provided by the data source we are accessing.

Luckily, as a user of a cursor, we don't have to create the cursor directly. We are really requesting it from some service provider, such as a relational database or a cursor library.

So think of a cursor as being the *manipulator* of a set of data. This data is prepared by a service such as Jet, and it uses the resources of the owner of the cursor. So a cursor manages our data: it has the ability to retrieve a portion of that data in the recordset. When the user us using our grid control to move from record to record, a request is made by the user of the cursor to retrieve a piece of data. This, in cursor lingo, is called **scrolling**.

While cursors were always with us when we were using DAO, we didn't need to concern ourselves with them. In fact, if you take a look at the intrinsic data control, a choice of cursors is there as plain as day:

Why Cursors are Important in ADO

So cursors are the beasts that let you move from row to row and maintain the contents of the grid as the user scrolls through the rows. Cursors come in many sizes and colors. Take a look at the data control property above. The DefaultCursor is always selected - this is the most powerful cursor. It permits the user to scroll forward and backwards in the recordset as well as update and delete records. This is the most expensive (in terms of memory and speed) type of cursor. After all, the cursor has to be prepared for any eventuality. Consequently, this default cursor can actually slow down your application. Why? Because it has to keep track of all of the things we just talked about. This takes time and memory.

With ADO, the understanding of cursors is extremely important. In fact, it is critical in order to get our recordset to do the things we want. We need to open certain ADO recordsets with specific types of cursors - in order to get the `.RecordCount` property, for example. Well, every time a new Recordset object is created, a cursor is automatically opened. But before we open a recordset, we can *specify* the type and location of cursor to use when retrieving our results. The `.CursorType` property allows us to set a cursor as forward-only, static, keyset-driven, or dynamic. Each type of cursor has its pros and cons. In the next chapter we will cover each of these and why they are used.

This is very important because the type of cursor we use determines whether a Recordset object can be scrolled forward/backward or updated. The type of cursor also affects who can see changed records. Keep in mind that the most efficient cursor is used by default. This is read forward only. If you only need to read the data, one time, and only move forward, this cursor is for you and there is no need to change the default. But if you need something a bit more robust, you need to bypass the default. Let's summarize the cursor options.

Types of Cursors

Cursors can be either **updateable** or **non-updateable**. If you only need to display information and not diddle with it, the non-updateable is the fastest. The provider simply passes you the data and forgets about it! There is no need to keep tabs on the data to see if it has been changed. Therefore, this is the fastest cursor to use.

Scrollable cursors, which can be updateable or non-updateable, permit you to move (scroll) back and forth in the recordset. If you only need to blast out some data to a grid or HTML page, a non-scrollable cursor will give a performance boost. This is because there is no need to track where you are in the recordset.

Keyset-Driven cursors take note of a key you may have in your database. Under normal circumstances, when you request records from a data source, you get the entire package. However, when a Keyset cursor is selected, only the keys are returned, giving a performance boost. Then, when you scroll through the recordset, the data for the keys is retrieved. However, when you first invoke the cursor, both keys and data are returned so you can see something in your bound control. When you scroll, and the data is not in the current batch of data, the Keyset fetches the next block. This way it only has to manage small keys rather than large chunks of data.

Dynamic and **Static** cursors determine what data is available in the cursor at any point in time. As the name implies, Static cursors only contain data that was placed in the cursor when it was created. However, with a Dynamic cursor, any new records that are added to the recordset are available. It's like a living cursor.

We can use our old friend the Object Browser to see the cursor types available to us:

With ADO, we have the choice of four types of cursors. We can simply use constants to tell the recordset which to use:

Cursor type	Constant
Static cursor. This is the one to use for generating reports or finding data. Additions, changes, or deletions by other users are not visible.	adOpenStatic
Forward-only cursor. This is the default. It is identical to the Static except that you can only scroll forward. The fastest cursor this side of the Pecos Mountains.	adOpenForwardOnly
Dynamic cursor. Additions and deletions by others are visible. All movement is supported. But some providers don't support this cursor type.	adOpenDynamic
Keyset-driven cursor. This is similar to a Dynamic cursor except you can't see records others add. If another user deletes a record, it is inaccessible from your recordset.	adOpenKeyset

We can also tell the recordset how to lock our data while it's being manipulated via the cursor:

Lock Type	Description
AdLockReadOnly	Default. Read-only: you cannot alter the data.
AdLockPessimistic	Pessimistic locking, record by record - the provider does what is necessary to ensure successful editing of the records, usually by locking records at the data source immediately upon editing.
AdLockOptimistic	Optimistic locking, record by record - the provider uses optimistic locking, locking records only when you call the Update method.
AdLockBatchOptimistic	Optimistic batch updates - required for batch update mode as opposed to immediate update mode.

Opening ADO Recordsets - Syntax

The syntax for opening an ADO recordset is like this:

```
adoRecordset.Open Source, ActiveConnection, CursorType, LockType, Options
```

The **Source** argument is Optional. This is a valid command object variable name, or it might be an SQL statement, a table name, or a stored procedure call

The **ActiveConnection** is also optional. This is either a valid Connection object variable name, or a String that contains our ConnectionString

The **CursorType** is also Optional. This is simply one of the cursor constants that tells the provider the type of cursor to use when opening the Recordset.

ConnectionString Options

There are several other options that we can provide the recordset as well. You may recall that when we build the connect string in our ADO data control, these options were provided in a drop down box. They may have looked a bit cryptic back then, but now we can see what they mean:

Description	Constant
The provider should take the source as a text description of a command, such as a SQL statement.	**adCmdText**
ADO should generate an SQL statement to fetch all rows from the table in Source.	**adCmdTable**
The provider should return all of the rows from the table named in Source.	**adCmdTableDirect**
The provider should treat the Source as a stored procedure.	**adCmdStoredProc**
The type of command in Source is unknown. **You should not use this! It is the slowest of all cursors.**	**AdCmdUnknown**
A saved recordset should be restored from the file names in Source.	**adCommandFile**
Source should be executed asynchronously.	**adFetchAsync**
After the initial quantity of records specified in CacheSize is fetched, any remaining rows should be fetched asynchronously.	**adFetchAsync**

When might you use some of these options? Well, a good illustration would be when using a **transaction**.

Transactions and You

Transactions are useful or even necessary when you need to make several changes at once. Think of a transaction as a **logical unit of work**. And if any part of the transaction fails, the whole thing is **rolled back** (i.e. any changes made since the beginning of the transaction are undone). The example often used in computer books is one drawn from banking. For example, let's say that you go to the bank to pay a bill. The funds are drawn from your account and placed in the electric company's account. So two things happen. First the funds are debited from your account and second, the funds are credited to the electric company's account. If the funds are not drawn from your account but *are* credited to the electric company, you are happy but the bank is not. If the funds *are* drawn from your account but *not* placed in the electric company's account, you are mad and the electric company is not that happy either. So both parts of the transaction must occur properly (i.e., the transaction is committed) or both part of the transaction are not executed (i.e., the transaction is rolled back).

Computer scientists use the acronym **ACID** to define the characteristics of a transaction.

▶ **Atomicity** - Although the changes may include several records, if anything fails the entire transaction fails. The system goes back to a pre-transaction state.

▶ **Consistency** - A transaction never leaves the database in an inconsistent state. If a change is made, it can be undone if the transaction fails at a later point.

▶ **Isolation** - A transaction behaves as if it were in complete isolation from other transactions in the system.

▶ **Durability** - Once a transaction's changes are committed, they persist beyond any system failure. If the system crashes (or GPF's!) after the transaction is committed, the transaction's results are still maintained.

An ADO Transaction

Let's look at an ADO example of a transaction that uses a few of the optional constants described above for opening our recordset. In this example, we examine the syntax for using a transaction. We just append a ` "" ` to each of the more than 8,500 titles in the Titles table. But if there is an error anywhere, the entire enchilada is rolled back and the original table is returned to its fresh as the new-driven snow state (mmm, enchilada's in the snow!). The transaction is sandwiched between the **.BeginTrans** and **.CommitTrans** method calls on the connection object:

```
Dim myConnection As ADODB.Connection
Dim myRecordset As ADODB.Recordset

Set myConnection = New ADODB.Connection
Set myRecordset = New ADODB.Recordset

myConnection.ConnectionString = _
          "Provider=Microsoft.Jet.OLEDB.3.51;Data Source=c:\BegDB\Biblio.mdb"
```

```
'—Open the connection --
myConnection.Open

'Determine if we conected.
If myConnection.State = adStateOpen Then

   myRecordset.Open "SELECT * FROM TITLES", myConnection, _
                                  adOpenDynamic, adLockOptimistic, adCmdText
Else
   MsgBox "The connection could not be made."
   myConnection.Close
   Exit Sub
End If

'—just to be sure --
myRecordset.MoveFirst

On Error GoTo transError

'—here is the top of the transaction sandwich --
myConnection.BeginTrans

While Not myRecordset.EOF
    mcounter = mcounter + 1
    myRecordset!Title = myRecordset!Title & ""  'so we don't really change it
    myRecordset.Update
    myRecordset.MoveNext
Wend

'—if we got here ok, then everything is written at once
myConnection.CommitTrans
myRecordset.Close
myConnection.Close

Exit Sub

transError:
myConnection.RollBack
myRecordset.Close
 myConnection.Close
MsgBox Err.Description
```

How It Works

After the connection is established, this example begins a transaction. The data changed in this transaction is either all committed at the end of the transaction, or it is all rolled back to the pre-transaction state. Let's take a look at the important parts of the code.

After we dim and initialize our connection and recordset objects, we build our connection string as we have been doing so far. The connection is then opened by invoking the `.Open` method of the connection object:

```
myConnection.ConnectionString = "Provider=Microsoft.Jet.OLEDB.3.51;Data
Source=c:\BegDB\Biblio.mdb"

'—Open the connection --
myConnection.Open
```

Then, as a precaution, we check out the **.State** property of the connection. Recall the general syntax of opening an ADO recordset:

adoRecordset.Open Source, ActiveConnection, CursorType, LockType, Options

Well, in our example, if the connection is open, we pass the **.Open** method of the recordset an SQL query string as the **Source**. It is requesting all of the records for the Titles table as the first parameter. Next, we pass in the **ActiveConnection** connection object, **myConnection**. Next, we specify the **CursorType** as an **adOpenDynamic** cursor for the recordset. This type of cursor permits all movement backwards and forwards, allows the user to make changes to the current record, and even will dynamically update if another user updates any records in the database that are included in our recordset. We will actually see any additions or deletions as they occur by others! We then specify the **LockType** as **adLockOptimistic**. This locks record by record and only occurs when the **.Update** method is called. Since we know this is a table, we pass in the **Options** parameter as **adCmdTable**. Now ADO does not have to spend time figuring out what it is going after. We have fully specified the type of recordset we want by passing each parameter.

```
'Determine if we connected.
If myConnection.State = adStateOpen Then

  myRecordset.Open "SELECT * FROM TITLES", myConnection, _
                        adOpenDynamic, adLockOptimistic,adCmdTable
Else
   MsgBox "The connection could not be made."
   myConnection.Close
   Exit Sub
End If
```

Once our recordset is opened, we want to perform an edit/update on each record in the recordset. Edit/update is very expensive in terms of processing time. So we sandwich our edit/ updates inside a transaction. When the **.BeginTrans** method is called, everything until the **.Commit** or **.RollBack** method of the connection object is reached:

```
'—here is the top of the transaction sandwich --
myConnection.BeginTrans
```

Now we do our processing. We loop through the recordset as we usually would. With ADO, no **.Edit** method is required as it is in DAO. Remember when we discussed ADO being slimmed down by having many redundant methods removed? Well, this is one of them. By simply changing the data, an Edit is assumed. So an Edit still occurs, but it is implicit. We don't have to explicitly call the method. So we modify (edit) each record and then call the **.Update** method. However, since we are in the transaction sandwich, the results are written to a temporary file. They are not yet committed to the database:

```
While Not myRecordset.EOF
    mcounter = mcounter + 1
    myRecordset!Title = myRecordset!Title & ""    'so we don't really change it
    myRecordset.Update
    myRecordset.MoveNext
Wend
```

If everything goes as planned, when we exit the loop we then call the `.CommitTrans` method of the connection object. Now, all of the changes are written to the data source **at one time**. So we are not hitting the disk for each record, writing the changes, then moving to the next record. The changes are kept, where possible, in memory and then blasted all at once to the data source. So instead of doing - say - 700 writes (one for each record), we only do a single bulk write which is much, much faster.

As I said, this technique can be used when you are not 'technically' performing a transaction. In other words, when you are not hitting two tables that require both to be changed simultaneously. When you only need to update a single table as in our simple example, this will be orders of magnitude faster than updating each individual record. Then we close the recordset and the connection when we are finished and exit the sub:

```
'—if we got here ok, then everything is written at once
myConnection.CommitTrans
myRecordset.Close
myConnection.Close
```

> *If we were going to perform the same task on several records such as appending an "" to each title, it would be much faster to just use the* `.Execute` *method and use SQL. But we wanted to show an example of the transaction method that you might be able to use in your every day programming.*

If we run into a snag, an error is generated. Since we have an active error handler, our VB code jumps to the **transError** label, which is the start of the error handler. Here we roll back everything that has occurred up to this point. The `.RollBack` method will bring the system back to the point of the `.BeginTrans` method. None of the records in the transaction sandwich will be changed. We then close the recordset and connection and display a description of the error from the global **Err** error object:

```
transError:
    myConnection.RollBack
myRecordset.Close
    myConnection.Close
MsgBox Err.Description
```

Using Transactions in Everyday Life

Now this is a cool tip. You can use transactions whenever you have to update several records in a coordinated manner. VB keeps as much in a cache as possible to reduce costly disk writing activity. With a transaction, everything gets written at once, instead of on every `.Update` method. The speed benefit can be enormous. I use this whenever possible when adding or editing records in a large recordsets

One caveat. If you attempt to do this with the ODBC connection we established earlier, you get the friendly message shown below:

Why? Because the ODBC driver we used does not support transactions. The moral of the story is: know your data source capabilities.

Summary

We covered a lot of ground in this chapter. We noted how ADO really evolved from DAO's inability to retrieve non-relational data. We saw how the need to access non-relational data was largely driven by the rise of the Internet, and by the problems of accessing the wealth of legacy data stored in a variety of formats.

We noted how the move to ADO was really evolutionary, not revolutionary. ODBC was a first attempt to permit a single interface to work with many database providers products. But ODBC, while still powerful, was limited to relational data. ADO breaks these bounds and allows us to access **everything** we could get hold of with ODBC, plus much more.

The basic way to retrieve an ADO recordset is by first opening a **connection** to the database. We examined the ins and outs of a **connection string** and even built our own **Data Source Name (DSN)**, and we opened an ADO connection using that.

Next we used ADO to examine the data provider's tables and fields by using the `.OpenSchema` method. This permitted us to see exactly how the data source was made up. We then went on to look at the **Errors** collection and how it is used in the ADO object model.

Moving on to **cursors**, we caught a glimpse of what really happens under the hood when data is returned to us in a recordset. An example was shown opening a recordset with a specific cursor.

We then ended up with transactions and discussed how they can not only help when we need to update several tables simultaneously, but can also really speed up our code when we have more 'garden variety' tasks such as updating several records.

What We Learned

- ▶ Programming **ADO** is very similar to DAO
- ▶ We program to ADO, but it is the **OLE DB provider** that does the real work of taking the ADO commands and translating them to work with the data source
- ▶ The **Connection Wizard** can be used to seamlessly create the connection string
- ▶ Once we are connected to an OLE DB data source, we can access data almost exactly like DAO
- ▶ **Declaring an object variable** implicitly or explicitly requires us to handle the variable differently when bringing it to life
- ▶ **Transactions** are not only useful when working with several recordsets, but can speed up everyday data access tasks

And now we will move on to another cool use of ADO – **building our own bound ADO ActiveX control**.

Exercises

1 When declaring a variable to represent an object from the ADO object model what must you do to ensure that your variable refers to an ADO object rather than a DAO object?

2 In the ADO object model what property of the **Connection** object specifies the data source to work with? What is the format that you use to identify the data source?

3 What is the difference between explicitly setting an object variable and letting Visual Basic implicitly set it for you?

4 Why is it important to use transactions when creating database applications?

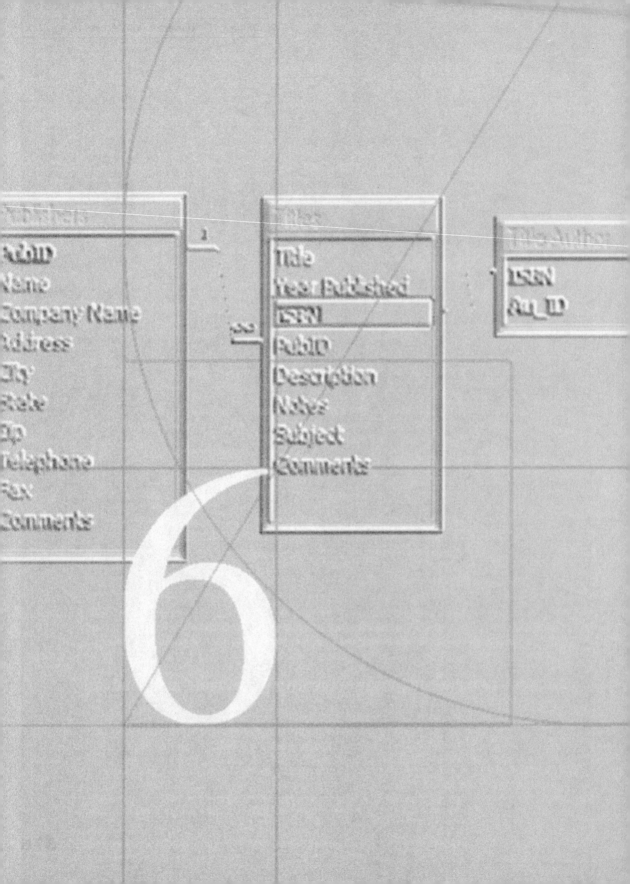

Creating ADO Data Bound ActiveX Controls

Well, we have already seen that VB 6.0 gives us some new and exciting database controls and tools. But what is really exciting is that we now have the ability to **create our own data bound ActiveX controls**, just like the controls on your tool palette! These controls can be used by yourself or any other programmer you wish to share them with.

In this chapter we're going to build our own data control and add code to it to make it a universally useful tool. Then we're going to package it up as a distributable file so that we can send it off into the wide world for other programmers to use. In many ways this is the same kind of process we went through when we built our class module, only this time we are creating reusable functionality for an ActiveX control that can be used over and over.

Here's the topics that we'll cover in this chapter:

- The background to the development of ActiveX controls
- The principles of binding
- How to create our own data control
- Adding code to build our control's functionality, including catering for interactions with command buttons and different types of record source
- Building documentation about our control that can be packaged up with it for other users
- Creating a distributable **.ocx** file and letting others share our new control

First, let's reflect on why the ability to build ActiveX controls is so significant.

We Could Create ActiveX Controls Before, Couldn't We?

Sure, we could create ActiveX controls before this release of VB. If we knew ahead of time which fields we wanted to bind, we could create controls that bound to fields. But these fields had to be *hard coded* in the control. So it we wanted to bind the Title field from the Titles table in a control, we could do that – it was simple. However, to do this we had to know what database fields would be bound to which controls in advance.

This is not quite the generalized approach most of us require in our day-to-day programming activities. And it certainly won't permit us to create a bound control that can be used in just about any situation. For example, with the bound grid data control, we just draw a data control on our form and set its properties. The data control is responsible for creating the recordset. Then we can use a DBGrid, hook it up to the data control, and we are fixed up. The data control can retrieve any recordset and the DBGrid can visually display the recordset retrieved by the data control.

What if we wanted to create our own generalized ActiveX control that could be used with **any** data source, like the ADO data control can? The ADODC control does not know ahead of time what data source or fields you might want to retrieve, but by setting a few properties such as the **ConnectString** and **RecordSource**, you can easily retrieve any arbitrary recordset of data.

If you wanted to create a control like that in VB prior to version 6, it could be done - but it was far from easy. In fact, you had to know C++ and something called the Microsoft Interface Definition Language (MIDL). You also had to create your own 'ClassID' using a program called **guidgen.exe**. It was far from simple, and consequently most VB programmers passed on this option and lived with the controls that came with VB or could be purchased from the hundreds of third party suppliers.

The Holy Grail of Code Reusability

The great news is that VB 6.0 gives us the ability to create new controls that can be bound not only to a few predefined fields, but to an entire record in the database - and we don't need to specify these fields in advance! This means that you can create your own ADO Data Control, just like the one in your tool palette! This is real power. So let's say that we wanted to create a new ActiveX control that we could simply draw on a form that would manage all of our data input requirements. How? It's simple!

Remember the data class we wrote a few chapters back that manages all of the bound fields on a form for us? The class was smart enough to know which fields were bound to the data control. The class locked the fields when they were not in use so the user could not enter any information unless the class was in an Edit mode. Then, when the user pressed Edit or Add, the class unlocked the fields and handled all of the editing for us. This was a great exercise and certainly cut down on our programming time by handling the complexity of managing the user input.

However, we must include the class with each program we write. Or if you want to give the class to an associate, the source code has to be distributed because the class code gets compiled right into the source of the program. There was always the risk that the user of our class might tweak the code for the current project, thus making it non-standard and therefore not reusable.

So if we wanted to distribute the functionality of our class in a compiled form so the programmer couldn't change it, we were out of luck. Or if we wanted to provide the functionality of a generalized data bound control to a C++ or Delphi programmer, we just couldn't do it. Until now.

VB 6.0 allows us to create our own bound controls, just like the controls found on your tool palette. And best of all, they can be compiled into real **.OCX** files so that you can distribute the binary files to programmers that use **any** language that can use bound controls.

C++ and Visual Basic - a Short (and Partial) History

In the early 1990s, it appeared that C++ was going to take the world by storm. This is because C++ permitted programmers to create classes that could be reused and extended by other programmers within the organization. In theory, this seemed like the silver bullet that corporate IS departments were looking for. To switch metaphors, this was the 'Holy Grail' of code reusability, meaning we didn't have to rewrite functionality from scratch for each project. However, in practice, things didn't quite work out this way. C++ classes are very abstract and difficult to use. And so programmers would change the classes for each project making reuse more of a dream than a reality.

Visual Basic then came on the scene with 16-bit **.VBX** controls - such as the text box. As the language evolved and we got to VB 3.0, we saw the birth of a remarkable control that came bundled with the language - the data control. A huge third party cottage industry sprang up to develop these controls. Then with VB 4.0, 32-bit **.OCX** controls were introduced that were even *more* powerful. These generalized visual controls were pre-built, and came with tons of functionality. Programmers simply drew the pre-configured controls on a form and could then concentrate on writing the application.

As such, these controls were a huge success. So much so, in fact, that the **.OCX** controls actually accomplished what the C++ classes failed to produce - true code reusability. And these controls are attributed with making VB the most popular Windows programming language ever - with more than a million VB programmers worldwide.

Just before we set about creating our custom ActiveX data control, let's take a minute to consider the important concept of **data binding**.

Time Out to Discuss Data Binding

Since we are going to be discussing binding fields of ActiveX controls to ADO recordsets, now is probably a good time to discuss **data binding**. Data binding is one of the more powerful uses of ActiveX controls. Essentially, using data binding allows a **property** of the ActiveX control to bind with a **specific field** in a database.

When the bound control property (such as the text box's **Text** property) is modified by the user of our control, the control actually notifies the database that the value has changed. It then requests that the relevant field of the current record be updated. This process takes place, and in return the database notifies the control of the success or failure of the update. Hmmm...sounds like a data control to me.

> *So in a nutshell, data binding allows a database entry, such as a record field, to be linked to a property of an ActiveX control.*

Our ActiveX control is typically hosted in a VB 6.0 form. This form and the bound controls provide the visual interface to the current record. The figure below illustrates a conceptual view of this binding:

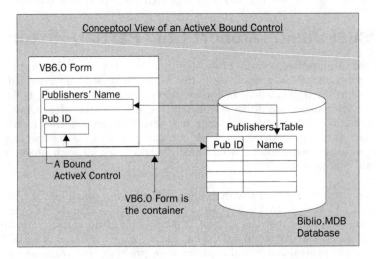

Conceptool View of an ActiveX Bound Control

VB6.0 Form

Publishers' Name

Pub ID

A Bound ActiveX Control

VB6.0 Form is the container

Publishers' Table

Pub ID | Name

Biblio.MDB Database

In this example, the ActiveX control has two text boxes, each of which has bound its **Text** property to the fields of a record. When the user makes changes to either text box, the modifications are made to the control's **Text** property. These changes are communicated to the database.

Remember earlier on when we mentioned than an ActiveX control is 'hosted' by a form? An ActiveX control needs a form to live on. Data binding is a notification mechanism that links our ActiveX control's **properties** - through the **container** (i.e. our form) to a **data source** (i.e. a database field).

When we bind an ActiveX control property, we must make sure that the control is able to send notifications to the database whenever the property changes. That notification is sent to the control container (i.e. the hosting VB form), which processes it and returns the database's response to the control.

In order to see the brand-new features that VB 6.0 offers database programmers, we are going to create three projects in this chapter:

> **First**, we will build a simple form that uses the new VB 6 **bindings** collection to get a feel for how this is done. We will simply bind two fields in the Publishers table to two text boxes. This will get your mind around how to accomplish this, and it will certainly provide you with food for thought. Next, we will **actually create our own ActiveX ADO Bound control**. This **.OCX** control will manage a recordset for us. You will be able to compile this control and give it to other programmers to use, or you might want to use it in your next project.

> **Second**, we will use the brand new **Data Repeater** control that comes with VB 6.0.

> **Finally**, we will build a data-aware **class**. This approach gives us the ability to use a class module to bind database fields to controls in a form – *without* an ADO data control! That's right, with VB 6.0 we can now bind database fields **directly** to bound controls on a form without the mediation of a data control.

VB 6.0 has really provided database programmers with a wealth of possibilities. Let's take a look.

Binding Datafields to Controls

Let's start with a very simple example, using an uncomplicated form, and a class module that we'll construct. We're going to create a class that will encapsulate the code to handle an ADO recordset for us. What we'll do here is bind two text boxes on our simple form to two fields in the Publishers table - a single button on the form will move us on to the next record. This is all pretty simple in terms of the functionality we'll use, but the principles involved will provide us with a good idea of how to extend this method.

Take another look at this illustration:

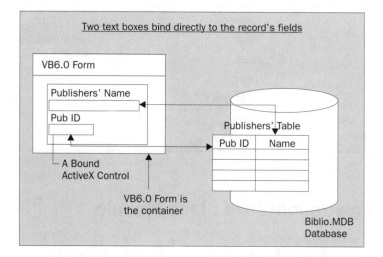

This is what our first program will accomplish without an ADO data control. So let's get on with the coding!

Try It Out - Create a Simple Bindings Collection

1 Start a new project called **\Chapter12\Bindings.vbp**. Name the default form **frmBoundExample**. Add a class module and name it **myBoundClass**. Your Project Explorer should now look like this:

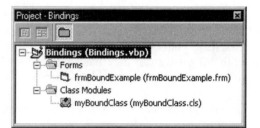

2 Add two text boxes, a check box, and a command button to the form. Lay out the controls like this:

Control	Property	Value
Text box	**Name**	txtPubID
	Text	txtPubID
Text box	**Name**	txtName
	Text	txtName
Checkbox	**Caption**	Show Message
Command Button	**Name**	cmdMoveNext
	Caption	&Move Next

So much for the form. Next - the class module.

Coding the myBoundClass Class Module

The next thing we're going to do is start building our class module. New with VB 6.0 is the ability to set up a **class** as a **data source**. This is very cool because we can now encapsulate recordset management in a class.

Try It Out - Building the myBoundClass Class Module

1 The first thing we need to do is let VB know that we want our class to be a **data provider** – that is, it's a resource that we use to get at some underlying data. We do this by setting the **DataSourceBehavior** property. VB is now smart enough to add a brand new sub to our class, **Class_GetDataMember**, as soon as we set the **DataSourceBehavior** property to **vbDataSource**. To set this up, bring up the property window for **myBoundClass** change the property to 1 as shown here:

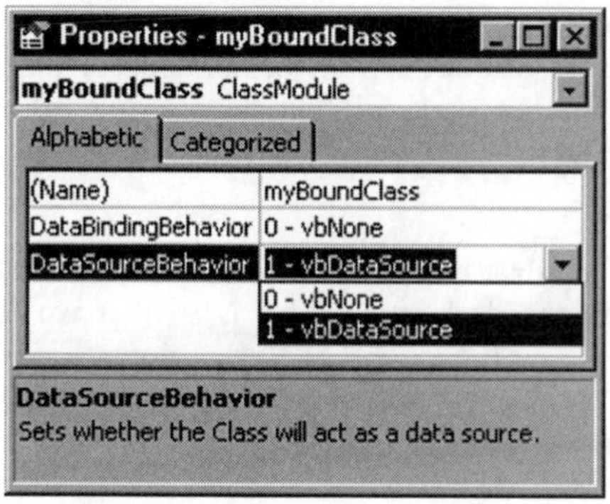

2 Click Project-References from the main VB menu and select the Microsoft ActiveX Data
Objects 2.0 library and the ActiveX Data Objects Recordset 2.0 library. Also add the
Microsoft Data Binding Collection type library:

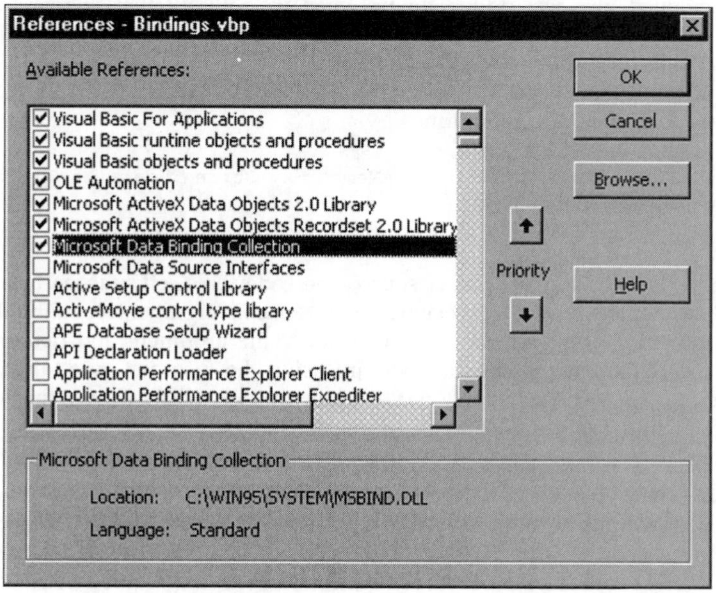

Now our project will understand not only what an ADO connection and recordset is, but
also how to deal with data binding **collections**.

3 Let's add some code to our **myBoundClass** class module. In the **General
Declarations** section, add the following:

```
Option Explicit
Private showInfo As Boolean
Private WithEvents adoPublishers As ADODB.Recordset
Private adoConnection As ADODB.Connection
```

What will this do for us? Well, first we declare a private variable, **showInfo**, that we will set with a property **displayMoveComplete** from the outside of our class. When the user checks or unchecks the check box on the form, we will set the variable **showInfo** to 'true' or 'false'. When it is true, we will show the status of the recordset after a move to the next record has been completed successfully.

Next, we declare an ADO recordset object variable called **adoPublishers**. Notice that we use the keyword **WithEvents** in the declaration. This is so that we can actually define ADO recordset events in our code. These events will then automatically fire because we have used the **WithEvents** keyword. Our code will include a **MoveComplete** ADO recordset event. Now, by simply using this keyword, this event will fire when the current record pointer of the recordset has moved to the next record.

Finally, we declare an object variable **adoConnection**. This will hold the connection to the database.

Now we're going to set up the **GetDataMember** sub that VB automatically placed in our class module. As mentioned, this was added for us when we told VB that the class is a data provider (by setting the class property). A data **provider** - such as our class - can have multiple sets of data that a data **consumer** (our form) can choose to bind to. Each set of data is called a **data member**. VB will set a **DataMember** to our recordset, **adoPublishers**. Add the highlighted code to the **Class_GetDataMember** subroutine:

```
Private Sub Class_GetDataMember(DataMember As String, data As Object)
    Set data = adoPublishers
End Sub
```

When we use a class module as a data source, we code the **GetDataMember** to return an appropriate data member value. The event's **DataMember** argument contains the value of the **DataMember** property. This way our code can query the argument and determine which data member is being requested. In this case, we are using the recordset **adoPublishers**. This can be passed back to the caller using the **data** argument. We will see how this will be called next, in the class initialization event.

4   Recall that when you open the code window for a class module, you must click the left hand drop down box to get to the class events – **Initialize** and **Terminate**. This code will execute exactly once in the life of the class. When the class is instantiated into an object in our form, this event fires. Add the following highlighted code to the **Class_Initialize** event now:

```
Private Sub Class_Initialize()

    showInfo = False
    DataMembers.Add "Publishers"

    Set adoPublishers = New ADODB.Recordset
    Set adoConnection = New ADODB.Connection

    With adoConnection
        .Provider = "Microsoft.Jet.OLEDB.3.51"
        .Open "C:\BegDb\Biblio.mdb"
    End With
```

```
adoPublishers.Open "Select * FROM Publishers", _
adoConnection, _
adOpenStatic, _
adLockOptimistic
```

End Sub

As we mentioned earlier, a **data provider** - such as our class - can have many sets of data that a data **consumer** (our form) could elect to bind to. These sets of data are called **data members** and each one is identified by a unique string. Here we are adding the string **"Publishers"**. The **DataMembers** collection contains the names of all data members accessible to the data consumer. In our simple program, we only have a single entry in **DataMembers**, **"Publishers"**:

```
DataMembers.Add "Publishers"
```

We then go on to create new instances of our connection and recordset object variables. We are already familiar with how to do that. But here, we are using a slightly different method of setting up our connection; instead of setting a connection string that contains everything the connection needs to open itself, we chose to set the **.Provider** property separately. We then pass in the location and name of the database to the **.Open** method of the connection. This is just to illustrate how you can set up the connection in various ways. As long as it has enough information, the connection can open successfully:

```
With adoConnection .Provider = "Microsoft.Jet.OLEDB.3.51"
  .Open "C:\BegDb\Biblio.mdb"
End With
```

Finally, we open the recordset to be managed by our class. For simplicity, we just select all records from the **Publishers** table:

```
adoPublishers.Open "Select * FROM Publishers", _
adoConnection, _
adOpenStatic, _
adLockOptimistic
```

So when the **Initialization** code is complete, we have a datamember added to the **DataMembers** collection, an open connection to the database, and an open recordset.

The Move Complete Event

The next stage is to add our **MoveComplete** event. Here, we will be defining a standard **MoveComplete** that is built into an ADO data control. If you drew an ADO Data control on your form and double-clicked to open the code window to look at the code, this event would be there. Here, we are simply adding this same event to our code. And since we declared the recordset with the keyword **WithEvents**, this event will fire in our class just as it would if you used an ADO data control. We must get the 'signature' correct, so be sure you add this exactly as shown.

5 Add the following code to the **adoPublishers_MoveComplete** private subroutine in our class module. Even though this looks like a lot of code, we are simply reading the values of the **adReason** and **adStatus** parameters that are passed into the event by VB, and displaying them to the user if they have checked the check box on the **frmBoundExample** form. Add the highlighted code now:

```
Private Sub adoPublishers_MoveComplete(ByVal adReason As ADODB.EventReasonEnum, _
ByVal pError As ADODB.Error, adstatus As ADODB.EventStatusEnum, _
ByVal pRecordSet As ADODB.Recordset)

Dim sMessage As String
Dim iIndx As Integer

If showInfo = True Then

  sMessage = "Reason: "
  Select Case adreason
    Case adRsnAddNew
      sMessage = sMessage & "Adding New Record" & vbCrLf
    Case adRsnClose
      sMessage = sMessage & "Closing Recordset" & vbCrLf
    Case adRsnDelete
      sMessage = sMessage & "Deleting Record" & vbCrLf
    Case adRsnFirstChange
      sMessage = sMessage & "First Change" & vbCrLf
    Case adRsnMove
      sMessage = sMessage & "Move" & vbCrLf
    Case adRsnMoveFirst
      sMessage = sMessage & "Move First Record" & vbCrLf
    Case adRsnMoveLast
      sMessage = sMessage & "Move Last Record" & vbCrLf
    Case adRsnMoveNext
      sMessage = sMessage & "Move Next Record" & vbCrLf
    Case adRsnMovePrevious
      sMessage = sMessage & "Move Previous" & vbCrLf
    Case adRsnRequery
      sMessage = sMessage & "Requering" & vbCrLf
    Case adRsnResynch
      sMessage = sMessage & "Resynch" & vbCrLf
    Case adRsnUndoAddNew
      sMessage = sMessage & "Undo Adding New Record" & vbCrLf
    Case adRsnUndoUpdate
      sMessage = sMessage & "Undoing Update" & vbCrLf
    Case adRsnUpdate
      sMessage = sMessage & "Updating record" & vbCrLf
  End Select

  sMessage = sMessage & "Status: "
  Select Case adstatus
    Case adStatusCancel
      sMessage = sMessage & "Cancel" & vbCrLf
    Case adStatusCantDeny
      sMessage = sMessage & "Cant Deny" & vbCrLf
    Case adStatusErrorsOccurred
      sMessage = sMessage & "Errors Occured" & vbCrLf
    Case adStatusOK
      sMessage = sMessage & "Ok" & vbCrLf
    Case adStatusUnwantedEvent
      sMessage = sMessage & "Unwanted Event" & vbCrLf
  End Select
```

```
      iIndx = MsgBox(sMessage, vbOKOnly + vbInformation, _
"Bound Data Class MoveComplete")

End If

End Sub
```

So as you can see, the only real code here is in the two **Select** statements. We are checking the enumerated values of the **adReason** and **adStatus** variables passed into the event and displaying them to the user (I just wanted to show you what these items were and how you can grab them if you need to read them).

The MoveNext Procedure

To keep things simple so we can concentrate on the code, we only have a **MoveNext** procedure. When the user clicks the single button on the form, the **MoveNext** procedure is called.

6 Add the following (new) **MoveNext** subroutine to your class module:

```
Public Sub MoveNext()
If adoPublishers.EOF Then
        adoPublishers.MoveFirst
Else
        adoPublishers.MoveNext
End If

End Sub
```

There is no magic here. When the button on the form is clicked, this procedure checks to see if we are at the end of the recordset. If yes, then we cycle back to the first record. If not, we move to the next.

Showing the Status of theOperation

7 Now we'll add a write-only property called **displayMoveComplete** to the class – it will ensure that the user is shown the status of the operation that they're performing. Add this property now:

```
Public Property Let displayMoveComplete(ByVal vNewValue As Boolean)
showInfo = vNewValue
End Property
```

When the user checks or unchecks the check box on the form, we pass in a true or false. When the box is checked, we set this property to true. In turn, the private variable **showInfo** is set to true. Notice that when the **MoveComplete** event fires, it checks the value of **showInfo**. If it is true, then the enumerated reason and status of the move is displayed in a message box. Sure, we could have just declared the **showInfo** variable as public and set it directly, but we would have violated the encapsulation approach. Using the standard property approach to set a private variable ensures that we use 'data hiding' through encapsulation.

587

Coding the frmBoundExample form

OK, we just need a few lines in our form to connect to the class and make it work.

8 Please add the following in the **General Declarations** section of the form:

```
Option Explicit
Private clsBoundClass As New myBoundClass
Private bndPublishers As New BindingCollection
```

Here, we first dim an object variable, **clsBoundClass** of type **myBoundClass**. When we instantiate this class, it will become an object in memory. Notice the **New** keyword. This means that we will not use the **SET** keyword to set a reference to the class. The first time we touch (reference in any way) the class, it will spring to life.

Next we dim another object variable, **bndPublishers** of data type **BindingCollection**. In our sample program, we use the **BindingCollection** object to bind a data source to two text box controls. So this line of code will permit us to create an instance of a **BindingCollection** object.

The **Binding** object represents a property of an object bound to a data field of a data source. We are using the **BindingCollection** object to bind a data source that has no design-time interface (our class module that is configured as a data source), to a data consumer (the two text boxes on our form).

Coding the Form Load Event

When our form loads, we can configure the **BindingCollection**. To do that we add some code to the **Form_Load** event.

9 Add the following subroutine to the form's **Load** event:

```
Private Sub Form_Load()
With bndPublishers
.DataMember = "Publishers"
Set .DataSource = clsBoundClass
.Add txtPubID, "Text", "PubID"
 .Add txtName, "Text", "Name"
  MsgBox "Number of items bound:  " &  .Count
End With
End Sub
```

What happens here? First, we set the **DataMember** property of the **bndPublishers BindingCollection**. Remember the **GetDataMember** procedure in our class? Well, **GetDataMember** sets the *source* of the data for the class. We must provide a unique string because a class might have several **DataMember**s. Here, again, we are only interested in one – the one that refers to the **Publishers** table.

Next, the **DataSource** of the **BindingCollection** is hooked up to our class, **clsBoundClass**, which we set as a data provider. Now we can add items to be bound. We are adding our two text boxes to the **BindingCollection** using its **Add** method. The general syntax of the **Add** method looks like this:

```
object.Add(object, PropertyName, DataField, DataFormat, Key)
```

The table shows the options for the **BindingCollection**'s **Add** method:

Parameter	Required/Optional	Description
Object	Required	The control or other data consumer which will be bound. Here we use the names of the two text boxes for each **Add**.
PropertyName	Required	The property of the data consumer to which the data field will be bound. We want the **Text** property of the textboxes to be bound.
DataField	Required	The column of the data source that will be bound to the property specified in the *PropertyName* argument. We insert the data field from the Publishers database that we wish to be bound to the text box.
DataFormat	Optional	A **DataFormat** object or a reference to a **DataFormat** variable that will be used to format the bound property.
Key	Optional	A unique string that identifies the member of the collection.

So we are simply initializing our **BindingCollection**, then adding the text boxes to the collection. You could add as many as you wish. Again, we wanted to concentrate on the code so we stuck with only two. Next, we interrogate the **Count** property of the collection and display this in a message box. When we run our program, we should see two bound items (i.e. both of the text boxes we inserted using the **Add** method).

Showing the Reason and Status of the ADO Recordset MoveComplete Event

This simply sets the Boolean variable, **showInfo**, in our class to true or false. When the user checks the check box, we set the **displayMoveComplete** property to true (the value of the check box). Now when the user moves to the next record, our message box in the class will be displayed.

10 Add this code to the form's **Check1_Click** event:

```
Private Sub Check1_Click()
clsBoundClass.displayMoveComplete = Check1.Value
End Sub
```

An Easy Choice for the User

11 To keep things fairly simple, we just permit the user to move to the next record in the recordset. Add the following code to the **cmdMoveNext** button's **Click** event:

```
Private Sub cmdMoveNext_Click()
clsBoundClass.MoveNext
End Sub
```

When the **cmdMoveNext** command button is clicked, we call the **MoveNext** event in our class. The record pointer is moved to the next record and the two bound text boxes display the contents of the **PubID** and **Name** fields for that record.

Running the Program

12 OK, be sure to save your project. Press *F5* to run the program:

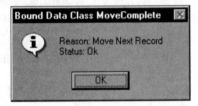

When the BindingCollection is initialized, we display how many items are in the collection in the form's **Load** event. As we expected, there are two (because we have added two text boxes to the collection).

13 Click OK to dismiss the message box and allow the form to display itself. The user can click the <u>M</u>ove Next button to display the two fields from the next record.

Now check the check box. Each time the <u>M</u>ove Next button is clicked, the following message box is displayed:

We are intercepting the enumerated values for both the **Reason** and **Status** variables passed into the **MoveComplete** event in our class.

14 Now close down the program. When you end the program, press *F2* to bring up the Object Browser:

Select the **ADODB** choice in the top drop-down box. I bet you were wondering how to find the enumerated constants for the **Reason** and **Status** but were afraid to ask. Well, this is yet another example of where the Object Browser is invaluable.

> *I remember when the Internet Explorer 3.0 came out. You could program it using VB, but the documentation was as scarce as hen's teeth. So I simply created an object variable of type IE and looked at the object browser. Everything was there in plain view! You could see all of the events, properties, methods and constants. Its helpful to think of the Object Browser as your universal reference for any object you may need to program.*

Let's Recap

Let's just take a moment to reflect on what we have just accomplished. We created a class module. New with VB6, we can have the class be a data provider by simply setting the **DataSourceBehavior** property. VB then automatically adds a **GetDataMember** sub for us. We can then set up an ADO connection and recordset within the class, build a few properties, and then instantiate the class in a form. Using the built-in **BindingCollection**, we can add controls to be bound, using our class module as the **DataSource** of the collection. Not too shabby!

The downside, of course, is that if you want to use something like this in a production environment, you probably need to do more than move forward a single record at a time. We might want to go backwards, edit, add, delete and all of the things that our users might want. Well, let's go to the next step and create our own data control that will actually do all of those things for us.

Creating Our Own Data Control

What we are going to do now is create our own **ActiveX ADO bound data control** that is based on the data class we developed earlier in this book. We will build it and compile it into an **.ocx** file that can be readily distributed to anyone - on disk or even over the Internet.

Try It Out - Building Our Own Data Control

1 Start a new project. But this time, instead of selecting a Standard EXE, be sure to choose ActiveX Control as the project type, as in this screenshot:

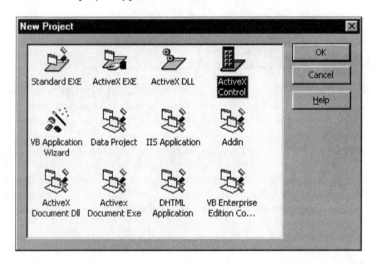

When you select this option, VB 6.0 places what is called an **ActiveX designer** form on the screen. While it looks like a standard form, it is actually the foundation for our new control:

VB also creates a new Project Explorer file with an icon of an ActiveX control. There is also a single folder, User Controls, with a single UserControl designer added:

2   Click on the UserControl1 to give it focus and press *F4* to bring up the Properties box. Change the name of **UserControl1** to **dbCtl**. Save the new project as **dataCtl.vbp**. And when you are prompted to save the control, save it as **dbCtl** as well (keeping the name of the control and the file used to store it the same makes things easier to manage).

3   We will be using ADO recordsets within our control. So from the VB main menu, select Project | References. Again, be sure to choose the Microsoft ActiveX Data Objects 2.0 Library so our control has reference to this library:

If we don't do this, our control won't know what an ADO recordset is.

OK, back to our control. In order to attach all the capabilities we need for this control, we want to create a control array of command buttons on the ActiveX Control designer form. This should be familiar to you from when we built our class module earlier in the book.

4   Draw a command button on your form (Oops! I mean *designer*) from the tool palette and change the name to **cmdButton**. Then highlight the button, copy it, and then paste it back to the designer form. You will be asked if you want to create a control array of **cmdButton** controls:

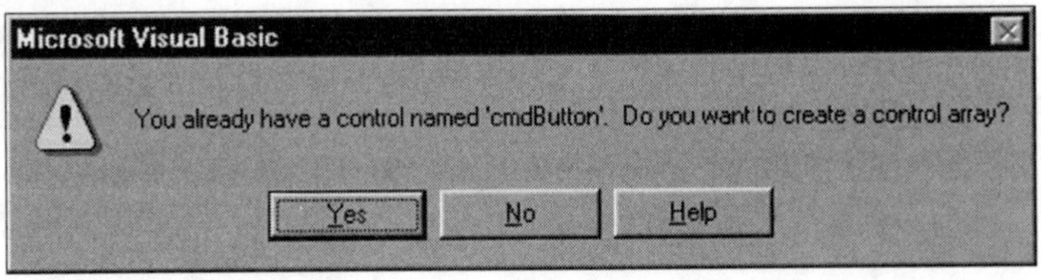

> **Microsoft Visual Basic**
>
> ⚠ You already have a control named 'cmdButton'. Do you want to create a control array?
>
> [Yes]   [No]   [Help]

Click on <u>Y</u>es.

5 Repeat the button-copying process until you have nine **cmdButtons** on the form, numbered 0 through 8, and lay them out as shown. Then draw a label on the designer and name it **lblControl**. Change the label's caption so that it's blank, and set its BorderStyle to 1 – Fixed Single.

> **dataCtl - dbCtl (UserControl)**
>
> | |<< | << | >> | >>| | |
> | Add New | Edit | Save | Delete | Undo |

6 Set the **Caption** properties of the buttons according to the table below:

Control	Caption Property
cmdButton(0)	|<<
cmdButton(1)	<<
cmdButton(2)	>>
cmdButton(3)	>>|
cmdButton(4)	&Add New
cmdButton(5)	&Edit
cmdButton(6)	&Save
cmdButton(7)	&Delete
cmdButton(8)	&Undo

7 When the buttons and the label are arranged, resize the designer as shown in the screenshot above. This will be the size of the control when a user (another programmer) draws it on a form. When we complete the control, it will actually show up as an icon in the programmer's tool palette right alongside the others.

Now we're going to write some code to enhance the control.

8 The control has a general area, just like a standard form. In the general area of the form, add the following code:

```
Option Explicit
'-- Default Property Values
Const m_def_connectionString = ""
Const m_def_recordSource = ""

'-- Property Variables. These will be read from the property bag
Dim m_connectionString As String
Dim m_recordSource As String
Dim m_form As Object          '—the form that hosts our control
Dim lTotalRecords As Long     '—holds the current number of records

'-- Keep our control a constant size
Private Const m_def_Height = 80
Private Const m_def_Width = 452

'--Values for our navigation and editing buttons
Public Enum cmdButtons
  cmdMoveFirst = 0
  cmdMovePrevious = 1
  cmdMoveNext = 2
  cmdMoveLast = 3
  cmdAddNew = 4
  cmdEdit = 5
  cmdSave = 6
  cmdDelete = 7
  cmdUndo = 8
End Enum

'--Values for our current edit status
Private Enum editMode
  nowStatic = 0
  nowEditing = 1
  nowAdding = 2
End Enum

Dim editStatus As editMode


'Declare our object variables for the ADO connection
'and the recordset used in the control
Private adoConnection As ADODB.Connection
Private adoRecordset As ADODB.RecordSet
Public Event validateRecord(ByVal operation As String, ByRef cancel As Boolean)
```

How It Works

Controls are special animals in a few respects. First, they must remember certain properties. For example, in a standard project say you draw a button on a form and in design mode, you change the caption to "Hello". Well, when the program is run, we expect the caption to be there, right? There must be some way for a control to remember properties that are set during design time that will be remembered when the control is run.

> *Actually, as mentioned earlier in the book, controls are 'always' running. Yes, when you are in design mode, the controls you are using are actually running chunks of code. You set properties in design mode and then, when you run the program, the control saves the new property values, destroys itself, and reincarnates itself on the running form. When it springs to life in run mode, it reads the properties the programmer set and uses those instead of the default values. That's how a caption property, for example, will say "Hello" in run mode instead of the default "Command1". The control provides a means of saving those properties with something called a PropertyBag. We will examine this shortly.*

Notice that when you draw a command button on a form, it has some default properties. For example, the default **Caption** is **Command1**. Likewise, for our own new bound data control, we must set some default properties. We will allow the user to specify a **ConnectionString** and **RecordSource**. So these two properties need default properties. The convention for control variables is **m_** for member, **def_** for default, followed by the name of the property:

```
'-- Default Property Values
Const m_def_connectionString = ""
Const m_def_recordSource = ""
```

When the user of our control sets these properties, the value gets assigned to working variables. These are named as **m_*variableName***. This way we can differentiate between the default and working variable values:

```
'-- Property Variables. These will be read from the property bag
Dim m_connectionString As String
Dim m_recordSource As String
Dim m_form As Object          '--the form that hosts our control
Dim lTotalRecords As Long     '--holds the current number of records
```

We will use the variable **lTotalRecords** to hold the number of records in the current recordset managed by our control. Since we will be using this variable often, for updating a label, it's much quicker to read a variable than to reference the **RecordCount** property of the ADO recordset.

Keeping the Control at a Constant Size

When the user draws our ActiveX control on a form, we want it to be a specific size. In other words, we don't want the user to shrink the control so some of the buttons are cut off, or to stretch it so the control takes up more form real estate than is really required. We will set the size to a constant value when the control is resized. This will permit our control to act like the timer control. It is a fixed size and can't be changed:

```
'-- Keep our control a constant size --
Private Const m_def_Height = 80
Private Const m_def_Width = 452
```

9 Your mileage may vary on the exact size of the control. Once you have it laid out the way you want, bring up the property box of the control. Set the ScaleMode to 3-Pixel. Then note the **ScaleHeight** and **ScaleWidth** sizes and set your constants **m_def_Height** and **m_def_Width** variables to the sizes shown in the property box. The control above has a **ScaleHeight** of **80** and a **ScaleWidth** of **452**:

Now no matter how much the user tries, whenever the control is first drawn or resized, it will snap back to the size that we have defined:

In the code, we then just have a few additional variables and the now familiar enumerated values for the command buttons. So you already know how they work.

Another thing we must also do is manually track the edit status of the recordset. Why can't we just check the **adoRecordset.EditMode** as we normally do? Good question! Since we are really operating in a level of indirection (the bound control actually holds the data field and we don't have any control over what fields will be bound), the **EditMode** is not always set when we need it. This can lead to erratic results. In all other cases, we could just read the **EditMode** and be done with it - letting ADO do the work. But in our control we must track the current state of the recordset. So the easiest way to accomplish this is to create enumerated constants for each of the three possible states of the recordset:

```
'--Values for our current edit status
Private Enum editMode
  nowStatic = 0
  nowEditing = 1
  nowAdding = 2
End Enum
```

To make our life as easy as possible, we define a form level variable, **editStatus** of type **editMode**. This means that the variable can only hold one of the three states we defined:

```
Dim editStatus As editMode
```

One of the really handy features of using enumerated constants is that not only will VB stop us setting it to a wrong value, but it is smart enough to display the 'legal' options available. Since we dimensioned **editStatus** as a type **editMode**, the three **editMode** options are displayed for us:

```
dataCtl - dbCtl (Code)

cmdButton                      Click

    Private Sub cmdButton_Click(Index As Integer)


    if editstatus =
                      nowadding
                      nowEditing
                      nowStatic
```

Neat, eh?

But the workhorses of the control will be the ADO **connection object** and the ADO **recordset object**. Our control will create the ADO recordset and use it internally to manage the data requested by the user. So we create two private variables to hold both of these objects:

```
'Declare our object variables for the ADO connection
'and the recordset used in the control
Private adoConnection As ADODB.Connection
Private adoRecordset As ADODB.RecordSet
```

We need some way to notify the host when a data operation is taking place. For example, the programmer using our control needs some place to enter data validation code to cater for when the user attempts to save a record. Let's say that the user tries to save a record with a blank field. Well, we will raise the event **validateRecord** on certain data events, such as saving a record. The programmer can then cancel the operation if the entries in the text boxes don't meet the specified data validation criteria. So by defining this event, we can raise it within the host form. Just like the normal events on other controls, we now have the ability to raise an event in the host.

A Word on Declaring and Raising Events

It used to be that 'Events' were acts of God. By that I mean that events were givens – they were just 'there'. If we wanted to add another event, we were out of luck. But since VB 5.0, we now have the ability to raise our own events. We first declare the event 'signature' that we wish to raise. This is **Public**, and is placed in the General Declarations section of the code module:

```
Public Event validateRecord(ByVal operation As String, ByRef cancel As Boolean)
```

You can declare event arguments just as you do arguments for procedures. However, there are just a few exceptions. For example, events cannot have named arguments, optional arguments, or ParamArray arguments. Events do not have return values like functions do.

So this declaration will permit us to raise an actual event, called **validateRecord**, in the form that is hosting our control. Whenever we want to raise this event from within our class, we can simply use the **RaiseEvent** function. For example, a bit later in the code we raise an event when the user attempts to add a record. We raise the **validateRecord** event and pass the string **"Add"** and a Boolean **bCancel** as parameters:

```
RaiseEvent validateRecord("Add", bCancel)
```

When we raise the event, the **validateRecord** event 'fires' in the form hosting our control. The string literal **"Add"** is passed to the form so the programmer knows which database operation raised the event. We also pass in **bCancel** so the user can either permit the add operation to proceed normally, or set **bCancel** to false to cancel the operation. We pass **bCancel** to the host form's event **ByRef**. This means that we pass in the memory location of the variable. This way, from within the form itself, the user can change the actual value of this variable. This way, when the code returns to our class module, we can interrogate the value of **bCancel**. If it is false, we proceed with the code in the class module. If false, we can abort the **Add**.

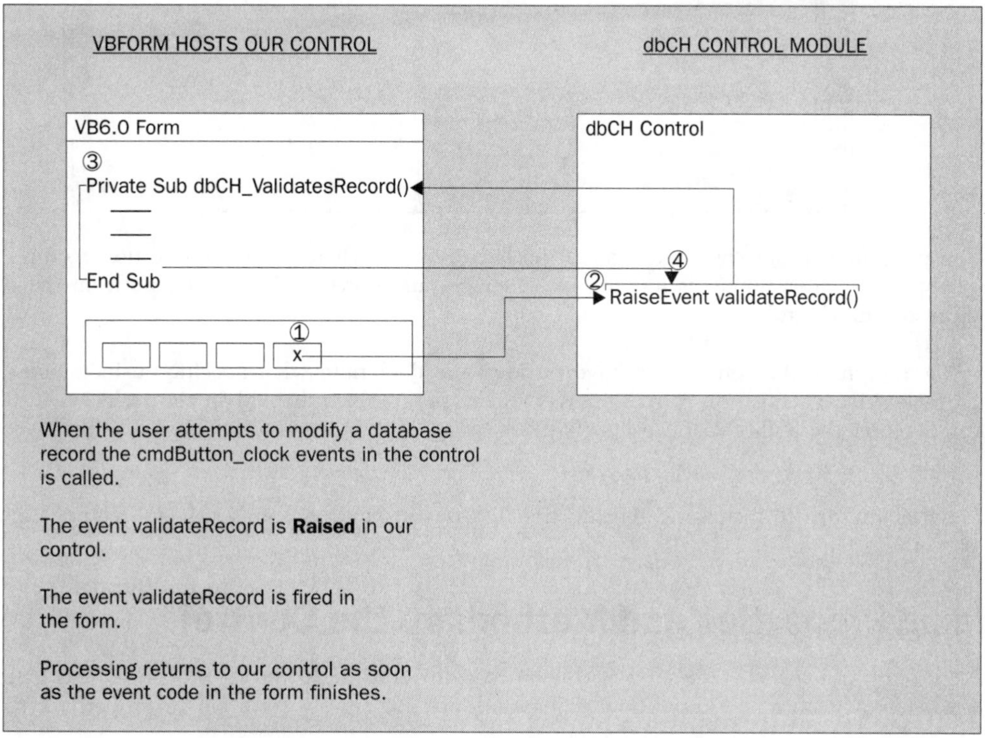

When the user attempts to modify a database record the cmdButton_clock events in the control is called.

The event validateRecord is **Raised** in our control.

The event validateRecord is fired in the form.

Processing returns to our control as soon as the event code in the form finishes.

By adding this event, the programmer can place code in the **validateRecord** event that will now be automatically placed within the form itself. The programmer can place form-specific code to validate the **Add** operation. If the validation passes, the programmer allows the add to take place. If they wish to disallow the add, the programmer (within the form itself) simply takes evasive action by setting **bCancel** to false.

Once our control is added to the form, the **validateRecord** event is automatically added as shown - the programmer can take any action that may be required for that particular form. This way, we can provide a generalized control that gives the programmer total control over it's operation - right from the form! Cool. This screen shot shows how the event shows up in the host form:

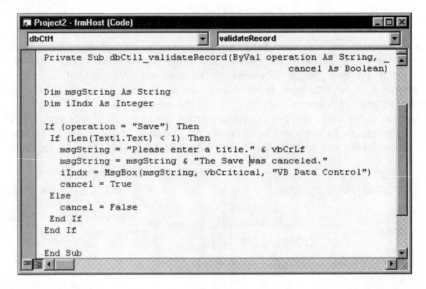

The programmer can choose to ignore the event, or do whatever the application requires. In this example, the programmer is looking for when the user presses the <u>S</u>ave button on the control array of our control.

While designing the control, we have no idea ahead of time what specific business rules might be required. So we simply turn this over to the programmer to add in the form event. So you can see that the ability to raise events gives us an extra dimension of flexibility that we can add to our control.

Now let's return to increasing the functionality of our control, and set up its methods and properties.

Adding Properties and Methods to the Control

Now our variables are defined, we can proceed to write the control's properties and methods. In order for our control to know how to handle data, we simply set a single property. Let's do it.

Try It Out - Adding a Property to Our Control

1 Bring up the property box for the **dbCtl** control and set the DataSourceBehavior property to 1 – vbDataSource:

As in the previous example that we worked through with our simple bound controls, setting this property will automatically add a new subroutine to our control - the **GetDataMember** subroutine. This is the main routine for creating our connection and recordset. We need to put some detail into this subroutine.

2 Bring up the **UserControl_GetDataMember** subroutine and add the following code:

```
Private Sub UserControl_GetDataMember(DataMember As String, Data As Object)
Dim iReturn As Integer

On Error GoTo ohno

'--Reasonability test --
If (adoRecordset Is Nothing) Or (adoConnection Is Nothing) Then
  If Trim$(m_connectionString) = "" Then
    iReturn = MsgBox("There is no connection string!", _
              vbCritical, Ambient.DisplayName)
    Exit Sub
  End If

  If Trim$(m_recordSource) = "" Then
    iReturn = MsgBox("There is no recordsource!", vbCritical, _
                      Ambient.DisplayName)
    Exit Sub
  End If

Set adoConnection = New ADODB.Connection
adoConnection.Open m_connectionString

Set adoRecordset = New ADODB.RecordSet
adoRecordset.CursorLocation = adUseClient
adoRecordset.CursorType = adOpenDynamic
adoRecordset.LockType = adLockOptimistic

adoRecordset.Open m_recordSource, adoConnection, , , adCmdTable

lTotalRecords = adoRecordset.RecordCount
```

```
      adoRecordset.MoveFirst

      Call cmdButton_Click(cmdMoveFirst)

      End If
      Set Data = adoRecordset
      Exit Sub

      ohno:
      MsgBox Err.Description
      Exit Sub
```

```
End Sub
```

How It Works

As mentioned, when our control is run, this sub will be invoked to create the ADO recordset based on the user's parameters. We first do a reasonability test to ensure that there is indeed a connection string and record source. If not, we notify the user. If you wish, you could raise an error to accomplish the same thing. But the message box serves our purposes here.

If, however, our reasonability test is passed, we go ahead and create a new ADO connection and open it using the **m_connectionString** variable. Of course, this won't be called until the control is in design mode. When the user sets the connection string, the variable **m_connectionString** will be set. Then, the connection will be opened:

```
Set adoConnection = New ADODB.Connection
adoConnection.Open m_connectionString
```

We must set the various properties of the recordset before we actually open it so our control can use it:

```
Set adoRecordset = New ADODB.RecordSet
adoRecordset.CursorLocation = adUseClient
adoRecordset.CursorType = adOpenDynamic
adoRecordset.LockType = adLockBatchOptimistic
```

Notice that we set the **CursorType** as **adOpenDynamic** because we need the **RecordSource** to be scrollable backwards and forwards, as well as being updateable.

Once these properties are set, we open the recordset. The ADO recordset is opened using the value of the variable **m_recordSource**, which will also be set by the user of our control:

```
adoRecordset.Open m_recordSource, adoConnection, , , adCmdTable
```

Notice that we open the recordset as type **adCmdTable**. This is done so we can get the **RecordCount** property and read the **AbsolutePosition** property to update our **lblCaption** as the user navigates the recordset:

```
adoRecordset.Open m_recordSource, adoConnection, , , adCmdTable

lTotalRecords = adoRecordset.RecordCount

adoRecordset.MoveFirst
```

Once our recordset is created, a call to **cmdButton_Click (cmdMoveFirst)** will move the recordset to the first record. And the code will enable/disable the appropriate buttons on our control, just like our data class did. Then, finally, we set the **Data** object variable to our new open recordset. This is what VB uses to permit our control to work with the recordset automatically:

```
Call cmdButton_Click(cmdMoveFirst)

Set Data = adoRecordset
```

What About When Our RecordSource Isn't a Table?

Since we are opening a table, all of the properties we need are available to us. However, if we opened the ADO recordset as **adCmdText** so we would pass an SQL command, we would not know ahead of time if these properties were available from the data source. If we did not know, we could use the **Supports** property of the ADO record source and test for what we need. VB will show us the list of enumerated Cursor options for that recordset. We would then have to test for each of the particular options we needed. If the property were not supported, we would have to write code to handle it:

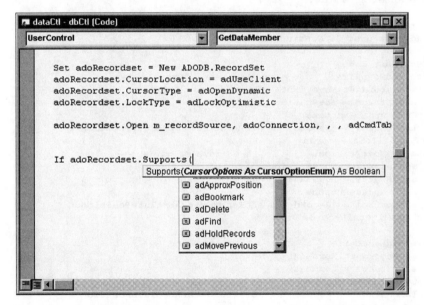

So instead of adding a lot of extra code that would take away from the essence of the control, for now we will permit the user to only select tables. Once the control is working, you could easily test to see if the recordset supported bookmarks, etc. using this property. Then you could enhance the control to handle *any* SQL statement. But since we are opening a table, we know that the properties we need are supported.

On To the cmdButton Control Array

Remember the interesting thing about control arrays - they all share the same code. So bring up the code window and select the **Click** event for the **cmdButton** control array. When the user clicks any of our nine buttons, this code will be invoked and the number of the button pressed will be passed to this sub from VB. We then handle each button individually just as we did in our data class a few chapters back.

This is the longest sub for our control, but it does an awful lot of work for us. After we have added the code we will discuss what is going on in each part of this sub.

Try It Out - Adding Code to the cmdButton_Click Event

1 Bring up the code window for the **cmdButton_Click** event and add the following code:

```
Private Sub cmdButton_Click(Index As Integer)
Static vMyBookmark As Variant
Dim bCancel As Boolean

'-- sanity check here --
If adoRecordset Is Nothing Then Exit Sub

Select Case Index
 Case cmdMoveFirst                 '--- move first ---
    adoRecordset.MoveFirst
    editStatus = nowStatic
    Call updateButtons
    lblControl = "Record " & adoRecordset.AbsolutePosition & _
" of " & lTotalRecords
 Case cmdMovePrevious              '--- move previous ---
    adoRecordset.MovePrevious
    editStatus = nowStatic
    Call updateButtons
    lblControl = "Record " & adoRecordset.AbsolutePosition & _
" of " & lTotalRecords

 Case cmdMoveNext                  '--- move next ---
    adoRecordset.MoveNext
    editStatus = nowStatic
    Call updateButtons
    lblControl = "Record " & adoRecordset.AbsolutePosition & _
" of " & lTotalRecords

 Case cmdMoveLast                  '-- move last ---
    adoRecordset.MoveLast
    editStatus = nowStatic
    Call updateButtons
    lblControl = "Record " & adoRecordset.AbsolutePosition & _
" of " & lTotalRecords

 '-- Now we are modifying the database --
 Case cmdAddNew                    '-- add a new record
    RaiseEvent validateRecord("Add", bCancel)
    If (bCancel = True) Then Exit Sub
```

```
      editStatus = nowadding
   With adoRecordset
      If (.RecordCount > 0) Then
         If (.BOF = False) And (.EOF = False) Then
            vMyBookmark = .Bookmark
         Else
            vMyBookmark = ""
         End If
      Else
         vMyBookmark = ""
      End If
      .AddNew
      lblControl = "Adding New Record"
      Call updateButtons
   End With

Case cmdEdit '-- edit the current record
   RaiseEvent validateRecord("Edit", bCancel)
   If (bCancel = True) Then Exit Sub
   editStatus = nowEditing
   With adoRecordset
      vMyBookmark = adoRecordset.Bookmark
      'We just change the value with ado
      lblControl = "Editing Record"
      Call updateButtons
   End With

Case cmdSave '-- save the current record
   Dim bMoveLast As Boolean
   RaiseEvent validateRecord("Save", bCancel)
   If (bCancel = True) Then Exit Sub

   With adoRecordset
      If .editMode = adEditAdd Then
         bMoveLast = True
      Else
         bMoveLast = False
      End If
      .Move 0
      .Update
      editStatus = nowStatic
      If (bMoveLast = True) Then
         .MoveLast
      Else
         .Move 0
      End If
      editStatus = nowStatic
      lTotalRecords = adoRecordset.RecordCount
      updateButtons True
      lblControl = "New Record Saved"
   End With '

Case cmdDelete   '-- delete the current record
   Dim iResponse As Integer
   Dim sAskUser As String

   RaiseEvent validateRecord("Delete", bCancel)
   If (bCancel = True) Then Exit Sub
```

```
          sAskUser = "Are you sure you want to delete this record?"
          iResponse = MsgBox(sAskUser, vbQuestion + vbYesNo _
                      + vbDefaultButton2, Ambient.DisplayName)
      If (iResponse = vbYes) Then
        With adoRecordset
            .Delete
            If (adoRecordset.RecordCount > 0) Then
              If .BOF Then
                 .MoveFirst
              Else
                 .MovePrevious
              End If
              lTotalRecords = adoRecordset.RecordCount
              lblControl = "Record Deleted"
            End If
        End With
      End If
      editStatus = nowStatic
      Call updateButtons '

  Case cmdUndo '-- undo changes to the current record
      RaiseEvent validateRecord("Undo", bCancel)
      If (bCancel = True) Then Exit Sub

      With adoRecordset

        If editStatus = nowEditing Then
            .Move 0
            .Bookmark = vMyBookmark
        End If
        .CancelUpdate
        If editStatus = nowEditing Then
            .Move 0
        Else
          If Len(vMyBookmark) Then
              .Bookmark = vMyBookmark
          Else
            If .RecordCount > 0 Then
                .MoveFirst
            End If
          End If
        End If
        lblControl = "Cancelled"
      End With
      editStatus = nowStatic
      updateButtons True

  End Select
End Sub
```

How It Works

Since we are using the enumerated values for our command buttons, we can use the familiar **Case cmdMoveFirst** instead of **Case 0**. Most of this code is familiar from our data class, but a few points are worth mentioning. The navigation buttons, 0 through 3 are self-explanatory. We navigate the recordset, enable/disable the appropriate buttons, and display our location within the recordset in the **lblCaption**. This is keeping with our philosophy of giving the user visual feedback. But we added another variable here, the **editStatus**:

```
editStatus = nowStatic
```

This just sets the form-level variable to **nowStatic**, essentially telling our program that there is
no adding or editing taking place. This is needed in our **updateButtons** helper routine so it
knows how to behave.

Next comes the code for adding a new record to the database from our ActiveX Control:

```
Case cmdAddNew           '-- add a new record
   RaiseEvent validateRecord("Add", bCancel)
   If (bCancel = True) Then Exit Sub

   editStatus = nowadding
   With adoRecordset
     If (.RecordCount > 0) Then
       If (.BOF = False) And (.EOF = False) Then
         vMyBookmark = .Bookmark
       Else
         vMyBookmark = ""
       End If
     Else
         vMyBookmark = ""
     End If
     .AddNew
     lblControl = "Adding New Record"
     Call updateButtons
   End With
```

With each of the operations that can change the database, we want to raise an event to the host
form. As we mentioned earlier, this will permit the programmer to cancel the operation if they
choose. So if the event in the form sets the **bCancel** variable to **True**, we just exit the routine.
In this case if we exit, then the status will be what is was before. There *might* be a case where
the programmer does not want a record added for some reason – for example, certain users
aren't allowed to add records, for security reasons perhaps. Well, if the user profile does not
permit this, the programmer just sets the cancel variable to **True** within the **validateRecord**
event and the user can't add a record.

If the user does in fact wish to add a new record, next we tell our program that we are adding
a record by setting the form level variable **editStatus**. Next, we see if there is a valid record.
If there is, we set the locally scoped variant **vMyBookMark** to the current record bookmark. We
do this so that if the user thinks better of adding the record and decides to cancel the add, we
can return to the record that was current *before* the add took place. (Many programs just move
to the first record in the recordset in cases like this, but the user will appreciate this nice touch.)

We also check to ensure that both the **.bof** and **.eof** properties of the recordset are not false.
This will happen if the user Adds then Cancels twice in a row - there will be no current record!
And VB will be kind enough to provide our user with a polite error message. These are the
types of error situations we must keep our eyes peeled to find and handle before our control
gets out in the wild:

607

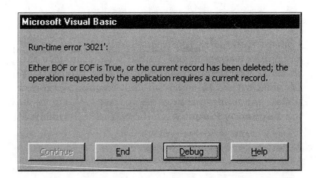

With a bit of forethought and testing we can shield our users from these nasty things.

The next part of the sub is for editing a current record from our control. One of the differences between DAO and ADO recordsets was that when we wanted to edit a record using DAO, we needed to invoke the **Edit** method of the recordset. This was seen as redundant, or superfluous in ADO. With ADO, we just make a change to the field and there is no need to call the **Edit** method. ADO calls this type of editing **Immediate Mode**. This makes sense, but we must take care to determine if the user is actually editing. Why? Because of our indirection again, when we are editing a record, the ADO **Recordset.EditMode** is set to **adEditNone**! Our recordset is not notified immediately when an edit takes place, whereas it is when we are working directly with a recordset. You might remember that in the general declarations section of the control we dimensioned our variable **editStatus** as type **editMode**:

```
Dim editStatus As editMode
```

This handy little variable is used to inform our program of the editing state of the program. It's kind of a pain that we have to do this, but I think you will agree that it's a small price to pay for the power of creating a data bound ActiveX control.

Here's the next significant code – it caters for when the user is editing a record:

```
Case cmdEdit '-- edit the current record
    RaiseEvent validateRecord("Edit", bCancel)
    If (bCancel = True) Then Exit Sub
    editStatus = nowEditing
    With adoRecordset
        vMyBookmark = adoRecordset.Bookmark
        'We just change the value with ado
        lblControl = "Editing Record"
        Call updateButtons
    End With
```

Again, we set the **vMyBookMark** to the current record in case the user decides to cancel the edit. As usual, we tell the user what is happening by way of the **lblControl** and then **updateButtons** will enable/disable the appropriate buttons on our control.

The next stage of the sub caters for saving an edited or added record to the database:

```
Case cmdSave '-- save the current record
    Dim bMoveLast As Boolean
    RaiseEvent validateRecord("Save", bCancel)
    If (bCancel = True) Then Exit Sub
```

```
    With adoRecordset
        If .editMode = adEditAdd Then
            bMoveLast = True
        Else
            bMoveLast = False
        End If
        .Move 0
        .Update
    editStatus = nowStatic
        If (bMoveLast = True) Then
            .MoveLast
        Else
            .Move 0
        End If
     editStatus = nowStatic
    lTotalRecords = adoRecordset.RecordCount
    updateButtons True
    lblControl = "New Record Saved"
End With '
```

You will recall that when a new record is added to our recordset, it is placed at the end. So if the user edited a current record, we stay where we are, but if it is a brand new record, we will move to the end of the recordset to display it. Notice that we have a **.Move 0** right before the **.Update** method is called. This might look strange, moving **0** records. However, in our control this is needed to force the **adoRecordset.EditMode** into **adEditAdd**. We need this so the **.Update** will work correctly for edited records. Again, because we are a level removed from the data, we need to gently coerce the **.EditMode** to ensure the record gets saved correctly. This is not needed when working directly with ADO recordsets. There, we can use code such as:

```
adoRecordset!myField = "New Value"
adoRecordset.Update
```

But since we don't know the fields ahead of time, and they are updated via bound controls, we need this extra **.Move 0** step.

Then we proceed to change the editStatus value, update the form level **lTotalRecords** to ensure our display is in sync, and update our buttons. Of course, we want to reassure the user that the record was indeed successfully saved.

The next chunk of code handles deleting a record from the database using our control:

```
    Case cmdDelete    '-- delete the current record
        Dim iResponse As Integer
        Dim sAskUser As String

        RaiseEvent validateRecord("Delete", bCancel)
        If (bCancel = True) Then Exit Sub

        sAskUser = "Are you sure you want to delete this record?"
        iResponse = MsgBox(sAskUser, vbQuestion + vbYesNo _
                        + vbDefaultButton2, Ambient.DisplayName)
        If (iResponse = vbYes) Then
          With adoRecordset
              .Delete
              If (adoRecordset.RecordCount > 0) Then
```

```
            If .BOF Then
                .MoveFirst
            Else
                .MovePrevious
            End If
            lTotalRecords = adoRecordset.RecordCount
            lblControl = "Record Deleted"
        End If
    End With
End If
editStatus = nowStatic
Call updateButtons '
```

There is no magic here. We just provide a message to the user that a record is about to be deleted. They can choose to proceed or cancel if they have had a change of mind. Notice that the title of the message box will be **Ambient.DisplayName**. Each and every control has access to various **Ambient** properties. One of them is the name of the current control, which is in the **DisplayName** property.

If the user proceeds with the deletion, we move to the previous record, or the first if there is only one left. If there are no records, our **updateButtons** routine will handle that for us.

Next, we code for canceling a change to an add or an edit:

```
Case cmdUndo '-- undo changes to the current record
    RaiseEvent validateRecord("Undo", bCancel)
    If (bCancel = True) Then Exit Sub

    With adoRecordset

        If editStatus = nowEditing Then
            .Move 0
            .Bookmark = vMyBookmark
        End If
        .CancelUpdate
        If editStatus = nowEditing Then
            .Move 0
        Else
            If Len(vMyBookmark) Then
                .Bookmark = vMyBookmark
            Else
                If .RecordCount > 0 Then
                    .MoveFirst
                End If
            End If
        End If
        lblControl = "Cancelled"
    End With
    editStatus = nowStatic
    updateButtons True
```

Notice that we must call the **.Move** method again to get the **.editMode** in sync. We aren't going anywhere - just moving zero records. But this is enough to ensure the **.editMode** is set. Then we call the **.CancelUpdate** method of the **adoRecordset** that will either get rid of a new record or cancel any editing to the current record. When we say new record, the record wasn't really added yet. The fields are stored in a buffer in memory and this command just throws the information away:

610

Here is where our **vMyBookMark** really shines. If the user was simply editing an existing record, we cancel the update and stay put. But if a new record was added, we move to the record we were on prior to the add. As a safety net - if no bookmark was set, the recordset moves to the first record. As usual, we tell the user what happened via the **lblControl** label, update the current **editStatus** and let the **updateButtons** routine spruce up the interface.

So next, let's add our code for the **updateButtons** routine.

Updating the User Interface

Just like our data class, this routine is responsible for enabling/disabling the command buttons. We have been talking about it, so let's take a closer look and code for this feature.

Try It Out - Coding the updateButtons Subroutine

1 Add a private subroutine called **updateButtons** and add an **Optional** variant parameter called **bLockem**:

```
Private Sub updateButtons(Optional bLockem As Variant)

'-------------------------------------
'Position    Button
'   0        move first
'   1        move previous
'   2        move next
'   3        move last
'   4        add a new record
'   5        edit the current record
'   6        save the current record
'   7        delete the current record
'   8        undo any current changes
'-------------------------------------
'

'Either we are Editing / Adding or we are not
If (editStatus = nowEditing) Or (editStatus = nowadding) Then
   Call lockTheControls(False)
   navigateButtons ("000000101")
Else
   If (adoRecordset.RecordCount > 2) Then
      If (adoRecordset.BOF) Or _
                   (adoRecordset.AbsolutePosition = 1) Then
          navigateButtons ("001111010")
      ElseIf (adoRecordset.EOF) Or _
                   (adoRecordset.AbsolutePosition = lTotalRecords) Then
          navigateButtons ("110011010")
      Else
          navigateButtons ("111111010")
      End If
   ElseIf (adoRecordset.RecordCount > 0) Then
      navigateButtons ("000011010")
```

611

```
        Else
            navigateButtons ("000010000")
        End If

        If (Not IsMissing(bLockem)) Then
            lockTheControls (bLockem)
        End If

    End If

End Sub
```

How It Works

This should look familiar – it mirrors what we did when we were building our data class. This routine is called from the **cmdButton_Click** routine. Whenever a button is clicked, this routine is called and is responsible for figuring out which buttons should be enabled or disabled. It checks the **editStatus** and record count. Once it knows the current state of the program, our handy routine calls the **navigateButtons** helper sub that actually does the work of enabling or disabling the appropriate buttons.

And if the state of the program is **nowStatic** (not adding or editing a record), then the optional parameter of **bLockem** is checked. If it is there, the controls either get locked or unlocked.

Next, we'll take a peek at the **navigateButtons** sub that does the enabling and disabling for us.

Enabling/Disabling the Buttons on Our Control

We're now going to add the code that will manipulate the buttons on our control.

Try It Out - Coding the navigateButtons Subroutine

1 Add a new private sub routine to your control and call it **navigateButtons**. Add the parameter **buttonString** as type **String**. This **buttonString** will simply be a string of 0's and 1's. Depending on the position of the 0 or 1, the appropriate button will be enabled or disabled. The brains of this operation was in the **updateButtons** routine that we just looked at. It determines which buttons should be enabled or disabled, builds the string, and sends it to **navigateButtons** to execute. Enter the code below:

```
Private Sub navigateButtons(buttonString As String)

    ''-------------------------------------------------
    ''-- This routine handles setting the enabled    --
    ''-- to true / false on the buttons.             --
    ''-------------------------------------------------
    ''-- A string of 0101 passed. If 0, disabled     --
    ''-------------------------------------------------

    Dim indx As Integer
```

```
buttonString = Trim$(buttonString)

For indx = 1 To Len(buttonString)
  If (Mid$(buttonString, indx, 1) = "1") Then
    cmdButton(indx - 1).Enabled = True
  Else
    cmdButton(indx - 1).Enabled = False
  End If
Next

DoEvents

End Sub
```

How It Works

Again, nothing out of the ordinary here. We have seen this before as well in our data control class.

So, if our control doesn't know in advance the names of the bound controls that will be used with it, how can it refer to them to lock and unlock them during editing? Here's how:

Locking/Unlocking the Bound Controls (Eliminating the Tag Property!)

Of course, one way we could notify our control which controls are associated with it is via the **Tag** property of the control. You may recall that in our data class, we just added a unique number to the tag property of each control that used our class. We will be able to eliminate that here by thinking a bit about what information is available to an ActiveX control. Our control knows its own name, so it will just check the **DataSource** property of each control in the host collection. If the **DataSource** name is equal to our control name, we know it is bound! This is how our control knows which controls to lock or unlock.

Remember that we only permit the user to edit data when they press the Edit button, or add when the Add New button is pressed. It is only then that we unlock the controls for data entry. This routine handles that task for us.

Try It Out - Coding the lockTheControls Subroutine

1 Add another sub routine to your control called **lockTheControls** with a Boolean parameter called **bLocked**). Passing in either True or False as the parameter will lock or unlock each of the controls that are bound to our ActiveX control.

```
Private Sub lockTheControls(bLocked As Boolean)

On Error Resume Next

Dim iindx As Integer

With m_form
  For iindx = 0 To .Controls.Count - 1
```

613

```
        If (.Controls(iindx).DataSource = Ambient.DisplayName) Then
            If (TypeOf .Controls(iindx) Is TextBox) Then
                If (bLocked) Then
                    .Controls(iindx).Locked = True
                    .Controls(iindx).BackColor = vbWhite
                Else
                    .Controls(iindx).Locked = False
                    .Controls(iindx).BackColor = vbYellow
                End If
            End If
        End If
    Next
End With

End Sub
```

How It Works

It is worth pointing out that our private variable, **m_form** of type Object, holds the reference to the current host of our control. This property will be set automatically by our control. Once our control knows about its host, this routine can just iterate through the collection of controls on the host form.

```
With m_form
    For iindx = 0 To .Controls.Count - 1
        If (.Controls(iindx).DataSource = Ambient.DisplayName) Then
```

Now this is a cool tip. Remember in the data class, we had to use the **Tag** property to determine which controls were linked to our class? This meant that the user had to set the **Tag** property in our class and then add that same number to the **Tag** property of each control that used the class. Well, it was simple, but still another step for the programmer not to forget.

Here, as our control iterates through the controls, it looks at the name of the **DataSource**. If our control is bound, it will have the name of our control tucked away there. We just check that name against the **Ambient.DisplayName** of our control. If they match, we know that the control is bound. Here we are able to deduce yet another piece of information, thus eliminating the user of our control to keep track of something. These are the little things that we always want to be on the look out for. By adding this little feature, we just made our control that much easier to use!

Containers, such as our host form, provide ambient properties that give controls hints about how they can best display themselves and other tidbits of information about the container. For example, the **ambient.BackColor** property tells a control what color it might set its own **BackColor** property so the control could read it and automatically blend in with the back color of the container.

Visual Basic makes these various ambient properties available to your ActiveX control through an **AmbientProperties** object. The ambient property of your **UserControl** returns a reference to the AmbientProperties object. One of the ambient properties is the value of the **DisplayName**. By reading the **DisplayName**, our control can identify the name of the specific data control. Remember that a single class can have several objects instantiated from it. The programmer will name each instance of the control with a different name. Our control needs to know which specific object it is working on. By reading the **Ambient.DisplayName**, we simply find out what the user named this instance of our control. And if the user has two or more instances of our control on the form, we know which one 'this one' is.

The UserControl Properties

Each and every ActiveX control already has some built in properties. Open the code window in your control and select UserControl from the drop-down window. Notice the various event procedures on the left drop-down box. We will add some code to a few of these now to get our control set up.

Try It Out - Coding the UserControl Properties

1 Please add the following code to the predefined **UserControl_Initialize** event procedure:

```
Private Sub UserControl_Initialize()
    editStatus = nowStatic
End Sub
```

We want to initialize the current **editStatus** of our control whenever it is initialized. The initialize event fires whenever our control either goes into design-time or run-time.

2 Now add this piece of code in the **UserControl_InitProperties** event:

```
Private Sub UserControl_InitProperties()
    m_recordSource = m_def_recordSource
    m_connectionString = m_def_connectionString
End Sub
```

The **InitProperties** event is fired only once - when the ActiveX control is first drawn on the host form. When it is drawn, the default properties for the **RecordSource** and **ConnectionString** are set to the default values, which we earlier fixed as **""**. At this point, the user of our control has a new instance and can set these properties to open any table desired.

3 Here's the next chunk of code – please add it to **UserControl_Resize** event:

```
Private Sub UserControl_Resize()
    Width = UserControl.ScaleX(m_def_Width, vbPixels, vbTwips)
    Height = UserControl.ScaleX(m_def_Height, vbPixels, vbTwips)
    Set m_form = UserControl.Parent
End Sub
```

Our control gets resized whenever it is drawn on the host form, or whenever the user attempts to physically resize it by stretching or shrinking the sizing handles. By setting the **Width** and **Height** properties of our control to our size constants (the ones we set up in the general area of the control) we take power away from the user; If the user attempts to stretch or shrink our control, it snaps right back to the size we defined. This is also a perfect place to **Set** our

m_form object variable to the name of the parent - which is the host of our control. Remember that since this is an object variable, we must use **Set**, because we are setting a reference to the object variable. A simple assignment of **m_form = UserControl.Parent** will generate our friend, the Run-time error '91':

```
Microsoft Visual Basic

Run-time error '91':

Object variable or With block variable not set

    Continue        End        Debug        Help
```

Remember, when using objects, we must always set a reference to them.

4 Another built-in event procedure is the **Terminate** event. When the user closes the form that is hosting our ActiveX control, the **Terminate** event fires. It is good practice to **Set** the references to both our **adoRecordset** and **adoConnection** to **Nothing**, as this ensures that all memory is freed up. In reality, this will occur without our intervention, but again, we don't want to rely on the default behavior of VB 6.0. It's much better to do this ourselves.

To achieve this, add the following code to the **UserControl_Terminate** event:

```
Private Sub UserControl_Terminate()
On Error Resume Next
If Not adoRecordset Is Nothing Then
  Set adoRecordset = Nothing
End If

If Not adoConnection Is Nothing Then
  Set adoConnection = Nothing
End If

Err.Clear
End Sub
```

The last two built in properties we will add code to are the **ReadProperties** and **WriteProperties**. These are critical to the operation of our control. When a control is initialized, the **ReadProperties** event is fired. This is what initializes our internal control variables. VB takes care of actually storing and retrieving the information for us. We simply must tell VB which properties to read and write, and it does the rest for us.

5 Add the following code to the **UserControl_ReadProperties** event:

```
Private Sub UserControl_ReadProperties(PropBag As PropertyBag)
    m_recordSource = PropBag.ReadProperty("RecordSource", _
                        m_def_recordSource)
    m_connectionString = PropBag.ReadProperty _
                        ("ConnectionString", m_def_connectionString)
End Sub
```

The **ReadProperties** event attempts to read the value stored in the name of the property. So in our code we are setting the private variable **m_recordSource**. The property is stored with the name **"RecordSource"**. If a value has been previously set for this, it is read and assigned to **m_recordSource**. If the property has not yet been set, as in a new control that is drawn on a form, the default value is read. So if a value is present, it is retrieved and assigned to our variable, otherwise the default value we defined in the general section is assigned.

The reciprocal event is the **WriteProperties** event. Whenever a property gets changed, this event is called and the new value is stored in the **PropertyBag** for us. These two events, **ReadProperties** and **WriteProperties** are responsible for making the properties of our ActiveX control persistent. So when a programmer adds a value for a **RecordSource**, it is written to the **PropertyBag**. Then when the program is run, the control is destroyed and recreated in the running program. As it gets initialized, the **RecordSource** property is read from the property bag and assigned to our internal variable. This is how the magic of property persistence occurs, even though our control is constantly getting destroyed and brought back to life through the cycle of design and run.

6 Add the code below to the **UserControl_WriteProperties** event:

```
Private Sub UserControl_WriteProperties(PropBag As PropertyBag)
    Call PropBag.WriteProperty("RecordSource", _
                        m_recordSource, m_def_recordSource)
    Call PropBag.WriteProperty("ConnectionString", _
                        m_connectionString, m_def_connectionString)
End Sub
```

The first parameter is the property to be written. This property is in quotation marks. If there is a value for the property, it gets written as the value. Otherwise, the default value gets written. So in the first example, if the user has defined a record source and it is different from the default value, this gets written as the current value. Otherwise, the default value gets written.

For optimization purposes, VB compares both the value of the variable (such as **m_recordSource**) *and the default value (such as* **m_def_recordSource**). *If they have the same value, the property does not get written. If they are different, VB knows that the value has been changed. In our example, it means the user entered a* **RecordSource** *for our control. In this case, the new value gets written and it is now persistent.*

---

7 Now take a minute to add two final properties, **RecordSource** and **ConnectionString**. These will be the only two properties that the user must enter to use our control. Choose <u>T</u>ools | Add <u>P</u>rocedure from the main VB menu. Ensure the properties are Pu<u>b</u>lic so the user can access them from outside of our control:

Adding the properties will just add templates to your control. You will have to do some tailoring of both the parameters and return values. Add the following code and please take special care that the parameters and return values are *exactly* as shown below:

```
Public Property Get RecordSource() As String
    RecordSource = m_recordSource
End Property

Public Property Let RecordSource(ByVal New_RecordSource As String)
    m_recordSource = New_RecordSource
    PropertyChanged "RecordSource"
End Property
```

8 Now add a **ConnectionString** property to our class. Add the following code:

```
Public Property Get ConnectionString() As String
    ConnectionString = m_connectionString
End Property

Public Property Let ConnectionString(ByVal New_ConnectionString As String)
    m_connectionString = New_ConnectionString
    PropertyChanged "ConnectionString"
End Property
```

The **Let** part of the property is fired when the user changes the value. So when the user changes the **RecordSource** property, the **Let_RecordSource** event gets fired. The new entry is passed in as the parameter **New_RecordSource** and is assigned to the internal variable **m_recordSource**. However, since this property has changed, we must inform VB so that it gets written to the **PropertyBag**. We simply add **PropertyChanged "RecordSource"** and it will be taken care of for us. Take care to ensure the name of the property, in this case **"RecordSource"** is spelled the same in the **Let**, **ReadProperties**, and **WriteProperties** event procedures. This is the string literal that VB uses to identify this specific property for reading and writing.

OK, now let's add some finesse to our property pages.

Property Pages - The Professional Touch

We're going to create some customized property pages to make our control easier to use for the programmer. Custom **Property Pages** not only make our control look professional, but they make it very easy for the user to set up our control. Property Pages are a snap to add. Before we use another Wizard to create the page for us, let's take a look at the finished product. Then as we walk through the steps, you will already have a good feel for what the end result looks like.

When the user draws our control on the form, by clicking on our control to give it focus and pressing *F4* they bring up the Properties box:

Notice that the highlighted choice is (Custom) with an ellipsis. Pressing this will bring up the Custom Property Page that we will build - our own **customized** property page. The user can now simply add the values for these two properties to set up our control for use:

We have really made it easy to use. Now when the user enters a property, the Apply button automatically becomes enabled. Pressing this will write the property to the **PropertyBag** and keep the form displayed. Pressing OK writes the property and dismisses the Property Page. But I think you will agree that this is a nice touch. We place the only two properties the user must enter on a single page.

> *If the user does not select (Custom) but instead clicks on either of these properties in the control property box, our customized Property Page is automatically displayed.*

Now that we've seen the end result that we're aiming for, let's build those custom property pages.

Try It Out - Creating the Property Page

1 If the Property Page Wizard is not currently on your drop down menu of Add-Ins, select Add-In Manager... from the Add-Ins menu. This will display a dialog box of all available Wizards loaded on your PC. Click the VB 6 Property Page Wizard. Be sure the Loaded/Unloaded check box in the Load Behavior frame is checked. Press OK and it will now be available from the Add-Ins menu.

2 Now that the Property Page Wizard is loaded, select it from the Add-Ins menu and click Next> to move on from the Introduction screen. Press Add to add a new property page. We will call this page VBDBDataControl:

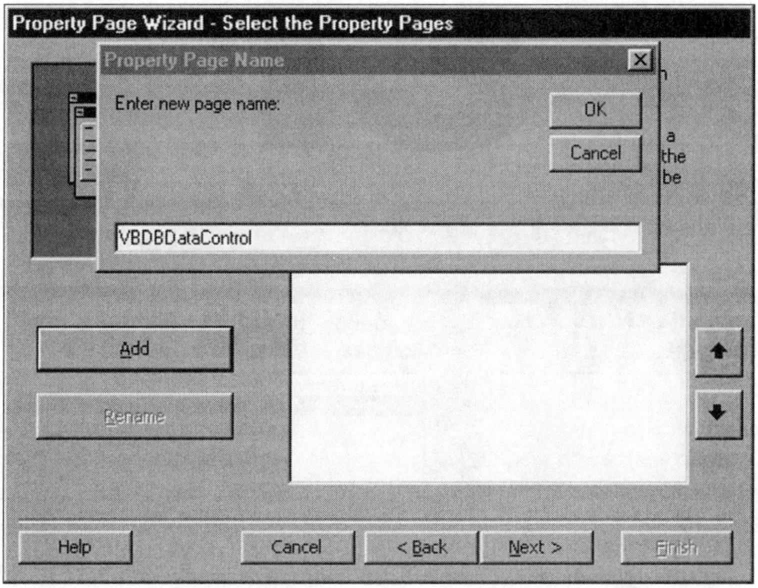

Click OK to add the page. Then press Next>.

The next screen in the Wizard permits us to select the properties we wish to add on our property page. The Wizard reads our ActiveX **dbCtl.ctl** file to see which properties we are reading and writing. Remember when we added these two properties to the **PropertyBag**? Well, the Wizard now knows that these are **persistent** properties, so it offers them as options to display on our new property page:

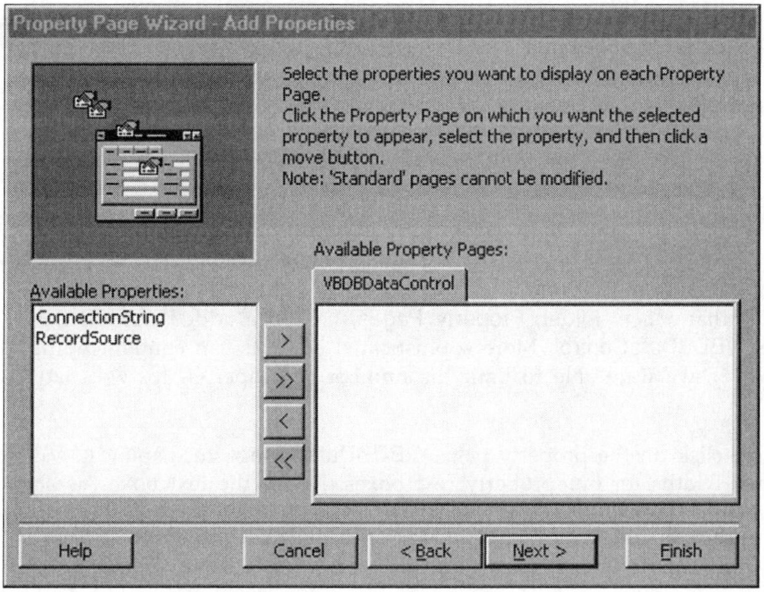

3 Select both of the available properties by clicking the >> button:

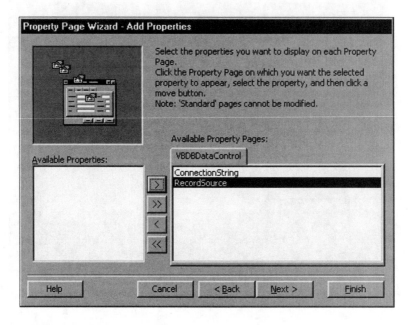

This will now make them available on our new property page.

4 After the properties are added, click <u>F</u>inish to dismiss the Wizard. You will get a Property Page Wizard Summary Report.

5 Now take a look at your Project Explorer:

Notice that a new folder, **Property Pages**, has been added. Within this folder is our single page, VBDBDataControl. More sophisticated controls can contain multiple property pages. However, we were able to limit the number of properties to two that the user must enter.

6 Double-click on the property page, VBDBDataControl, to display it. VB provides some default widths for our property text boxes. Resize the text boxes as shown:

We know that the **ConnectionString** can be long, so by making this text box wider the user will be able to see the entire string at a glance.

That's it. The Wizard now has linked in our customized Property Page and it will automatically be available for the users who program using our data control. VB has some additional standard Property Pages that could be used if necessary. For example, if you wanted to permit your users to change the color of the control, you would write a **BackColor** property and select the **StandardColor** Property Page. Bring up the Properties window for your data control and click on PropertyPages:

It makes sense for our control only to have our own customized Property Page. However, if you build other controls, you can simply select any of the predefined Property Pages available here and VB 6.0 will automatically add them for you.

The user need to know what version they're using, so let's add an informative About box to our control.

Adding an About Box

All good programmers are proud of their work. So let's add an About box for our control. It's very easy, but goes a long way in providing the look and feel of a real production application.

Try It Out - Adding an About Box

1 Simply add a new form to your **dataCtl** ActiveX control using Project-Add Form from the main VB menu. When the Add Form dialog is displayed, select the About Dialog form type:

2 Selecting the About Dialog will automatically add this form to your project. When it is added, change the Title Bar's **Icon** property:

624

I simply selected a disk drive icon from those provided with VB. This is important because this is the icon that will show up when the user selects your file in the Project Explorer. While you are at it, use the same icon for the picture in the upper left-hand side of the about box by changing the **Picture** property of **picIcon**.

The Application Title and Version will automatically be added when the ActiveX control is compiled into a **.ocx** file. However, you must manually change the App Description and Warning labels on the form. This is a good opportunity to provide a description of your control. The form adds the code to bring up the System Info box if it is installed on the user's computer.

3 The form is named **frmAbout**, so let's keep this descriptive name. We now must add a procedure to display the About box. Add a public sub routine to your control called **showAbout**. It's pretty straightforward. Here's the code to add:

```
Public Sub showAbout()
    frmAbout.Show vbModal
End Sub
```

When this sub is called, our new About form will be displayed modally.

4 For us to get the About box to show up in our ActiveX control's property box, we must wire in the procedure. Simply select Tools | Procedure Attributes... from the main VB menu. In the Name drop-down box, select our new subroutine, showAbout. Add a brief description of our procedure here as well. This description will show up in the Object Browser. So when programmers look at our control with the Browser, they will see descriptions of the procedures.

5 Click the Advanced>> button and select AboutBox as the Procedure ID for showAbout.

625

6 When you are finished, press OK. This will wire our About box into the Properties box of our control. Then when the user selects About, the **showAbout** sub will be executed and our About box will be shown modally. Let's take a look at how this will look when our control is compiled into an **.ocx** file.

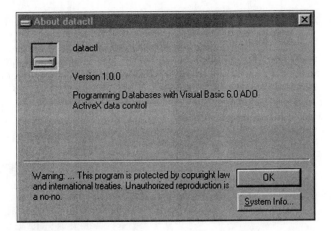

Our previous step, that of wiring in the **showAbout** procedure, automatically added (About) to our control's Properties box. We now have both an (About) and (Custom) selection for our control. When the user selects (About), our new about form is displayed in all its glory:

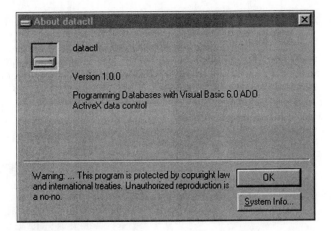

While we're adding functions that help the user out, let's add an enhancement that center-stages our control on the user's tool palette.

The ToolboxBitmap

In addition to our About box, another way to set our program apart from the others is to show a special bitmap in the tool palette. VB provides the standard blue control bitmap, but we want to make our control stand out. No problem. Read on!

1   Bring up the Properties box of the control and select ToolboxBitmap. Clicking the ellipsis will display the file dialog box. Select a **.bmp** file from one of the bitmaps that ships with VB 6.0 - or any other bitmap that you might like. If you are unlike me and have artistic abilities, you might even use PaintBrush and draw your own. For now though, just select a bitmap and press OK. This will automatically provide that bitmap as the picture that shows up for your control on the programmer's tool box when our control is compiled.

Then when you let the mouse linger over your control, the name of the control is displayed in the tool tip box, right under your new bitmap.

Testing Our Program

As you know, our control can't work by itself. We need to have a form to host it. VB provides us a simple and easy way to do that. We can actually add another project to our existing project. VB will then take these two projects and create a Project Group. So now instead of having two instances of VB running - one to build the control and another to test it, we can simply add another project to the existing one and switch between them in the same session.

1   From the main VB menu, select File | Add Project... Be sure **not** to select New Project! When you select Add Project, choose a Standard EXE type. Add a new project and name it **hostPrj**. This will distinguish it from our **dataCtl.vbp** that holds the control. Both visual basic projects are now included in the same group. From the main VB menu, select File | Save Project Group As... and follow through the save dialogs. Save the new project's form as **frmHost**, and save the project as **hostPrj**. Save the project group itself as **GRPACTIVEX**. Now when you return to your program, just load in the new group **GRPACTIVEX**. When you select this, both of the **.vbp** project files will also be loaded. Your Project Explorer should now look like this:

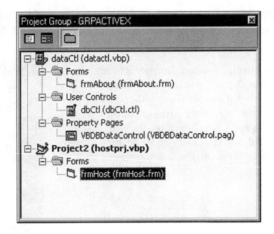

Notice how our dataCtl project has three folders: Forms, User Controls and Property Pages. When we create our control, all of these will be bundled into the final **.OCX** file.

2 Close all the windows related to the **dataCtl** project. Click on the frmHost and draw a copy of our new control and a text box. Try to stretch or shrink our control. It will bounce back to the size we specified because when the user changes the shape, the **Resize** event fires in our control and we placed code to resize the control there. So they can try to resize this till the sun goes cold - it will always retain its correct shape:

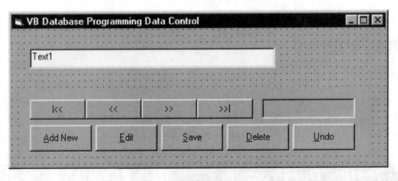

3 Now bring up the Properties window for our new control and select the (Custom) page we created:

Add Titles as the RecordSource and the key in the ConnectionString as shown. These are the only two properties the user of our control must set. It really can't get any easier than that! (If you need a refresher on how to create a connection string, please refer back to the last chapter under the heading *Review of steps to set up the ADODC ConnectionString*).

Click on OK.

One of the things I encountered when entering a **ConnectionString** is that if it is not exactly correct, VB provides this extremely verbose and descriptive message (not!) telling us exactly what went wrong when the program is run:

So if you get this message, it's a good bet that the **ConnectionString** was typed in wrong. Take a look at it and try again.

How It Works

Just so you can get a better sense of how the **PropertyBag** works, here is how the form (the host of our control) stores the properties of our control. As you probably know, VB forms are stored in ASCII text. Later we will add a form to host our control. But if you opened a form that was hosting our control in **Notepad.exe** and took a peek, you would see the handy work of the **Read** and **Write Properties** routines:

```
Object = "*\Adatactl.vbp"
Begin VB.Form frmHost
   Caption          =    "VB Database Programming Data Control"
   ClientHeight     =    4125
   ClientLeft       =    2355
   ClientTop        =    3810
   ClientWidth      =    7335
   LinkTopic        =    "Form1"
   ScaleHeight      =    4125
   ScaleWidth       =    7335
   Begin dataCtl.dbCtl dbCtl1
      Height        =    1200
      Left          =    360
      TabIndex      =    1
      Top           =    2520
      Width         =    6780
      _ExtentX      =    11959
      _ExtentY      =    2117
   RecordSource     =    "Titles"
   ConnectionString=    "Provider=Microsoft.Jet.OLEDB.3.51;" _
      & "Data Source=c:\BegDb\Biblio.mdb"
   End
   Begin VB.TextBox Text1
      BackColor     =    &H00FFFFFF&
      DataField     =    "Title"
      DataSource    =    "dbCtl1"
      Height        =    375
      Left          =    360
      Locked        =    -1    'True
```

```
        TabIndex        =    0
        Text            =    "Text1"
        Top             =    360
        Width           =    4815
     End
  End
```

Notice the two properties **RecordSource** and **ConnectionString**. These are the string titles we gave the properties when reading and writing. So the property bag works something like the old **.INI** files. It has a key - the string name of the property - and finds it in the host, which is the form. It then either reads or writes the property there. So again, it is the host of our control that is really responsible for storing the properties. Notice the highlighted areas and you can see the various property values. Our two custom properties are stored at the end of the **dataCtl** area.

The Bound Text Box

Now that we have our ActiveX ADO data control up built, we need to connect it to a bound control. Like a standard ADO data control, the only piece missing is the visual representation of the database field values. Let's bind a text box to our new control and test everything out.

Try It Out - Binding a Text Box

1   Click on the text box to provide focus, then bring up the Properties box. Select the **DataSource** property and voila! Our control is there as a data source for our text box, just like the data control. Now even we VB 6.0 database programmers can create any sort of data bound control we can think of.

Since the control is data aware, by clicking the **DataField** property of the text box, all of the available fields are listed. Our control knows about all of the fields in the **Titles** table of the **Biblio.mdb** file:

2 Select Title.

> *When you try to run the program, you must remember this is in a Project Group.*
> *Right click on the* **hostPrj.vbp** *and click* Set as Start Up. *Even when you do this,*
> *when you run the project you will get this enigmatic error:*

Wait! Didn't we just set the project with our form, **frmHost** as the startup for the project? Yes, but the default startup for our control is **Sub Main()**. Since there is no **Sub Main()**, you must select the <u>S</u>tartup Object for **dataCtl.vbp** and set it to None. This has caused many programmers to pull out whatever hair they have left.

Validating Our Data

As smart as our data control is, we still must handle data validation for each form. Remember when we raised the **validateRecord** event from our control whenever the user attempts to Add, Edit, Save, Delete or Undo a database operation? Well, click on the **dbCtl1** in the left-hand drop down box in the code window of **frmHost**. Notice that **validateRecord** is listed as an event! We have now raised our own events! This is where the user can enter any form-specific data validation. We have provided a handy single routine to handle this.

Let's customize some code for this (now) built-in event.

1 Please enter the following in the form **dbCtl1_validateRecord** event procedure that will be fired from our ActiveX control:

```
Private Sub dbCtl1_validateRecord(ByVal operation As String, cancel As Boolean)

    Dim msgString As String
    Dim iIndx As Integer

    If (operation = "Save") Then
      If (Len(Text1.Text) < 1) Then
        msgString = "Please enter a title." & vbCrLf
        msgString = msgString & "The database operation was canceled"
        iIndx = MsgBox(msgString, vbCritical, "VB Data Control")
        cancel = True
      Else
        cancel = False
      End If
    End If

End Sub
```

How It Works

Notice that we pass in the current operation. We are testing for when the user tries to **Save** a record. If the length is **<1**, then we won't permit the user to save the record. The programmer can test for any of the operations and then handle them as they see fit. For our example, we simply validate the length of the text box whenever the user attempts to save either a new or edited record. When the <u>S</u>ave button is pressed, the **cmdButton** in our control is fired and within our control, the event is raised and fired at the host. The code in the control that does this is:

```
    RaiseEvent validateRecord("Save", bCancel)
    If (bCancel = True) Then Exit Sub
```

The control fires the event and we simply perform our validation within the form routine. The code in our form tests for the operation, which is **"Save"**. If the user is trying to save the record but the length is **<1**, we display our message box and set **cancel = True** in our form event procedure.

```
    If (operation = "Save") Then
      If (Len(Text1.Text) < 1) Then
```

If we set **cancel = True** the save operation is effectively halted. Why? Because back in the control, when the event procedure completes within the form, we test for the value of **bCancel**. If **bCancel** is **True**, it means that our **validateRecord** found something it didn't like and canceled the operation. So our control simply exits the code and does not permit the save operation to take place.

Here we display our message informing the user what they need to do and cancel the operation. You could make this a bit more fancy by setting focus to the offending text box:

If you have your thinking caps on, you might be wondering how the cancel gets passed back to the control? We just set **cancel = True** in our form and the control knows about it. How does this work? Good question.

Well, it has to do with the way we created our event within the code. Recall that we defined the event like this:

```
Public Event validateRecord(ByVal operation as String, ByRef cancel as Boolean)
```

The **ByRef** (which is the VB default) is the answer. If we pass in the cancel variable **ByVal** (by value), then a copy of the variable is sent to the **validateRecord** event in the form. This is just a copy, so any changes made in our form would be discarded. The original variable would be unaffected.

However, by passing in the variable **ByRef** (by reference) we are actually passing the memory location of that variable. This means that our event procedure in the form has access to the physical memory location of the 'cancel' variable. So if that variable is changed, we can pick up that change in our control. Why? Because both the form event and the control are now both working with the exact same memory location that is holding the value of the variable cancel.

Our New ActiveX ADO Data Control in Action

Let's run our program; right click on the **hostPrj.vbp** project in the Project Explorer and select Set As Startup. Then press *F5* to run the new control.

Of course, you would want to add additional text boxes for other fields. When the form is loaded, our control looks for each of the controls that are bound to our data control and locks them. Using our control, we have effectively recreated our **State Machine** that we discussed earlier. The user can't make a mistake. Once our control has all of the bells and whistles we wish to add, then making up a nice human/machine interface - the window between the database and the user - becomes a snap.

Next, let's look at how we package up our control so that we can let other people use it.

Building the .OCX for Distribution

When you are satisfied with your control, it's time to build it into an **.OCX** file.

Try It Out - Making Our Control into a Distributable File

1 Select the **dataCtl.vbp** project so it gets focus. Next, select File-Make dataCtl.ocx... from the VB menu. The Make Project dialog is displayed:

2 Keep the name dataCtl. Press the Options... button to bring up the Project Properties box:

3 This is where we put the final touches on the attributes of our **.ocx** control. Since we added the disk drive icon to our frmAbout form, we will select that in the Icon drop-down box. It is also a good idea to add information for each of the Type choices in the Version Information frame. This is so a user can right click on our **.ocx** file and get information on our program. When you are finished, press OK. Then press OK on the Make Project dialog box.

> *At this point, anything that the compiler does not understand will be shown to you.*
> *Many programmers periodically compile their control during the development*
> *phase. This is because it does a thorough job of ensuring the program is tight and*
> *well constructed. When everything is as it should be, the compiler will convert your*
> *code to a .ocx file. Nothing in the source is changed; it just creates another file, one*
> *with an .ocx extension.*

Now when the user finds your **.ocx** file in on the hard drive using Windows Explorer, simply right clicking brings up the control properties. These have been compiled right into the program. When you right click on your brand new **dataCtl.ocx** file within the File Explorer, you will be greeted with the following:

Our Control in the Registry

When you distribute your control, you can use the Setup Wizard that comes with VB 6.0. This program will ensure that the control gets registered in the registry. Of course, when you compile the **.ocx**, VB registers it for you. So if you ran **Regedit.exe** and did a find on **dataCtl**, the control would be found. VB takes care of generating a unique **CLASSID** so that the Registry can identify the control and its location:

Luckily we don't have to worry about this - VB 6.0 takes care of it for us. If you decide to take a look at your compiled control in the Registry - **Please do not make any changes**! There are many cases of a single small change that ended up in not being able to reboot the PC. So please, **look but don't touch**.

Now when you take a look at the ActiveX components that are available to your project, notice that dataCtl now shows up prominently.

We'll now take a close look at one of the really useful new controls in VB 6.0 – the DataRepeater.

The Brand New VB 6.0 Data Repeater Control

OK, now you are an expert in creating ActiveX data bound controls so I think you will like this new tool. In keeping with the tradition of providing cool new tools, Visual Basic 6.0 has not let us down. There is a new tool called the **data repeater** that can be used with ADO. Since it is brand new and you have never seen this before, let's take a look.

Using the New Data Repeater Tool

The **data repeater** is specifically designed for use with ADO. Essentially the data repeater control acts as a **data-bound container** for any user control you create. So if you create an ActiveX control, the repeater can **host** it for you. At run time, the data repeater displays several instances of your user control - each in its own row. After you compile the control into an **.OCX**, the data repeater control's **RepeatedControlName** property is set to your new user control. The data repeater is then bound to a data source, in our case the ADO data control, which sets up a connection between your control and the **Publishers** database. Amazingly, each is bound to a different record in the database. I know that the explanation above sounds like a mouth full, but don't worry. We will take each part step by step. So that you have an idea of what the control looks like in action, here's a preview:

As you can see, the data repeater control can display several records simultaneously. This is pretty cool, I think you will agree. By just scrolling on the data repeater, you can look at any and all records that you select. We are going to use the data repeater control to create a data bound ActiveX control from our **Publishers** table.

In the next exercise, we will create another ActiveX control. This control will then show up as an icon in your tool palette, just like the other tools at your disposal.

Try It Out - Creating a Control to Work with the Data Repeater

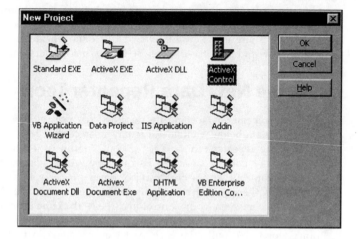

1 The first thing we want to do is start a new project of type ActiveX Control:

When you select the ActiveX Control type of project, a new control project will be created as shown in the Project Explorer. Notice that the icon is that of a control. This is a visual cue that we are now building a control:

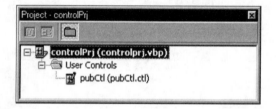

2 First of all, name the project `controlPrj` and the control `pubCtl.ctl`. We want to name these with a descriptive name because we will be using a feature that was added in VB 5.0 – the **project group**. As you know, an ActiveX control is worse than useless if there is not a host to run it in. A control can't have a life of it's own - it needs a host to care for it and feed it.

Essentially, in a project group, one executable project (the Standard EXE project in our case) serves as the startup project. When you have a project group open and select Start from the Run menu, the startup project is executed.

In the Professional or Enterprise editions, you can use the project group to create and debug multiple component applications. If you don't have the Professional version then, alas, you will have to run two instances of VB 6.0, but you can accomplish the same thing but with a few more keystrokes.

3 Let's draw the control. Click on the control from the Project Explorer and you will notice the 'control designer' appear. Again, you draw the interface to an ActiveX control just as you would create a standard form. Add three textboxes and three labels to the control as shown and then resize the form so there will be no wasted space. Try to get it close to the example shown. That is because the control, when complete, will be as large - or as small - as the form you have drawn it on:

4 We have three text boxes. Give them the following names:

Control	Name property
Text1	txtName
Text2	txtCompany
Text3	txtPubID

5 Now add the following code to the control as shown in the listings. We drew intrinsic controls - text boxes and labels - on our new control. So the text boxes have the **Change** event procedure built in. For the three text boxes, add the following line of code. We are calling the built-in **PropertyChanged** method and passing it the parameter of the variable name we wish to save. By providing the name of the variable in quotes, VB handles saving any data in the text boxes whenever the normal **Change** event is fired.

Add this code to the **Change** events of the respective text boxes:

```
Private Sub txtCompany_Change()
PropertyChanged "Company" 'automatically makes this persistent
End Sub

Private Sub txtName_Change()
PropertyChanged "Name"
End Sub

Private Sub txtPubID_Change()
PropertyChanged "PubID"
End Sub
```

How It Works

You may remember when we were discussing ActiveX controls in the earlier chapters that the host (a.k.a. the form) is responsible for saving the properties of the controls. Well, our control is no exception. There is a built-in mechanism that automatically saves any properties we choose. By simply calling `PropertyChanged` and the name of the variable, VB 6.0 takes care of saving that value in the host for us. We don't need to worry about the details. So we can save the values for the three variables by simply calling `PropertyChanged` and passing the variable in quotation marks.

As you know, the `Get` property reads the value of the text box while the `Let` property updates the text box with the new value. These values will be read directly from the database. From the outside of our control, when an assignment to a property is made, we handle it as any other property for any other object, using the syntax:

```
myControl.myProperty = newValue
```

Well, under the hood when an assignment is made, VB knows this and automatically fires the `Let` event for that particular property. Likewise, when we need to read a value, it is done by reversing the items on either side of the equal sign:

```
NewValue = myControl.myProperty
```

Again, VB recognizes that we want to retrieve a value from our control, so it automatically invokes the `Get` procedure for the property. So when we see a `Get` something, we are returning a value. When we see a `Let myProperty`, we are assigning an internal private ActiveX control variable with a new value. When the user of our control wants to read the value of an internal ActiveX control variable, the `Get myProperty` is fired. So you can see that the `Get` does not take a parameter, because we are just reading and returning the value of a variable. However, `Let` does take a parameter. The parameter will be the value we want to change the internal variable to.

Adding Properties to Our Control

Now we're going to add some properties to our control. The easiest way is to let VB do the grunt work of adding the property templates for us.

Try It Out - Adding a few Properties to the pubCtl

1   Click on the control form to bring up the code window. Then from the main VB menu, select <u>T</u>ools | Add <u>P</u>rocedure... to bring up the Add Procedure window. We want to add some public properties so that they can be accessed from outside of our control. When we select <u>P</u>roperty as the type of procedure, VB is kind enough to add both a `Let` and `Get` property for us:

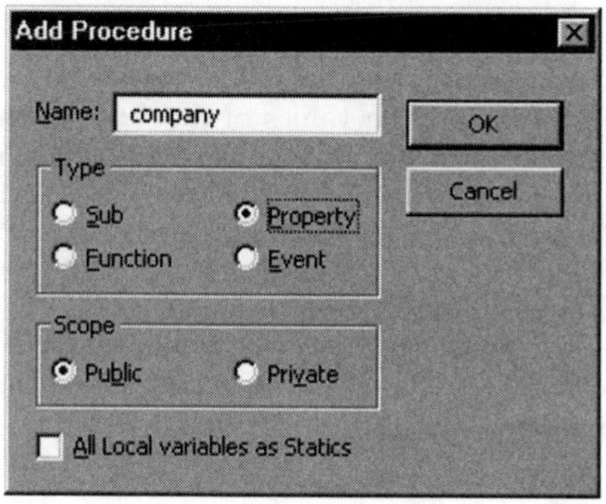

2 Add three new public properties, called **company**, **name** and **id**. Because these are just templates that are added (it is up to us to add the code to make the control do something) VB puts in default values for parameters and return values. Please take a look at what VB puts in and change the values accordingly to those shown below.

3 Be sure to change the default **names** of the parameters of the properties and to change the default **types** of the parameters from **Variant** to String for the **txtName** and **txtCompany** text boxes' **Get** properties. Change the return type to **String** from **Variant** as well. Change the **txtPubID** data types from **Variant** to **Long**:

```
Public Property Get company() As String
company = txtCompany
End Property

Public Property Let company(ByVal newCompanyName As String)
txtCompany = newCompanyName
End Property

Public Property Get name() As String
name = txtName
End Property

Public Property Let name(ByVal newName As String)
txtName = newName
End Property

Public Property Get id() As Long
id = txtPubID
End Property

Public Property Let id(ByVal newPubID As Long)
txtPubID = newPubID
End Property
```

How It Works

Notice that we have both a **Get** and a **Let** for the **company**, the **name** and the **id** properties. The **Get**s are responsible for retrieving the values of the **txtCompany**, **txtName** and **txtPubID** text boxes and assigning the values to our private variables. Likewise, the **Let**s are responsible for assigning the values from the new record to our text boxes. When the data repeater needs to display a new record, it simply invokes the **Let** properties of the text boxes and displays the new values as the user scrolls through the recordset. So by using the data repeater, our class is made pretty simple. For each text box we have in our control, we simply write code for the **Change** event of each text box. Then we write a **Let** and **Get** for each text box and we are finished with the class. Voila! The data repeater does all of the grunt work of retrieving and displaying the correct fields of the correct record in each instance of our class displayed.

Setting the Procedure Attributes

All right, now that all of the properties have been added, we now need to do something special. Because our control will be data aware - remember it will be taking data from an ADO data control - we must set up the text boxes to be able to talk to the recordset so that its values can be displayed. We want to bind the text boxes to the data fields in the recordset. It's very simple to do this, but it is a critical step.

Try It Out - Setting the Procedure Attributes

1 From the main VB menu, click on <u>T</u>ools |Procedure <u>A</u>ttributes... The names of the three properties we added will be in the <u>N</u>ame drop-down box. Click on name and then click the Ad<u>v</u>anced>> button to expose the rest of the dialog box. For the name, check the Property is da<u>t</u>a bound in the Data Binding frame. Then check Sho<u>w</u> in DataBindings collection at design time.

> *As you can see, VB 6.0 allows us to mark properties of our ActiveX control as bindable. This lets us to create data-aware controls. We can associate bindable properties with fields in any data source, making it easier to use our control in database applications.*

2   Click <u>A</u>pply to make the changes. Now do the same thing for the other two properties, the **id** and **company**. When you are finished, click on OK to save the changes and dismiss the box.

Now we are ready to make our control.

3   From the main VB menu, click <u>F</u>ile | Ma<u>k</u>e and name the control **pubCtl**. The default will be **controlPrj.ocx** reflecting the name of our project. So the name **pubCtl** is a bit more descriptive of what our control is doing. Now press OK. This step does a couple of things for us. It will create the **.OCX** file and also register it in the registry. Now Windows will know how to find our control when we need it:

When you press OK you will hear some disk activity. When it stops, the control is ready to use. As in the previous project, an **.OCX** file is created and can be included in any project. Like any ActiveX control, it does not do us much good until there is a host to use the control. So we want to add another project to the existing one. Adding a new project to the existing one will automatically create a project group for us.

4   From the main menu, select <u>F</u>ile | A<u>d</u>d Project. Select a Standard EXE project. This will host our newly minted control. We will select the **ctlHost** project as our startup and it will host our control. This way we can easily go between projects until our control is working the way we want it to.

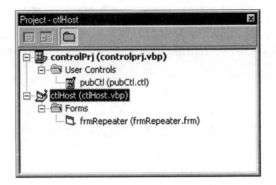

5 Rename the new project and form as shown to **ctlHost.vbp** and **frmRepeater.frm**. Bring up the **frmRepeater** form. You will actually see your new control in the tool palette. Neat, eh?

6 OK, we want to add the data repeater control to our project. This new project, **ctlHost**, will be responsible for hosting our new ActiveX control. Right-click on the tool palette and bring up the Components dialog box and select both the Microsoft DataRepeater Control 6.0 and the Microsoft ADO Data Control 6.0:

Press OK.

The data repeater control icon looks like this:

7 OK, now both the data repeater control and the ADO data control have been added to your tool palette. Once the controls are on your palette, draw each of the controls on your form as shown in the next screenshot.

Since we have a project group, we cannot work on the control while the host is open. So if you need to go back and tweak the control, be sure to close the host form.

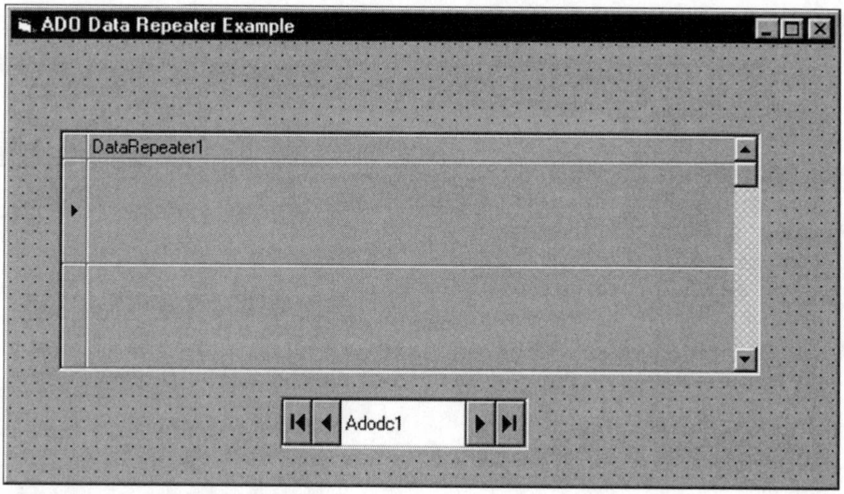

8 The first thing we want to do is wire up our ADO data control to the **Biblio.mdb** database. We went over how to create the connection string in the last chapter under the heading *Review of steps to set up the ADODC ConnectionString*. So just repeat those steps and connect the ADO data control to the **Biblio.mdb** database and select the **Publishers** table.

9 Next, set the **Visible** property of the ADO data control to **False**. We will use it to link to the database, but we will navigate the recordset using the data repeater control. So the ADO data control is important to our project, but it does not need to be seen by our users.

Now we need to tell the data repeater which data control it will be using. Right-click on the control and set the DataSource property to Adodc1.

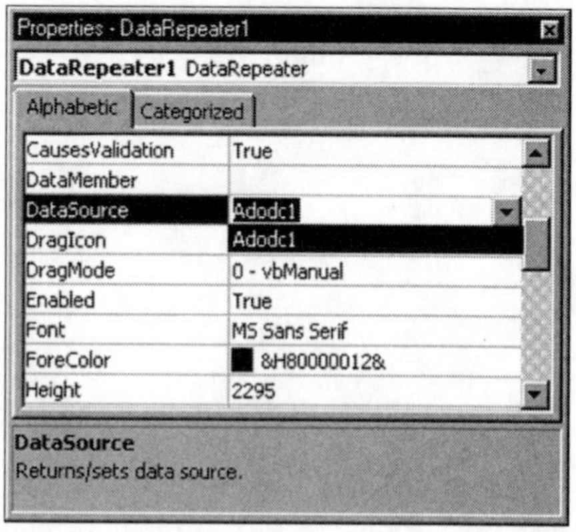

Now we have linked the control to the database. Notice how this is exactly the same as the standard data control set up.

10 Next, we need to tell the data repeater which control it will be **repeating**. Of course, it will be the new control we just created. So click the drop-down button for the RepeatedControlName property and you will see all of the registered controls on your machine. Since our control (controlPrj.pubCtl) was automatically registered when we made the **.OCX**, it will be in the list. There will probably be a ton of controls that will be displayed. So you can see why it is important to provide our control with a descriptive name so we can easily find it.

By the way, ensure that the **IntegralHeight** property is set to **True**. This handy property tells the control only to show another record if another entire version of the control can be shown. This ensures that we won't be seeing only half of our control in the data repeater:

Properties · DataRepeater1		
DataRepeater1 DataRepeater		▼

Alphabetic | Categorized

Index		▲
IntegralHeight	True	
Left	480	
MouseIcon	(None)	
MousePointer	0 - drpDefault	
RepeatedControlName	controlPrj.pubCtl	▼
RowDividerStyle	ComCtl2.Animation.1	▲
RowIndicator	ComCtl2.Animation.2	
ScrollBars	ComCtl2.DTPicker.2	
	ComCtl2.FlatScrollBar.2	▼
	ComCtl2.MonthView.2	
RepeatedControlNan	ComCtl2.UpDown.1	
Returns/sets program II	ComCtl2.UpDown.2	
	controlPrj.pubCtl	▼

11 The last thing we need to do is bind our user control properties to the ADO data control. Once our control is contained by the data repeater, we want to bind the control's properties to the record source which is, of course, **Publishers**. So this time we want to look at the custom property box for the data repeater. Right-click on the data repeater control and select P̲roperties.

12 Click on the R̲epeaterBindings tab. The P̲ropertyName drop-down box will contain the three properties we added to our control. Remember when we told our control to display the properties in the bound properties collection? Well, here they are. For the PropertyName company, select Company Name in the DataF̲ield drop-down box. This will map our **company** property to the **Company Name** field in the database. Click A̲dd to add the grouping.

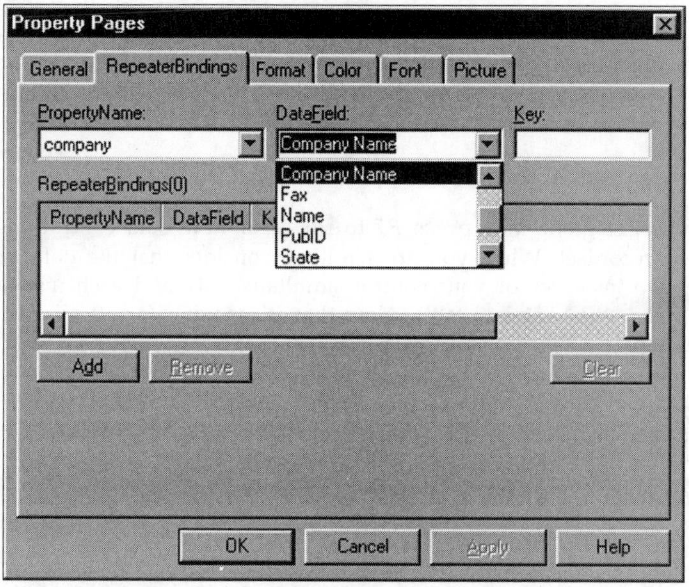

13 Now map the **id** property to the **PubID** data field and the **name** property to the **Name** data field. Be sure to add each one. When the three properties are mapped, press OK. That's it!

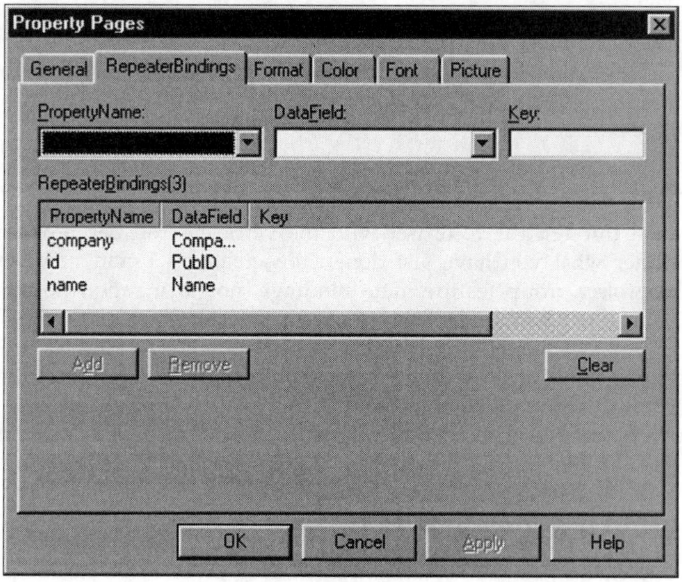

When each of the property names have been bound to the data field, your property page should look like the screen shot above.

14 Since we have two projects in a single project group, we must tell VB which project to use for startup. Right-click the **ctlHost.prj** in the Project Explorer and click Set as Start Up. Now click on controlPrj and select Properties, select (None) from the drop-down box under Startup Object.

15 Save your project group and press *F5* to run your new data control. Use the scroll bar to navigate the recordset. While you are scrolling, consider that the data repeater is actually displaying two instances of your control simultaneously and each instance is holding a record from the **Publishers** table. Now that is amazing for 10 minutes work! OK, maybe 15 minutes tops.

This next screenshot shows the data repeater in action:

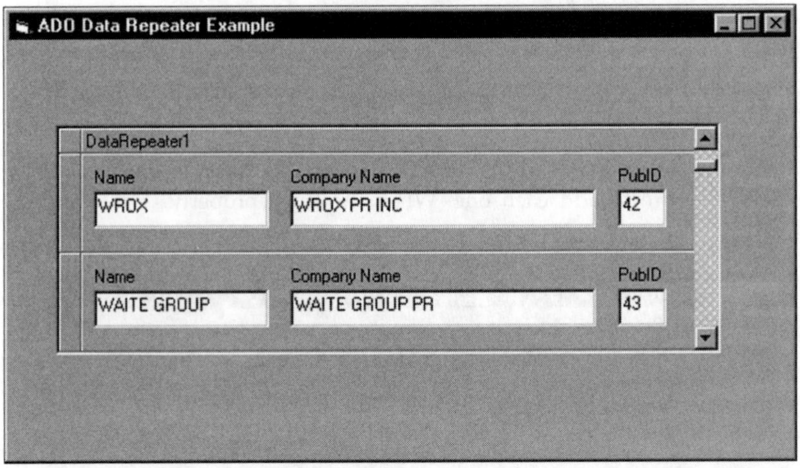

Go ahead and scroll through the recordset with the vertical scroll bar provided by the data repeater, and consider what you have just done. You created a brand new **.OCX** ActiveX control, learned about the project group feature, data bindings, not to mention how to use the data repeater control. That's not bad; and all using ActiveX Data Objects.

I'm sure that you can think of all sorts of uses for the data repeater control. We built a pretty straightforward control. You could easily build a control that displays images in a database, or tracks your personal finances. The uses of this new control are really only limited by your imagination.

Check Out the Object Browser Again!

Now click on the controlPrj in the Project Explorer. This gives focus to our project that holds the control. Then select View-Object Browser from the main VB menu and select the controlPrj as shown. The entries in the Members box that are in bold are properties that have code in them:

Summary

Well, once again we have covered a lot of ground. We discussed how VB 6.0 permits us to build reusable database components by looking at the data binding capabilities. In order to permit our control to communicate back to the host form, we reviewed declaring and raising events. Events permit our ActiveX control to actually raise any event within the host whenever needed. Of course, like every event for every control, the programmer can choose to ignore the event.

While concentrating on controls, we tapped into the Ambient properties to read the **Name** property to determine which instance of the control our code was operating on. We put a finishing touch on the control by adding customized property pages. Finally, we built an ActiveX control that was embedded in the new data repeater control.

What Have We Learned?

▶ How to create a **data bound ActiveX ADO control**.

▶ How to **raise an event in the host** from our control.

▶ How to add **customized property pages** to our control.

▶ How to wire in an **About form** to the control's property box.

▶ How to add a customized bitmap for the tool palette.

▶ How to build the final **.OCX version** of the control.

▶ How the compiled control is entered in the Registry on the user's machine. This is how VB locates our control.

In the next chapter we'll continue exploring ADO by looking at how we can use it to interact with **Active Server Pages (ASP)** in order to build database applications for the Internet.

Exercises

1   What are some of the benefits of building and using ActiveX Controls in Visual Basic?

2   How can a control contact the form on which it has been placed?

3   What is the significance of the procedure ID for a procedure in an ActiveX control? Which procedure ID do we specify for a procedure that we want to execute when the developer selects (About) in our Properties window?

4   What purpose does the `PropertyBag` serve in an ActiveX control?

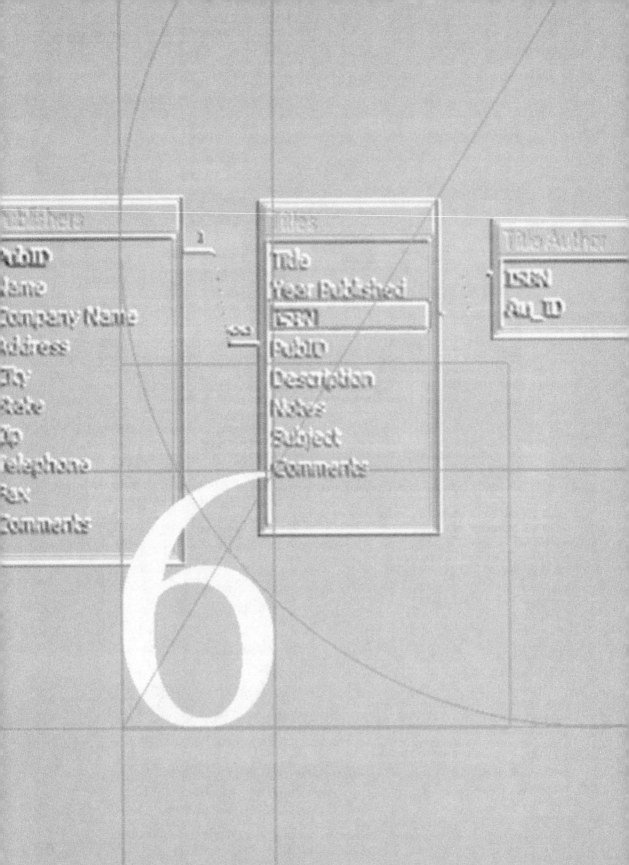

ADO and Active Server Pages

We have spent some time learning about ADO, opening connections, creating recordsets, and navigating around between records. By now you might be asking yourself "Hey, what's the fuss about?" It's not really that much different from DAO. Well, we are going to now use ADO in the way it was intended - to send data over the Internet. That's right, we are going to create our own Active Server web pages using ADO.

Don't worry. You don't need a fancy server, your own domain name, or anything like that. In fact, all you need is the free Personal Web Server from Microsoft and a standard Internet connection from any provider. We will discuss how to get set up in a minute. But first, let's talk about Active Server Pages, what they are, and how they are used with ADO.

Active Server Pages

Before we talk about exactly what Active Server Pages (**ASP**) are, imagine being able to have users request information from your database over the Internet. Recall that the Internet is a huge client-server architecture. The client is the web browser. It is requesting a web page, data, a file, or whatever from some computer somewhere - anywhere - in the world. The server is that computer that holds the information you want. It *serves* the data back to the requesting client.

For example, let's say that you wanted to display information to a user about several book titles that were published by Apress. Well, you could take the request from the user (though a web browser client) and then use ADO on your server to actually retrieve the information from your database.

But then what? How can we take the information from the recordset that we created and send it back to the user's browser? After all, each and every request will probably have different values, records, etc. Each request can be unique.

Servers send information to web surfer clients using Hyper Text Markup Language (**HTML**). And HTML is static. In some ways, HTML is like the page of a book: once the page is printed, it's tough to change. Likewise, once an HTML page is built to send from a client to a server, it's static and unchanging. But we want to use HTML because every browser on the planet can understand it. So how in the world can we use HTML on one hand but provide dynamic information on the other?

Well, that's where Active Server Pages come in. By using ADO to get the information from a database we then use ASP to actually format the page, in-flight, while the application is running. We package up the information that the client requests and transmit it to them. We have no way of knowing precisely what a user will ask for on each visit to our site, so we use ASP to take their requests and dynamically generate an HTML-coded web page to display to them. This way, we can easily send back a unique HTML page that looks like this:

Cool, eh? And you will be surprised at how easy it is. Don't worry, we are going to walk through each and every step. So by the end of the chapter you will be comfortable with creating your own ASP pages using some of the more advanced features of ADO. You will be able to do this in the comfort of your own PC - without any fancy server. Your PC and an Internet connection are all that you will need. Interested?

Let's begin by reviewing some important Internet technologies. We'll start with the language used to create web pages – HTML.

Hyper Text Markup Language - or HTML

I know most of you will probably be at least a little familiar with Hyper Text Markup Language, or HTML. When you want to go to a web site, you typically enter a Universal Resource Locator, or URL. This might be something like **http://www.apress.com**. The HyperText Transfer Protocol (HTTP) tells the browser that you will be retrieving an HTML page from that web site. If no page is specified, as in our example, the **default.html** page is downloaded from the domain - **www.apress.com**.

So when we retrieve a page from a web site by specifying a URL, we are really providing our browser three pieces of information:

▶ the protocol – **http**

▶ the host – the unique location of the resource we want - **www.apress.com**

▶ the page on that host that we want to download - in this case **default.html**.

So the URL is really **http://www.apress.com/default.html**. We provide our browser with the protocol, the location of the **.html** file, and the name of the file to retrieve. The URL specifies a unique **.html** file somewhere in the World Wide Web - there is a fully qualified URL that is unique to each and every web page on the planet.

An HTML file is really just an ASCII file that uses HTML **tags** to tell the browser how to render the text. For example, the HTML page might have something like:

```
<B>This text will be displayed in bold</B>
```

The text we will see on the page when we view it with our browser is sandwiched between the two tags: there's a 'Bold' tag - **<B>**, and an 'End Bold' tag - **</B>**. The tags are enclosed in **<>** brackets. If you know the meanings of the various tags, it is actually pretty easy to figure out what the resulting page will look like.

In this case the **<B>** tag tells the browser to make everything that follows it in bold until the delimiting tag, **</B>** is encountered. As you can see, most tags come in pairs and act – conceptually - as containers. Another tag will do something like:

```
<C>This text will be centred in the browser display</C>
```

That's all there is to it in principle. Now a single ASCII, human-readable HTML file can be rendered to look almost the same in any browser, running on any type of computer, anywhere in the world. It is the individual browser's responsibility to render the tags in the way that browser does best. So the beauty of HTML is that it is browser-independent - we can display an HTML page in the Netscape Browser, the Microsoft Internet Explorer, or any software browser. Any browser running on an Apple, IBM, Sun, or whatever is responsible for rendering the HTML to the screen. As long as we serve up the HTML page correctly, it is the browser's responsibility to make it look good.

> *When you get a second, fire up your browser and access any web page on the Internet. Then from the main menu of the browser, select View-Source. The browser will start up a notepad window and actually show you the HTML code for the web page that it is currently displaying. This exercise is very informative. You can see just how simple most web pages really are.*

The problem is that HTML pages are like the old 8-millimeter movies of the 1950s. They are quaint, but can't do anything beyond displaying static text. Of course, there are tags to include graphics, such as **.GIF** files. Other tags permit the downloading of sound in **.WAV** files or even movies in **.AVI** files. But once an HTML page is defined by writing it in the tag-based HTML language, that's it. It is essentially static.

Well, what happens if we need to present specific information depending on who is asking for it? Well, up until recently only gurus could accomplish this magic. They would write what are called CGI scripts typically in a very arcane scripting language called PERL. This approach usually worked, but was very esoteric and error prone.

Enter Active Server Pages

An ASP file is just an HTML file with extended features. ASP files usually contain some HTML tags that are interpreted by the browser, just like those of a standard HTML file. But an ASP file also contains what are called **Server Side Scripts**. In other words, the ASP file uses code (the scripts) to generate an HTML file with dynamic content. In our example above, we used an ASP file to generate (on the web server - hence server side scripts) a dynamic HTML page that is sent to the browser. When the browser receives the page from the server, all it sees is the HTML page that the server generated - it just plain old HTML, so the browser doesn't need any special features to read and render the server's output. The Active Server Page did all the intelligent work - it used ActiveX Data Objects to retrieve specific content from the database and then created a page that any old browser could read.

That is the real beauty of ASP: the work gets done on the server. The script takes the dynamic information from our database and formats it into standard HTML, and the browser independent, universally readable results are sent to the browser. In our example above showing Wrox titles, the output would certainly look different if we retrieved titles from some other publisher. So ASP, using ADO, formats the page with the specific information we want to show and sends it to the browser.

So ASP uses server-side scripting. This is where the server interprets and executes the script in the **.ASP** page **before** it delivers the HTML page to the browser. Like client-side scripting, the script source code is coded in the ASP page. The beauty is that this code is never sent across the wire to the browser! Instead, the server interprets and executes the code and sends the resulting HTML stream to the browser. The HTML stream contains the information that tells the browser what to display (the data) and how to display it (the HTML tags).

This means that we can use ASP and ADO to create HTML files that can be read with any old garden-variety browser - there are no special plug-ins required at the client browser. So even the oldest browsers can read ASP files! Your audience is now everyone on the Internet, on any platform, using any browser. And that translates to a planet-wide audience. Cool! By now hopefully you are getting comfortable with this alphabet soup of ASP, ADO, and HTML.

Running Active Server Pages

In order to run ASP pages on your local PC, you will need the Microsoft Internet Explorer version 3 or higher. Since the price is right for this powerful software - free - I highly recommend downloading the most current version. The examples in this book use version 4.0.

We have been discussing client and server concepts. We can now make your PC act as a server that can create and display ASP pages. The pages can be used on the same machine, or you can even allow others to access your ASP pages via the Internet. In order to accomplish this feat, we will need to use the Microsoft Personal Web Server (**PWS**). The PWS is similar to any other Web server, except that it is compact enough to run on Windows 95, but powerful too: PWS 4.0 is a scaled-down version of Microsoft's Internet Information Server. PWS does not require a high-end server machine and, what's more, it's free.

If you have a later version of Windows 95 or 98, or Front Page, the Microsoft Personal Web Server (PWS) is fully integrated into the Windows taskbar and Control Panel, allowing users to start and stop HTTP and FTP services, administer the server, or change general options.

The PWS is required to run our ASP files. If you don't have the Personal Web Server currently installed, you can easily download the latest version from Microsoft. Here's how.

How to set up PWS on Your Machine

The first thing you must do is install the free Microsoft Personal Web Server. If you have the Windows NT4 Option Pack CD you can install from there. If you haven't got the disk, you can get hold of PWS by logging on to Bill's homepage and downloading the PWS software from there:

Try It Out - Downloading PWS

1   Fire up your web browser of choice and go to the following URL:

`http://www.microsoft.com/ie/sitemap`

When the web page has loaded, click Downloads, and then click the Personal Web Server choice.

2   On the next screen, choose Personal Web Server 4.0 for Windows or NT 4.0 (Part of the NT 4.0 Options Pack). Click the Next button. The Microsoft Windows NT 4.0 Option Pack screen is then displayed. Yes, this is under Windows NT - go figure!

3   Click the Download button on the right hand side of the screen. The Windows NT 4.0 Option Pack screen is displayed. You will be asked to answer a few questions. There are two pages of questions. Once answered, press Next.

4   On the third page, you will be asked "Which components of the Windows NT 4.0 Option Pack do you intend to download today?" Check the box for "Microsoft Windows NT 4.0 Service Pack 3" and click the Finish button.

5   On the next page, the Windows NT 4.0 Option Pack page presents two options for downloading. Click Option 1. This will auto-install the software for you. Follow through the rest of the steps as directed.

> *Note: You will see " Reminder: The Windows NT 4.0 Option Pack requires Microsoft Internet Explorer 4.01 or later and Windows NT 4.0 Service Pack 3." Don't worry if you are running Windows 95/98. This is the right place. But be sure to download the latest version of the Internet Explorer – 4.01. Again, this is also free.*

6 Be sure to remember the directory the **download.exe** file is being downloaded to. It will take about 5 minutes or less. When the download is complete use the Windows File Explorer to find the file, **download.exe**, and double click. *Be sure to stay connected to the Internet*. This is the program that will handle the automatic installation for you. When you double click, you will see the licensing screen:

7 Read the agreement and click OK. This will start the process.

8 The good news is that this great piece of software is free - the bad news is that it could take over 4 hours to download - this depends on the speed of your Internet connection. Also, if you have the NT4 Option Pack CD, you can install PWS directly from that. But the time spent is well worth the wait:

You might as well get a cup of coffee and read through the rest of the chapter while this is downloading. The set up will painlessly guide you through the process.

9 When all the installation files have downloaded, you'll be presented with the install screen shown below:

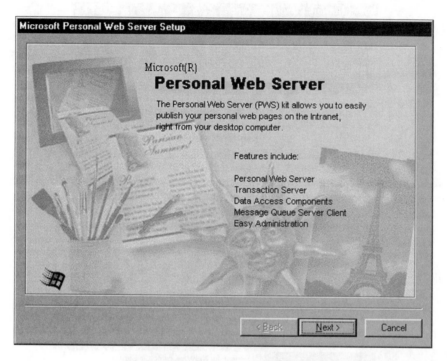

10 Simply follow the instructions on the screen and the software will install itself on your machine:

Depending on how your machine is set up, you may need to go through the following steps too:

11 Go to Network in the Control Panel in Windows and press Add, select Service:

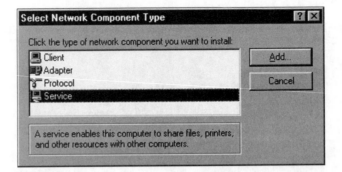

Press Add, select Microsoft from the Manufacturers column, double click on Personal Web Server, and press OK on the network control panel:

12 When the installation is complete, all that is left is for us is to start up the Personal Web Server. The installation process will have added a new icon on your task bar - usually it will be next to the time display. Click on the icon (or start PWS up from Start | Programs, and the Main window for the server will be displayed. Press the Start button:

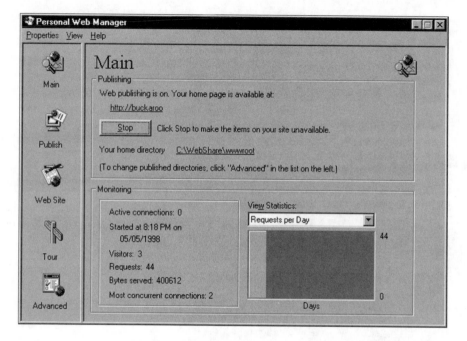

PWS will now allow you to publish ASP pages.

Notice that the name of your computer is available in the Publishing frame. My computer is named 'buckaroo', so my web site is **http://buckaroo**. However, if you don't have a dedicated Internet connection and use a dial up service such as AOL, Netcom, Mindscape, or some other Internet Service Provider, you are actually provided an Internet address each and every time you log on. Why? Because every computer connected to the Internet needs an address. However, each time you log on, the address is different. The network provider has a bunch of numbers reserved and issues you a new one each time you long on.

This 32-bit number used for the address is given to you for the duration of your connection. If you are interested in seeing the number, simply run **Winipcfg.exe** from the Windows Start-Run box. This will bring up a handy utility showing the current Internet Provider (IP) address. You don't need to know it, but it's fun to see the connection. From it, I can see that my IP Address for the current session is 206.217.104.199. Now if you wish friends to log in to your computer over the Internet to test out the ASP pages on your PC, you can give them this IP address and they can access the ASP pages you create. They would simply put **http:// 206.217.104.199/myPage.asp** in their browser and would see your cool page from their machine. Of course, you have to check the IP address each and every time you log in because it will be different:

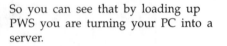

So you can see that by loading up PWS you are turning your PC into a server.

Setting up a Directory for Our Examples

When the PWS is installed, it adds a directory called **Webshare** (on NT, the directory is called **InetPub**). PWS then adds a few subdirectories underneath. We want to place all of our ASP pages we write in the subdirectory **\Chapter13**. We'll also create a **Virtual** directory within PWS that will refer to our *physical* **Chapter13** directory. All of the cool ASP pages you write will be in the (physical) **Chapter13** directory, and PWS will be able to find them.

Try It Out - Creating a Virtual Directory

1 Click on <u>V</u>iew | A<u>d</u>vanced from the main menu on the Web server:

2 When you have <Home> highlighted, click Add.

3 In the Add Directory window, use the Browse button to find your **BegDB\Chapter13** directory, and add it. In the Alias box, enter Ch13:

4 Click OK.

Now, we can use the Ch13 alias to get to the files we'll store in the **Chapter13** directory. To do this, we'll type in the URL in our browser in this form:

```
http://my_server_name/Ch13/filename
```

Note that PWS uses the alias **Ch13** to refer to the physical directory **[drive letter]:\BegDB\Chapter13**

So all the ASP pages you write should be in **\Chapter13**.

> *When you run an ASP page that your write, you must type its URL in the browser's address window. You can't load the file into the browser because it won't execute the ASP features unless you access it via PWS.*

ASP, Scripts and HTML

Without further ado (no pun intended), let's create a simple ASP script - the ASP 'code' that makes ASP really dynamic and differentiates it from static HTML. ASP scripts can be written in any scripting language, such as Visual Basic Scripting Edition (VBScript), JScript, or JavaScript. A script can be inserted anywhere in an HTML document, that is, anywhere between the **<HTML>** and **</HTML>** tags (these demarcate the start and end points of the HTML page). You will find that ASP Scripts are an easy way to begin creating interactive pages. Using scripts and ASP, for example, you can collect information from an HTML form, and generate an HTML document personalized with a customer's name that can then be returned to their browser. Since this is a book about database programming, we will be using a database to display customized information to users over the Internet. I think you will find that ASP provides a compelling approach to accomplishing these tasks.

Previously, to collect information from an HTML form, you would have had to learn a complicated programming language to build a Common Gateway Interface (CGI) application. Now you can collect and analyze data from a form by using simple instructions that you embed directly into your HTML/ASP documents. The good news is that you do not need to learn a full programming language or compile programs separately to create interactive pages.

We will be using VBScript because it is very simple and is really a subset of Visual Basic - this means you already know it. VBScript is a programming language that looks and feels like Visual Basic! You can send VBScript embedded in an HTML page to a client's browser to perform some tasks (the limitation of this particular technique is that VBScript is not supported at all on any browser other than Microsoft's Internet Explorer). We will use VBScript on the server side, so that the limitations of the client-level browsers don't matter - VBScript is the perfect choice for server-side script no matter what browsers your users have.

What Does an ASP Script Look Like?

Let's start out with our first ASP script, written in VBScript. It does nothing stunning, but simply prints out numbers from 1 to 5. This is a straight text file. This means that we won't be using the Visual Basic IDE for a while, just the trusty **Notepad** program that comes with Windows. We will be simply adding a bit of text written in VBScript to create our ASP script file.

Our First ASP Script

As mentioned, the best tool for writing ASP scripts is not Visual Basic, but **Notepad.exe**. Yep. We need to write these in ASCII and nothing beats Notepad (unless of course you have a copy of Microsoft Visual InterDev 6.0). But if you don't - no problem. Notepad.exe will serve our purposes, and it has the benefit of helping us clearly see what we're doing - some of the proprietary HTML editors complicate things with colors and automatic formatting 'behind our backs'. Notepad keeps things clear and simple, which is what we want when we're learning ASP.

Let's write that script.

Try It Out - Writing a Simple ASP Script

1 Open up NotePad.exe - or any other text editor of your choice - and type in the following code. Save the file as **FirstScript.asp**. Be sure it is saved in your **\Chapter13** directory. Remember, this is the directory where we'll ask PWS will go to find our files:

```
<HTML>
<HEAD><TITLE>Our First ASP Script</TITLE></HEAD>
<H1><B>Our First ASP Script</B></H1>
<BODY>

Let's count up to 5.

<BR>
<HR>
<% For iCounter = 1 to 5
   Response.Write(iCounter) %>
<BR>
<% Next %>
<HR>
</BODY>
</HTML>
```

We will run this in a few minutes. First, we'll discuss some of the ins and outs of HTML and then talk about PWS some more.

How It Works

To start out with, each page must start with the tag **<HTML>** and end with **</HTML>**. Our page is sandwiched between these tags. These tell the browser that this is a web page and, armed with this knowledge, it knows what to do and how to show it:

```
<HTML>
<HEAD><TITLE>Our First ASP Script</TITLE></HEAD>
<H1><B>Our First ASP Script</B></H1>
<BODY>

Let's count up to 5.

<BR>
<HR>
<% For iCounter = 1 to 5
   Response.Write(iCounter) %>
<BR>
<% Next %>
<HR>
</BODY>
</HTML>
```

Everything between the **<HEAD>** and **</HEAD>** tags contain general information about the document, such as the title:

```
<HEAD><TITLE>Our First ASP Script</TITLE></HEAD>
```

Within these tags we place the **<TITLE>** and set it to **Our First ASP Script**. This is what shows up in the title of the browser. Titles should be descriptive because this is often used as a reference to visited sites. As a rule of thumb, you should be able to guess the contents of the page from the title alone.

Next comes the <BODY> tag:

```
<BODY>
```

Everything between this and the </BODY> tag encloses the HTML that is to be displayed in the browser, as well as our ASP code in our case here. Our ASP script is not *dependent* on the HTML tags. We are just adding them here for correctness. But we will see later on that some ASP specific commands come at the very top of the page.

Next we are using the **<H1>** tag:

```
<H1><B>Our First ASP Script</B></H1>
```

This stands for 'level-1 heading'. Headings come in six levels, H1 through H6, decreasing in importance. Next we sandwich our heading text **Our First ASP Script** between the **<B>** and **</B>** tags. This tells the browser to render any text between these two tags in bold. So, this HTML tells the recipient browser that we want to render a first level heading in bold text on the page.

Then we simply instruct the browser to display **Let's count up to 5.** We just type it in. Finally, we have a **
** tag and a **<HR>** tag.

```
Let's count up to 5.

<BR>
<HR>
```

This is known as a Line Break and acts just like a hard carriage return. So the next thing rendered will be on the next line directly under the line with the **
** tag. Lastly, for some gratuitous effects, we add the HTML tag **<HR>** for Horizontal Rule. This will draw a nice recessed line across the screen for us.

The % is the Magic!

Now we get into the ASP part of our script. The key character is the **%**. Everything between the **%** tags is VBScript:

```
<% For iCounter = 1 to 5
  Response.Write(iCounter) %>
  <BR>
<% Next %>
<HR>
</BODY>
</HTML>
```

All of the scripts we will be writing are written in VBScript. Everything enclosed between the `<% %>` tags is Active Server Page code. The VBScript variety of server code, which we are now writing, can have the `%` tags sprinkled throughout a standard HTML page. And just like HTML tags, every script opening tag `<%` must have a corresponding script closing tag `%>`. VBScript is the default scripting language of Active Server Pages. Active Server Pages will process any legitimate commands that are between the `<%` and `%>` tags.

Here's the first chunk of script again:

```
<% For iCounter = 1 to 5
   Response.Write(iCounter) %>
```

So we are writing VBScript code here between the `%` tags. Using VB syntax, we are just looping 5 times. For each iteration through the loop, we are writing the result of **iCounter** to the browser. We use the **.Write** method of the ASP **Response** object to send information to the browser. Whatever we write is treated as a variant. Notice that we did not dimension **iCounter**. Any variable defaults to a variant, just like in Visual Basic 6. So if you wrote a script that had a line such as:

`<% Response.Write now %>`

you would get the following result rendered on the browser:

7/19/98   11:50:22 PM

After we output the value of **iCounter** to the browser, we send the HTML tag `<BR>`, for a hard break. So we must delimit our VBScript code with the `%>` right after we send the response - **Write now %>**.

Here's the next part of this page's script component:

```
<BR>
<% Next %>
<HR>
```

Here we place the HTML `<BR>` tag which will place the next number produced by our loop right underneath. And then we need the ASP code **Next** to complement our **For** loop. So the **Next** keyword must be enclosed in `<%  %>` because it is VBScript, not HTML. You get the idea. We bracket the ASP specific commands within the `%` tags and leave the standard HTML code out in the open. When each of the five numbers are printed, we place another `<HR>` tag to give a nice effect. And to wrap things up, we end our page - as all HTML pages are ended with this:

```
</HTML>
```

There, you have written your first ASP page. And that's all there is to it. Of course, we will get a bit fancier with the output in the next example, but you now have the essence of an ASP page.

You have probably noticed that HTML commands are really designed to specify the logical structure of the document, far more than the physical layout. For example, our HTML tags tell the browser what the heading should be by enclosing it within the **<H1></H1>** tags, but the *browser* can find its best way of displaying the heading. If we shrink or stretch the browser window, it is responsible for reformatting as best it can to adapt to the new size.

Let's Run Our First ASP Script

Remember, you must save the text file **FirstScript.asp** file in the **\Chapter13** Directory. In order to run each of our programs in this chapter, we need to have our web browser running and have PWS started up. Fire up your connection to the Internet and then start the Personal Web Server. From the Main screen, click Start (if you haven't already done so):

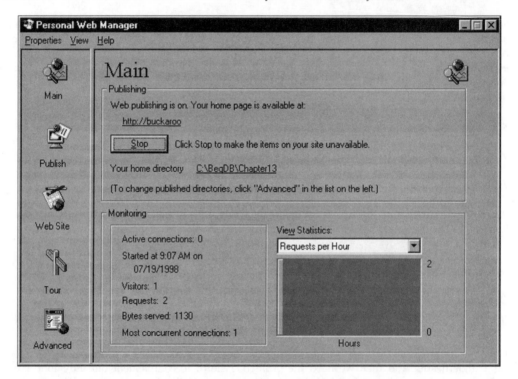

Notice that the name of my machine is http://buckaroo. Note the name that appears on your screen, because that is how the PWS will locate the **FirstScript.asp**.

Since everything is a go, you can minimize the PWS and it will operate for you in the background.

Try It Out - Running the ASP Script

1 Now bring up your Internet Browser. In the address box, you must enter the fully qualified name of the machine and the file in the browser dialog box. So you should enter **http://mycomputer/Ch13//FirstScript.asp** in the address line.

The *mycomputer* should be whatever showed up in the PWS main screen where it says where your home page is located. Again, my machine is **buckaroo**. Please use whatever shows up for your machine. Also, do **not** choose File-Open to load your ASP file because it will not run this way. You must type in the complete URL of **FirstScript.asp** directly in the browser itself.

> *If you change the file in Notepad as you are debugging you can just press the Refresh button on the browser to reload the page you just modified and saved.*

If you are logged into the Internet but forget to start the Personal Web Server, you will be greeted by the following message:

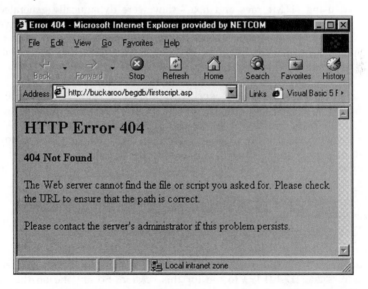

If you misspell the name of the file, the PWS can't find what you are looking for. In this case, you will get the famous Error 404. If you get this, please ensure the name is entered in the address box correctly.

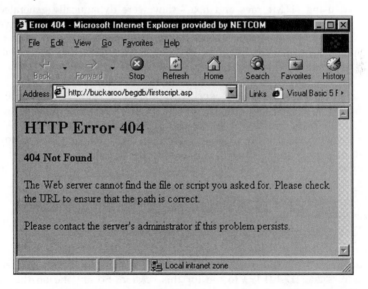

Ok, now when we run **FirstScript.asp** file that contains the ASP script, the output is rendered in the browser as shown below. Cool!

OK, let's take a closer look at the script that generated this page. Now here is the important part. If we take a look at the View-Source from the browser, we can see what it actually received. Notice that the ASP script actually generated dynamic HTML code! In other words, the VBScript generated HTML code, on the fly, that was sent to the browser. The numbers displayed weren't hard-coded using HTML tags and text - they were dynamically generated by the ASP script that was run when the `.asp` page was accessed. The browser then received the page as if it were simply standard HTML - which it is, of course, in the sense that what is sent to the browser when ASP has finished its magic is straight HTML. The ASP runs on the server and generates HTML that can be displayed by any browser anywhere.

You now you have an idea of how ASP works from 50,000 ft. The ASP script on the server generates dynamic HTML code and simply 'serves' the browser something it can understand - HTML. Neat, eh? That is the beauty of server side VBScript used to generate ASP code. We can send any customized information at all to any browser. Now it's easy to see how we could extract any arbitrary database information and send it to the client. We don't need to know in advance what to send, we simply use VBScript to generate the specific HTML code - on the fly.

> *One of the things to keep in mind is that every variable or constant used in an Active Server Page is a variant.*

If you now wish one of your friends to access your machine over the Internet to see your page, this is where you need the IP address. When I logged in to the Internet, my service provider issued the IP address 206.217.104.199 to me for this session. So anyone on the planet can log into your site to see your page if they entered. **http://206.217.104.199/FirstScript.asp**.

ASP Scripting Languages

We have seen that Active Server Pages are really a combination of VBScript and HTML tags. Processing these scripts on the server generates the dynamic HTML that can be rendered in any browser. VBScript is the default scripting language, although you could use JScript. All of our examples use the native VBScript. Everything within the `<%  %>` is written in VBScript, which has almost identical syntax to VB.

A More Robust ASP Example Using ADO

Ready to move on to a more exciting example? We will now write a simple ASP script that will display all of the book titles that are in the Titles table of the **Biblio.mdb** file. The real benefit to us, the database programmer, is to be able to use ADO for retrieving data and making it available over the Internet. Here is what the result of our next program will look like in your browser:

Try It Out - Creating the Simple.asp File

1 OK, get out your trusty **Notepad.exe** program and enter the following code. When you are finished, save the file as **Simple.asp** in the **\Chapter13** directory:

```
<HTML>
<HEAD>
<TITLE>Database Programming with Visual Basic 6.0</TITLE>
</HEAD>
<BODY>
```

```
<CENTER>
<H1><FONT size=4>
Using ADO in a Visual Basic Script Web Page
</FONT></H1>
<H2>Database Programming with Visual Basic 6.0</H2>
<HR>

<! Begin server side script here>

<%

dim myconnection
dim rsTitleList

set myConnection = Server.CreateObject("ADODB.Connection")

myconnection.open "Provider=Microsoft.Jet.OLEDB.3.51;" _
                  & "Data Source=C:\begdb\biblio.mdb"

SQLQuery = "SELECT title FROM titles"

set rsTitleList = myConnection.Execute(SQLQuery)

do until rsTitleList.eof
  Response.Write rsTitleList("Title")  %>
  <BR>
  <%
  rsTitleList.movenext
loop

rsTitleList.close
set rsTitleList = nothing
%>
<! end server side script>
<HR>

</CENTER>
</BODY>
</HTML>
```

2 After you enter the code in Notepad, ensure that you save the file as **Simple.asp** to the **\Chapter13** directory. Now, in your browser, type in the name of the file in your address field, using the alias for the Chapter13 directory. You will see the results in your browser, similar to this:

How It Works

That's it. Now let's take a closer look at what is going on here. The first part of our file is pure HTML:

```
<HTML>
<HEAD>
<TITLE>Database Programming with Visual Basic 6.0</TITLE>
</HEAD>
<BODY>
<CENTER>
<H1><FONT size=4>
Using ADO in a Visual Basic Script Web Page
</FONT></H1>
<H2>Database Programming with Visual Basic 6.0</H2>
<HR>
```

This part of the file should be second nature to you now. We are just using standard HTML tags. We display two headers, **H1** and **H2**, then delimit the headers with a horizontal rule command, **<HR>**. This command draws a horizontal line across the browser.

Next we have:

```
<! Begin server side script here>
```

This is just a comment. We enclose comments in **<! >**. However, since the comment is not embedded in the VBScript brackets, it gets sent to the client. Here the source is viewed as it was received at the client browser. Notice the comment:

```
┌─────────────────────────────────────────────────────────────────────┐
│ ▤ tri2190.TMP - Notepad                                    ▄ □ ☒    │
├─────────────────────────────────────────────────────────────────────┤
│ File  Edit  Search  Help                                            │
├─────────────────────────────────────────────────────────────────────┤
│<HTML>                                                            ▲   │
│<HEAD>                                                            ▒   │
│<TITLE>Database Programming with Visual Basic 6.0</TITLE>         ▒   │
│</HEAD>                                                           ▒   │
│<BODY>                                                                │
│<CENTER>                                                              │
│<H1><FONT size=4>                                                     │
│Using ADO in a Visual Basic Script Web Page</FONT></H1>              │
│<H2>Database Programming with Visual Basic 6.0</H2>                  │
│<HR>                                                                  │
│                                                                      │
│<! Begin server side script here>                                    │
│                                                                      │
│dBASE III : A Practical Guide                                        │
│  <BR>                                                                │
│  The dBASE Programming Language                                      │
│  <BR>                                                                │
│  dBASE III Plus                                                      │
│  <BR>                                                                │
│  Database Management : Developing Application Systems Using Oracle   │
│  <BR>                                                                │
│  Wordstar 4.0-6.0 Quick Reference Guide                        ▼    │
│◀                                                            ▶  //   │
└─────────────────────────────────────────────────────────────────────┘
```

So here we are just making a note in the source code that the server side scripting is starting next.

Here's the next part of the functional code:

```
<%

dim myconnection
dim rsTitleList

set myConnection = Server.CreateObject("ADODB.Connection")

myconnection.open "Provider=Microsoft.Jet.OLEDB.3.51;" _
                & "Data Source=C:\begdb\biblio.mdb"

SQLQuery = "SELECT title FROM titles"

set rsTitleList = myConnection.Execute(SQLQuery)
```

OK, look familiar? Well, it is the same ADO syntax we used earlier to open a connection and then a recordset. We are just using the **.Execute** method of the connection object to create the recordset. The same ADO commands you used earlier in the book can be used here. We build an SQL query requesting all titles form the Titles table. The result will be placed in our recordset **rsTitleList**. This part of the code is considered VBScript. In fact, anything between the **<%** and **%>** brackets is VBScript, and is treated specially by our PWS server, because it 'speaks ASP'. And the server must be 'Active Server Page ready' (for example, running PWS, as we are) to be able to understand VBScript. Otherwise, you would just see the VBScript right on the web page.

Now we loop through the recordset normally. Remember that the `<%` from earlier is in effect. So we are still executing VBScript here:

```
do until rsTitleList.eof
  Response.Write rsTitleList("Title")  %>
  <BR>
  <%
  rsTitleList.movenext
loop

rsTitleList.close
set rsTitleList = nothing
%>
```

As in the earlier example, we just use the `.Write` method of the Response object to send the value of the field "`Title`" to the browser. When the current record is printed, we call the `.movenext` method of the `rsTitleList` recordset and print out the next record. When the recordset has been traversed, we just close the recordset and set it to **nothing**. With the exception of enclosing the VBScript commands in `<%` `%>`, there is not much difference between VBScript and VB syntax.

```
<! end server side script>
<hr>

</CENTER>
</BODY>
</HTML>
```

We wrap things up by adding a comment and a horizontal rule line.

Let's now consider how ASP, ADO and HTML are interrelated.

VBScript Gets the Data and HTML Displays it

Let's say that we wanted to show the user all of the books published by Wrox Press. We will create a page called **wrox.asp**. The **.asp** extension tells the browser that this is an Active Server Page. We also might want to make the output a bit more fancy. So we will have to use HTML to do that. We can use simple VBScript and ADO to create the recordset, but will need HTML to send it to the browser in a formatted way. So take a look at this screen:

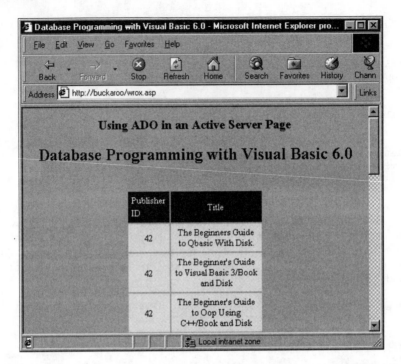

This screen is the result of the ASP page we will create next. Ready? We will create an ASP page by using a combination of VBScript and HTML for accessing and displaying an ADO recordset! How's that for alphabet soup of technologies? And the best part of all is that you understand what the acronyms mean and how they are used.

Try It Out - Displaying the Titles from a Publisher

Now lets look at the code that generated the page in the screenshot above. Open your trusty **Notepad.exe** and get to work!

1 Create a new .asp file called Wrox.asp and save it in the \Chapter 13 directory. Key the following code into this file:

```
<HTML>
<TITLE>Database Programming with Visual Basic 6.0</TITLE></HEAD>

<CENTER>
<H1><font size=4>Using ADO in an Active Server Page</H1></font>
<H2>Database Programming with Visual Basic 6.0</H2><br>

<%
dim myConnection
dim connectString

connectString = "Provider=Microsoft.Jet.OLEDB.3.51;" _
        & "Data Source=C:\begdb\biblio.mdb"
```

```
Set myConnection = Server.CreateObject("ADODB.Connection")
Set RSTitleList = Server.CreateObject("ADODB.Recordset")

myConnection.Open connectString

Set RSTitleList = myConnection.Execute( "Select * From titles WHERE PubID = 42")
%>

<TABLE align=center COLSPAN=8 CELLPADDING=5 BORDER=0 WIDTH=200>

<!-- Begin our column header row -->
<TR>
    <TD  VALIGN=TOP BGCOLOR="#800000">
      <FONT STYLE="ARIAL NARROW" COLOR="#ffffff" SIZE=2>       Publisher
      ID</FONT>
    </TD>
    <TD ALIGN=CENTER BGCOLOR="#800000">
      <FONT STYLE="ARIAL NARROW" COLOR="#ffffff" SIZE=2>       Title
      </FONT>
    </TD>
</TR>

<!-- Ok, let's get our data now -->
<% do while not RStitleList.EOF %>   <TR>
    <TD BGcolor ="f7efde" align=center><font style ="arial narrow" size=2>
          <%=RStitleList("PubID")%></font>   </TD>

    <TD BGcolor ="f7efde" align=center><font style ="arial narrow" size=2>
          <%=RSTitleList("Title") %>    </font>    </TD>   </TR>

    <% RSTitleList.MoveNext%>
<%loop %>

</TABLE>
</CENTER>
</BODY>
</HTML>
```

Be sure to save the file. Now open the file in your browser and view the results.

How It Works

We start by setting up our HTML page as before. Notice that the **
** is the last HTML tag here. We have placed it on the same line to show you that white space is not important. You can place the tags anywhere - it is the *sequence* of tags that is important to the browser:

```
<HTML>
<TITLE>Database Programming with Visual Basic 6.0</TITLE></HEAD>
<CENTER>
<H1><font size=4>Using ADO in an Active Server Page</H1></font>
<H2>Database Programming with Visual Basic 6.0</H2><BR>
```

Next, we start our VBScript to get the data from the database. Since the block of code below is all VBScript, we enclose the entire thing in **<% %>** brackets:

```
<%
dim myConnection
dim connectString

connectString = "Provider=Microsoft.Jet.OLEDB.3.51;" _
& "Data Source=C:\begdb\biblio.mdb"

Set myConnection = Server.CreateObject("ADODB.Connection")
Set RSTitleList = Server.CreateObject("ADODB.Recordset")

myConnection.Open connectString

Set RSTitleList = myConnection.Execute( "Select * From Titles WHERE PubID = 42")
%>
```

There is nothing special here. We are just building a connection string and then setting reference variables to a new connection and a recordset. The connection is then opened and we execute the SQL statement that retrieves all of the titles from the **Titles** table where the PubID = 42. In our database, the PubID for Wrox Press is 42. The result of the query is placed in the **RSTitleList** recordset.

Now, on to the scary HTML

Well, this stuff does *look* a bit scary. But we are just creating a table in HTML and displaying the information in various colors. It's interesting how the ADO code is second nature to us, but if you have not seen HTML before, it might look just a bit strange. Well, here we are just creating a table, which contains tabular data. We want the items centered in the table. The border attribute tells the browser to draw a border, but our output looks good without one:

```
<TABLE align=center COLSPAN=8 CELLPADDING=5 BORDER=0 WIDTH=200>
```

Next we set up our headers to display the string literal "Publisher ID" in the first column and "Title" in the second. The Table Row **<TR>** tag defines the end of a row in the table and the start of a new one. Once we have a new row, we add data using the Table Data **<TD>** tag. Within the tag, we give it background color attributes, font size, and font color. Then we provide the data, such as "Publisher ID" to be displayed. Next, the Table Data is delimited by **</TD>** for both the first and second cells that make up the header:

```
<!-- Begin our column header row -->
<TR>
<TD  VALIGN=TOP BGCOLOR="#800000">
  <FONT STYLE="ARIAL NARROW" COLOR="#ffffff" SIZE=2>      Publisher ID
  </FONT>
</TD>

<TD ALIGN=CENTER BGCOLOR="#800000">
  <FONT STYLE="ARIAL NARROW" COLOR="#ffffff" SIZE=2>      Title
  </FONT>
</TD>

</TR>
```

And we finish off the row of two header cells above with the **</TR>** tag, telling the browser that this row is complete. So now that we have our fancy header displayed, let's grab the data from the recordset and output it to the browser:

```
<!-- Ok, let's get our data now -->
<% do while not RStitleList.EOF %>    <TR>
    <TD BGcolor ="f7efde" align=center><font style ="arial narrow" size=2>
        <%=RStitleList("PubID")%></font>    </TD>

    <TD BGcolor ="f7efde" align=center><font style ="arial narrow" size=2>
        <%=RSTitleList("Title") %>    </font>    </TD>    </TR>

    <% RSTitleList.MoveNext%>
<%loop %>

</TABLE>
```

The **do while** looks familiar. Then we start another table row using the HTML tag **<TR>**. As above, we add table data using the **<TD>** tag. We simply provide a background color and tell the browser to center the data field within the cell. Once we format the cell the way we want, we output the recordset field. For the first cell in this row, we output the "PubID" field. And notice the tag **<%=** below. This is a special variation of the **<%,** which tells the browser to output the value immediately:

```
<%=RStitleList("PubID")%>
```

Then we do the same with the second row. Once we output the Title field, we delimit the row with a **</TR>**. We then use the VBScript command to move to the next record and then loop to display that record. Finally, when the end of the recordset is reached, we end the table with the **</TABLE>** tag. We then finish off the script file in the usual way, by ending the **Center**, **Body**, and **HTML** commands tags:

```
</CENTER>
</BODY>
</HTML>
```

So I think you will agree that with this example the ADO part was easy. It's getting the HTML right that causes us the headache here. But I think you can now see how Active Server Pages work and how elegant a solution it is. By being able to blend standard HTML tags with VBScript commands, the final output is straight HTML. As we discussed, any and every browser on the planet can render HTML. No plug-ins or latest versions required. A very nice solution.

A Simple Client/Server ADO Application

OK, ready for some really interesting stuff? Let's create a form where a web surfer anywhere on the planet can request information from the database on your server. We will allow the surfer to request a form that permits the user to request all of the titles from a specific Publisher. The web surfer will be asked to enter a publisher ID number. Now of course, this could be any sort of request you can think of. Possibly you will let your employees in Europe access the corporate telephone book in Washington DC, for example. The possibilities are only limited by your imagination. Our server will get information from the user and use an ADO connection and recordset to retrieve the data. Then we will use the already familiar HTML tags to display the data the user requested.

We will create two pages. The first will be called `request.htm`. This is a standard HTML page so we use the extension `.htm`. Now when a user logs into your server, they can specify the page `http://yourcomputer/request.htm`. However, if you named the form `default.htm`, then this is the form that would be displayed as soon as the surfer logged into your site.

The second page will be an Active Server Page that we will call `results.asp`. The server will use ADO to retrieve all of the records that meet the request and then ASP scripting will be used to format the display of those records. If no records meet the request, then the requester will be notified.

Requesting Data From the Server

Here is what the web surfer on the other side of the globe will see:

The user just enters a Publisher's ID number and clicks Submit PubID. If the user wishes to try again, a click of Reset Form will clear the entry. This is what is known as a 'thin' client - all of the software and database files are on the server. The only software needed at the client site is a web browser. The client will request information and our server will serve it up!

The Request Form Code

Let's take a look at the HTML tags required to create this form. Using straight HTML we can create the buttons and text box. Each and every browser will be able to create these. So when the user logs into your site, they receive this HTML page and the browser creates the form to display.

Try It Out - Getting Data from the User

1 Open Notepad and create a new file called **request.htm**. Save the file in the **\Chapter13** directory. Now, please add the following code to this file:

```
<HTML>
<HEAD>
<TITLE>Request information from the server</TITLE>
</HEAD>
<BODY>

<H1><FONT size="5">Please enter the Publisher's ID</FONT></H1>

<HR>

<FORM NAME="request" Action="Results.asp" method="POST">
    <P>Enter the ID
    of the Publisher for retrieving titles:</P>
    <BLOCKQUOTE>
        <TABLE BORDER="0">
            <TR>
                <TD ALIGN="right"><I>Publisher ID</I></TD>
                <TD><INPUT TYPE="text" size="25"
                name="PubID"> </TD>
            </TR>
        </TABLE>
    </BLOCKQUOTE>
    <P><INPUT TYPE="submit" value="Submit PubID">
        <INPUT TYPE="reset" value="Reset Form"> </P>
</FORM>

<HR>

<H5>Copyright: Programming Databases with Visual Basic 6.0.<BR>
Last revised: July 19, 1998</H5>
</BODY>
</HTML>
```

Please be sure the file is saved and then enter the name of the file in your browser. Your final product should look like the example in the screenshot above.

How It Works

The key to this is the **FORM** tag. This tag allows you to solicit user input by building HTML documents that contain fill-in forms. We are building a text box and two buttons, but you can also create check boxes, radio boxes, pull-down lists, and even menus:

```
<FORM NAME="request" Action="Results.asp" method="POST">
```

Essentially, the form will send the data to a particular program on the server, namely **Results.asp** that we have yet to write. Of course, in our examples the client and server happen to be on the same machine.

In our case, the data gathered from the user in the form will be sent to the server to invoke the **Results.asp** Active Server Page. So this line says that the name of our form is **request**, that we want it to call **Results.asp**, and that it will **POST** the data to the server. The server will take the information the user enters in the text box and grab the requested data from the database.

```
<P>Enter the ID
   of the Publisher for retrieving titles:</P>
```

Here, we just output some text to the user asking them to input the ID of the Publisher. Now we are ready to build the text input box that will accept the input from the user:

```
<BLOCKQUOTE>
      <TABLE BORDER="0">
         <TR>
            <TD ALIGN="right"><I>Publisher ID</I></TD>
            <TD><INPUT TYPE="text" size="25"
            name="PubID"> </TD>
         </TR>
      </TABLE>
   </BLOCKQUOTE>
```

To make the form nice and neat, we build a table with two elements. The first is the text "**Publisher ID**" We display the text "**Publisher ID**" between the **<I>** tags. **<I>** tells the browser to italicize any text between these tags.

The second table element is an **INPUT TYPE="text"** box of **size = "25"**. We also give this text box the name **"PubID"**. This serves to distinguish this text box from any others that might be on the form. Also, we will retrieve the information that the user submits in this text box at the server, when the form is posted.

Now we create two standard HTML buttons, a submit and reset button:

```
<P><INPUT TYPE="submit" value="Submit PubID">
      <INPUT TYPE="reset" value="Reset Form"> </P>
</FORM>
```

HTML knows about these types of buttons, so we just define the input type as **"submit"** and give it the value (which is the caption) of **"Submit PubID"**. The other button knows how to reset the fields in the form and has the caption **"Reset Form"**. That's all we need to do to create these built-in types of buttons. The browser knows how to construct them when it receives this HTML code.

Not too bad. Please take a minute to digest the code above. It might look a bit strange if you are not familiar with HTML, but it will all start to make perfect sense shortly. So here we just created an HTML page that will get information from the user, who could be anywhere on the planet. The form will submit the client's request to the server. Now, let's move on to scooping up the request on the server and displaying the results to the client.

2 Please type the name of the **request.htm** form into your browser now. Be sure it looks like the example. Don't try and submit any information yet, or you will get the dreaded HTTP Error 404 - remember, we haven't built the server side code as yet. When you are satisfied with how the form looks, let's move on to the next step.

The Server Side

Before we start coding, let's take a look at the finished product. This is how the results will look to the client that requests the data from our server. Here is the form that the client will see after they submit the Publisher's ID (using the value "4") to the server:

Each of the titles from the Publisher with the PubID submitted will be displayed.

All right, now let's now move on to building the server code. We can cut and paste most of the code from the **Wrox.asp** previous example for the **Results.asp** form. In this example, we will grab the number that the user requested and retrieve the appropriate records. Recall in the **request.htm** page we just wrote, the user enters a Publisher's ID and submits this.

Try It Out – Retrieving and Displaying the Data for the Client

1 OK, open up your trusty **Notepad.exe** and create a new file called **Results.asp** and save it in the **\Chapter13** directory. Add this code (you can adapt some of it from Wrox.asp):

```
<HTML>
<HEAD>
<TITLE>Database Programming with Visual Basic 6.0</TITLE>
</HEAD>

<CENTER>
<H1><FONT size=4>Requesting Publisher's Titles</H1></FONT>
<H2>Database Programming with Visual Basic 6.0</H2><BR>
```

```
<%

dim myConnection
dim rsTitleList
dim connectString
dim sqlString
dim requestPubID

connectString = "Provider=Microsoft.Jet.OLEDB.3.51;" _
& "Data Source=C:\begdb\biblio.mdb"

Set myConnection = Server.CreateObject("ADODB.Connection")
Set rsTitleList = Server.CreateObject("ADODB.Recordset")

myConnection.Open connectString

requestPubID = Request.Form("PubID")

sqlString = "Select * From titles WHERE PubID = " & requestPubID

Set RSTitleList = myConnection.Execute(sqlString)

If (RSTitleList.BOF) AND (RSTitleList.EOF) then
  Response.Write("Sorry, but Publisher Number " & requestPubID _
        & " was not found.")
ELSE
%>

<TABLE align=center COLSPAN=8 CELLPADDING=5 BORDER=0 WIDTH=200>
<!-- BEGIN column header row -->
<TR>
   <TD  VALIGN=TOP BGCOLOR="#800000">
     <FONT STYLE="ARIAL NARROW" COLOR="#ffffff" SIZE=2>
        Publisher ID
     </FONT>
   </TD>
   <TD ALIGN=CENTER BGCOLOR="#800000">
     <FONT STYLE="ARIAL NARROW" COLOR="#ffffff" SIZE=2>
        Title
     </FONT>
   </TD>
</TR>
<!-- Get Data -->
<% do while not RStitleList.EOF %>
<TR>
   <TD BGcolor ="f7efde" align=center>
     <font style ="arial narrow" size=2>
        <%=RStitleList("PubID")%>
     </font>
   </TD>
   <TD BGcolor ="f7efde" align=center>
     <font style ="arial narrow" size=2>
       <%=RSTitleList("Title") %>
     </font>
   </TD>
</TR>
<% RSTitleList.MoveNext%>
<%loop %><!-- Next Row -->
```

684

```
</TABLE>
</center>
</BODY>
<% End if %>
</HTML>
<HTML>
```

2   Be sure to save the file. Next, load up the Request.htm form in your browser. Enter a publisher's ID, such as 4, and this form will be called. It will retrieve and display all of the titles for that publisher.

How It Works

We are familiar with most of this code from the earlier **Wrox.asp** example. So let's just concentrate on what is different.

The main difference is that we are getting data from the requesting form. We use the **Request.Form()** to retrieve the value(s) from the form elements posted to the HTTP request. To use this, we use this format:

Request.Form(parameter)

Here the parameter is the name of the item on the form we want to retrieve. You can also get the count of the items in the collection. But in our example, we are just retrieving a value from the name of the field ("PubID") in the form's collection. Remember in the **request.htm** form we gave the text box used to get user input the name "PubID"? Well, that name is now accessible as a member of the requesting form's collection (these are built-in features of the ASP object model.) So we just ask for the value of the requesting form's text box named "PubID" and assign the result to our local variable **requestPubID**. This variable now holds the number of the publisher the user requested:

```
requestPubID = Request.Form("PubID")
```

Many web programmers create hidden fields that hold information and pass this information back to the server. So if you ever need to get any information for the client, you can simply place the value in a text box and make that hidden. This way you can get much more information than the client sees. This keeps for a simple, clean requesting form.

In our example, we are taking the user's entry for the text field "PubID" on the **request.htm** form. We then assign it to a variable, **requestPubID**. Once we have the value, we simply embed it into a standard SQL statement. Once the string is assigned to the variable **sqlString**, we again use the **Execute** method of the ADO connection and assign the results of the recordset to **RSTitleList**.

```
sqlString = "Select * From titles WHERE PubID = " & requestPubID

Set RSTitleList = myConnection.Execute(sqlString)
```

The only eventuality we must cater for is that the user puts in a number that is not a valid Publisher ID. This is easy to check. If the recordset's **.BOF** and **.EOF** is true, we know that no records were returned. If that is the case, we simply inform the requester that the publisher number was not found. And as this is all done within VBScript, it is included within the **%** tags:

```
If (RSTitleList.BOF) AND (RSTitleList.EOF) then
  Response.Write("Sorry, but Publisher Number " & requestPubID _
       & " was not found.")
ELSE
%>
```

We covered displaying the output, if there is indeed output, in the earlier example. The only new element is the `<% END IF %>` line. This permits us to either display the message that there were no records, or display all of the records that were found:

```
</BODY>
<% END IF %>
</HTML>
```

So now, if the user enters a bogus ID number, such as 4444, they will be shown the following message:

Depending on how your browser security is set up, you might see the following Security Alert:

This just tells you that you are sending information over the local Intranet - in our case where both the client and server reside on the same machine. That is because we are **POSTING** data - or sending it to the server. Usually you are just retrieving HTML pages, but not sending any user information.

So there you have it. We have just built an Internet client-server system! We allowed anyone anywhere to access your server, ask for records on a publisher, and then displayed the results using VBScript. I hope you realize just how powerful this principle is. In just a single chapter, we build an Internet client-server system permitting database access. Powerful applications beckon.

Persistent Client Side Data Using Cookies

You are going to like this next example. It shows the reason that ADO is the wave of the future.

On the Internet, when you request a web page using Hyper Text Transfer Protocol (http), this connection is known as 'stateless'. When you request a web page, a connection is opened, the HTML code is downloaded to your browser, and the connection is closed. The server has no memory of you being there. It just served the HTML page to the client browser and then went about its business. If you came back to that server, it had no idea if this was your first visit or your twentieth.

There has got to be some way for the server to 'remember' if you were there. Why? Well consider some of the surveys you fill out to gain access to a site. You fill out the text boxes, get registered, and the next time you log in the survey is bypassed. It's a good thing too, because if you had to fill out the survey every time you logged in to the site, you would never go back.

There is also the notion of 1 to 1 marketing. Let's say that my web site sells a new product called an Oscillating Overthruster as an aid to entering the 8th dimension. Well, if you ordered one from my site, the next time you return I might want to display accessories for the product, or notify you of version 2.0 that is much better. I can tailor the HTML page for an individual user.

But wait. How can this be done after we just discussed the statelessness of each and every HTTP connection? Well, we can easily accomplish this by using what is known as a **cookie**. What are cookies? Essentially, they are just simple text files that can be written to the user's hard drive by the server. So when you download an HTML page, there can be a command right in the page that writes the cookie file to your PC. It can contain any information the server wishes to place in it. And then it can be read the next time you log in to that server. So the server could take your response to a survey and when you successfully complete it, a cookie with a unique identifier is written to your PC. The next time you log in to that site, the HTML page that is downloaded to your PC looks for a cookie. If it finds it, the unique identifier is read and the server knows you have already responded to the survey, so the survey process is bypassed. If no cookie is found, it assumes you are new and presents the survey before you can move on.

> *Cookies written by a server to your machine can **only** be read by that self-same server.*

All right. Lets' say that we build a web site where we wish to track each and every visitor. The first time the surfer logs in, we ask for the Big Kahuna's First and Last name. We then send that information to the server. The server stores that data using ADO, and generates a unique ID number. This unique ID number is now associated with this individual surfer. We send another page back to the browser confirming that the information was successfully saved. However, we also take the liberty to write a cookie to the surfer's PC. In the cookie, we store the unique number. Now the next time the user logs into our server, we read the cookie from the user's PC, grab the unique number and send it to the server. Using ADO, we retrieve the information about that user. This way we can track each and every visitor to our site and store any information we care to about this person. This is how all of the large professional web sites perform this magic. Like custom configuration of a page, or customized news stories, or just about any individualized page. It's done with cookies.

> *Hysteria was generated a few years back when surfers found out that servers could actually write to their hard drives. The Wall Street Journal even had a front page article about this. People felt their machines were being violated. They also feared that servers could read the contents of their hard drive to find any illegal copies of software that might be there. However, this is not the case. And cookies proved so useful that the World Wide Web Consortium has endorsed a cookie standard.*

Building an Application for Persistent Data

Here is our strategy. We will create four web pages and a .DLL for our purposes:

▶ **login.asp**. This page will be the first one that a user sees when they visit our site. It will look for a cookie and if one is present it will be sent to the next page, visitor.asp.

▶ **visitor.asp**. This page checks for the value of the cookie. If there is a valid value, then this page will instantiate a DLL that will open an ADO connection. A recordset of data about that user will be updated and then displayed. If there is no valid value for the cookie, we know this is a new user. Then control will be redirected to the page **newUser.asp**.

▶ **newUser.asp**. This page will prompt the new user for their first and last name. The user submits this information to the **updateNewUser.asp** page.

▶ **updateNewUser.asp**. This page retrieves the First and Last name from the user, instantiates a DLL that opens an ADO connection and creates a new user record. The DLL returns a unique number that is then written to the user's PC inside a cookie. The form then notifies the user that their data has been successfully updated.

▶ **visitors.dll**. This will open the connection and handle all of the database operations for us.

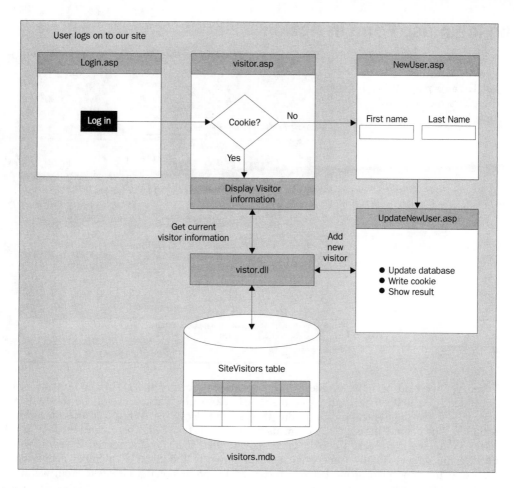

Let's begin with the `login.asp` file.

The login.asp Form in Action

Ready to get started? Let's start by creating the `login.asp` page. When complete, the page will look like this:

Programming databases with VB6 Cookie Example - Microsoft Internet Explorer...

File   Edit   View   Go   Favorites   Help

Back   Forward   Stop   Refresh   Home   Search   Favorites   History   Channe

Address http://buckaroo/login.asp   Links   Visual Basic 5 For Progran ▸

Welcome to the ADO Cookie Web Site

Press Enter to log in to my web site

Log In

Copyright: Programming Databases with Visual Basic 6.0.
Last revised: July 19, 1998

Local intranet zone

Whenever we read or write cookies, that code must be before the HTML code or an error is generated. OK, first off we will create the **Login.asp** file. This form will be the first form a user sees when they enter your site. But this is a bit deceiving. Why? Because the user only sees a button, but behind the scenes we are using a hidden text box. Our page will look on the user's PC to see if there is a cookie previously written there by the server. If yes, it will be sent back to the server - totally transparent and unknown to the client. Remember above we discussed the concept of a hidden text box used by professional web sites? Well, we are gong to implement this technique ourselves.

First, we'll handle writing the cookie to the user's PC.

Try It Out - Writing Cookies to the Client's Browser

1   Ready? OK, open your **Notepad.exe** and create a file called **login.asp**. Again, this is a straight text file so just type in the following:

```
<!-- Notice that the cookie code is before the HTML tag -->
<%
dim cookieValue
cookieValue = Request.Cookies("visitorNumber")
%>
```

```
<!-- Now we start the actual page -->
<HTML>
<HEAD>
<TITLE>Programming databases with VB6 Cookie Example</TITLE>
</HEAD>
<BODY>
<CENTER>
<H1>Welcome to the ADO Cookie Web Site</H1>
<HR>


<FORM NAME="login" Action="visitor.asp" method="POST">
    <INPUT TYPE="hidden" NAME="cookieValue" VALUE="<%=cookievalue%>"><P>
    <P>Press Enter to log in to my web site</P>
    <P><INPUT TYPE="submit" value="Log In">
</FORM>
</CENTER>
<HR>
<H5>Copyright: Programming Databases with Visual Basic 6.0.<BR>
Last revised: July 19, 1998</h5>
</BODY>
</HTML>
```

Be sure to save the file in **\Chapter13** as **login.asp**.

How It Works

As always, we bracket our VBScript between **<% %>** tags. The first thing we want to do is see if the user has visited our site before:

```
<%
dim cookieValue
cookieValue = Request.Cookies("visitorNumber")
%>
```

We are calling our cookie file **"visitorNumber"**. We then use the **.Cookies** method of the ASP **Request** object to retrieve a value (if any) and assign it to our variable cookieValue. If I were you, I'd be wondering just what the heck does a cookie file look like? Well, here is how the cookie is stored on my PC:

When we write the code to place a cookie on a client's machine, these weird numbers will make more sense. But as you can see, we are reading the value of **visitorNumber**. It just so happens that this web surfer was assigned the number **3**. Now when the user accesses our site again, the above code reads the value of this cookie, which in this case happens to be 3. This number is sent to the next form that will look up the record that has **3** in the key field. The user's information will be stored in this database record. Again, we will discuss this a bit more when we write the cookie, but you can see how the data is stored in a plain text file. My cookie was written (by the server) to **\Windows\Profiles\Buckaroo\Temporary Internet Files**.

The next part of our code defines a form that contains a button on our page. When the user presses the button to post the data, we want the Action to invoke the **visitor.asp** page. Notice that we have added a hidden field that we are calling **"cookieValue"**. This is a common technique that allows us to send this information to the server without the user having to even know it is there. We are setting the value of the hidden field to **<%=myCookie%>**. Remember that this variable - that contains a value for the cookie, is a VBScript variable. So we set the value to whatever was returned from the cookie - if anything.

```
<FORM NAME="login" Action="visitor.asp" method="POST">
   <INPUT TYPE="hidden" NAME="cookieValue" VALUE="<%=myCookie%>"><P>
   <P>Press Enter to log in to my web site</P>
   <P><INPUT TYPE="submit" value="Log In">
</FORM>
```

We then add a submit button with the caption of **"Log In"**. When the user clicks this, all of the values within the form are **POST**ed to the **visitor.asp** page. So at this point, there may or may not be a cookie value. The **visitor.asp** page that includes more VBScript will figure this out and what to do. Notice that in the code snippet above we are calling the **visitor.asp** when the current form is **POST**ed. This will automatically call the visitor.asp form as soon as the user clicks the Log In button.

Be sure your new file is saved. Now enter the name of the **login.asp** page in your browser. Make sure that it looks like the example. Again, actually trying to log in using this form at the moment would generate a HTTP Error 404. When you are satisfied, let's move on to the workhorse of our example, the **visitor.asp** page.

The visitor.asp Page in Action

As mentioned, the **visitor.asp** form will be called when the user clicks the button on the previous form. This next form will grab the hidden text from the cookie, look up the number in a database, and determine if this user has been here before. If the user is in our database already, the **visitor.asp** screen will actually be displayed when they log in. Because our code checks and finds a valid cookie, the information for that user can be retrieved. After the user has logged into our site at least once, they will see the **visitor.asp** form:

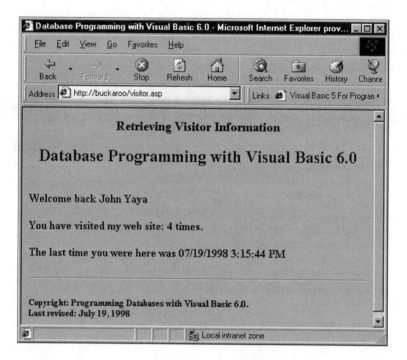

So here, the database successfully retrieved the user. But if no cookie is found, our program assumes that this is a new client. Of course, if the user deletes the cookie, or refuses to accept it, our program has no way to track them. But if this is the first time someone logs into your site, here is what they will see:

OK, let's see how this is done. This form will take a bit of work because we are going to create a database to hold user information. We will use ADO to manage the database. However, we are going to encapsulate all of the data management into a dynamic link library (DLL) file. This file can then be called upon just as if it were part of our program. Let's do it!

Try It Out - The Application's Workhorse - visitor.asp

1 Open Notepad and add this code. Save the file in **\Chapter13** as **visitor.asp**:

```
<%
visitorCookie = Request.Form("cookieValue")
if visitorCookie = "" then
  response.Redirect "newUser.asp"
End If
%>

<HTML>
<HEAD>
<TITLE>Database Programming with Visual Basic 6.0</TITLE>
</HEAD>

<BODY>
<CENTER>
<H1><font size=4>Retrieving Visitor Information</font></H1>
<H2>Database Programming with Visual Basic 6.0</H2>
</CENTER>
<BR>
<B>

<%
dim myDll
dim myArray
dim firstName
dim lastName
dim previousVisit
dim totalVisits
dim secondsAgo

Set myDll = Server.CreateObject("trackVisitors.visitors")

myArray = myDll.getvisitor(visitorCookie)

firstName = myArray(0)
lastName = myArray(1)
previousVisit = myArray(2)
totalVisits = myArray(3)

Response.Write("Welcome back ")
Response.Write(firstName)
Response.Write(" ")
Response.Write(lastName)
%><P>
```

```
<%
Response.Write("You have visited my web site: ")
Response.Write(totalVisits)
Response.Write(" times.")
%><P>
<%
Response.Write("The last time you were here was ")
Response.Write(previousVisit)
%>
<P>

</B>
<HR>
<h5>Copyright: Programming Databases with Visual Basic 6.0.<br>
Last revised: May 24, 1998</h5>
</BODY>
</HTML>
```

How It Works

As with reading and writing cookies, the **.Redirect** method of the Request object must be called before any HTML code. So we check for the value of **cookieValue** from the hidden text box, **cookieValue**, in the **login.asp** form. If there is no cookie value we know this is a new surfer to our site. In this case, we simply redirect control to the **.asp** file we use to get information from the user. Namely, we pass control to the **newUser.asp** form we just examined. If however, the user has a valid cookie, our code continues normally:

```
<%
visitorCookie = Request.Form("cookieValue")
if visitorCookie = "" then
  response.Redirect "newUser.asp"
End If
%>
```

If the user does have a cookie on their machine, we want display the header on the form and to instantiate an instance of our DLL. We will write this **.DLL** file as soon as we finish reviewing how this form works. But as you can see, we set a reference to our DLL with the object variable **myDLL**. And our DLL will handle all of the ADO data access:

```
Set myDll = Server.CreateObject("trackVisitors.visitors")
```

Next, we call the **.getVisitor** method of our DLL. We pass in the **visitorCookie** which holds the unique ID of this particular user. The DLL retrieves the user record and places the information in a variant array. We retrieve the array of information from our DLL in an array we call **myArray**.

```
myArray = myDll.getvisitor(visitorCookie)
```

Next, we extract the fields from the array that is returned from our DLL and place the element data in our variables for easy display:

```
firstName = myArray(0)
lastName = myArray(1)
previousVisit = myArray(2)
totalVisits = myArray(3)
```

Now we just write the information to the page normally:

```
Response.Write("Welcome back ")
Response.Write(firstName)
Response.Write(" ")
Response.Write(lastName)
```

That's it for the VBScript code. Now we need a database to work with! Let's start with building a customized database to hold the information on all of the hundreds of thousands of surfers that will be visiting our site every day.

Creating the Visitors Database

In order to store information about our site visitors, create a simple database called Visitors. I just used Access to whip up this five-field table named **siteVisitors**. Notice that the cookieID field is type AutoNumber. This will ensure a unique entry for each new visitor to your site. We're going to quickly create this simple database.

Try It Out - Create the Visitors.mdb Database

1 Use Access to create the database and place it in your **C:\BegDB** subdirectory. Of course if you don't happen to have Access on our machine, simply fire up Visdata and create the table.

Call the database **Visitors.mdb** and create a table called **siteVisitors**.

2 The database is very simple. Please add the following fields to the siteVisitors table:

Field Name	Data Type	Description
FirstName	Text	50
LastName	Text	50
CookieID	AutoNumber	Primary Key
PreviousVisit	Date/Time	
TotalVisits	Number	Long Integer

3 Now close the file and quit Access.

Now we are ready to build our .DLL file that will manage all data access for us.

Creating Our visitors.dll File

Are you tired of using **Notepad.exe** to create the VBScript yet? Well, finally we can jump back to our familiar VB development environment and create a new DLL. Start a new project. This time we are going to create an ActiveX DLL file that will handle all of our database accesses.

Try It Out - Creating Our DLL

1 Start a new project of ActiveX DLL type:

2 Call our new project visitor.vbp and save it in **\Chapter13**. Name the DLL file **visitors.cls**. This will hold the code for us.

Our DLL will expose two functions to the outside world. And remember that functions look like methods to the outside world. The **setVisitor** function will add a new user to our database and the **getVisitor** function will retrieve information about existing users. Our DLL will have no visual face to the world, so there will be no forms. Just a DLL file with two functions. And remember we have to add the ADO references for our DLL to be able to access the components it needs.

3 So now is a good time to add the ADO references to our file. Bring up the References dialog in your new project and add the references as shown in the screenshot:

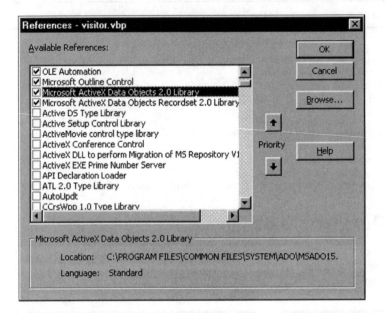

Now we'll add the relevant methods to our DLL.

The setVisitor Function

The first thing we need to code is the **setVisitor** function. This function will allow us to add a new visitor when they visit our new web site. Notice the signature of the function. We will pass in both the first and last name of the new user as a variant. This is important!

Remember, everything must be a variant so we can have consistent VB and ASP data types.

Also, note the return value is a variant. When we add our new user to the database, we will grab the **AutoNumber** value that the database assigns to the **cookieID** field and return that to the caller, **visitor.asp**. This will be used to identify the user the next time they log in.

Try It Out - Saving New Visitors to Our Site

1 Let's start by adding a function to our .DLL. Add this function to our **visitors.cls** module. Please enter the code as shown:

```
Public Function setVisitor(ByVal firstName As Variant, ByVal lastName As Variant)
As Variant

Dim adoConnection As ADODB.Connection
Dim adoRecordset As ADODB.Recordset
Dim connectString As String
```

```
connectString = "Provider=Microsoft.Jet.OLEDB.3.51;" & _
                "Data Source=C:\BegDB\visitors.mdb"

Set adoConnection = CreateObject("ADODB.Connection")
Set adoRecordset = CreateObject("ADODB.Recordset")

adoConnection.Open connectString
adoRecordset.Open "SELECT * FROM SiteVisitors", adoConnection, _
                             adOpenDynamic, adLockOptimistic

With adoRecordset
   .AddNew
   !firstName = firstName
   !lastName = lastName
   !previousVisit = Now()
   !totalVisits = 1
   .Update
End With

'-- Return a unique ID so we can set the cookie
setVisitor = adoRecordset!cookieID

'-- Close the recordset and the connection
adoRecordset.Close
adoConnection.Close

End Function
```

How It Works

We are now familiar with opening an ADO connection and creating a recordset consisting of all visitors to our site. So we are just retrieving the records from the database and adding a new one for this user. First, we call the **.AddNew** method of the recordset that creates the record for us. Then we add the first and last names of the new user that were passed in when this method was called. The **previousVisit** field is set to the system time using **Now()**. And since this is the first visit, set the **totalVisits** field to 1 and then we update the record to commit it to the database:

```
With adoRecordset
   .AddNew
   !firstName = firstName
   !lastName = lastName
   !previousVisit = Now()
   !totalVisits = 1
   .Update
End With
```

Once the record is added, Jet adds the unique AutoNumber in the **cookieID** field. Since we are at the end of the recordset, and all new records are added to the end, we just take that new value and assign it to the return value of our function, **setVisitor**. And remember, the return value is a variant. This is the number that will be added to the cookie we write to the user's PC:

```
'-- Return a unique ID so we can set the cookie
setVisitor = adoRecordset!cookieID
```

If this were a production system, we would **movelast** so we don't rely on the default behavior of the recordset. But for the sake of clarity we know we will be at the end of the recordset, so we just take the value. We then proceed to close the ADO recordset and connection as usual. Not too bad.

Next, we need to code the **getVisitor** method. This is used when our form, **visitor.asp**, gets a valid cookie from the **login.asp** form. The unique number is passed into the **getVisitor** method (Ahmm, function) and is used to locate the information on the current visitor.

The getVisitor Method

Again, this method is called from the **visitor.asp** form when the user already exists in our database. Here we will return a variant array with the fields of data that we stored. This will allow us to present the user with pertinent information such as their name, the last time they visited, and how many times they have surfed into our site in the past.

Try It Out - Retrieve Information about Visitors in our Database

1 Add another method, **getVisitor**, to the DLL file. Again, note the both the input and the output of the function - as shown in the signature - a variant. This is important!

```
Public Function getVisitor(ByVal visitorNumber As Variant) As Variant

Dim adoConnection As ADODB.Connection
Dim adoRecordset As ADODB.Recordset
Dim connectString As String
Dim sqlString As String
Dim visitorArray() As Variant    'must be a variant

connectString = "Provider=Microsoft.Jet.OLEDB.3.51;" & _
                "Data Source=C:\begdb\visitors.mdb"

Set adoConnection = CreateObject("ADODB.Connection")
Set adoRecordset = CreateObject("ADODB.Recordset")

adoConnection.Open connectString

sqlString = "Select * From SiteVisitors WHERE CookieID = " & visitorNumber

adoRecordset.Open sqlString, adoConnection, adOpenDynamic, adLockOptimistic

If (adoRecordset.BOF) And (adoRecordset.EOF) Then
  ReDim visitorArray(1)
  visitorArray(0) = "Not Found"
Else
  ReDim visitorArray(4)
  visitorArray(0) = adoRecordset!firstName
  visitorArray(1) = adoRecordset!lastName
  visitorArray(2) = adoRecordset!previousVisit
  adoRecordset!previousVisit = Now()
  adoRecordset!totalVisits = adoRecordset!totalVisits + 1
```

```
      adoRecordset.Update
      visitorArray(3) = adoRecordset!totalVisits
   End If

   adoRecordset.Close
   adoConnection.Close

   getVisitor = visitorArray
   End Function
```

How It Works

When this method is called, the **visitorNumber** is passed in as a parameter of type variant. We retrieve the record from our database where the **CookieID** field equals the **visitorNumber** passed in. Of course, the visitorNumber is the cookie value of the current user:

```
sqlString = "Select * From SiteVisitors WHERE CookieID = " & visitorNumber
```

We know that the record will be there, but for safety we check the **.BOF** and **.EOF** properties to ensure the recordset is not empty. If there was some error and the user was not found, we redim our array to 1 element and add the text "**Not Found**".

Assuming the record is there - and we know it will be - we just redim our **visitorArray** to have four elements. We then add the fields that we want our DLL to return to the calling ASP form. These are taken from the record that was retrieved from our recordset for the current user.

```
   ReDim visitorArray(4)
   visitorArray(0) = adoRecordset!firstName
   visitorArray(1) = adoRecordset!lastName
   visitorArray(2) = adoRecordset!previousVisit
   adoRecordset!previousVisit = Now()
   adoRecordset!totalVisits = adoRecordset!totalVisits + 1
   adoRecordset.Update
   visitorArray(3) = adoRecordset!totalVisits
```

Remember when we earlier discussed the immediate update method of ADO? We don't need to invoke a **.Edit** method - in fact one does not exist. We just update the fields we want and call the **.Update** method to save the changes. Once we extract the **previousVisit** time and place it in the third element (2) of our **visitorArray**, we then update the field to **Now()** which reflects the last time this surfer visited our web site. Remember that our array is starting at base 0, not 1.

We then add 1 to the number of visits and update the recordset. Next, we assign the new **totalVisits** to the fourth element (3) of our array. If we had an on-line store, we could have stored the last purchase made. Or if our **newUser.asp** was more involved, we could have added all kinds of survey information and stored it as well. You get the idea.

We then close the recordset and connection normally. Finally, we assign the **visitorArray** with our information to the return value of our function, **getVisitor**. Again, this must be a variant:

```
   getVisitor = visitorArray
```

Saving the DLL

Well, there was not too much to that - but we need to store our `.dll` in usable format. Let's do that now.

Try It Out - Compiling our DLL for action!

1 In VB, rename the project to **trackVisitors**:

2 Now save the class module as **visitors.cls**, and the project as **visitor.vbp**. When we compile the `.DLL`, it will ask us to compile **visitor.dll**, which is the name of our project.

Your project explorer will now have the project and class module within the DLL named correctly:

3 Select Project | trackVisitors Properties... from the main VB menu. Be sure to add a Project Description so you can identify your DLL in the Project References dialog box:

Now we need to compile the **.DLL**. Again, it's always a good idea to place a descriptive name in the Project Description. This will show up in our references later on.

4 Select File-Make visitor.dll and press **OK** to compile. This process also registers your new .DLL in the registry. Now if you want to use this in any other VB projects, it is there for you to select. However, now that it is registered, our VBScript files can find it when we create an instance of it:

Now we have got a DLL file and a new database, we can move on to our newUser form. You might remember that in our **visitors.asp**, we check to see if there is a valid cookie. If now, we redirect the control to the form newUser.asp. This will actually display the form to the user asking for their name. Let's build this form now.

The newUser.asp Form in Action

When the user presses the Log In button of the login.asp form above, the **visitor.asp** form is called. The first thing the **visitor.asp** does is check to see if the cookie has a valid ID number. If it does not, then control is redirected to the **newUser.asp** form. This is what a new visitor to our web site sees the first time they log in:

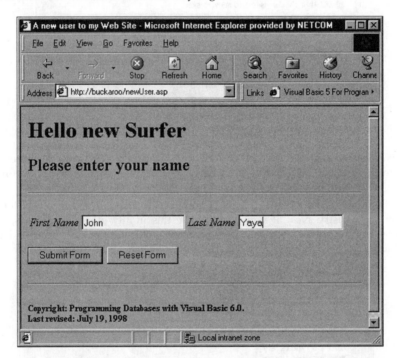

1 OK, take out the trusty Notepad.exe once more. Create a text file called newUser.asp and save it in \Chapter13. Please add the following code:

```
<HTML>
<HEAD>
<TITLE>A new user to my Web Site</TITLE>
</HEAD>
<BODY>

<H1>Hello new Surfer</H1>
<H2>Please enter your name<H2>
<HR>
```

```
<FORM NAME="request" Action="updateNewUser.asp" method="POST">
  <TABLE BORDER="0">
    <TR>
      <TD align="right"><I>First Name</I></TD>
      <TD><INPUT TYPE="text" size="20" name="firstName"> </TD>
      <TD align="right"><I>Last Name</I></TD>
      <TD><INPUT TYPE="text" size="20" name="lastName"> </TD>
    </TR>
  </TABLE>
  <P><INPUT TYPE="submit" value="Submit Form">
    <INPUT TYPE="reset" value="Reset Form"> </P>
</FORM>

<HR>

<H5>Copyright: Programming Databases with Visual Basic 6.0.<BR>
Last revised: July 19, 1998</H5>
</BODY>
</HTML>
```

Be sure to save the file. When it's saved, enter the name in your browser to ensure it looks like the sample.

How It Works

We just place two text boxes between **FORM** tags. As usual, we tell the form to call the **updateNewUser.asp** form when the data is **POST**ed. There are two input text boxes of size 20 displayed. And we name the first text box **firstName** and the second one **lastName**:

```
<FORM NAME="request" Action="updateNewUser.asp" method="POST">
  <TABLE BORDER="0">
    <TR>
      <TD align="right"><I>First Name</I></TD>
      <TD><INPUT TYPE="text" size="20" name="firstName"> </TD>
      <TD align="right"><I>Last Name</I></TD>
      <TD><INPUT TYPE="text" size="20" name="lastName"> </TD>
    </TR>
  </TABLE>
  <P><INPUT TYPE="submit" value="Submit Form">
    <INPUT TYPE="reset" value="Reset Form"> </P>
</FORM>
```

So this is just a standard data gathering form. The information the user enters into the text boxes can then be retrieved in the **updateNewUser.asp** form that we will write next. The **updateNewUser** form is called when the user completes this and clicks the Submit button. If this were a real application, we would use VBScript on the client side to ensure that the fields were filled out. However, VBScript does not run in every browser. Alas, we would probably then use JScript. But for now, we will just take what the user enters. Otherwise, we could check on the server when the user submits the form, but this causes a round trip if indeed the fields were not correctly filled out. We would have to check on the server and resend the form. However, if the editing were done within the ASP form itself, it would not be sent until it was correct. As mentioned this would permit us to check right at the client's browser instead of submitting the data to the server and letting it check. This approach saves bandwidth and is much faster than having a round trip to the server and back if the fields are not complete.

When the user clicks on the Submit button, the `updateNewUser.asp` form adds the user to the database and then writes a cookie to the surfer's browser. If the security on the browser is set to notify when cookies are about to be written, a message such as this is displayed:

The data we are writing to the cookie is "**3**". This is the unique number that our DLL generated to identify this new user. Notice that the name of the cookie is `visitorNumber`. When we write the cookie, we also must give it an expiration date, otherwise it disappears at the end of the session. So we will have the cookie stick around on the users machine until December 30, 2000. Of course, if the user declines the cookie, then we have no way of knowing the user was here before and they will always be presented with the new user screen. Let's write the final form, `updateNewUser.asp` that will write this cookie.

The updateNewUser.asp Form in Action

As soon as a new user clicks the Submit button, this form is displayed. However, the new cookie is written before the form is displayed. That is why the user would see the cookie alert before this form is displayed. When the `updateNewUser` form is displayed, the user information has been written to the database, a new unique ID has been generated, and the cookie has successfully been written to the user's browser!

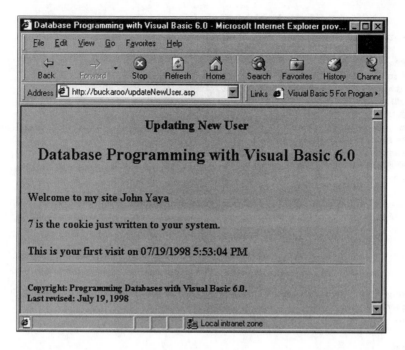

As mentioned above, whenever we read or write cookies, this must be done before any HTML code is generated.

Try It Out - Confirming User Registration

1 OK, this is the last form. Fire up **Notepad.exe** and create a new file called **updateNewUser.asp**. Be sure to save this in **\Chapter13** with the rest of the ASP and DLL files. Now enter this code as shown:

```
<%
Dim myDll
Dim myArray
Dim cookieID
dim firstName
dim lastName

firstName = Request.Form("firstName")
lastName = Request.Form("lastName")

Set myDll = Server.CreateObject("trackVisitors.visitors")

cookieID = myDll.setvisitor(firstName, lastName)

Response.Cookies("visitorNumber") = cookieID
Response.Cookies("visitorNumber").Expires = "December 30, 2000"

%>
```

```
<HTML>
<TITLE>Database Programming with Visual Basic 6.0</TITLE></HEAD>

<CENTER>
<H1><font size=4>Updating New User</font></H1>
<H2>Database Programming with Visual Basic 6.0</H2><BR>
</CENTER>
<B>
Welcome to my site
  <% Response.write(firstName)
     Response.Write(" ")
     Response.Write(lastName) %>
     <P>
     <%
     Response.Write(Request.Cookies("visitorNumber"))
     Response.Write (" is the cookie just written to your system.")
   %>
<P>
This is your first visit on <%=now %>
</B>
<HR>
<h5>Copyright: Programming Databases with Visual Basic 6.0.<BR>
Last revised: May 24, 1998</H5>
</HTML>
```

How It Works

Within the **%** VBScript tags, we first extract the information from the **firstName** and **lastName** text boxes on the **newUser** form and assign them to local variables. Recall that when that form was posted, it called the **updateNewUser.asp** form. So by using the **.Form** method of the Request object and passing it the name of the field we are interested in, we can retrieve that value. So we just grab the first and last name from the text boxes in the **newUser.asp** form.

```
firstName = Request.Form("firstName")
lastName = Request.Form("lastName")
```

Here we use the DLL that manages all of our database access. We instantiate our DLL and assign it to our object variable **myDll**:

```
Set myDll = Server.CreateObject("trackVisitors.visitors")
```

Once we have created an instance of our **visitors.dll**, we call its **.setVisitor** method and pass in the **firstName** and **lastName** as parameters. This is, of course, the name of the user who just filled out the **newUser** form. We call **setVisitor** for new users. This method updates the database and returns a unique number that we will use to write the cookie. This unique value is assigned to the variable **cookieID**:

```
cookieID = myDll.setvisitor(firstName, lastName)
```

We pass in the first and last name of the surfer to the **.setVisitor** method of our DLL. The DLL updates the database and return the unique **cookieId** to us.

When the new user has been written to the database, we then write the cookie to the user's PC. We give it the value of **cookieID** which in our example is "**7**". We then set the **.Expires** property so the cookie does not disappear when the user leaves our site. If we did not set the **.Expires** property, the cookie would only last for the session. So we place it there to last for a while:

```
Response.Cookies("visitorNumber") = cookieID
Response.Cookies("visitorNumber").Expires = "December 30, 2000"
```

After the VBScript code executes, we jump into the HTML code and display the results. Of course, we bracket our VBScript code within the HTML code in **<% %>** as usual:

```
<B>
Welcome to my site
  <% Response.write(firstName)
     Response.Write(" ")
     Response.Write(lastName) %>
     <P>
     <%
     Response.Write(Request.Cookies("visitorNumber"))
     Response.Write (" is the cookie just written to your system.")
  %>
```

The Application in Action

OK, let's try the whole thing out. Fire up the **login.asp** page and click on Log In. Enter your details in the resulting data entry page and submit the form. You'll receive the confirmation that the cookie has been written to your machine.

Next, go back to the **login** page and refresh it (or close down your browser, restart, and open up the login page again). When you click on Log In this time, you'll be shown the details stored about you in the **visitors.mdb** database. ASP has interrogated the cookie on your PC, recognized you, and found your details in the database. This is only a very basic application, but it gives you some idea about the ability of ASP to interact with the user, VBScript, DLLs and databases.

As you've probably gathered, all we've done here is scratch the surface of what ASP is capable of in conjunction with databases. But the client/server principle and the use of ADO within the ASP scripts are a powerful demonstration of how simple the baseline interactions can be.

Summary

There you have it. You have just written an Internet client server system. And we learned about the PWS in the process. To accomplish this task, we discovered and wrote a few Active Server Pages. We wrote forms that took information from a web surfer, saw how to store and retrieve the data in a database using ADO, and how to display it to the user. We learned how to write cookies to the client browser so we can easily identify repeat visitors, and we covered posting data from one form to another. Finally, we built an in-process DLL file that managed all of the data access for us. Now if we need to tweak the DLL file, we can simply update it and recompile it - and not have to change any of the `.asp` files. Not too bad for a single chapter. We hope that this has whetted your appetite for using ASP with ADO.

What We've Learned

▶ Active Server Pages allow the generation of dynamic HTML code to be sent to a browser

▶ We can write ASP pages using VBScript

▶ The Personal Web Server permits us to run and test our programs on the Internet

▶ We can embed a DLL in a server side `.asp` file. We built one that used ADO to manage visitors to our site

▶ Your server can write a cookie file to a client's browser

▶ Either HTML or ASP files can take data from a user and pass it back (i.e., POST) it to the server

In the next chapter we're going to take a look at another powerful technique - data mining.

Exercises

1 What is the default language used to create server-side scripts in Active Server Pages? How similar is it to Visual Basic?

2 What is the standard way to allow a web client to send information to be used by an Active Server Page? What functionality does it support?

3 What is a "cookie"? How do "cookies" benefit a web developer?

4 Describe how building a DLL and using it from an ASP can help a web developer.

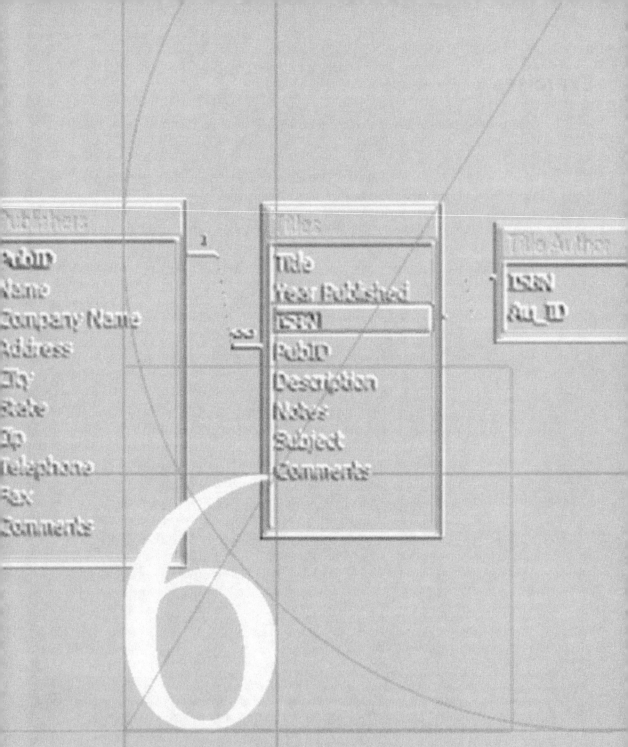

14

Advanced ADO Programming - Data Mining

In this chapter we're going to explore **data mining** This is an exciting technique that uses the power of databases to help us extract meaningful knowledge from a mountain of data. We'll talk about the ideas behind data mining before moving on to code our own example of a data mining program. Let's begin by discussing just what data mining is.

Data, Data, Everywhere...

John Naisbett's famous phrase "We are drowning in information, but starving for knowledge" takes on more truth with each passing day. Most corporate legacy systems have years of data on purchases, clients, products, etc. But it is just that - so much data - on its own it is meaningless. It is up to us our users to make sense of it, and turn it into meaningful and useful **information**. So, ironically, as more and more data piles up around us, we face a paradox: "the more data there is, the less information we have."

So the real question for us in this chapter is how can we distill useable knowledge from that mountain of data? For example, how can product managers at a company take all of the information that is in the various databases and use it to market products smarter? Or how can they see subtle trends that will permit a better use of limited advertising funds?

To take this to an extreme, consider the American Stock Exchange. With all of the data and all of the investment companies employing sophisticated algorithms to gain an edge, to a large extent securities trading has become a game of computers against computers. Humans are there to advise only at a "meta" level.

In this chapter we are going to go beyond the opening and closing of recordsets. Here we are actually going to create our own simple data mining program. Using the data in the **Nwind.mdb** table, we will apply our programs to the data to see if there are any underlying trends. We will aggregate all of the detail from the orders and products table and distill it into a single table that we can apply our algorithms to. Yes, there is a bit of coding, but you will learn quite a few things along the way in this chapter.

Data Mining

Well, you might say, why not just create a SQL statement with joining operations to retrieve specific information from our data tables? That is a good start, but with SQL we can only uncover shallow data. This is information that is easily accessible from our data sources. While query tools and data mining tools compliment each other, straight query tools can't find any hidden data they can only find what we know how to ask for. The truth of the matter is that 80% of all interesting information can be abstracted from a data source using SQL if the user really knows and understands the data. But the remaining 20% of hidden information requires more advanced techniques. And from a small local company to a large, multi-national corporation, this 20% can prove to be the vital link between being a leader and struggling to meet the bottom line.

There's a cliché that says "if you know what you are looking for, use SQL. But if you only have a fuzzy idea, or a hunch, then use data mining". It's in this context that the power of the computer really shines. Consider that the computer can do both more and less than humans can. A computer can easily compare millions of data elements in seconds. No human can come close. Any three-year-old child can pick out a tree instantly, but it takes many CPU cycles for a computer to discern a tree. And even then, the computer won't know if it is a real tree or just a picture of one. So while computers excel in number crunching, humans excel in pattern recognition.

Another way to look at data mining is to consider the medieval laborer walking across a field. He might be walking over hidden coal deposits that in several hundred years could be mined to power machines that he could never conceive of. We want to mine for data in our various data sources, and we will permit the strength of the computer to sift through the data in search of the hidden gem. But only a human can tell if what is found is really a gem, or fools' gold. Much of the history of computer science has been deeply involved with the collection, manipulation, and dissemination of data - and the newest rage is data mining. We want to extract some knowledge from all of that data.

There is a wider term called **Knowledge Discovery in Databases (KDD)** that is used for the process of - logically enough - the discovery of knowledge in data. This term includes finding relationships and patterns in data. The term was generally agreed to mean this by the attendees at a KDD conference held in Montreal in 1995. The group also agreed that data mining should be used for only the discovery stage of the KDD process. KDD is not a new process, but has been on the minds of researchers for quite some time. The field includes statistics, artificial intelligence, data visualization, machine learning, expert systems, neural networks, and other disciplines. Phew! Where do we start with these concepts in a Beginning VB6 database programming book? We'll begin by thinking about an algorithm that will model how to extract knowledge from data.

The ID3 Algorithm

There are many schools of thought on how to extract knowledge from data. Esoteric areas of genetic algorithms and neural networks are pushing the frontiers of this field on a daily basis. However, there is a relatively simple technique that can be used to extract knowledge from data. Back in the 1960's, Dr. J. Ross Quinlan developed a technique that has evolved into the most commonly used method in expert systems that employ **induction methods** to generate rules - this is programming that tries to learn from generalized examples. Essentially the program looks at a ton of data and distills rules from it. The best part about this is that the program does not need to know anything about the data in advance. It will just look at the pieces and determine which ones are the most important to whatever outcome you are looking for. The **ID3 algorithm** can essentially look at a stack of data and determine which pieces are more important than the others.

Let's take a look at a reasonable example. In the **Nwind.mdb** file that comes with VB 6.0, there are several tables that simulate a small company's business. It has orders, products, customers, etc. Well, assume that you are the head of IS for the Northwind company. The product manager comes to you and asks you if you could set up a query form in VB so she can easily retrieve information. She is working on a project to determine how best to spend next year's marketing budget. She says that if she only had SQL capability, it would be possible to retrieve the information that she thinks might be important. She has in her mind what she intuitively thinks is important and wants to go ahead and put together a bunch of known relationships.

During this discussion, you start explaining about this great ID3 algorithm that you have been reading about. It can find important relationships in mountains of data. She looks at you as if you were the answers to her dreams! "Can you build me one of those?" she challenges. "Yes indeed," you reply.

The Product Analysis Tool

Our project will take the data from the **Nwind.mdb** file that comes with VB 6.0. We will display the various Categories, and the Products within the categories to analyze. Our program will use a combination of SQL and add a dash of the ID3 algorithm to find any hidden meaning in the data. The product manager can click on a category of product. Then, only the products for that category will be displayed in the Products list box. Then the user clicks the Analyze button and the ID3 program attempts to find any possible hidden relationships in the data. I think you will like this one.

However, before we start to work, let's look at the finished product so you can get an idea of where we are going:

What does this all mean? Well, the product manager can select a category from the list box. When a category is selected, all of the relevant products are placed in the Products list box. When the Analyze button is clicked, our program goes to work. It takes a look at the selected data as well as some handy extra data we placed in the database. So instead of a garden-variety, one-line SQL statement that might retrieve the top 10% of revenue generating products, our program will do much more. It will determine how important each country is to a specific product, and it also looks at regions of the world. It could be that growth is experienced in the Mediterranean countries in general. Or, possibly, Spanish speaking countries are scooping up our product. This might mean that in Spain and Venezuela - two opposite parts of the world, our new pasta is really taking off. These are things that probably wouldn't be easily found by the product manager on their own. For our program though, it's a snap! So our program will look for that hidden data we were talking about earlier.

The program considers the various countries, country regions, and languages as part of its analysis. It then generates a number, called **entropy**, which indicates the relative importance of each of these categories to our sales growth. Like a golf score, a lower number here is better than a higher one. The user simply clicks on another product and the analysis can be run again.

Once we get our program in shape, in the next chapter we will create an export feature that will permit the product manager to send the data to a spreadsheet, the corporate Intranet, or any package that accepts a **comma delimited file** (such as Access, Excel or just about any analysis package).

The first step in this project is - as ever - to build our prototypical user interface.

Try It Out - Building the ID3 User Interface

1 Start a new project. Name the project \Chapter14\ID3.vbp. Rename the default form for the project frmID3.

2 For the user interface, we need to add two list boxes to display the Categories and Products. Then, we add two MSFlexGrid controls. One will display the various regions, languages and countries, and the other will display the results of our ID3 algorithm's results. Another text box will provide the product manager with English-like text on how to best proceed with the results. And of course, our status bar will keep the user informed as the program is working. For good visual measure, we add a progress bar. We can update this as our program is crunching those numbers to ensure the product manager that all is well. Create your visual interface now using the following screenshot and the table that follows for guidance:

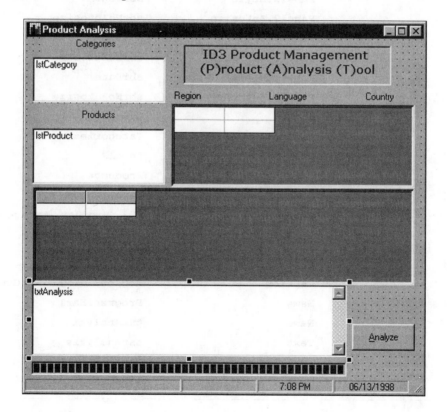

Control	Property	Value
List Box	Name	lstCategory
List Box	Name	lstProduct
MSFlexGrid	Name	miningGrid
	FixedCols	0
	FixedRows	0
MSFlexGrid	Name	resultsGrid
	AllowUserResizing	1- FlexResizeColumns
	FixedCols	0
Command Button	Name	cmdAnalyze
Status Bar	Name	sbStatus
	Panel1.Style	sbrText
	Panel1.Autosize	sbrSpring
	Panel2.Style	sbrText
	Panel2.Autosize	sbrNoAutosize
	Panel3.Style	sbrTime
	Panel3.Autosize	sbrNoAutosize
	Panel4.Style	sbrDate
	Panel4.Autosize	sbrNoAutosize
Label	Name	Label1
	Caption	Categories
Label	Name	Label2
	Caption	Products
Label	Name	Label3
	Caption	ID3 Product Management (P)roduct (A)nalysis (T)ool
Label	Name	Label4
	Caption	Region Language Country
Progress Bar	Name	ProgressBar1
Text Box	Name	txtAnalysis
	Text	txtAnalysis
	MultiLine	True
	ScrollBars	2-Vertical

One of the things that we do with data mining is to **re-aggregate** much of the information we spent a lot of time breaking down into various tables. Recall how we took pains to break our data into small tables during the normalization process earlier in the book? Well, now we find ourselves in the position of taking data from several tables and lumping it together (i.e. re-aggregating) so our program can look at a lot of data at one time.

3 Rather than change any data in existing tables, add another table to your copy of the Nwind.mdb database and call it ID3. We will be aggregating much of the information extracted from various tables and placing the results here. We will be discussing how each of the fields will be used, but please add this table now.

If you have Microsoft Access, just open the [Drive letter]\BegDB\Nwind.mdb. Notice that there are several normalized tables that are included. Each of the tables contains data on the fictitious Northwind company:

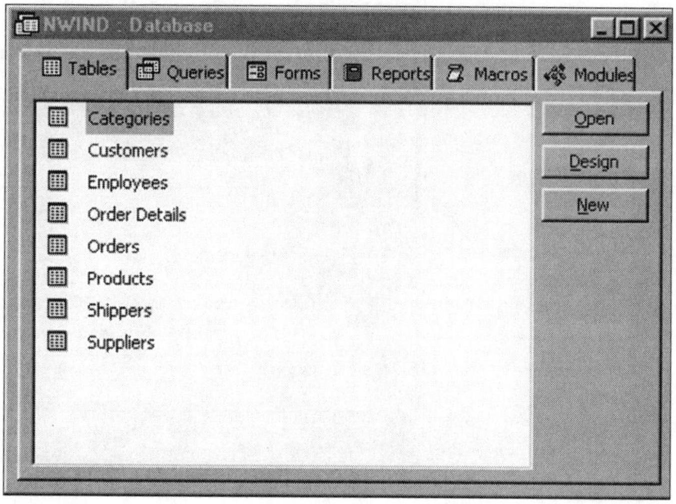

4 Click on the New button that is to the right-hand side of the tabbed form. We want to add a new table to the Nwind.mdb database. The New Table dialog box is presented. Select the Design View and click OK. This will bring up the view that permits us to add our fields to the new table.

Add the fields and data types as shown below. As you can see, what we will be doing is aggregating data and entering the results in the ID3 table. This way we don't have to modify any of the data in the Nwind tables. We will group information we retrieve from these tables using SQL and aggregate the results in our own ID3 table:

5 When you are finished, select File-Save from the main Access menu. You will be prompted with a Save As dialog box. Give your new table the name ID3 and click OK:

The new table will now be added to the **Nwind.mdb** database.

6 If you aren't using Access, create the new table using VisData. We already know how to add a new table using VisData. Open the database and right-click inside the Database Window. From there select New Table. We covered this process earlier in the book, so it should be familiar to you:

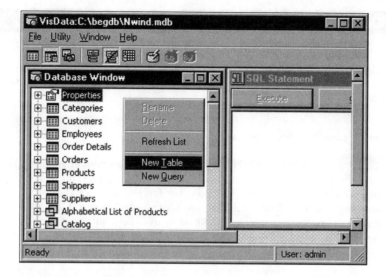

Use this table to lay out the new VisData **ID3** table:

Field	Type	Length
Category	Text	50
Product	Text	50
OldQuantity	Number	Long Integer
NewQuantity	Number	Long Integer
Country	Text	50
SalesUp	Yes/No	
UpByHowMuch	Number	Single
CountryRegion	Text	50
CountryLanguage	Text	50

Now that we have a table all to ourselves, we can start to write some code to see if there are any patterns that can be deduced. And from this exercise, you will get some ideas on how to apply this approach to any real world problem that you might need to solve.

ID3 Project Form and Code Initialization

We'll begin by creating the code that will help set up the functionality of our user interface.

Try It Out - Coding the User Interface

1 In the General area of the frmID3 form, declare a form-level variable that we will use for our connection to the database. Once we set it in the Form_Load event, we can then use it throughout the program:

```
Dim adoConnection As ADODB.Connection
```

When the form is loaded, we want to first show the user what is going on. So sprinkled throughout the program we will update the **sbStatus** panel. Since some of the initialization code can take a few seconds, we force a show of the form, with **Me.Show**. To ensure that the **Show** method is forced, we issue a **DoEvents**. Of course, this will process all pending CPU tasks - of which **Me.Show** is one. So while our form is loading, the user has something to look at. Otherwise, we can get half-drawn forms on the screen, which does not look very professional.

> *If you recall, earlier in the book we discussed putting all visual components in the Form's Activate event. While this is generally true, in this program we are opening a database, which might take a few seconds. So we will make a design decision and violate this rule here. Why? Because we want the user to actually see something while we are initializing our program. In this case, it does make sense to force the form to be visible by using Me.Show. If the user has the database on a local area network somewhere, you might have to add another few seconds to open the table and display the list boxes. So by forcing the form to show itself here, we provide a quick, crisp interface to the user immediately upon loading our program.*

2 Add the following code to the form's Form_Load event:

```
Private Sub Form_Load()

'-- Show what we are doing here --
sbStatus.Panels.Item(2).Text = "Loading..."

Me.Show
DoEvents

'---------------------------------------
'-- Open the database with ADO --
'---------------------------------------
sbStatus.Panels.Item(1).Text = "Opening the database..."
If (Not openTheDatabase()) Then
  sbStatus.Panels.Item(1).Text = "Database failed..."
  sbStatus.Panels.Item(2).Text = "Error."
  Exit Sub
End If

Call setupID3

sbStatus.Panels.Item(1).Text = "Updating list boxes..."
```

```
        Call updateListBoxes

        sbStatus.Panels.Item(1).Text = ""
        sbStatus.Panels.Item(2).Text = "Ready."
```

End Sub

How It Works

We call our function **openTheDatabase** to establish the connection to the database. If we are successful, we call **setupID3**, which is responsible for updating the Region - Language - Country flex grid. Finally, we make a call to **updateListBoxes** that fill the two list boxes with categories and products. We will look at each of these subs in detail. But you can see that the **Load** event is clean and crisp. We just call a few subs and update the status bar.

Opening the Database Connection

The **openTheDatabase** function is short and sweet. We simply set a reference to our form-level **adoConnection** variable. Once we set up our connection string, we open the database connection. If we are successful, then the form-level **adoConnection** object variable is available to any recordset that might need it. Notice that we can get away with a single connection to the database. We return a Boolean to indicate if we were successful or not. If there was an error of some sort, our minimal error handler will tell the user what is wrong and the calling routine will simply exit. Of course, in a real program, you would place a much more detailed error handler in this procedure.

Try It Out - The openTheDatabase Function

1 Add a new function to our frmID3 form. We wrap up the code to open the connection to the database in a straightforward function. And since the adoConnection variable has form-level scope, once we open the connection here, we can use it anywhere in the form.

```
    Public Function openTheDatabase() As Boolean

    '-- Here we want to open the database
    Dim sConnectionString As String

    On Error GoTo dbError

    sbStatus.Panels.Item(1).Text = "Opening the database."

    '-- Set reference to a new connection --
    Set adoConnection = New ADODB.Connection

    '-- Build the connection string
    sConnectionString = "Provider=Microsoft.Jet.OLEDB.3.51;" _
                    & "Data Source=C:\BegDB\Nwind.mdb"

    adoConnection.Open sConnectionString

    openTheDatabase = True
```

```
Exit Function

dbError:
MsgBox (Err.Description)
openTheDatabase = False
sbStatus.Panels.Item(2).Text = "Could not open database."
End Function
```

How It Works

There is no magic here. This function, which is called from the **Load** event of **frmID3**, will simply open the connection to the database for us and return a Boolean of **True** or **False** indicating success or failure. Of course, we will also take advantage of our status bar to provide the user with valuable visual feedback in the process.

Initializing Our ID3 Table

This is the table that we will use for generating the results of the ID3 algorithm. Here we are going to take liberty with our data. After doing a bit of research on our markets, we have decided that each country has its own language and each belongs to a region of the globe. We can use our ID3 algorithm to decide if the country, region, or language is important to new sales for each individual product.

While our database has all of the details of each sale, the products purchased, etc., we want to take a broader look. So instead of just looking at each order, we might get the results that price is important to the quantity of products sold. While this is helpful, this type of 'literal' information can be quickly retrieved with an SQL statement. We want to work a bit smarter, through. So we will add some **meta-information** (i.e. information about information) about the sale of our product. We might wish to know what language our purchasers speak. Or what region of the globe they live. This will provide our ID3 algorithm with more to work with.

We will update our table by looking at each market our customers are in and associating each with a region and language. So we are adding these additional parameters to our table. We have no way of knowing if they will be important - that is for the algorithm to tell us. As mentioned, we could have just run the ID3 algorithm on the data as-is. But this simply illustrates how you might be able to add simple meta-data to provide additional insight on the underlying data.

Take a look at the following diagram. This is how the core of our application will operate. A lot of this won't make much sense to you right now, but keep this chart in mind as you work through the rest of this chapter.

Select Product from list box

User pressed cmdAnalyze

```
setupID3 ──┬──── empties the ID3 table from last query
           │     adds Language/Region to ID3 table
           └──── calls gridID3 ──────────────────────► updates the country/language grid

buildID3 ──┬──── retrieves product/order detail from Nwind.mdb
           └──── aggregates (summarizes) data in ID3 table

determineEntropy ──┬──── builds two dimensional array with classifications
                   ├──── calls getEntropy ──────────► determines entropy for each classification
                   ├──── calls qsort ───────────────► sorts entropy in ascending order
                   └──── calls gridTheResults ───────► displays the results of the ID3 analysis
```

Try It Out - Coding the setupID3 Subroutine

1 Please add the following sub to the frmID3 form. This is a routine that will simply update our ID3 table with the region of the globe and the language spoken in each of the countries where we have customers. We will simply look at each country where we have a customer and add the region of the globe where the country is located and the language spoken by its inhabitants.

```
Public Sub setupID3()

Dim adoTempCountry As ADODB.Recordset
'holds each unique country

Dim adoTempid3 As ADODB.Recordset
'holds a recordset for ID3

Dim sCountry As String
Dim sSql As String

'------------------------------------------------------
'-- Get the unique countries and place in temp --
'------------------------------------------------------
Set adoTempCountry = New ADODB.Recordset
sSql = "SELECT DISTINCT Country FROM Customers"
Set adoTempCountry = adoConnection.Execute(sSql)
'------------------------------------------------------


'------------------------------------------------------
'-- Clean out all of the data from the ID3 table --
'------------------------------------------------------
adoConnection.Execute ("DELETE * FROM ID3")
```

```
'---------------------------
'-- Now set up the ID3 --
'---------------------------
Set adoTempid3 = New ADODB.Recordset
adoTempid3.CursorType = adOpenKeyset
adoTempid3.LockType = adLockOptimistic
adoTempid3.Open "ID3", adoConnection


'----------------------------------------------------------
'-- Iterate through the country table and add each     --
'-- unique entry to the Country field of ID3.          --
'----------------------------------------------------------


While Not adoTempCountry.EOF

    sCountry = adoTempCountry!country

    With adoTempid3
      .AddNew
      !Country = sCountry

    Select Case UCase(sCountry)
        Case "ARGENTINA"
          !CountryRegion = "South America"
          !CountryLanguage = "Spanish"
        Case "AUSTRIA"
          !CountryRegion = "Europe"
          !CountryLanguage = "German"
        Case "BELGIUM"
          !CountryRegion = "Europe"
          !CountryLanguage = "Dutch"
        Case "BRAZIL"
          !CountryRegion = "South America"
          !CountryLanguage = "Portuguese"
        Case "CANADA"
          !CountryRegion = "North America"
          !CountryLanguage = "English"
        Case "DENMARK"
          !CountryRegion = "Scandinavia"
          !CountryLanguage = "Danish"
        Case "FINLAND"
          !CountryRegion = "Scandinavia"
          !CountryLanguage = "Finnish"
        Case "FRANCE"
          !CountryRegion = "Europe"
          !CountryLanguage = "French"
        Case "GERMANY"
          !CountryRegion = "Europe"
          !CountryLanguage = "German"
        Case "IRELAND"
          !CountryRegion = "British Isles"
          !CountryLanguage = "English"
        Case "ITALY"
          !CountryRegion = "Europe"
          !CountryLanguage = "Italian"
        Case "MEXICO"
          !CountryRegion = "North America"
          !CountryLanguage = "Spanish"
```

```
                  Case "NORWAY"
                     !CountryRegion = "Scandinavia"
                     !CountryLanguage = "Norwegian"
                  Case "POLAND"
                     !CountryRegion = "Europe"
                     !CountryLanguage = "Polish"
                  Case "PORTUGAL"
                     !CountryRegion = "Mediterranean"
                     !CountryLanguage = "Portuguese"
                  Case "SPAIN"
                     !CountryRegion = "Mediterranean"
                     !CountryLanguage = "Spanish"
                  Case "SWEDEN"
                     !CountryRegion = "Scandinavia"
                     !CountryLanguage = "Swedish"
                  Case "SWITZERLAND"
                     !CountryRegion = "Europe"
                     !CountryLanguage = "German"
                  Case "UK"
                     !CountryRegion = "British Isles"
                     !CountryLanguage = "English"
                  Case "USA"
                     !CountryRegion = "North America"
                     !CountryLanguage = "English"
                  Case "VENEZUELA"
                     !CountryRegion = "South America"
                     !CountryLanguage = "Spanish"
                  Case Else
                     !CountryRegion = "Unknown"
                     !CountryLanguage = "Unknown"
               End Select
               .Update
            End With
         adoTempCountry.MoveNext
       Wend
     adoTempCountry.Close
     adoTempid3.Close

     Call gridID3

     End Sub
```

How It Works

We will open two locally scoped recordsets in this routine, **adoTempCountry** and **adoTempid3**. First, we wish to find out all of the individual countries where our clients reside. So by selecting a group of records that have a distinct country from the customers table, we know that there will only be one entry per country. Even though we might have 100 clients in Spain, by using the **DISTINCT** keyword we are assured we will only get one record for Spain. In this example, we are using the **Execute** method of the connection object to return our recordset and assign it to **adoTempCountry**.

```
sSql = "SELECT DISTINCT Country FROM Customers"
Set adoTempCountry = adoConnection.Execute(sSql)
```

The product manager will probably be doing analysis on many products. So each time a new analysis is done, we will delete all previous entries from the **ID3** table so we can start fresh.

```
adoConnection.Execute ("DELETE * FROM ID3")
```

Now we are ready to open a recordset for the currently empty **ID3** table. Again, we are still using the single form-level **adoConnection** object here. So we set a reference to our **adoTempid3** table, set two properties, and open the table. We can then update the **adoTempid3** table with information that will populate the underlying **ID3** table.

```
Set adoTempid3 = New ADODB.Recordset
adoTempid3.CursorType = adOpenKeyset
adoTempid3.LockType = adLockOptimistic
adoTempid3.Open "ID3", adoConnection
```

Now we can add our data to the **ID3** table. We take the first record of the **adoTempCountry** table that contains a record for each individual country where we have customers. Since we know the **ID3** table is empty, we add a record with the **.AddNew** method and assign the new country to the **Country** field. Now here is where we add our new perspective on the country. Depending on the country, we add both a **CountryRegion** and a **CountryLanguage** to that record. So now each country belongs to a region and language. Why is this important? Well, our ID3 algorithm might determine that all Spanish-speaking people are just craving our new beer. Or that the South American region is not buying as much of our Boysenberry, or that the Mediterranean region is starting to take off. This could provide the product manager with valuable information on how to spend those advertising dollars.

```
While Not adoTempCountry.EOF

    sCountry = adoTempCountry!Country

    With adoTempid3
      .AddNew
      !Country = sCountry

    Select Case UCase(sCountry)
        Case "ARGENTINA"
           !CountryRegion = "South America"
           !CountryLanguage = "Spanish"
```

We can see that a new record is added to the **ID3** table for each record in the **adoTempCountry** recordset. We know that **adoTempCountry** will contain a unique record for each and every country. So we walk through the **adoTempCountry** recordset. For each record in the **adoTempCountry** recordset we add a new record to the **adoTempid3** recordset with our additional information. Once we reach the end of the **adoTempCountry** recordset, we close both of them and then call **gridID3**, which will actually display the results in a flex grid.

```
adoTempCountry.Close
adoTempid3.Close

Call gridID3
```

Populating Our Region, Language, Country Flex Grid

This grid is really a reference for the product manager. You can see how our program is grouping countries. So this can easily be scrolled through for quick reference by the user.

Try It Out - Displaying the Results of Our Geographic Groupings

1 Add another sub to the frmID3 form named gridID3. We will update the geographic groupings in this single sub routine. We noticed above that this is called as soon as the setupID3 routine finishes grouping the countries by region and language. We now display the results here.

```
Public Sub gridID3()

Dim adoID3 As ADODB.Recordset
Dim sSql As String
Dim iRows As Integer
Dim iCols As Integer
Dim iRowLoop As Integer
Dim iColLoop As Integer


sSql = "SELECT CountryRegion, CountryLanguage, Country"
sSql = sSql & " FROM ID3 GROUP BY "
sSql = sSql & "CountryRegion, CountryLanguage, Country"

Set adoID3 = New ADODB.Recordset
adoID3.CursorLocation = adUseClient

adoID3.Open sSql, adoConnection, , , adCmdText

adoID3.MoveFirst

iRows = adoID3.RecordCount
iCols = adoID3.Fields.Count

miningGrid.Rows = iRows
miningGrid.Cols = iCols


'---------------------------
'-- Set up the grid here --
'---------------------------
miningGrid.Row = 0
miningGrid.ColAlignment(0) = 7

For iColLoop = 0 To miningGrid.Cols - 1
  miningGrid.Col = iColLoop
  miningGrid.MergeCol(iColLoop) = True
  miningGrid.ColWidth(iColLoop) = 1500     'Set column's width
Next
miningGrid.MergeCells = flexMergeRestrictColumns
```

```
    For iRowLoop = 0 To iRows - 1
      For iColLoop = 0 To iCols - 1
        miningGrid.Row = iRowLoop
        miningGrid.Col = iColLoop
        miningGrid.Text = adoID3.Fields(iColLoop)
      Next
      adoID3.MoveNext
    Next

    adoID3.Close

    Set adoID3 = Nothing

    End Sub
```

How It Works

We wish to retrieve the geographic information that was just placed in our **ID3** table. However, we want to retrieve the ADO recordset in a specific order. So we select the three fields we want and then group them together. This will ensure they show up correctly on our flex grid when cells are merged together.

```
    sSql = "SELECT CountryRegion, CountryLanguage, Country"
    sSql = sSql & " FROM ID3 GROUP BY "
    sSql = sSql & "CountryRegion, CountryLanguage, Country"
```

Again, rather than hard coding anything we can dynamically size our grid. We use the current recordset's **RecordCount** property to tell us how many rows and the **.Fields.Count** property to determine how many columns. This is a good technique for subs like this. We can create generalized routines that dynamically resize themselves. You could easily make this a routine where you pass in a recordset and the code automatically formats everything.

```
    iRows = adoID3.RecordCount
    iCols = adoID3.Fields.Count
```

Next we want to loop though the fields in our **miningGrid** grid to initialize them for size and merging. This next section simply loops through the columns in our recordset and updates the top row (row 0) of our grid. This places the heading on our grid. Each time through the loop - once for each field in the recordset - we set the **Col** property to the current column we want to format. We then tell it to merge and set its width. When we are finished, we set the **MergeCells** property to permit columns to merge if they have the same value. This is one of the powerful features of the grid - it will determine when and how to merge for us. That is why we retrieved the recordset using the **GROUP BY** clause in the SQL statement. We want like regions to be grouped together, and within those, the language. This way, countries in a region that have the same language will be grouped together. Of course, each country has a unique name, so there will be no grouping here. But we tried to look at the data to see which values could have identical values and placed them together.

```
    miningGrid.Row = 0
    miningGrid.ColAlignment(0) = 7

    For iColLoop = 0 To miningGrid.Cols - 1
      miningGrid.Col = iColLoop
      miningGrid.MergeCol(iColLoop) = True
      miningGrid.ColWidth(iColLoop) = 1500  'Set column's width
```

730

```
    Next
    miningGrid.MergeCells = flexMergeRestrictColumns
```

Next, we want to add some data to our grid. To lay out the grid so it looks nice and neat, we just set the **Text** of the current field to be the contents of the ordinal position of the field in the recordset. The first time through the loop, the **iRowLoop** is set to **0**. Next the program control moves to the inner, **iColLoop** and loops from **0** to how many columns there are in the recordset - 1. Since we are starting at 0, we want to go one less. If there are, say, five fields, and we loop from 0 to 4 that gives us the five fields. So the first time through the **iColLoop**, the value is **0**. We tell the grid which cell we are interested in by setting the **Row** and **Col** properties. Next we take the field in ordinal position 0 from **adoID3** and place it in the grid. We then loop through the rest of the fields in that record. When finished, we move on to the next record and repeat the process.

```
For iRowLoop = 0 To iRows - 1
  For iColLoop = 0 To iCols - 1
    miningGrid.Row = iRowLoop
    miningGrid.Col = iColLoop
    miningGrid.Text = adoID3.Fields(iColLoop)
  Next
  adoID3.MoveNext
Next
```

When complete, we close the recordset. Remember that this sub was called from **setupID3**. In turn, that was called from the **Form_Load** event procedure. There is one more initialization routine that we call from the **Load** event. This one, **updateListBoxes**, updates the list boxes with **Categories** and **Products** within the categories. Now you can see why we forced a refresh at the beginning of the **Load** event.

Try It Out - Displaying Our Categories and Products

1   Add a new sub to the frmID3 from called updateListBoxes. Here we are just updating the two list boxes to display the legitimate categories and products. This is helpful because we only show legitimate choices. Again, keeping the man/machine interface design in mind, we display a lot of information to the user. However, there is no data-entry required! The user simply clicks choices from the list boxes. Cool!

```
Public Sub updateListBoxes()

Dim adoTempRecordset As ADODB.Recordset
Dim sSql As String

'-- Let the user know what we are doing here ---
sbStatus.Panels.Item(1).Text = "Updating list boxes."

'-------------------------------------
'-- Set up the Categories list box --
'-------------------------------------
Set adoTempRecordset = New ADODB.Recordset
adoTempRecordset.CursorLocation = adUseClient
```

```
adoTempRecordset.Open _
   "SELECT * FROM Categories ORDER BY CategoryName", _
   adoConnection

ProgressBar1.Max = adoTempRecordset.RecordCount

lstCategory.Clear
With adoTempRecordset
   If .RecordCount > 0 Then .MoveFirst
   While Not .EOF
      ProgressBar1.Value = .AbsolutePosition
      lstCategory.AddItem !CategoryName
      lstCategory.ItemData(lstCategory.NewIndex) = !CategoryID
      .MoveNext
   Wend
End With
lstCategory.ListIndex = 0
ProgressBar1.Value = 0

adoTempRecordset.Close


'--------------------------
'—Set up the Products -
'--------------------------
sSql = "SELECT ProductName, ProductID FROM Products"
sSql = sSql & " WHERE CategoryID = " & _
lstCategory.ItemData(lstCategory.ListIndex)

adoTempRecordset.Open sSql, adoConnection

ProgressBar1.Max = adoTempRecordset.RecordCount

lstProduct.Clear
With adoTempRecordset
   If .RecordCount > 0 Then .MoveFirst
   While Not .EOF
      ProgressBar1.Value = .AbsolutePosition
      lstProduct.AddItem !ProductName
      lstProduct.ItemData(lstProduct.NewIndex) = !ProductID
      .MoveNext
   Wend
End With

lstProduct.ListIndex = 0
ProgressBar1.Value = 0

sbStatus.Panels.Item(1).Text = ""

End Sub
```

2 Press *F5* and run the program. All we have done so far is to add the region, language and country to our grid, and updated our list boxes. At this point, though, your project should look like this:

How It Works

We want to populate the Categories list box first. We know there is a one-to-many relationship between category and product. One category has many products associated with it. We want to have the recordset return the categories in alphabetical order, so the **ORDER BY** does that job for us. Again, please keep little things like this in mind. In the absence of any other logical grouping for returned records, it's better to group them in alpha order. It displays order and security to the user, rather than having the categories returned in a hap hazard way.

```
adoTempRecordset.Open _
    "SELECT * FROM Categories ORDER BY CategoryName", _
    adoConnection
```

We are then planning on looping through the **adoTempRecordset** and stuffing the category name into the **lstCategory** list box. But first, notice that we are setting the **Max** property of the progress bar to the **RecordCount** property of the recordset. This will permit us to graphically show the user the progress. By now you are noticing that showing the user progress is our standard Modus Operandi - our MO. This is a very good habit to get into. The graphical tools really lend themselves to this, so we should use them wherever possible.

We then clear out any previous contents of the **lstCategory** list box by calling its **Clear** method. Then we loop through the recordset, and, as a sanity check, we ensure that the current record pointer is pointing to the first record.

We then loop through and update the progress bar. If there were eight records in the recordset, then the **Max** property would have been set to 8 and when we set the value, the progress bar would now be 1/8th filled in. Next, we add the **CategoryName** to our list box. Finally, we use

733

the **ItemData** property of the list box. This permits us to add a hidden value along with the visible value the user sees in the list box. Then, we move to the next record in the **adoTempRecordset** and do the same thing until we reach the end.

```
ProgressBar1.Max = adoTempRecordset.RecordCount

lstCategory.Clear
With adoTempRecordset
  If .RecordCount > 0 Then .MoveFirst
  While Not .EOF
    ProgressBar1.Value = .AbsolutePosition
    lstCategory.AddItem !CategoryName
    lstCategory.ItemData(lstCategory.NewIndex) = !CategoryID
    .MoveNext
  Wend
End With
lstCategory.ListIndex = 0
ProgressBar1.Value = 0

adoTempRecordset.Close
```

Let's spend a minute discussing the **ItemData** property of the list box. The **ItemData** property is an array of long integer values. It has the same number of items in it as the control's **List** property. So we can use the list box's index number to identify the items. This is hidden from the user. For the visible entry we place in the list box using the **AddItem** method, we can place a hidden value the **ItemData** property. So when the user clicks on an entry in the list box, say the 5th element, we can retrieve the value in the **ItemData** property. In our case, when the user clicks on a category, we are going to retrieve the hidden **CategoryID** value so we can refresh the Products list box with all of the products for this category.

Once the list box is populated, the **ListIndex** is set to **0**. This highlights the first item in the list box (remember that collections start at 0?). We also zero out the progress bar.

> *I use the ItemData property when displaying items such as employee names. Each name is added to the list box with the AddItem method as expected. But I then add the employee ID to the ItemData property of that list box. Since an employee database would be keyed on an employee number (which might be a social security number), that is used as the unique primary key. For example, we might have five John Smiths in the database and hence the list box, but in the ItemData property is the unique identifier for each of the Smiths. So when the user clicks on a name, the unique identifier for the name in the ItemData property is retrieved. This is what is used to hit the database and retrieve the employee record. The employee number means nothing to the user, but the name does. However, we can't retrieve a guaranteed unique record only by the name, so the unique employee ID, hidden from the user, does the trick.*

We then go on to update the Products list box in exactly the same way. In the **ItemData** property, we stuff the **ProductID** value for each product. We will be using these values in a bit to embed in SQL queries to retrieve records from the database.

We are not quite finished with the list boxes. When a user clicks on a selection in the **Categories** list box, we refresh the Products list box with all products for only that category. Let's look at how this is done.

734

Try It Out - Retrieving Products for a Category

1 In the Click event of the lstCategory list box, add the following code. When the user clicks on the Categories list box, we simply build a SQL query that will retrieve all of the products where the CategoryID is equal to the CategoryID for the currently selected category. In other words, when the user clicks on an item in the Categories list box, we grab the CategoryID that we placed in the ItemData property and round up all of the products that have this same ID. These are then displayed in the Products list box.

```
Private Sub lstCategory_Click()

Dim adoTempProducts As ADODB.Recordset
Dim adoTempPicture As ADODB.Recordset

Dim sSql As String

sSql = "SELECT ProductName, ProductID FROM Products"
sSql = sSql & " WHERE CategoryID = "
sSql = sSql &  lstCategory.ItemData(lstCategory.ListIndex)

Set adoTempProducts = New ADODB.Recordset
adoTempProducts.CursorLocation = adUseClient

adoTempProducts.Open sSql, adoConnection


If adoTempProducts.RecordCount > 0 Then _
 adoTempProducts.MoveLast
ProgressBar1.Max = adoTempProducts.RecordCount
adoTempProducts.MoveFirst

lstProduct.Clear
With adoTempProducts
   If .RecordCount > 0 Then .MoveFirst
   While Not .EOF
     ProgressBar1.Value = .AbsolutePosition
     lstProduct.AddItem !ProductName
     lstProduct.ItemData(lstProduct.NewIndex) = !ProductID
     .MoveNext
   Wend
End With
lstProduct.ListIndex = 0
ProgressBar1.Value = 0
adoTempProducts.Close

sbStatus.Panels.Item(1).Text = ""

Call showAnalysis

End Sub
```

How It Works

The following SQL statement is the brains of the operation. When the user clicks on a selection in the Categories list box, we dynamically generate a SQL statement. We want to retrieve the products associated with the selected category; so we can grab the **ProductName** and the **ProductID** from the Products table where the **CategoryID** is the value we stuffed in the **ItemData** property of the list box. This way, we only retrieve products that have the required **CategoryID**.

```
sSql = "SELECT ProductName, ProductID FROM Products"
sSql = sSql & " WHERE CategoryID = "
sSql = sSql &  lstCategory.ItemData(lstCategory.ListIndex)
```

We retrieve that recordset based on the above SQL, clear the list box of old entries, and blast in the new products and IDs. Since the code is the same as above, we don't need to go over it here. But the great thing is that when the user clicks on a category, only relevant products will be displayed.

If you had your thinking hats on, you might have remembered that just a while ago in the **updateListBoxes** routine, we set the **ListIndex** property to **0**. This has the effect of clicking and highlighting the first item - item 0. When this happens as the program is initialized, the **Click** code is executed and only the products for the first category will be displayed. So by setting the **ListIndex** property using code, we simply simulate someone clicking the first item.

```
Call showAnalysis
```

You might have noticed the call to **showAnalysis** at the end of the routine. Quite simply, this places some English text in the **txtAnalysis** box so the user can see the criteria that will be used when the Analyze button is clicked. This is a simple visual conformation of what items will be analyzed if the Analyze button gets clicked.

Try It Out - Displaying What Will be Analyzed

1 Please add a new sub to the frmID3 form. Name the sub showAnalysis and enter the following code.

```
Public Sub showAnalysis()

Dim sAnalysis As String

sAnalysis = "Search / Analysis Criteria:  " & vbCrLf
sAnalysis = sAnalysis & " Category:  " & lstCategory & vbCrLf
sAnalysis = sAnalysis & " Product:  " & lstProduct & vbCrLf
txtAnalysis = sAnalysis

End Sub
```

2 Now place this single line of code in the lstProduct_Click event. This will just update the **txtAnalysis** text box.

```
Private Sub lstProduct_Click()

Call showAnalysis

End Sub
```

3 Press *F5* to test our list boxes and the **showAnalysis** sub. The Categories and Products list boxes should be populated. The first item in each should be highlighted because we set the ListIndex property to 0 for each of them.

How It Works

Since we set the Products list box's **ListIndex** to **0** when the program is initialized, a call to **showAnalysis** is made - just as if the user clicked an item. Our routine just takes the current item in the Categories and Products list boxes and displays them in the **txtAnalysis** text box. Since we set the **MultiLine** property to **True**, the built-in VB constant **vbCrLf** (for carriage return/line feed) places each string of text on its own line in the text box. We will be using this text box to show the results, but it was too much screen real estate to waste while the user made a selection. So here we just provide a bit of reinforcement.

Now we have the infrastructure of our program down. The user interface looks good. So now let's write the code that actually does the grunt work and performs the analysis.

Performing the Analysis

The **cmdAnalyze** button starts the process rolling. We simply empty out the **txtAnalysis** text box and call three routines. We have already examined the first routine, **setupID3**. This deletes all records in the **ID3** table that might have been left over from a previous analysis and resets the country information. So now it's time to look at the code for the analysis.

Try It Out - Performing the Analysis

1 In the Click event of the cmdAnalyze button, please add the following code. Notice that we are clearing out the txtAnalysis box and then calling three routines, one after the other. We already wrote the setupID3 routine. As you recall, that routine added the region and language to our ID3 table. So that is called each time the user wishes to analyze another product. So now we need to write the next two routines, the buildID3 and determineEntropy routines.

```
Private Sub cmdAnalyze_Click()

txtAnalysis = ""
Call setupID3
Call buildID3
Call determineEntropy

End Sub
```

2 Add another sub to your **frmID3** form with the name **buildID3**. This is rather long, but it actually populates the rest of our **ID3** table. Essentially, we are gong to use some monster SQL statements to retrieve information from the existing tables and make some deductions about the contents. This is the aggregation we were discussing earlier. Don't worry if this looks a bit scary. We will go over it piece by piece. But for now, please enter the code into the **buildID3** sub.

```
Private Sub buildID3()

Dim sSql As String
Dim sCriteria As String
Dim sCurrentCountry As String
Dim sCurrentLanguage As String
Dim sCurrentRegion As String
Dim adoRequestedData As ADODB.Recordset
Dim adoID3 As ADODB.Recordset

sbStatus.Panels.Item(1).Text = "Building Query."
sbStatus.Panels.Item(2).Text = "Working..."

'-------------------------------------------------------------
'-- This SQL will retrieve the Category Name, Total,
'-- Order Date, Country, and Product Name for the categories
'-- requested.
'-------------------------------------------------------------
```

```
sSql = "SELECT DISTINCTROW Categories.CategoryName, "
sSql = sSql & " SUM([Order Details].Quantity) AS Total,"
sSql = sSql & " Orders.OrderDate, Customers.Country,"
sSQL = sSQL & " Products.ProductName "
sSql = sSql & " FROM (Customers INNER JOIN Orders ON "
sSql = sSql & " Customers.CustomerID = Orders.CustomerID)"
sSql = sSql & " INNER JOIN ((Categories INNER JOIN Products"
sSql = sSql & " ON Categories.CategoryID ="
sSql = sSql & " Products.CategoryID) INNER JOIN "
sSql = sSql & " [Order Details] ON Products.ProductID = "
sSql = sSql & " [Order Details].ProductID) ON "
sSql = sSql & " Orders.OrderID = [Order Details].OrderID "


'----------------------------
'-- Now check the criteria --
'----------------------------
sCriteria = ""
sCriteria = sCriteria & " Categories.CategoryID = " & _
    lstCategory.ItemData(lstCategory.ListIndex)
sCriteria = sCriteria & " AND "
sCriteria = sCriteria & " Products.ProductID = " & _
    lstProduct.ItemData(lstProduct.ListIndex)

sSql = sSql & " WHERE " & sCriteria

sSql = sSql & " GROUP BY "
sSql = sSql & " Categories.CategoryName, "
sSql = sSql & "[Order Details].Quantity, Products.ProductName,"
sSql = sSql & " Orders.OrderDate, Customers.Country "
sSql = sSql & " ORDER BY Categories.CategoryName "

'MsgBox sSql

'-----------------------------------------------------
'-- Open a recordset with the results of the query --
'-----------------------------------------------------
Set adoRequestedData = New ADODB.Recordset
adoRequestedData.CursorLocation = adUseClient
adoRequestedData.CursorType = adOpenDynamic
adoRequestedData.Open sSql, adoConnection


'---------------------------------------------
'-- If there were no records, exit the sub --
'---------------------------------------------
With adoRequestedData
   If (.RecordCount < 1) Then
     MsgBox "No records"
     Exit Sub
   Else
     ProgressBar1.Max = .RecordCount
     .MoveFirst
   End If
End With

sbStatus.Panels.Item(1).Text = "Determining Sales Information"

'------------------------------------------------------------
'-- Now, create the ID3 table and prepare to refresh --
'------------------------------------------------------------
```

```
  Set adoID3 = New ADODB.Recordset
  sSql = "SELECT * FROM ID3"
  adoID3.Open sSql, adoConnection, adOpenDynamic, _
    adLockOptimistic, adCmdText
  '----------------------------------------------------------
  '-- Loop through all of the records in the recordset
  '-- returned by the query and update the ID3 table based
  '-- on the results.
  '----------------------------------------------------------
  With adoRequestedData
   While Not .EOF

     ProgressBar1.Value = .AbsolutePosition
     DoEvents
     sCurrentCountry = !Country
     adoID3.Filter = "Country = '" & sCurrentCountry & "'"
     If ((Not adoID3.BOF) And (Not adoID3.EOF)) Then
       adoID3!Category = !CategoryName
       adoID3!Product = !ProductName
       If (Year(!OrderDate) = "1995") Then
               adoID3!OldQuantity = adoID3!OldQuantity + !Total
       ElseIf (Year(!OrderDate) = "1996") Then
               adoID3!NewQuantity = adoID3!NewQuantity + !Total
       End If
       If (adoID3!OldQuantity < adoID3!NewQuantity) Then
               adoID3!SalesUp = True
       Else
               adoID3!SalesUp = False
       End If
       If (adoID3!NewQuantity > 0) And (adoID3!OldQuantity > 0) _
           Then
         adoID3!UpByHowMuch = _
CSng(Format((adoID3!NewQuantity/adoID3!OldQuantity), "##.###"))
       End If
       '-- There were only sales in the current year --
       If (adoID3!NewQuantity > 0) And (adoID3!OldQuantity < 1) _
           Then
         adoID3!UpByHowMuch = CSng(Format(1, "##.###"))
       End If
       '-- There were only sales in the previous year --
       If (adoID3!NewQuantity < 1) And (adoID3!OldQuantity > 0) _
           Then
         adoID3!UpByHowMuch = CSng(Format(-1, "##.###"))
       End If
       adoID3.Update
     End If
     .MoveNext
   Wend
  End With

  adoConnection.Execute _
  ("DELETE * FROM ID3 WHERE ((OldQuantity = 0)" _
   & " AND (NewQuantity = 0))")
  sbStatus.Panels.Item(1).Text = ""
  sbStatus.Panels.Item(2).Text = "Ready."
  ProgressBar1.Value = 0

  Exit Sub
```

```
    myError:
    MsgBox (Err.Description)


    End Sub
```

How It Works

While this looks crazy, we are really just doing something rather simple. First, we are retrieving the details on all of the orders placed for the product requested to be analyzed. We then loop through the recordset and add all of the sales for 1993 into the old quantity field for a specific country and all of the 1994 sales into the new quantity field. We then determine if the sales have gone up or down from year to year, and by how much. So we will have all of this data for each country for the specific product in our **ID3** table. See, we are aggregating the sales from several years and storing the data in our **ID3** table. Let's walk through the code and discuss how we are doing this. But in a nutshell, here is what this routine is doing:

> An SQL statement retrieves all of the relevant information on the product to be analyzed.

> That information is placed in the recordset **adoRequestedData**.

> We then open the **adoID3** recordset. Remember now there is a record for each country, but the rest of the fields are empty.

> We then loop through each of the **adoRequestedData** records.

> The sales figures for each country are summed in the **adoID3** table. All sales for 1995 are summed in the **oldQuantity** field and 1996 sales are summed in the **NewQuantity** field for that country's record.

> When all records in the **adoRequestedData** for each country have been reviewed, we determine if the sales of the product in 1996 was greater than 1995. We then determine the growth between years. The fields **SalesUp** and **UpByHowMuch** are then calculated for that country's record in the **adoID3** recordset.

Let's look at the code and examine how each of these steps works.

The Big Kahuna of SQL Statements

First, we need to retrieve fields from the tables where the records meet the criteria the user selected to be analyzed. We want to build an SQL statement to get the raw data we need to update our **ID3** table. Since the statement is a bit longer than what we have previously built, the easiest way is to build the statement in three sections.

The first part of the SQL statement explains the fields that we want to retrieve. We ask for the **CategoryName**, next we create a derived field that provides the total quantity of the orders for that category, then the date, the country, and finally the product name.

We must then provide SQL join operations so the relations between the tables can be exploited. We are retrieving data from the **Categories, Order Details, Orders, Customers** and **Products** tables in a single recordset.

```
    sSql = "SELECT DISTINCTROW Categories.CategoryName, "
    sSql = sSql & " SUM([Order Details].Quantity) AS Total,"
    sSql = sSql & " Orders.OrderDate, Customers.Country,"
    sSQL = sSQL & " Products.ProductName "
```

741

```
sSql = sSql & " FROM (Customers INNER JOIN Orders ON "
sSql = sSql & " Customers.CustomerID = Orders.CustomerID)"
sSql = sSql & " INNER JOIN ((Categories INNER JOIN Products"
sSql = sSql & " ON Categories.CategoryID ="
sSql = sSql & " Products.CategoryID) INNER JOIN "
sSql = sSql & " [Order Details] ON Products.ProductID = "
sSql = sSql & " OrderDetails.ProductID) ON "
sSql = sSql & " Orders.OrderID = [Order Details].OrderID "
```

Since the SQL statement is really a single string, we keep concatenating the string **sSql** that will provide the query. To give you a visual sense of how we are going to retrieve the fields, if you have Microsoft Access, you can see the relationships. As a personal opinion, if you don't have Access, this feature alone is well worth the price. As I mentioned before, you can experiment until you get your query right in Access, then cut/paste the SQL statement it generates and tweak it.

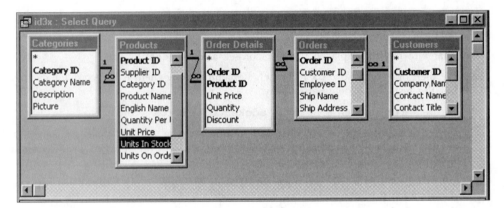

Once we have defined the fields required, we establish the criteria by using the **WHERE** clause. Notice that we are retrieving records where the **CategoryID** is equal to the **ItemData** value of the selected field. Remember when we stuffed this value in there when we populated the list box. Now we take that ID value that is associated with the user selection. Likewise, we also want the **ProductID** to be equal to the **ItemData** value of the **lstProduct** list box. Once we build that string, we append it to the first part of the SQL statement and preface it with the **WHERE** clause.

```
sCriteria = ""
sCriteria = sCriteria & " Categories.CategoryID = " & _
    lstCategory.ItemData(lstCategory.ListIndex)
sCriteria = sCriteria & " AND "
sCriteria = sCriteria & " Products.ProductID = " & _
    lstProduct.ItemData(lstProduct.ListIndex)

sSql = sSql & " WHERE " & sCriteria
```

Finally, we want the data returned to us in a specific order. By using the SQL **GROUP BY** clause, we can get the records returned grouped by **CategoryName**, then **Quantity**, then **ProductName**, then **OrderDate**, and finally **Country**. The SQL **ORDER BY** clause sorts items in **CategoryName** sequence.

```
sSql = sSql & " GROUP BY "
sSql = sSql & " Categories.CategoryName, "
sSql = sSql & "[Order Details].Quantity, Products.ProductName,"
sSql = sSql & " Orders.OrderDate, Customers.Country "
sSql = sSql & " ORDER BY Categories.CategoryName "
```

When you are testing out the SQL statement, you might want to add a message box right after the statement is built. You could just add:

```
MsgBox sSql
```

This line will show you the fully built SQL before you try to open a recordset with it. You can check that the values are set. Notice in the **WHERE** clause the **Category ID = 1** and the **Product ID = 1**. This ensures that the correct values are being embedded in the statement.

However, your eyesight must be pretty good to read this thing! Remember when we discussed re aggregating data from several tables? You can see that is exactly what we are doing here. The individual tables are nicely normalized. But since we are trying to draw some conclusions from data that resides in each of them, we round up all of the fields needed from each of the tables and place the results in a recordset **adoRequestedData**. Now we are ready to execute the query and create the recordset.

We set properties on the **adoRequestedData** recordset and pass the **Open** method the **sSql** statement. Notice that on this recordset, we are setting properties before we open the recordset. We want the client-side cursor so we can get the **RecordCount** property. We are setting the **CursorType** property instead of passing it as a parameter to the **Open** method of the recordset just to show you that it can be done this way.

```
Set adoRequestedData = New ADODB.Recordset
adoRequestedData.CursorLocation = adUseClient
adoRequestedData.CursorType = adOpenDynamic
adoRequestedData.Open sSql, adoConnection
```

The **adoRequestedData** recordset holds all of the relevant information on the specific product the product manager wants to analyze. If there are records returned from our request in the **adoRequestedData** table, we are ready to go to work on our **adoID3** recordset. Again, the **adoID3** recordset will hold the results of our analysis on the data returned in the **adoRequestedData** recordset.

We set a reference to our **adoID3** recordset and then open it, selecting all records to be returned. Remember that we will have as many records in our **ID3** table as we had unique countries. However, there are still a few fields in each record that we now need to fill out, such as the sales numbers - are the current sales greater than previous sales, etc.

```
Set adoID3 = New ADODB.Recordset
sSql = "SELECT * FROM ID3"
adoID3.Open sSql, adoConnection, adOpenDynamic, _
    adLockOptimistic, adCmdText
```

We are now ready to build the rest of our **ID3** table. We can now attempt to deduce any sales patterns by summing the sales information from the **adoRequestedData** recordset and placing it in the **adoID3** recordset.

Aggregating Data in Our ID3 Table

The **adoRequestedData** recordset will be walked through one record at a time. As we loop through the **While Not .EOF** loop, we first update the progress bar. Users love this and they feel important as it progresses. Just watch them puff out their chests as the blue blocks progress.

Next we take the country out of the current record of the **adoRequestedData** recordset. Remember that we returned the records on the product being analyzed, and the sales information includes multiple sales from multiple countries. However, if we had 100 sales of our new beer to France, each of the sales figures will be distilled to a single record for France in our **ID3** table.

We take the first record in the **adoRequestedData** recordset and assign its country, say it's France, to the variable **sCurrentCountry**. Remember that there might be 100 records of sales of our product to France in the **adoRequestedData** recordset.

We want to find the **adoID3** record for that country, France. There are two ways to do this. First, we could execute an SQL statement against the **adoID3** table to retrieve all records **"WHERE Country = '"** & sCurrentCountry & **"'"**. But you already know how to do this, so here we are using a new ADO 2.0 feature - the **Filter** property.

```
With adoRequestedData
  While Not .EOF

    ProgressBar1.Value = .AbsolutePosition
    DoEvents
    sCurrentCountry = !Country
    adoID3.Filter = "Country = '" & sCurrentCountry & "'"
```

The **Filter** property can be used to select specific records in a recordset object when using client-side cursors. The filtered recordset becomes the current cursor. By setting the property, the current record becomes the first record that satisfied the values for the filter. Remember that **adoID3** was opened with all records in the table. By setting the filter, we are isolating only those records that satisfy a criterion. In this case, we only want those that equal the country in the current record of **adoRequestedData**. Of course, there will only be one record returned from **ID3**, because each **ID3** record has a unique country.

> *It would probably be just a tad faster to create a SQL statement against the ID3 table to get the specific record. However, this is a good place to illustrate this new property. It works just fine for our purposes.*

Let's assume that **sCurrentRecord** = "France". If a record was returned from the filtered **ID3** - and we know it will - we add the **CategoryName** and **ProductName** to the record. Remember that we can only analyze a single product at a time, so this will be the same for each record in the **ID3** table.

```
If ((Not adoID3.BOF) And (Not adoID3.EOF)) Then
        adoID3!Category = !CategoryName
        adoID3!Product = !ProductName
```

The year is plucked from the date of the order from the current **adoRequestedData** record. If it is 1995, we add it to the **OldQuantity**, else if the order was placed in 1996, we add it to the **NewQuantity**. So if there are 100 orders for this product from France, all of the orders are summed in either of the two fields. For example, if there were 50 orders placed in 1995 and 50 placed in 1996, the totals for each year will be in the respective fields in the single **adoID3** record. This will permit us to compare the growth rates of the two years.

Now we can simply update our binary field, **SalesUp**, in the **ID3** table. If the quantity sold of the product being analyzed in 1995 was less than the quantity sold in 1996, then we set the **SalesUp** to **True**. This simply tells us that there is an upward trend. Otherwise, we set **SalesUp** to **False**. We are simply deducing a new piece of data that is not in our existing tables anywhere. This is clearly a helpful piece of information for the product manager.

```
If (adoID3!OldQuantity < adoID3!NewQuantity) Then
    adoID3!SalesUp = True
Else
    adoID3!SalesUp = False
End If
```

We are now in a position to determine the relative growth of the product over the two years. If both of the quantity fields have a value, then we calculate the **UpByHowMuch** field. A value of 1.0 means that sales were steady. Any value greater than 1 tells us how much growth. A value less than one, say 0.80 tells us that sales were down from one year to the next. Quite simply, we divide the **NewQuantity** (1996 sales) by the **OldQuantity** (1995 sales). To ensure that we have the values stored in a standardized way in the **ID3** table, we first **Format** the field. Finally, we convert (cast) the result to a single using **CSng**. This value is then placed in the **UpByHowMuch** field in the **adoID3** recordset.

```
If (adoID3!NewQuantity > 0) And (adoID3!OldQuantity > 0) _
        Then
            adoID3!UpByHowMuch = _
    CSng(Format((adoID3!NewQuantity/adoID3!OldQuantity), "##.###"))
End If
```

Thinking About Exceptions

It could be that we are analyzing a new product and there are only sales in 1996 but not 1995. Or, the product could have been discontinued in 1995, so there are no 1996 numbers. If we only had sales in one of the two years, we simply hard code in a 1 or -1 in the field. This will tell us if we went up or down. So if there were no sales in 1995 but some in 1996, we place a 1 telling us that there was some growth, but we don't have a relative measure yet because there is no history. However, if there were no sales in 1996 but some in 1995, we add a –1. Finally, we call the **Update** method of the recordset and write the results to the database.

```
'-- There were only sales in the current year --
If (adoID3!NewQuantity > 0) And (adoID3!OldQuantity < 1) _
        Then
    adoID3!UpByHowMuch = CSng(Format(1, "##.###"))
End If
'-- There were only sales in the previous year --
If (adoID3!NewQuantity < 1) And (adoID3!OldQuantity > 0) _
        Then
    adoID3!UpByHowMuch = CSng(Format(-1, "##.###"))
End If
adoID3.Update
```

There are some records in the database where sales for both years are 0. Why? Remember when we initialized the **ID3** table we created a record for each country. Well, if the product we are analyzing did not have any sales to a specific country, we want to delete that record from the **ID3** table. Otherwise, we would not get an accurate picture of what is really happening with sales. We just 'clean' the data to eliminate those records that could skew our results. Data mining technologists call this cleaning, or scrubbing the data prior to analysis.

```
adoConnection.Execute _
("DELETE * FROM ID3 WHERE ((OldQuantity = 0)" _
& " AND (NewQuantity = 0))")
```

So if we ran a query on, say the Carnarvon Tigers product in the Seafood category, the **ID3** table might look like this when the **buildID3** routine is complete. Notice the sales to France. There were a total of 98 orders placed from France in 1995 but only 36 placed for 1996. So the SalesUp check box is not checked, so we know sales were down. We calculated sales to be only 36 percent of the previous year! We also see examples of no sale in 1995 for Italy, but a total of 8 for 1996. This is a case where we place a 1 in the UpByHowMuch field. Likewise, there were 8 products sold to Norway in 1995 but none in 1996, so a –1 is placed here.

Category	Product	OldQu	NewQu	Country	Sales	UpByH	CountryRegion	CountryLan
Seafood	Carnarvon	9	35	Austria	☑	4	Europe	German
Seafood	Carnarvon	24	29	Brazil	☑	1	South America	Portuguese
Seafood	Carnarvon	98	36	France	☐	0	Europe	French
Seafood	Carnarvon	64	10	Germany	☐	0	Europe	German
Seafood	Carnarvon	25	8	Ireland	☐	0	British Isles	English
Seafood	Carnarvon	0	8	Italy	☑	1	Europe	Italian
Seafood	Carnarvon	8	0	Norway	☐	-1	Scandinavia	Norwegian
Seafood	Carnarvon	33	30	USA	☐	1	North America	English
Seafood	Carnarvon	0	25	Venezuela	☑	1	South America	Spanish

Record: 1 of 9

Now that we have aggregated our data in the **ID3** table, let's see if we can make any deductions from the results. Everything we have done up to now has been to build this **ID3** table. This table represents the re-aggregation of data we have been discussing.

Determining the Entropy of the Values We Added

This next procedure, **determineEntropy**, is the last one called from the **cmdAnalyze** button. What we want to do here is calculate something called (surprise!) **entropy**. The term comes from communication theory and is a precise measurement of information. Remember that we added the fields **CountryLanguage**, **CountryRegion** and **Country** to our **ID3** table? What we now want to do is determine the relative impact of each of these categories on total sales growth. Entropy is a measure of the uncertainty of the classification. The smaller the number, the less 'uncertainty' that the specific classification is important to the result, sales growth. As the number increases, the more uncertainty there is that this classification really does influence the sales growth.

We want to see how the three categories: **CountryLanguage**, **CountryRegion** and **Country** compare in importance to sales growth. We will do that by calculating the entropy factor for each. The lesser of the three numbers indicates the factor that is the most important in sales growth.

Try It Out - Determining which Factors Impact Sales the Most!

1 Please add another sub to the **frmID3** form called **determineEntropy**. Add the following code to that procedure.

```
Private Sub determineEntropy()

Dim adoTemp As ADODB.Recordset
Dim sSql As String
Dim totalSamples As Integer
Dim entropyCountry As Single
Dim entropyCountryLanguage As Single
Dim entropyCountryRegion As Single
Dim Position(2, 1) As Variant 'holds the classifications

sbStatus.Panels.Item(1).Text = "Determining Entropy..."
sbStatus.Panels.Item(2).Text = "Working..."

adoConnection.Execute("DELETE * FROM ID3 WHERE Category = NULL")
'-----------------------------------------------------
'-- Determine how many records are in the ID3 Table --
'-----------------------------------------------------
Set adoTemp = New ADODB.Recordset
sSql = "SELECT count(*) as HowMany from ID3"
adoTemp.Open sSql, adoConnection
totalSamples = adoTemp!HowMany
adoTemp.Close
```

```
'-------------------------------------------------------------
'-- Determine the relative Entropy on each of the fields --
'-------------------------------------------------------------
entropycountryLanguage = getEntropy _
    ("CountryLanguage", totalSamples)
Position(0, 0) = entropycountryLanguage
Position(0, 1) = "CountryLanguage"
entropyCountryRegion = getEntropy("CountryRegion", totalSamples)
Position(1, 0) = entropyCountryRegion
Position(1, 1) = "CountryRegion"
entropyCountry = getEntropy("Country", totalSamples)
Position(2, 0) = entropyCountry
Position(2, 1) = "Country"

Call qsort(Position, LBound(Position), UBound(Position))

txtAnalysis = "ID3 Analysis of the Category " & lstCategory & _
    " and the Product " & lstProduct & vbCrLf
txtAnalysis = txtAnalysis & "The lesser the entropy, the more "
txtAnalysis = txtAnalysis & "important is this Attribute "
txtAnalysis = txtAnalysis & "to overall Sales" & vbCrLf
txtAnalysis = txtAnalysis & Position(0, 1) & " Entropy: " & _
    Position(0, 0) & vbCrLf
txtAnalysis = txtAnalysis & Position(1, 1) & " Entropy: " & _
    Position(1, 0) & vbCrLf
txtAnalysis = txtAnalysis & Position(2, 1) & " Entropy: " & _
    Position(2, 0) & vbCrLf
txtAnalysis = txtAnalysis & "Product Manager - Review sales to: "
txtAnalysis = txtAnalysis & Position(0, 1) & vbCrLf

Call gridTheResults

sbStatus.Panels.Item(1).Text = ""
sbStatus.Panels.Item(2).Text = "Ready."

End Sub
```

How It Works

We will essentially determine the entropy factor on each of our three classifications and present the results to the product manager. But we want to ensure we are working with clean and valid data. In our effort to scrub the data, we want to delete any records from our **ID3** table that could have a **NULL** value in the **Category** field. Remember that we are working with legacy data here. We can never assume that it is perfect. We must be on guard to ensure the data we are working with is clean. Once we do that, we just determine how many records are left in our **ID3** table. This number, **totalSamples**, is used to see how each of the categories we are looking at did compared with all of the samples.

```
adoConnection.Execute ("DELETE * FROM ID3 WHERE Category = NULL")
'-------------------------------------------------------
'-- Determine how many records are in the ID3 Table --
'-------------------------------------------------------
Set adoTemp = New ADODB.Recordset
sSql = "SELECT count(*) as HowMany from ID3"
adoTemp.Open sSql, adoConnection
totalSamples = adoTemp!HowMany
adoTemp.Close
```

Now we have a clean **ID3** table. It only contains records where we have valid sales data for each country that actually ordered this product we are analyzing. Now that the table is clean, we are prepared to determine the entropy factor for the **CountryLanguage**, **CountryRegion** and **Country**. We have another routine, **getEntropy**, that will do the calculations for us.

```
entropyCountryLanguage = getEntropy _
    ("CountryLanguage", totalSamples)
Position(0, 0) = entropyCountryLanguage
Position(0, 1) = "CountryLanguage"
entropyCountryRegion = getEntropy("CountryRegion", totalSamples)
Position(1, 0) = entropyCountryRegion
Position(1, 1) = "CountryRegion"
entropyCountry = getEntropy("Country", totalSamples)
Position(2, 0) = entropyCountry
Position(2, 1) = "Country"
```

We call the **getEntropy** routine and pass it two parameters, the classification we want to get the entropy factor on and **totalSamples** - just how many records are in the recordset.
So in the first line, we call the **getEntropy** routine and pass in **"CountryLanguage"** and the **totalSamples**. We assign the value that is returned to us to **entropyCountryLanguage**. We then update the local variant array, **Position**. In the first row, first position **(0, 0)** put in the entropy value that was returned for the **CountryLanguage**. Then in the first row, second position **(0, 1)** we add the title, **"CountryLanguage"**. We then do this for the **CountryRegion** and then **Country**. Now we don't know how the values should be ranked.

In order to sort our array, I have included a modified quick sort routine that will sort the contents of our array, **Position**, from the lowest entropy factor to the highest. We simply call this routine and pass in the array with its lower and upper bounds. This routine, which we will write in a minute, will place the lowest entropy value first. As mentioned, the lower the score, the better. This means that this particular classification has the least uncertainty.

```
Call qsort(Position, LBound(Position), UBound(Position))
```

Once the array has been sorted, we display the results in the **txtAnalysis** text box. We also instruct the product manager to look at the value in the lowest category - whatever that might be. This is the category that is the most relevant to sales growth for that particular product.

```
txtAnalysis = "ID3 Analysis of the Category " & lstCategory & _
    " and the Product " & lstProduct & vbCrLf
txtAnalysis = txtAnalysis & "The lesser the entropy, the more "
txtAnalysis = txtAnalysis & "important is this Attribute "
txtAnalysis = txtAnalysis & "to overall Sales" & vbCrLf
txtAnalysis = txtAnalysis & Position(0, 1) & " Entropy: " & _
    Position(0, 0) & vbCrLf
txtAnalysis = txtAnalysis & Position(1, 1) & " Entropy: " & _
    Position(1, 0) & vbCrLf
txtAnalysis = txtAnalysis & Position(2, 1) & " Entropy: " & _
    Position(2, 0) & vbCrLf
txtAnalysis = txtAnalysis & "Product Manager - Review sales to: "
txtAnalysis = txtAnalysis & Position(0, 1) & vbCrLf
```

Finally, we call our generalized routine, **gridTheResults**. This will display the details of the ID3 algorithm to the user so she can visually see the relationships between the classifications.

```
Call gridTheResults

sbStatus.Panels.Item(1).Text = ""
sbStatus.Panels.Item(2).Text = "Ready."
```

Let's add the **gridTheResults** subroutine now!

Try It Out - Displaying Results in the resultsGrid FlexGrid

1 Add the following new subroutine called **gridTheResults** to the **frmID3** form.

```
Public Sub gridTheResults()

'-------------------------------------------------
'-- Now let's update the grid with the regions --
'-------------------------------------------------
Dim adoID3 As ADODB.Recordset
Dim sSql As String
Dim iRows As Integer
Dim iCols As Integer
Dim iRowLoop As Integer
Dim iColLoop As Integer

sSql = "SELECT UpByHowMuch, OldQuantity, NewQuantity,"
sSql = sSql & " CountryRegion, CountryLanguage, Country FROM"
sSql = sSql & " ID3 ORDER BY UpByHowMuch DESC,"
sSql = sSql & " CountryRegion, CountryLanguage"

Set adoID3 = New ADODB.Recordset
adoID3.CursorLocation = adUseClient

adoID3.Open sSql, adoConnection, , , adCmdText

adoID3.MoveFirst

iRows = adoID3.RecordCount
iCols = adoID3.Fields.Count

resultsGrid.Rows = iRows
resultsGrid.Cols = iCols
'--------------------------
'-- Set up the grid here --
'--------------------------
resultsGrid.Row = 0

For iColLoop = 0 To resultsGrid.Cols - 1
  With resultsGrid
     .Col = iColLoop
     .ColWidth(iColLoop) = 1400
     .ColAlignment(iColLoop) = 7
     Select Case iColLoop
```

```
            Case 0
              .Text = "Growth Factor"
              .MergeCol(iColLoop) = True
            Case 1
              .Text = "Previous Qty"
              .MergeCol(iColLoop) = True
            Case 2
              .Text = "Recent Qty"
              .MergeCol(iColLoop) = True
            Case 3
              .Text = "Country Region"
            Case 4
              .Text = "Country Language"
            Case 5
              .Text = "Country"
        End Select
      End With
  Next

  resultsGrid.MergeCells = flexMergeFree

  For iRowLoop = 1 To iRows - 1
    For iColLoop = 0 To iCols - 1
      resultsGrid.Row = iRowLoop
      resultsGrid.Col = iColLoop
      resultsGrid.Text = adoID3.Fields(iColLoop)
    Next
    adoID3.MoveNext
  Next

  adoID3.Close

  Set adoID3 = Nothing

End Sub
```

How It Works

This code is very similar to that in the **gridID3** subroutine so I won't discuss this subroutine in much detail.

We build an SQL statement taking the **UpByHowMuch**, **OldQuantity**, **NewQuantity**, **CountryRegion**, **CountryLanguage** and **Country** fields from the **ID3** table. We then **ORDER BY UpByHowMuch** (in **DESC** order), **CountryRegion** and **CountryLanguage**.

```
sSql = "SELECT UpByHowMuch, OldQuantity, NewQuantity,"
sSql = sSql & " CountryRegion, CountryLanguage, Country FROM"
sSql = sSql & " ID3 ORDER BY UpByHowMuch DESC,"
sSql = sSql & " CountryRegion, CountryLanguage"
```

As with the **gridID3** code, we loop through all the rows and columns in our **adoID3** recordset. We use a **Select Case** statement to set up the headings for the columns - renaming **UpByHowMuch** as **Growth Factor**, **OldQuantity** as **Previous Qty** and **NewQuantity** as **Recent Qty**. We allow the cells for **UpByHowMuch**, **OldQuantity** and **NewQuantity** to be merged by setting their **MergeCol** properties to **True**.

```
Select Case iColLoop
    Case 0
        .Text = "Growth Factor"
        .MergeCol(iColLoop) = True
    Case 1
        .Text = "Previous Qty"
        .MergeCol(iColLoop) = True
    Case 2
        .Text = "Recent Qty"
        .MergeCol(iColLoop) = True
    Case 3
        .Text = "Country Region"
    Case 4
        .Text = "Country Language"
    Case 5
        .Text = "Country"
End Select
```

Getting all the Entropy We Can Eat!

This next routine, **getEntropy**, is the main routine for determining which classification is the most important for sales growth. We will turn to communication research and rip off one of their discoveries. As mentioned, entropy is a precise measurement of information.

> *In a nutshell, entropy is a measure of uncertainty in an observation. The entropy explains the amount of uncertainty about a particular outcome.*

This is used a lot in determining information that comes over noisy data lines. We, however, have hijacked it for our marketing purposes.

We will be using logarithms, which happen to be a built-in function in VB 6.0. If you are a bit rusty on them, it simply means that $\log x = y$ where (2 to the power y) = x, in this case log has base 2. In English, this means that the log to base 2 of any number is any bits that it would take to represent that many numbers. For example, $\log 2(16) = 4$. This tells us that it takes 4 bits to uniquely represent 16 different values. So we will explain this in the code below. But hey, don't worry. We will just use the VB built-in log function to do the dirty work for us.

Try It Out - Determining the Entropy of a Classification

1   Please add another function to the **frmID3** form. Name the function **getEntropy** and enter the code as shown. This routine will determine the entropy for the classification and return the entropy to the calling routine, **determineEntropy**.

```
Public Function getEntropy(ByVal sField As String, itotalRecords As Integer) As
Single

'----------------------------------------------------------------
'-- First, determine how many unique values of this field are
'-- in the table. Store them and determine the entropy for each
'----------------------------------------------------------------
```

```vb
Dim sSql As String
Dim adoHoldGroup As ADODB.Recordset
Dim totalUp As Integer
Dim totalDown As Integer
Dim totalSamples As Integer
Dim fractionalEntropy As Single
Dim entropy As Single
Dim searchValue As String

fractionalEntropy = 0

Set adoHoldGroup = New ADODB.Recordset
adoHoldGroup.CursorLocation = adUseClient

'-- grab the info here--
sSql = "SELECT * FROM ID3 ORDER BY " & sField
adoHoldGroup.Open sSql, adoConnection
If (adoHoldGroup.BOF) And (adoHoldGroup.EOF) Then
  MsgBox "No records in the ID3 Table"
  Exit Function
End If

totalSamples = adoHoldGroup.RecordCount
adoHoldGroup.MoveFirst

searchValue = adoHoldGroup.Fields.Item(sField)

With adoHoldGroup

  While Not .EOF
      totalUp = 0
      totalDown = 0
      '----------------------------------------------------
      '-- Loop through all of the records with like values
      '----------------------------------------------------
      Do While (searchValue = .Fields.Item(sField))
          If !SalesUp = True Then
            totalUp = totalUp + 1
          Else
            totalDown = totalDown + 1
          End If
          .MoveNext
          If (.EOF) Then Exit Do
      Loop
      '----------------------------------------------------
      '-- Now determine the entropy for that group --
      '----------------------------------------------------
      If (totalUp = 0) Then
        fractionalEntropy = -1#
      ElseIf (totalDown = 0) Then
        fractionalEntropy = -1#
      Else
          fractionalEntropy = _
-(totalUp / totalSamples) * Log(totalUp / totalSamples) - _
(totalDown / totalSamples) * Log(totalDown / totalSamples)
      End If
      fractionalEntropy = (fractionalEntropy / itotalRecords)
      entropy = entropy + fractionalEntropy
```

```
            If (.EOF) Then
              getEntropy = entropy + fractionalEntropy
            Else
              searchValue = adoHoldGroup.Fields.Item(sField)
            End If
      Wend
  End With


  End Function
```

How It Works

We want all of the records sorted by the particular field we will be examining. So if we are determining the entropy on the **CountryLanguage** classification, for example, all of the records that have **English** in the **CountryLanguage** field will be lumped together.

So what we want to do is loop through the recordset and determine the entropy on each of the records that have the same value in the CountryLanguage field. When the value of the field changes to, say, **German**, we will stop and calculate the value for **English** because we know we have looked at each of those. So by returning the records sorted by the classification field, we can be sure that all like records are together. An easy way to do this is to take the first value passed into our **getEntropy** function, **sField**. We can dynamically build our SQL statement instructing the recordset to be returned ordered by that field. So if we were determining the **CountryLanguage**, all entries for **English** would be together, etc.

```
'-- grab the info here--
sSql = "SELECT * FROM ID3 ORDER BY " & sField
adoHoldGroup.Open sSql, adoConnection
```

We start by opening the recordset **adoHoldGroup**, which gives us all of the records in the **ID3** table. Now that the recordset is opened, we to know which classification we will be working with. After all, it might be **CountryRegion**, **CountryLanguage** or **Country**. Well, we passed in the value as a parameter to the function, **sField**. Let's say that **sField** contains **Country**. So we use that variable and pass it to the recordset's **Fields.Item()** as a parameter. This will return the current value of that field (**Country**) in the current record. That value, say **Spain**, is assigned to the variable **searchValue**. Please notice that this is another example of a generalized routine. We don't hard code in a value, but permit a parameter passed into the routine, **sField**, to determine what we will be searching on. This allows us to use the same routine to examine each of the three classifications.

```
adoHoldGroup.MoveFirst

searchValue = adoHoldGroup.Fields.Item(sField)
```

As mentioned, we want to handle each category. Let's assume that we passed in **CountryLanguage** as the classification to be evaluated. If the **CountryLanguage** of the current record is **English**, then **English** is assigned to **searchValue**. As long as the value of the current record's **sField** (**CountryLanguage**) is equal to **English**, we loop through the recordset and increment the **totalUp** and **totalDown** fields. We are simply incrementing the **totalUp** or **totalDown** fields if that particular record shows that sales were either up or down. So if we had 4 records from four countries that speak English, and three of the countries experienced sales growth while the fourth did not, **totalUp** would be 3 and **totalDown** would be 1. As long as the **searchValue** (say **English**) is equal to the field being examined

754

(`CountryLanguage`), the `Do` loop looks at each record and increments the `totalUp` or `totalDown`. In addition, since all of the records with like languages are grouped together, we know we will get them all. Now say the `MoveNext` goes to the next record and the `Fields.Item(CountryLanguage)` is now `German`. The code exits the `Do` loop and continues.

```
While Not .EOF
     totalUp = 0
     totalDown = 0
     '----------------------------------------------------
     '-- Loop through all of the records with like values
     '----------------------------------------------------
     Do While (searchValue = .Fields.Item(sField))
        If !SalesUp = True Then
          totalUp = totalUp + 1
        Else
          totalDown = totalDown + 1
        End If
        .MoveNext
        If (.EOF) Then Exit Do
     Loop
```

The Scary Part

Essentially, we want to see how many records for countries that speak English had sales that were up and how many were down. So we are going to calculate something called `fractionalEntropy`.

What we want to look at here is the `fractionalEntropy` when both the `totalUp` and `totalDown` are not 0. If one of these were indeed 0, we would get a divide by zero error. So right away this tells us that we want to have enough samples so that typically both the `totalUp` and `totalDown` will have a number greater than zero. We calculate the `fractionalEntropy` because this is currently being calculated for a single, for example, language. However, we still need to calculate the number for Spanish, French, German, etc. So we call this `fractionalEntropy` because it is a piece of the total.

```
If (totalUp = 0) Then
   fractionalEntropy = -1#
ElseIf (totalDown = 0) Then
   fractionalEntropy = -1#
Else
   fractionalEntropy = _
   -(totalUp / totalSamples) * Log(totalUp / totalSamples) - _
   (totalDown / totalSamples) * Log(totalDown / totalSamples)
End If
```

What we want to do is look at the frequency of an "up" value out of the total values. Let's say that there were 10 countries with the language of English. If 5 were up, then the probability of the language classification having a positive sales growth is 5 out of 10, or 5/10. Likewise, the probability of the language classification having a negative sales growth is also 5/10. In general terms, we can look at the formula like so:

```
Outcome = - Probability(up) log Probability(up) - Probability(down)
                    log Probability(down)
```

755

In our example we would then have

```
Outcome =  -5/10 log (5/10) - 5/10 log (5/10)

Outcome = 1     (i.e. no change. We can't discern anything here)
```

The outcome represents the uncertainty of sales going up, based on the information we placed in the `ID3` table. This is NOT meant to be a math book, but only to add an element of interest in data mining and show a simple technique on how we can add another dimension to our knowledge of data mining.

```
fractionalEntropy = (fractionalEntropy / itotalRecords)
entropy = entropy + fractionalEntropy
If (.EOF) Then
   getEntropy = entropy + fractionalEntropy
Else
   searchValue = adoHoldGroup.Fields.Item(sField)
End If
```

We then divide the **fractionalEntropy** by the number of records in the recordset and assign this to **fractionalEntropy**. Now that we have calculated the **fractionalEntropy** for say, the English language, we add that to the variable **entropy** which represents the entire classification. So we would loop through to the next record in the **ID3** table and determine the **fractionalEntropy** for all countries that speak Spanish. When finished, this **fractionalEntropy** factor for Spanish would be added to the **entropy** variable. So **entropy** is cumulative. Each of the **fractionalEntropy** factors for each language is just added to the variable **entropy**, which is the sum of each of the similar records.

If we have reached the end of the recordset, we assign the result to the name of the function, **getEntropy**, and return that value for the recordset based on the criteria we just analyzed. Otherwise, we update the value of **searchValue** with the current record. The code then jumps to the top of the loop, initializes the variables, and looks at the next group. Notice how we update the **fractionalEntropy** with the results from each grouping of say, **CountryLanguage**.

The final value is then returned to the calling routine, **determineEntropy**, and placed in the array for sorting and display. Let's now take a look at how to sort our array to ensure the lowest entropy value is stored in the first position.

Try It Out - Sorting Our Multi-Dimensional Array

1 Add a final sub to our **frmID3** form called **qsort**. We will call this to sort the array, **Position**, so the least entropy factor is in the lowest position. Essentially, this will sort our array in ascending order.

```
Public Sub qsort(ByRef myArray() As Variant, ByVal iLowBound As Integer, ByVal
iHighBound As Integer)

Dim intX As Integer
Dim intY As Integer
Dim intMiddle As Integer
Dim sHoldString As String
Dim varMidBound As Variant
Dim varTmp As Variant

If iHighBound > iLowBound Then
    intMiddle = ((iLowBound + iHighBound) \ 2)
    varMidBound = myArray(intMiddle, 0)

    intX = iLowBound
    intY = iHighBound

    Do While intX <= intY
        '-- if a value lower in the array is > than one --
        '-- higher in the array, swap them now          --
        If myArray(intX, 0) >= varMidBound _
            And myArray(intY, 0) <= varMidBound Then
                varTmp = myArray(intX, 0)
                sHoldString = myArray(intX, 1)
                myArray(intX, 0) = myArray(intY, 0)
                myArray(intX, 1) = myArray(intY, 1)
                myArray(intY, 0) = varTmp
                myArray(intY, 1) = sHoldString
                intX = intX + 1
                intY = intY - 1
        Else
          If myArray(intX, 0) < varMidBound Then
              intX = intX + 1
          End If
          If myArray(intY, 0) > varMidBound Then
             intY = intY - 1
          End If
        End If
    Loop
    Call qsort(myArray(), iLowBound, intY)
    Call qsort(myArray(), intX, iHighBound)

End If
End Sub
```

How It Works

We call this sub from the **determineEntropy** routine. Notice that we are passing in the array **ByRef**, or by reference. This is so that **qsort** actually has the memory location of the array. Passing in the array by reference permits the **qsort** routine to work on the actual array - not a copy of the array in memory. Passing in by reference is the default behavior of VB. It can make the changes for us here. A quick call to **qsort** from **determineEntropy** will sort the array. We can then print the array from **determineEntropy** and it will now be sorted for us.

The **qsort** routine works on the divide-and-conquer principle. It splits the array into two groups and then sorts both the top and the bottom. It does this by calling itself to sort each group. When a routine calls itself, that process is called **recursion**.

```
   If iHighBound > iLowBound Then
      intMiddle = ((iLowBound + iHighBound) \ 2)
      varMidBound = myArray(intMiddle, 0)

      intX = iLowBound
      intY = iHighBound
```

If the upper bound of the array is greater than the lower bound, we want to grab the middle. When we call **qsort** from **determineEntropy**, **iHighBound = 2** and **iLowBound = 0**. In the next line we determine the middle of the array – which will be 1. Recall that the entropy value is in position 0 of the array and the classification is in position 1. So **varMidBound** is assigned the value from **myArray(1, 0)** which is the entropy value of the classification.

Now we loop as long as the lower bound **<=** the upper bound variables. If the entropy value stored in element **intX** (which will be 0 the first time though) is **>=** the entropy value stored in the middle value **And** the entropy value stored in the **intY** element (which will be 2) is **<=** the middle entropy value, we have some switching to do.

```
Do While intX <= intY
      '-- if a value lower in the array is > than one --
      '-- higher in the array, swap them now          --
      If myArray(intX, 0) >= varMidBound _
            And myArray(intY, 0) <= varMidBound Then
```

So now we just swap what's in position **intX** with what is in position **intY**. Then we move the lower and upper boundaries towards each other and do the same test.

```
            varTmp = myArray(intX, 0)
            sHoldString = myArray(intX, 1)
            yArray(intX, 0) = myArray(intY, 0)
            myArray(intX, 1) = myArray(intY, 1)
            myArray(intY, 0) = varTmp
            myArray(intY, 1) = sHoldString
            intX = intX + 1
            intY = intY - 1
```

When **intX > intY**, the code moves down and calls itself - recursion. The routine is called on the lower part of the array to sort it, then the upper part. This is the divide-and-conquer principle.

```
      Call qsort(myArray(), iLowBound, intY)
      Call qsort(myArray(), intX, iHighBound)
```

Now don't worry if this part looks a bit cryptic. Years are spent in some computer science courses discussing the various sorts and the math behind them. Luckily we can learn from the masters. It's unfortunate that VB does not have any built-in sorting capabilities like **qsort**. They are built into other languages, such as C.

> *To sort strings, instead of numbers, some programmers add a hidden list box to the
> form. The Sorted property is set to True. They just use the AddItem method to add
> strings in any order. When all of the strings are added, they start at position 0 of the
> list box and retrieve each of the items. They will of course now be in sorted order.
> The list box is not visible so the user never sees it, but this is a quick and dirty way
> to get some quick string sorting done. Unfortunately this will not work for numbers.
> A 2 would come before a –3, for example. Not exactly precise for our needs!*

OK, finished! Press *F5* to run your program. Don't forget to add a reference to the Microsoft
ActiveX Data Objects 2.0 Library if you haven't done so already. Try the analyzing the various
products and see how the results stack up. You are now ready to turn this beauty over to the
product manager.

One word on the results. Since we only have a single country for each entry, this usually has
the lowest entropy. So we can assume that the country is important. What really makes sense to
look at is what is in the second position - after country. In this example for Hokkien Fried Mee,
our program says that this is really on the decline in not a single country - but Europe in
general! Now this is great information. The product manager might be wondering why sales are
down in Germany, without realizing that sales across Europe for this product are in a nose-dive!

I think you can see the value of data mining and hopefully there is enough information
provided for you to apply this technique to your real world problems. We re-aggregated the data

into a single table. We then tried to find some logical classifications and applied the entropy approach to determine which one of them provided the least uncertainty about sales growth. We tried to illustrate a non-traditional use of database information.

A Word on Creating THAT SQL Statement

The long SQL statement in **buildID3** probably looked a bit scary. By far the easiest way to get complex SQL statements right is to use the Microsoft Access query builder. You graphically select the tables you are interested in. Access then automatically links the tables. Notice the 1-to-many relationships. You can then easily run your queries and see the output right in Access. This gives you a quick and easy way to get complex SQL statements right. You can immediately see the results.

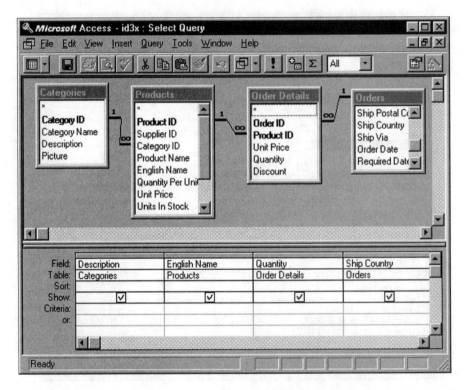

Once the data returned is correct, simply select View-SQL View from the menu and you can see the statement that Access used to generate your output. A quick cut and paste and you have your SQL statement. The only thing left to do is 'stringize' it and add the variables you wish that specify the **WHERE** clause. This alone is well worth the price of Access.

```
Microsoft Access - id3x : Select Query                          _ □ X
File  Edit  View  Insert  Query  Tools  Window  Help            _ 8 X

SELECT DISTINCTROW Categories.Description, Products.[English Name], [Order
Details].Quantity, Orders.[Ship Country], Orders.[Order Date]
FROM Orders INNER JOIN [[Categories INNER JOIN Products ON
Categories.[Category ID] = Products.[Category ID]] INNER JOIN [Order Details]
ON Products.[Product ID] = [Order Details].[Product ID]] ON Orders.[Order ID] =
[Order Details].[Order ID];

Ready
```

And as a note, whenever you are concatenating strings, always use the **&** character. Yes, the **+** will work, but that also works for math. When we say 2 + 2, VB knows this will be a math operation. However, if we say **"Hello " + "World"**, VB first has to figure out if this is a math operation or a string operation. Not only can you get unpredictable results in many cases, it is just plain slower. So whenever you need to concatenate two strings, always use the **&** character.

What We Learned

While there are mountains of data available in databases all over the planet, we need a way to determine any underlying meanings or trends. We examined one of these methods, the ID3 algorithm, which looks at the relative importance of a classification. We can set up our own criteria if we wish - such as region of the globe and language spoken - and let ID3 tell us if these are valid to consider when looking at sales growth. We also set up a two dimensional array to store an entropy value and a classification. By writing a variation of the standard quick sort routine, we were able to sort our array in ascending order based on the entropy value of the classification.

We concentrated a bit on the user interface, by designing a sophisticated system that requires absolutely no user input. The product manager simply points and clicks to get results. We also learned a bit more about the MSFlexGrid control. We used two of these in the program to their best advantage. They can group items together automatically to provide a powerful and compelling way to look at reams of complex data.

Finally, we went beyond the literal approach to database access. Not only did we use ADO recordsets, cursors, and filters, but we also used the data in a new and meaningful way by creating the **ID3** table. This is the future of data processing - being able to distill meaning from all of the data that is around us.

Exercises

1 For what reason would we want to create a database that was not structured into a normalized format?

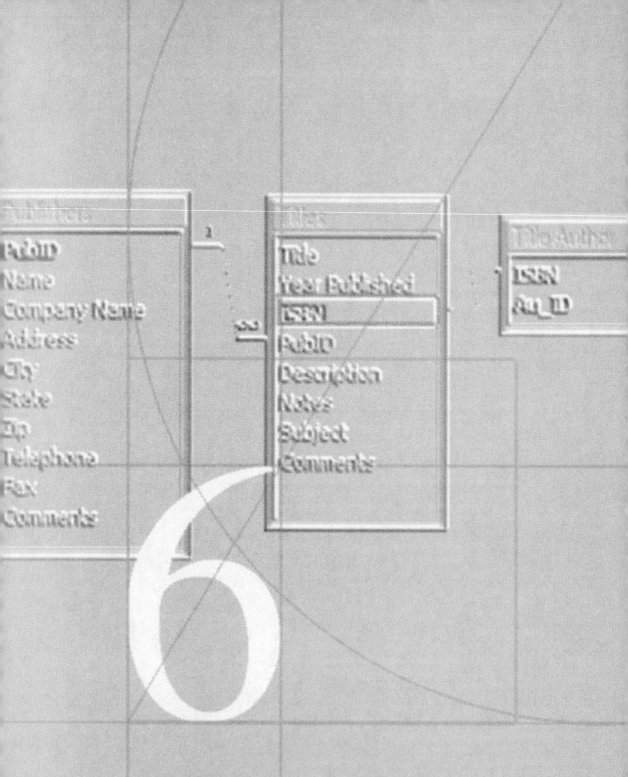

Making our Data
Available Universally

In this final chapter, we are going to examine a few of the more advanced ADO techniques and discuss how they may change computing as we know it. However, the end game of any database program is to be able to get at the data and use it wherever it is needed. In this chapter we're going to look at some more advanced techniques for accessing and sharing data.

Here's a summary of what we're going to cover:

> ▶ Exporting data in a variety of formats, including Excel and HTML

> ▶ Sending **disconnected** recordsets across a network for updating and return

> ▶ Making recordsets persistent (giving them a life beyond their transient existence in memory)

So first, we are going to look at a few ways of exporting ADO recordsets from our VB 6.0 programs. This way, we can move the data to *any* program that might need it. Let's get started.

Exporting Recordsets to other Programs

No matter how well we may design any application that we build, there will always be a need to export data to another application. For example, we may wish to place our data in a spreadsheet for a quick analysis, or we might want to put it in a graphics package for that big meeting this afternoon. Or the boss might want to import the data into a Project Management software package. You get the idea.

Personally, I have been involved in writing and selling financial software to large corporations since the early 1980s with the advent of PCs. In the mid 80s clients would ask "What is this big red switch for?" - meaning how do you turn on the computer. However, as we reach the end of the 1990s clients now ask "How easy is it to import data?" Business people have become incredibly systems-literate. Many used computers in college and grad school, so they know how to exploit their power for increased productivity. Almost always, they assume your software will work as advertised, and they have moved beyond the obvious - they are now asking questions at the level of shuttling data back and forth between applications. They don't want to handle the data more than once – or not at all if possible. Gone are the days of re-keying data output from one system into another. No, today's business people want to shepherd the data from app to app and handle any exceptions. But it is the kiss of death if your modern business application can't import and export data. Hopefully these examples will be of use in your development initiatives.

So we are going to look at a few generalized routines that will accept an ADO recordset and export the contents for you. The data can be easily exported either in a Comma Delimited, EXCEL, or HTML format. Please feel free to incorporate these routines into your production projects. It is one of those design details we discussed earlier that can make all of the difference in how users perceive your application. Let's begin with Comma Delimited files.

Comma Delimited Files

The most common method of exporting data is in a **comma delimited** format, also known as 'comma separated values' (csv). This format simply means taking each row in our recordset and separating each field with a comma. If there is no data in the field (i.e., it is NULL), we simply delimit the field with a comma, indicating that the field is blank. A csv file is the lingua franca of file transfer. In other words, it is the most common method used to share data between two dissimilar file formats. Most programs can speak csv. For example, you can import and export csv files to both Excel and Access.

> *An early attempt at a universal data format was the Data Interchange Format (DIF Files). This format was developed by the US Navy in the 1960s and presented the data in ASCII tuples. It was a good first statement, but looked pretty weird and never caught on in the corporate world. The csv format was introduced soon afterwards and took off like a rocket. It was simple to understand and easy for programmers to parse.*

HTML Exporting

You should be pretty familiar with HTML from our Active Server Page chapter. But here, in this current chapter, we just write the data to a file while strategically incorporating HTML tags. This way, you can dynamically create an HTML file that can be rendered in any browser. A server is not required for this example. Essentially we will take our data and write a file that contains HTML codes. Many times a company will have a corporate Intranet. We can just export our data and send it to a common directory where anyone with LAN access can render our file in a browser.

Both of our file export choices, the csv and HTML options, will present the user with the Windows Common Dialog box. This permits them to name the file as anything they like and save it anywhere, even over a network. And we add defaults to the common dialog box so that, many times, all that is required of the user is to accept the defaults and click a mouse button.

Excel Exporting

We will also send data to Microsoft Excel. This is the standard spreadsheet program used in corporations. Sure, we could create a csv file and just import it into Excel - but there is a much more elegant solution. We can use ActiveX Automation and send the data directly to the spreadsheet. No muss, no fuss, no home assembly. The user just presses a button and the data gets written directly to the spreadsheet.

Try It Out - Preparing to Export Data

1   Create a new project called **\Chapter15\export.vbp**. Name the default form for the project **frmExport**. We will use a single form to demonstrate the three methods of exporting data from an ADO recordset.

2   Add three command buttons to the **frmExport** form. Name then **cmdCsv**, **cmdHTML**, and **cmdExcel** and set their captions as shown in the screenshot below. Then add a common dialog box to the form, and make sure that you change its name to **CD1**.

The common dialog box is not an intrinsic control, so you must add it to your tool palette. Right click the tool palette and select Components... Select the Microsoft Common Dialog Control 6.0 that is stored in **comdlg2.ocx**:

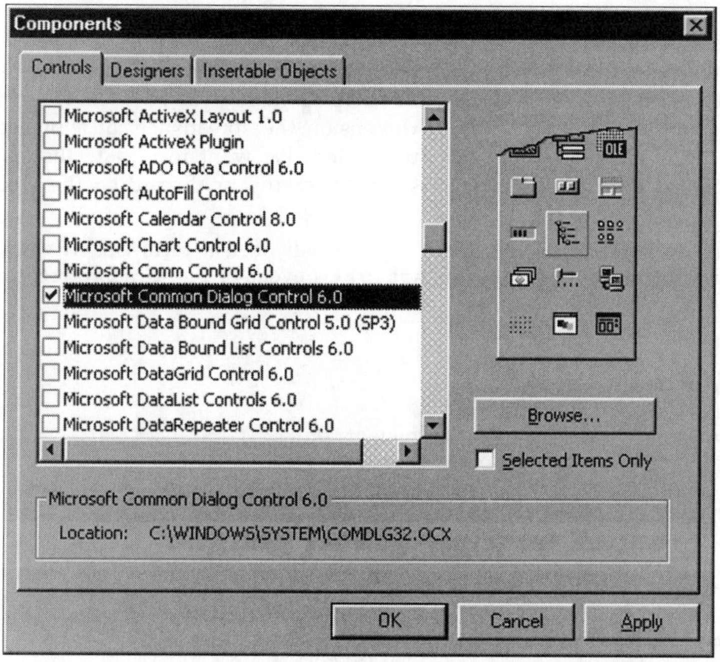

3   You'll also need to ensure that you set up your Project-References to include the Microsoft ActiveX Data Objects 2.0 Library and the Microsoft ActiveX Data Objects Recordset 2.0 Library.

4 When you draw a common dialog box on your form, you will see it at design time, but it is invisible at run time. Lay the form out like this:

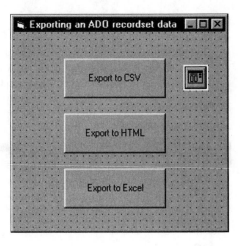

5 In the general area of the form, add the following code:

```
Option Explicit
Dim adoConnection As adodb.Connection
Dim adoRecordset As adodb.Recordset
Dim connectString As String
Dim objExcel As Object
Dim objTemp As Object
```

Essentially, we are creating a recordset that is visible at the form level. This way we can open the recordset when the form loads and then pass the recordset to our various export routines. And the two objExcel and objTemp items will be used when we use Excel as an automation server. If we were to dimension the spreadsheet at a procedure level, it would go out of scope when the procedure exited. We want to update the spreadsheet and leave it displayed until the user dismisses it by saving or discarding the worksheet.

6 In order to run our export examples, we will need a recordset to work with. Please add the following code to the **Form_Activate** event of the **frmExport** form:

```
Private Sub Form_Activate()

Dim sSqlString As String

Set adoConnection = New adodb.Connection
Set adoRecordset = New adodb.Recordset

connectString = "Provider=Microsoft.Jet.OLEDB.3.51;" _
                & "Data Source=C:\begdb\biblio.mdb"

sSqlString = "SELECT * FROM Publishers where PubID <= 50"

adoConnection.Open connectString
adoRecordset.CursorLocation = adUseClient
adoRecordset.Open sSqlString, adoConnection
MsgBox adoRecordset.RecordCount

End Sub
```

We are simply opening the form-scoped **Connection** and **Recordset** objects. In our example, we are going to retrieve all of the records from the Publishers table that have a **PubID** value **<=** **50**. This recordset will be available throughout our program.

Exporting Our Data in a Comma Delimited File

Of course, we want our programs to have the look and feel of professional programs. Likewise, we don't want to spend time writing acres of code to make that happen. So by using the pre-built Common Dialog Box control, we can easily display the Save File box just like sophisticated Spreadsheet or Word Processor programs. Users are used to these common boxes. In fact, they go a long way towards making Windows look consistent across applications - hence the name Common Dialog box. So Windows has done the work to give us this control. We just have to set a few properties.

When a user wishes to create a Comma Delimited Export File, the Common Dialog box is presented. Here the user can name the file to whatever makes sense. Not only that, if the file needs to be sent from the Finance Department over to Accounting, the user can simply select the appropriate sub-directory on the Local Area Network and send the file to another building.

Notice that we provide a default name, **Export.csv**, and a Save as type of .CSV:

So we can really customize the dialog box for any application.

Once the file is named and its location set in the Common Dialog box, the user clicks Save. This creates the csv file. And when our routine is finished, a message box is displayed showing the user that the operation was successful:

And if you were wondering exactly what a Comma Delimited File format looks like, here is an example:

While this might not look very comprehensible to you, Excel, Access, or just about any modern program that can import a file can easily read it. Yes, it is ugly - but it is not meant for human consumption. In fact, users will never actually see the file. They just export it from our program and import it into another.

Creating a CSV Export File

Let's write a generalized routine that will create a csv file from an ADO recordset. We pass in an **ADODB.Recordset** and return a Boolean that indicates the success or failure of the operation.

Try It Out - Creating Our CSV Export File

1 In the **frmExport** form, add a new function called **csv**. We will pass in a recordset and this function will create the csv file. Upon completion, it will return a Boolean true or false indicating success or failure. Add the following code now:

```
Public Function csv(adoRecordset As adodb.Recordset) As Boolean

Dim iTotalRecords As Integer
Dim sFileToExport As String
Dim iFileNum As Integer
Dim msg As String
Dim iIndx As Integer
Dim iNumberOfFields As Integer


Screen.MousePointer = vbDefault


On Error Resume Next
```

```
With CD1
  .CancelError = True
  .filename = "Export.csv"
  .InitDir = App.Path
  .DialogTitle = "Save Comma Delimited Export File"
  .Filter = "Export Files (*.CSV)|*.CSV"
  .DefaultExt = "CSV"
  .Flags = cdlOFNOverwritePrompt Or cdlOFNCreatePrompt
  .ShowSave
End With


'-------------------------------
'-- User cancels the operation --
'-------------------------------
If (Err = 32755) Then  'operation canceled
   Screen.MousePointer = vbDefault
   Beep
   msg = "The export operation was canceled." & vbCrLf
   iIndx = MsgBox(msg, vbOKOnly + vbInformation, _
         "Comma Delimited Export File")
   csv = False
   Exit Function
Else
  On Error GoTo expError
End If


'--------------------------------------
'-- Let's save the data now.         --
'-- Get the name of the file to save. --
'--------------------------------------
Screen.MousePointer = vbHourglass

iTotalRecords = 0
sFileToExport = CD1.FileName
iFileNum = FreeFile()
Open sFileToExport For Output As #iFileNum 'Open file for output


'-------------------------
'-- Stream out the data --
'-------------------------

iNumberOfFields = adoRecordset.Fields.Count - 1

adoRecordset.MoveFirst
Do Until adoRecordset.EOF
 iTotalRecords = iTotalRecords + 1
 For iIndx = 0 To iNumberOfFields
  If (IsNull(adoRecordset.Fields(iIndx))) Then
   Print #iFileNum, ","; 'simply a comma delimited string
  Else
   If iIndx = iNumberOfFields Then
    Print #iFileNum, Trim$(CStr(adoRecordset.Fields(iIndx)));
   Else
    Print #iFileNum, Trim$(CStr(adoRecordset.Fields(iIndx))); ",";
   End If
  End If
 Next
```

```
   Print #iFileNum,
   adoRecordset.MoveNext
   DoEvents
Loop


'----------------
Close iFileNum
Screen.MousePointer = vbDefault
Beep
msg = "Export File " & sFileToExport & vbCrLf
msg = msg & "successfully created." & vbCrLf
msg = msg & iTotalRecords & " records written to disk." & vbCrLf
iIndx = MsgBox(msg, vbOKOnly + vbInformation, _
         "Comma Delimited File")
csv = True
Exit Function

expError:

Screen.MousePointer = vbDefault
MsgBox (Err & " " & Err.Description)
csv = False

End Function
```

How It Works

Of course, we set our mouse cursor to an hourglass, as we should whenever our program is beavering away. We then set a few properties on our Common Dialog box that is called **CD1**. By setting the **CancelError** property to true, we are telling **CD1** to generate an error if the user cancels the Save process. Why? When all of our properties are set we invoke the **ShowSave** method to display the box. If the user cancels, we can check the error number:

```
On Error Resume Next

With CD1
   .CancelError = True
   .filename = "Export.csv"
   .InitDir = App.Path
   .DialogTitle = "Save Comma Delimited Export File"
   .Filter = "Export Files (*.CSV)|*.CSV"
   .DefaultExt = "CSV"
   .Flags = cdlOFNOverwritePrompt Or cdlOFNCreatePrompt
   .ShowSave
End With
```

We set the various properties and then invoke the **ShowSave** method. When **ShowSave** is invoked, the Common Dialog is displayed modally. You will recall that this means that the user must respond to the dialog before it is dismissed - which means in our case that the file must either be saved or the operation must be canceled. Nothing else in our program can happen until one of these two choices is made.

If the user cancels the operation, we can determine if the error was from pressing the cancel button. If yes, then we can display an informational message and gracefully exit the function. Otherwise some strange and unexpected error must have occurred, and we can jump to the error handler.

The **Flags** properties are **Or**'d together - this sets both flags to be true. They tell our control not to overwrite a file with the same name and then to provide a prompt for the user. This way the user can't accidentally overwrite an existing file that happens to have the same name as the new file. Nice touch, eh?

Now if the file is to be saved, or the operation is canceled, the CD1 box is dismissed and the code moves to the next section:

```
If (Err = 32755) Then    'operation canceled
   Screen.MousePointer = vbDefault
   Beep
   msg = "The export operation was canceled." & vbCrLf
   iIndx = MsgBox(msg, vbOKOnly + vbInformation, _
            "Comma Delimited Export File")
   csv = False
   Exit Function
Else
   On Error GoTo expError
End If
```

If the user decides to cancel the operation, they get a customized dialog box that informs them exactly what has happened. Clear, concise, and reassuring:

However, let's assume that the user pressed the <u>S</u>ave button to create the file. We now have to actually name and create the file. The **FileName** property of **CD1** will return the name the file is to be called. So if the user wants to save the file to the X drive over in accounting, the **FileName** might return something like "**X:\accounting\September\Export.csv**". So the file name will be fully qualified with the drive, directory, and file name.

Windows needs a number to refer to an open file – a so-called file handle. We use the **FreeFile()** function that returns an integer representing the next file number available for use by the **Open** statement. We don't care what the number is, but using **FreeFile()** will assure us that whatever it is - it will be unique. I have seen programmers hard-code in the number 1. Someone might use something like **fileNum = 1**, then proceed to use the **fileNum** value in opening the file. This is great if there is only a single file open, but can lead to strange and terrible behavior if more that one file is open concurrently. So always use the **FreeFile()** function to ensure that we never run into hard to debug problems here.

We then open the file. This might seem obvious, but you must open a file before any I/O operation can be performed on it. Calling **Open** allocates a buffer for I/O to the file. It also determines the mode of access to use with the buffer. And be sure to use the **#** in front of the **#fileNum** variable:

```
iTotalRecords = 0
sFileToExport = CD1.FileName
iFileNum = FreeFile()
Open sFileToExport For Output As #iFileNum 'Open file for output
```

Taking Care of Business

Now we enter into the business end of our function. Remember that the ADO recordset is passed in to our function as a parameter. This means that we don't have to worry about creating and opening it. The recordset is handed to us on a silver platter.

Recall that we want to delimit every field with a comma. Well, we don't know ahead of time how many fields there will be in the recordset. So we can just grab the **Count** property of the **Fields** collection of the recordset:

```
iNumberOfFields = adoRecordset.Fields.Count - 1
```

For each individual record, we are going to loop through each of the fields. This is a great approach because there can be an arbitrary number of fields - we certainly don't know ahead of time how many there might be. So by looking at the **Count** property of the **Fields** collection we can determine just how many fields we should write, separating each with a comma.

We just put in a safety net and ensure that the current record of the ADO recordset is the first record:

```
adoRecordset.MoveFirst
Do Until adoRecordset.EOF
 iTotalRecords = iTotalRecords + 1
 For iIndx = 0 To iNumberOfFields
  If (IsNull(adoRecordset.Fields(iIndx))) Then
   Print #iFileNum, ","; 'simply a comma delimited string
  Else
   If iIndx = iNumberOfFields Then
    Print #iFileNum, Trim$(CStr(adoRecordset.Fields(iIndx)));
   Else
    Print #iFileNum, Trim$(CStr(adoRecordset.Fields(iIndx))); ",";
   End If
  End If
 Next
 Print #iFileNum,
 adoRecordset.MoveNext
 DoEvents
Loop
```

Notice that the outer loop, the **Do Until** loop, will loop through each record in the recordset. The inner loop, **0 To iNumberOfFields**, will loop through each of the fields in the current record. Since we are starting at field position 0, we want to read up to 1 less than the number of fields. If our recordset has 10 fields, we read from position 0 through 9, which gives us the 10 fields. So when we set our variable, it's important to subtract 1 from the total.

Since the number of fields won't change within the recordset we are working on, we always want to assign the value of the **Fields.Count** property to a variable. If we wrote the code to loop from **0 To adoRecordset.Fields.Count -1** , we would be asking VB to evaluate this property for each and every field in every record. So we only evaluate this once and stuff the value in a variable. Remember that it is much faster to read the memory location of a variable than to retrieve an object's property value. Also, using the 'read property approach' would mean that we would have two dots to resolve. So our approach is certainly the best and cleanest.

As we loop through each of the fields in the current record, we first determine if the value is NULL. If this is the case, there is of course no data in the field, so we just delimit it with a comma. This designates an empty field. If the field is not NULL, we then test to see if this is the last field in the recordset. If it is, we simply print the field to the file. Otherwise, we append a **","** to the field to separate it from the next field.

Because **Print #** writes an image of the data to the file, you must delimit the data so it prints out correctly. By appending a "**;**" to the end of the print statement, we tell VB to continue on the same line. If we omitted the "**;**", each print statement would send the output to a new line. We, however, only want this to happen at the end of a record.

Finally, be sure to close the file after everything is written. When you close the file that was opened for Output, any final data in the operating system buffer for that file is written to disk. All buffer space associated with the closed file is released. This ensures that the buffer is purged and everything gets written correctly to disk. When the **Close** statement is executed, the association of our file with its file number ends:

```
Close iFileNum
```

That's it. We then display the results in our never-ending attempt to provide useful feedback to the user.

One other thing. There could be commas embedded in the fields we are trying to delimit. For example, let's say that we are exporting fields that contain palindromes. Palindromes are words or sentences that are spelled the same way forewords and backwards, such as wow, or mom, or dad. OK, let's say that one of the fields has a very long palindrome: "A man, a plan, a canal, Panama" (go ahead and try it if you don't believe me - it really is spelled the same forwards and backwards). But anyway, even though this phrase would be the contents of a single field, when it was written to disk, there would be three extra commas. The program importing the record would see "A man" as a single field because there is a comma embedded in it. This is not good. What most programs do is embed all text fields within quotation marks "". So you might wish to enhance this routine to do this. Then when the palindrome field is written to disk it would look like "A man, a plan, a canal, Panama". Now the importer will not confuse it with being four fields, but will know it is one because the "" marks make it a string literal – to be taken whole.

Let's export our file.

1 In order to test out our new procedure, add this line in the **cmdCSV** button's **Click** event:

```
Private Sub cmdCSV_Click()

Call csv(adoRecordset)

End Sub
```

Since the recordset has already been opened in the form's **Activate** event and has form level scope, we just pass in the open recordset as a parameter to our procedure. Cool.

Running the Code

Let's run our code and look at how some standard applications can deal with csv files that we create.

1 Run your **frmExport** form. You'll be presented with a dialog box that confirms the number of records that have been read into the recordset:

2 Click on OK to continue:

3 Now click on the Export to CSV command button:

4 Click on <u>S</u>ave to save the file to your **Chapter15** directory:

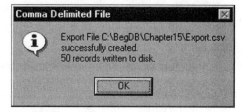

5 Click on OK to close the dialog. The file has been created.

Now you might be asking yourself, "Hey what's the big deal?" Well, that strange-looking csv file is a known quantity to programs such as Excel, as mentioned. Once the file is created, you can go to Microsoft Excel, open a file, and set the Files of type drop down box to Text Files (*.prn, *.txt, *,csv). See, even Excel has this type defined:

Now if we were to select the **.CSV** file that our VB program has made, Excel will import it automatically. Each field is placed in it's own cell:

	A	B	C	D	E	F
1	1	SAMS	SAMS	11711 N. Colle	Ste 140	Carmel
2	2	PRENTICE	PRENTICE HALL	15 Columbus C	New York	NY
3	3	M & T	M & T BOOKS			
4	4	MIT	MIT PR			
5	5	MACMILL/	MACMILLAN CO	11 W. 42nd St.	3rd flr.	New York
6	6	HIGHTEXT	HIGHTEXT PUBNS			
7	7	SPRINGEI	SPRINGER VERLAG			
8	8	O'REILLY	O'REILLY & ASS	90 Sherman St	Cambridge	MA
9	9	ADDISON-	ADDISON-WESL	Rte 128	Reading	MA

Of course, the commas are used to delimit the fields. So Excel just reads the file and takes care of the rest. Now if you have a program and need to send data between programs, this is an option.

Let's say that you have some data in several databases scattered around the enterprise. You could read them all in your VB program, distill the information, and write a csv file that could be sent to just about any database, and imported. For example, having seen how easy it was to import a csv file into Excel let's take a look at how we would bring it into Access.

Similarly, if you have Microsoft Access, you can perform this simple exercise. First, create a new empty database, calling it **importcsv**. Then save the file as **\Chapter15\importcsv.mdb**. Next, choose File-Get External Data-Import from the main Access menu, where you're greeted with the Import dialog box. Just like with Excel, we select ***.CSV** as the type of file to display in our **Chapter15** directory:

Clicking on the Export.csv gives us the Import Text Wizard screen. This wizard exists precisely because csv files are used so much in business:

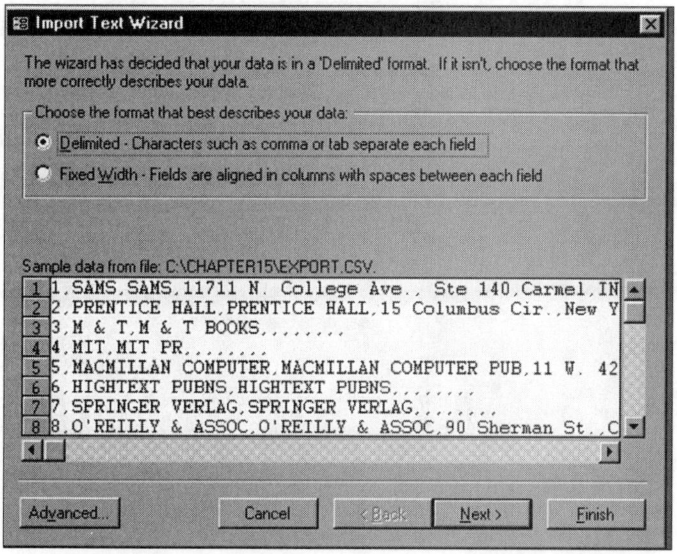

Leaving the default as Delimited and clicking Next you'll see:

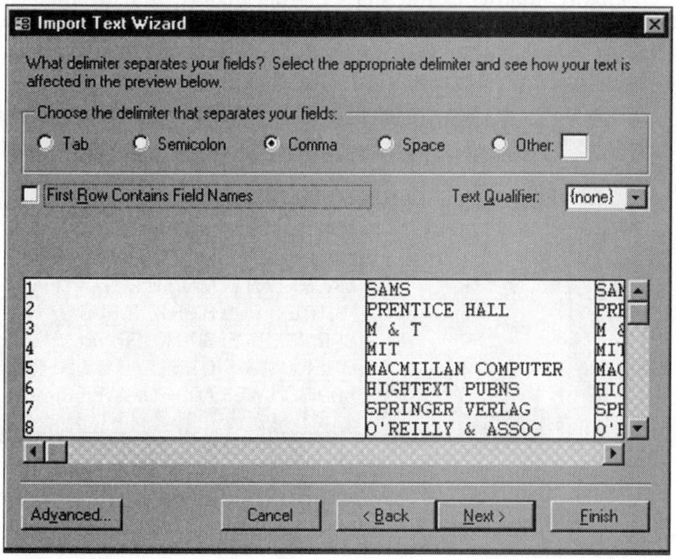

Make sure you click on the First Row Contains Field Names check box. Just like all Wizards, when it has enough information to do something, the Finish button becomes enabled. However, we would click on Next so we can tell the Wizard that we would like to have a new table created:

Finally, following the steps of the wizard, it will create a new table, using the name of the import file (ironically called export because we exported the data from an ADO recordset in VB6.0). And now the data from our csv text file has been imported:

Voila! Now you can go into Access design mode and change the names of the fields, data types, etc. But by importing the data we just saved days of manual data input.

These illustrations are just to show you how flexible the csv file format can be. When you are in a bind and need to shuttle data between programs, this might just be the ticket.

The Power of CSV

I recently wrote a financial production program in Visual Basic that is currently in use in over 200 companies in the United States. This program retrieves same day information (on paper checks) from a bank sent to a company's lockbox (you know, when you mail in a check to P.O. Box 12345). The VB program retrieves the check and invoice information in a file from the bank and updates an Access database. Previously, the company had to wait until the next day to get the physical items. Now the data is sent, same day, to the VB program. This timely information permits the credit manager to make shipping decisions. If the check is really there – and not just in the mail – the product can be shipped. Also, the treasury people use the same data to determine cash flow. And finally, the accounts receivable people use the data to update the Accounts Receivables (A/R) system. So instead of manually writing journal entries, a file gets exported from the software to the company's A/R system. The problem is that companies have several A/R systems from several vendors - and no two accept the same format. So this program exports the remittance data in a csv file, making it easily importable into a wide variety of A/R systems. In these situations, csv has proved to be the lingua franca in big business IT departments.

We'll now turn our attention to using another useful and universal file format - HTML.

Exporting Our Data in HTML

We also might wish to provide the ability to export a recordset using Hyper Text Markup Language. With the rise of corporate Intranets, many users might wish to export data from your program and make it available to others through a browser. Fortunately, this is fairly straightforward. We can display the same Common Dialog box as in our previous example:

When the data from the recordset is saved, it has a **.HTM** extension. This way, a user can simply load this file into a browser to view the data. Or if the PC has the **.HTM** extension associated with the browser, simply clicking on the file name fires up the browser and the data will be rendered there.

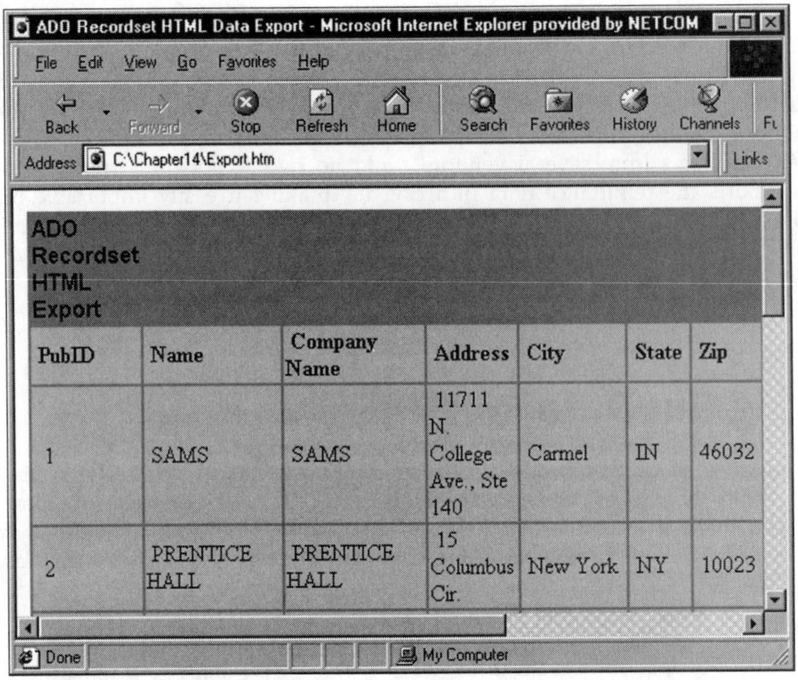

Let's examine how we can translate our data into browser-friendly format.

Try It Out - Creating an HTML Export Routine

Let's take a look at the code. Most of this should be second nature now, after writing our ASP files earlier.

Add another function to the **frmExport** form. Enter the code as shown below. Yes, this code looks a little bit intimidating, but it is generalized - so we can pass in any ADO recordset and it will generate the HTML file for us. Add the code for the **html** function now:

```
Public Function html(adoRecordset As adodb.Recordset) As Boolean

Dim fileToExport As String
Dim iFileNumber As Integer
Dim outerloop As Integer
Dim innerloop As Integer
Dim sMsg As String
Dim iIndx As Integer

Screen.MousePointer = vbDefault

On Error Resume Next
```

```
With CD1
  .CancelError = True
  .filename = "Export.htm"
  .InitDir = App.Path
  .DialogTitle = _
"Save (H)yper (T)ext (M)arkup (L)anguage Export File"
  .Filter = "Export Files (*.HTM)|*.HTM"
  .DefaultExt = "HTM"
  .Flags = cdlOFNOverwritePrompt Or cdlOFNCreatePrompt
  .ShowSave
End With


'--------------------------------
'-- User cancels the operation --
'--------------------------------
If (Err = 32755) Then   'operation canceled
  Screen.MousePointer = vbDefault
  Beep
  sMsg = "The export operation was canceled." & vbCrLf
  iIndx = MsgBox (sMsg, vbOKOnly + vbInformation, "HTML Export File")
  html = False
  Exit Function
Else
  On Error GoTo htmlError
End If


'----------------------------------------
'-- Let's save the data now.          --
'-- Get the name of the file to save. --
'----------------------------------------
Screen.MousePointer = vbHourglass

fileToExport = CD1.filename
iFileNumber = FreeFile()

Open fileToExport For Output As #iFileNumber

adoRecordset.MoveFirst

Print #iFileNumber, "<HTML><HEAD><TITLE>ADO Recordset HTML" & _
                    " Data Export</TITLE></HEAD>"
Print #iFileNumber, "<BODY BGCOLOR=""FFFFFF"">"
Print #iFileNumber, "<TABLE BGCOLOR=""00AAFF"" WIDTH=""100%"">"
Print #iFileNumber, "<TR><TD>"
Print #iFileNumber, "<FONT FACE=ARIAL SIZE+=3><B>ADO " & _
                    "Recordset HTML Export</B></FONT></TD></TR>"
Print #iFileNumber, "<TR>"
For iIndx = 0 To adoRecordset.Fields.Count - 1
  Print #iFileNumber, "<TD BGCOLOR=CCCCC>"
  Print #iFileNumber, "<B>  "; adoRecordset.Fields(iIndx).Name; "  </B>"
  Print #iFileNumber, "</TD>"
Next
Print #iFileNumber, "</TR>"

With adoRecordset
  .MoveFirst
```

```
      While Not .EOF
        Print #iFileNumber, "<TR>"
        For innerloop = 0 To .Fields.Count - 1
          Print #iFileNumber, "<TD BGCOLOR=CCCCC>"
          Print #iFileNumber, " "; .Fields(innerloop); " "
          Print #iFileNumber, "</TD>"
        Next
        Print #iFileNumber, "</TR>"
        .MoveNext
      Wend
    End With

    Print #iFileNumber, "</TABLE></BODY></HTML>"

    Close #iFileNumber

    MsgBox "Done"
    Screen.MousePointer = vbDefault
    html = True

    Exit Function

    htmlError:
    Screen.MousePointer = vbDefault
    MsgBox Err.Description
    html = False

    End Function
```

How It Works

We know that the common dialog part of the routine - it's just like what we covered above. So let's concentrate on the HTML specific code.

The first thing we want to do is place a nice header on our file, so we start by creating a table, setting its colors, and then placing our title in it. This segment of code simply adds the fancy top portion of our HTML output:

```
Print #iFileNumber, "<HTML><HEAD><TITLE>ADO Recordset HTML" & _
                    "Data Export</TITLE></HEAD>"
Print #iFileNumber, "<BODY BGCOLOR=""FFFFFF"">"
Print #iFileNumber, "<TABLE BGCOLOR=""00AAFF"" WIDTH=""100%"">"
Print #iFileNumber, "<TR><TD>"
Print #iFileNumber, "<FONT FACE=ARIAL SIZE+=3><B>ADO " & _
                    "Recordset HTML Export</B></FONT></TD></TR>"
```

The next part of the code prints the Titles of the fields. Each column will have the title of the field. In this example, we didn't assign the field count to a variable just to illustrate the other method of counting fields. Each field is printed in bold using the **<B></B>** tags. When each field is finally printed, we delimit the table record **</TR>** indicating that the record has been finished:

```
    Print #iFileNumber, "<TR>"
    For iIndx = 0 To adoRecordset.Fields.Count - 1
      Print #iFileNumber, "<TD BGCOLOR=CCCCC>"
      Print #iFileNumber, _
                   "<B>  "; adoRecordset.Fields(iIndx).Name; "  </B>"
      Print #iFileNumber, "</TD>"
    Next
    Print #iFileNumber, "</TR>"
```

Now that our HTML table has been set up, we can just add data:

```
    With adoRecordset
      .MoveFirst
      While Not .EOF
        Print #iFileNumber, "<TR>"
        For innerloop = 0 To .Fields.Count - 1
          Print #iFileNumber, "<TD BGCOLOR=CCCCC>"
          Print #iFileNumber, " "; .Fields(innerloop); " "
          Print #iFileNumber, "</TD>"
        Next
        Print #iFileNumber, "</TR>"
        .MoveNext
      Wend
    End With

    Print #iFileNumber, "</TABLE></BODY></HTML>"
```

Here we use the same outer loop/inner loop combination to loop through each of the fields in each of the records. We just print the HTML tags to format the data when it is loaded into a browser. When we start a new record in the **adoRecordset**, we instruct the HTML table that a new table record is starting by printing the **<TR>** tag. We then add each field using the table data **<TD>** tag, delimiting the field with **</TD>**. Finally, when each of the fields for the current record is printed, we close off the record with the table record **</TR>** HTML tag indicating that this table record is complete. The code then moves to the next record and does the same thing over again.

We then close the table and close the file. A new HTML file has just been created on an arbitrary recordset. How about that?

Creating the HTML File

So much for words - let's see this process in action.

Try It Out - Exporting an HTML File

1   In the **cmdHTML** button's **Click** event, please add this single call to the **html** routine. Again, we are just passing in the recordset:

```
Private Sub cmdHTML_Click()

    Call html(adoRecordset)

End Sub
```

Since VB already knows the type of parameter the procedure requires, it is nice enough to give us a tip on what to pass:

Go ahead and create a **.HTM** file.

2 Open up the form, go through the informational dialog box, and click the Export to HTML button. When the HTML file is created, load it into your browser:

PubID	Name	Company Name	Address	City	State	Zip	Telephone	Fax	Comments
1	SAMS	SAMS	11711 N. College Ave., Ste 140	Carmel	IN	46032	Null	Null	Null
2	PRENTICE HALL	PRENTICE HALL	15 Columbus Cir.	New York	NY	10023	800-922-0579	Null	Null
3	M & T	M & T BOOKS	Null	Null	Null	Null	Null	Null	Null
4	MIT	MIT PR	Null	Null	Null	Null	Null	Null	Null
5	MACMILLAN COMPUTER	MACMILLAN COMPUTER PUB	11 W. 42nd St., 3rd flr.	New York	NY	10036	212-869-7440	Null	Null
6	HIGHTEXT PUBNS	HIGHTEXT PUBNS	Null	Null	Null	Null	Null	Null	Null
7	SPRINGER VERLAG	SPRINGER VERLAG	Null	Null	Null	Null	Null	Null	Null
8	O'REILLY & ASSOC	O'REILLY & ASSOC	90 Sherman St.	Cambridge	MA	02140	Null	Null	Null
9	ADDISON-WESLEY	ADDISON-WESLEY PUB CO	Rte 128	Reading	MA	01867	617-944-3700	617-964-9460	Null
									DATABASES MICROCOMPUTER SOFTWARE

3 Since we exported the file in straight HTML, it can be rendered in *any* browser. So if the company has a corporate Intranet, your program might write the file to a publicly accessible directory and make it available to anyone that needs the data.

Here is a text file generated with our **html** routine:

As you can see, it simply formats our recordset data and places HTML tags in the correct places. Now this simple text file can be seen in any browser.

Remember in Chapter 14 we built the ID3 program for the product manager to analyze sales trends? Well, you did such a great job that she is now asking you if you could export the data to Microsoft so she can further analyze the results. While you tell her, "This will be a tough one. Let me think about it", you are actually thinking – "This couldn't be easier". You're a sly one, all right. Here's how you'll accomplish what you've implied will be a daunting task:

Using Objects to Send ADO Data to an Excel Worksheet

Many times it is useful to send database information directly to an excel spreadsheet. While Visual Basic has many mathematical functions, nothing can beat Excel for mathematical prowess. Or since most users already have Excel on their PC, some users just feel more comfortable using a spreadsheet. Luckily, it is very easy to take any information from an ADO recordset and send it directly to an Excel spreadsheet.

Let's start by discussing how to create objects. We will be using ActiveX Automation to communicate directly with Excel 8.0 from Visual Basic 6.0. The way this magic is accomplished is by **binding**.

787

Essentially, binding is the way that VB accesses objects in another application. An application, like Excel for example, exposes properties and methods for other applications to use. In this respect, Excel is not only a program in its own right, but we can also program it from VB. In this case, Excel becomes an **ActiveX Automation Server**. We can completely control Excel, just like a remote control robot, from Visual Basic.

To achieve this usage of Excel, we create an object variable that points to an object supplied by the ActiveX Automation Server. When we use any of the properties or methods of the object that the object variable points to, Visual Basic must be sure that the object actually exists. It must then go through the work of ensuring that the properties (and we – the client) specify the correct form for using the methods. This verification process, which ensures that everything is correctly specified, is known as binding. There are two types of binding available to us - 'late' and 'early'. Let's discuss them in reverse order.

Late Binding

Late binding takes place at run time. When the client program (our VB application) runs, Visual Basic must look up the object as well as its properties each and every time a line with that object is run within our application. Because the object is late bound, a reference to the specific object as a 'type of object' does not exist. In other words, VB does not know if the object is an instance of Excel, or a bowl of oatmeal. Therefore, VB must continually check the object and its methods to ensure they are specified correctly, and must check with the operating system and the application (such as Excel) that supplies the object. As you can imagine, this can really slow things down.

You can think of late binding as having to type in the URL of your favorite web site in the browser each and every time you wish to visit the site. Each time you must enter the exact address. However, it is much easier to simply add the URL to our list of favorites. This way we simply click the name of the site, instead of typing in the entire address. Typing out the entire address is much slower that simply clicking the selection off the list of favorites. However, the end result is the same.

Here is an example of late binding:

```
Dim objExcel as Object
Set objExcel = CreateObject("Excel.Application")
ObjExcel.Workbooks.Add
```

Here we dimension an object variable, **objExcel**, and tell VB it will be the generic type **Object**. Here, our program does not know anything about what the **objExcel** object variable will ultimately be like. However, it must set aside memory for this unknown object. This is considered a **weakly typed** variable. It does not really tell VB much about what the object variable will ultimately contain.

In the second line, we are actually setting the object variable to a brand new instance of Excel. However, before this can take place, VB has to check the system registry to find out what an Excel Application is. Once it does the homework to find out, the next line of code is executed. Now, VB must go to the work of looking up the Workbooks collection of the Excel Application. After it confirms that the collection indeed exists, it must then check out the **Add** method to ensure it also exists and that we have referenced it the correct way. That is a lot of work. Not only that, each and every time you use the object variable `objExcel`, the same steps must be taken. As you can imagine, these time-consuming look-ups can really impact performance. And not only does each reference at run time require at least 50% more work by Visual Basic, but at compile time you get no error checking. So if there was any syntax error or reference to a mistyped method, it will only show up when we run our program.

Early Binding

The way to get around this performance problem is to use **early binding** where possible. When we add references to our project, from the Project-References, we are really adding a **type library** to our project. Application type libraries (`.TLB` files) define all of the objects, properties, and methods that are exposed by an application. Since these definitions are added to our project, VB now has advance information on the properties and methods of the objects that we want to reference.

For example, Microsoft Excel has a type library describing all of its exposed spreadsheet and chart objects - the Microsoft Excel 8.0 Object Library.

So type libraries enable us to perform early binding. This provides faster, design-time syntax checking of the VB code that refers to these objects. Of course, we have been doing this all along when we added references to ADO and DAO 3.51 to our projects.

Essentially, to use early binding, we must strongly type all object references in our Visual Basic code. As you know, a strongly typed object is one that is created with a specific object type. For example, you can't create objects with object types of Object or Variant when you wish to use early binding.

> *As a rule of thumb, you should always early bind objects if possible. In fact, the only time you should really have to declare a variable* As Object *is if you do not have a type library available for the object. Another exception is if you need to be able to pass any kind of object as an argument to a procedure.*

Since we added the Excel type library to our project, you might want to open up the Object Browser for the Excel lib and have a look around. It has been said that Excel is the most complicated program ever written for Windows. Additionally, since it exposes more functionality than any other windows program, it makes Excel a perfect candidate for programming remotely. We can leverage all of its functionality with just a few lines of code. With VB, you can program Excel using any of the properties and methods that are exposed and shown in the browser:

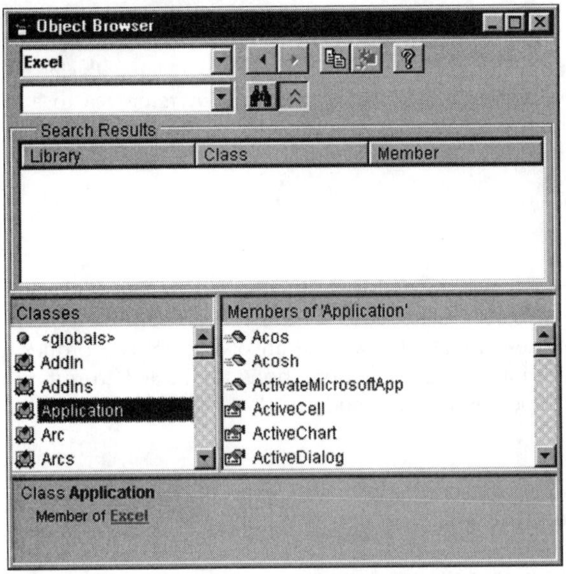

Let's get back to coding our project.

Sending ADO Recordset Information to Excel

Now that we know that we can directly control an Excel spreadsheet, we can easily pass the contents of our recordset to Excel. The screenshot below shows our ADO recordset data after it has been directly sent to an Excel spreadsheet:

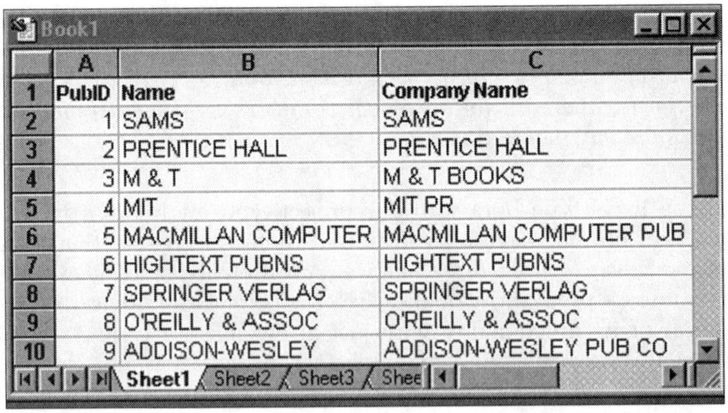

Let's add the code that will let us actually interact directly with Excel from our VB 6.0 program. We can create an instance of Excel from within our software and actually program Excel from VB!

Try It Out - Calling Excel from VB

1 Firstly, be sure to add the Microsoft Excel 8.0 Object Library to your program:

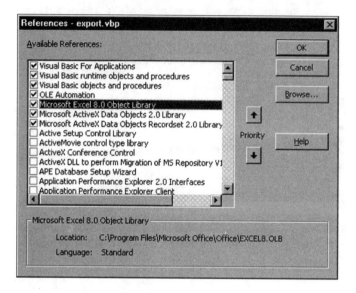

Now the program can reference and fully qualify all of the references to Excel. The references are bound early, during design time. So if there is any problem with syntax, we find out about it while still in the design time environment.

2 Add a new sub routine to the **frmExport** form called **excel**. Then add the following code:

```
Public Sub excel(adoRecordset As adodb.Recordset)

Dim iIndx As Integer
Dim iRowIndex As Integer
Dim iColIndex As Integer
Dim iRecordCount As Integer
Dim iFieldCount As Integer
Dim sMessage As String
Dim avRows As Variant
Dim excelVersion As Integer

'-- Read all of the records into our array
avRows = adoRecordset.GetRows()

'-- Determine how many fields and records
iRecordCount = UBound(avRows, 2) + 1
iFieldCount = UBound(avRows, 1) + 1
```

```
'-- Create reference variable for the spreadsheet
Set objExcel = CreateObject("Excel.Application")
objExcel.Visible = True
objExcel.Workbooks.Add

'We need this line to ensure Excel remains visible if we switch
'to the Active Sheet
Set objTemp = objExcel

excelVersion = Val(objExcel.Application.Version)
If (excelVersion >= 8) Then
 Set objExcel = objExcel.ActiveSheet
End If

'-- Place the names of the fields as column headers --
iRowIndex = 1
iColIndex = 1
For iColIndex = 1 To iFieldCount
  With objExcel.Cells(iRowIndex, iColIndex)
      .Value = adoRecordset.Fields(iColIndex - 1).Name
    With .Font
      .Name = "Arial"
      .Bold = True
      .Size = 9
    End With
  End With
Next

'-- memory management --
adoRecordset.Close
Set adoRecordset = Nothing

'-- Just add data --
With objExcel
  For iRowIndex = 2 To iRecordCount + 1
    For iColIndex = 1 To iFieldCount
     .Cells(iRowIndex, iColIndex).Value = avRows _
       (iColIndex - 1, iRowIndex - 2)
    Next
  Next
End With

objExcel.Cells(1, 1).CurrentRegion.EntireColumn.AutoFit

End Sub
```

How It Works

The first thing we do is read the contents of the recordset into our variant array in one fell swoop. The **GetRows** method of the **adoRecordset** passes all of the fields of all of the records to an array in one blur of action. We dimmed the **avRows** as a variant. Remember that this is an arbitrarily sized recordset - we don't know ahead of time how many fields or records there might be. However, we want to make this routine generalized so that it will work with any recordset we pass in.

So by using the **UBound** function we can easily get the information we need about the recordset's size. And remember that the array will start at 0 so we need to add 1 to each of the variables:

```
'-- Read all of the records into our array
avRows = adoRecordset.GetRows()

'-- Determine how many fields and records
iRecordCount = UBound(avRows, 2) + 1
iFieldCount = UBound(avRows, 1) + 1
```

Now that we have the contents of the recordset safely stored in the **avRows** array, we can create an instance of an Excel worksheet. We set the reference, make the reference visible, and add a workbook. This will give us a new workbook with sheet 1 displayed. However, there are a few ways to display an instance of Excel:

Function	Behavior
`CreateObject("Excel.Application")`	This always loads a new invisible instance of Excel
`GetObject("","Excel.Application")`	This always load a new visible instance
`GetObject(,"Excel.Application")`	This will return an already running instance of Excel or fails with an "OLE Automation" error

Depending on your needs, you can use any of these. Notice that in our code we are using the **CreateObject**.

> *Since Excel has such a wealth of built in functions, many programmers use Excel in the background to perform complicated math. For example, they will create an invisible instance of Excel from VB. Then they feed the spreadsheet data from their VB program to perform forecasting, regression, or other complicated mathematical functions. Finally, they grab the results from Excel and dismiss the spreadsheet. The user never even knows that it was Excel that did the heavy lifting. In cases such as these, Excel was used an automation server. It ran in it's own process space and served the VB program (the client) results on demand. You may find a need to accomplish this when analyzing database information.*

Back to our code.

We set a reference to our Excel spreadsheet and then make the application visible:

```
'-- Create reference variable for the spreadsheet
Set objExcel = CreateObject("Excel.Application")
objExcel.Visible = True
```

If we left this line out, Excel would be chugging along in the background but we would not know it because its **Visible** property is set to **False** by default. We must always set it to **True** when using the **CreateObject()** method. Next, we add a new workbook to the **Workbooks** collection:

```
objExcel.Workbooks.Add
```

Unfortunately, the **CreateObject** and **GetObject** methods of automation work a bit differently in Excel 97 than in earlier versions. We, of course, want our code to work with any version of Excel the user might have on their PC. We can do that by checking the version of Excel and assigning it to the variable **excelVersion**:

```
'We need this line to ensure Excel remains visible if we switch
'to the Active Sheet
Set objTemp = objExcel

excelVersion = Val(objExcel.Application.Version)
If (excelVersion >= 8) Then
  Set objExcel = objExcel.ActiveSheet
End If
```

First, we assign **objTemp** to the object variable **objExcel**. This will ensure that **objExcel** will remain visible if we need to switch to the **ActiveSheet**. If the version of Excel is **>= 8**, we reset the **objExcel** reference to refer to the active sheet.

Once we have the **objExcel** reference variable set correctly, we can now add the names of each of the fields to the first row in each column:

```
For iColIndex = 1 To iFieldCount
  With objExcel.Cells(iRowIndex, iColIndex)
     .Value = adoRecordset.Fields(iColIndex - 1).Name
     With .Font
       .Name = "Arial"
       .Bold = True
       .Size = 9
     End With
  End With
Next
```

We set the **.Value** property of **.Cells(row,column)** to the name of the field. It is worth pointing out here that we are using the **With...End With** syntax to minimize the dots. So this next section simply sets up the titles of each column by printing the name of each field in the recordset.

Recall that when we reference another application's objects from Visual Basic, we use the dot syntax "**.**" to navigate that object's hierarchy of collections, objects, properties, and methods. Typically, it becomes fairly common to create very lengthy navigation strings. In the example above, we would have to write **objExcel.Cells(iRowIndex, iColIndex).Font.Name = "Arial"**. It takes us three dots to reach the name property of the font collection of the specific cell in the **cells** collection of the Excel object. Phew! Again, this can be time consuming.

Now, we have all of our data from the recordset in the variant array **avRows**. So we can go ahead and close the recordset and set its reference to **Nothing**:

```
'-- memory management --
adoRecordset.Close
Set adoRecordset = Nothing
```

This ensures that we reclaim the memory used by the recordset. Now we are ready to add our recordset data (which is now safely stored in the **avRows** array) to the spreadsheet. Again, we use the outer loop to move from record to record and the inner loop to move from field to field within each record:

```
'-- Just add data --
With objExcel
  For iRowIndex = 2 To iRecordCount + 1
    For iColIndex = 1 To iFieldCount
```

```
      .Cells(iRowIndex, iColIndex).Value = avRows(iColIndex - 1, iRowIndex - 2)
    Next
  Next
End With
```

Just another quick glance at the finished product so that these row and column assignments will make more sense:

	A	B	C
1	PubID	Name	Company Name
2	1	SAMS	SAMS
3	2	PRENTICE HALL	PRENTICE HALL
4	3	M & T	M & T BOOKS
5	4	MIT	MIT PR
6	5	MACMILLAN COMPUTER	MACMILLAN COMPUTER PUB
7	6	HIGHTEXT PUBNS	HIGHTEXT PUBNS
8	7	SPRINGER VERLAG	SPRINGER VERLAG
9	8	O'REILLY & ASSOC	O'REILLY & ASSOC
10	9	ADDISON-WESLEY	ADDISON-WESLEY PUB CO

Notice that we are looping from row 2 through the total count of the records + 1:

```
For iRowIndex = 2 To iRecordCount + 1
```

Why? Take a look at the spreadsheet. We have added the headers in the first row - the headers are the field names of the ADO recordset. Since the headers are in row one, we start in row two. Now the inner loop starts printing fields starting in column 1. This is because we want to start in the left-hand field.

Also, you might be wondering why the coordinates don't start at zero. After all, don't these collections always start there? Well, remember we are placing our data on a spreadsheet. Also, it uses the Cartesian coordinates (remember from 8th grade?) to locate a place on the grid. So (1,1) means the first row, first cell. So when we print our first piece of data, we are printing it at (2,1): the second row, first column.

Finally, as long as we have a reference to the spreadsheet, we tell it to format the fields so each field is as wide as the longest entry. It will look at the entire contiguous region and fit the longest entry:

```
objExcel.Cells(1, 1).CurrentRegion.EntireColumn.AutoFit
```

Notice row 29, which is PubID 28:

	A	B
26	25	CORIOLIS GROUP
27	26	Prentice-Hall
28	27	South-Western Educational
29	28	INTL THOMSON COMPUTER PR(SHRT DISC)
30	29	PRENTICE HALL
31	30	MARCEL DEKKER
32	31	DUKE COMMUNICATIONS
33	32	INST OF ELECTRICAL &

This is the longest entry so our command stretched the B column to fit it. As you can see, you can program Excel from VB 6.0 just as if you were within Excel itself.

Of course, we could have dispensed with copying the ADO recordset to the array and just iterated though the recordset like we did when writing the csv and HTML export files. But this method is faster, under the circumstances. If we decided to grab data straight from the recordset, we would have to navigate the object hierarchy of both the ado recordset as well as the Excel object. But the **avRows** array data is stored in memory, so access to the data we want to write is much quicker.

> *Note: If we were using DAO instead of ADO, there is a great method called* `CopyFromRecordset`*. With this method, You can copy an entire result set to a range on a worksheet at once. This method begins to copy at the current row of the result set. Then, when the transfer is completed, the* `Recordset` *object pointer is positioned just past the last row, or at EOF. So it essentially blasts the information to the worksheet all at once instead of writing to each cell like we had to do with ADO The syntax looks like this:*

```
Worksheets("Sheet1").Range("A2").CopyFromRecordset myRecordset
```

Try It Out - Running the Program

1 Add the following code to the **Click** event of the **cmdExcel** command button:

```
Private Sub cmdExcel_Click()
Call excel(adoRecordset)
End Sub
```

2 Go ahead and run the program. Export the data into Excel. After the program runs you'll see something like:

If you run this with the entire Publishers table, the operation could take several minutes. If you cancel the Excel spreadsheet after getting tired of watching it update, you will be greeted with this error message:

It's telling us that the ActiveX Automation failed - we were trying to communicate with Excel and it was no longer available.

You can see how easy it would be to add these three new export procedures to the data mining program in the last chapter. A drop-down menu could show the three methods of exporting the returned recordset, and it could then be sent to a spreadsheet for the product manager to analyze the results. Alternatively, an HTML file could be created and placed on the corporate Intranet for Product Managers in other locations to review the results for their marketing campaign.

The Completed Project

You now have the ability to export an ADO recordset data to a csv file, an HTML file, or send it directly to Excel. We put a user interface on the project so we could explain it to the user:

But since you have learned how to make classes, this would be a good candidate for a class module. Simply cut and paste the code into the class module, set a few properties, and you are there. Then you could include this **export.cls** class in any project you are working on. Simply instantiate an instance of the class in your VB program and pass it any ADO recordset! Imagine how powerful you can make your programs now. Users will be amazed if you provide them menu choices to export their data in any of these three formats. By including this code in any of your programs, you have just made your data universally usable. Not a bad goal.

Next, let's take a look at some advanced ADO techniques that will help us really get the most out of our data.

Advanced ADO Techniques

Now, we are going to look at some of the more advanced ActiveX Data Object topics. While this is a beginning book, these topics are really very straightforward, and we want to cover them so you will know all about the new and exciting capabilities of ADO. I am sure you will find applications for using what we cover here in your new programming assignments.

Learning about Advanced ADO Topics

Well, so far we have seen how we can use ADO with Active Server Pages and then data mining. We have exported our ADO recordset data to csv and HTML, then directly into Excel. Just when you think that you have got the hang of what can be done with a recordset, along comes a totally new and exciting idea - the notion of a **disconnected or remoted recordset**. One of the fundamental tenets that designers of business objects came up with is to partition application logic and business rules. And to take this a step further, they want to protect business rules and data from redistribution. Now throw in the Internet to the pot and you have quite a mix. To handle all of these seemingly conflicting goals and rules, the disconnected recordset concept was born.

Using the disconnected recordset idea, you can actually create an ADO recordset and ship it off somewhere, say over the Internet to another division across the globe. You can think of a disconnected recordset as a sort of space ship: it gets sent off somewhere, gathers data, and then returns to earth to reveal what it has found.

This type of recordset is not connected to the database, but is a self-contained unit. Embodied in the recordset is the knowledge of how to update itself when the user adds, deletes, or modifies any of the records. When the remote user has finished updating the disconnected recordset, it is sent back and 'docks' with the original database. Once reconnected, it updates the underlying database just as a normal recordset would. It does sound a bit like science fiction, no? Let's take a look at these exotic and exciting creatures.

Disconnected ADO Recordsets

What can disconnected ADO recordsets do for us? Well, let's say we want to place the price schedule of our product line on the Internet. We might permit clients to log in and see our product line and the associated prices so that they can place orders to us over the Web. However, depending on who logs in, we may wish to change the prices we display for our products. For example, if we have some preferred clients, we might read their cookie that we placed on their machine and display a 'preferred' price list using Active Server Pages. We might also have a tiered discount structure in place. So if a client orders more that 500 widgets, they get a 20% volume discount. We might also have some rules that govern tax rates on the widgets based on the location of the purchaser. These are all examples of business rules that would manage the operation of our business.

Many of these business rules could be fluid: the Marketing Department might wish to offer a promotion, which means that our tiered discount structure must be changed. Or maybe one of the states modifies a tax rate. Those sorts of things. We certainly don't want our customers having access to our business rules - we don't want customers that only order 1 widget seeing the prices we give to larger customers that might order 5,000. So these business rules should be stored on a remote computer where the client has no knowledge of its logic. Also, we would like to have the ability to update our rules easily and without our clients being aware of the changes.

Business Objects

The way that this is done is to use **Business Objects**. Business objects are a perfect way to separate the business rules that our company uses from the client computer that accesses our web site. Our business objects would exist on a remote server and be invoked and used when the client hits our site.

Let's say that we have a preferred customer that logs into our web site. Using the ASP example we wrote in chapter 13, we could easily identify the client as the ABC Company, a large consumer of our widgets based in Austin, Texas. The cookie then permits our server to use ADO to retrieve the purchasing habits of the ABC Company. Based on the ABC Company's last purchase of 10,000 widgets and their prompt payment for the order, our business rules could display an attractive price to the ABC Company. So our business rules might have a tiered discount structure that factors in the credit worthiness of the purchaser as well. When the user logs in to make a purchase, the business rules are consulted prior to displaying the price per unit for this particular customer. OK, what does a remote recordset have to do with all of this? Good question. Let's take a look.

Remoting a Recordset

Let's say that we have just received an order from the ABC Company for another 5,000 widgets. However, the purchasing agent just realized that all 5,000 should not be red, but 2,000 of them must be blue. We could easily design a system that would permit the purchasing agent to actually do the data entry and make the changes on the order.

Consider this scenario. The purchasing agent logs into our Web site and we determine they are from the ABC Company by reading the cookie on their PC. One of the specialized screens for purchasing agents provides a 'Modify Order' button. The agent presses this button and the command gets sent to our server.

Back at our location (i.e., the server), our **ModifyOrder.Asp** page would build a dynamic SQL statement that would retrieve all outstanding orders for the ABC Company. The SQL statement is passed to an ADO recordset object. Now here is the totally amazing part: the ADO recordset object can become disconnected from the database connection and be sent over to the client's browser. Here the purchasing agent could review the Widgets that are on order in a grid rendered right on their browser. The changes are then made, right to the ADO recordset. When the agent has changed 2000 of the widgets to Blue, pressing a 'Submit Change' button would send the disembodied ADO recordset back to our server. There we reconnect it with the data source and update the database with the changes made remotely by the purchasing agent.

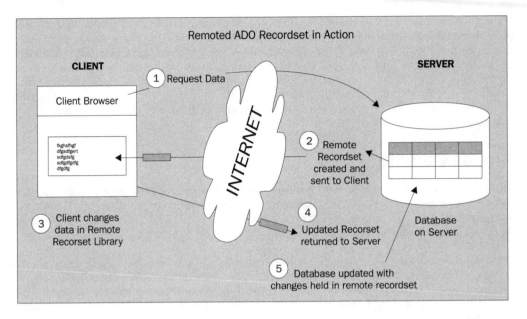

Any records that have been modified on the client by the purchasing manager are written back to our Web server through a technique called **marshaling**. Marshaling is the process of packaging and sending ADO recordset interface method parameters across thread or process boundaries. So ADO recordset data can be marshaled within a single program, between executable programs, or even over the Internet. Now in my opinion, that is amazing!

Creating a Disconnected Recordset

Before we can remote a recordset, that recordset has to be able to live on its own. By that I mean that it must be able to function as a recordset without a live connection to the database. Think of the disconnected recordset as a space ship. It can be fired off by itself, it can sustain life on its own, be sent out to space and function normally, then return to home base and dock up.

Likewise, we can create an independent disconnected recordset that lives on its own. A disconnected recordset can exist without a live connection to the database server. It knows how to remember changes and edits. It can be navigated. And when the changes are complete, the disconnected recordset is marshaled back to the server, reconnected to the data source, and the database is updated.

Creating a Disconnected Recordset is Simple

All we have to do to create a disconnected record is to set the **CursorLocation** property of the Recordset object. Essentially, the **CursorLocation** property allows us to tell the Recordset object two things. First, we can specify whether to use client or server cursors. And secondly, but most importantly, we can instruct the recordset to allow changes to be made in a batch mode. So just setting these properties permits the creation of a remote ADO recordset.

It's all in the Cursor

If we set the **CursorLocation** property to the constant **adUseClient** , then any updates to the disconnected record set are executed in a batch mode. The client-side cursor is used to cache the unique identification for the record set. Once the client makes the updates to the recordset, our data then gets marshaled back to our server for redocking with an ADO connection to our database.

Before remoting a record set, the record set has to be able to function as a Recordset object without a live connection to the database server. After a recordset is marshaled to a client computer, the data connection can't be marshaled with the record set; therefore, the record set must be disconnected from the database server. A disconnected recordset is thus a recordset without a live connection to a database server.

Updating Our Database from the Remoted ADO Recordset

After the changes are made to our recordset, the client computer has two options when it comes to returning the data to the server. It can choose to marshal the whole recordset back, or send back only the data that has been changed. In fact, the **MarshalOptions** property of the ADO record set was designed just for this purpose. Let's take a look at some sample code to see just how this magic is accomplished.

Please refer to the illustration to see what our next project is going to accomplish. We are going to actually build a remoted recordset and simulate sending it back and forth across the Internet.

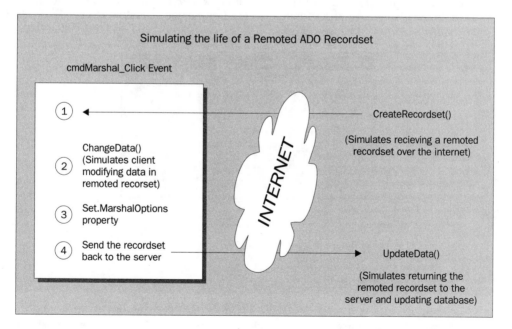

Even though we only creating a single VB 6.0 form here, we can actually build and send a remoted ADO recordset. All of the action takes place in the click event of a button on the form.

There are three functions we will write. Two of them, **createRecordSet()** and **UpdateData()** simulate operations on a remote server. The third, **changeData()** simulates a client making changes to the recordset locally, right on a browser. Although all of the functions happen to reside in a single form, the process would be the same if we were actually sending the remoted recordset over the Internet rather than simulating this part of the operation.

Calling **createRecordSet()** builds a remoted recordset for us and returns it to the **cmdMarshal_Click** event. The recordset is assigned to a locally scoped recordset. Next, a simple routine **changeData()** changes a single field in the recordset. The **.MarshalOptions** property is set that tells the recordset to return everything (or just the *modified* records) to the server. Finally, we call **updateData()** which simulates sending the remoted recordset back to the server and updating the database.

Ready? OK, let's write some code.

Try It Out - Remoting a Recordset

1 Be sure to add the ADO references (Microsoft ActiveX Data Objects 2.0 Library and the Microsoft ActiveX Data Objects Recordset 2.0 Library) to your project before you start. Create a new project called **\Chapter15\marshal.vbp**. Name the default form **frmMarshal**. Add a command button to the form, name it **cmdMarshal** and caption it as shown in the screenshot:

2 Now in the **General** section of the form, add the following code:

```
Option Explicit
Dim sConnString As String
```

The **sConnString** will hold our connect string. Since the variable is dimensioned at the form level, it is of course visible throughout our program. This way we can set it once and use it in any sub within our form.

3 Now, in the **Load** event of the **frmMarshal** form, please add the following code:

```
Private Sub Form_Load()

    sConnString = "Provider=Microsoft.Jet.OLEDB.3.51;" & _
                  "Data Source=C:\begdb\Biblio.mdb"

End Sub
```

How It Works

When the **cmdMarshal** button is clicked, the process starts in motion. In the **cmdMarshal_Click** event we are simulating a Web client communicating with our server. We simulate building a remote business object on our server to get a recordset using **createRecordSet()**. We then simulate a user modifying some of the data in the remoted recordset in the function **changeData()**. Then, finally, we reconnect the remoted recordset with the database in the function **updateData()**. This simulates sending the recordset back to the server and reconnecting it with the database.

Let's build the rest of the code.

Try It Out - Building a Remote Recordset

1 In the **cmdMarshal** click event of the **frmMarshal** form, please add the following code:

```
Private Sub cmdMarshal_Click()

    Dim adoMainRecordset As ADODB.Recordset
    Dim strMessage As String
    Dim iIndx As Integer

    Set adoMainRecordset = createRecordSet()

    Set adoMainRecordset = changeData(adoMainRecordset)

    '-The data has been changed. Which marshaling option?

    strMessage = "Edit in progress." & vbCr
    strMessage = "Would you like to update the database?"

    iIndx = MsgBox(strMessage, vbYesNo + vbQuestion, _
            "MarshalOptions")

    If (iIndx = vbYes) Then

        strMessage = "Would you like to send all the rows " & _
                     "in the recordset back to the server?"

        iIndx = MsgBox(strMessage, vbYesNo + vbQuestion, _
                "MarshalOptions")
```

```
        If (iIndx = vbYes) Then
           adoMainRecordset.MarshalOptions = adMarshalAll
        Else
           adoMainRecordset.MarshalOptions = adMarshalModifiedOnly
        End If

        If (updateData(adoMainRecordset)) Then
          If (iIndx = vbYes) Then
             MsgBox "Database updated - All records marshaled."
          Else
             MsgBox "Database updated - Modified records marshaled."
          End If
          Exit Sub
        Else
         MsgBox "Not updated."
        End If

    Else

      MsgBox "Database not updated."
    End If

    End Sub
```

How It Works

We dimension a locally scoped **ADODB.Recordset**. Then we call the function **createRecordSet**. This simulated business object actually creates a local remoted recordset and returns it to us. We then set our local recordset to the returned remoted recordset:

```
Set adoMainRecordset = createRecordSet()
```

This function simulates how a remote business object, **createRecordSet ()**, can build on the server and returned to us. The **createRecordSet** returns a remoted ADO recordset to us. We can visualize this being as if we - the client - are asking for the recordset in an ASP page and the server returns the records for (say) our company's purchases. We set a reference locally to that recordset by setting our locally scoped **adoMainRecordset** to the returned remoted recordset:

```
Set adoMainRecordset = changeData(adoMainRecordset)
```

In this example, we happen to be grabbing a remoted recordset within the same process (our VB program). But this could just as easily be another program or a client browser requesting the remoted recordset using VBScript. And of course, there is no database connection for the recordset, as we will soon see.

Once the recordset is created and returned to us from **createRecordSet()**, the **changeData()** function simulates a remote user modifying the recordset. In **changeData()** we are just changing one of the fields. But this could just as easily be a user modifying several records. The modified recordset is then sent back to us.

Now, when we want to update the underlying database with the changes in the remoted **adoMainRecordset**, we have the option to send the entire recordset back to the server, or only the records that were modified. We present a message box to permit the user to choose which option. If the user only wants the modified records to be sent, we set the **.MarshalOptions** property to **adMarshalAll**. Otherwise, we set it to **adMarshalModifiedOnly**:

```
    If (iIndx = vbYes) Then
          adoMainRecordset.MarshalOptions = adMarshalAll
    Else
          adoMainRecordset.MarshalOptions = adMarshalModifiedOnly
    End If
```

Finally, we will reattach the remoted recordset to the data source in the **updateData()** function. Here we will update the underlying database. We are still in the **cmdMarshal_Click** event so we are simulating being on the client PC. Here we can select to return all of the records in the remoted recordset to the host or just those that have been changed by the user. The remoted recordset, since we just set its **MarshalOptions** property, is smart enough to handle and remember all of the changes.

By simply setting the **MarshalOptions** property on the remoted recordset object we instruct the recordset how to return the data to the server. Once we set the **MarshalOptions** property, we then return the recordset for it to be reconnected:

```
    If (updateData(adoMainRecordset)) Then
```

Now our recordset has been sent back to the server and the underlying database has been updated. Now let's move on to the supporting routines that make this magic happen.

The createRecordset Function

OK, now for the fun stuff. The **createRecordSet()** function simulates our business object that creates a remoted ADODB recordset. First, notice the return in the 'signature' of the function. We will be returning a recordset. So when this is created, it will be disconnected from a connection object and then returned from this function to the caller – which in our case it the cmdMarshal button. Again, this button is simulating a client's browser at the other end of the world.

Let's hit the code trail once more.

Try It Out - Building the Supporting Functions

1 Please add this function to the **frmMarshal** from. Name the function **createRecordSet** and be sure the return value is type **ADODB.RecordSet**. Of course, we will create a recordset and return it to the calling function in **cmdMarshal**:

```
Public Function createRecordSet() As ADODB.Recordset

Dim adoRecordset As ADODB.Recordset
Dim sSqlString As String

On Error GoTo createError:

sSqlString = "SELECT * FROM Authors"

Set adoRecordset = New ADODB.Recordset
```

```
        adoRecordset.CursorType = adOpenKeyset
        adoRecordset.LockType = adLockOptimistic
        adoRecordset.CursorLocation = adUseClientBatch

        adoRecordset.Open sSqlString, sConnString

        Set createRecordSet = adoRecordset
        Exit Function

        createError:
        MsgBox Err.Description
        Set createRecordSet = Nothing
        Exit Function

        End Function
```

How It Works

There are a few points to note here. Of course, we are just creating a recordset with all of the records from the Authors table. This could have just as easily been anything at all. For example, what if you had several divisions of your far-flung company sprawled around the globe. However, headquarters in New York maintained all employee records. When the division in Stuttgart Germany logged in, an ASP script could be downloaded to the client browser from our server in New York. The VBScript code reads the cookie, determines that this is a legitimate user from Stuttgart, and our business object dynamically generates a remoted recordset of all employees in Germany.

So here we build a new ADO recordset and set a few properties. We must ensure that the recordset is updateable on the client, so we can't use the default cursor. A cursor that permits updating must be selected, so we choose **adOpenKeyset**:

```
    Set adoRecordset = New ADODB.Recordset

    adoRecordset.CursorType = adOpenKeyset
    adoRecordset.LockType = adLockOptimistic
    adoRecordset.CursorLocation = adUseClientBatch
```

The critical piece of this code is the **CursorLocation** property. By providing the constant **adUseClientBatch**, we are effectively creating a remoted ADO recordset.

Now comes the interesting part – we open the recordset without a connection object! That's right – no connection object is used here:

```
    adoRecordset.Open sSqlString, sConnString
```

We provide the SQL query string as usual. And again, this string could easily have requested any arbitrary grouping of records based on the request from the client browser. So when we open the recordset, we pass in the **sSqlString** to tell it what records to retrieve. Next, we pass in the **sConnString**, which defines the connection! We do not pass in any 'open connection object' code.

Then we take the newly minted recordset and return it to the caller of our business object:

```
    Set createRecordSet = adoRecordset
    Exit Function
```

Since the return type is an **ADODB.Recordset** object, we need to use the **Set** keyword to set a reference to the object.

Now the remoted recordset has been returned to the caller from our simulated server. The connectionless recordset using the **CursorLocation** property set to **adUseClientBatch**. makes it remotable. Way cool!

Changing Some Data on the Client Side

Our next function simulates changing some data in the remoted recordset by the client. We do this by passing in the recordset to a function, **changeData** – change a field it – and return it to the caller.

Try It Out - Add the changeData Function

1 Please add this next function, **changeData**, to the **frmMarshal** form:

```
Public Function changeData(adoRecordset As _
                           ADODB.Recordset) As ADODB.Recordset

On Error GoTo changeError:

With adoRecordset
    !author = "New Data"
End With

Set changeData = adoRecordset
Exit Function

changeError:
MsgBox Err.Description
Set changeData = Nothing


End Function
```

How It Works

This function is pretty simple. We simply pass in the remoted recordset, change a single field, and return the recordset to the caller in **cmdMarshal**. We only modify the first record here by changing the Author field to **"New Data"**. Then the function name is **Set** to the modified recordset and it is returned to the caller:

```
With adoRecordset
    !author = "New Data"
End With

Set changeData = adoRecordset
```

The data in the remoted ADO recordset has been changed and returned to the **cmdMarshal** which is simulating the remote client. Now that the information is changed, we set the **MarshalOptions** to either return all of the records or only those modified. It is a good idea to send only those records that have been modified. The bandwidth savings can be tremendous. Imagine if you sent a 10,000 ADO recordset to a client and only one record was modified. If you set the **MarshalOptions** to **adMarshalModifiedOnly**, then only the single record is returned, not the entire 10,000.

Now that the remoted recordset has some data changed, we simulate passing it back to the database on the server. We have just one more function that takes care of this for us.

Try It Out - Updating the Database from the Remoted Recordset

1 Add another function to the **frmMarshal** form. Name the function **updateData**. Here's the code to add to this function:

```
Public Function updateData(adoRecordset As ADODB.Recordset) As Boolean

Dim adoTemp As ADODB.Recordset

On Error GoTo updateError:

Set adoTemp = New ADODB.Recordset

adoTemp.Open adoRecordset, sConnString
adoTemp.UpdateBatch
updateData = True
Exit Function

updateError:
MsgBox "In Update:  " & Err.Description
updateData = False

End Function
```

How It Works

This is the interesting part of the updating process. First we create a local ADO recordset. Then we open the local recordset using the remoted ADO recordset in the place of the SQL statement. And then using the **sConnString**, the local recordset is opened and updated:

```
Set adoTemp = New ADODB.Recordset

adoTemp.Open adoRecordset, sConnString
adoTemp.UpdateBatch
```

So in our simple program we have called a function that creates a remoted ADO recordset. We modify the data. Finally we return the recordset, permitting the user to return all records or just those changed by setting the **MarshalOptions** property. We have also shown how we can pass a recordset around by setting one recordset to another.

Run the Program

Please save and run the program.

Of course, you just get to press a button on this one – nothing flashy in terms of a user interface. But under the hood we are performing magic. It's easy to see how, by using remoted recordsets, you could make your data available to anyone in the world. And with business objects on the server acting as a traffic cop to ensure only the proper information goes to each requester, we have a pretty powerful mix. I've said this before, but I think those people up in Redmond are truly Wizards.

Now that we have sent recordsets flying over the Internet, let's take a closer look at the **AbsolutePosition** property of an ADO recordset. Many beginners stumble on this because the cursor property must be set correctly to be able to read this property.

Getting the AbsolutePosition Property

In order to get the **AbsolutePosition** property to show where we are in a recordset, we need to use client-side cursors.

Try It Out - How to Get the AbsolutePosition Property

1   Add a new form to your current project. Name the form **frmClient**. Add a command button, name it **cmdClient**, and caption it as shown in the screenshot. Add a progress bar and change the name to **progressBar1** (remember, you'll need to add the Microsoft Windows Common Controls 6.0 component to get the progress bar icon in your toolbox). Finally, add a label and change the name to **lblAbsolute**. Lay the form out like the screenshot:

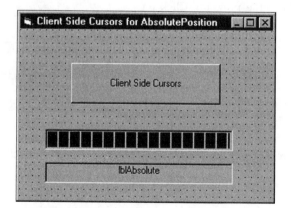

This is a fairly simple, one-procedure program. We will open an ADO recordset, iterate through it, and display our current position using both a progress bar and a label.

2 Please add the following code to the **cmdClient_Click** event procedure:

```
Private Sub cmdClient_Click()
Dim adoRecordset As ADODB.Recordset
Dim sConnectionString As String
Dim sMessage As String

sConnectionString ="Provider=Microsoft.Jet.OLEDB.3.51;" & _
                    "Data Source=C:\begdb\Biblio.mdb"


Set adoRecordset = New ADODB.Recordset
adoRecordset.CursorLocation = adUseClient
adoRecordset.Open "Titles", sConnectionString, , , adCmdTable

ProgressBar1.Min = 0
ProgressBar1.Max = adoRecordset.RecordCount

While Not adoRecordset.EOF
    ProgressBar1.Value = adoRecordset.AbsolutePosition
    lblAbsolute = "Record: " & adoRecordset.AbsolutePosition & _
                   " of " & adoRecordset.RecordCount
    DoEvents
    AdoRecordset.MoveNext
Wend

End Sub
```

3 Now, save and run the program. Click on the Client Side Cursors command button:

How It Works

There is no magic here. We are just setting the cursor location to the client:

```
adoRecordset.CursorLocation = adUseClient
```

Of course we are violating all of our rules about reading object properties each time through the loop. Here we read the **AbsolutePosition** twice and the **RecordCount** once. We do this just to slow down the display. Remember, each "**.**" read must be resolved by Visual Basic:

```
ProgressBar1.Value = adoRecordset.AbsolutePosition
lblAbsolute = "Record: " & adoRecordset.AbsolutePosition & _
             " of " & adoRecordset.RecordCount
```

Of course we would read the **Recordcount** before entering the loop and assign the value to a variable. Since it won't change for the duration of the loop, we don't need to read a property. Reading a property is *always* slower than reading a variable. Then we would assign the **Recordcount** to a variable once and read the value for the **ProgressBar1** and the **lblAbsolute**.

If you were to change the **CursorLocation**, like this:

```
adoRecordset.CursorLocation = adUseServer
```

both of these properties return –1:

So when you want to read the **AbsolutePosition** property to update your fancy doodads, be sure to set the **CursorLocation** to **adUseClient**. The default uses server side cursors and this can cause you to pull out your hair if you don't know this tip.

After our little diversion, we'll now have a look at making ADO recordsets persist beyond their memory lifespan.

Another ADO 2.0 Wonder - Persistent Recordsets

Well, we covered remoting recordsets just a while ago. There is another advanced property that is available to us in ADO 2.0, that of persistent recordsets. That's right, up to now we have been working with recordsets that just reside in memory. But when we exit the program, or the recordset object variable goes out of scope, phoof! The recordset is gone. You might consider this a tad volatile. We now have another option when working with ADO – persistent recordsets: you can now create a recordset and save it right to your local hard drive! This will allow you to connect to a server, request a recordset, and save the recordset to your hard drive. Then you can shut down the computer, power up at some later time, and resuscitate the recordset just where you left off! Let's write a simple program to illustrate how this is done.

Try It Out - Creating Persistent Recordsets

1 Add a new form to your project and name it **frmPersistent**. Rename the project **Persist** and save it as **Persist.vbp**.

2 Add two command buttons named **cmdSave** and **cmdRetrieve** as shown:

What we are going to do is add code to each of the buttons. OK, I know this is not fancy either, but the code will impress you, guaranteed. It's simple to create a persistent recordset.

3 Please add this code to the **cmdSave** button's **Click** event. This will create a recordset and save it to your hard drive:

```
Private Sub cmdSave_Click()
```

```
Dim adoConnection As ADODB.Connection
Dim adoRecordset As ADODB.Recordset
Dim sConnString As String
Dim sSqlString As String
Dim sMyFile As String

On Error GoTo createError:

sConnString =    "Provider=Microsoft.Jet.OLEDB.3.51;" & _
                 "Persist Security Info=False;" & _
                 "Data Source=C:\begdb\Biblio.mdb"

Set adoConnection = New ADODB.Connection
adoConnection.Open sConnString

sSqlString = "SELECT * FROM Authors"

Set adoRecordset = New ADODB.Recordset

adoRecordset.CursorType = adOpenDynamic
adoRecordset.LockType = adLockOptimistic
adoRecordset.CursorLocation = adUseClient

adoRecordset.Open sSqlString, adoConnection
```

```
      ChDir App.Path

      sMyFile = Dir(App.Path & "\myAdoRecordset")
      If (Len(sMyFile)) Then
        Kill sMyFile
      End If

      adoRecordset.Save ("myADORecordset")

      MsgBox ("Recordset successfully saved")

      Exit Sub

      createError:
      MsgBox Err.Description
      Set adoRecordset = Nothing
      Set adoConnection = Nothing
      Exit Sub

End Sub
```

How It Works

We know how to open an ADO recordset, so let's jump right to the properties. For this to work, you must use client side cursors. So be sure to set the **CursorLocation** to **adUseClient**. Then the recordset is opened normally:

```
      adoRecordset.CursorType = adOpenDynamic
      adoRecordset.LockType = adLockOptimistic
      adoRecordset.CursorLocation = adUseClient

      adoRecordset.Open sSqlString, adoConnection
```

If you don't explicitly change the default directory, then the operating system sets it to the location of the VB 6.0 executable. Any recordset that we attempt to save will also be stored in the same place. So let's save the recordset to the directory of the application, which will be **\Chapter15**. This way we can isolate the recordset and retrieve it. If we did not take this step, it would be saved to the VB directory. Then, if another program changed the directory and the default **dir** was somewhere other than VB, we would not be able to retrieve the recordset even though it was on the hard drive. So we use the VB function **ChDir** and explicitly change the default directory to our applications path:

```
      ChDir App.Path

      sMyFile = Dir(App.Path & "\myAdoRecordset")
      If (Len(sMyFile)) Then
        Kill sMyFile
      End If
```

We have to take a precaution before saving the recordset. Since we are going to name it **"myAdoRecordset"**, if we try to save another recordset, VB will give us this very helpful message informing us that a file by that name already exists:

To prevent that, we use the VB **Dir** function to see if a file (recordset) by the name
"**myAdoRecordset**" already exists in the current directory. If it does, the fully qualified path and
name is placed in the variable **sMyFile**. If the length of **sMyFile** is > 0, we know that the file
exists. So we just use the built in **Kill** function do delete the file. We use **Kill** and pass it
sMyfile, which of course has the name and path of the recordset we want deleted. This
ensures that we can always save a recordset. For production code, you might wish to save
several recordsets. In this case, you would have to manage the names so there would not be
any conflicts.

Now, all that is required to save an open recordset to your hard drive is to use the **Save**
method of the recordset and pass in a string with the name to save it under. That's it! So the
recordset will be saved and we display a message acknowledging all is well:

```
adoRecordset.Save ("myADORecordset")

MsgBox ("Recordset successfully saved")
```

Now that we have the recordset safely tucked away on our drive, we can power down and
grab some lunch. When we return, we can very easily reanimate the recordset. Let's add the
code that will allow us to do that:

Try It Out - Adding the Retrieval Code

1 Now, in the **Click** event of the **cmdRetrieve** button, please add the following code. This
will take care of reconstituting the dormant recordset:

```
Private Sub cmdRetrieve_Click()

Dim adoRecordset As ADODB.Recordset

On Error GoTo retrieveError

Set adoRecordset = New ADODB.Recordset

ChDir App.Path

adoRecordset.Open "myADORecordset", , , , adCmdFile
MsgBox ("Recordset successfully retrieved")
Exit Sub

retrieveError:
MsgBox Err.Description
Exit Sub

End Sub
```

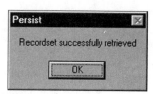

2 Run the program and click the <u>R</u>etrieve Recordset button:

How It Works

Quite simply, we just dim a local **ADODB** recordset and **Set** it to new as we normally do. To ensure we can find the recordset, we use the **ChDir** again to make sure that the default current directory points to our application's directory. Then we use the **Open** method as we usually do. However, this time we pass in the string of the name we used to save the recordset. Be sure to use the **adCmdFile** in the options position of the **Open** method:

```
adoRecordset.Open "myADORecordset", , , , adCmdFile
MsgBox ("Recordset successfully retrieved")
```

Then when the file is brought back into memory, we display a message box saying all is right with the world.

Life is good.

You can now go back to work on your recordset.

Wrapping Up

We've introduced some powerful new techniques in this chapter. Before winding up the book in chapter 16, let's review the things we saw in this chapter that can help us make our data more widely available and more flexible to use.

Summary

Well, in this chapter we really focused on areas that extend the powers of the database programmers beyond anything that has been previously possible. First, we covered how to export data from our ADO recordset to a csv file and showed how to import the results into Excel (or any spreadsheet for that matter) and Access. And in fact, the data can now be imported into just about any software program: any program worth it's salt can import a csv file. Next, we covered how to export the same data to an HTML file. We simply formatted the data in the text file using HTML tags, and now these unassuming straight text files can be rendered in any web browser on the globe. We then used ActiveX automation to program the exposed methods of Excel; we created an instance of Excel and programmed it with our ADO recordset data.

Finally, we then went on to explore some of the advanced ADO techniques, such as remoting a recordset, ensuring that the **AbsolutePosition** property works correctly, and persisting an ADO recordset right on your hard drive. Not a bad note to end this chapter on.

What We Have Learned

▶ We can easily export our recordset information to a comma delimited, HTML or Excel file so the data can be used in other programs

▶ A disconnected recordset permits us to shuttle the recordset across the globe and when it returns, update our database.

▶ We can now not only send disembodied, connectionless recordsets across the enterprise or the world, we can now also make them persist on a local drive. This will give several people in the business organization that need to review/update the data, the ability to do so locally. Users can now exit your application without fear that the recordset will be destroyed.

In the final chapter we'll take a step back from the maelstrom of code and recordsets and offer some reflections on the journey that we've taken in this book and where the future destinations of database programming might be found.

Exercises

1 Why is it important to allow users to export information from our applications?

2 Explain the difference between early and late binding. Give an example of when you would want to use late binding.

3 What is the advantage of using a disconnected recordset? When might you want to use one?

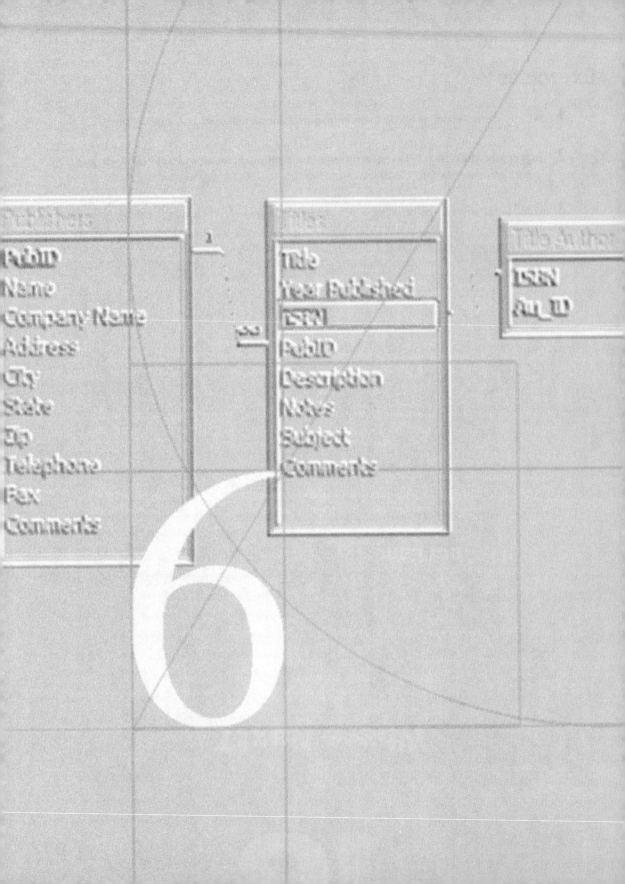

Where Next?

It would be crazy to attempt to summarize a book of this size in just a few pages, so rather than do that we'll take a relaxed excursion to the land of 'Where we've been, where we are now, and where we might be going next'.

This short final chapter aims to help us ground ourselves after our headlong flight through a lot of complexity and hard work. I'm no astrologer - these are just some personal reflections on the world of database programming.

This Land is Your Land

As we said right at the start of this book, the territory that we've been exploring - programming databases - is a large and complicated one, so any one itinerary will never be able to cover the whole map in detail. But we can make sure that we've seen the really important sights.

Where We've Been

We started out at the beginning of this book by introducing some database concepts, and talked at some length about relational databases, taking the supplied **Biblio.mdb** database as our example.

By now, any discussion of records/rows and fields/columns should be second nature to you. We saw how important these concepts were throughout the book, since an understanding of how the data looks schematically gives us a real insight into how to get hold of that data and manipulate it programmatically. Without the background knowledge, you can quickly be reduced to thrashing around in the dark - or in the half-light at least.

We used the Jet database engine to retrieve the underlying database records and make them available to our VB programs in recordsets. Once we have got hold of the recordset from the underlying data store - whatever its nature - we can use VB and its components to manipulate them programmatically. We did this using both DAO and ADO.

The ADO object model flattens our perspective somewhat, and makes it easier to visualize data access in terms of the objects that we need to be able to interact with. For example, we can create recordset objects, open connections with them, and process the data held in the recordset.

Working at the object level makes life simpler for us by abstracting us further and further away from the physical idiosyncrasies of different data stores - all we need to do is code for them as objects and use platform-specific drivers to handle all the knuckle-barking work under the hood. This approach takes us closer to the nirvana of being able to access data stores of all types from any type of user interface. Obviously, as VB programmers, our interface of choice is a VB program that presents the user with a friendly, intuitive, and highly functional face.

Being committed to using VB as our interface builder and operator implicitly means that we're swimming in the Microsoft ocean, and there's no getting away from the fact that if you program with VB you need to be aware of where the Microsoft strategy is headed. As we mentioned several times, the goal is Universal Data Access (UDA), where layers of data providers and technologies give our VB front-end seamless access to all the world's data stores. The architecture that is helping shape these developments is embodied in the Component Object Model (COM). Although the tools and platforms to fully implement this ideal are still some way off for many garden-variety applications, a sketch of the finished article has been drawn up.

> *Take a look at the Microsoft Web Site and you'll find plenty of discussion papers about the Microsoft interpretation of the future of data access.*

Where Are We Now?

We're clearly at an important transition point in the evolution of VB-centric database programming. We have a number of established technologies available to us, and newer ones developing all the time.

In this book we've focussed on the two most VB-friendly data access technologies - DAO and ADO. As we've often repeated, DAO is out there, running countless applications all over the world. This is a technology that is well established and proven. We also said that DAO wouldn't be developed any further than it is now - it is a technology that will be frozen, Peter Pan-like. So there will be plenty of opportunity to work with DAO into the foreseeable future.

The coming technology is ADO, which will work closely with OLE DB to serve us up simplified data access to different platforms. These two technologies are well integrated with VB, and seem destined to become even more closely linked. We looked at a lot of examples of how to use ADO and get hold of information held in Access databases using the Microsoft **Jet OLEDB.3.51** provider, and we saw that there were other providers available to handle access to other types of data store. This looks to be the way the world is headed, with code encapsulated and called when needed. Interoperability and encapsulation are two of our most important programming watchwords.

Where Are We Going Next?

This is a tricky question. Anybody who sticks their neck out and predicts the future in the computer industry is constrained by the pace of change and by the sheer complexity of the landscape.

However, what does seem clear is that there is now an established trend towards thinner clients, whereby the processing power moves back onto the server. One example of this that we worked with here was in ASP - all the intelligence and memory is on the server - the client is just a browser! These kinds of developments mesh nicely with the conception of networks (in general) and the Internet (in particular) as the major vehicles for technological and commercial development.

In this context, you might also consider how VB's ability (through ADO) to interact with all of these technologies - ASP, the Internet, and databases - makes for exciting possibilities for interface and program development.

A Word of Caution

With all the excitement about the opportunities available to us through the digitalization of the planet, it's easy to lose sight of some of the more prosaic issues: privacy, integrity, and security - those sorts of things.

We read every day how corporate Intranets are quickly becoming the most effective way to share information for many different business tasks. So the need for security and enhanced privacy is growing as we see electronic forms of identification replace face-to-face and paper-based IDs. With the amazing emergence of the Internet, and companies rushing to move their businesses outside the firewall to obtain 'customer intimacy', there is a tremendous demand for sophisticated public-key technology. To address these needs, we are seeing the emergence of so called "Smart Cards" - these credit card-sized devices are used to unmistakably identify a user. One variety are the integrated circuit cards (ICCs). These are interesting to PC developers because they are able to perform very sophisticated security processing.

So the next book on databases for VB 6.0 and above will probably contain a section on how to encrypt data being sent over the Internet, and how to ensure that the data can only be viewed by using some kind of smart card access attached to the PC. We have been discussing remote access of data over the Internet for inter-business communication. In fact, this business use is rapidly driving the evolution of security technology. So stay tuned. While we want to send our data everywhere, anywhere – we also want to be sure that only the intended recipient can see it. These are the kind of paradoxes and problems that ensure that we, as database programmers, always live in interesting times.

Next Steps

As a programmer, you'll no doubt want to explore some of the subjects that we've covered in this book. There are a number of areas of study that follow on logically from looking at programming databases using VB6, among these are VB/ActiveX Objects, Databases/ADO, and ASP.

Finally

We hope that you have found this book useful, informative and rewarding. We have covered a lot of ground for a beginner's book, and we expect that you'll have found some sections of the material more interesting than others. Inevitably, given the subject matter, your favorite subject wasn't covered the way that you'd prefer it to be. Help us create the next Apress database book by offering your comments and suggestions.

It seems like a long time ago that we asked 'What Is a Database?', and we trust that you have a far better understanding of what you can do with databases using VB. We have given you a start, and now the initiative lies with you. There are mountains to climb and problems to solve, and you now have many of the tools to tackle them.

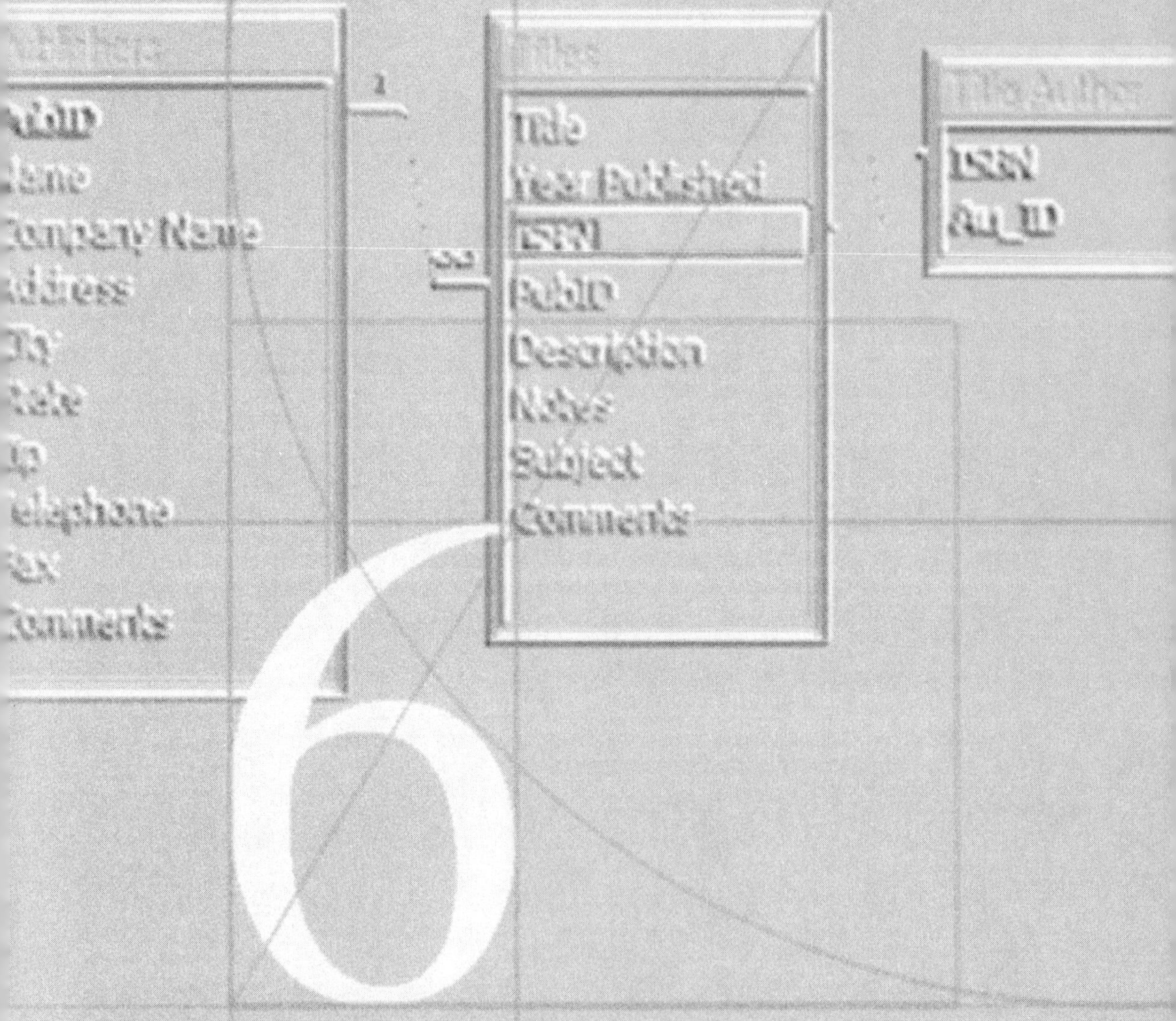

Publishers

- PubID
- Name
- Company Name
- Address
- City
- State
- Zip
- Telephone
- Fax
- Comments

Titles

- Title
- Year Published
- ISBN
- PubID
- Description
- Notes
- Subject
- Comments

Title Author

- ISBN
- Au_ID

6

One Standard, Many Flavors...

Standards are, theoretically, a wonderful thing - everyone does the same thing the same way, according to an agreed-upon practice. However, since you and I live in RealWorldLand, we know that standards are made to be broken. And "standard" SQL is no exception, which means that what we as developers prepare for one SQL database will *almost* work in any other SQL database.

Microsoft Access, and the Jet database engine that powers it, were created years ago for the specific purpose of serving applications that run on the desktop. Implicit with that purpose was the absence of any need to maintain strict compatibility with "larger" databases that run on bigger, faster systems. As a result, Jet's flavor of SQL implements many of the same features of bigger database systems, but implements them *differently*. Worse still is that some implementation differences don't result in actual errors, but merely different results for the same query.

Although Access has matured to support multi-user capability and other features like those of its bigger, older cousins, it is clearly a little brother to Microsoft's enterprise database, SQL Server. As Microsoft points its data access direction toward larger-scale databases through Universal Data Access via OLEDB and ActiveX Data Objects (ADO), it becomes clear that developers will need to be conversant in the details of more than one dialect of SQL. Things become even more complicated if you consider the "generic" flavor of SQL used by Microsoft's ODBC standard.

How do they all differ? It would be nearly impossible to describe all the subtleties in each variation of SQL in wide use. However, it is possible to describe a few of the more important differences that relate to specific examples in this book. As you gain experience with any one flavor of SQL, these subtleties magically become natural, and therefore somewhat less annoying in the long run.

The [Field Name] Syntax

You can't qualify the name of a field in a query with brackets in SQL Server. This isn't so much of a problem, because SQL Server by default doesn't allow spaces in the field names of its tables, which is usually why you need that syntax in the first place. If you have a field name that contains special characters, you typically must access the field by enclosing the reference in double-quotes.

The BETWEEN Clause

In Jet SQL, the order of the values in a **BETWEEN** clause is not important. However, in SQL Server, they must be in ascending order. For example:

```
SELECT Age FROM StudentList WHERE Age BETWEEN 20 AND 18
```

will work in both Jet SQL and SQL Server's Transact-SQL, but they will produce different results. In the Jet case, the query will work as you and I might expect; it will return a list of **Age** values that fall between 18 and 20. However, in SQL Server, because the high end of the range is specified first, a higher value is anticipated for the end range; the list will therefore be empty but no error will be generated.

Column Aliases

The primary method for column aliasing in Jet works in SQL Server version 6.5 with no problem:

```
SELECT ColumnName AS AliasName FROM TableName
```

SQL Server supports an aliasing syntax that is **not** supported in Jet SQL:

```
SELECT ColumnName 'AliasName' FROM TableName
```

Joins

It was not until the release of SQL Server 6.5 that this flavor of SQL supported the full set of ANSI-style joins. However, support for **OUTER JOIN**s still has a small but important caveat.

We understand that an **OUTER JOIN** is to return all the records of one table, and the records of a second table that match a particular criteria related to the first table. If you qualify the second table with a **WHERE** clause, things get tricky. In fact, a query that performs a **JOIN** might present two different results if applied to the same tables in JET and SQL Server.

Here are the particulars. If you specify an **OUTER JOIN** on two tables using Jet SQL, and include a **WHERE** clause on the second table, Jet will apply the **WHERE** clause after the **JOIN** is completed. On the other hand, the same query in SQL Server will be interpreted to apply the **WHERE** clause before the **JOIN** is completed.

You might think it wouldn't make any difference - but it does. Think of the **WHERE** clause as a filter, and a **JOIN** as glue. In this example, if I filter the second table, I still have all the records in the first table. When I glue the records together, I have all the records from the first table to glue to the matching records in the second table. Conversely, if I glue the records together first, then apply my filter, my filter applies to records in the glued table. If I note that a new record in my joined table includes a record that should be filtered out, I have to throw out the entire record - including the one from the first table of my join.

You may ask, "Why don't they work the same way?" Keep asking questions like that and we'll have you removed. The difference arises from the fact that the Jet engine constructs **JOIN**s in compliance with the ANSI SQL-92 standard, which includes a specification for the construction of **OUTER JOIN**s. SQL Server, on the other hand, implemented its own style of **OUTER JOIN**s before the ANSI SQL-92 spec was released. You could make arguments on both sides that either is the correct implementation. From the ANSI SQL-92 perspective, the Jet implementation is correct. From another, the SQL Server implementation makes sense in the context of how you might think a **JOIN** should work.

For specific information on this behavior, you might want to check out Microsoft Knowledgebase article Q124152.

Summary

The point here is that SQL to one vendor isn't necessarily SQL to every other vendor. Although the basic syntax is common among most implementations, there are subtle differences that are typically only realized through experience. The better you know the target system, the less likely you are to encounter problems.

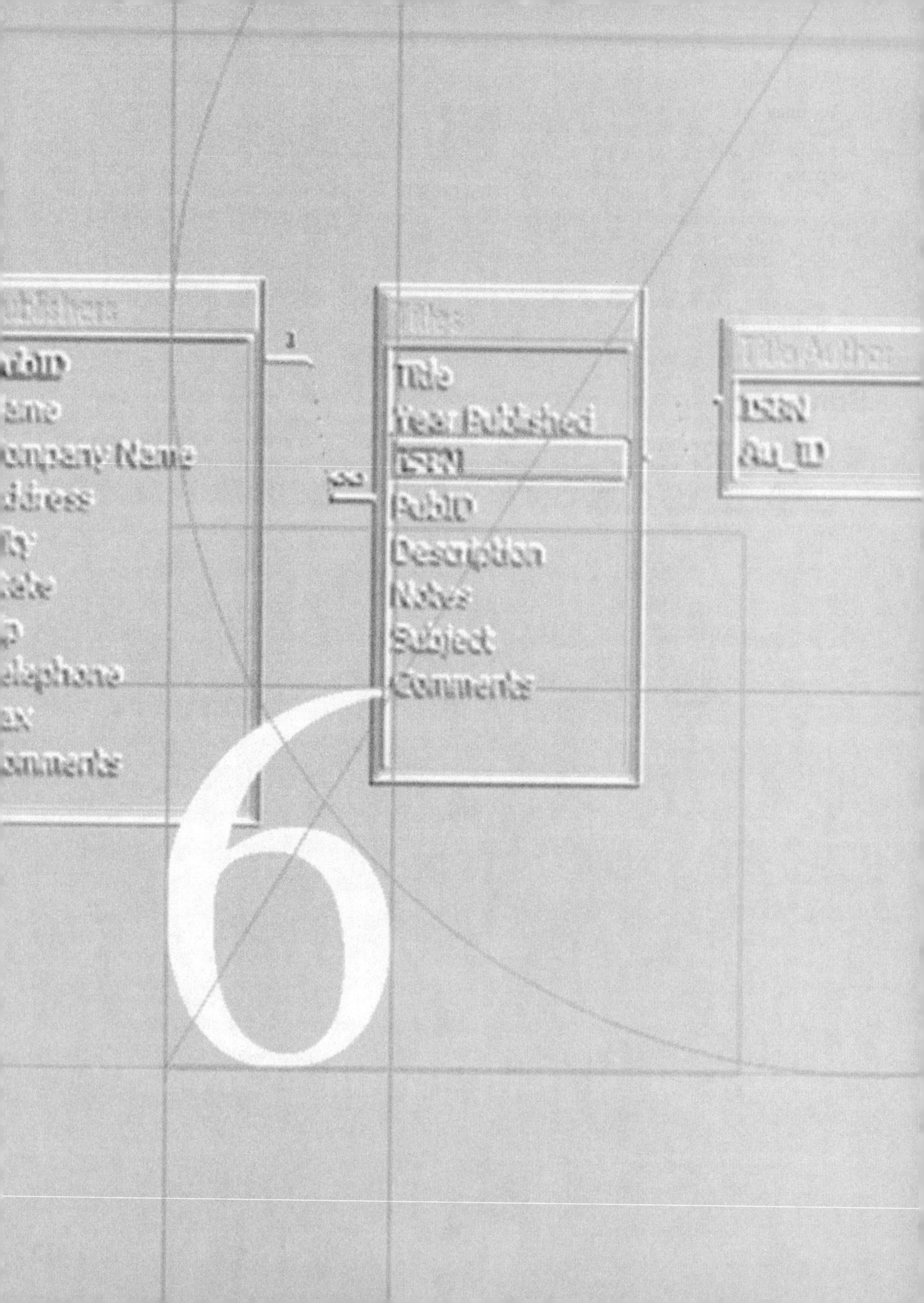
Title
Year Published
ISBN
PubID
Description
Notes
Subject
Comments
ISBN
Au_ID

6

Solutions

The next few pages provide solutions to the questions that were included at the end of each chapter.

Chapter 1 - What Is a Database?

1 A table is used to store information in the database. It usually contains information that relates to a single type entity for which we are keeping information. There are rules of normalization, which we will talk about that help to identify the contents of a table.

A record contains the information for a single entity. Where a table may hold information about publishers, a record holds information about one publisher like Apress.

A field is one item of information kept for each record in a table. For the record that identifies Apress in the Publishers table there is a field that contains the phone number.

2 The database engine is the "brains" of a database system. The engine responds to requests for outside to manage the information in the data store. The data store is where the information is actually kept. A data store does not need to be a traditional database. It could be a web page, email message or anything that has information that is used by an application.

3 A primary key is a field, or set of fields that can uniquely identify a record in a table. Often an arbitrary number is used as the primary key so that it can be guaranteed to be unique. This number is then often called an ID. An example of this is the PubID in the Publishers table in the **Biblio.mdb** database. Here an AutoNumber field is used to automatically increment the PubID for each new record saved in the table.

A foreign key is used to create a link between the table it is in and another table. Again using the **Biblio.mdb** database as an example there is a foreign key named PubID in the Titles table. This foreign key links the title record to the publisher record, which describes the publisher of the title.

The relationship between a primary and foreign key is that a foreign key in one table "points" to a primary key in another table to create a link or relationship between a record from each table.

4 A database schema is a map of the database. It identifies the structure used to store information in the database. A schema is useful in many ways. First it gives us a document that we can review with others to ensure that the database will allow all of the needed information to be stored. Second it gives us a document to reference as we begin to develop the application that will manage the data in the database. The database schema helps us to show other developers how the information is stored and helps them to understand our application in a more timely manner.

Chapter 2 - Meet the ActiveX Data Object (ADO) Data Wizard

1 A data control gives us a jump-start on accessing the information in our data store. It manages the connection to the database and leaves the developer free to focus their efforts on the user interface. It is a very good tool to use for creating a quick prototype to help users understand the application that is being build and allow them to give feedback very early in the development process.

2 A profile in the Data Form Wizard saves some of the information that we enter. This information can then be reused to help us create similar forms in the future without having to reenter the information. The information that is saved includes the database type, database name, form layout, binding type and the available controls. By using a profile it is very easy to duplicate the style of the data viewing forms that you create. These profiles are available not only within the project where they are created, but within any project created on that machine.

3 The first thing that the user must do to add a record is to click on the Add button. This blanks the form allowing for the user to enter the required information. The user must then click on one of the text boxes to move the focus to that field. Next the user enters the information in each of the desired fields on the form. No information should be entered into the PubID field because it is an AutoNumber. Now the user must click on the Update button or move to a different record to cause the new record to be saved.

One of the good things about this method is that is does allow the user to easily add a record to the database. Simply selecting one button gives them a clean form that can be used to enter the information for a new record. Then by navigating to a new record or by selecting the Update button they can cause the new record to actually be saved in the database.

830

One of the bad things about this method is that it is not always intuitive to a new user that they must actually select the <u>A</u>dd button prior to entering in the information for the new record. Many novice users expect that the <u>A</u>dd button will actually cause the information on the form to be added to the database as the new record. Also if the user exits that application with navigating to a new record, or selecting the <u>U</u>pdate button the new record is not saved and the user is not informed that the information is discarded.

Chapter 3 - Programming the Data Control

1   An intrinsic control is built into the Visual Basic environment. The control is available to the developer at anytime and will always be included with the delivered application, even if it is not explicitly used in the application.

An ActiveX control is a control that is added to the Visual Basic environment. These controls are available from many sources; you can even create your own. They provide functionality that is not included in the intrinsic controls and can help to make the creation of an application easier and allow for the reuse of code. The developer should be careful to only add the ActiveX controls that they are using in a Visual Basic project. Any control that is added to the environment will be distributed with the application even if it is not used. This causes the application to be larger than is required.

2   The `ConnectionString` and the `RecordSource`.

The `ConnectionString` property identifies the data source that is to be used for retrieving and storing the information manipulated by the data control. It includes information OLE DB provider used to communicate with the data source.

The `RecordSource` property identifies the information to be managed by the data control. This could relate to all of the information in a single table, some of the information from a single table or information stored in multiple tables in the data source.

3   First the developer must add a data control to the form. This data control must be setup indicating the `ConnectionString` and `RecordSource` to identify the data that is available to the bound controls on the form. The developer then adds a data aware control to the form and sets the `DataSource` property to be the data control. The `DataField` property of the data aware control is then set, from a list of the fields that are included in the `RecordSource`, to be the information that is to be displayed in that bound control.

4   The command type `adCmdText` allows the developer to enter an SQL command to identify the information that is to be made available from the data control. This SQL command is very flexible in allowing us to specify the data that we want to manage.

The command type `adCmdTable` allows the developer to name the table in the data source that will be made available from the data control. When this option is selected all of the records and all of the field in each record will be available through the data control.

Chapter 4 - Designing a User Interface for the Data Control

1 Properties allow the developer to view or set the attributes or characteristics of an object. Properties are often said to describe the object.

Methods used by the developer to cause an action to occur on, or with the object. Methods are the actions that can be performed on or by the object.

2 This description is the basis of event programming in Windows. Windows senses that the mouse button was clicked and where it was clicked. It identifies the event as an event for your application. It places a message into the queue for your application. Visual Basic processes the message and executes the code in the event procedure that relates to the mouse click event. In this case the event procedure would be the **commandbutton_Click** event handler.

3 Following is a listing of the code for this exercise:

```
Option Explicit

Private Sub Form_Activate()
    Debug.Print "Form_Activate"
End Sub

Private Sub Form_Initialize()
    Debug.Print "Form_Initialize"
End Sub

Private Sub Form_Load()
    Debug.Print "Form_Load"
End Sub

Private Sub Form_Paint()
    Debug.Print "Form_Paint"
End Sub
```

Following is a copy of the information found in the Immediate window after running the application:

```
Form_Initialize
Form_Load
Form_Activate
Form_Paint
```

As a further exercise you might want to play with this application while switching between it and other applications. You might also add code to the **Form_Deactivate**, **Form_GotFocus**, **Form_LostFocus**, **Form_QueryUnload**, **Form_Terminate** and **Form_Unload** event handlers. It is good to get familiar with the order in which these and other events are called.

4 The **RecordCount** property only gives a count of the records that have already been processed by the **Recordset**. The **Recordset** only processes records as required. To ensure that the **RecordCount** property is giving an accurate count of the records represented by the **Recordset** you must first ensure that all records have been processed. It is common to use two methods of the **Recordset** to ensure that all of the records have been processed. By executing the **MoveLast** method followed by the **MoveFirst** method you ensure that the **Recordset** has processed all records and that the current record has been reset to the first record in the **Recordset** allowing processing to begin.

Chapter 5 - Programming a Bulletproof User Interface

1 The **BOFAction** property tells the data control what to do if the current record pointer moves to the BOF "record" which is prior to the first record in the recordset. The possible values and their meanings are:

0 - MoveFirst. Moves the current record pointer to the first record in the recordset

1 - BOF. Leaves the current record pointer on the BOF "record".

2 To create a new record in the recordset you must call the **AddNew** method. This will create a blank record, which you may use to enter the desired information. Once the record has been populated you must call the **Update** method to cause the new record to be written to the database.

To edit an existing record you must call the **Edit** method. This will allow you to change the values of the fields associated with the current record. Once all desired changes have been made you must call the **Edit** method to save the changes to the database.

3 The **BookMark** property allows the developer to mark a record to be returned to later. The bookmark uniquely identifies a record and allows the current record pointer to be returned quickly and easily to that record.

To save a bookmark do the following:

```
Dim vLastRecord As Variant

vLastRecord = Data1.Recordset.Bookmark
```

To return to the bookmarked record:

```
Data1.Recordset.Bookmark = vLastRecord
```

4 The `CancelUpdate` method of the recordset causes all changes to the current record to be discarded and the record be returned to the state it was in prior the call to the `Edit` method. The code to handle the `Click` event of the command button is shown below.

```
Public Sub cmdCancel_Click()
'cancel the update of the current record
Data1.Recordset.CancelUpdate
End Sub
```

Chapter 6 - Completing the User Interface

1 Here's one solution:

```
Option Explicit
Private Sub Form_QueryUnload(Cancel As Integer, UnloadMode As Integer)
Select Case UnloadMode
   Case vbFormControlMenu
      MsgBox "The form was closed from the Control Menu", _
         vbOKOnly, "QueryUnload Test"
   Case vbFormCode
      MsgBox "The form was closed from the code", vbOKOnly, "QueryUnload Test"
   Case vbAppWindows
      MsgBox "The form was closed because Windows is ending", _
         vbOKOnly, "QueryUnload Test"  Case vbAppTaskManager
      MsgBox "The form was closed from the Task Manager", _
         vbOKOnly, "QueryUnload Test"  Case vbFormMDIForm
      MsgBox "The form was closed with its MDI parent window", _
         vbOKOnly, "QueryUnload Test"
End Select

End Sub
```

2 Windows standards dictate that the *Tab* key should be used to move from one control on a form to the next. The *Enter* key should cause the `Click` event of the default button, if one is one designated, to be executed. For these reasons it is often best to follow the standards so that users of your application are treated as they are with most other Windows applications.

You might want to consider changing the standard behavior in the case where you are upgrading an existing application and your users are accustomed to these features. It might also be acceptable to add these features when the users of your application will be spending most of their time entering data and these features would minimize the number of keystrokes required to enter a record.

3 Windows assigns handles when an application is running. These are the keys that Windows uses to identify and communicate with the various parts of an application. A Windows handle is not even available to us when we are writing the program and even if it were they are very dynamic. The handle to a window will be different each time you run the application. Therefore it is not possible to hard code a handle into your program.

As a Visual Basic programmer most of the work that must be done with a Windows handle is hidden from us. The most common reason that we must reference a handle is when we are making a call to the Windows API.

4 The **NoMatch** property allows the developer to inquire of the recordset if it was able to locate a record based on the criteria set in a call to one of the **Seek** or **Find** methods.

Chapter 7 - Building a Data Control Class Module

1 A class often called the cookie cutter and an object the cookie. The class defines all of the methods and properties of an object, and it is what we build using a class module in Visual Basic. An object is an instance of a class that is used by another module in the program. When we declare a variable of the type of a class we are creating an object variable.

2 A member of a class can be a variable, a sub procedure, a function or a property procedure. Each of these members can be declared as either **Private** or **Public**. A **Private** member is only visible and available for use within the class. A **Public** member is visible outside of the class and becomes part of the interface to that class. **Private** members are used to manage the work in the class and **Public** members are used to expose the information and functionality of the class to its users.

3 The property procedures are used to create properties for a class that can be exposed to the outside world. The **Let** and **Set** procedures take a value from the user of the object and use that value as the new value for the property. A **Let** is used for intrinsic data types while a **Set** is used for object data types. The **Get** procedure returns the value of the property to the user of the object.

Property procedures are useful for many reasons. The two most important are:

▶ They allow the developer of the class to cause code to be executed prior to changing or returning the value of a property

▶ They allow the developer of the class to create either read only or write only properties

By using property procedures the developer of the class has much greater control over how the user of the class is allowed to interact with it.

4 There are two basic ways that you can declare and setup a new variable from a class, there is a third but we won't be talking about it now. You must dimension a new variable of the type **dtaClass** and you must tell Visual Basic that you want the variable set to a new object of that class. This can be done in either one or two statements as shown below:

One statement:

```
Dim objNewObject As New dtaClass
```

Two statements:

```
Dim objNewObject As dtaClass

Set objNewObject = New dtaClass
```

Using a single statement will cause Visual Basic to implicitly create the object just prior to the first reference of the object that it encounters in the application. Using two statements allows the developer to explicitly create the object when and where they desire.

Chapter 8 - SQL - Getting the Data You Want from the Database

1 To create this **SELECT** statement we will have to explicitly identify the columns to be returned and also indicate the column that we want the results sorted by. The statement is as follows:

```
SELECT Title, [Year Published]
FROM Titles
ORDER BY Title
```

The **Year Published** field name is enclosed in brackets because SQL does not understand field names with spaces in them. It is best to not use spaces in your field names when creating tables.

2 A **JOIN** causes two or more tables to be aggregated together to produce a result that includes information from each of the tables. An **INNER JOIN** is used to return only information for which there is a match in each table. An **OUTER JOIN** is used to return all of the records from one of the tables even if there are no corresponding records in the other table.

For instance an **INNER JOIN** between the Publishers and Titles tables might return records for all titles that have been published and the information about the publisher of the title. If there is a record for a publisher with no corresponding records in the Titles table the information for that publisher would not be returned. If on the other hand an **OUTER JOIN** was executed you could cause information for all publishers in the Publishers table to be returned regardless of whether there were any corresponding books for the publishers in the Titles table.

3 To do this exercise we need to use many of the skills that we learned in this chapter. It requires us to do an **INNER JOIN**, use an aggregate function and a **GROUP BY** clause. It is good to do exercises like these because in the real world much of the work you will do with SQL will require you to solve problems like this. The **SELECT** statement is shown below:

```
SELECT Publishers.Name, Count(*)
FROM Publishers INNER JOIN Titles ON Publishers.PubID = Titles.PubID
GROUP BY Publishers.Name
```

4 A relational database has a value known as **Null**. This value is different to any other value. It is not an empty string, it is not a 0 and it is not **False**, rather it is **Null**. The only way for a developer to test to see if a field retrieved from the database is **Null** is to use the **IsNull** function. It is important to handle a **Null** because some of the things that we do with data in Visual Basic will cause an error to be raised if we try to use a **Null** value.

Chapter 9 - Database Design, Construction and Analysis

1 The first three levels of database normalization are:

First Normal Form - Eliminating repeating groups. Requires the removal of any fields or set of fields that are repeated in a table.

Second Normal Form - Eliminate Redundant data. Requires any fields that do not fully depend on the primary key of the table to be moved into a table where that dependency exists.

Third Normal Form - Eliminate data that is not dependent on the key. Requires any fields that are dependent on more than just the primary key to be moved to another table.

2 A recordset that is opened as a **Snapshot** does not allow the user to change the information contained in the records that are returned. This reduces the overhead of creating and maintaining the recordset and will improve performance. Any time that you are retrieving data that will not be updated you should consider using a **Snapshot** type of a recordset.

A **ForwardOnly** recordset does not allow the user to backup through the records that is holds. Once the user has moved to the next record they can no longer view any prior records. Once again this reduces the overhead associated with the recordset and will improve performance. You should watch for opportunities to use both the **Snapshot** and **ForwardOnly** recordsets to decrease the overhead in your applications and provide a friendlier interface for your users.

3 A relational database uses an index to find records in the table. An index on a database is much like the index of a book; it will point to the place where record with the specified value exists and speed up the process of returning information to the user. If there are no indexes that would be useful to help find a record the database must do a table scan which will cause each record in the table to be checked. A table scan is very slow and should be avoided when possible.

The disadvantage of creating an index is that the database must maintain the index. If you create an index for each field in every table the database will require time and resources to maintain them. It is likely that it would require fewer resources to do a table scan when you ask it to search for a record with a value for a field that does not have an index. Be careful when you design your databases to use indexes wisely.

4 Creating relationships within a database will allow the database to enforce rules that we set up when designing our data structures. These rules might include a rule requiring that a related record exist in one table if records are to exist in another table. For example there must be a publisher record if there are titles that relate to it. Access, as well as other databases, can enforce these rules and raise an error if a query would cause a rule to be broken. By placing this knowledge in the database we can reduce the burden of some of the data validation on the developer and allow them to only respond to an error if the database complains.

Chapter 10 - Programming The Address Book

1 You must first add the component to your project. Select Project-Components and turn on the check box for Microsoft Windows Common Controls 6.0 and select OK.

Select the tool bar icon from the toolbox and draw a toolbar on your form. It will automatically be moved to the top of the form. Next select the image list icon from the toolbox and draw an image list control on your form.

Right-click on the image list control and select Properties. Select the Images tab. Select the Insert Picture command button and add a picture to the image list control. Repeat until you have all of the desired pictures in the image list.

Right-click on the tool bar and select Properties. On the General tab select your image list control from the combo box labeled ImageList. Select the Buttons tab. Select the Insert Button command button. Add a Caption for the button. Type the index number of the picture in the image list control as the value of the Image. Repeat until you have defined each of the desired buttons.

This will give you a tool bar with the desired buttons and the corresponding images.

2   A tree view control is very useful when displaying information of a hierarchical nature to the user. This control is very useful for giving order to data. It could be used to show which authors have written a title for each publisher. To do this you might place the name of each publisher as root nodes on the tree view control and when the user opens a node it would display the authors associated with the publisher as child nodes.

3   A pop-up menu must be defined on the form that it will be displayed on. The menu might be accessible from the menu bar of the form or it might only be available as a pop-up menu. To define the menu, select the Menu Editor from the Tools menu. Add My Menu as the Caption and mnuMyMenu as the menu Name. If you wish the menu to be visible on the form leave the Enabled check box checked otherwise clear it. This will only be used if the menu is visible on the menu bar. Next indent the menu hierarchy and add three new menu items as follows:

Caption	Name
Add	mnuAdd
Delete	mnuDelete
Save	mnuSave

This will set up your menu.

Next create an event procedure for the **MouseDown** event on the form. The procedure should be as follows:

```
Public Sub Form1_MouseDown(Button As Integer, Shift As Integer, _
        X As Single, Y As Single)
If Button = vbRightButton Then
        PopupMenu mnuMyMenu
    End If
End Sub
```

4   This will require that we use the **WHERE** clause to identify the record that we want to delete. The statement is as follows:

```
DELETE
FROM HotContacts
WHERE FirstName = "Phred"
AND LastName = "Friendly"
```

Chapter 11 - Universal Data Access Using ADO

1 Because many of the objects in the DAO and ADO object models have the same name you must preface a reference to an ADO object with **ADODB** and follow that with a period (**.**) and the object. Here is an example:

DAO

```
Dim rsRecordset as Recordset
```

ADO

```
Dim rsRecordset as ADODB.Recordset
```

2 The property that you use to specify the data source to connect to is the **ConnectionString**. This property allows you to identify both the **OLEDB Provider** to use and the **Data Source** to have the provider access for you. In the case of an Access database the **ConnectionString** property might look like the following:

```
adoConnection.ConnectionString = _
"Provider=Microsoft.Jet.OLEDB.3.51;" _
& "Data Source=C:\Program Files\CoolApplication\CoolData.mdb"
```

This would use the Microsoft OLE DB provider for Access and open an access database named **CoolData.mdb** found on the **C** drive in the **Program Files\CoolApplication** directory.

3 If you explicitly create the object you have full control as to when it is created and you can easily set the debugger to check the state of the application prior to, or immediately after the object has been created. If you allow Visual Basic to implicitly create the object it will be created when Visual Basic first encounters a reference to the object in the code. By explicitly creating the object you maintain more control over how your application behaves. The following two examples show the difference between and implicit and explicit declaration.

Implicit:

```
Dim objMyObject As New CoolObject

objMyObject.NeatProperty = "Hello World"
'here the object is created because the
' programmer used the object
```

Explicit:

```
Dim objMyObject As CoolObject

Set objMyObject = New CoolObject
' here the programmer creates the object

objMyObject.NeatProperty = "Hello World"
```

4   A transaction will ensure that a series of steps are either completely executed and committed to the database or that none of the steps are completed. This is important when one step will leave the data in an inconsistent state if the other step(s) are not completed. The classic example is a bank transfer. If you request that $1000 dollars be moved from your savings account to your checking account you want to ensure that the entire transfer is completed or that none of it happens. You would not be very happy at all if the money were removed from your savings account but never added to your checking account. By placing multiple SQL commands into a transaction you can ensure that the data in the database remains in a consistent state.

Chapter 12 - Creating ADO Data Bound ActiveX Controls

1   ActiveX controls provide one of the few successful means of reuse in the programming world today. There are many ActiveX controls that you can buy which will allow you to add functionality to your applications without having to develop the features yourself. Visual Basic 5.0 was the first version of Visual Basic to allow a developer to create an ActiveX control. It is now very easy to encapsulate commonly used functionality into an ActiveX control and reuse the control in all of your applications. The benefits will not be seen on the first project, in fact it will take you a little longer to create the controls than it would to just place the functionality directly into your application. Once you start to reuse the control in other applications you will see the great benefits that it will bring.

2   Normally a control allows its host, the Visual Basic form in this case, to control what it does. There are times when the control needs to contact the host to inform it of something that has happened. Visual Basic allows the developer of the control to define events that it can raise to the host to inform the host that something has happened. To add an event to one of your controls you must define the event and then at the appropriate time raise the event so that the host can respond if it so desires.

3   Visual Basic has a set of predefined procedure IDs that it uses in certain ways. One of these is the (Default) Procedure ID. The procedure in our code that has been identified with the (Default) Procedure ID will be the procedure that is executed when a developer specifies our object without a property or method defined. Visual Basic will assume that the developer wants the functionality associated with the procedure that has been declared to be the (Default).

Another predefined Procedure ID is the (About) ID. This ID is used to specify the procedure that we want to execute when the developer selects (About) in the Properties window. Most often this procedure will show a form with information about our control to the user.

4 The `PropertyBag` is implemented by Visual Basic and allows the control developer to save information associated with the setup of a control by the application developer at design time. When the application developer sets properties at design-time we want to be able to save the values to be reloaded each time the program is executed. A Visual Basic User Control has events that allow these values to be written to and read from the `PropertyBag`. This gives our control the ability to maintain some state information between design-time and run-time of the application.

Chapter 13 - ADO and Active Server Pages

1 The default language used to create server sides scripts in ASPs is VBScript. VBScript is a derivative of Visual Basic. In some ways it has somewhat less functionality, but in others it is more powerful. VBScript has been tuned for creating Web applications and it is very helpful when you want to create useful and interactive web sites. Knowing Visual Basic will give you a jump-start in the world of VBScript.

2 The simplest way to allow a web client to send information to be used by and ASP is to create a standard HTML form. This form can be setup so that once the information is submitted by the user the ASP will execute and can retrieve the information that was entered onto the form by the client. This information can then be used to make decisions while creating the web page that will be displayed to the client. This information can be used to build dynamic SQL request to show information to the client.

An HTML form allows many controls to be placed on the form for the user to send us information. These controls include, but are not limited to text boxes, check boxes, radio buttons, command buttons, menus and lists. You can even create your own ActiveX controls to be used on an HTML form. This gives us great flexibility in creating web applications. It also provides us an example of a true "thin" client.

3 A cookie, on the Internet, is simply a text file that is written to your hard drive when you access a web site. The developer of the web site can put information in this cookie that will allow them to recognize you when you return to the site at a later date. This information can be used to customize the information that is displayed to you when you return to that site.

The fact that this information exists is very useful to both the web developer and the web surfer. First the developer can track information about the people that visit the web site and can even create customized versions of the site for those that return at a later date. The surfer can identify their interests when they first visit a web site and from that point on they can be presented with the information that is most useful to them without having to wade through piles of information that they are not concerned about. You see that this can be a win-win situation!

4 One of the benefits of VBScript is that it allows us to call procedures that are contained within DLLs. These DLLs can be created by the web developer or by other programmers. The DLLs can be written in languages that are more powerful than VBScript and provide that power to the ASP. By creating a DLL the developer can create a reusable component that can be called from both the Web application and a Visual Basic application. This allows the logic of the application to be created one time and ensures that a function performed from one user interface (the Web) will give the same results as when the same function is performed from the other user interface (the Visual Basic Application). There are many benefits that can be realized by creating a DLL.

Chapter 14 - Advanced ADO Programming - Data Mining

1 When we create an application whose job it is to maintain data, it is important to do our best to normalize the database. Recall that we discussed the rules of normalization earlier in the book. By structuring our database in this manner it is far easier to ensure that the information stored in the database does not become corrupt and invalid. When we create an application whose job it is to analyze information that has been gathered in some other manner we often want to consider breaking the rules of normalization. This is often done to increase the speed at which the application can return data to the user. When the program must join tables together to get a full picture of the data it slows down the process. If the data is not going to be changing we not longer need to worry about the consistency and validity of the data and we can break all the rules of normalization. This can reduce the amount of work that the database must do to return the information that we request.

Chapter 15 - Making our Data Available Universally

1 Most often the information that we maintain in our applications belongs to the user. It is information that they collect in the process of doing their everyday business. When we create an application we try to supply all of the functionality that we foresee the users needing, but we will almost always fall short. By providing a means through which the user can extract their data from our application we will help the user to do their job by allowing them to utilize other tools to do the things that our application will not do. A knowledgeable spreadsheet user will be able to extract mountains of information from the data that we have locked up in our application if we will give them the opportunity to do so. This will make our application more useful to them and in turn will make our application successful. Remember that the job of our application is to help the user to do their work, not to allow them to use our application.

2 Early binding is accomplished by explicitly telling Visual Basic the class of an object when you write the program. Late binding allows you to create a generic object variable that can be used to reference any class of object at run-time. Early binding has many advantages over late binding. With early binding, Visual Basic can ensure that you are using the object properly prior to running the application. With early binding Visual Basic knows the calls that you are making to the members of an object before running the application and is more efficient when making those calls.

Late binding has its advantages as well. When you declare a generic object variable you are free to let it reference any class at run-time, even a class that did not exist when the original application was developed. Late binding provides flexibility that is not possible through early binding, but the cost comes in performance and error checking capabilities.

You would want to utilize late binding if you did not know the class of object that you would need to process when you create the application.

3 A disconnected recordset allows us to create a recordset that can be wholly managed on the client side until we are ready to send the changes back to the server to update the database. By allowing the client to manage the recordset we reduce the traffic between the client and server and increase the performance of our application.

The ability to have a disconnected recordset is very valuable when working with clients over the Internet. Because traffic between the client and server can be very slow when working over the Internet anything that can reduce the interactive communication between the client and the server will greatly improve the performance of the application. This is a great example of when you might want to use a disconnected recordset.

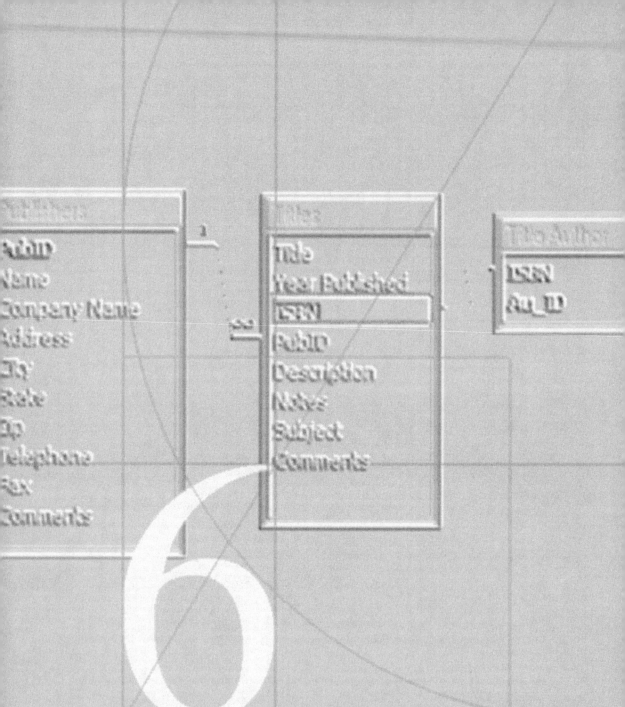

Summary of Microsoft Access Field Types

The Table fields column displays the **Type** properties available in Design View in Access, along with the six **FieldSize** properties available for the Number data type.

The second and third columns display the corresponding Visual Basic data types and DAO field object types respectively.

Table Fields	Visual Basic	DAO Field Object Type
Yes/No	**Boolean**	**dbBoolean**
Number (**FieldSize** = Byte)	**Byte**	**dbByte**
AutoNumber (**FieldSize** = Long Integer)	**Long**	**dbLong**
Currency	**Currency**	**dbCurrency**
Date/Time	**Date**	**dbDate**
Number (**FieldSize** = Double)	**Double**	**dbDouble**
Number or AutoNumber (**FieldSize** = Replication ID)	*Not supported*	**dbGUID**
Number (**FieldSize** = Long Integer)	**Long**	**dbLong**
OLE Object	**String**	**dbLongBinary**
Memo	**String**	**dbMemo**
Number (**FieldSize** = Single)	**Single**	**dbSingle**
Number (**FieldSize** = Integer)	**Integer**	**dbInteger**
Text	**String**	**dbText**
Hyperlink	**String**	**dbMemo**
Not supported	**Variant**	*Not supported*

Beginning
Visual Basic 6 Database Programming

A

About Boxes
   adding to custom-built ADO control 624-626
AbsolutePosition property
152, 158, 170, 809
accelerator keys 174
Access (Microsoft) 24, 400
   Access system (MSys) tables 50
   advantages 35
   building SQL queries with 376-379
   connecting to 151
   database types 169
   default user name 523
   field lengths 159
   importing into 776
   ISAM files 411
   limits of Access 167
   multi-table queries 31, 32
   Query Builder 760
Action argument 263
Activate event 152
Active Server Pages (ASP). *see* **ASP**
ActiveX automation 767, 787
ActiveX automation server 788
**ActiveX Data Object (ADO)
controls.** *see* **ADO**
add-ins 42
   API Viewer 241
   Application Wizard 42
   locating available add-ins 43
   Wizards 43
Address Book example 390
   1st Normal Form 394

2nd Normal Form 395
3rd Normal Form 397
creating the database with DAO 418
creating the tables 400
eliminating columns 397
eliminating repeating groups 394
splitting tables 395
The Database Analyzer 425
un-normalized fields 392
**ADO (ActiveX Data Objects)
33, 34, 35**
   see also ADO object model and ADO data control
   advanced techniques 798
     disconnected recordset 798, 800
     marshalling recordset method parameters 800, 801
     recordsets disconnected from database 799
   advantages of ADO 518, 519, 520
   analysing data sources 548, 549
   analyzing schema 549
   object model of ADO 520
   obtaining data source schema 549-553
   obtaining data type information 553-555
   transactions 569-573
   UDA (Universal Data Access), using 518
ADO Data Control (ADODC)
   see also ADO and ADO Data Control object model
   adding About Box 627
   adding to programs 90, 520-528
   adding to toolbox 85, 105
   adding validateRecord event 632, 633

binding data 579, 581
   overview 580
building 593, 595
connecting to database 522-525
connecting with recordset 525, 527
connection option
   OpenSchema method 548, 549, 550-555
connection strings 521
   Data Link property box 522-525
   options list 568
custom-built 578, 592-600
   adding About Box 624-626
   adding properties 600- 603
   bound control connections 630, 631
   converting to .ocx file 634, 635
   locking control size 596, 597
   non-tabular record sources 603
   recordset object creation 598
   Registry listing 635
database connections 135, 151
display 528
features 87, 90
handling multiple records using 106
icons 106
identifying record position 528
initializing 528
OLEDB indicator 106
properties 529
   comparison with DAO data control properties 529, 530
Property Pages 619-623
Properties window 107
RecordSource property 111
testing database connection 109
text boxes 527, 528
when to use 134
with DataCombo control 107-113

ADO Data Control object model 530

see also ADO Data Control

command object 531-532

connection object 530-531

methods 531

properties 531

object interactions 531

recordset object 531

ADODC. *see* **ADO Data Control**

ADO data repeater. *see* **data repeater**

ADO object model

see also ADO and ADO Data Control

collections 561

command objects 562

DAO object model , compared 562

aggregate functions

SQL (Structured Query Language) 361

combining with WHERE clause 365

COUNT 362

NULL values 364

aliasing, SQL 362, 363

Alignment property 142, 162

AllowUserResizing property 100

ANSI (American National Standards Institute) standard 344

API (Application Programmer's Interface) 238-240

see also DLLs (Dynamic Link Libraries)

calls 239, 240, 253

API Viewer 241-243

App object 222

arithmetic operators 363

AS clause (SQL) 362, 363

Asc() function 78

ASCII (American Standard Code for Information Interchange) 76-78

ASP (Active Server Pages) 653, 656

hidden fields 685

HTML 654

object model 685

Request object 691

Response object 667

server side scripts 656

B

BackColor property 305

bang notation 103

symbol for 103

BETWEEN operator (SQL) 357

binding 787

early 789

late 788

binding collections 581, 582

BOF (beginning of file) 148, 169-170

pointers for 148

properties 149

BOF property 170

BOFAction property 169

BookMark property 170, 200

Boolean operators 358

BorderStyle property 223

Bound Column property 112

bound controls 40, 84, 88.

altered records 145

check box (DAO) 89

combo box (DAO) 89

creating custom 579

DataCombo (ADO) 90, 105, 106

DataFields property 143

DataGrid (ADO) 89, 106

DataList (ADO) 89, 106

DataRepeater (ADO) 90

DataSource property 143

DateTimePicker (ADO) 90

empty fields 145

fields 171

hierarchical FlexGrid (ADO) 90

image (DAO) 89

label (DAO) 89

list box (DAO) 89

list of 89

locking/unlocking 613

masked edit (ADO) 89, 104

MS HFlexGrid (ADO) 89, 106

comparison with standard grid 122

OLE-container (DAO) 89

picture box (DAO) 89

properties 93-100

read-only 88

refreshing current record 170

relationship with data controls 84, 122

saving data from 170

text box (DAO) 88, 89, 91-94

text boxes 630, 631

adding to forms 138-143

labeling 142

bound list boxes 238

BoundClass module 582-591

BoundColumn property 115-119

business objects 798, 799, 804

remote 804

business rules 798, 799

C

Cancel property 223

cancel state 172

Caption property 155, 162

CGI (Common Gateway Interface) 664

charts 49

creating using Data Form Wizard 70 - 75

MS Chart 69

child records 49, 65

Chr() function 78

Class Builder

Add New Method 295

Method Builder 295

Class Module Builder 277

menu icons 279

Methods tab 296

screen components 276

updating file changes 281

variable declarations 285

class modules 168, 797

see also classes and objects

as data providers 591

classes 27, 797

encapsulation 272-275

inheritance 274

parent/child objects 274

methods 274

objects as instances of 273

overview 273-275

polymorphism 274

properties 274

client side scripting 656

client/server system 409-411, 653, 679, 799

Close method 171
connection object 531
connection/recordset objects 548
code modules 238
adding to projects 238, 239
collections 412, 442
ADO object model 561
and objects 412
binding 581, 582
control collections 195
Count property 195
database 413
Errors 412, 458
Parameter objects 563
Workbooks, Excel 788
Workspaces 412, 458
columns 16
fields as 52
comma delimited files
embedded commas 775
exporting data 769
comma separated values (csv) 766
embedded commas 775
exporting 770
command buttons
adding Case Statements 176
control arrays for 173
disabling 184
navigating recordsets using 177
Command object 531
Parameter object collection 563
using with multiple connection objects 562
CommandTimeOut property 531
CommitTrans method 531
common dialog box 766, 769
compound primary keys 30
Connect property 169
default 151
connection objects
ADO Data Control 530
interactions with recordset object 531
methods 531
properties 531
custom ADO Data Control 598
Execute method 545, 546, 547
obtaining provider information using 559-560
OpenSchema method 548-555

ConnectionString property 107, 531
connection string display format 110
instructions for building connection strings 108-110
connection strings 110
ADO data control 108-110
ODBC (Open Database Connectivity) 543
options for 568
ConnectionTimeOut property 531
constants, enumerated 175
adding to class modules 286
lists of 590, 591
control arrays 138
creating 139
indexes for 139, 147
controls
see also ADO control
ADO vs. DAO 106
collections of 195
focus 225
intrinsic 84, 86
lightweight 174
locking size of 596, 597
MS HFlexGrid 119
OLEDB 106
ProgressBar 160
read-only 119
Tab 449
tree view control 425, 451
cookies 798, 806
magic. see handles
reading and writing 690
COUNT function (SQL) 362
Count property 195
CursorLocation property 531
cursors
ADO 563, 564
default 566
read-only 565
read/write 565
recordset management 564, 565, 566
I-Beam
focus indicator 229
in disconnected recordsets 801
types of
Dynamic 567
Forward-only 567
Keyset-driven 565, 566, 567
Scrollable 565, 566

Static 567
updateable/nonupdateable 566
CursorType property 566-567

D

DAO data control 84-87, 134-137, 151
see also DAO and DAO object model
accessing databases 135
database-connection options 151
DatabaseName property 136
properties 148, 151
RecordCount property 154
RecordSource property 137
when to use 134
DAO (Data Access Objects) 33
advantages 34
history 513
Jet interface 409,
limitations 514
object hierarchy 412
using to create a database 409
when to use 33, 388, 411
DAO object model 412-413
ADO object model, compared 562
data
see also databases
aggregation 399
binding 579-581
denormalizing 399
encapsulation 287
entry
forms 225-232, 281-285
validating 261, 326
mining 399, 713, 714
data re-aggregation 718
entropy 716, 747, 752
ID3 Algorithm 715
modeling 393
normalization 24, 392-399
redundancy 392
warehousing 399
data bound controls. *see* **bound controls**
data controls. *see* **ADO and DAO data controls**
Data Form Wizard 39
Data Link property box 522-525

data mining 399, 713, 714
  data re-aggregation 718
  entropy 716, 747, 752
  ID3 Algorithm 715
data modeling 393
data repeater 637-648
Data Source Name. see DSN
data warehousing 399
data-aware controls. see bound
controls
Database collection 413
database engines
  ISAM 411
  Jet 28, 388
DatabaseName property 168, 169
databases
  see also recordsets
  Access (Microsoft) 24-25
  analysis 387
  analyzing data types in 553-555
  analyzing fields in 548-553
  as data stores 29
  components 11
  constructing 387
    with DAO 409
    with VisData 400
  database engines 27, 28
  designing 387, 393
  fields 145, 158, 685
  flat-file 14
  interfaces, ODBC 47
  ISAM (Indexed Sequential Access
  Method) 515
  mechanics of 144
  normalization 24, 392-399
  ODBC (Open Database
  Connectivity) 516-518
  relational 9, 14-16
    advantages 15
    components 15
    joining tables in 367-369
DataChanged property 95, 96
DataCombo control (ADO)
90, 105, 106
  BoundColumn property 114
  using with ADO data control 106
DataFields property 143
DataGrid control (ADO) 89, 106

DataList control (ADO) 89, 106
DataRepeater control (ADO) 90
DataSourceBehavior property 591
DataSource property 143
data warehousing 399
date interchange format (dif) 766
dates, converting 477
DateTimePicker (ADO) 90
dBase databases, accessing 514
DBEngine 412, 415, 458
  Errors collection 412
  Workspaces collection 412
Debugging 189, 555-559
  error-identification, ADO 555-559
  time-saving tips 189
delete anomaly 395
Delete method 171
DELETE statements (SQL) 359
denormalizing data 399
dif (date interchange format) 766
disconnected recordsets 798
  ADO 798
  creating 800
DISTINCT keyword (SQL) 359
DLLs (Dynamic Link Libraries)
27, 28, 85
  see also API and type libraries
  as references 209
  filename extensions 86, 106
  how to use 86
  ISAM drivers 515, 516
DoEvents 191
dot notation 131
DSN (Data Source Name)
  connection string code 543
  creating 537- 543
  testing 543-545
DSN-less connections 537
dynamic cursors (ADO) 567
dynamic linking 86
dynamic SQL (structured query
language) 345
dynasets 146

E

early binding 789
  see also binding
Edit method 171
  limitations 374
EditMode property 170, 184
  built-in constants 184
  checking during unloading 221
encapsulating data 286-287
  hiding data using 587
encapsulation (OOP) 275
engines, database 27
  ISAM 411
  Jet 27, 28
entropy 716, 747, 752
enumerated constants 175
  action arguments 263-264
  features 597
EOF property 170
EOFAction property 149, 150, 169
error messages
  see also errors
  database connection failures 524
  invalid data 265
  invalid procedure call/argument
  191
  invalid property value 230
  moving off recordset 178
  no current record 178
  unusable names 197
errors
  see also error messages
  accidental file overwrites 320
  avoiding 172
  BOF and EOF related 148, 150
  compile errors 322
  data editing errors 184
  data entry errors 104, 105
  global variables errors 244
  handling errors 96
    data entry 104, 105
    SQL query-related 383
  Identifying errors 555-559
  incorrect property values 144
  run-time errors 157, 227
  SQL errors 349, 350
  type-mismatch es 197
  unloading during editing 220

Errors collection 412, 458, 555-559
events 84
  Activate 152
  declaring/raising 598, 599
  executing 134, 157
  Form_Load 96
  Form_MouseMove() 132
  Form_Unload events 223
  initialization sequence 229
  overview 131, 132, 133, 134
  Public vs. Private 181
  Query Unload 220, 221
  raising events 599
  Reposition 152
    adding field highlights 227, 228
    firing 158
    testing 227
    updating current records in 261
  Resize event 64
  Unload event 223
Excel 789
  ActiveX automation server 788
  as an automation server 793
  calling from VB 791
  exporting 767
  importing a csv file into 776
  invisible instances of 793
  object 794, 796
  object variable 788
  sending ADO recordsets 790
  sending data via ActiveX
  automation 767, 787
  type library 789
  using objects to send ADO data 787
  Workbooks collection 788
Exclusive property 169
Execute method 531, 545-547
  function 545
  testing 546, 547

F

fields 11, 15, 16, 24
  accessing 547
  altered records 145
  attributes 18
  data types 18
  duplicate fields 21, 24
  eliminating
    inconsistent dependency 392

    redundancy 392
  empty 145
  field types 312, 313
  hidden fields 685
  key fields 22
  length 158
  linking 15
  locking 234, 235
  NULL values 30, 358
  required fields 264
  searching 312, 313
  selecting fields
    Data Form Wizard, using 50, 51
    RecordSource property (ADO) 111
  sorting fields
    ASCII order 76, 79
    Data Form Wizard, using 52
    SQL queries 76
  table columns 52
  unnormalized 392
files
  BOF/EOF pointers 148
  comma delimited files 766
    embedded commas 775
    exporting the data 769
  comma separated values (csv) 766
    embedded commas 775
    exporting the data 769
  data files , ADO 525, 527
  data stores 29
  data-storage 16
  date interchange format (dif) 766
  DLLs (dynamic link libraries) 27, 28
  ISAM 411
FindFirst method 171
  locating records using 237
FindLast method 171
FindNext method 171
FindPrevious method 171
flat-file databases 14
focus
  forms (form objects) with 229
  highlighting controls with 226
  I-Beam cursor as indicator 229
  overview 225
  setting prematurely 228
foreign keys 23, 24
form templates 330, 332-336
  creating parent/child forms
  330, 332-336

forms
  as templates 168
  creating via HTML 681
  generating 42
  initializing 102
  profiles 53
  purpose of 27
  type of 48, 49
forms (form objects)
  accessing 129
  active 130
  BorderStyle property 223
  Caption property 131
  GUIs (graphical user interfaces) 138
  intrinsic features 129
  modal/non-modal 256
  parent/child 330-336
  properties 130, 131
  resizing 129
    preventing 247
  Show method 256
  standard features 129
FreeFile function 773
FROM clause (SQL) 345, 346
functions
  aggregate
    using in SQL queries 361, 362
    WHERE clause with 365
  API 239-241
  Asc() 78
  Chr() 78
  FreeFile 773
  MsgBox 221
  Public vs. Private 181
  statistical, SQL 365, 366

G

General Declarations section
  connecting class modules with forms
  283
  Option Explicit statements 175
global modules 319
global variables 243-249
  advantages 249
  limitations of 244
  when to use 243-245
graphical user interfaces. *see* **GUIs**
Grid (Datasheet) layout forms 49

creating 58-60
Show Data Control option 60
grids
controls for 100, 120-122
resizing 100, 120
navigating 119
GROUP BY clause (SQL) 345, 366-367
GUIs (Graphical User Interfaces) 51, 138

H

handles 253
HAVING clause (SQL) 345, 367
heterogeneous joins 409
Hierarchical FlexGrid control. *see* MS HFlexGrid control
HTML (HyperText Markup Language) 653, 656, 654, 781
adding script s 664
and ASP 654
ASCII file 655
browser independence 655
cookies 687
reading and writing 690
exporting 766, 781,785
HTTP (HyperText Transfer Protocol) 654
stateless connection s 687
static language 653, 655
streams 656
tags 655
URL (Uniform Resource Locator) 654
web sites 654
hWnd property 240, 253

I

ID3 Algorithm, data mining 715
IIf statements 351
image control (DAO) 89
IN operators, SQL 357
Index parameter (control arrays) 139, 147
Indexed Sequential Access

Method. *see* ISAM
indexes 13, 24
advantages 19, 20
creating 19
guidelines 407
index variables 190
overview 18-19
primary keys 23
using 76
inheritance (OOP)
parent/child objects 274, 332-336
Initialize event, class modules 284
INNER JOIN approach, SQL 368-369
instantiating objects 273
integer variables, naming 190
IntelliSense 156-157
Internet 653
cookies 687
data access requirements 517, 518
stateless connection 687
Intranet applications, using ADO 34, 35
intrinsic controls 84, 86
see also bound controls
IP Address 661
IS NOT NULL clause, SQL 364
ISAM (Indexed Sequential Access Method) 410
accessing with intrinsic data control 515
data access 411
data sources 411
database support 515, 518
drivers 515, 516
file types 513

J

JavaScript 664
Jet database engine
and ISAM 411
bypassing with ODBCDirect 516
DAO-support 513, 515
DLLs (Dynamic Link Libraries) 28
flexibility of 28, 410
limits of 167
overview 27-28

programming Jet
ADO (ActiveX Data Objects) approach 33-35
DAO (Data Access Objects) approach 33-34
recommendations for use 388
relation to other engines 400
security 109
JOIN keyword, SQL 345
JScript 664

K

key fields
defining 22
linking tables using 21
keys 24
basing relationships on 21, 23
foreign 23
primary 22
compound 30
features 23
unique 21
Keyset-driven cursors 565- 567
Knowledge Discovery in Databses (KDD) 714

L

label control (DAO) 89
late binding 788
legacy data 748
accessing 514
databases 102
libraries
ADO reference 520
application type 789
dynamic link (DLLs) 85, 86, 209
statically-linked 85, 86
type libraries 789
adding to projects 209
components 209, 210
Excel 789
LIKE operator, SQL 356
list box control (DAO) 89
Locked property 192, 235
locking
bound controls 613
control sizes 596-597

fields 234-235
records 192-194
logic rules 798
Lotus spreadsheets 514

M

machine states 179, 180
magic cookies. *see* **handles**
many-to-many relationships 20
  see also relationships
many-to-one relationships 21
  see also relationships
marshalling 800-801
  MarshalOptions property 801
Mask property 105, 453
masked edit control (ADO) 89, 451
  features 104
  idiosyncracies of 487
master records 49
Master/Detail layout forms 49, 61
  creating 61, 62, 63
  displaying 64
  navigating 64, 65
MDB database files 513
  analyzing using DAO 425
  data controls for 134
merging data 66
message boxes, syntax 221
meta-information 724
Method Builder 295
Microsoft Jet 3.51 OLE DB Provider 108
  see also Access and OLE databases
Microsoft Access 400
  see also Access
Microsoft Excel. *see* **Excel**
Microsoft Hierarchical FlexGrid control
  see MS HFlexGrid control
Microsoft Masked Edit Control 6.0
  see masked edit control
Microsoft DAO 3.51 Object Library 209
modal displays 256

modules 27
  class 238, 591
  code modules 238
  templates 319
month view control (ADO) 90
MousePointer property 250, 294
MoveFirst method 149, 171
MoveLast method 162, 171, 176
MoveNext method 149, 171, 176
MovePrevious method 149, 150, 171, 176
MS Chart layout forms 49, 69-75
MS HFlexGrid control (ADO) 89, 106, 119
  DataSource property 122
  using 119-122
MS HFlexGrid layout forms 49
  creating 65-69
MsgBox function 221
MSys tables 50
multi-table relational searches 31-32
mvar prefix 286

N

naming conventions 189
nested conditions, SQL 358
New keyword (for objects) 283, 560-561
nodes 431, 467
  collection 467
  root 431
  tree 431
non-relational data 514, 518
normalization 24, 392-397
  denormalizing 399
NULL values 30, 250, 358

O

Object Browser 277, 648
  accessing 209
  advantages of using 212
  examining classes in 327
  searching 210-211
  window components 209-210

object variables 788
  see also recordsets
  declarations 283
  dimensioning 560-561
  recordsets 811
Object-Oriented Programming (OOP)
  overview 273-275
  polymorphism 274
  Visual Basic approach 275
objects
  accessing via binding 788
  and collections 412, 413
  App 222
  as class instances 273
  business 798-799
    remote 804
  command objects 562
  parameter objects 563
  recordsets 417, 796, 801
    disconnected type 799-800
    overview 145-147
    types of 146
ODBC (Open Database Connectivity) 410, 516
  and Jet 409
  data sources 537-543
  drivers 572
  ODBCDirect 409, 516, 517
  ODBC interface 47
ODBC DSN connection 543-545
OLE DB
  ADO, using with 520
  controls 106
  providers
    identifying errors 555-559
    getting schema 549, 550-553
    obtaining data type information 553-555
    obtaining source information 549
OLE-container control (DAO) 89
one-to-many relationships 20-21
  see also relationships and tables
one-to-one relationships 20-21
  see also relationships and tables
OOP. *see* **Object-Oriented Programming**
Open Database Connectivity. *see* **ODBC**
Open method
  connection object 531
  recordset object 547

OpenSchema method 548-553
  analyzing data types 553-555
operating systems (OS)
  Windows 132
Oracle databases
  connecting to using Data Form
  Wizard 47
ORDER BY clause (SQL)
345, 360, 361
ordering
  see also sorting
  recordsets 360
orphaned records 23
OUTER JOIN approach, SQL 369,
371

P

Paradox databases
  accessing 514
  updating files from 515
Parameter object collection 563
parent records 65
  see also master records
parent/child forms
  avoiding design problems 336
  creating 98-101, 330-336
  example 102
parent/child relationships 98
passwords, adding to connection
strings 109
paths, fully-qualified 169
pattern matching, searching
records using 238, 255
PercentPosition property
158, 162, 170
persistent recordsets 811
Persistent Data Application with
ASP 688-709
  getting information on a new surfer
  704
  retrieving information about visitors
  700
  writing cookies to the Client's
  browser 690
Personal Address Book example
390
  creating the address book 444

creating the database with DAO 418
creating the tables 400
normalization issues 392-397
programming 441
splitting tables 395
Personal Web Server (PWS) 656
  setting up 657
  virtual directories 662
picture box control (DAO) 89
place markers 170
pointers
  BOF (beginning of file) 149
  EOF (end of file) 150
  Mouse 250, 294
  record pointers, 171
polymorphism 274
Posting data 686
primary keys 22, 24
  See also keys
  compound 30
  editing 114
  features 23
Private scope 181
Procedures Attributes dialog 327
Production Analysis Tool 715-722
programming
  DAO vs. ADO 33-35
  data controls 154-155
  encapsulated code 272-273
  event-driven 131-134
  induction methods 715
  languages 579
  levels of indirection 180, 181, 197
  modular approach 180
  object-oriented. *see* OOP
  reusable components 272
  user interfaces 27
programs
  see also applications and databases
  data-return speed 146
  designing programs 172
  exporting recordsets to 765
  memory conservation 222
  overheads 147
  resources 176
  self-contained 28
  speed 155, 185
  state machine approach 172
  user interfaces 127

progress bars
  adding 160-162
  when to use 161
ProgressBar control 160
ProgressBar property 280
Project Explorer window 284
properties 84
  AbsolutePosition 152, 158, 170, 809
  AddCaption 248
  ADO Data Control 529
  ADO data repeater 640, 641, 642
  Alignment 142, 162
  AllowUserResizing 100
  assigning values with Property Let
  288
  BackColor 194, 234, 305
  BOF 170
  BOFAction 149, 169
  BookMark 170
  BorderStyle 223
  BoundColumn 112, 114
  BoundColumn property 118
  Cancel 223
  Caption 131, 155, 162
  Connect 151, 169
  connection object (ADO) 531
  Connection String (ADO) 107, 110
  Count 195
  custom-built (ADO) 600-603
  customized properties 248
  DAO (Data Access Object) 135, 148,
  151
  data controls 92, 169
  DatabaseName 168, 169
  DataChanged 95, 96
  DataFields 138, 143
  DataSource 138, 143
  DataSourceBehavior 591
  EditMode 170, 184, 221
  Enabled 188, 190, 249
  EOF 170
  EOFAction 150, 169
  Exclusive 169
  FindFieldMatch 314
  ForeColor 142
  Hidden 212
  hWnd 240, 253
  Let RecordSource 329
  Let/Get templates 247
  ListField 112

Locked 192, 235
MarshalOptions 801
Mask (masked edit control) 105
MousePointer 250, 294
Multiline 161
PercentPosition 158, 162, 170
Property Let/Get 287
Public vs. Private 181
ReadOnly 169
RecordCount 149, 154
Recordset 169-170
RecordsetType 169
RecordSource 145, 168
TabIndex 229, 230
TabStop 232
ToolTip Text 193
UnloadMode 220
Updatable 351
UserControl 615
**Property Pages, ADO Data
Control 619-623**
prototyping 56, 127, 128
Provider property 531
Public scope 181

Q

queries
see also SQL
databases , discussed 145
tables, discussed 31
Query Builder 760
Query Tester program 352-354
QueryUnload event 220
**queues, Windows operating
system 132**

R

raising events 598- 599
RDO (Remote Data Objects) 518
ODBC support 518
read-only controls 88
read-only cursors (ADO) 565
read-only recordsets 169
read/write cursors (ADO) 565
read/write rights 169
ReadOnly property 169

record counts 286
**RecordCount property
149, 154, 170**
ADO recordsets 566
initializing 155
records 11, 15, 16, 24
see also recordsets
accessing 28, 32
adding 200
background color cues 194
BookMark property for 200
counting 149
current record operations
deleting 171
displaying 84, 175, 637
editing 171
identifying position of 170
moving pointer for 176
refreshing 170
grouping records 366
handling multiple records 106, 112
indexing 13
linking using key fields 21
locating 237-238
locking/unlocking 192-194
manipulating 87
marshaling 800-801
master/detail 49
non-unique records 359
ordering records 360
orphaned 23, 205
parent/child 65
pointers 170
position of 528
ranges 357
retrieving records 84
searching for records
limiting query returns 354
multi-table relationships for 31-32
pattern matching 255
sorting records
ASCII order 76, 79, 114
indexes for 76
source fields 51
table rows 52
updating records 572
viewing multiple records 58
recordsets 40
see also records and databases
acccessing 148
accessing fields 547
adding data to 114, 117

connecting ADO Data Control to
525, 527
CopyFromRecordset method 796
data ranges 357
determining state 182
disconnected 798
EditMode 597
Empty recordsets 145
exporting to other programs 765
formatting 313
locating records 237, 238
managing 564, 566
MarshalOptions property 801
methods 176, 800
modifying data 384
navigating
ADO controls for 57-58
command buttons for 177, 179
options for 158
scrollbars for 60
text box controls 94
VCR buttons for 150, 152
objects 417, 796, 801
object types
dynasets 146, 291
snapshots 146
tables 146
object variables 811
opening recordsets 418, 568
persistent recordsets 811
properties 168-170, 801, 809
querying recordsets 145
record position 152
referencing recordsets 563
remote 799, 802, 803, 809
Refresh method 170
searching recordsets 354
sorting recordsets 360, 361
updating recordsets 371-375
Recordset property 169
**RecordSource property 94, 145,
168-170, 280**
ADO data control 111
data controls 87, 137
masked edit control example 105
parent/child form example 99
simple text box example 92
text box control 97
references
ADO libraries 520
DAO libraries 389
adding to projects 209

dimensioning object variables 560
fully-qualified 155
object references 209
type libraries 389
identifying available 208
References dialog box 208
referential integrity 423
**Refresh button, Data Form Wizard
53**
Refresh method 169-170
opening/reopening databases 250
refreshing controls 170
Registry, Windows 635
relational databases 9, 14-16
see also databases
advantages 15
components 15
relationships
defined 20
key-based 21, 23
many-to-many 20
many-to-one 21
multi-table 31-32
one-to-many 20-21, 61
one-to-one 20-21
parent/child 98
referential integrity 423
structure of 21
Remote Data Objects (RDO) 518
ODBC support 518
remote recordsets 799, 802-803, 809
updating the database from 801
repeating groups 393
required fields 264
Resize event 64
Response object, ASP 667
result sets 563, 564
retrieving data. *see* searching
RollBackTrans method 531
rows 16, 52
RowSource property 112
run-time errors
incorrect focus-setting 227
initialization failures 157
no current record 178
NULL value errors 250
records with apostrophes 258
.RWP filename extension 53

S

saving data
data values 170
files 320
records 202-204
Wizard Profiles 53
scope
Public vs. Private 181
variables 152
screen flicker, reducing 249
Screen object 195
screen objects, accessing 211
scripting languages 664
ASP 664
JavaScript 664
JScript 664
VBScript 664
Scrollable cursors (ADO) 565, 566
Scrollbars 119, 161
adding to text boxes 161
navigating tables using 119
Scrollbars property 161
scrolling 565
**Search Text box (Object Browser)
209, 210**
searching
data field types 312-313
Object Browser 210-211
multiple table s 31-32
records 238, 253
recordsets 171, 354
sound-alike names
pattern matching for 238
Soundex routine for 237
tables 18-24
Select Case statements 176, 185
**Select screens (Data Form Wizard)
66, 71, 72**
SELECT statements, SQL 353-362
aggregate functions 362
arithmetic operators 363
DISTINCT keyword 359
FROM clause 346
GROUP BY clause 366, 367
HAVING clause 367
IS NOT NULL clause 364
joining tables 367-368
INNER JOIN 368-369
OUTER JOIN 369, 371

keywords list 345
ORDER BY clause 360-361
SELECT clause 345-346
statistical functions 365
servers
server side scripting 656
using VBScript 664
your PC as 656
Set keyword 283
SetFocus method
correct event for 228
features 229
premature execution 228
Show method 256
Snapshots 146
sorting
data 76
records 113-114
recordsets 360-363
strings 759
source code 85
**SQL (Structured Query Language)
28, 32**
aggregate functions 361-365
aliasing column headers 362-363
avoiding syntax errors 349
error handler for 350
Boolean operators 358
building with Access 376-379
comparison operators 355
DELETE statements 359
DISTINCT keyword 359
dynamic queries 345, 380-381
building generator for 380-383
features 344-345
filtering results 354
BETWEEN operator 357
IN operator 357
LIKE operator 356
nested conditions 358
NOT IN operator 358
WHERE clauses 355
general format 346
grouping identical records 366
joining tables
INNER JOIN approach 368-369
OUTER JOIN approach 369, 371
table.field approach 367, 368
keywords 345
modifying data using SQL 384
NULL values 358

ordering recordsets 360-361
recordsets, querying with SQL 145
SELECT statements 346-362
  aggregate functions 362
  arithmetic operators 363
  DISTINCT keyword 359
  GROUP BY clause 366, 367
  HAVING clause 367
  INNER JOIN approach 368, 369
  IS NOT NULL clause 364
  joining tables 367, 368
  ORDER BY clause 360, 361
  OUTER JOIN approach 369, 371
  statistical functions 365
  UPDATE statement 375
sending commands 545
servers, connecting to 47
shallow data 714
sorting data 113
statistical functions 365, 366
updating recordsets 371-375
SQL 7.0 database
  programming-related warning 134
  using as a desktop 388
SQL Query Tester 347-354
startup object, customizing 55, 284
state machine programming model 179-180, 207
State property 531
stateless connections 687
static cursors (ADO) 567
static linking 85, 86
static properties 155
static variables 461
  declaring 200
statistical functions (SQL) 365-366
Status Bar Control 450, 461
STDEV (Standard Deviation), SQL 365-366
STDEVP (Standard Deviation of Population), SQL 365-366
string properties 131
string variables 190
strings
  conditional 355
  connection strings 568
  matching 355
  passing 185-188, 247
  safeguarding passing of 251

subroutines
  see also methods
  adding to forms 181
  automatic record locking/unlocking 194
  code modules in 180
  comparison with functions 182
  Dim statements in 152
  Public vs. Private 181
  templates for 182
Supports property 603
synchronizing data 23

T

Tab control 449
TabIndex property 229-234
tables 15, 16, 24
  adding data to 141, 147
  changing data in 103
  columns 52
  Delete method for 171
  home tables 23
  joining 368
    JOIN approach 368
    table.field approach 368
  layout formats 49
  linking 21
  multi-table relationships 31-32
  multiple tables 112
  recordset object type 146
  relationships
    design considerations 21
    key-based 21, 23
    many-to-many 20
    many-to-one 21
    one-to-many 20, 21
    one-to-one 20, 21
    parent/child 98
    referential integrity 423
    structuring 21
  rows 52
  searching 18-24
  splitting 395
  table.field approach 367
  viewing 58
tabs
  Alphabetic 130-131
  automatic tabbing 236-237
  Categorized 112, 130

data entry forms 229-232
ordering 231-232
TabStop property 232-234
Tag property 193-194, 280
templates
  see also class modules
  Class Builder, using 287
  creating data entry forms from 323
  forms 168, 330-336
  Let/Get properties 247
  storing 317-318
  subroutine templates 182
temporary objects 145-146
Terminate event 284
terminating.. *see* closing
text box control (DAO) 88-89
  binding to data control 91-94
  how it works 96-97
text boxes 88-89
  adding scrollbars to 161
  adding to forms 138-143
  control arrays 139-140
  labeling 142
  locking and unlocking 180
  multiple 138
  TabIndex property 230-234
  TabStop property 232-234
text variables 313
toolbox
  adding an ADO data control 85, 105, 521
  adding controls to 98
  built-in controls 84, 86
  Components dialog box 90
  Icons 86, 104, 106, 627
ToolTip text property 193
transactions
  ADO (ActiveX Data Objects) 569-573
  atomicity 569
  consistency 569
  features 569
  isolation 569
  updating records using 572
trees 431
tree view control 425, 442, 451
  Add method 431
  node objects 468

type libraries 789
see also DLLs (Dynamic Link
Libraries)
application 789
DAO (Data Access Object) 389
adding to projects 209
Classes list box 210
searching for components 210
Excel 789
identifying components 209
TypeOf methods 196

U

**UDA (Universal Data Access)
514, 518**
ADO, using 518
Advantages of UDA 519
Components of UDA 519
Unload event, using 223
unloading forms 218-223
UnloadMode 220
unlocking
bound controls 613
records 192-194
Updatable property 351
update anomaly 395
Update method 171
limitations 374
**Update Project button (Class
Builder) 281**
**UPDATE statements (SQL) 375,
376**
UpdateRecord method 170
updating
records 200
recordsets 114, 117, 169, 371-375
**URL (Uniform Resource Locator)
654**
host 655
protocol 655
user controls
adding properties, ADO 615

user interfaces 27
BoundClass module 589
Cancel button 170
canceling operations 254
command buttons 611
data entry 229-238
data entry forms 281-325
designing 127
enhancing forms 168
adding records 200, 201
data manpulation 200
deleting records 204, 205
editing records 202
instructions for 173-178
run-time display 206-208
saving records 202-204
undoing record changes 206
professional appearance 142
safeguards 172, 179-180
accidental deletions 205
accidental edits 192
avoiding SQL syntax errors 349-350
invalid data entries 265
naming database locations 245
premature form closing 219
preventing form resizing 247
*preventing unwanted field changes 234-
235*
QueryUnload event 219-220
recordset navigation errors 177, 184
SQL query generators 383
unwanted form resizing 223-224
validating data entry 326
separating code from 238
simplifying 177
user controls 615
visual cues
background color changes 194
background colors 234
current field highlights 227-228
enabled/disabled controls 207
highlighting current controls 225-226
hourglass mouse pointer 250, 294
importance of 179
visual feedback
progress bars 158
Windows' effect on 128
**UserControl properties, ADO 615-
618**

V

Validate event 261-265
validateRecord event 633
**VAR (variance) function (SQL)
365-366**
variables
adding to code 152
declaring 200
form/module level 182, 494
formatting 313
Jet requirements for 313
global
advantages 249
when to use 243-245
local 181
naming conventions 189
object references 209
object variables 788
see also recordsets
private 301-305
scope 152, 460
importance of limiting 244
static 461
storing properties as 131
strongly typed 789
text 313
weakly typed 788
**VARP (Variance of the Population)
function, SQL 365, 366**
**VB 6.0 IDE, add-ins and Wizards
43**
VBScript 664, 806
**Version property (connection
object) 531**
virtual directories 662
VisData 24, 390, 400
accessing 400
creating a database with 400
Visual Basic
calling Excel 791
early editions 152
history 579
language, limitations of 389
programming approaches
object-oriented programming 275
reusable components 272

prototyping using 127-128
sample databases
   Biblio.MDB 25
   Nwind.MDB 25
template directory 317-318
   modules subdirectory 319
version 5.0
   code facilitating features 156
   code syntax improvements 153
version 6.0
   new controls 89-90

W

web browsers 653, 656
host 655
protocol 655
tags 655
WHERE clauses (SQL) 355
aggregate functions with 365
BETWEEN operator 357
comparison operators 355
IN operator 357
LIKE operator 356
nested conditions 358
NOT IN operator 358
wildcard (*) symbol 346, 353, 356
**windows, handles to (hWnd)
240, 253**
Windows (Microsoft)
features 132
messages 132
queues 132
**Windows Application
Programming Interface. see API**
Wizards
adding to Visual Basic 43- 44
Application Wizard 42
Data Form Wizard 39
   ADO control problems 75
   code limitations 75
Import Text (MS Access) 779
Profiles, saving 53
Workspaces collection 412, 458
**wrapping lines, Multiline
property 161**
write-only properties 247